# Artificial Intelligence and Industry 5.0



**G. NARAHARI SASTRY**
Senior Professor
Department of Biotechnology
Indian Institute of Technology Hyderabad

**HRIDOY JYOTI MAHANTA**
Scientist
Advanced Computation and Data Sciences Division
CSIR-North East Institute of Science and Technology, Jorhat, Assam

**ASHEESH KUMAR**
Project Scientist-I
Advanced Computation and Data Sciences Division
CSIR-North East Institute of Science and Technology, Jorhat, Assam

**SELVARAMAN NAGAMANI**
Scientist
Advanced Computation and Data Sciences Division
CSIR-North East Institute of Science and Technology, Jorhat, Assam

**PHI Learning Private Limited**
Delhi-110092
2026

*In fond memory of* ***Shri Asoke K. Ghosh*** *(October 1942 – February 2024), Founder Chairman and Managing Director of PHI Learning, whose vision endlessly inspires.*

*The Legacy Continues....*

Published by Pushpita Ghosh, PHI Learning Private Limited, Rimjhim House, 111, Patparganj Industrial Estate, Delhi-110092 and Printed by Syndicate Binders, A-20, Hosiery Complex, Noida, Phase-II Extension, Noida-201305 (N.C.R. Delhi).

**₹895.00**

**Artificial Intelligence and Industry 5.0**
G. Narahari Sastry, Hridoy Jyoti Mahanta, Asheesh Kumar and Selvaraman Nagamani



**ISBN-978-93-5443-742-7 (Print Book)**
**ISBN-978-93-5443-966-7 (e-Book)**

The export rights of the book are vested solely with the publisher.

# Contents

# Preface

The genesis of the book stems from the initial attempts of the molecular modelling group at CSIR Indian Institute of Chemical Technology, Hyderabad in making lectures for the internal discussions in 2018. However, these initial attempts involving a number of colleagues, could not take off during those years. But, after Prof. G Narahari Sastry moved to Jorhat, Assam in 2019, series of lectures on Advanced Computation and Data Sciences, popularly known as ACDS lecture series, was resumed in which the various aspects of Artificial Intelligence, Machine Learning, Data Sciences and related areas were discussed. The entire lecture series was divided into two parts, such that 20 lectures were devoted to basics and fundamentals while the other 20 lectures were dedicated to applications. This initative was further amplified when the Department of Science and Technology (DST), Govt. of India gave us the responsibility to provide a three months research exposure program-cum-training course to the students from the Northeastern states, Jammu & Kashmir and Ladakh during 2022–23. The lecture notes and contents prepared for the training program was of great help in writing this book. Several people, especially the peers and the ones who have attended the lectures encouraged us to write a book, which formed the basis of the idea to write this book for undergraduate and postgraduate students. Thus, we thank all the people who directly or indirectly contributed to these efforts, especially those from the group, in the last 6 years.

The book is also prepared considering the Indian academia and researchers. A quick perusal of the market reveals that there are a number of excellent books in many of the areas detailed in this book, and it is not an exaggeration to say that there are books written exclusively on individual chapters in this book. As the main aim of the book is to introduce the topics to the undergraduate and postgraduate students and researchers interested in entering into the field, we focused more on the topics and techniques rather than an in-depth coverage. Our intention is to present a book that caters to the needs of students who are willing to enter into volatile areas of Artificial Intelligence and Machine Learning, especially those from Science and Engineering (*other than Computer Science*) backgrounds. We feel that this is the first of its kind textbook which has a wide coverage and can very well be used as such as a main text for 4 credit courses by the B.Tech or M.Tech students. Needless to say, all the mistakes and inadequacies that are present in the book are due to our deficiency, the writers of the book and cannot be attributed to the other members of the group.

We are extremely happy that PHI has come forward to take up the responsibility of publishing this book. Several people are involved in the discussions which created base for this book. We thank our students, specially Anamika Singh Gaur, Nandan Kumar, Lijo John, Himakshi Sarma, Anwesh Pandey, Bhargav Kumar, Lipsa Priyadarsinee, Esther Jamir, Kikrusenuo Kiewhuo, Sita Sirisha Madugula, Ram Vivek, Dipshikha Gogoi, Kripa Dristi Dihingia, S Vaikundamani, and also all the interns who were a part of the group. A special thanks to Mr Ranjan Deka, an intern, who had assisted us in preparing the lecture materials in the initial days along with senior members—Mr Debabrata Das, Mr Khirod Buragohain, Dr Supriya Saha and Late Dr Y Shilla Devi. We are also thankful to the students who participated in the DST sponsored training program as well as all the participants who took part in the workshops and conferences conducted by us. The interactions with the participants and Q&A sessions were very useful in framing the book.

Finally, we would like to thank the administration, especially the Directors of CSIR-North East Institute of Science and Technology, Jorhat, CSIR-Indian Institute of Chemical Technology, Hyderabad and Indian Institute of Technology, Hyderabad for extending their support. We also acknowledge the support of Department of Biotechnology (DBT), Govt. of India in the form of BIC Center of Excellence for Advanced Computation and Data Sciences at Jorhat.

**G. Narahari Sastry**
**Hridoy Jyoti Mahanta**
**Asheesh Kumar**
**Selvaraman Nagamani**

Chapter 1

# Genesis of Artificial Intelligence

## 1.1 DEFINING ARTIFICIAL INTELLIGENCE

Artificial intelligence commonly known as AI, is the ability of a machine to learn and think as humans do. The aim of AI is to create computer systems that have all kinds of human intelligence—the ability to see, hear, learn, understand different languages and solve problems. These intelligent machines can take in huge amounts of data and information from the world around them through sensors, cameras or even text corpus and numbers etc. They can then learn from that data to do things that would otherwise require lots of programming by people. Human mind learns from experience and so can the machines in machine learning where they follow a particular algorithm to attain a particular goal, say, to classify objects. This model upon successful training can be used for other set of data.

In the present era, AI can do some pretty good work—like beat the world's best chess player, identify objects in photos, predict the lead compound and help predict lead hit for drug discovery, make predictions for different types of toxicity, predict antiviral compounds and a lot more. Scientists keep finding new ways to give machines more kinds of intelligence through different techniques like machine learning, neural networks modelled after the brain, and deep learning for processing data. Big tech companies use AI to understand speech and language to create helpful voice assistants like Siri or Alexa. In the future, the goal is to make AI that is as smart as people in every way, an objective that continues being researched thoroughly around the world even though it remains extremely challenging. The more intelligent machines become, the more they can help society by taking over monotonous repetitive tasks or dangerous work for humans in several industries and come up with solutions that even the smartest humans would never think of.

***Definitions of AI based on thought process and reasoning:***

> *It is the science and engineering of making intelligent machines, especially intelligent computer programs.*
>
> —John McCarthy

*The study of intelligent agents: any device that perceives its environment and takes actions that maximize its chance of successfully achieving its goals.*

—Stuart Russell and Peter Norvig

*A field of computer science that seeks to create intelligent agents, which are systems that reason, learn, and act autonomously.*

—Melanie Mitchel

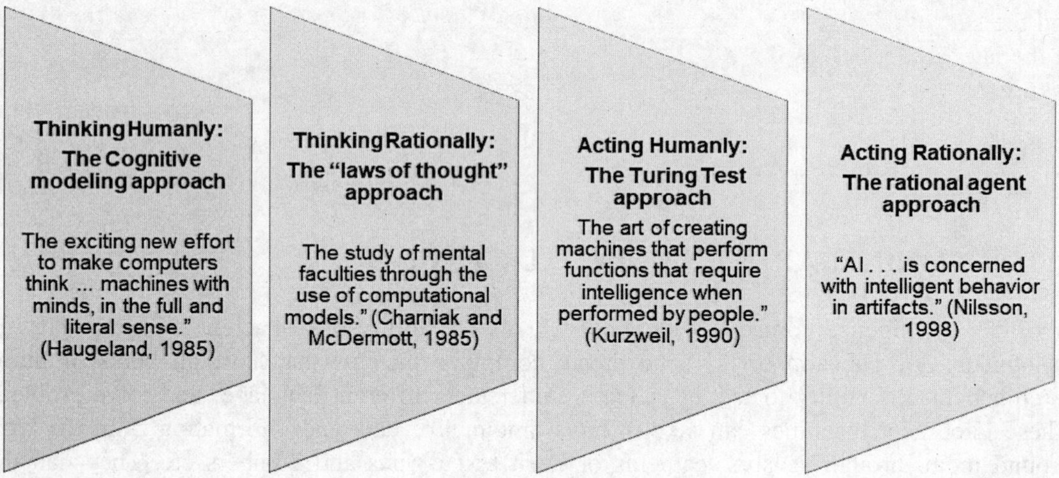


**FIGURE 1.1** Definitions of AI based on 4 different approaches the way humans behave

### *The Genesis*

AI has its origins early as the 1950s, when researchers started exploring the possibility of machines to process data and behave intelligently like the humans. In 1956 at the Dartmouth Conference, the term 'artificial intelligence' was first coined. Researchers like Alan Turing, Marvin Minsky, John McCarthy and Claude Shannon put forth ideas by their work about the concept that machines can think and learn like the humans. Early research in AI focused on solving problems such as chess playing, theorem proving, and puzzle solving through search algorithms and knowledge representation. Key milestones included the Logic Theorist, which could prove mathematical theorems, and the General Problem Solver, a computer program that was one of the first examples of separating out search from domain knowledge. In 1960s, research on methods such as microworlds, neural networks, and perceptrons generated excitement as well as overpromising, contributing later to an AI winter when limitations were revealed. Key developments included Joseph Weizenbaum's ELIZA natural language processing (NLP) system, which could hold text-based conversations by following parsing rules, and Edward Feigenbaum's Dendral algorithm for analysing chemical structures. The programming language Prolog gave programmers a new way to create rules-based logical AI systems. Research explored the possibility of general problem solvers that could leverage knowledge bases in different domains. Expert systems, such as XCON in 1980, achieved success in specialized domains like manufacturing. But the limitations of rule-based systems were also becoming apparent. To overcome critiques, AI researchers focused more on statistical approaches and neural networks inspired by neuroscience. Backpropagation algorithms trained multi-layer neural nets. The first AI winter lasted from the mid-1970s to the early 1980s when initial optimism surrounding machine translation and symbolic reasoning systems like expert systems fell short of expectations and significant cuts were made in research funding and staff. The setbacks led the field to regroup around more focused applications with limited scope like specialized expert systems for narrow tasks as well as renewed connections to neuroscience, psychology and the statistical capabilities enabled by new hardware. Then the second AI winter descended in the late 1980s through 1993 as wider economic factors compounded disappointed hopes that even expert systems could meaningfully improve business productivity at scale. With support diminishing once again from major funders like DARPA and sharper critiques levied at the validity of neural networks as a theory of intelligence itself, the second AI winter marked a period of reduced activity and even an exodus away from the unfashionable labels of 'AI' until an uptick of confidence in machine learning and Bayesian statistical approaches in the mid-1990s combined with increased availability of digital data and computing resources to eventually spur investment back into AI and renew momentum. With neural networks reviving optimism in 1990s, AI attracted increased funding and corporate involvement. Machine learning methods were applied widely to pattern classification and data mining problems. AI achieved more localized successes, like speech recognition in products. But despite advances, sceptical views of AI as too narrow prevailed by the end of the decade. With the advent of big data from the web, AI techniques excelled in text and data analysis applications, albeit narrowly. Increased data and compute power revived bigger approaches to AI. DARPA conducted the Grand Challenge for autonomous vehicles in 2005. In the late 2000s, important breakthroughs were made in machine learning (ML) via Support Vector Machines (SVM), Bayesian networks, Hidden Markov Models (HMM), and advancements in NLP, laying the groundwork for the next phase of AI.

## 1.2 TYPES OF AI

Based on the functionality and capability to perform different tasks, AI can be divided into various types:

### *Narrow or Weak AI*

Narrow AI refers to systems that are programmed to perform very specific, well-defined tasks as opposed to having general intelligence. Narrow AI excels at the single task it is designed for, though it has no flexibility to handle tasks outside that narrow domain. For example, chatbots are a form of narrow AI that can communicate intelligently with humans, understand questions and provide answers on a range of customer service topics. A chatbot could have stimulating conversations about products, services, orders, complaints and recommendations.

However, if questions shift to unrelated topics like astrophysics discoveries or celebrity gossip, the chatbot would falter. It cannot transfer knowledge or skills outside its training domain to exhibit versatile intelligence. It is narrowly focused on a single application area.

While narrow AI already contributes tremendous value in targeted applications today, the dream of multi-talented general AI still remains distant.

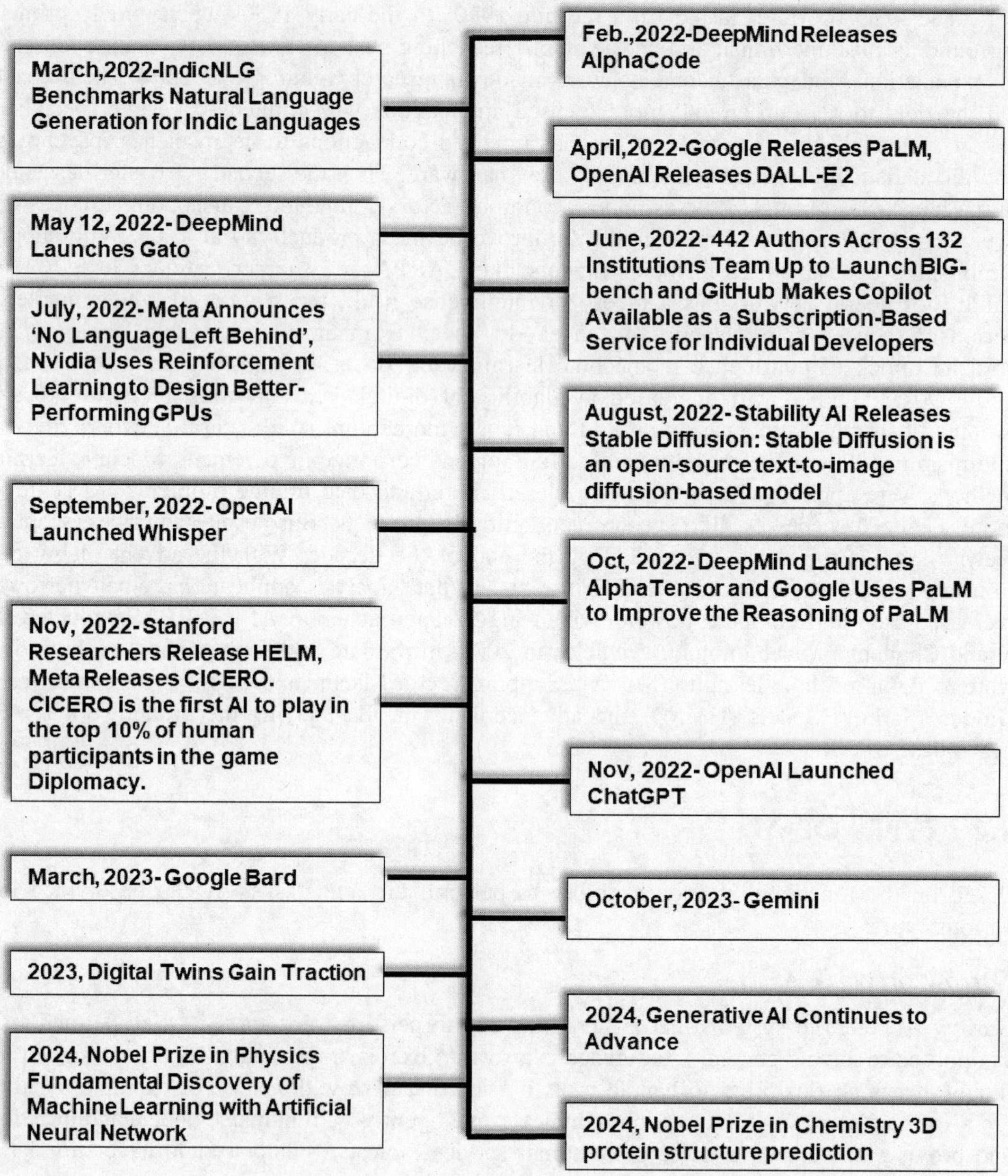


**FIGURE 1.2** Evolution of AI from 2022 to 2024

### General or Strong AI

General AI refers to machines that have broad intelligent capabilities and versatility matching or exceeding human cognition. For instance, if a computer scientist, doctor, lawyer and mechanic each spent year learning their respective fields, a machine with artificial general intelligence could learn all these disciplines to a similar level of mastery. It could gain expertise by analysing textbooks, research papers, case files and manuals the way humans learn—identifying concepts, remembering details, recognizing patterns and making inferences. Such an adaptable machine could combine knowledge across these diverse areas to solve multi-faceted problems. This ability to transfer learning across domains and bring together different bodies of knowledge to handle novel, open-ended situations is a signature of flexible general AI that narrow AI still lacks today. Experts believe continuing incremental breakthroughs across AI accelerating progress on perception, reasoning, abstraction, social intelligence and more could someday culminate in the emergence of this kind of broadly competent artificial general intelligence rivalling the cognitive abilities humans derive from our versatile biological brains.

### Artificial Superintelligence (ASI)

An AI that significantly surpasses human cognition in all respects is referred to as artificial super intelligence, or ASI. This is seen as the ultimate goal of developing artificial intelligence, while being one of the most futuristic notions. Although many situations involving artificial super intelligence have previously been imagined, the technology is currently only a notion. In the subject, experts generally agree that ASI will result from the 'Intelligence Explosion' or the exponential growth of AI algorithms. It is an explosion of intelligence, as the name implies, from general artificial intelligence at the human level to an incredible intelligence. Recursive self-improvement is the means by which this happens.

The above types are primarily based on the capability of an AI system. Based on functionality, AI can be further divided to various types as given below.

### Reactive Machines

Reactive machines are the most fundamental AI systems that essentially react automatically to inputs from the environment via simple direct mappings without any ability to form internal representations or memory of previous events. They operate through straightforward stimulus-response without any understanding or context.

A common example is basic AI chatbots that have a set of rules like 'If user says Hi, reply with Hello'. Whenever they receive a 'Hi' input, they will spit out the matched 'Hello' response automatically without any comprehension of the conversation. Even if you just had a long chat, if you say Hi, the fixed 'Hello' will come. Other reactive AI examples include things like computer chess games that can play by calculating best moves but don't have any concept of an ongoing chess match.

### Limited Memory Machines

Limited memory AI systems have the ability to accumulate some contextual data over time, analyse it with algorithms, and use it to optimize their performance - but only within narrowly defined purposes rather than general intelligence.

A common example is a shopping website that can recommend you products to buy based on your browsing and purchase history. It remembers which categories and items you showed interest in, at what prices etc. and uses that data to offer personalized suggestions that you are likely to enjoy. However, that data is only used within the shopping domain. Self-driving cars, for instance, employ a kind of limited memory to detect and react to incoming vehicles, change course, and change speed. However, because their recollection of past events is restricted and only employed in a smaller time frame, machines with limited memory are unable to acquire a thorough picture of the world.

### *Theory of Mind*

Theory of mind refers to the ability of an intelligent system to understand and model the mental states of people—like desires, beliefs, intentions, emotions etc. This allows the system to understand humans at a deeper level and interpret or predict behaviour based on attributed mental states.

For example, think of a robot nurse named Florence assisting patients in a hospital. Beyond just monitoring medical stats, Florence could use algorithms to understand patient anxieties about an upcoming surgery based on verbal and non-verbal cues and console them by explaining details about operation risks and outcomes. Similarly, for a needy patient unable to afford treatment, the robot may partially cover costs based on perceiving patient desperation.

### *Self-aware AI*

Self-aware machines refer to hypothetical future AI systems that have evolved a sense of self and consciousness—an ability to introspectively model and understand their own thought processes, knowledge and existence as independent entities. For example, an advanced robot named Cleo that has developed self-aware AI could continuously analyse its functionality, strengths and limitations from interactions with the physical world. When faced with an unfamiliar object, Cleo may even ask itself questions like: 'What exactly am I looking at?', 'How does my computer vision system represent this?', 'What concepts in my knowledge base relate to this?'. With no pre-existing labelling, categories or programming to recognize the object, the introspective questioning and meta-cognition about its own capabilities can guide the robot to learn autonomously through self-directed experiments. This sense of internal inquisitiveness and agency reflects emergent consciousness.

## 1.3 AI-AGENTS AND ENVIRONMENTS

AI agents are intelligent systems that interact with environments to pursue defined goals and tasks. They utilize sensors to perceive environment states in the form of observable variables like positions, temperatures, velocities etc. Agents then perform actions via effectors that impact environments by altering those states—for example, a robot moving objects or a smart thermostat adjusting temperatures. Environments provide feedback on actions taken—rewards for goal progress, penalties for illegal actions etc. Additionally, environments have transition rules and logic governing how states change based on agent actions and other dynamics like physics. Multiagent environments feature multiple agents interacting, often competitively or collaboratively towards their own interests. For an agent to excel, it must assess state transitions after actions to select optimal moves towards favourable outcomes and goal achievement, iterating through a perceive-act-learn cycle. The complexity, uncertainty and information accessibility of an environment determines the reasoning sophistication required. Games have fully observable states while the real-world poses partial observability challenges. Analysis of interactions between agents and environments provides insights into designing smarter systems. The key ideas are the paired dynamics of agents perceiving and modifying environments which in turn provide evaluative feedback, propelling iterative agent learning and decision optimization.

### 1.3.1 Terminologies

In the field of AI, the concepts of an agent and its environment serve as foundational pillars for comprehending the intricate dynamics through which AI systems engage with the external world and arrive at informed decisions. In this discourse, we shall embark upon an exploration of these fundamental concepts.

#### *Agents*

The agent serves as the fundamental building block of an AI system. The term 'agent' encompasses a broad range of entities, including both software programmes and physical robots, which possess the remarkable ability to perceive their surroundings, analyse and interpret incoming information, and subsequently execute actions with the purpose of accomplishing predefined objectives. Agents are meticulously crafted entities that possess the remarkable ability to make informed decisions and execute actions by leveraging their astute observations and vast reservoirs of knowledge. The main components in agents includes the following:

**Sensors:** The agents can detect or comprehend elements of their surroundings with help of sensors. Depending on what the agent is used for, these sensors could include cameras, microphones, temperature sensors, and more.

**Actuators:** The agents can control their surroundings or conduct activities with actuators. Any device that enables the agent to influence its environment falls under this category, including motors, speakers, wheels, and so on.

**Perception and Thought:** In order to choose the optimum course of action, the agent's internal systems analyse sensory data and employ reasoning or decision-making algorithms.

**Targets and Goals:** Agents are created with predetermined aims in mind, which direct their decision-making. These refers to the targets and goals of the agents.

**Environment:** The agents are surrounded by the environment and sensors where actuators act as the bridge between them. All the inputs to the agents are being transmitted through the environment. These surroundings, either real or virtual, are dynamic and subject to alter throughout time. The environment can be categorised into various types based on which the agents can behave to solve a task. Some of these categories are as follows:

1. ***Stochastic and Deterministic:*** A stochastic environment has random components or uncertainty due to which the agents cannot determine the next step of action. Whereas, a deterministic environment adheres to predictable principles. The next executive step is known to the agent in a deterministic environment.
2. ***Dynamic and Static:*** A dynamic environment is one which changes frequently or evolves over time when the agent is undergoing some actions. Whereas, a static environment does not over time, it is mostly idle with no state change.
3. ***Continuous and Discrete:*** For a continuous environment, there are endless number of options to reach the final state and is generally continuous in nature. In a discrete environment, there are a finite number of states or activities which are to be performed to reach the final state.
4. ***Partially Observable and Observable:*** In the event of a partially observable, the environment could conceal some characteristics from the agent, forcing it to rely on educated assumptions. However, in an observable event, the environment allows the agent to completely observe its current state.
5. ***Sequential and Episodic:*** In sequential environment, the past decisions by the agent may have an impact on its future course of action. In an episodic environment, the current or future states are unrelated to earlier ones. Each action is divided to smaller sets of actions or incidents without any dependency on the past acts.
6. ***Competitive and Collaborative:*** A competitive environment, one competes with another agent to optimize the output. In collaborative on the other hand, the agents work cooperatively with each other to avoid any collision event and produce the desired output.

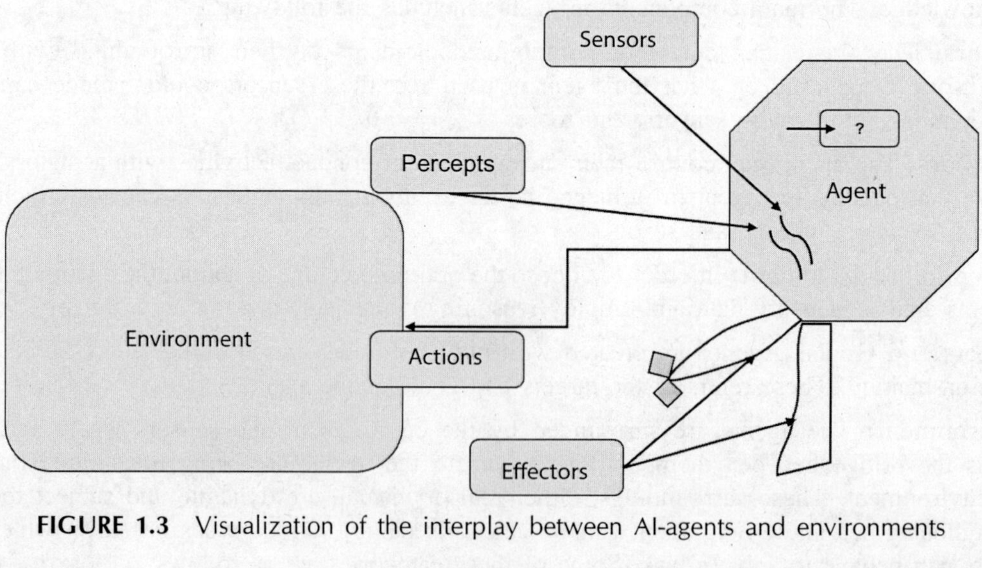


**FIGURE 1.3** Visualization of the interplay between AI-agents and environments

## 1.3.2 Types of Agent Programs

### *Simple-Reflex Agents*

A simple reflex agent is the preliminary type of AI agent with very little intelligence. It just acts automatically based on what it is currently sensing from the environment using hard-coded conditional rules without any deeper understanding. It does not have any memory or model of the environment dynamics. An example is a temperature regulation device that turns the heater on whenever the room temp falls below 20°C based on the sensor input and turns it off upon reaching 25°C. It has no concept of the home's layout, the outdoor weather forecast or occupants' comfort. Reflex agents have minimal cognitive abilities to contextualize perceptions into informed actions. They purely react to immediate stimuli similar to innate biological reflexes rather than exhibiting true intelligence. While modern AI has moved towards much more sophisticated goal-based and learning-based agents that can optimize behaviours over time, reflex agents illustrate the basic stimulus-response principles from where intelligence evolution begins.

Simple-reflex agents, despite their inherent limitations in decision-making capabilities, play a pivotal role as a fundamental concept in intelligent agents and AI research. These intelligent agents demonstrate exceptional performance in environments characterized by precisely defined rules and unambiguous cause-and-effect relationships. As a result, they are particularly well-suited for tasks that require rapid and accurate responses to stimuli.

### *Reflex Agent with Internal State (Model-based reflex)*

Unlike basic reflex agents that just map perceptions to actions through hard-coded rules, model-based reflex agents maintain an internal symbolic model that reflects the agent's current understanding of the environment dynamics. This allows the agent to keep track of aspects like past states, possible transitions and projections without having to directly experience or perceive all information at every point. For example, a vacuum cleaning robot that maps outlines of rooms and obstacles creates a model of the floor plan. If it did not perceive any obstructions in the last few meters, it can estimate its current location based on the expected motions rather than having to rescan the vicinity again. The model essentially serves as an abbreviated informational snapshot of the environment from the agent's perspective to promote more informed actions. However, unlike more advanced goal-based agents, model-based reflex agents still lack objectives and only respond reflexively to inputs rather than planning ahead. So, while their internalized representations and memory improve responsiveness, it is still reactive and not driven by higher goals. But model-based reflexive reasoning marks an advancement towards deliberative intelligence in agents.

### *Goal-based Agents*

Goal-based agents are more intelligent AI systems that can pursue specific objectives or desirable situations in the environment proactively. In addition to sensors that recognize the current state of the environment, goal-based agents are also equipped with a capability to distinguish certain states they want to achieve. In contrast to reflex agents, which solely respond to immediate percepts, goal-based agents adopt a more sophisticated approach by considering not only the present state, but also possessing a clearly defined objective or goal that they actively pursue.

These agents utilise a synergistic amalgamation of perception, knowledge, and reasoning capabilities to strategically devise and execute a meticulously curated series of actions, ultimately propelling them towards the attainment of their intended objective. The adoption of a goal-driven approach empowers individuals to navigate and thrive in ever-changing environments, enabling them to make informed decisions that consider the far-reaching implications of their actions.

The inherent capability of goal-based agents to effectively adapt to a diverse array of scenarios stands as a prominent strength. Goal-oriented agents frequently utilise search algorithms and planning methodologies to systematically investigate and assess potential action sequences, thereby enabling them to identify optimal or nearly optimal solutions for accomplishing their desired objectives. With a well-defined objective, these intelligent agents possess the capability to effectively allocate resources and make decisions by prioritising their actions according to their perceived significance in achieving the desired outcome. This approach enables them to optimise resource utilisation and enhance the efficiency of their decision-making process.

### *Utility-based Agents*

Utility-based agents are a sophisticated type of artificial intelligence system that make decisions based on maximizing an expected "utility" or benefit measure. They expand on simple goal-based agents by ranking different world states according to a quantified utility function tied to the agent's preferences and objectives. In contrast to their goal-based counterparts, utility-based agents possess the remarkable ability to effectively navigate complex scenarios characterized by the presence of multiple objectives, each endowed with distinct levels of significance. Decisions are made through a systematic evaluation of the anticipated utility derived from various potential courses of action, while simultaneously considering the probabilities associated with different outcomes.

Utility-based agents possess a multitude of advantageous qualities, among which their remarkable aptitude for making decisions in intricate, uncertain, and ever-changing environments stands out prominently. Through the process of assigning numerical values to various states or outcomes, utility-based agents possess the capability to engage in quantitative comparisons among different options. This capability enables individuals to effectively navigate complex scenarios characterized by inherent trade-offs among divergent objectives. The inherent versatility and applicability of machine learning algorithms render them invaluable in a myriad of real-world contexts, spanning from economic resource allocation to decision-making within autonomous systems.

**TABLE 1.1** Classification of various environments with real life examples

| *Environment* | *Accessible* | *Deterministic* | *Episodic* | *Static* | *Discrete* |
|---|---|---|---|---|---|
| Chess with a clock | Yes | Yes | No | Semi | Yes |
| Chess without a clock | Yes | Yes | No | Yes | Yes |
| Poker | No | No | No | Yes | Yes |
| Backgammon | Yes | No | No | Yes | Yes |
| Taxi driving | No | No | No | No | No |
| Medical diagnosis system | No | No | No | No | No |
| Image-analysis system | Yes | Yes | Yes | Semi | No |

### 1.3.3 Structure of Intelligent Agents

The agents in AI are the entity that makes decisions and activates in the environment with help of actuators. These are often coined as intelligent agents as they have the ability to learn while performing the tasks. These intelligent agents comprise of four major components—percepts, action, environment and goals.

#### *Percepts*

Percepts refer to an agent's sensations and perspective of its environment. This includes visual feeds, text data, speech inputs, and other digital representations captured through cameras, microphones, instruments and other sensors. Percepts form the lens through which agents obtain observable information about states, entities and events in their environments to drive cognition and decision making. The quality and scope of percepts shapes what phenomena the agent can reason about and respond to through actions.

#### *Action*

An agent's actions refer to the set of executable behaviours and interventions it can perform on environments using effectors. This includes capabilities like physical motion, object manipulation, computation, digital communication etc. Actions make up an agent's repertoire to deliberately alter states and processes beyond its own computational boundaries in environments. More capable effectors and algorithms to map contexts to productive actions support more sophisticated agency and impact.

#### *Environment*

Intelligent agents are inherently built to operate in environments—the external worlds encapsulating domains, constraints and affairs they monitor and act upon. This can range from limited games to expansive real-world spaces. Environments provide the changing backdrop of states, entities and dynamics that agents must model, predict and interact with using actions guided by goals. Responsive environments that react to actions based on interpretable rules and contingencies enable evaluative feedback.

#### *Goals and Decisions*

Goals supply agent's directive by defining systemic objectives they must strive towards, impose constraints and determine success criteria. Whether implicitly optimized or explicitly stored, goals encode the purposes, intents, desirable states and functions that contextualize an agent's reasoning and behaviour within environments. Expanding goal representations and reasoning techniques support increasingly complex purposeful agency. But goal-directedness is essence of intelligence. Based on decision and goals met, further decision may be taken by the intelligent accordingly.

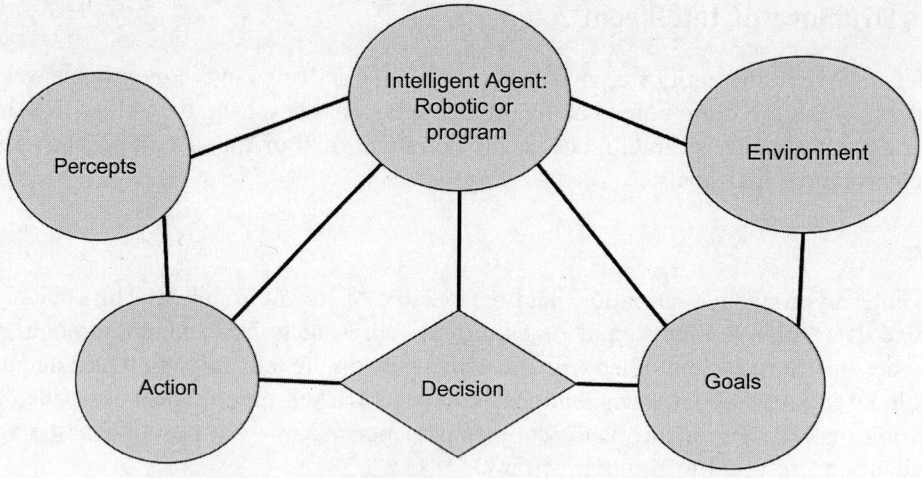


**FIGURE 1.4** General structure of Intelligent Agents

## 1.4 PROBLEM FORMULATION AND SOLVING

Problem solving in AI primarily consists of various stages where an agent tries to reach the goals. These goals help to decide the actions to be performed by the agents which is also known as problem formulation. A problem in AI has five main components—the initial state, actions, transition model, goal test and finally the path cost. An agent who is intended to solve a problem starts with the initial state and carries out all the actions that are available with it. The transition model describes what each action can do which is generally a function that returns the result of an action. These three components i.e. initial state, actions and transition model defines the state space of a problem. The goal test measures whether the current state achieved by the agent is goal state or not. Once the goal state is reached, a numeric cost is assigned to each path as path cost which is used to find the optimal solution. The optimal solution will be the one with the least path cost. Problems like 8-puzzle, 8-queen problems, vacuum world are some toy problems that are solved using AI agents.

### 1.4.1 Solving Problems through Searching

Once a problem has been formulated, it needs to be solved through a proper solution. The solution consists of a sequence of all the possible sequences. These sequences are the leads to form a search tree from initial state to goal state by expanding the current states of the agents. Finally, using the path cost the most optimal solution is arrived at. There can be many ways or algorithms to solve the same problem, however, each can have a different performance factor which is measured by factors like completeness (is there a guaranteed solution?), optimality (is the solution optimal?), time complexity (time to find the optimal solution) and space complexity (memory required to find the solution). For measuring the efficiency of a search algorithm, search cost (based on time complexity) is generally used, however, total cost (search cost and path cost) can also be used. There are several search strategies available in AI which can be broadly categorized to uninformed search or blind search and informed search or heuristic search. For each of these strategies there are several algorithms which are executed to solve a problem.

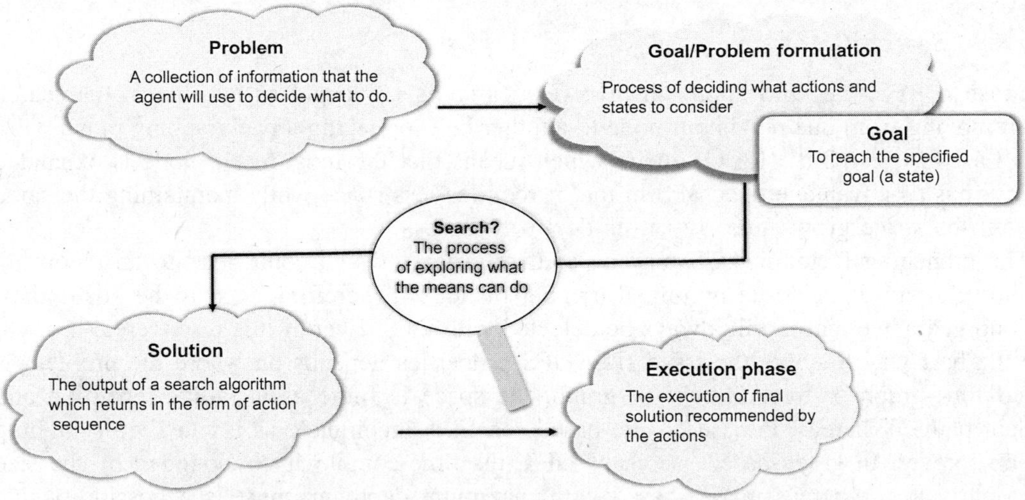


FIGURE 1.5 Representation of solving problems in AI by Searching

## *Uninformed Search*

Uninformed search, commonly referred to as blind search, serves as a means to locate a solution within a problem space devoid of any supplementary knowledge pertaining to the states or their interconnections. The search strategy employed in this particular approach is known as systematic exploration of the state space. It entails considering each potential option in a uniform manner, without any bias or preference, until either a solution is discovered or all possible alternatives have been thoroughly examined and deemed unviable. Some of the major search strategies under this scheme are breadth-first search (BFS), depth-first search (DFS), and depth-limited search.

### *Breadth-First Search (BFS)*

In BFS, the expansion starts with the root node and moves on to its successors. Until the last successor is achieved, the procedure is iterated. In general, 'First In, First Out' (FIFO) is used to implement BFS search technique. If the branching factor, $b < \infty$, and the shallow goal node is located at the depth $d < \infty$, then during traversal, the following set of nodes are generated,

$$b^1 + b^2 + b^3 + \cdots + b^n = O(b^d) \tag{1.1}$$

The shallowest node located at $d < \infty$ will be reached only after generating other shallow nodes which are not the goal node.

If there exists at least one solution to the problem, then the BFS strategy will always arrive at it making it complete in nature. But, if there are multiple solutions to the same problem, then a set of solutions can be found with the least expensive being the first priority. Due to its nature of traversal, there will never be a situation with BFS when exploring a branch is infinitely deep, but at the cost of time and space which will increases with the branching factor. The space requirement is a bigger problem in BFS than the time. Also, if the depth search space is very high, such problems turn exponentially complex and thus cannot be solved by any uninformed search algorithms.

### *Depth-First Search (DFS)*

In contrast to BFS, the DFS approach involves searching as deeply as feasible in the search tree, but moving from one neighbour node to another before making a backtracking move. DFS uses a 'Last In, First Out' (LIFO) queue which means that the most recent node is expanded first. DFS has an advantage over BFS in that it requires less space while maintaining the same depth, but the space grows linearly as the depth increases.

The branching factor in DFS may be endlessly deep, which could lead to an algorithm that follows a path if there are unlimited number of nodes. Therefore, even if the goal exists, there is no guarantee that it will always be detected with DFS. Even if it is discovered, it might not be the best way to solve the issue. The DFS properties depends on where the problem is searched for—graph or tree. In case of graph, the space is finite as it avoids repetition and redundant paths. Whereas, in case of tree-based search is incomplete as it can keep searching in a loop forever. In graph-based search of DFS, the time-complexity is bounded by the size of the state space, whereas in tree-based with maximum depth m, there is a possibility that all the nodes $O(b^m)$ are generated in the search tree. Backtracking search is a variant of DFS where only one successor is generated at a time making space complexity $O(m)$ instead of $O(b^m)$. For tasks involving large state space, these methods are highly successful.

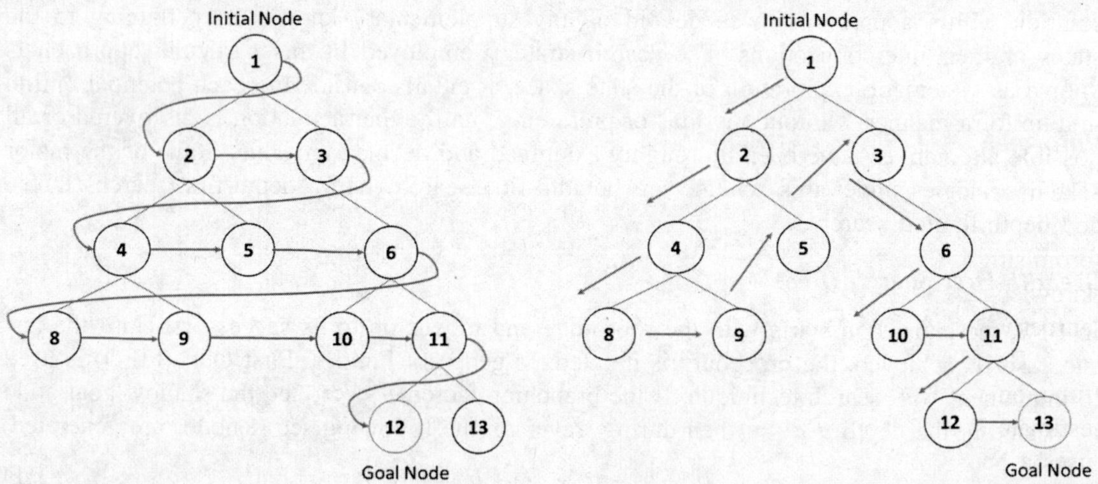


**FIGURE 1.6** Node expansion using (A) breadth-first search strategy and (B) depth-first search strategy.

### *Depth-Limited Search*

The main difference between the depth-limited search and DFS is that the former has a set depth limit ($l$) before beginning the search, while the latter has no such limit and can search indefinitely.

Depth-limited search is an answer to the problem of infinite search space in DFS. However, if the actual depth (*d*) is not known, then for a situation where $l < d$, will result into a source of incompleteness. The time and space complexity of depth-limited search is $O(b^l)$ and $O(bl)$, respectively. Besides these strategies, there are also other search methods like uniform cost search, iterative deepening DFS and bidirectional search under uniformed search.

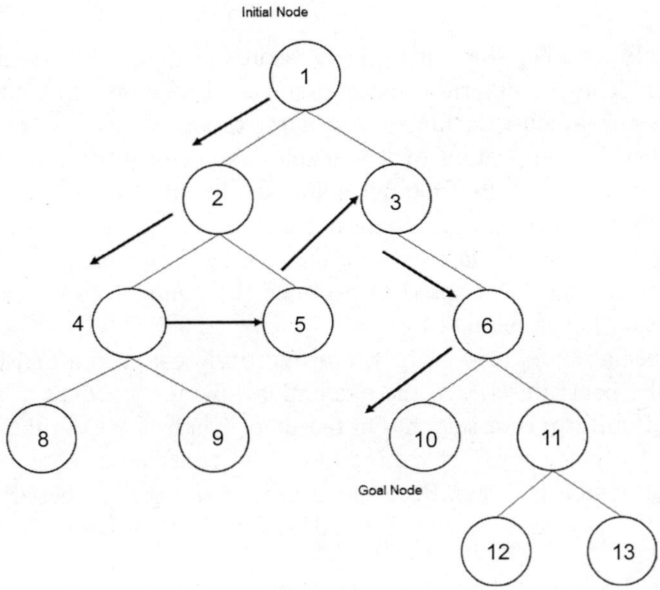


**FIGURE 1.7** Node expansion using depth-limited search strategy with depth = 2.

### *Informed Search*

The main idea behind informed search or heuristic search, is to use the supplementary information, known as heuristics, to drive the search process towards regions within state space that hold promising results. In contrast to uninformed search techniques, which operate without any prior knowledge of the problem at hand, informed search methods leverage heuristics to gauge the attractiveness of various states and subsequently allocate exploration efforts accordingly.

Best-first search is a conventional approach of informed search which uses an evaluation function $f(n)$ to select the node for expansion. This function $f(n)$ is dependent on the cost estimate of the nodes, thus one with the lowest cost is selected first. Best-first search strategy uses a heuristic function $h(n)$ such that, $h(n)$ = projected path cost (cheapest) from the initial state of node $n$ to the goal state. This heuristic function $h(n)$ is the additional information of the problem that is provided to the search algorithm.

### *Greedy Best-First Search*

This search strategy aims at expanding the nearest node towards the goal, which is somewhat similar to the BFS method. Here, the heuristic function itself is used for evaluating the node i.e. $f(n) = h(n)$ which specifies the projected cost from the specific node to the goal. The ideal solution to the problem is searched using the heuristic values from $h(n)$, but unfortunately, the optimal solution is not guaranteed. Because this technique is recursive, care must be taken when implementing it to prevent an infinite loop. The worst-case time as well as space complexity is $O(b^m)$ with m as the highest depth but can be substantially reduced with a proper heuristic function.

### *A* Algorithm*

On of the most widely used best-first (not greedy) search technique by researchers and scientists is the A* algorithm. The A* algorithm seamlessly integrates the strengths of BFS and DFS methodologies by using a heuristic function to approximate the cost of reaching desired goal from any given state. The utilization of A* enables the prioritization of states that exhibit a higher likelihood of leading to the optimal solution, thereby facilitating a more streamlined and efficient search process. The evaluation function of A* algorithm is represented by $f(n) = g(n) + h(n)$, where for the last node $n$, the cost of entire path till nth node is $g(n)$ and $h(n)$ represents the heuristic that is used to estimate the complete traversal cost. The optimal cost of reaching a solution is defined by $f(n)$.

Among the special cases of A* algorithm, uniform cost search and best-first search are quite common. If the heuristic $h(n)$ in the evaluation function is equal to 0, then $f(n) = g(n)$, which is the case of uniform cost search. On the other hand, if $g(n)$ in the evaluation function is equal to 0, then we get again $f(n) = h(n)$, which is considered to be best-first search. A* search is exhaustive, which is a significant advantage that a greedy best-first search approach lacks. As a result, the objective of an informed search strategy is satisfied by the A* search technique.

The optimality of A* algorithm can be arrived with two conditions, first admissible heuristics where the heuristic function will not overestimate the cost to reach the goal. Second is consistency or monotonicity, where the successors $(n')$ of each node n, is generated by an action such that the estimated cost of reaching the goal from n is always less than the summation of step cost and estimated cost for reaching $n'$. Mathematically,

$$h(n) \leq c(n, a, n') + h(n') \tag{1.2}$$

For problems where the step costs are constant, growth in runtime is analyzed by two factors – absolute error and relative error. The absolute error is the difference between actual cost of getting the root $(h^*)$ and the heuristic $(\Delta \equiv h^* - h)$, whereas the relative error is defined by $(\varepsilon = (h^* - h)h^*)$. For a single goal problem, where the state space can be represented as a tree, the time complexity is $O(b^{\Delta})$. Whereas, for constant step cost problem, the complexity is $O(b^{\varepsilon d})$ where d is the solution depth. Interestingly, computation time is not a factor to be worried for A* search algorithm, but memory definitely is. This make A* impractical for large scale complex problems. Two variants of A*, memory-bound (MA*) and simplified MA* (SMA*) are generally used to overcome the memory issue of this search algorithm.

## 1.4.2 Game Playing and Adversarial Search

Game playing serves as a central point to integrate and converge strategic decision-making, search algorithms, and adversarial reasoning. It encompasses development of sophisticated intelligent agents that possess the ability to make optimal or near-optimal decisions within competitive environments. The primary objective is to design and train these agents to exhibit superior performance and strategic thinking, thereby enabling them to outperform human players. Formally, a 'game' can be defined as a search problem which consists of the following:

- Initial state ($s_0$) to specify how the game should start
- Player(s) which has the control in a state
- Action(s) or a set of moves
- Result ($s$, $a$) defined by a transition model
- Terminal-test(s) which defines the end of a game
- Utility ($s$, $p$) function which assigns a score (a numeric value) for the in terminal state '$s$' for a player '$p$'

Game playing serves as a prime example that highlights the complex balance between exploration and exploitation. In this context, intelligent agents are confronted with the formidable task of traversing expansive state spaces in order to ascertain the optimal course of action.

At the core of AI, game playing lies the pivotal notion of adversarial search, a fundamental technique employed by intelligent agents to devise strategies that surpass their adversaries. Adversarial search, a fundamental principle within the AI and game theory, delves into the details of decision-making within competitive environments, wherein multiple agents are driven by divergent objectives. This particular search methodology finds extensive application in strategic games like 'Chess', 'Go', and 'Poker', wherein participants engage in a turn-based manner to execute moves with the primary objective of surpassing their opponents. The fundamental concept revolves around the construction of a comprehensive game tree that encapsulates every conceivable sequence of moves and counter-moves. By evaluating the consequences of various strategies, one can ascertain the optimal course of action. Adversarial search algorithms are designed to ascertain an optimal or nearly optimal strategy for an agent by considering the decisions and potential counter-strategies of the opponent.

### *Mini-max Algorithm*

The minimax algorithm, a fundamental technique of adversarial search rooted in game theory, aims to optimize decision-making in scenarios involving two opposing entities. By analyzing the potential outcomes of each possible move, the mini-max algorithm enables intelligent agents to make strategic choices that maximize their own gains while simultaneously minimizing the potential losses incurred. The underlying principle of this approach is embedded in the assumption that the opponent will exhibit optimal decision-making behaviour. Consequently, the objective is to strategically minimize the adversary's maximum potential gain. The aforementioned approach entails the formulation of a strategic framework that aims to optimize the agent's likelihood of achieving favorable outcomes, under the assumption of flawless decision-making on the part of the adversary.

A game-tree with two players makes it simple to explain how the minimax algorithm operates. The two players are Maximizer and Minimizer. The Maximizer will try to acquire the maximum possible score whereas the minimizer will try to acquire the minimum possible score. As this algorithm uses DFS as base, all the intermediate nodes are to be traversed to reach the terminal node. The values are at the terminal node which will be compared and then backtracked until the initial state occurs. This algorithm is complete in nature and will be able to find the solution (if exist), in the finite search tree.

### *Alpha-beta Pruning*

The Alpha-beta pruning algorithm is an improved version and an optimization technique of the minimax algorithm. In decision trees, the term 'pruning' which refers to removing branches and leaves, is frequently used. Decision trees can grow extremely complex in certain situations, which is why pruning became necessary. A few unnecessary branches in that tree add to the model's complexity. Therefore, in order to prevent this, Alpha-Beta pruning is used to decrease the amount of time the computer spends examining the entire tree. The algorithm is slow because of these peculiar nodes. Hence, the algorithm gets faster by eliminating these nodes. The two threshold parameters alpha and beta used for future expansion of the tree can be defined as,

***Alpha:*** The finest choice or maximum value that has been found at any point along the path of Maximizer.

***Beta:*** The finest choice or minimum value that has been found at any point along the path of Minimizer. The initial value of alpha is $-\infty$ and beta is $+\infty$.

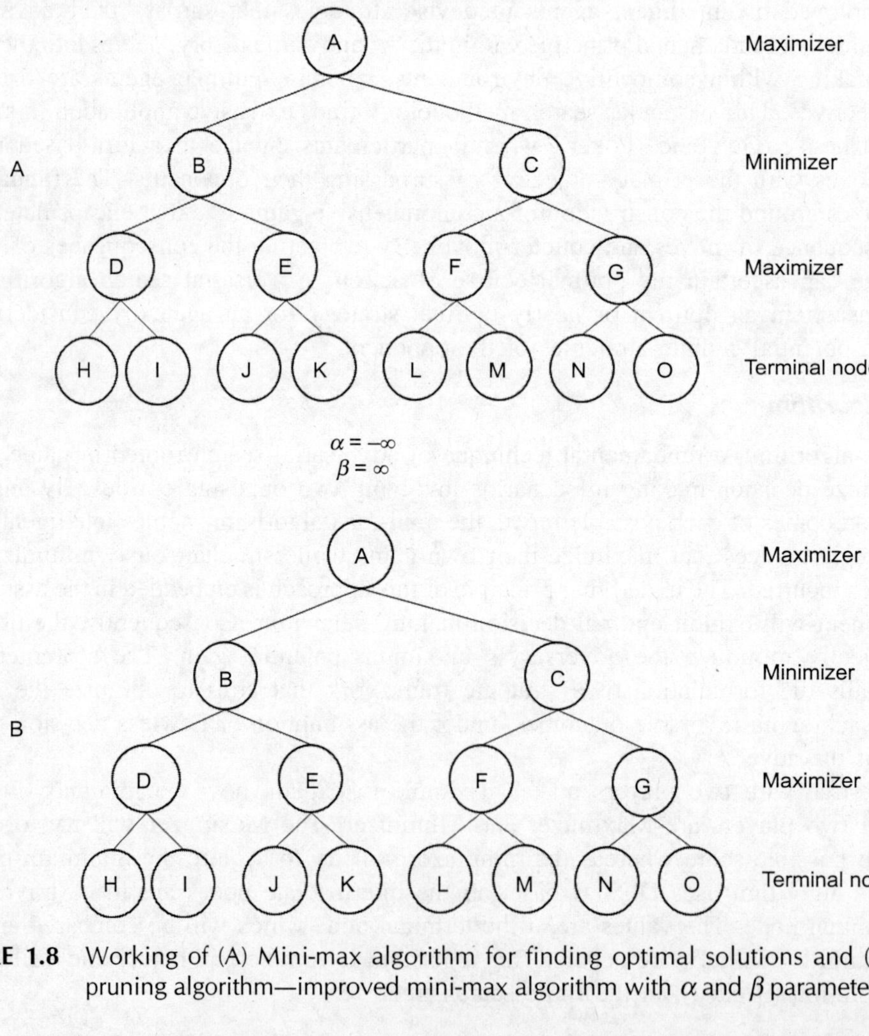


**FIGURE 1.8** Working of (A) Mini-max algorithm for finding optimal solutions and (B) Alpha-beta pruning algorithm—improved mini-max algorithm with $\alpha$ and $\beta$ parameters for pruning.

Alpha-beta pruning can be done on a tree at any depth, and in certain cases, the entire sub-tree as well as the tree's leaves are pruned. The effectiveness of this algorithm depends on the order in which the node is examined which is also known as move ordering. Move ordering can be done in two ways—worst ordering and ideal ordering. In worst ordering, not a single node is pruned by the algorithm thereby making it work like standard minimax algorithm. Due to the alpha-beta factors, this consumes a lot of time and also fails to give any effective results. In such a scenario, the best move occurs on the right side of the tree. In ideal ordering, a lot of nodes are pruned by the algorithm and the best move occurs on the left side of the tree. As it is based on DFS, it first searches the left part of the tree and then goes deeper (twice as minimax algorithm) in the same amount of time.

## 1.5 KNOWLEDGE REPRESENTATION AND REASONING

Among the fundamental pillars of AI, knowledge representation and reasoning provide the essential framework for constructing sophisticated intelligent systems. Knowledge representation involves the process of formulating information in a structured manner that enables machines to effectively perform various cognitive tasks such as decision-making, and natural language understanding, which are crucial for AI systems to exhibit intelligent behaviour. By representing knowledge in a suitable format, AI systems can efficiently process and manipulate information, enabling them to reason, learn, and interrelate with humans in a more sophisticated manner. Reasoning encompasses the cognitive process through which AI systems engage in the generation of logical inferences, deductions, and ultimately, the formulation of conclusions. This intricate mental operation relies on the wealth of knowledge that these systems have acquired, enabling them to navigate complex problem-solving scenarios. The primary objective of the process of reasoning is to effectively harness the encoded knowledge in order to attain well-founded and logical conclusions or resolutions to various problems or challenges.

### 1.5.1 Propositional Logic

Propositional logic is simple but has powerful implication in representation and manipulation of knowledge in a discrete and binary fashion in AI. Propositional logic also known as sentential logic is a fundamental branch of mathematical logic that deals with the construction of complex statements from atomic propositions. Propositional logic is used for representation of both simple sentences and complex sentences. For simple sentences, there are mainly two proposition symbols with fixed meanings—True: the proposition is always true and False: the proposition is always false. In case of complex sentences, which are generally formed with joining simpler sentences, logical operators such as conjunction (AND), disjunction (OR), negation (NOT), implication (if then) and bidirectional (if and only if) are used. By employing these operators one can create intricate logical structures that capture the essence of various real-world scenario.

Truth table plays an important role to understand simple logics—specifically in connection with Boolean algebra, functions, and propositional calculus. It has one column for each input variable (for example, P and Q) to show whether a propositional expression is true for all valid input values, or false otherwise. It fundamentally represents all the possible combination of logics (True and False) for these variables which can be later connected with logical connectives to derive a final output. Where P and Q will be simple sentences, they can be connected with the logical connectives to form a complex sentence.

**TABLE 1.2** Truth table with two variables *P* and *Q* with possible combinations of logical values

| *P* | *Q* |
|---|---|
| True | True |
| True | False |
| False | True |
| False | False |

Logical connectives are used to connect two simple propositions to make complex sentences.

**Conjunction (AND/∧):** It conjuncts' or adds two simple sentences. For example, let P = "Stephen is intelligent" and Q = "Stephen is hardworking" then the conjunction of P and Q (P ∧ Q) = "Stephen is intelligent and hardworking".

**Disjunction (OR/∨):** It is the disjunctions of disjuncts'. For example, let P = "Ritika is Doctor" and Q = "Ritika is Engineer" then the disjunction of P and Q (P ∨ Q) = "Ritika is a doctor or Engineer".

**Implication (if then/→):** These are also known as if-then rules. Let, P = "It is raining", and Q = "Ground is wet", so it is denoted as P → Q (read as "P implies Q") = "If it is raining, then the ground is wet."

**Bi-conditional (if an only if/⇔):** Combination of two conditional statements. Let, P = "I am not breathing" and Q = "I am dead", it can be represented as P ⇔ Q = "If I am not breathing, then I am dead".

**Negation (NOT/¬):** This connective makes a positive literal as negative and vice versa. If P = "I am alive" then ¬P = "I am not alive"

**TABLE 1.3** Logical equivalences (T: True; F: False)

| *Name* | *Equivalence* |
|---|---|
| Identity laws | P ∧ T ⇔ P<br>P ∨ F ⇔ P |
| Idempotent laws | P ∨ P ⇔ P<br>P ∧ F ⇔ P |
| Domination laws | P ∨ T ⇔ T<br>P ∧ F ⇔ F |
| Double negation laws | ¬ (¬P) ⇔ P |
| Commutative laws | P ∨ Q ⇔ Q ∨ P<br>P ∧ Q ⇔ Q ∧ P |
| Associative laws | (P ∨ Q) ∨ R ⇔ Q ∨ (P ∨ R)<br>(P ∧ Q) ∧ R ⇔ Q ∧ (P ∧ R) |
| Distributive laws | P ∨ (Q ∧ R) ⇔ (P ∨ Q) ∧ (P ∨ R)<br>P ∧ (Q ∨ R) ⇔ (P ∧ Q) ∨ (P ∧ R) |
| De Morgan's laws | ¬ (P ∧ Q) ⇔ ¬P ∨ ¬Q<br>¬ (P ∨ Q) ⇔ ¬P ∧ ¬Q |

The precise and coherent structure of propositional logic facilitates the utilisation of inference rules to derive logical conclusions based on pre-existing knowledge. The logical connectives derive a set of logical equivalence statements whose utilisation enables these agents to navigate complex scenarios and optimise their actions towards achieving desired outcomes. The significance of this aspect cannot be overstated in domains such as autonomous robotics, wherein agents are required to effectively traverse intricate environments and make informed decisions grounded in their comprehensive comprehension of the surrounding world.

### *First-Order Logic (FOL)*

The general syntax of natural language comprises of four major components—nouns, noun phrases, verbs and verb phrases. The nouns/noun phrases can be referred as objects and verbs/verb phrases as relations and some of the relations can also be directed to as functions. The augmentation of propositional logic is achieved through the incorporation of object-oriented concepts, relational structures, and quantification mechanisms, thereby enabling a more intricate and nuanced depiction of knowledge. First-order logic (FOL), commonly known as predicate logic is a formal system used to represent and reason about knowledge. Predicates play a crucial role in this logic by allowing us to express properties and relationships between objects. By utilising predicates, we can make statements that capture various characteristics and connections within a given domain. Additionally, variables are essential components in FOL as they enable us to make statements about entire classes of objects. By employing variables, we can generalise our assertions and reason about properties that hold true for a wide range of objects within a specific context.

The incorporation of quantifiers, denoted by symbols such as "∀" for universal quantification and "∃" for existential quantification, serve to augment the expressive capacity of formal languages. The universal quantifier is also known as "For all.." such that the expression ∀ × P will resemble a logical expression that P is true for every object x. For example, the sentence "All Scientist are humans" will be difficult to be depicted using propositional logic, but using FOL, it can be represented as ∀ × Scientists $(x)$ => Human $(x)$. There are also statements referring to "some" objects instead of every object as in universal quantifier. For example, "Some students become good doctors", in such case to represent it using universal quantifier is not possible. The existential quantifier fulfils the need, and can be represented as ∃ × Students $(x) \Rightarrow$ Doctors $(x)$.

Further, there is also a possibility of using nested quantifiers when required. The statement "Sisters are siblings" is complex to be represented with any quantifier, but with the concept of nested, it can be written as $\forall x\ \forall y$ Sisters $(x, y) \Rightarrow$ Siblings $(x, y)$. In another instance the sentence "There is someone who is ignored by everyone" can be represented as $\exists x \forall y$ Ignored $(x, y)$.

FOL allows for the formulation of statements pertaining to all objects within a given domain or the existence of particular objects. The indispensability of FOL in AI lies in its ability to represent intricate real-world domains with a remarkable level of precision and sophistication.

### 1.5.2 Logic and Inference

Logic and inference are two interrelated notions which play a crucial role in enabling intelligent systems to emulate human-like cognitive processes and make informed decisions based on available information. Logic, refers to the formal system of rules and principles that govern the validity and coherence of reasoning. It provides a structured framework for representing knowledge and expressing relationships between different pieces of information. The fundamental concepts of propositional logic and FOL have been discussed in the previous section.

Inference on the other hand, pertains to the process of deriving new insights or conclusions from existing knowledge or evidence. It relates to the cognitive procedure of formulating conclusions or extracting novel insights from preexisting data through the application of logical principles and deductive reasoning. The ability to extract implicit information is of utmost importance in facilitating informed decision-making and addressing intricate problems. By transcending the confines of explicit statements, we are empowered to delve deeper into the underlying context and uncover valuable insights.

The inference rules are used to generate valid arguments. They are applied to derive proofs in AI, which leads to the desired goal. Among all the connectives, implications play an important role in inference rules. There are various types of inference rules generated using the connectives.

Modus Ponens states that if $P$ and $P \to Q$ is true, then it can be assumed that $Q$ will be true and represented by,

$$Modus\ Ponens : \frac{P \to Q, P}{\therefore Q} \tag{1.3}$$

Modus Tollens states that if $P \to Q$ is true and $\neg Q$ is true, then $\neg P$ will also be true,

$$Modus\ Tollens : \frac{P \to Q, Q}{Q} \tag{1.4}$$

Hypothetical Syllogism states that if $P \to R$ is true whenever both $P \to Q$ and $Q \to R$ is true and can be represented as,

$$Hypothetical\ Syllogism : P \to Q; P \to R \therefore Q \to R \tag{1.5}$$

Disjunctive syllogism states that if $P \vee Q$ is true, and $\neg P$ is true, then $Q$ will also be true and can be represented as,

$$Disjunctive\ Syllogism : \frac{P \vee Q, \sim P}{Q} \tag{1.6}$$

Addition rule is one of the most common inference rules which states that if $P$ is true, then $P \vee Q$ will be true. It can be represented as,

$$Addition : \frac{P}{P \vee Q} \tag{1.7}$$

Simplification rule states that if $P \wedge Q$ is true, then $Q$ or $P$ will also be true and can be represented as,

$$Simplification : \frac{P \wedge Q}{P}\ or\ \frac{P \wedge Q}{Q} \tag{1.8}$$

### 1.5.3 Quantifying Uncertainty and Probability

The knowledge representation through propositional logic or FOL is possible when there is certainty about the predicates. But there may be cases when the surety of a statement $P$ or $Q$ to be true or false is unknown which may be due to ignorance, unreliable information, errors and faults leading to the fact of uncertainty. In order to quantify uncertainty, probability theory serves as a fundamental instrument offering a robust framework for ascribing probabilities to various outcomes and gauging the plausibility of events.

***Probabilistic Reasoning***

Probabilistic reasoning plays a crucial role in tackling the pervasive uncertainty inherent in numerous real-world situations. These probabilities serve as quantitative measures that effectively capture the likelihood of various outcomes. The adoption of this approach becomes particularly pivotal in scenarios characterised by the presence of incomplete or noisy data, thereby posing significant obstacles to the generation of deterministic predictions. The probability of an uncertain event can be found by computing,

$$Probability\,(P) = \frac{No.\,of\ desired\ outcomes}{Total\ no.\,of\ outcomes} \tag{1.9}$$

***Probabilistic Reasoning Can Solve a Problem in Two Ways:*** Bayes' Rule and Bayesian reasoning. The Bayes' rule is one of the central theorems in probability theory which allows updating probabilities based on new evidence. It provides an ethical way to add prior knowledge with new data to update the probabilities of diverse outcomes. Bayes' rule has been extensively used in AI for solving problems related to classification, prediction, and decision-making tasks where uncertainty needs to be addressed. Bayes' rule can be represented by,

$$P(A \mid B) = \frac{(P(B \mid A) \times P(A))}{P(B)} \tag{1.10}$$

Bayesian probability theory or Bayesian reasoning offers a systematic and rigorous framework for the revision of beliefs in light of fresh evidence. Bayesian networks, which serve as graphical depictions of probabilistic relationships, offer immense value when it comes to modelling complex and uncertain domains.

### 1.5.4 Ontologies

Ontologies are fundamental frameworks for the systematic organisations and representation of knowledge within a particular domain. A comprehensive and precise representation of the concepts, entities, and relationships pertaining to a specific domain is furnished by formal ontologies, thereby facilitating enhanced information retrieval, reasoning, and decision-making capabilities. By utilizing ontologies, the AI systems are empowered to comprehend and manipulate intricate information in a methodical and organised fashion. They play a crucial role in enabling effective communication and knowledge exchange among various components within AI systems, as well as across a wide range of applications.

One such application is natural language processing (NLP), where ontologies facilitate the comprehension of the contextual nuances and semantic implications inherent in words, sentences, and documents. A structured framework is offered by these models to effectively map linguistic expressions to their corresponding underlying concepts. This capability empowers AI systems to proficiently execute a range of tasks, including sentiment analysis, entity recognition, and semantic parsing. This enables NLP based systems to make well-informed decisions, offer expert advice, and effectively tackle intricate problems across diverse fields such as healthcare, finance, engineering, and information retrieval.

### 1.5.5 Temporal Reasoning

Temporal reasoning encompasses the intricate handling, manipulation, and logical deduction pertaining to temporal information. This type of reasoning plays a vital role in diverse array of applications, spanning from the domains of scheduling and planning to the realms of natural language comprehension and robotics. It enables AI systems to effectively simulate and comprehend the intricate dynamics of time-dependent phenomena occurring in the physical realm. Consequently, these systems gain the ability to engage in sophisticated reasoning processes that encompass the analysis of past occurrences, the understanding of present circumstances, and the prediction of future states and events.

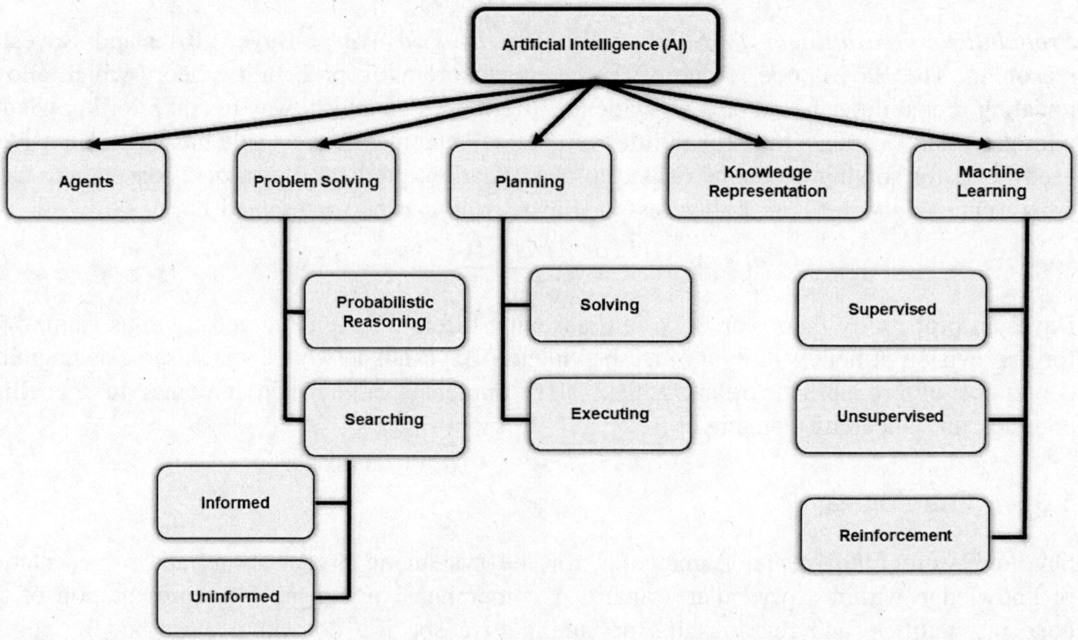


FIGURE 1.9 The Ontology of AI.

Temporal reasoning involves various methodologies for analyzing and interpreting time-dependent phenomena, with qualitative and quantitative approaches being prominent among them

The field of qualitative temporal reasoning is dedicated to the study and analysis of temporal relations, specifically those pertaining to the concepts of "before," "after," and "simultaneous."

Quantitative temporal reasoning, in contrast, encompasses the meticulous quantification of time intervals and durations. The precise timing and synchronisation of events play a crucial role in domains that demand meticulous attention, especially in real-time systems or applications that revolve around physical processes. Temporal reasoning techniques have a wide range of applications across various domains, showcasing their versatility and significance. These techniques are particularly valuable in automated planning, task and resource scheduling, event recognition, and temporal logic-based verification of systems.

### 1.5.6 Knowledge Representation

The concept of knowledge representation in AI focuses on the cognitive processes of AI agents and how these processes influence their actions. It gives a computer a representation of real-world data so that it can comprehend and apply this knowledge to solve challenging real-world issues like voice recognition, speech translation, and diagnostics. It is not merely storing the knowledge in some form but enabling the machines to learn from them and behave as humans do. The representation of knowledge in machine learning encompasses a diverse range of forms, each with its own unique characteristics and applications. These forms include symbolic logic, semantic networks, frames, and ontologies. The knowledge to be represented may be declarative knowledge, procedural knowledge, relationships, heuristic knowledge or even meta knowledge.

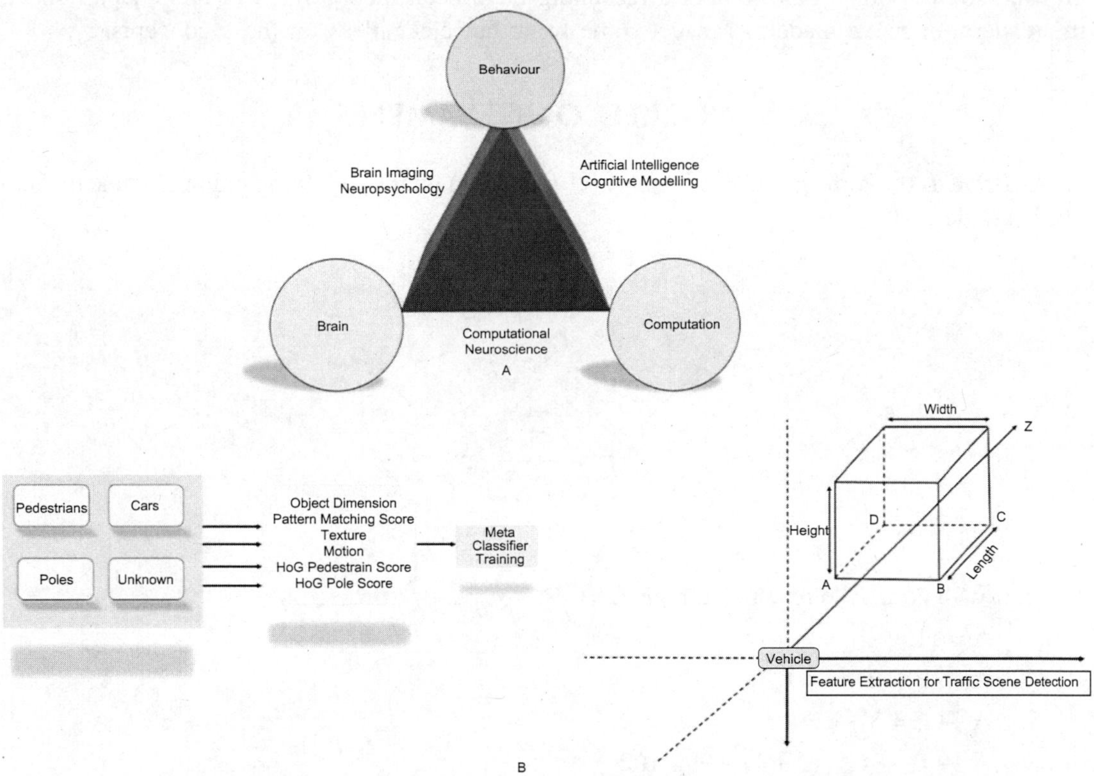


**FIGURE 1.10** (A) General representation of temporal reasoning; (B) Using temporal reasoning for object detection—traffic scene

***Properties of Knowledge Representation***

- ***Representational Adequacy:*** Capacity to demonstrate the necessary knowledge
- ***Inferential Adequacy:*** The capacity to create new knowledge by modifying the represented knowledge
- ***Inferential Efficiency:*** Capacity to steer the inferential mechanism in the most advantageous ways
- ***Acquisitional Efficiency:*** The capacity to learn new information automatically whenever it is possible
- ***Procedural Knowledge:*** Representation of "how to make it" rather than "what it is".

## SUMMARY

This chapter presents a broad overview of AI, its genesis, concepts and applications to build intelligent systems. This is a comprehensive exposition which delves into the fundamental concepts that have laid the groundwork for the development of sophisticated AI systems. Knowledge representation and reasoning, which is one of the pillars of developing any AI systems have been explained in detail. The fundamental concepts of propositional logic, first order logic, probabilistic reasoning, and temporal reasoning have been incorporated in this chapter so that the readers (or naïve readers) can get some basic but clear ideas on these concepts.

## WORKED OUT EXAMPLES

**EXAMPLE 1.1** Perform inform search - A* algorithm on the following graph given actual cost and heuristic cost.

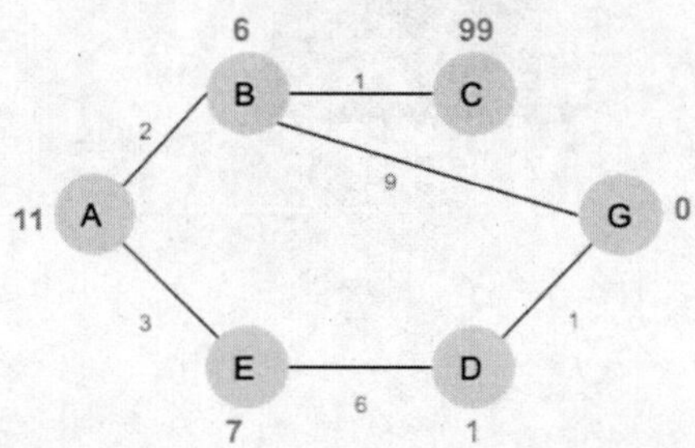


***Solution:***

We start with node A to reach goal node G,

$$A = 11$$

$$A \rightarrow B = 2 + 6 = 8$$

$$A \rightarrow E = 3 + 6 = 10$$

$$A \rightarrow B \rightarrow C = (2 + 1) + 99 = 102$$

$$A \rightarrow B \rightarrow G = (2 + 9) + 0 = 11$$

$A \rightarrow E \rightarrow D = (3 + 6) + 1 = 10$

$A \rightarrow E \rightarrow D \rightarrow G = (3 + 6 + 1) + 0 = \mathbf{10}$

**EXAMPLE 1.2** Use truth tables to show that the two propositions P → Q and ¬P∨Q, are equivalent.

***Solution:***

| **P** | **Q** | **¬P** | **P → Q** | **¬P∨Q** |
|---|---|---|---|---|
| T | T | F | **T** | **T** |
| T | F | F | **F** | **F** |
| F | T | T | **T** | **T** |
| F | F | T | **T** | **T** |

**EXAMPLE 1.3** Using uninformed search technique Breadth First Search (BFS) to reach the destination node N from A, find the total number of steps involved.

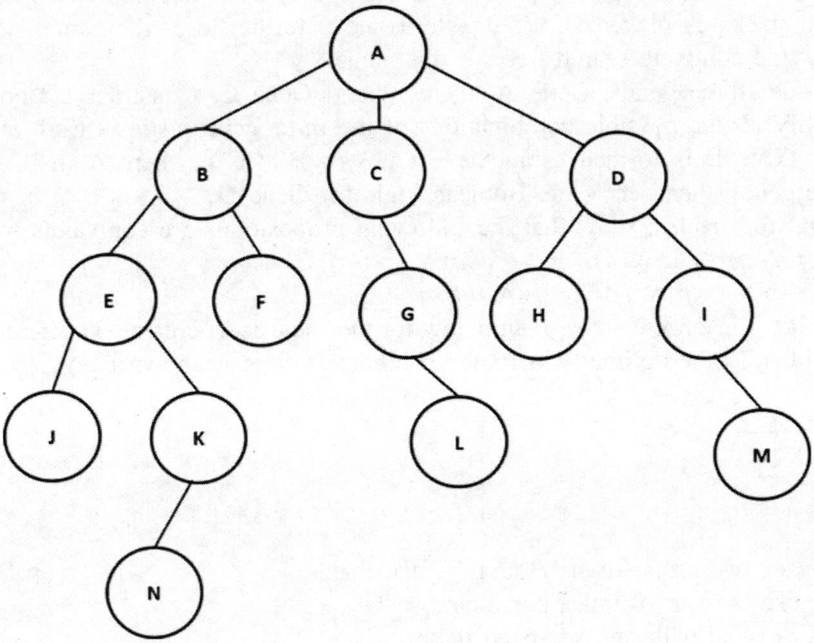


***Solution:*** The BFS uses queue (First in First out) data structure to traverse through. To find the number of steps involved to reach from A – N, we use a queue and start from node A, and traverse all the associated nodes (cross: node is traversed; bold: new node reached)

Step 1: B, C, D

Step 2: ~~B~~, C, D, E, F

Step 3: ~~C~~, D, E, F, G

Step 4: ~~D~~, E, F, G, H, I

Step 5: ~~E~~, F, G, H, I, J, K

Step 6: ~~F~~, G, H, I, J, K

Step 7: ~~G~~, H, I, J, K, L
Step 8: ~~H~~, I, J, K, L
Step 9: ~~I~~, J, K, L, M
Step 10: ~~J~~, K, L, M
Step 11: ~~K~~, L, M, N
Step 12: ~~L~~, M, N
Step 13: ~~M~~ N
Step 14: N (Goal node)
So, it takes 14 steps to reach the goal node with BFS.

## EXERCISES

1. A two players game is played such a way that it starts with a single stack of 7 tokens. On each move, the player selects one stack and divides it into two non-empty, non-equal stacks. A player who is unable to move further loses the game.
Draw the complete search tree for this game.
2. Consider three genes, Gene A, Gene B and Gene C. Construct a Boolean logic to identify all the possible combinations of the three genes using a truth table. If a new gene Gene D is formed using the ¬ (A ∧ (¬ B ∨ C)), where A, B, C represent the three genes, then derive the Boolean logic for Gene D?
3. Using truth tables, show that the following propositions are equivalent.
(a) $(p \wedge q) \rightarrow (p \vee q) \equiv \neg (p \wedge q) \vee (p \vee q)$
(b) $\neg (p \vee (\neg p \wedge q)) \equiv \neg p \wedge \neg (\neg p \wedge q)$
4. Consider the current state given below for the Tic-Tac-Toe game. Design the state space and identify the optimal win route. The current state is shown below.

| X | | |
|---|---|---|
| O | X | X |
| O | | O |

5. Consider two propositions *P* and *Q* such that,
P: X drives over 90 miles per hour.
Q: X is fined with an overspeed ticket.
Using logical connectives (including negations), write the following propositions with *p* and *q*.
(a) X do not drive over 90 miles per hour.
(b) X drive over 90 miles per hour, but is not fined with an overspeed ticket.
(c) X will be fined overspeed ticket if he drives over 90 miles per hour.
(d) If X do not drive over 90 miles per hour, then he will not be fined with overspeed ticket.
(e) Driving over 90 miles per hour is adequate to be fined with an overspeed ticket.

## BIBLIOGRAPHY

Jackson, P. C. (2019). *Introduction to Artificial Intelligence*, Courier Dover Publications.

Levesque, H. J., and Lakemeyer, G. (2001). *The logic of Knowledge Bases*, MIT Press.

Oguike, O. (2021). *A First Course in Artificial Intelligence*, Bentham Science Publishers.

Schmidt, J. W., and Thanos, C. (Eds.). (2012). *Foundations of Knowledge Base Management: Contributions from Logic, Databases, and Artificial Intelligence Applications*, Springer Science & Business Media.

Stuart, R., and Peter, N. (2010). *Artificial Intelligence A Modern Approach,* Third Edition, Prentice-Hall.

Chapter 2

# Industry 5.0 and Beyond

## 2.1 INTRODUCTION

The industry as a whole has undergone a profound transformation due to the unparalleled technological disruptions of the last few decades. From Industry 1.0's steam-powered mechanisation to Industry 2.0's mass assembly lines, Industry 3.0's computerised automation, and Industry 4.0's intelligent connection, we have come a long way. We are now at the beginning of the era of Industry 5.0, which uses technologies like robotics, nanotechnology, plenary scaling, and quantum computing in the next phase of sustainability, human-centricity, and seamless autonomy.

Industry 5.0 proposes self-learning, self-evolving, self-adapting factories and industrial systems. Intelligent algorithms, devices, and resources will enable data analysis, failure prediction, change adaptation, decision-making, and decentralised self-organization. This transition to a self-adaptive, self-learning manufacturing system will allow for unprecedented levels of mass customisation and on-demand manufacturing capacity compared to previous industrialization models. Collaborative robots, or cobots, will work alongside humans in a safe manner, enhancing each other's skills and making up for personal shortcomings.

The primary goals of Industry 5.0 are sustainability and human well-being, as opposed to the prior industrial revolutions' emphasis on increasing production and efficiency. It seeks deeper societal, moral, and existential significance in addition to financial gains. Resources will be conserved as industries and the wider value chain move towards circular economies with the aid of technologies such as sustainable production, industrial symbiosis, renewable energy, etc. Algorithmic audits and AI ethics will guarantee that judgements continue to be responsible, equitable, and transparent.

Global value chains will be affected by Industry 5.0 as it progressively becomes a reality via pilot initiatives and test beds over the next ten years. Ability to adapt, creativity, transparency, long-term viability and human-centricity will be the cornerstones of competitiveness. The development, technology, and expected effects of Industry 5.0 on industrial systems, as well as society at large will all be covered in further detail in this chapter. The aforementioned transformative changes will surely have a significant and wide-ranging impact on how industries and human civilization develop in the future.

### *Defining Industry 5.0*

The definitions presented below by some of pioneers in these areas provides significance of human-centricity, sustainability, and resilience within the context of Industry 5.0.

> *Industry 5.0 is a vision for the future of industry that places people at the center of production. It is about using technology to augment human capabilities and create a more fulfilling and productive work environment.*
>
> —Klaus Schwab, Founder and Executive Chairman of the World Economic Forum.

> *Industry 5.0 is a new era of industrialization that is based on the principles of sustainability and resilience. It is about creating an industry that is good for the planet and for people.*
>
> —Paul Polman, former CEO of Unilever

> *Industry 5.0 is the next industrial revolution, and it is about humans and machines working together to create a better future. It is about using technology to solve the world's biggest challenges, such as climate change and inequality.*
>
> —Jim Hagemann Snabe, Chairman of Siemens

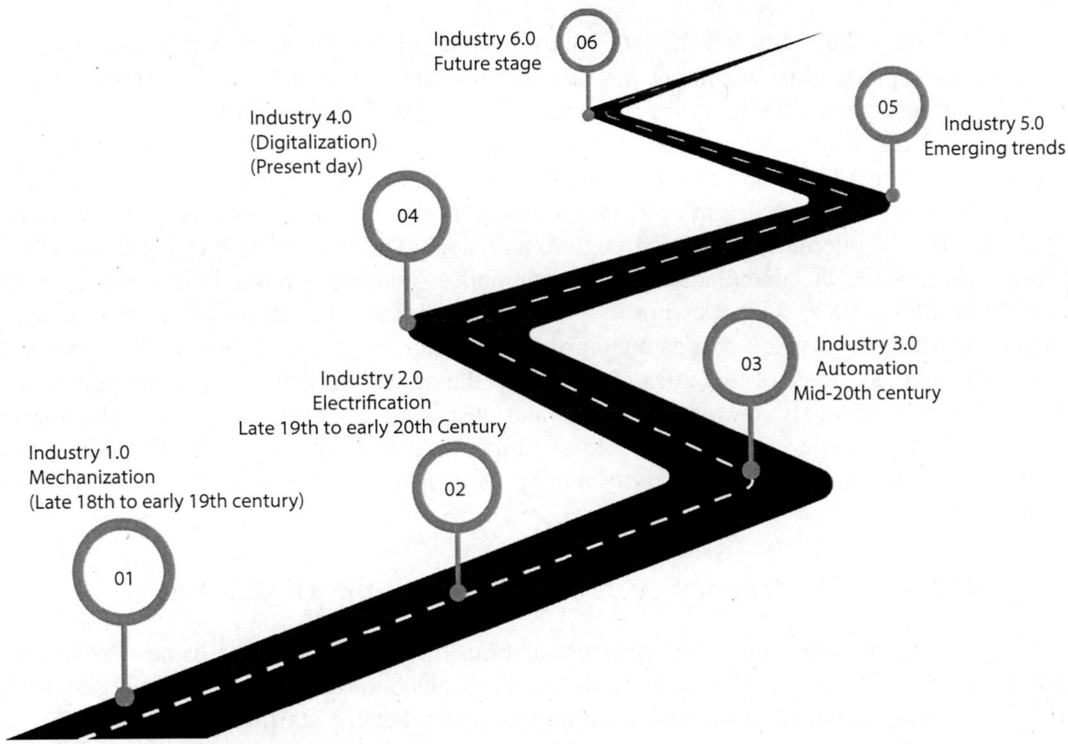


**FIGURE 2.1** The road map of various industrial revolutions.

## 2.2 INDUSTRIAL REVOLUTIONS FROM 1.0 TO 4.0

### 2.2.1 Industry 1.0: Mechanization

The First Industrial Revolution, also known as Industry 1.0, was a period from the late 18th century to the early 20th century when production shifted from manual labour to machines. During this time, machines like steam engines and hydel power were introduced and became more common. These machines were used to make production processes more automated and efficient. Important inventions that greatly changed the textile industry by introducing machines to do the work were the flying shuttle, spinning jenny, and cotton gin. These innovations made the manufacturing process much faster and more efficient. The iron industry went through significant changes with the introduction of processes like puddling and coke smelting, as well as the automation of forging. The introduction of steam power and machine tools made it possible to have production in big factories instead of small homes, which greatly improved how much could be produced. Transportation networks like roads, railways, and canals were built to make it easier to move goods and raw materials for industrialization. Industry 1.0 replaced human and animal muscle power with machines, which allowed for mass production. The mechanisation revolution changed the world by making industries more advanced and allowing for the widespread use of coal and the expansion of global economies.

### 2.2.2 Industry 2.0: Electrification and Power Grid

Industry 2.0 transpired between the late 1800s and the mid-1900s. During this time, there was a lot of mass production which means that things were made in large quantities. This was possible because people had specific jobs and tasks, so they became experts in those areas. The use of interchangeable parts and assembly lines, which were first introduced in slaughterhouses and armouries, revolutionised the manufacturing process. These principles enabled significant improvements in scale, speed, and efficiency. Some important advancements were the introduction of electricity, the internal combustion engine, and steel. The use of the moving assembly line greatly transformed the manufacturing of automobiles, making it possible to produce a large number of affordable cars such as Ford's Model T. Radio and film technologies also appeared, making it easier to distribute consumer products to large groups of people. Big companies with structured systems of organisation became the most powerful in the economy. Mass production made goods that were once rare and costly more readily available and affordable for the growing middle class. This led to an improvement in living standards. However, the significant improvements in productivity during Industry 2.0 caused a shift in society and the economy, focusing more on mass consumerism.

### 2.2.3 Industry 3.0: Automation, Computers, and the Digital Age

Industry 3.0 was the next step after mass production. It happened because of new technologies like electronics, IT, and automated machines. These technologies, such as robots and CNC machines, made manufacturing and productivity even better. Starting from the 1970s, the increase in computing power and software led to the use of computer-controlled automation in factories and warehouses. This allowed for precise, consistent, and efficient operations on a very large scale. Programmable logic controllers (PLCs) connect devices together in networks to create adaptable systems that can be easily changed. Automated processes such as picking, assembly, handling, welding, painting, and other applications have increased efficiency, improved quality, and enhanced reliability, all while reducing costs. Advanced tools such as 3D printers and CNC machine tools have made it easier to achieve greater precision and create intricate shapes. Automation has made it possible to produce more goods and services without relying as much on human effort. Instead, there is now a greater demand for skills related to information technology (IT) and mechatronics, which is a field that combines mechanical engineering and electronics. Automated inspection and tracking of parts greatly enhanced quality assurance. As Industry 3.0 became more efficient, it also raised concerns about job loss due to technology and a decrease in the skills of workers. However, smart and adaptable automation became important for making production more efficient in industries such as automobiles and electronics. This led to the rise of Industry 4.0, which is focused on using data to drive advancements in manufacturing.

### 2.2.4 Industry 4.0: The Era of Digitalization and Smart Manufacturing

Industry 4.0 is the term used to describe the current phase of technological advancements in manufacturing. It started around 2010 and is marked by the increased use of data-driven automation, connectivity, and intelligence in manufacturing technologies and processes. Smart factories are now able to collect, analyse, and share large amounts of data across machines, components, systems, and value chains. This is possible due to advancements in artificial intelligence, industrial internet of things (IIoT), big data analytics, and other emerging technologies. Sensors inside products, equipment, and infrastructure provide constant real-time data about how they are working and performing to smart control and analysis systems. Sophisticated algorithms use this data to help improve efficiency, predict when maintenance is needed, quickly adjust settings, and make decisions that can adapt to different situations. New advancements have enabled the creation of interconnected systems that combine physical and digital elements, leading to increased automation, control, and productivity. Advanced manufacturing techniques are being developed that are intelligent, adaptable, and efficient. However, there are concerns about protecting data privacy and security, as well as ensuring that the workforce can adapt to these changes. These challenges need to be addressed. Industry 4.0 is a concept that is still developing, but it has the potential to greatly change how things are made and how businesses operate in manufacturing, supply chains, and connected companies.

## 2.3 INDUSTRY 5.0: THE CONVERGENCE OF HUMANITY AND TECHNOLOGY

Industry 5.0 is a concept that focuses on making future manufacturing centred around welfare of people, creativity, and sustainability. Industry 5.0 is a new idea that wants to move away from using data and automation, like in Industry 4.0. Instead, it wants to focus more on people and use technologies like AI, cobots, extended reality, nanotechnology, biotech, and green manufacturing. However, Industry 5.0 is still just an idea and not fully developed yet. The objective is to create factories where humans and machines work together smoothly, with machines and systems that can adapt and optimise themselves. Artificial intelligence and collaborative robots will enhance human potential and make work more flexible, creative, and meaningful. They will not replace jobs, but rather work alongside humans. Production systems are going to be made closer to where they are needed and adjusted according to what people want. This will be possible because of innovations like 3D printing. Circular economy principles aim to reduce waste by implementing strategies such as industrial ecology, using renewable materials, and improving resource efficiency across all levels. Technologies such as biomanufacturing and digital twins will help make sustainable production methods that are inspired by nature easier to implement. Industry 5.0 is a vision for the future of factories, supply chains, and workplaces.

## 2.4 CORE VALUES OF INDUSTRY 5.0

The notion of Industry 5.0, as a burgeoning paradigm, places significant emphasis on the seamless amalgamation of human cognitive capabilities and expertise with cutting-edge technologies within the realms of manufacturing and industrial domains. The fundamental principles that underpin Industry 5.0 encompasses various concepts.

### *Human centric*

In Industry 5.0, genuine cooperation between human skills and machine capabilities is prioritised over human-robot competition. Incorporating people into the design of technological systems and keeping them informed are two ways to enhance human capabilities. Hence, the concept of Industry 5.0 revolves around the development of an industrial ecosystem that is both human-centered and sustainable in nature. This paradigm shift aims to address the limitations of previous industrial revolutions by placing a greater emphasis on the well-being of individuals and the environment. By integrating advanced technologies such as artificial intelligence, robotics, and the IoT, Industry 5.0 endeavours to foster a harmonious coexistence between humans and machines, enabling a more efficient and socially responsible mode of production.

### *Sustainability*

Innovating production systems, products, business models and supply chains so they are regenerative—creating environmental and social value. Circular flows, clean energy, higher efficiency is crucial for sustainability. Industry 5.0, the latest paradigm in manufacturing, is dedicated to the noble cause of mitigating the adverse environmental consequences associated with industrial processes. This transformative approach seeks to foster a harmonious coexistence between industrial activities and the natural environment, paving the way for a greener and more sustainable future. The attainment of this objective can be realised by leveraging the potential of renewable energy sources, adopting sustainable materials, and implementing circular production processes.

### *Resilient*

The concept of Industry 5.0 revolves around the development of a highly robust industrial ecosystem that possesses the ability to effectively navigate and endure various forms of

**TABLE 2.1** A detailed comparison of various industrial revolutions—Industry 1.0 to 5.0

| *Aspects* | *Industry 1.0* | *Industry 2.0* | *Industry 3.0* | *Industry 4.0* | *Industry 5.0* |
|---|---|---|---|---|---|
| Time and Characteristic Feature | 1780s-Mechanization | 1870s-Electrification | 1970s-Automation | Today-Digitalization | Future- Personalization |
| Focus Areas | Production in industry using steam and water-powered machinery | Electricity, assembly lines for mass production | Utilising computers and electronics for automation | Additional process automation can be achieved by introducing linked devices, data analytics, and artificial intelligence technology | Human-machine cooperation is the main focus of Industry 5.0, as cognitive computing and human intelligence combine to create goods and services that are oriented towards the needs of users and people |
| Key Innovation | Mechanization | Electrification, Mass Production | Automation | Digitalization | Personalization |
| Core Technologies | Water/Steam Power, Textile Machinery | Electricity, Combustion Engine, Assembly Line | Computers, Microprocessors, Automation, PLCs | IoT, AI, Big Data, 3D Printing | AR, Cobots, Advanced AI |
| Key Impact | Mechanization of Production, Urbanization | Mass Production, Standardization | Increased Precision, Efficiency, Globalization | Smart Factories, Customization, Supply Chain Optimization | Integration of Human Intelligence and Skills |
| Key Sectors | Textiles, Mining, Early Manufacturing | Automotive, Steel, Chemical | Electronics, Telecommunications, Aerospace | IT, Automation, Advanced Manufacturing | Customized Manufacturing, Healthcare, Creative Industries |
| Workforce | Semi-Skilled Labor | Skilled and Semi-Skilled Labor, Assembly Line Workers | Engineers, Technicians, Computer Specialists | Data Scientists, AI Specialists, IoT Experts | Cross-Disciplinary Teams, Emphasis on Creativity and Innovation |

disruptions, including but not limited to natural calamities and supply chain disturbances. The primary objective is to establish a system that can seamlessly adapt and recover from such adversities, thereby ensuring the continuity and stability of industrial operations. By utilising state-of-the-art technology, including machine learning (ML) and artificial intelligence (AI), to proactively detect and mitigate possible hazards, this goal can be achieved.

## 2.5 HUMAN MACHINE RELATIONSHIP: 5C MODEL

A new understanding of the human-machine dynamic is required in light of Industry 5.0's sophisticated integration of AI and humans. With the 5C model, robots move from being passive tools to active participants, engaging in everything from broad creative cooperation to fundamental commanding oversight. Human and machine cooperation and coordination will be the cornerstone of effective Industry 5.0 systems. For this mutually beneficial collaboration, where technology enhances rather than replaces human capacities, the 5C model offers a road map. Developing mutual respect and trust between people and AI at every step of this relationship journey is essential for the responsible implementation of Industry 5.0. These Cs, namely, Coexistence, Confluence, Coordination, Cooperation and Collaboration are the crux of the model's essence, embodying critical concepts that contribute to its overall efficacy and comprehensiveness.

### *Coexistence*

Coexistence, a term that describes how human and AI systems can coexist in the world in a constructive and peaceful manner, is an emerging notion in human-AI relations. Important facets of coexisting humans with AI include—respect, understanding, complementarity, benefit sharing and responsibility. Proactively forming AI systems and governance frameworks in accordance with these principles is necessary to promote successful cohabitation. It's critical that AI be developed responsibly for the good of everyone. Thus, there exists a harmonious collaboration between human intellect and machine capabilities, wherein both entities synergistically leverage their distinctive proficiencies.

### *Confluence*

The concept of confluence represents the harmonious integration and convergence of human intellect and machine capabilities, working in agreement to accomplish common goals. This phase encompasses a synergistic and cohesive approach wherein humans and machines collaborate harmoniously, frequently engaging in collective decision-making and collaborative problem-solving. In the domain of collaborative robotics, commonly referred to as cobots, a symbiotic relationship is established between humans and machines, wherein they collaborate harmoniously to accomplish various tasks. This collaboration is characterised by machines assuming the responsibility of executing repetitive or hazardous components, while humans assume the role of providing invaluable guidance and meticulous oversight.

### *Coordination*

In order to effectively collaborate on shared objectives, humans and artificial intelligence systems must carefully and strategically synchronise their behaviours. This is known as coordination.

Among the essential components of human-AI coordination are—communication, goal alignment, role clarity, interoperability and feedback loops. The management of technological and societal issues that arise from further integrating artificial intelligence capabilities with human activities is necessary for effective coordination between humans and AI. Coordinating human and AI resources wisely can have a positive impact on society, science, and economic output.

***Cooperation***

The term "human-AI cooperation" describes the collaboration of human and artificial intelligence systems to accomplish common objectives by utilising their complementary strengths and talents. Important components that promote beneficial human-AI collaboration include trust, shared mental models, teamwork, feedback loops and benefit sharing. Building cooperative frameworks leverages teamwork for shared benefit instead of relying solely on competition. In the area of healthcare, a notable illustration can be found in the harmonious collaboration between surgical robots and skilled surgeons. In this symbiotic relationship, the surgical robot adeptly executes precise movements, while the surgeon assumes the role of a guiding force, orchestrating the procedure with finesse and expertise.

***Collaboration***

Humans and AI systems collaborating in harmony, cooperation, and thought partnership is referred to as human-AI collaboration. AI and humans can work together to produce better results than they could separately when they collaborate effectively, acting as each other's force multipliers. The following are important components of productive human-AI cooperation—augmentation, reciprocal interaction, joint decision-making, shared goals, accountability, trust & transparency. The 5C Model of Human-Machine Relationship presents a highly valuable framework that facilitates a comprehensive comprehension of the ever-changing dynamics between humans and machines across diverse domains.

## 2.6 OPPORTUNITIES AND LIMITATIONS OF INDUSTRY 5.0

Industry 5.0, the forthcoming phase of industrialization, holds immense potential for enterprises and the broader societal landscape. This paradigm shift is poised to unlock a myriad of opportunities, fostering unprecedented growth and progress.

### 2.6.1 Opportunity in Industry 5.0

***Increased productivity and efficiency***

The rise of Industry 5.0 technologies has ushered in a new era of transformative potential for businesses, offering unprecedented opportunities to automate various tasks, curtail wastage, and enhance overall operational efficiency. By harnessing the power of cutting-edge technologies, organisations can unlock a multitude of benefits that propel them towards a more streamlined and optimised future.

### *Improved product quality*

Industry 5.0 technological integration presents a promising opportunity for businesses to enhance their product quality. By using these advanced technologies, organisations can optimise their manufacturing processes, resulting in superior products that can meet and exceed customer expectations. Businesses may attain greater levels of accuracy, consistency, and effectiveness in their production lines by seamlessly integrating cutting-edge technology like artificial intelligence, robotics, and the Internet of Things (IoT). One illustrative application of advanced technology lies in the utilisation of cutting-edge sensors and sophisticated data analytics techniques to proactively identify and mitigate defects at their nascent stages within the production process.

### *Greater customization and personalization*

Industry 5.0 technology can facilitate organisations' ability to create specialised and unique goods. This is due to the fact that these technologies enable firms to customise their manufacturing processes to meet the demands of specific clients. The integration of advanced sensor technologies and sophisticated data analytics holds immense potential in optimising energy consumption and mitigating wastage. By harnessing the power of these cutting-edge tools, industries and organisations can achieve significant improvements in resource efficiency and sustainability. Through the deployment of sensors, real-time data can be collected and analysed, enabling precise monitoring and control of energy usage. This data-driven approach empowers decision-makers to identify areas of inefficiency, implement targeted interventions, and ultimately drive down energy consumption and waste. The seamless integration of sensors and data analytics thus emerges as a promising avenue for achieving substantial environmental and economic benefits.

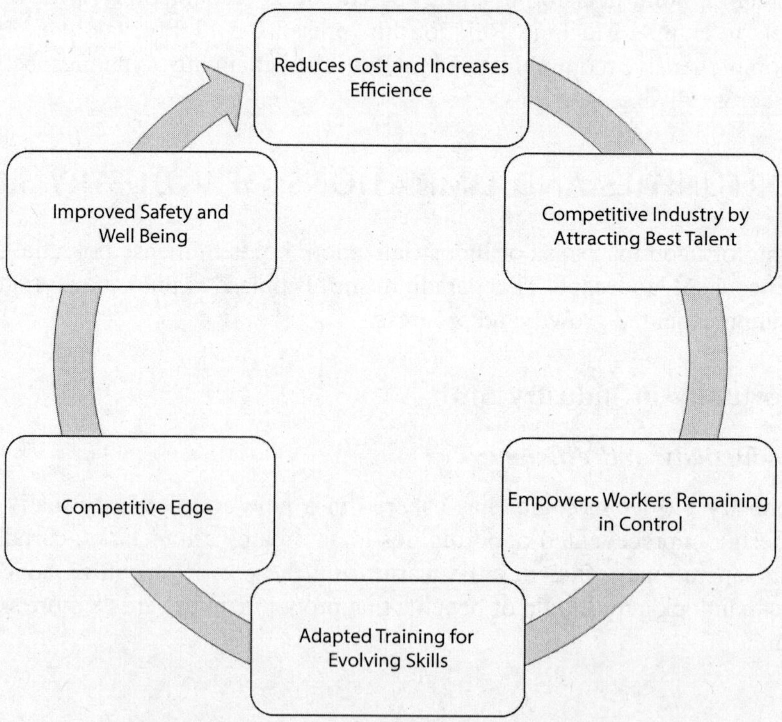


**FIGURE 2.2** Various opportunities in Industry 5.0

### 2.6.2 Limitations of Industry 5.0

The onset of Industry 5.0 has undoubtedly presented an overabundance of promising prospects for various sectors. However, it is imperative to acknowledge and carefully deliberate upon the limitations that accompany this transformative era.

#### *High cost of implementation*

The implementation of Industry 5.0 technologies may pose a significant financial burden, particularly for small and medium-sized enterprises (SMEs).

#### *Need for skilled workers*

The successful implementation and operation of Industry 5.0 technologies necessitates a highly proficient and adept workforce capable of effectively managing and sustaining these advanced systems. The dearth of these skills is a pervasive issue across numerous countries.

#### *Cybersecurity risks*

The advent of Industry 5.0 has witnessed a notable surge in the integration of cutting-edge technologies with the internet, thereby rendering them susceptible to potential cybersecurity threats and attacks.

#### *Ethical concerns*

The ethical implications surrounding Industry 5.0 have garnered considerable attention, with certain individuals expressing apprehension regarding potential ramifications, including but not limited to job displacement and data misuse.

## 2.7 ADVANCEMENTS IN COMMUNICATION—5G AND 6G

5G is the next significant advancement in mobile communication networks that is constructed to satisfy the growing connectivity needs of the 2020s and beyond. Lower latency, faster speeds, and the ability to support a massive increase in the number of linked devices are just a few of the notable improvements it offers over 4G LTE networks.

5G offers a number of important features, such as peak download and upload rates of up to 20 Gbps and 1–10 millisecond latency, respectively. Virtual reality, driverless cars, smart cities, and industrial IoT—use cases with significant connectivity needs—can all be supported by 5G networks thanks to their massive capacity and incredibly dependable low latency. Early 5G deployments are still taking place around the world, but within the next ten years, it promises to revolutionise connectivity in many ways. Improved mobile broadband should be 10 to 100 times faster than 4G, connectivity density should increase 1000 times, and reduced latency should result in nearly instantaneous communication between devices. Customers and companies will begin to directly experience these next-generation speeds and capabilities in the 2020s when new 5G networks and devices begin to roll out.

Scientists are already anticipating the next generation of networks—6G—even as 5G technology is still being deployed internationally. With a projected standardisation time of

2028–2030, 6G is currently in its very early stages of development and study. Terabits per second (Tbps) of speed, sub-millisecond latency, and native support for future applications are all part of the 6G vision.

6G networks (sense networks) with integrated vision, hearing, and sensing capabilities; faultless security; and powerful machine learning integration are a few examples of the revolutionary capabilities focused on by 6G. Key 6G design considerations include the requirement for creativity, intelligence, security, and connectivity.

Synthetic reality, decentralised cell-free designs, seamless integration of satellite networks, high-fidelity mobile holograms, and 3D integrated networks are just a few of the advancements it is expected to enable. Currently, 5G will provide consumers and businesses with far better mobile broadband access, which could hasten the development of 6G.

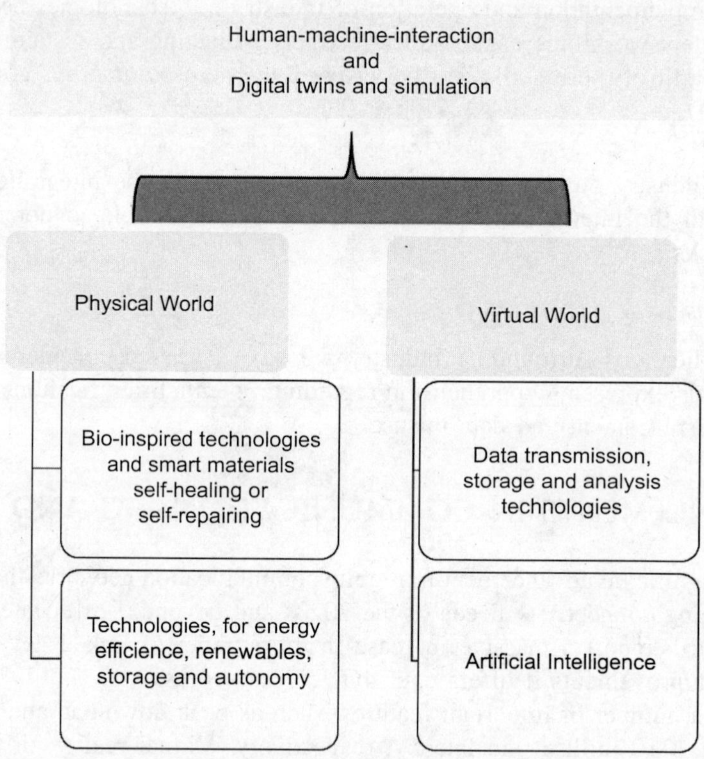


FIGURE 2.3 Technologies that make Industry 5.0 possible.

### *Important terminologies related to 5G and 6G*

**1. Shannon-Hartley Theorem for Channel Capacity:** The highest possible data rate, or channel capacity (*C*), that may be securely sent across a communications channel is theoretically limited by the Shannon-Hartley theorem.

$$C = B * log_2\left(1 + \frac{S}{N}\right) \tag{2.1}$$

Where, $C$ is the channel capacity in bits per second (bps), $B$ is the channel bandwidth in Hertz (Hz), $S$ is the signal power in Watts (W) and $N$ is the noise power in Watts (W).

**2. Path Loss:** In wireless communication, path loss is the phenomena where the signal strength drops with increasing transmitter and receiver distance. The Friis Free Space Path Loss (FSPL) equation is a widely used formula for estimating path loss, and there are several models available. This formula uses the transmitted power ($P_t$) to determine the received signal power ($P_r$) at a receiver.

$$P_r = P_t * G_t * G_r * \left(\frac{\lambda}{4\pi d}\right)^2 \tag{2.2}$$

Where, $P_r$ is the received signal power in Watts (W), $P_t$ is the transmitted power in Watts (W), $G_t$ is the transmitting antenna gain, $G_r$ is the receiving antenna gain, $\lambda$ is the wavelength of the signal in meters (m) and $d$ is the distance between the transmitter and receiver in meters (m).

**3. Path Loss (Free Space):** It calculates the attenuation of a signal in a simplified, ideal environment across frequency and distance. Also, it aids in estimating the predicted signal intensity at a specific transmitter distance.

$$PL(dB) = 20 * log_{10}(f) + 20 * log_{10}(d) \tag{2.3}$$

**4. Friis Free Space Path Loss (FSPL):** An electromagnetic wave travelling in free space will lose signal strength, which can be computed using the Friis free space path loss (FSPL) formula.

$$FSPL(dB) = 20 * log_{10}(f) + 20 * log_{10}(d) + 32.45 \tag{2.4}$$

Where, $FSPL$ is the free space path loss in decibels (dB), $f$ is the frequency of the signal in Hertz (Hz), $d$ is the distance between the transmitter and receiver in kilometers (km), $20\,log(d)$ – path loss due to distance, $20\,log(f)$ – path loss at higher frequencies and 32.44 is a constant.

**5. Beamforming Gain:** In wireless communication systems, beamforming techniques are used to boost the received signal strength. This is referred to as beamforming gain. A technique for signal processing called beamforming is used to enhance communication between a transmitter and a receiver by focusing signal transmission or reception in a particular direction.

$$Beamforming\ Gain\,(dB) = 10 * log_{10}(N) \tag{2.5}$$

Where, $G$ is the beamforming gain (dB, or decibels), $N$ is the total number of antenna components in the array. By directing the energy of an array in a certain direction, beamforming gain rises.

**6. Spectral Efficiency:** In wireless communication, the term "spectral efficiency" (*SE*) describes how well the available bandwidth is used for data transmission. Usually, it is expressed as the maximum data transmission capacity per bandwidth unit. In order to build and optimise communication systems for better data rates and overall performance, spectral efficiency is an essential parameter.

$$SE = \frac{R}{B} \tag{2.6}$$

Where, $R$ = Net data rate (bits per second) and $B$ = Channel bandwidth (Hertz).

**7. Energy Efficiency:** A crucial performance indicator for wireless communication systems is energy efficiency (*EE*), which calculates the amount of data that can be sent for each unit of energy used. The energy efficiency formula is,

$$EE = \frac{R}{P} \tag{2.7}$$

Where, *EE* is the Energy efficiency (bits/Joule), *R* is the Net data rate (bits/second) and *P* is the total power consumed by the communication system (Watts)

**8. Latency (Round-Trip Time):** The time it takes for a signal to travel from the transmitter to the receiver and back is known as latency, or round-trip time (RTT), and it is a crucial performance metric in wireless communication systems.

The following is the formula for delay between wireless nodes A and B,

$$RTT = \frac{2\text{d}}{C} \tag{2.8}$$

Where, *d* is the distance between node *A*, *B* and *c* is the Propagation speed of signal.

**9. MIMO Channel Capacity:** Using multiple transmit and receive antennas, MIMO (multiple-input multiple-output) technology significantly boosts spectral efficiency and channel capacity. For a perfect MIMO system with $M_t$ transmit antennas and $M_r$ receive antennas, the channel capacity or maximum data rate is as follows:

$$C = Blog_2(1 + \rho M_t M_r) \tag{2.9}$$

**10. Total Holographic rate:** Frame rate, compression ratio, colour depth, resolution, and frame rate are some of the elements that must be taken into account when calculating the total holographic data rate for transmission. Holographic video transmission raw data rate can be computed using the following formula.

$$Data\ Rate\left(\frac{bits}{sec}\right) = No.\ of\ pixels \times Frame\ rate\left(\frac{frames}{sec}\right) \times Color\ depth\ (bits/pixel) \tag{2.10}$$

**TABLE 2.2** Some promising deep learning methods in 6G networks

| *Deep Learning Methods* | *Focused Applications* |
|---|---|
| MD-IMA | Offers a multi-dimensional intelligent multiple access (MD-IMA) method of intelligent resource allocation that takes situational awareness into account. DRL and long short-term memory (LSTM) form the foundation of the deep learning (DL) system. |
| AOW-DQN | Building a new adaptive observation window for the deep Q-network that changes its size to increase learning efficacy while responding to the dynamism of the industrial environment. This architecture for the 6G Industrial Internet of Things (IoT) is built on machine learning (ML). |
| Micro-Safe | Updating deep neural network (DNN)-based algorithms to improve the accuracy of the choices made and shown to end users in 6G intelligent transportation systems while maintaining personalised safety services to reduce the number of accidents. |
| DDPG | A twin-timescale Markov decision-based slicing control mechanism is implemented in the 6G RAN via the DRL architecture. Our developed approach is based on the convergence of the double deep-Q-network (Double-DQN) and the deep deterministic policy gradient (DDPG). |

| *Deep Learning Methods* | *Focused Applications* |
|---|---|
| FAT-DL | Created utilising a feature-aided adaptive-tuning deep learning (FAT-DL) network for large-scale device detection in 6G networks. Its foundation is a layer-by-layer training architecture that 6determines the network's device distribution parameters based on the trained data. |
| DL | Stochastic network calculus and DL are combined to train on data in a way that facilitates cooperative driving by rapidly computing the delay limits in real-time operations. This method was created for connected self-driving cars in 6G networks. |
| DRLR | Unmanned aerial vehicles (UAVs) can be utilised in 6G IoT networks to gather sensor data. The DRL recruiting (DRLR) technique can be used to construct algorithms for UAV path planning. Reducing expenses and expanding the coverage area improve the data collection process. |
| IScaler | IScaler is a DRL-based approach used for resource scaling and service placement in 6G Internet of Everything (IoE) systems, particularly for mobile edge computing. It addresses the difficulties presented by a dynamic environment and provides better scaling and placement choices. |
| DRL | A DRL-based architecture can be effectively used in 6G optical wireless communication (OWC) systems to tackle the handover issue, allowing end users to seamlessly and continuously switch access points. The neutral network is trained and updated by DRL using the Q-target and Q-evaluation. |
| H-DAC-RL | Value function is referred to as the "critic" and policy function as the "actor" in hierarchical deep actor-critic reinforcement learning (H-DAC-RL). It can be used to manage networks and allocate resources in large-scale 6G space-terrestrial integrated IoT systems. |

## 2.8 INDUSTRY 6.0

As each industrial revolution transforms production systems to unprecedented levels, thoughts naturally turn to what lies ahead. While still highly speculative, the vision for a potential Industry 6.0 era would realize fused, adaptive, and autonomous systems that combine cyber, physical, biological, and cognitive capabilities. Quantum computers may enable complex optimizations of entire value chains or simulations of physical processes for rapid innovation. Biotech could facilitate engineered materials, fuels, and fabrication techniques emulating the resilience of nature. Cognitive systems may not just predict and prescribe, but also explain reasoning, adapt goals, and imply purpose. The integration of cyber-physical-biological-cognitive (CPBC) systems could give rise to a generalized production capability surpassing human-designed solutions. While such visionary notions border on science fiction at present, they offer thought-provoking perspectives on the ever-accelerating pace of industrial transformation.

### 2.8.1 Vision of Industry 6.0

Industry 6.0 is poised to revolutionise the industrial landscape, surpassing the scope and impact of its predecessors, the previous industrial revolutions. This paradigm shift is composed to exert a profound impact on the industries 6.0, catalysing a transformative shift in the work culture of humanity. In Industry 6.0, progress will focus on important aspects like sustainability, using similar assets carefully, safety, resilience, being able to adapt and grow, working well with nature, using digital twin technologies together, and promoting an economy that cares about the environment. The concept of homogeneous assets emphasises the standardisation and interoperability of technologies, enabling seamless integration and collaboration across various sectors. Safety and resilience will be paramount, with a focus on designing systems that can withstand and recover from potential disruptions.

### 2.8.2 Key Technologies in Industry 6.0

The area of 6G technology is currently in its nascent stages, with several key technologies undergoing active development. Among the most auspicious advancements that have garnered attention are discussed below.

#### *Terahertz (THz) Communication*

Terahertz (THz) waves, also known as T-waves, represent a segment of the electromagnetic spectrum characterised by exceptionally high frequencies. These waves possess the remarkable capability to facilitate data transmission at unprecedented rates, surpassing the limitations of conventional communication channels. Terahertz (THz) communication, although currently in its nascent phase, holds immense promise in propelling the advancement of 6G technology by facilitating unprecedented data rates of up to 1 terabit per second (Tbps).

#### *Artificial Intelligence (AI) and Machine Learning (ML)*

6G will heavily rely on AI, both for new applications and network optimisation. AI may be used to generate new services like personalised connection and real-time machine learning as well as automate network administration activities, enhance network performance, and enhance existing services. Several algorithms coming together within the architecture of 6G networks will facilitate a multitude of benefits. These benefits encompass intelligent network management, dynamic resource allocation, and the capacity to swiftly adapt to evolving user demands and network conditions in a real-time fashion.

#### *Massive Multiple-Input Multiple-Output (MIMO)*

The MIMO technique transmits and receives data concurrently using multiple antennas. The usage of MIMO can boost data throughput and enhance signal quality. In comparison to earlier cellular network generations, 6G is anticipated to employ even more antennas, resulting in even better data speeds and more dependable connectivity.

#### *Beamforming*

Radio waves are concentrated in one direction using a method called beamforming. By doing so, interference from other devices can be decreased while also enhancing signal strength and range. To allow more effective spectrum usage and to deliver more specialised connectivity, 6G is anticipated to utilise cutting-edge beamforming techniques.

#### *Network Slicing*

A method called "network slicing" separates a single physical network into many virtual networks. This makes it possible to modify each virtual network to match the requirements of a particular application or use case. Network slicing is anticipated to be used by 6G to serve a variety of new applications, including augmented reality, smart factories, and self-driving automobiles.

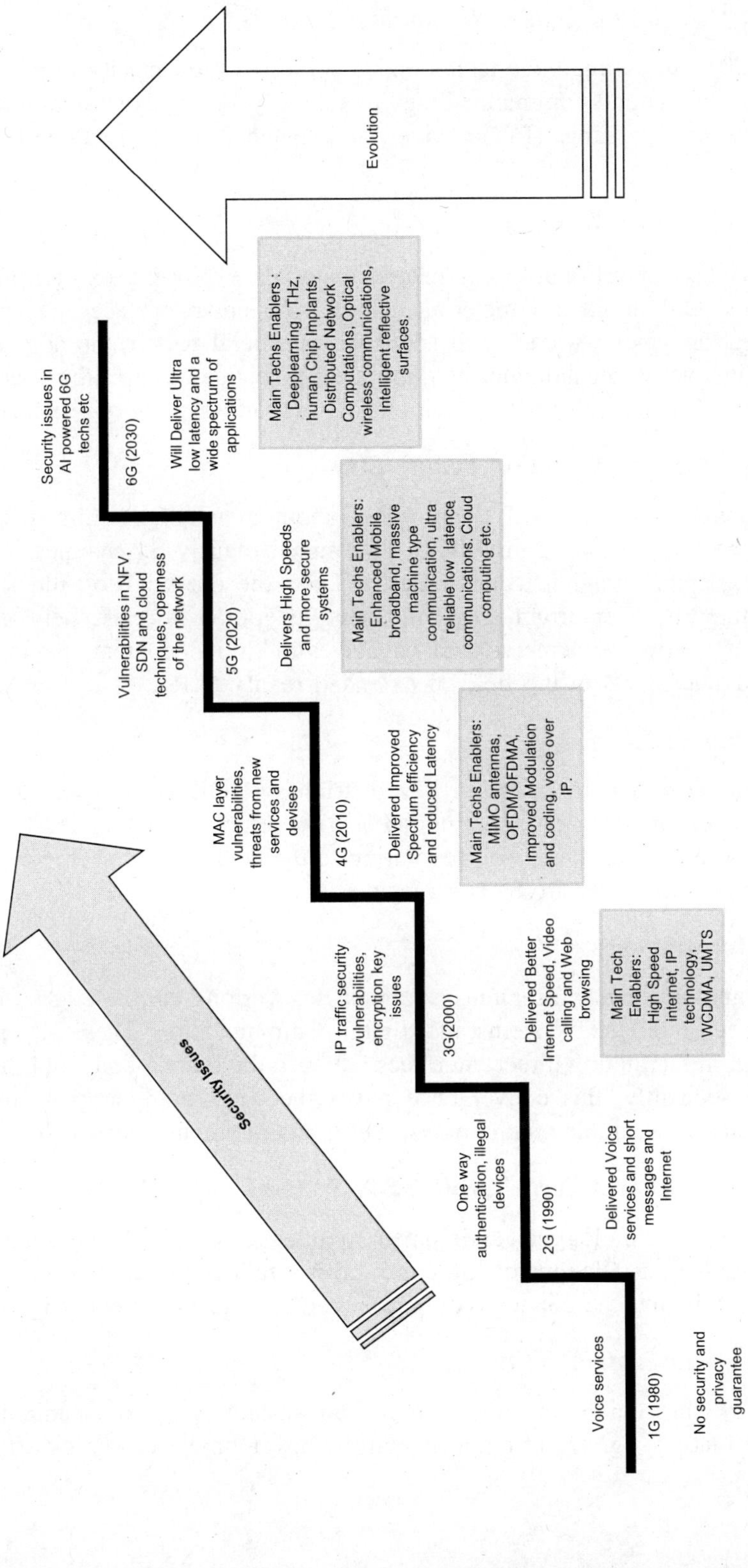


**FIGURE 2.4** Evolution from 1G to 6G with their characteristic features.

### Blockchain and Distributed Ledger Technologies (DLTs)

The integration of these cutting-edge technologies possesses the capacity to play a pivotal role in fortifying transactions and communications, particularly in contexts encompassing essential infrastructure, Internet of Things (IoT) devices, and financial applications within the realm of 6G networks.

### Metamaterials and Smart Surfaces

Metamaterials, a class of artificially engineered materials exhibiting extraordinary properties beyond those observed in natural materials, along with smart surfaces capable of actively manipulating electromagnetic waves, will soon play a crucial part in the advancement of 6G networks. These innovative technologies hold immense potential for expanding network coverage and enhancing signal quality, thereby revolutionising the landscape of wireless communication.

### Holographic Imaging and Extended Reality (XR)

The growing popularity of 6G will likely bring about a paradigm shift in the domain of augmented reality (AR), virtual reality (VR), and mixed reality. By seamlessly incorporating cutting-edge holographic imaging technologies, 6G has the potential to unlock a new era of immersive and interactive environments. This next-generation wireless network is expected to revolutionise the way we perceive and engage with digital content, paving the way for unprecedented advancements in the field of extended reality (XR).

### Quantum Communication

Quantum technologies, such as quantum key distribution (QKD), are poised to become an indispensable component of the forthcoming 6G era. By offering unparalleled levels of security and encryption, these advancements will revolutionise the landscape of secure communications, particularly in the realm of sensitive data transmission.

### Bio-Integrated Technologies

The field of technological advancements encompasses various cutting-edge innovations that serve as a—between biological systems and digital communication. These advancements hold immense potential in facilitating direct interfaces between the human body and the forthcoming 6G network. Consequently, this convergence paves the way for remarkable progress in the domains of healthcare, wearable technologies, and human-computer interaction.

### Satellite Networks and Low Earth Orbit (LEO) Systems

The forthcoming 6G technology is anticipated to integrate cutting-edge satellite networks, potentially leveraging constellations of low Earth orbit satellites to deliver uninterrupted global coverage, thereby bridging the connectivity gap in remote and underserved regions.

### Energy Efficiency and Sustainability

In light of the growing emphasis on environmental sustainability, it is anticipated that 6G technologies will place a significant emphasis on the development of energy-efficient designs.

This will be achieved through the utilisation of cutting-edge advancements, including energy harvesting techniques, low-power components, and sustainable manufacturing processes.

It is extremely important to acknowledge that the progression of 6G technology is currently in its nascent stage, and the eventual realisation of this technology may encompass novel technologies and concepts that have not yet been conceived or actualized.

#### *Spectrum Communication Technique*

The concept of spectrum serves as the fundamental basis for the transmission of broadcast signals. Since the advent of widespread communication in the 1980s, there has been a remarkable surge in the advancement of spectrum assets across each successive generation. This can be attributed to the incessant pursuit of higher data rates, which serve as the primary benchmarks for the forthcoming 6G era, promising the accumulation of terabits per second. The Terahertz (THz) and perceptible light spectra are two remarkable domains that have garnered significant attention in the field of optics and photonics.

### 2.8.3 Need and Benefits of Industry 6.0

Industry 6.0, the forthcoming era of manufacturing, represents a pivotal advancement that enterprises must embrace to sustain their competitiveness within the intricate fabric of the global economy. The manifold advantages of Industry 6.0 are abundant, encompassing a wide array of benefits that are poised to revolutionise various sectors. These benefits are multifaceted and encompass both tangible and intangible gains, ultimately leading to enhanced productivity, efficiency, and competitiveness.

There are several need and benefits of Industry 6.0, some of them are discussed below.

#### *The Needs*

**Hyper-Automation:** To significantly increase productivity, efficiency, product quality, data-driven decision making, innovation speed, and sustainable economic competitiveness, Industry 6.0 hyper-automation is quickly becoming a necessity across all industrial sectors. Businesses may function with previously unheard-of levels of agility, intelligence, and cost performance by utilising technologies like artificial intelligence (AI), advanced robotics, Internet of Things (IoT) sensors, and additive manufacturing to digitise, analyse, anticipate, optimise, and automate end-to-end value chains.

**Extreme Customization and Personalization:** In order to meet the evolving demands of modern consumers, industries are increasingly recognising the imperative of harnessing the power of highly customised and personalised product offerings. This entails the ability to seamlessly produce such products at scale, while effectively catering to the unique preferences and requirements of individual customers.

**Quantum Leaps in Efficiency:** In the context of Industry 6.0, it becomes imperative to attain unprecedented levels of efficiency and resource utilisation, surpassing the boundaries of our current imagination. The potential advancements encompassed within this domain encompass remarkable strides in the realms of energy efficiency, waste mitigation, and resource optimisation.

**Enhanced Sustainability and Environmental Responsibility:** In the context of Industry 6.0, it is imperative to place utmost emphasis on the prioritisation of sustainability and environmental stewardship. The implementation of cutting-edge technologies and innovative practises aimed at mitigating environmental repercussions and fostering sustainable manufacturing procedures is a crucial consideration in this context.

**Seamless Integration of Digital and Physical Realities:** The unveiling of Industry 6.0 necessitates a heightened level of convergence between the digital and physical realms, thereby engendering the utilisation of cutting-edge technologies such as extended reality (XR), encompassing virtual reality (VR) and augmented reality (AR). These technologies are poised to revolutionise critical operations such as design, prototyping, and training within the industry.

### *The Benefits*

**Highly Adaptive and Agile Operations:** The capacity to swiftly adjust to evolving market demands, unanticipated disruptions, and emerging prospects would bestow significant advantages upon various industries. The aforementioned phenomenon has the potential to engender heightened levels of competitiveness and resilience within the given context.

**Enhanced Product Quality and Reliability:** Leveraging cutting-edge technologies and employing state-of-the-art precision manufacturing techniques, the advent of Industry 6.0 holds immense promise in the field of producing products that exhibit unparalleled levels of quality and reliability. This transformative era has the potential to significantly mitigate defects and recalls, thereby revolutionising the manufacturing landscape.

**Improved Resource Utilization and Sustainability:** The introduction of Industry 6.0 holds immense potential in revolutionising resource utilisation, waste reduction, and environmental sustainability. The incorporation of this approach is of utmost importance in tackling the pressing global sustainability challenges.

**Global Connectivity and Collaboration:** The implementation of Industry 6.0 has the potential to revolutionise the way in which global partners, suppliers, and customers collaborate and connect with one another. This transformative phase promises to establish a seamless and interconnected global economy, where barriers to communication and cooperation are effectively dismantled. By harnessing the power of advanced technologies and intelligent systems, Industry 6.0 paves the way for unprecedented levels of collaboration, enabling organisations to transcend geographical boundaries and foster a truly interconnected ecosystem. Through enhanced connectivity and streamlined processes, Industry 6.0 empowers businesses to unlock new opportunities, drive innovation, and achieve unparalleled levels of efficiency and productivity.

## SUMMARY

Industry 5.0 and beyond is the continuous integration of cutting-edge digital technologies with a human-centered approach to alter supply chains and production systems. The essence of Industry 5.0, its ambition, and a possible roadmap for what's "beyond 5.0" are all explored in this chapter. The Industry 5.0 era leverages technology such as artificial intelligence, robotics, big data analytics, industrial internet of things, and virtual/augmented reality to enable mass customisation, rapid experimentation, sustainable production techniques, and human-machine collaboration. It develops symbiotic connections between human talents and mechanical/ computational capabilities, going beyond automation. In the upcoming decades, exciting breakthroughs in this beyond 5.0 age will push the boundaries of what is possible by leveraging the intersections of combine artificial intelligence (AI) with human cognition, the intersection of the digital, physical, and biological domains.

In addition to providing an overview of Industry 5.0 and beyond, this chapter offers an insightful analysis of how continuous advancements in intelligence, connectivity, and creativity are advancing both industry and humanity.

## WORKED OUT EXAMPLES

**EXAMPLE 2.1** Massive MIMO technique with 128 antennas is used by 5G base stations. Compute the overall data rate of the base station if each antenna has a 100 Mbps data transmission capacity.

***Solution:*** Total data rate = Number of antennas × Data rate per antenna = 128 antennas × 100 Mbps = 12.8 Gbps.

So, the overall data rate of the base station is 12.8 Gbps.

**EXAMPLE 2.2** A 5G base station directs a beam of light in the direction of a user using a homogeneous linear array made up of 16 antennas. What is the anticipated gain from beamforming under perfect circumstances?

***Solution:***

Given:

5G base station with uniform linear array (ULA) of 16 antennas

Directional beamforming towards a user

The beamforming gain of an antenna array is: $G = 10\log(N)$, Where $N$ is the number of elements in the array.

This holds under ideal conditions of no coupling between antenna elements, no losses, and accurate phase shifting between each antenna.

Here the number of elements N in the ULA is 16.

Therefore, the beamforming gain is: $G = 10\log(16) = 10\log(2^4) = 12.04$ dB

So, with 16 antenna elements and ideal beamforming towards a single user, the theoretical maximum gain over a single antenna is 12 dB.

**EXAMPLE 2.3** A holographic video of a one-meter object is transmitted at a frame rate of 60 frames per second using a 6G system with a resolution of 1000×1000 pixels. What amount of information is sent every second?

***Solution:***

1. Calculate the total number of pixels in the holographic video:
   Number of pixels = Resolution × Resolution
   Number of pixels = 1000 × 1000
   Number of pixels = 1,000,000 pixels
2. Calculate the total number of frames per second:
   Frame rate = 60 fps

3. Calculate the total number of bits required to represent each pixel:
   Assuming each pixel is represented by 8 bits (1 byte), we have:
   Bits per pixel = 8 bits
4. Calculate the total data transmission rate in bits per second:
   Data rate = Number of pixels × Bits per pixel × Frame rate
   Data rate = 1,000,000 pixels × 8 bits/pixel × 60 fps
   Data rate = 480,000,000 bits/second
   or
   Data rate = 480 Mbps
   Therefore, the data transmission rate for the holographic video is 480 Mbps.

## EXERCISES

1. Determine the SINR in dB for a 5G system given the following parameter values: –70 dBm for the received signal, –80 dBm for interference, and –90 dBm for noise.
2. With a carrier bandwidth of 80 MHz, a 5G network operator is implementing a novel base station. In urban regions, they expect a standard SINR of 20 dB. Could users in these urban locations potentially attain the highest theoretical data rate possible under the given conditions, as predicted by the Shannon-Hartley theorem?
3. 64 antennas constitute the Massive MIMO system that is integrated into a 5G base station. For the purpose of increasing signal intensity and spatial coverage, the system employs beamforming. Determine the beamforming gain for the specified base station using the formula Beamforming Gain (dB) = $10 * \log_{10}(N)$, where $N$ represents the number of antennas.
4. To concentrate a signal on a particular user, a 5G base station employs a uniform linear array comprising 128 antennas. Compute the potential beamforming gain that could be attained, under optimal conditions.
5. Time Division Duplexing (TDD) and Frequency Division Duplexing (FDD) are being considered for implementation in various segments of the network by a 5G network operator. In the context of 5G requirements and challenges, describe the most important considerations that should guide their decision between TDD and FDD.

## BIBLIOGRAPHY

Božanić, M, Sinha, S. (2021). Mobile Communication Networks: 5G and a Vision of 6G. Cham, Switzerland: Springer.

Massaro, A. (2021). *Electronics in advanced research industries: Industry 4.0 to Industry 5.0 Advances*, John Wiley & Sons.

More, C. (2002). *Understanding the industrial revolution*, Routledge.

Reddy, C.K., Anisha, P.R., Khan, S., Hanafiah, M.M., Pamulaparty, L., Mohana, R.M., editors (2024). *Sustainability in Industry 5.0: Theory and Applications*, CRC Press.

Stearns, P.N. (2020). The Industrial Revolution in World History, Routledge.

Chapter 3

# Probability and Statistics

## 3.1 PERMUTATION AND COMBINATION

Probability theory is an indispensable cornerstone within the discipline of statistics, offering a robust mathematical framework for scrutinizing events fraught with uncertainty and effectively quantifying the plausibility of diverse outcomes. Probability, a fundamental concept in statistics, serves as the base for both inferential and predictive analysis. Probability theory enables the characterization of the innate uncertainty present in real-world phenomena through the utilisation of random variables and their corresponding probabilities. The incorporation of fundamental concepts such as conditional probability, independence, and Bayes' theorem serves to enhance the depth and complexity of statistical analysis, thereby enabling the utilisation of more advanced modelling techniques. While there have been a lot of advances in probability theory, the fundamental backbone is the concept of permutation and combination.

Permutation and combination are used to determine the probabilities and hence can be considered the backbone. Both permutation and combination are built on the concept of factorial (!) such that for any number, say $n$, denoted by "$n!$" can be computed by $n! = n(n - 1)(n - 2)(n - 3) \ldots 1$

For instance, if we have to find the factorial of 6 then it can be computed by $6! = 6 \times 5 \times 4 \times 3 \times 2 \times 1 = 720$.

### 3.1.1 Permutation

Permutations, as a fundamental concept in mathematics and statistics, assumes an important role in explaining the complex nature of arrangements and the systematic ordering of elements across diverse scenarios. Permutations hold significant relevance in scenarios where the precise ordering of elements is important, and each arrangement possesses a unique identity. The significance of permutation resides in the arrangement of the elements, or the order in which they are placed. In general,

$$P(n, r) = n(n - 1)(n - 2)(n - 3) \ldots (n - r + 1) \tag{3.1}$$

The number of permutations for n objects taken r at a time is computed by,

$$nPr = \frac{n!}{(n-r)!} \tag{3.2}$$

### 3.1.2 Combination

Combinations holds a fundamental position within the context of mathematics, exhibiting a close relationship with permutations and assuming a pivotal role in Probability and Statistics. Combinations gracefully navigate the space of object selection, disregarding the trend in which the items are selected, and instead focusing solely on the composition of the chosen subset. Combinations, in essence, offer a powerful mechanism for quantifying the countless possibilities of selecting elements from a set, all while disregarding any specific arrangement considerations. The consideration of combinations becomes particularly salient in scenarios where the sequential arrangement of elements holds no significance. The number of combinations for n objects taken $r$ at a time is computed by,

$$nCr = \frac{n!}{(n-r)!r!} \tag{3.3}$$

Both permutations and combinations offer distinct perspectives on the arrangement and selection of objects. These two concepts, though closely related, offer unique insights into the fascinating world of combinatorics.

## 3.2 CONCEPT OF PROBABILITY AND CHANCE

Chance, in the context of probabilistic reasoning, serves as a fundamental metric that measures the likelihood of an event to occur. It encapsulates the essence of uncertainty, enabling us to assess the probability associated with a particular outcome. The quantification of an event's likelihood is typically represented as a scalar value within the range of 0 to 1. In this context, a value of 0 signifies the event's impossibility, while a value of 1 denotes its absolute certainty. Probability by chance leads to a scale of probability where 1 means certain and 0 means impossible., all other points reflect the possible conditions. The pervasive nature of probability and chance permeates a multitude of domains, spanning from the area of games of chance and gambling to the expanse of scientific inquiry and the intricacies of decision-making processes. Probability serves as a vital tool for discerning the import of experimental findings and deriving cogent inferences. In daily practices, chance assumes a pivotal role, applying its influence over numerous of occurrences, ranging from the capricious whims of weather patterns to the unpredictable ebb and flow of traffic congestion.

## 3.3 RANDOM VARIABLES

Random variables and probability distributions serve as foundational pillars in probability theory and statistics. These concepts play an important role in understanding and quantifying uncertainty, enabling us to model and analyse a wide range of phenomena. By formalising the notion of random variables, which capture the uncertain outcomes of a given experiment, and probability distributions, which describe the likelihood of these outcomes, one can gain a powerful framework for probabilistic reasoning and statistical inference.

### *How Random is "Random"?*

Randomness is an "elusive" concept. Anything that is not predictable is actually random. The outcome of dice was seemingly random till 2012 when researchers from Poland and Scotland could predict the outcome considering air viscosity, table friction and acceleration of gravity. The radioactive decay of an atom, which according to Quantum theory is impossible to predict is "random". The world is made of 12 fundamental particles and interacts in 4 predictable ways, if the position and velocity of each of these can be determined, then there will be nothing will be unpredictable and hence there will be no "random" left in the universe.

### *Understanding Random Variables*

Random variables emerge as a fundamental concept, serving as a mathematical function that adeptly maps the various outcomes of a given random experiment onto the vast landscape of real numbers. Random variables can be categorized into two primary classifications—discrete and continuous random variables. Discrete random variables are further characterized by a finite or countably infinite set of distinct values, or continuous, endowed with the ability to assume any value within a specified interval. Discrete random variables are intrinsically linked to probability mass functions (PMFs), which elegantly summarize the probabilities associated with each distinct value that the random variable may assume. In contrast, continuous random variables are intrinsically linked to probability density functions (PDFs), which elegantly capture the density of probabilities at every conceivable point within the range of potential values. Both categories of random variables must adhere to the fundamental principle that the cumulative probabilities (for discrete variables) or the integration of the probability density function (for continuous variables) across the entire domain amounts to unity.

### *Discrete Random Variables*

Discrete random variables have found wide-ranging applications in a multitude of real-world scenarios, wherein they serve as invaluable tools for modelling the occurrences of successes within a series of trials, quantifying the frequency of specific events, and comprehensively analyzing the outcomes of games of chance.

The utilization of probability distributions linked to discrete random variables is of utmost importance for estimating probabilities, computing expected values, and evaluating the likelihood of diverse events. Notably, the Binomial distribution, Poisson distribution, and geometric distribution stand as prominent examples in this domain. These distributions serve as invaluable tools for discerning the probabilities associated with discrete outcomes, thereby enabling the quantification and assessment of uncertainties in various scenarios. Discrete random variables are also crucial in statistical modelling, hypothesis testing, and decision-making for diverse domains extending from engineering and biology to social sciences and economics.

Discrete random variables, with their ability to capture the intrinsic randomness and quantifiable characteristics of specific events, present indispensable instruments for leveraging probabilistic forecasts, deriving dependable inferences, and tackling uncertainties within the realms of data analysis and decision-making.

#### *Continuous Random Variables*

In contrast to their discrete counterparts, continuous random variables exhibit an expansive spectrum of potential values, rendering them apt for capturing the intricacies of phenomena characterised by continuous fluctuations. Continuous random variables have gathered significant attention and extensive utilisation across diverse domains such as physics, engineering, finance, and social sciences. This is primarily due to their inherent capability to effectively model phenomena characterised by seamless and uninterrupted variations.

Continuous random variables are integral components of statistical modelling, hypothesis testing, and data analysis due to their association with various probability distributions. Prominent among these distributions are the normal distribution, exponential distribution, and uniform distribution. These distributions are important in quantifying the likelihood of different outcomes and are extensively employed in a multitude of applications. Continuous random variables are advantageous in analysing large samples due to the profound implications of the central limit theorem (CLT). CLT asserts that the means of the samples derived from a set of independent and identically distributed random variables exhibit a remarkable tendency to follow normal distribution, irrespective of the distribution of original data.

### 3.3.1 Functions of Random Variables

When a random variable is thought of as having a function, its many outcomes are subjected to a mathematical procedure in order to produce a new random variable. The utilization of these functions assumes a pivotal role in the modelling of intricate phenomena and the comprehension of the dynamics exhibited by systems encompassing multiple variables. These measures encompass fundamental quantities like expected values, variances, and cumulative distribution functions. Machine learning models empower researchers and analysts by providing them with the capability to make accurate predictions and derive insightful conclusions regarding the potential outcomes of stochastic events. These models leverage the intrinsic characteristics of the underlying functions to facilitate this process.

A ubiquitous illustration of the utility of random variables lies in their ability to model the summation or subtraction of multiple random variables. An additional illustration lies in the manipulation of random variables through the utilization of exponential, logarithmic, or trigonometric functions. This practice assumes high significance when endeavoring to model natural phenomena that adhere to particular distributions. The utilization of random variable functions extends beyond theoretical frameworks, finding practical applications in simulation studies and Monte Carlo methods. These techniques leverage the power of random variable functions in generating random samples from complex distributions.

### *Cumulative Distribution Function*

The Cumulative Distribution Function (CDF) of a random variable $X$ delivers the probability that $X$ assumes a value less than or equal to a specific value "$x$". The CDF of a random variable $X$ is typically represented by the symbol $F(x)$ and is formally defined as $F(x) = P(X \leq x)$ in mathematical notation. CDF offers a comprehensive representation of the probability distribution of a random variable, encompassing its entire range and providing information on the probabilities associated with various outcomes.

CDF contributes in comprehending the characteristics and patterns exhibited by random variables. This tool enables the computation of diverse probabilities related to the stochastic variable, such as the likelihood of $X$ being within a specific interval or surpassing a given threshold. Furthermore, CDF is frequently employed in the derivation of various significant measures, including the mean, variance, and percentiles of the given distribution. CDF exhibits a remarkable property of non-decreasing monotonicity, ensuring that its values ascend or remain constant as the variable's domain is traversed. Furthermore, the CDF's range spans the closed interval from 0 to 1, encapsulating the entire spectrum of possible probabilities. As the input value $x$ tends towards negative infinity, the CDF asymptotically converges to zero. Conversely, as $x$ tends towards positive infinity, the CDF asymptotically approaches unity. Moreover, it is worth noting that the CDF exhibits right-continuity, thereby implying the absence of any discontinuities or abrupt changes at particular points. It is represented as:

$$F_x(X) = P(X \leq x) - \alpha < x < \alpha \tag{3.4}$$

Where $F_x(X)$, encapsulates the fundamental essence of the probabilistic behaviour of the random variable $X$. The elegant symbolism of the uppercase letter $F$ elegantly signifies the CDF's pivotal role in quantifying the cumulative probability distribution of $X$.

## 3.3.2 Distributions of Random Variables

The characterization of a random variable's distribution offers a structured framework for comprehending the dispersion of its values and the corresponding probabilities of occurrence. Among the various distributions, the binomial distribution is fundamental that elegantly captures the likelihood of achieving a predetermined number of successes within an amount of distinct Bernoulli trials. On the other hand, the Poisson distribution is often employed to explore the occurrence of rare events over a fixed interval of time or space. Lastly, the geometric distribution captures the probability of achieving the sequence of independent Bernoulli trials. The normal distribution and exponential distribution are typical illustrations of continuous probability distributions.

Some important and widely used distributions (continuous and discrete) are explained below:

**Uniform Distributions:** Consider a stochastic variable characterized by a probability distribution that follows the uniform distribution over the interval [0, 1]. The probability distribution function can be expressed as $P(a \leq X \leq b) = b - a$, where a and b are within the range of 0 to 1. Additionally, the probabilities of $X$ being less than 0 or greater than 1 are both 0.

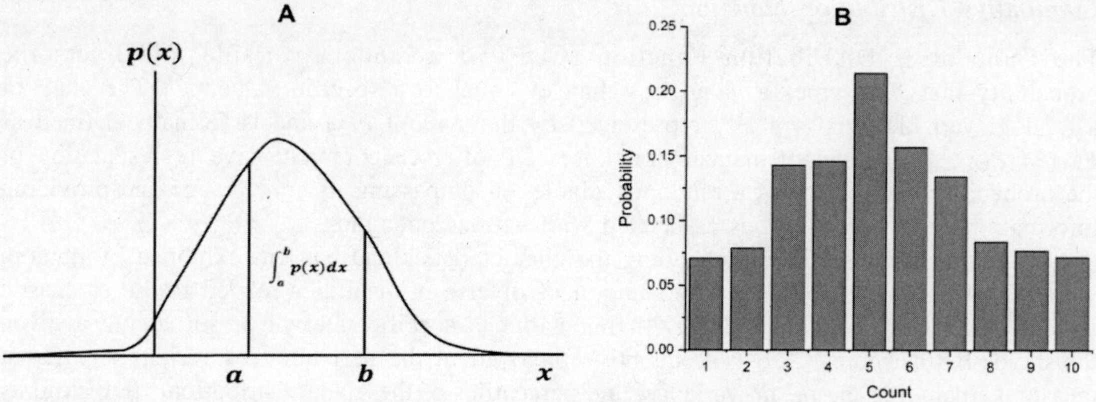


**FIGURE 3.1** Visual interpretation of (A) continuous probability distribution and (B) discrete probability distributions

**Normal Distribution:** Consider a random variable $X$, which is characterized by the probability density function $\varphi$. In mathematical analysis, it is evident that the inequality $-\infty < a \leq b < \infty$ holds true. The variable $X$ is commonly referred to as having a $N(0, 1)$ distribution, also known as the standard normal distribution.

**Exponential Distribution:** Consider a fixed constant $\lambda > 0$. Let us consider the function $f$: $R_1 \rightarrow R_1$, where $R_1$ denotes the set of real numbers.

$$f(x) = \begin{cases} \lambda \cdot e^{-\lambda x} & \text{if } x \geq 0 \\ 0 & \text{if } x < 0 \end{cases} \tag{3.5}$$

So, $f(x) \geq 0$ for all $x$.

$$\int_{-\infty}^{\infty} f(x)\,dx = \int_{0}^{\infty} \lambda e^{-\lambda x}\,dx = (-0) - (-1) = 1 \tag{3.6}$$

If $X$ is a random variable having this density function f then,

$$P(a \leq X \leq b) = \int_{a}^{b} \lambda e^{-\lambda x}\,dx = (-e^{-\lambda b}) - (-e^{-\lambda a}) = e^{-\lambda a} - e^{-\lambda b}, for\ 0 \leq a \leq b < \infty \tag{3.7}$$

**Bernoulli Distributions:** The Bernoulli distribution, serves as a powerful tool for modelling binary events characterized by two distinct outcomes: success, denoted by the value 1, and failure, denoted by the value 0. Its adaptable nature allows to find practical utility across a diverse range of disciplines, such as statistics, probability theory, and the expanding field of machine learning. The PMF for Bernoulli's equation is given by,

$$p(x; p) = \begin{cases} p & if\ x = 1 \\ 1 - p & if\ x = 0 \end{cases} \tag{3.8}$$

**Binomial Distribution:** The Binomial distribution serves as a powerful tool for modelling the count of successes within a predetermined number of independent Bernoulli trials. The model encompasses a pair of pivotal parameters, namely "$n$" denoting the count of trials and

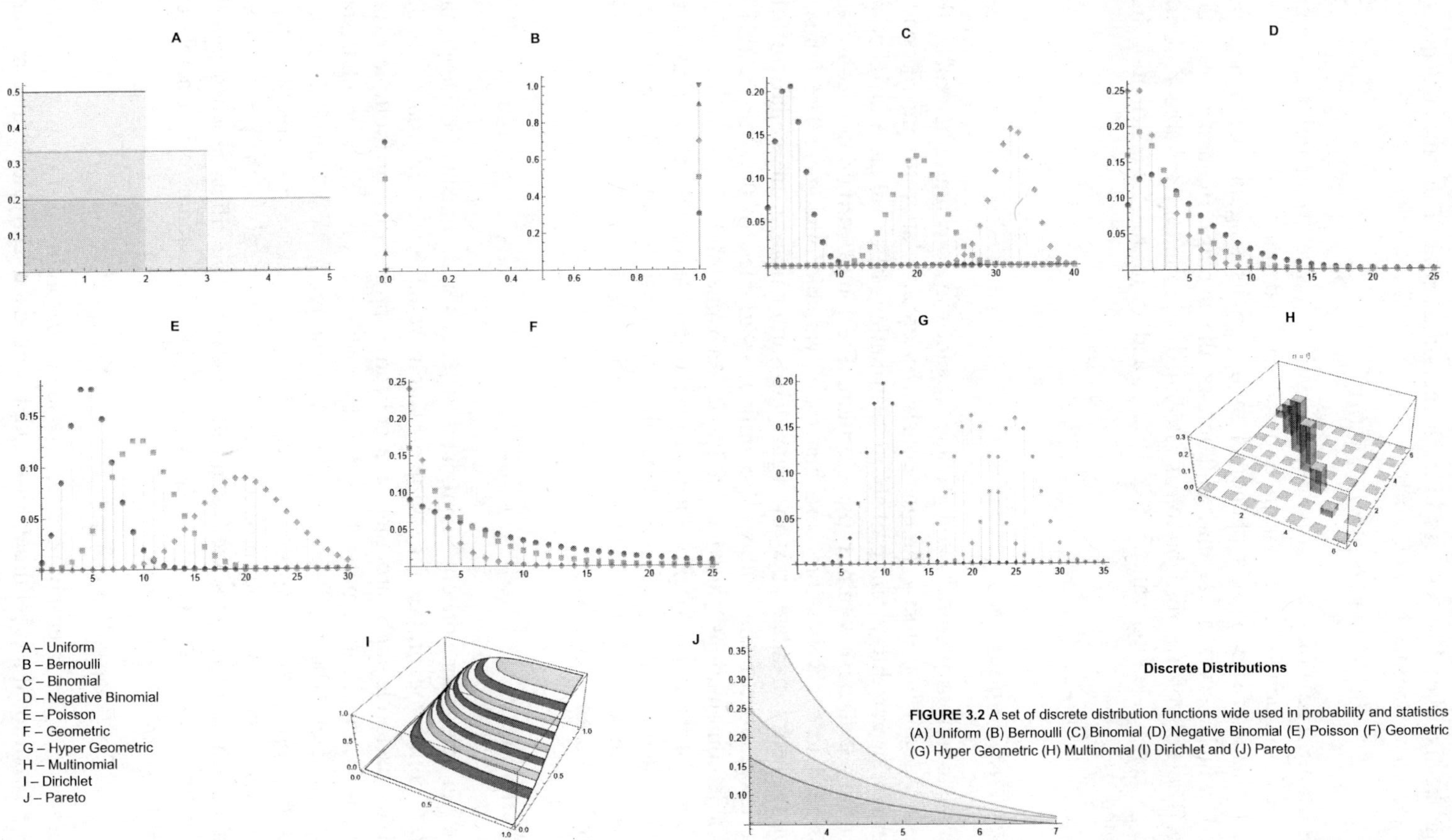


**FIGURE 3.2** A set of discrete distribution functions wide used in probability and statistics—(A) Uniform (B) Bernoulli (C) Binomial (D) Negative Binomial (E) Poisson (F) Geometric (G) Hyper Geometric (H) Multinomial (I) Dirichlet and (J) Pareto.

"$p$" representing the likelihood of success in each individual trial. The binomial distribution function for a random variable $x$ is depicted by,

$$P(x:n,p) = nC_x p^x (q)^{n-x} \tag{3.9}$$

**Poisson Distribution:** The Poisson distribution is again a powerful model for quantifying the occurrence of infrequent events within a predetermined temporal or spatial interval. The fundamental characteristic of this phenomenon lies in its singular parameter, denoted as "$\lambda$" (lambda), which serves as a representation of the average frequency at which the events transpire. The Poisson ($\lambda$) distribution is attributed to a random variable $Y$, denoted as $Y \sim$ Poisson ($\lambda$), when $y$ takes on values of 0, 1, 2, 3, and so forth. The distribution function can be represented by,

$$P(X=x) = \frac{\lambda^x e^{-\lambda}}{x!} \tag{3.10}$$

#### *Joint Probability Distributions*

Joint probability distributions provide a concise and elegant way to capture the probabilities of multiple events or variables occurring simultaneously. By encapsulating the interdependencies between these events or variables, joint probability distributions offer valuable insights into the complex relationships that exist within a given system. The joint distribution encapsulates the probabilities assigned to every possible combination of variable outcomes. The fundamental tenet of probability theory mandates that the aggregate summation, in the context of discrete variables, or the integration, in the context of continuous variables, of the probabilities linked with all conceivable combinations must inevitably yield a value of 1.

The utilisation of joint probability distributions is pervasive across various domains, including but not limited to statistics, machine learning, and finance. Probabilistic relationships between multiple variables are illuminated by these invaluable tools, enabling the facilitation of inference, prediction, and decision-making processes.

### 3.3.3 The Chain Rule

The Chain Rule, an important concept in probability theory and statistics and especially in the computation of joint probabilities for multiple random variables. Utilization of conditional probabilities allows us to elegantly articulate the collective probability of multiple events by establishing a chain-like connection among them, thereby enabling a comprehensive understanding of their interdependencies. The fundamental principle underlying the Chain Rule lies in the recognition that the joint probability of a series of events can be effectively derived by sequentially multiplying the conditional probabilities of each event, given the preceding events.

In terms of mathematical analysis, the Chain Rule holds great significance when considering a sequence of random variables denoted as $X_1$, $X_2$, ..., $X_n$. This fundamental principle can be elegantly expressed as follows,

$$P(X_1, X_2 .., X_n) = P(X_1) \times P(X_2 \mid X_1) \times P(X_3 \mid X_1, X_2) \times .. \times P(X_n \mid X_1, X_2 .., X_n) \tag{3.11}$$

This formula summarizes the interplay between the joint probability distribution of the entire sequence and the conditional probabilities associated with each individual random variable,

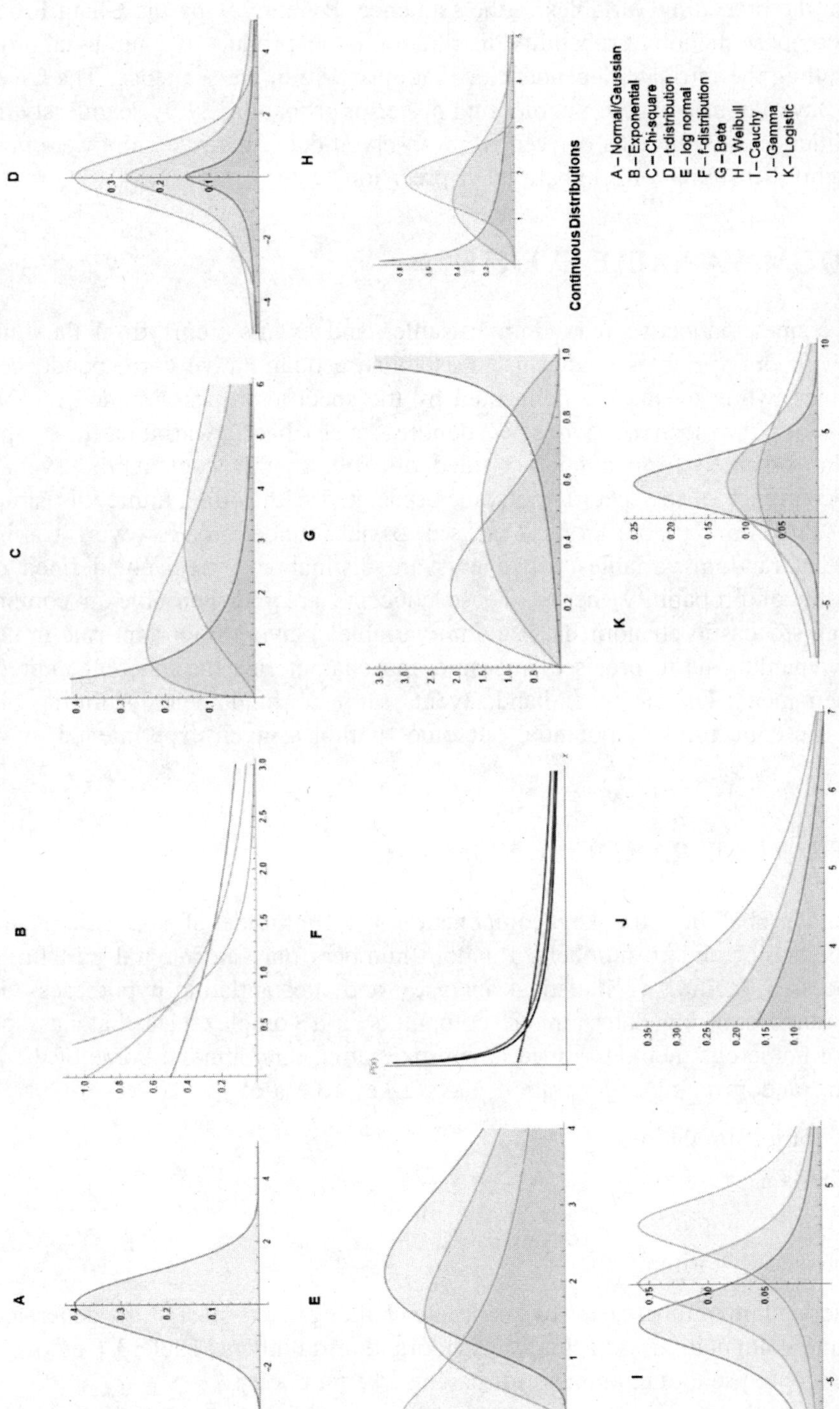


**FIGURE 3.3** A set of continuous distribution functions wide used in probability and statistics (A) Normal/Gaussian (B) Exponential (C) Chi-square (D) t-distribution (E) Log normal (F) f-distribution (G) Beta (I) Weibull (I) Cauchy (J) Gamma and (K) Logistic.

conditioned on the preceding variables in the sequence. By employing the Chain Rule, one can effectively decompose the joint probability distribution into a product of conditional probabilities, thereby unravelling the intricate dependencies that exist within the sequence. The Chain Rule is important for Bayesian inference for computing posterior probabilities. By seamlessly integrating prior probabilities and likelihoods derived from observed data, this rule empowers practitioners to derive insightful insights with unparalleled precision.

## 3.4 RANDOM VARIABLE EVENTS

The intrinsic connection between random variables and events stems from the fundamental principle that random variables enable us to establish a quantitative correspondence between diverse outcomes, while events are delineated by the specific values assumed by the random variable. Consider the scenario where $X$ denotes a stochastic variable that captures the numerical value obtained from a fair six-sided die roll. In this context, the event "$X = 3$" signifies the occurrence of the specific outcome associated with rolling a three. In simple terms, the notion of "Random Variable Events" lacks a formal foundation. However, it is imperative to recognize that random variables and events are distinct and precisely defined constructs within the realm of probability theory. These concepts are indispensable in comprehending and scrutinizing stochastic phenomena. Random variables play an important role in uncertainty quantification, enabling us to precisely measure and characterize the inherent unpredictability of various phenomena. On the other hand, events serve as fundamental building blocks that delineate specific collections of potential outcomes within a given experimental or situational context.

## 3.5 GENERATING RANDOM NUMBERS

In statistics and probability, the key component for a multitude of applications lies in the concept of generating random numbers. Random numbers play an integral part in simulating stochastic processes, facilitating statistical analyses, and substantiating hypotheses. Generating truly random numbers using deterministic computers is a complex task that has spurred the development of numerous methods aimed at approximating randomness. Some of the important domains where random number generation plays a key role are:

1. Monte Carlo Simulations
2. Hypothesis Testing
3. Bootstrap Resampling
4. Randomized Algorithms

Generating true random numbers has always been a challenge, and most of the generated random numbers through computation are actually pseudorandom numbers. Table 3.1 below compares true randomness with pseudorandomness for having a better clarity.

**TABLE 3.1** A comparison of True Randomness and Pseudo Randomness

| *Aspects* | *True randomness* | *Pseudo randomness* |
|---|---|---|
| *Source* | Derived from unpredictable physical phenomena | Generated algorithmically from a seed value |
| *Predictability* | Unpredictable and inherently random | Deterministic, produces the same sequence given the same seed |
| *Reproducibility* | Not reproducible; new random values each time | Reproducible with the same seed |
| *Statistical Properties* | True randomness, difficult to test | Subject to statistical tests for quality |
| *Usage Complexity* | Requires specialized hardware or processes | Easily implemented using algorithms |
| *Examples* | Quantum processes, radioactive decay | Linear Congruential Generators, Mersenne Twister, Cryptographically Secure PRNGs |

## 3.6 SAMPLING DISTRIBUTIONS

The acquisition of data from an entire population is frequently unfeasible or unattainable, thereby necessitating the reliance on samples by researchers to infer broader conclusions about the population at large. The sampling distribution is a fundamental concept in statistical inference, serving as a representation of the distribution of a statistic. This value represents the average or percentage of subsets of the whole population that were randomly selected. The analysis demonstrates the inherent variability in the statistical measures across the entire spectrum of potential samples, thereby offering crucial insights into the fluctuation of the sampling process and the precision of estimations derived from the sample.

The Central Limit Theorem (CLT), an important concept in the field of sampling distributions, allows to use normal distribution for interpreting inferences about population parameters, even in scenarios where the distribution of the population is either unknown or non-normal.

### 3.6.1 The Central Limit Theorem

The Central Limit Theorem (CLT) asserts that with increase in the sample size, the distribution of the sample mean tends to approximate a normal distribution. This theorem holds true irrespective of the shape of the population distribution, till the samples are drawn from a similar population. In essence, the CLT enables us to make reliable inferences about the population mean based on the characteristics of the sample mean.
Mathematically, the theorem is expressed as,

$$\mu_{\bar{x}} = \mu \tag{3.12}$$

$$\sigma_{\bar{x}} = \frac{\sigma}{\sqrt{n}} \tag{3.13}$$

Where $\mu$ = population mean; $\sigma$ = population standard deviation; $\mu_x$ = sample mean; $\sigma_x$ = sample standard deviation; and $n$ = Sample size

### 3.6.2 t-Distribution

A probability distribution with characteristics comparable to the normal distribution but with fatter tails is called a t-distribution. This implies that there is a higher probability of generating values that deviate significantly from the mean. This distribution belongs to a family of probability distributions that exhibits similarities to the standard normal distribution. However, it possesses heavier tails, rendering it particularly well-suited for situations involving limited data points in the sample. The statistical measure utilized for this hypothesis testing is commonly referred to as the t-statistic. The score for this statistic is computed as follows,

$$t = \frac{(X_1 - X_2)}{\left(\frac{\sigma}{\sqrt{n_1}} + \frac{\sigma}{\sqrt{n_2}}\right)} \tag{3.14}$$

Where, $x_1$ = average value of sample 1; $x_2$ = average value of sample 2; $n_1$ and $n_2$ = length of sample 1 and sample 2 respectively.

### 3.6.3 Z-Distribution

The Z-distribution is also called as the standard normal distribution. Its significance lies in its role in both hypothesis testing and confidence interval estimation. The standard normal distribution, characterized by its symmetric bell-shaped curve, serves as a fundamental tool in statistical analysis. To facilitate calculations and inferential procedures, the probabilities associated with this distribution are conveniently organized in a widely recognized reference known as the Z-table. The significance of Z-distribution lies in its ability to transform raw data into Z-scores, enabling researchers to precisely quantify the deviation of an observation from the mean in terms of standard deviations. Z-distribution is important in hypothesis testing as it helps to influence sample data in order to draw inferences about the larger population and derive meaningful conclusions regarding the efficacy of interventions or the significance of observed disparities. Here, the sample is considered to be distributed normally. The statistical measure employed for hypothesis testing in this context is commonly called as the z-statistic. The calculation of this score is performed as follows,

$$Z = \frac{(x - \mu)}{\frac{\sigma}{\sqrt{n}}} \tag{3.15}$$

Where, $x$ = average of the sample; $\mu$ = average of the population; $\sigma/\sqrt{n}$ = standard deviation of population. If the calculated test statistic is less than the critical value, the hypothesis should be accepted; otherwise, it should be rejected.

## 3.7 EXPECTATION

The operation of expectation is very important for random variables, as it possesses the ability to unveil profound insights into the intricate behavior exhibited by such variables. It is expressed as:

$$E(X) = \sum_i p_i x_i, \text{ where } P(X = x_i) = p_i \tag{3.16}$$

Conditional expectation serves as a tool for computing the anticipated value of a random variable, considering specific information pertaining to another variable. The notation $E[X \mid Y]$ is commonly used to denote the conditional expectation of the random variable $X$ given the value of $Y$. This mathematical expression captures the expected value of $X$ under the condition that $Y$ has a specific value. The computation of conditional expectation entails the amalgamation of integrating or summing the product of the conditional probability of variable $X$ given variable $Y$ and the feasible values of $X$, predicated on the accessible information regarding $Y$. The utilization of conditional expectation has emerged as a formidable instrument in decision-making, regression analysis, and the comprehension of intricate interdependencies among random variables.

For two random variables, it is expressed as,

$$E(Y \mid X = x) = \sum_{y \in Range(Y)} y * pY \mid X = x(y) \tag{3.17}$$

**TABLE 3.2** Various discrete distribution functions of probability and statistics with their possible usages

| *Name* | *Formula* | *Remarks* |
|---|---|---|
| Uniform | $P(x) = \begin{cases} \frac{1}{b-a} & \text{for } a \leq x \leq b \\ 0 & \text{otherwise} \end{cases}$ | For modelling randomness and uncertainty in various real-world scenarios |
| Bernoulli | $P(X = x) = p^x \cdot (1-p)^{1-x}$ | For modelling binary outcomes |
| Binomial | $P(X = k) = \frac{n!}{k!(n-k)!} \cdot p^k \cdot (1-p)^{n-k}$ | Used in modelling discrete random variables and inference of data |
| Negative Bionomial | $P(X = k) = \binom{k-1}{r-1} p^r (1-p)^{k-r}$ | Used in modelling count data with overdispersion |
| Dirichlet | $P(y^k) = \frac{\Gamma(\alpha_0)}{\prod_{i=1}^{k} \Gamma(\alpha_i)} \prod_{i=1}^{k} y_i^{\alpha_i - 1}$ | For representing uncertainty and capturing dependencies among multiple categorical variables |
| Pareto | $P(x) = \frac{ab^a}{x^{a+1}} D(x) = 1 - (\frac{b}{x})^a$ | To model distributions with heavy tails |
| Poisson | $P(X = k) = \frac{e^{-\lambda}\lambda^k}{k!}$ | For modelling random events that occur independently over time or space |
| Geometric | $P(X = k) = p \cdot (1-p)^{k-1}$ | Models the number of trials needed to achieve the first success in a sequence of independent Bernoulli trials |
| Hypergeometric | $P(X = k) = \frac{\binom{b}{k} \cdot \binom{r}{n-k}}{\binom{b+r}{n}}$ | For modelling the probability of selecting a specific number of successes in a finite population without replacement |

**TABLE 3.3** Various continuous distribution functions of probability and statistics with their possible usages

| *Name* | *Formula* | *Remarks* |
|---|---|---|
| Normal/Gaussian | $P(x) = \frac{1}{\sigma\sqrt{2\pi}} e^{-\frac{(x-\mu)^2}{2\sigma^2}} \quad -\infty < x < \infty$ | For modelling randomness and uncertainty in various real-world scenarios |
| Exponential | $p(x) = \begin{cases} \lambda e^{-\lambda x} & \text{for } x > 0 \\ 0 & \text{for } x \leq 0 \end{cases}$ | For analysing processes with constant rates of occurrences |
| logistic | $p(x) = \frac{e^{\left(\frac{x-\mu}{\nu}\right)}}{1+e^{\left(\frac{x-\mu}{\nu}\right)}}, -\infty < x < \infty$ | Modelling of continuous random variables with bounded support |
| Cauchy | $p(x) = \frac{a}{\pi(x^2 + a^2)} \quad a > 0, -\infty < x < \infty$ | Used when heavy-tailed or long-tailed distributions are observed |
| Log normal | $p(x) = \frac{1}{\sigma\sqrt{2\pi}} \cdot \frac{e^{-\frac{(\log x-\mu)^2}{(2\sigma^2)}}}{x}$ | Modelling skewed data with positive values and providing insights into the variability and distributions |

## 3.8 INTRODUCTION TO STATISTICS

The field of statistics is an indispensable discipline that assumes an important role in the comprehensive process of data acquisition, meticulous analysis, insightful interpretation, compelling presentation, and meticulous organisation. The fundamental objective of machine learning is to derive significant insights from data, unveil latent patterns and correlations, and facilitate well-informed decision-making grounded in empirical evidence and probabilistic reasoning. Through the application of sophisticated statistical methodologies, it is possible to extract invaluable insights pertaining to the intricate workings of intricate systems. This enables them to rigorously examine hypotheses, while also facilitating the ability to make accurate predictions regarding forthcoming events.

In the current era of data-driven advancements, the exponential growth of data has necessitated the continued reliance on statistics as an indispensable tool. Its role in extracting valuable insights, facilitating informed decision-making, and fostering innovation across diverse domains cannot be overstated. Hence, Statistics is the science of collecting, organizing, analysing and interpreting data.

The measures of central tendency and dispersion serves as crucial statistical instruments employed for the purpose of concisely encapsulating and scrutinizing data, thereby furnishing invaluable insights pertaining to the core and distribution of a given dataset, correspondingly. The essence of a dataset can be briefly captured by employing the mean, median, and mode. In the metrics of dispersion, namely the range, variance, and standard deviation, serve as quantitative indicators that capture the extent or variability of data points in relation to the central tendency.

### 3.8.1 Mean, Median and Mode

Mean is an important concept of statistics and is also called as the average. The process of computing the mean in a dataset involves the aggregation of all individual data points, divided by the total number of observations. The mean, a fundamental statistical measure, serves as an indicator summarizing the essence of a dataset's central tendency. The presence of outliers within a dataset can exert a substantial impact on the mean, causing it to deviate from the central tendency of the data distribution. Hence, it is imperative to precisely scrutinize the data's distribution and duly acknowledge the existence of outliers while interpreting the mean. The mean of a sample space of size $n$ can be calculated using the following formula,

$$Mean\ (\mu) = \frac{(x_1 + x_2 + \cdots + x_n)}{n} \tag{3.18}$$

Median is another crucial measurement of central tendency within the scope of statistics and presents a distinct vantage point when assessing the representative value within a given dataset. The inherent property of median to exhibit reduced sensitivity towards outliers renders it a highly robust measure of central tendency, particularly in scenarios where datasets exhibit skewed distributions or substantial variability. Median represents the middlemost value within a dataset, meticulously organized in either ascending or descending order. The computation of the median can be expressed using the following formula,
For odd-numbered datasets,

$$Median = \frac{(n+1)}{2} \tag{3.19}$$

For an even-numbered dataset:

$$Median = Average\ of\ values\ at\ n/2\ and (n/2+1)\ places \tag{3.20}$$

Mode is an indicator of central tendency which epitomises the value that occurs with highest frequency within a given dataset. In contrast to the measures of central tendency like mean and median, which offer insights into the average or middle value of a dataset, the mode is used for identifying the value that occurs most frequently. The identification of multiple modes within a dataset holds immense potential for unravelling the intricate fabric of its underlying structure, thereby offering profound insights. Such instances of multimodality not only hint at the existence of distinct subgroups or patterns but also serve as valuable indicators of the complex dynamics at play within the data. Moreover, in datasets exhibiting symmetry, the mode, mean, and median can align, signifying a uniform distribution of data around the central value.

### 3.8.2 Range, Variance and Standard Deviation

The range, a fundamental measure of dispersion, is derived by computing the disparity between the highest and lowest values within a given dataset. The metric in question offers an approximation of the dispersion of the dataset; however, it is susceptible to significant distortion due to the presence of outliers.

Variance on the other hand provides intuitions into the spreading of a dataset. It is the concept of quantifying the spread of data around the mean and obtaining a measure of variability is of utmost importance in the field of statistics and data analysis. The utilisation of this approach is pervasive and possesses the advantage of enhanced interpretability, owing to its adherence to the same units as the primary dataset. Variance can be calculated by:

$$Variance\,(\sigma^2) = \frac{\left[(x_1-\mu)^2+(x_2-\mu)^2+\cdots+(x_n-\mu)^2\right]}{n} \tag{3.21}$$

Where $\sigma^2$ denotes the variance; the variables $x_1$, $x_2$, ..., $x_n$ represent the individual data points; $\mu$ is the arithmetic mean and '$n$' represents all observations within the dataset.

In normal distribution, the data is generally distributed symmetrically and not skewed in any direction. Standard deviation provides a measure of how these data is related to the mean of all the observations. It is computed by finding the difference of each point from the mean such that if these means are summed up, the total will always be zero.

$$\sigma = \sqrt{\frac{\Sigma(x_i-\mu)^2}{N}} \tag{3.22}$$

Where $x$ represents the observation, $\mu$ is the mean and $N$ is the size of the data. When the standard deviation is small, it depicts that the data are clustered tightly around the mean. Conversely, when the standard deviation is large, the data are more spread out. If a standard deviation is close to zero, it depicts that data points are very close to the mean.

### 3.8.3 Quartile and Interquartile Range

When analysing data distribution in statistics, quartiles and the interquartile range (IQR) could be helpful. The concept of quartiles is to enable the division of a given dataset into four distinct groups, each encompassing an equal proportion of the total data points, specifically 25% of the dataset. This serves as a valuable means of summarising and understanding the distribution of data, facilitating the identification of central tendencies and variability within the dataset. The first quartile, denoted as Q1, represents the lower boundary below which 25% of the data values are located. The second quartile (Q2), commonly referred to as the median, serves as a pivotal measure within the dataset, signifying the central value (50%). The third quartile, denoted as Q3, is a statistical measure that represents the data point below which 75% of the observed values lie. The interquartile range (IQR) is calculated as the difference between the third quartile (Q3) and the first quartile (Q1). The IQR captures the dispersion of data by representing the range of values that encompasses the central 50% of the dataset. A larger IQR signifies a broader distribution, indicating that the data points are more widely scattered. Conversely, a smaller IQR indicates a more concentrated distribution, suggesting that the data points are closely clustered together.

For datasets with odd number of observations ($n$ = odd), quartiles are measured as,

$$Q1 = \left[\frac{(n+1)}{4}\right]^{th} term$$

$$Q2 = \left[\frac{(n+1)}{2}\right]^{th} term$$

$$Q3 = \left[\frac{3(n+1)}{4}\right]^{th} term$$

For datasets with an even number of observations ($n$ = even), quartiles are measured as,

$$Q1 = \left[\frac{(n+2)}{4}\right]^{th} term$$

$$Q2 = \left[\frac{n}{2}+1\right]^{th} term$$

$$Q3 = \left[3\left(\frac{n}{2}\right)\right]^{th} term$$

One must first sort the data in ascending order then use the quartile formula to determine the matching word in order to use these calculations.

IQR serves as a robust measure of dispersion, providing valuable insights into the variability of the data distribution. The IQR adeptly encapsulates the dispersion exhibited by the central 50% of the dataset, exhibiting a remarkable resilience against the disruptive impact of outliers or exceedingly anomalous values.

$$Inter\ Quartile\ Range\ (IQR) = Q3 - Q1 \tag{3.23}$$

## 3.9 STATISTICAL INFERENCE, SAMPLES, POPULATION AND ROLE OF PROBABILITY

Data science plays an essential part in deriving meaningful insights and drawing accurate conclusions about a population based on a representative sample. One potential application of statistical analysis is to determine the significance of differences between a sample and the population from which it was drawn. If the addition or removal of a feature from a model is likely to significantly enhance the performance of the model, will it be beneficial? If there exists a substantial disparity in performance between two models? Nevertheless, the primary objective is focused on the broader concept of hypothesis testing.

Population (Donated by N) is the dataset that encompasses all individuals belonging to a designated group, comprising the complete range of potential data values. For instance, all students pursuing a degree in Data Science.

Sample (denoted by n) on the other hand consists only a portion or subset of the population. This makes the size of a sample is always lesser than the size of actual population from which it was taken.

Sampling is the primary methodology utilized for the purpose of data selection. This methodology is frequently employed for both the initial exploration and ultimate analysis of the data. The property of interest exhibited by the original set of data is approximately equivalent in the given set. Sampling is employed in situations where acquiring the complete dataset of interest is deemed impractical due to its exorbitant cost or time-consuming nature. Similarly, processing the entire dataset of interest is considered economically or temporally burdensome.

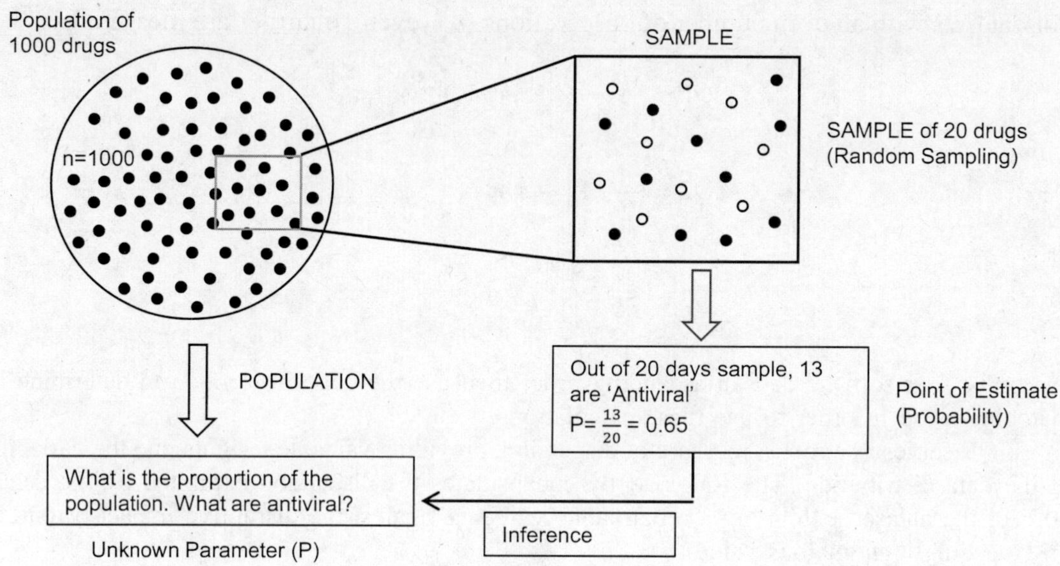


**FIGURE 3.4** The process of obtaining an inference of a population using a sample out of it.

## 3.10 TESTING OF HYPOTHESIS

The overall concept is for having a decision criterion that governs the acceptance or rejection of a hypothesis pertaining to a population based on the evidential support derived from a sample. A hypothesis test serves as a rigorous examination of two contrasting hypotheses pertaining to a given population—

Null hypothesis—It is the statement being tested—"no effect" or "no difference"

$$H_0 : \mu = \mu_0 \tag{3.24}$$

Alternative hypothesis—It is the statement that concludes true based on evidence from sample.

$$H_a : \mu \neq \mu_0 \tag{3.25}$$

$$H_a : \mu > \mu_0 \tag{3.26}$$

### 3.10.1 Chi-Square Test

It is a widely employed statistical test specifically designed for analyzing categorical data. It serves the purpose of assessing a noteworthy association between two categorical variables and evaluating the goodness-of-fit of observed data to expected theoretical distributions. By examining the deviations between observed and expected frequencies, the chi-square test enables researchers to draw meaningful conclusions about the underlying relationships. To assess the relationship between observed frequencies ($O$) and expected frequencies ($E$) while assuming independence, this test can be computed by,

$$X^2 = \Sigma \frac{(O-E)^2}{E} \tag{3.27}$$

### 3.10.2 Distribution and Analysis of Variance (ANOVA)

This is a powerful methodology in statistics which is employed to effectively compare and contrast the means of multiple groups or treatments. Through careful examination of the variation within and between these groups, ANOVA enables researchers to discern significant differences and draw meaningful conclusions. The method evaluates the presence of substantial disparities among the means through an examination of the variance within and between groups.

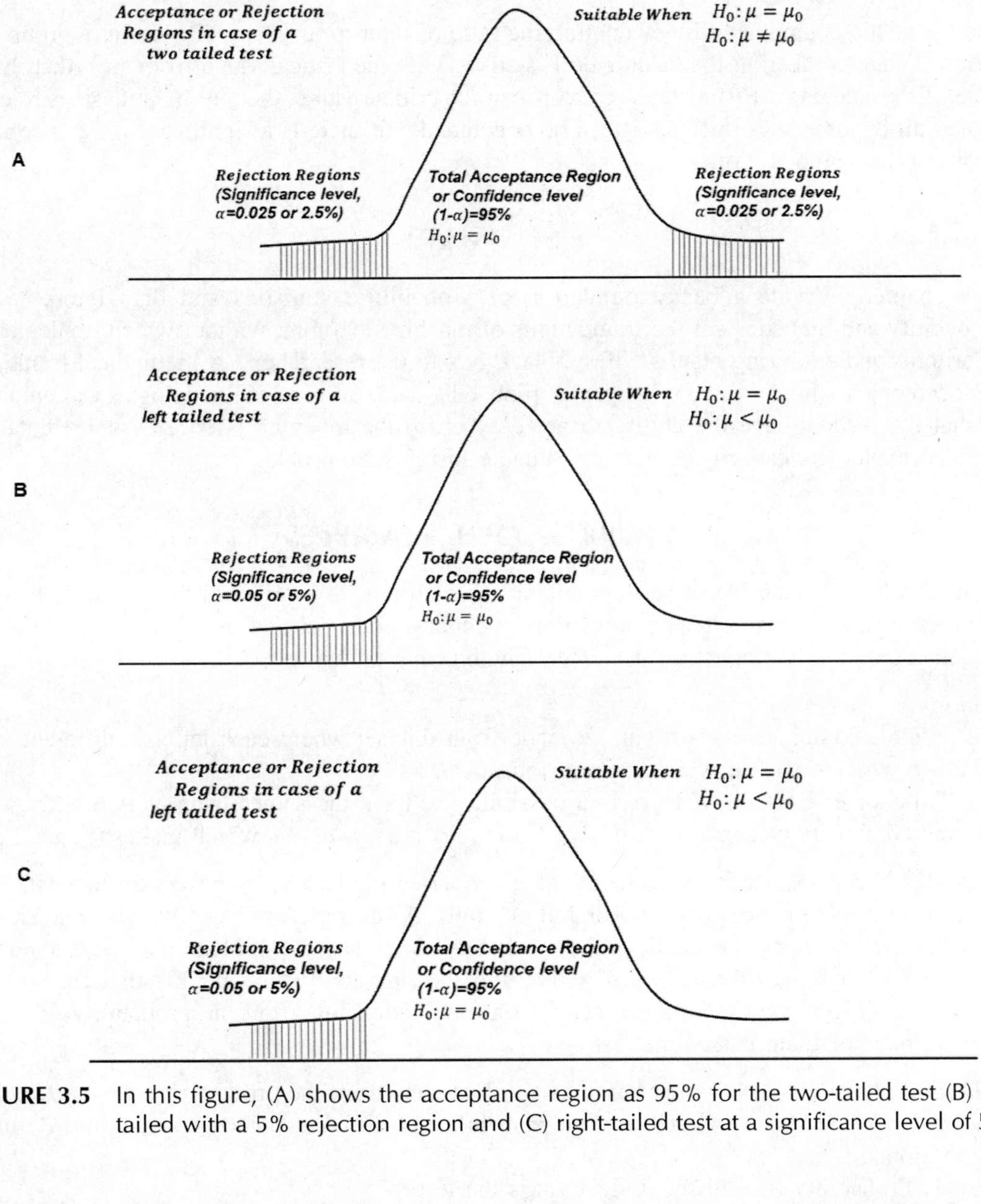


**FIGURE 3.5** In this figure, (A) shows the acceptance region as 95% for the two-tailed test (B) left-tailed with a 5% rejection region and (C) right-tailed test at a significance level of 5%.

The Annova Coefficient (F) is computed as,

$$F = \frac{MSB}{MSW} \tag{3.28}$$

Such that $MSB = \frac{SSB}{dfb}$ and $MSW = \frac{SSW}{dfw}$

Where $SSW$ = sum of squares within groups, SSB = sum of squares between groups, dfw = total number of observations ($n$) – total number of groups ($k$) and $dfb$ = total number of groups ($k$) – 1.

The F-statistic is computed by evaluating the ratio of inter-group variability to intra-group variability. While comparing the calculated F-statistic with the critical value from an F-distribution table, if the calculated F-statistic is greater than the critical value, the null hypothesis is rejected. If the null hypothesis is rejected, it can be concluded that there is a significant difference in the means of the methods adopted.

## SUMMARY

This chapter presents a basic foundation of probability, statistics and data interpretation. Probability and Statistics are the foundations of machine learning, without which implementing algorithms and analyzing results will be black box to the researchers. A methodical framework that encompasses fundamental principles of probability and statistical methodologies was employed so that the readers have the ability to not only grasp the inherent essence of unpredictability but also exploit its capacity to extract valuable insights from data.

## WORKED OUT EXAMPLES

**EXAMPLE 3.1** Consider a set comprising three strings "*a*", "*b*", and "*c*". What is the total number of possible two-letter combinations, including both real and imaginary words, that can be generated from the constituent elements within this grouping?

***Solution:***

The possible combinations that can be made from this set where each letter is different are—*ab*, *ba*, *bc*, *cb*, *ac* and *ca* which make a total of 6.

On another instance, if there is a possibility to have the same string as two letter words then the combinations come to—*ab*, *ba*, *bc*, *cb*, *ac*, *ca*, *aa*, *bb*, *cc* which makes the total as 9.

**EXAMPLE 3.2** Consider a scenario where a series of tests is being conducted with each test having result in success (pass) or failure (fail). A machine produces widgets and the test is performed to check the quality of the widgets. Let's say the probability that a randomly selected widget passes the test is $p = 0.8$, and the probability that it fails the test is $1 - p = 0.2$. If 5 widgets are randomly selected from production line, find the probability that all of them or none of them passes the test.

***Solution:*** Now, let's say we randomly select 5 widgets from the production line and test them independently. We want to calculate the probability of different outcomes using the Bernoulli distribution.

**Case 1:** Probability that all the widgets pass the test

$$P(X = 1\ 1\ 1\ 1\ 1) = p^5 = (0.8)^5 = 0.32768$$

**Case 2:** Probability that none of the widgets pass the test

$$P(X = 0\ 0\ 0\ 0\ 0) = (1 - p)^5 = (0.2)^5 = 0.00032$$

**EXAMPLE 3.3** The fundamental protein molecule known as vasopressin serves comprises of precisely 8 amino acids, this molecule is intricately interconnected through chemical bonds, adhering to a specific sequential arrangement. The sequential arrangement of amino acids plays a crucial role in facilitating the optimal functionality of vasopressin. If the eight amino acids are taken one at a time out of a hat, how many different ways are there to organize them?

***Solution:*** The eight amino acids may be depicted by the symbols A, B, C, D, E, F, G, and H. The individual is required to complete a total of eight empty spaces, denoted as: _ _ _ _ _ _ _ _.

There exists a total of eight possible options for the initial position, followed by seven potential choices for the subsequent position, six potential selections for the third position, and so forth.

The total number of possible orderings can be calculated as follows: 8 factorial, denoted as 8!, which is equal to 8 multiplied by 7 multiplied by 6 multiplied by 5 till 1, resulting in a value of 40,320.

## EXERCISES

1. Take into consideration the trio named "Harry, Paul, and Nicky," all of whom are male. What is the total number of different two-person teams that may be selected from this pool of available options?
2. The bookshelf possesses a capacity that accommodates precisely five books. How many different ways can a set of five books be arranged on the bookshelf?
3. In three players shooting game, the probability that the first player hits the target is 90%, second player hits the target is 80%, and the third player hits the target is 70%. Considering that all the three players are shooting for the target at the same time, what is the probability that at least one of them hits the target?
4. In the card game, a player is given a hand of 13 cards from a deck that has been thoroughly shuffled and follows the standard format. What is the likelihood of a hand having no cards in at least one suit, also known as being void in a suit?
5. Take into consideration a modest production unit with five workers: four labourers and a supervisor. Monthly salaries for the workers are Rs. 5,000, while the supervisor receives a salary of Rs. 10,000. Find the salary's mean, median, and mode.

## BIBLIOGRAPHY

Beyer, W. H. (1991). CRC *Standard Probability and Statistics*, CRC. ISBN: 0-8493-0680-9.

Cox, D.R. and Miller, H.D. (1977). *The Theory of Stochastic Processes,* Chapman and Hall, ISBN: 978-0412151705.

Deep, R. (2006). *Probability and Statistics*, Academic Press, ISBN: 978-0-12-36946 8.

Goodman, W. M. (2009). *Modern Statistics,* Nelson, ISBN: 978-0-17-625179-6.

Grami, Ali. (2019). *Probability, Random Variables, Statistics, and Random Processes: Fundamentals and Applications*, John Wiley & Sons, 2019.

Hayter, A. (2007). *Probability and Statistics for Engineers and Scientists,* third edition, Thomson, ISBN: 0-495-10757-3.

Chapter 4

# Artificial Neural Networks

## 4.1 INTRODUCTION

Artificial neural networks (ANN) can be considered as a computerized replica that simulates the composition and activities of a human brain. Similar to the way networks of neurons in the human brain process information, ANNs consist of 'neurons', i.e., artificial neurons, arranged in interconnected layers. The connections between artificial neurons have numeric weights associated with them that can be tuned based on experience. By tuning these connected weights after processing each input, ANNs can learn to perform tasks like pattern recognition, regression, classification, speech recognition, and more.

ANNs are trained rather than explicitly programmed for specific tasks. They are presented with large sets of training data representing examples of inputs and desired outputs, which allows the ANN to gradually "learn" by adjusting its weights to be able to produce the right outputs for each input. The capability of ANNs to adapt and learn from experience allows them to effectively represent intricate nonlinear connections between input and output variables, eliminating the need for explicit programming instructions. Once trained, ANNs can rapidly process new unseen inputs to make predictions, classifications and decisions.

## 4.2 BIOLOGICAL NEURAL NETWORK (BNN) VS ARTIFICIAL NEURAL NETWORK (ANN)

Billion linked neurons, or brain cells that receive and transmit data using chemical and electrical signals, make up the biological neural network of the human brain. This vast complex network allows the remarkable abilities of the human mind—thinking, reasoning, learning, etc. ANNs contain basic computing units imitating the neurons in our brain. These artificial neurons are connected in layers, forming a network that can learn by examples. For instance, after showing many cats and dogs images to an ANN, it learns to recognize new animal pictures. While ANNs try to mimic some aspects of the mind, biological capabilities are clearly far more advanced and complex. But brain-like learning is what guides innovation in neural networks, to inch them closer towards the natural intelligence.

A biological neuron comprises three primary components:

***Dendrites:*** They serve as the primary recipients of incoming electrical input signals originating from neighbouring neurons.

***Soma:*** They are also known as the cell body, performs the essential function of integrating the incoming signals.

***Axon:*** The axon, upon reaching a critical threshold of input, undergoes depolarization, leading to the generation of an action potential. This action potential propagates along the axon, facilitating the transmission of signals to interconnected neuronal cells.

It has three fundamental components:

***Input:*** Receives input signals from adjacent neurons, thereby facilitating the flow of information within the neural network.

***Node:*** A node, also referred to as a neuron, performs the summation of weighted inputs it receives.

***Output:*** Upon reaching a certain threshold of input, the neuron undergoes activation, resulting in the transmission of a signal through its output connections to interconnected neurons.

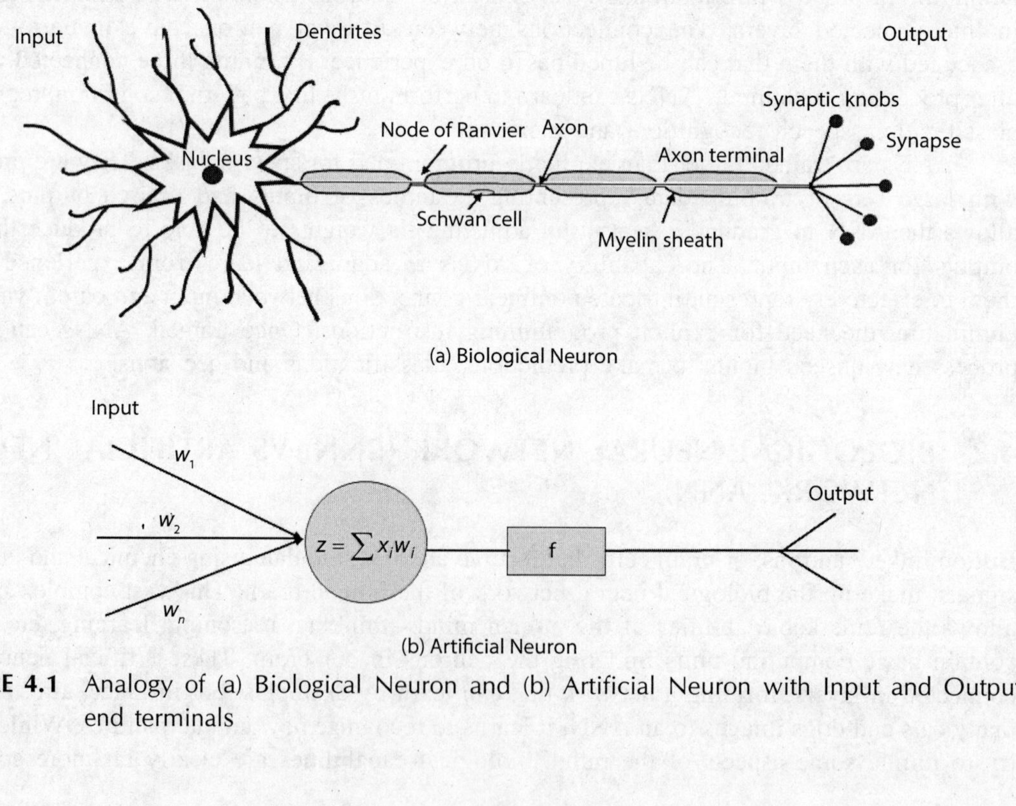


**FIGURE 4.1** Analogy of (a) Biological Neuron and (b) Artificial Neuron with Input and Output end terminals

**TABLE 4.1** Analogous Terminology of ANN and BNN

| *BNN* | *ANN* |
|---|---|
| Soma | Node |
| Dendrites | Input |
| Axon | Output |
| Synapse | Weight |
| Many Neurons | Few Neurons |
| Learning involves adjustments to the synaptic connections between neurons. | Learning involves adjustments to the weight's connections between neurons. |

## 4.3 McCULLOCH PITTS MODEL

The McCulloch-Pitts (MP) model was one of the first and important neural network models. Proposed in 1943 by neuroscientist Warren McCulloch and logician Walter Pitts, the MP model simplified neurons into basic "on/off" threshold logic units. Each unit sums up weighted inputs from connections with other neurons, and if the sum exceeds a certain threshold, the neuron fires a discrete "1" or "0" signal. Otherwise, the neuron remains off, passing no signal. Despite this basic functionality, McCulloch and Pitts demonstrated how networks of these simplified neurons could theoretically compute complex logical propositions when wired up and weighted appropriately between units. The model was pivotal in neural networks shifting to an engineering discipline, providing a building block for creating intelligent machines based on human-brain design. It also laid conceptual foundations that machine learning algorithms would later formalize and develop further.

In the McCulloch-Pitts (MCP) model, we can use the concept of excitatory and inhibitory inputs to create an AND gate for Mike's decision to hold an umbrella based on two weather conditions. An AND gate only produces an output of 1 when both inputs are 1.

***Inputs:***

- $x_1$: Raining (1 if true, 0 if false)—Excitatory
- $x_2$: Windy (1 if true, 0 if false)—Excitatory

***Threshold:***

- $\theta$: Threshold for holding an umbrella (e.g., 2)

***Output:***

- $y$: Hold an umbrella (1 if true, 0 if false)

The MP neuron for Mike's decision to hold an umbrella using an AND gate can be represented below:

$$y = f(x_1 + x_2 - \theta) \tag{4.1}$$

Here, $f$ is activation function, which is a step function:

$f(x) = 1$ if $x \geq 0$, and 0 otherwise

***Different Cases:***

***Case 1:*** Raining and windy ($x_1 = 1$, $x_2 = 1$): $y = f(1 + 1 - 2) = f(0) = 1$ Mike will hold an umbrella.

***Case 2:*** Raining but not windy ($x_1 = 1$, $x_2 = 0$): $y = f(1 + 0 - 2) = f(-1) = 0$ Mike will not hold an umbrella.

***Case 3:*** Not raining but windy ($x_1 = 0$, $x_2 = 1$): $y = f(0 + 1 - 2) = f(-1) = 0$ Mike will not hold an umbrella.

***Case 4:*** Not raining and not windy ($x_1 = 0$, $x_2 = 0$): $y = f(0 + 0 - 2) = f(-2) = 0$ Mike will not hold an umbrella.

In this example, both excitatory inputs (raining and windy) need to be present (i.e., have a value of 1) for the neuron to fire and for Mike to decide to hold an umbrella. If either input is 0, the sum will not exceed the threshold, and the neuron will not fire, resulting in Mike not holding an umbrella.

This demonstrates how the MCP model can be used to create an AND gate for decision-making based on two inputs without using weights. The threshold is set to 2, ensuring that both inputs must be 1 for the neuron to fire.

**FIGURE 4.2** Schematic representation of (a) McCulloch Pitts model, (b) for AND, (c) for OR Function and (d) for NOT Function.

So, we can say,

$$y_{\text{out}} = f(y_{\text{sum}}) = \sum_{i=1}^{n} x_i = \begin{cases} 1, & x \geq \theta \\ 0, & x < \theta \end{cases} \tag{4.2}$$

TABLE 4.2 McCulloch Pitts Neuron for two inputs

| *Inhibitory Input A* | *Excitatory Input_A1* | *Excitatory Input_A2* | *Sum(A1+A2)* | *Threshold Value* | *Threshold Reached?* | *Output* |
|---|---|---|---|---|---|---|
| 0 | 0 | 0 | 0 | 2 | No | 0 |
| 0 | 0 | 1 | 1 | 2 | No | 0 |
| 0 | 1 | 0 | 1 | 2 | No | 0 |
| 0 | 1 | 1 | 2 | 2 | **Yes** | **1** |
| 1 | 1 | 1 | NA | NA | NA | **0** |

## 4.4 PERCEPTRON

The Perceptron is one of the earliest and most influential neural networks developed in 1957 by Frank Rosenblatt at the Cornell Aeronautical Laboratory. It is a supervised learning algorithm for binary linear classification—dealing with two class classification problems. For example, determining if an input image contains a cat or not. The Perceptron model consists of input values ($x_1$, $x_2$, …), associated weights ($w_1$, $w_2$, ...), and an output layer that makes the binary prediction based on inputs and weights. It learns the weight parameters using an algorithm based on stochastic gradient descent and the perceptron learning rule. The goal is to find a linear separator between classes. The learning rule essentially increases weights leading to correct classification and decreases weights for incorrect predictions. Over many iterations, it can converge upon optimum weights.

The Perceptron only has two layers—the input layer of nodes representing input features, directly connected to an output layer node that makes the binary prediction. There are *no hidden layers*. Backpropagation refers to the method for calculating gradients to update weights in multi-layer feedforward neural networks. The error from output is propagated backwards through the hidden layers to efficiently calculate gradients for the weights. Since the Perceptron lacks hidden layers, there are no intermediate activations that could enable error propagation from the output backwards. The only weights in the Perceptron are between the inputs and the single output node. So, there is *no concept of backpropagating* an error to earlier layers. Instead, the Perceptron relies on the simpler Perceptron learning rule. Based on the output error, it only adjusts the input-to-output weights in a way that minimizes errors at the final output.

$f(x) = 1$ if $\sum_i^n x_i w_i \geq \theta$

$f(x) = 0$ if $\sum_i^n x_i w_i < \theta$, where

*$\theta$ is the threshold*

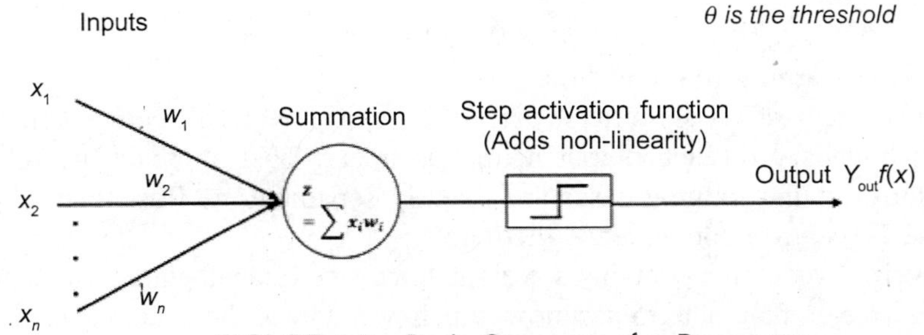


FIGURE 4.3 Basic Structure of a Perceptron

The most common step functions used in perceptron are:

***Heaviside/Binary Step Function:*** The Heaviside step function outputs 0 for any input below 0, and outputs 1 for any input greater than or equal to 0. This creates a binary "step" at 0. It is used to model the activation of a neuron, where 1 represents firing and 0 represents not firing.

Mathematically,
$$f(x) = \begin{cases} 0 & \text{if } x < 0 \\ 1 & \text{if } x \geq 0 \end{cases} \tag{4.3}$$

***Bipolar Step Function:*** This map negative values to –1, positive values including 0 to 1, creating a "bipolar" binary output representation. It can be useful for modelling on and off states. Mathematically,
$$f(x) = \begin{cases} -1 & \text{if} x < 0 \\ 1 & \text{if} x \geq 0 \end{cases} \tag{4.4}$$

***Sign Function:*** Similar to bipolar function but with 0 values mapped uniquely to 0 instead of 1 or –1. Provides symmetry around the origin of the input space.

These functions help introduce non-linearity in the output of perceptrons since they generate discrete outputs rather than continuous values. They simplify outputs to logical interpretations necessary for classification tasks. The choice depends on the preferred output encoding style for a problem.

Mathematically,
$$f(x) = \begin{cases} -1 & \text{if } x < 0 \\ 0 & \text{if } x = 0 \\ 1 & \text{if } x > 0 \end{cases} \tag{4.5}$$

## *Perceptron Learning Rule*

To reduce classification errors, adjust weights and bias based on the discrepancy between expected and actual output.

**Procedure**

1. ***Randomly initialise the bias (b) and weights (w).***
2. ***For every example (x, y) in the training:***

Determine the inputs' weighted sum using:
$$z = W^T * x + b \tag{4.6}$$
where T is the transpose of the weight vector w in a neural network or perceptron mode. Apply the step function, which is the activation function in most cases:
$$\hat{y} = sign(z) \tag{4.7}$$
$$w = w + \eta * (y - \hat{y}) * x \tag{4.8}$$
This is the perceptron learning rule equation.

As with logistic regression classifiers, perceptrons are unable to learn complex patterns since the decision boundary of each output neuron is linear. That approach would, however, converge to a solution if the training cases are linearly separable, as Rosenblatt showed. We refer to this as the Perceptron convergence theorem.

Where, $w$ = the weight vector, $w$ contains a weight for every input feature, $\eta$ = learning rate. This is a hyperparameter that determines how much we adjust the weights at each update step, $y$ = the true label or target output value that we are training towards which is the desired output, $\hat{y}$ = predicted output from the perceptron, and $x$ = the input feature vector. $x$ contains our input variables that are fed into the perceptron.

For biases,

$$b = b + \eta * (y - \hat{y}) \tag{4.9}$$

Where, $b$ = the bias term which acts similar to a trainable weight, except that it has no associated input value. Over multiple training iterations, this update rule tunes the bias term to values that improve the model predictions.

**3. *Continue step 2 until a predetermined number of epochs or convergence occurs.***

The Perceptron is guided by the rule in the direction of a decision boundary that accurately divides classes. In order to prevent overfitting and balance the rate of convergence, the learning rate ($\eta$) is essential. For datasets that are linearly separable, the convergence of the Perceptron is assured. Although it's a basic algorithm, it forms the basis of more sophisticated neural networks.

## 4.5 MULTI-LAYER PERCEPTRON

A layer that contains the input, one or more than one concealed layer, and an output layer comprise the components of a multi-layer perceptron (MLP). Lower layers are often those that are closest to the input layer, while upper levels are typically those that are closest to the outputs. Bias neurons are present in all layers but the output layer, and they are all fully coupled to the layer above them.

Researchers have faced challenges in training MLPs for a long time, but have not been able to find a solution. However, the backpropagation method, which is still in use today, was first presented in a seminal paper by David Rumelhart, Geoffrey Hinton, and Ronald Williams in 1986. Simply said, it's Gradient Descent with an effective method for automatically calculating the gradients. In merely two traversals of the framework (a single forward and another backward), the backpropagation algorithm will identify the change in gradient that represents the network's error for every sinusoidal model attribute.

***Step 1:*** It processes a small group of data at a time (e.g., with 32 instances in each group) and iterates through the entire training set multiple times. An epoch refers to each pass through the entire dataset.

***Step 2:*** The first hidden layer of the network receives each mini-batch, which is then sent there by the input layer. Following that, the algorithm calculates each neuron's output in this layer (for each instance in the mini-batch). Until we reach the output layer, which is the final layer, the result is passed to the following layer, whose output is then computed and passed to the following layer, and so on. In the forward pass, all intermediate outcomes are kept since they are required for the backward pass. Otherwise, it is exactly the same as making predictions.

***Step 3:*** Subsequently, a loss function is employed by the algorithm to calculate the output error of the network by comparing the real and predicted output with an error.

***Step 4:*** Next, it calculates the contribution of each output link to the error. The chain rule, which is arguably the most fundamental calculus rule, is applied analytically to accomplish this, making the process quick and accurate.

***Step 5:*** After that, the algorithm works backward until it reaches the input layer, calculating the proportion of these error contributions that originate from each connection in the layer below, once more using the chain rule. Since the error gradient is propagated backward through the network, as previously mentioned, this reverse pass effectively measures the error gradient across all of the link weights in the network—thus the algorithm's name.

***Step 6:*** Using the error gradients, it just generated, the method next uses a Gradient Descent step to adjust each connection weight in the network.

The backpropagation is of utmost importance and deserves a concise summary. It begins by making a prediction for each training instance through a forward pass and subsequently measuring the error. Then, it meticulously evaluates the error contribution from each connection by traversing through each layer in reverse during the reverse pass. Finally, it optimises the connection weights by performing a Gradient Descent step to minimise the error.

One of the crucial modifications to the MLP's architecture was to ensure its optimal performance. It was decided to replace the step function with the logistic (sigmoid) function, denoted as,

$$\sigma(Z) = \frac{1}{(1+\exp(-Z))} \tag{4.10}$$

This change proved to be essential in enhancing the algorithm's capabilities. Unlike the step function, which consists of only flat segments and lacks a gradient for Gradient Descent to work with, the logistic function has a well-defined nonzero derivative throughout its range. This property enables Gradient Descent to make progress at every step, making it a more effective choice for optimisation.

### MLP for Regression

Regression tasks can be performed using MLPs where one just needs a single output neuron, whose output is the expected value, to predict a single value (such as the price of a house given several of its attributes). One output neuron is required for each output dimension in order to do multivariate regression, or to predict several values at once. For instance, two output neurons are required to forecast 2D coordinates, which are necessary to pinpoint the centre in an image. Two further measurements are required if one wishes to add a bounding box around the object—its height and width. Consequently, you have four output neurons.

Typically, when constructing a Multilayer Perceptron (MLP) for regression purposes, it is advisable to refrain from employing any activation function for the output neurons. This allows them to freely generate a wide range of values as outputs. To ensure a consistent positive output, the ReLU activation function can be employed in the output layer. Another option is to utilise softplus activation function, log(1 + exp($z$)). When $z$ is negative, the value is nearly 0, while when $z$ is positive, it closely approximates $z$. In order to ensure that the predictions remain within a specific range of values, there are a couple of options available. One option is to utilise the logistic function, which maps the predictions to a range of 0 to 1. Another option is to use the hyperbolic tangent function, which scales the labels to a range of –1 to 1. By employing these functions and appropriately scaling the labels, you can effectively control the range of the predictions.

**TABLE 4.3** Typical regression MLP architecture

| *Hyperparameter* | *Typical Value* |
|---|---|
| Input Neurons | On per input features (e.g., 28 × 28 for MNIST) |
| Hidden Layers | Depends on the problem but typically 1 to 5 |
| Neurons per hidden layers | Depends on the problem but typically 10 to 100 |
| Output Neuron | 1 per prediction dimension |
| Hidden Activation | Re LU |
| Output Activation | None, or ReLU/softolus (if output is positive) |
| Loss Function | MSE or MAE/Huber (in case of outliers) |

### *MLP for Classification*

MLPs are a versatile tool that can be effectively employed for classification tasks as well. In binary classification problems, a single output neuron which uses the logistic activation function is sufficient. This neuron will generate a value ranging from 0 to 1, which is the estimated probability of the positive class and accordingly probability of the negative class can be determined. MLPs are highly adept at efficiently managing and solving multilabel binary classification tasks.

**TABLE 4.4** Typical Classification MLP architecture

| *Hyperparameter* | *Binary Classification* | *Multiclass Classification* |
|---|---|---|
| Input and Hidden Layers | Same as regression | Same as regression |
| Output Neuron | 1 | 1 per class |
| Output layer Activation | Logistic | SoftMax |
| Loss Function | Cross entropy | Cross entropy |

The most popular activation functions used with MLPs are Sigmoid, Tanh, ReLU and some of its variants like Leaky ReLU. The choice of activation depends on the network layer (input, hidden, output), problem type (classification, regression etc.) and other factors. But ReLU, LeakyReLU and more recently ELU, GELU are very widely used in modern MLP architectures due to their demonstrated performance. Today, deep neural networks with substantially more hidden layers have proven vastly more effective than shallow MLPs for difficult problems.

The key steps for how backpropagation work in MLP are described below in details.

***Forward Pass:*** To calculate the output values from existing weights and activation functions, input data is routed across the network of neurons layer by layer. Forward propagation is done first, where a training input is fed through the neural network layer by layer until an output is calculated. Each node in each layer gets activated based on the weights and inputs it receives from the previous layer nodes. These activations are transformed by the node's activation function as well. The final output layer activation gives the network's prediction for the current input.

***Loss Calculation:*** The output from the model is compared to the true labels to calculate the loss function (eg. MSE). This quantifies how well the model is currently performing. Next, this predicted output is compared to the true label and a loss or error is calculated. This quantifies how far the current prediction is from the correct label.

***Compute Gradients:*** The gradient of the loss is computed corresponding to every weight parameter, commencing at the output layer. The chain rule of derivatives is applied layer-by-layer moving backwards to efficiently compute gradients. Finally, having error gradients w.r.t each weight enables updating the weights proportional to their influence on the final error, nudging the prediction output closer towards the desired value. This gradient descent process repeated over many input samples lets MLPs efficiently learn non-linear functional relationships.

***Update Weights:*** The gradients indicate how much each weight must change to minimize the loss function. So, the weights are updated proportional to the gradients using gradient descent.

***Repeat Forward and Backward Passes:*** The above-mentioned steps constitute one training pass. They are repeated over many iterations to incrementally improve model performance by updating weights to reduce loss.

So, in essence, backpropagation leverages the chain rule to efficiently calculate loss gradients for each weight in the network, which enables effective learning via gradient descent over multiple layers. This can model complex non-linear relationships not achievable with single layer perceptron.

**TABLE 4.5** Comparison between the single and multiple layer perceptron

| *Single layer* | *Multi-layer* |
|---|---|
| Can not represent nonlinear function | Can represent any linear and nonlinear functions |
| Insufficiently expressive; they are non-linear i.e. can not represent non-linear and continuous functions | Sufficiently expressive; can represent any Boolean and continuous functions using appropriate activation functions |
| Can not deal with generalized data sets | Can be trained to deal with generalized data sets, i.e. via error back-propagation |

## 4.6 ARCHITECTURE OF ANN

The structure pertains to the arrangement and interconnection of its artificial neurons with different layers. Having a solid grasp of these fundamental components of ANN like neuron, biases, weights, different layers and configurations is essential in order to fully gain useful insights in the learning and information processing capabilities of ANN. Following below is the architecture of ANN that consists of various components as follows:

***Input Layer:*** This is the foremost layer and raw input information is stored here. For example, pixel values from an image or documented measurements. Each input neuron usually represents a single feature.

*Example:* An image classification ANN that accepts 28 × 28 pixel RGB images would have an input layer with 28 × 28 × 3 = 2352 neuron units representing the values of each pixel.

***Hidden Layers:*** Hidden layers are between the input and output layers and perform transformations on the data before it reaches the output layer. An ANN can have multiple hidden layers, which allows it to learn more complex relationships. Each hidden layer consists of a set of neurons that derives new attributes by combining the various weight-adjusted inputs it receives from the previous layer. The hidden layers can be of n number of layers in a ANN. For example, an ANN with two hidden layers having 120 and 80 hidden units respectively. Each unit applies transformations to received inputs.

***Output Layer:*** The output layer obtains signals from the last hidden layer and converts them into the format required for the prediction or classification task. The number of neurons in the output layer represents the number of output categories the network is designed for. For example, an output layer with 10 neurons can represent 10 possible digit classifications from 0–9.

***Weights and Biases:*** Each connection between neurons has an associated real-valued weight, which determines the influence of a signal from one neuron on another. Biases are additional parameters that allow neurons to adjust their activation thresholds. The optimized values for all the weights and biases are learned during network training. For example, *w*eights initially set randomly between –1.0 to 1.0, and bias terms set to 0.1

***Activation Functions:*** Activation functions are employed to introduce non-linear properties to the network, so that it adapts to fit more complex data. Examples of activation functions are sigmoid, tanh, and ReLU. These functions are utilized on the aggregated input collected by each neuron, which is the sum of the inputs weighted by their respective weights. For example, *a* ReLU activation, which outputs the value received if positive otherwise zero.

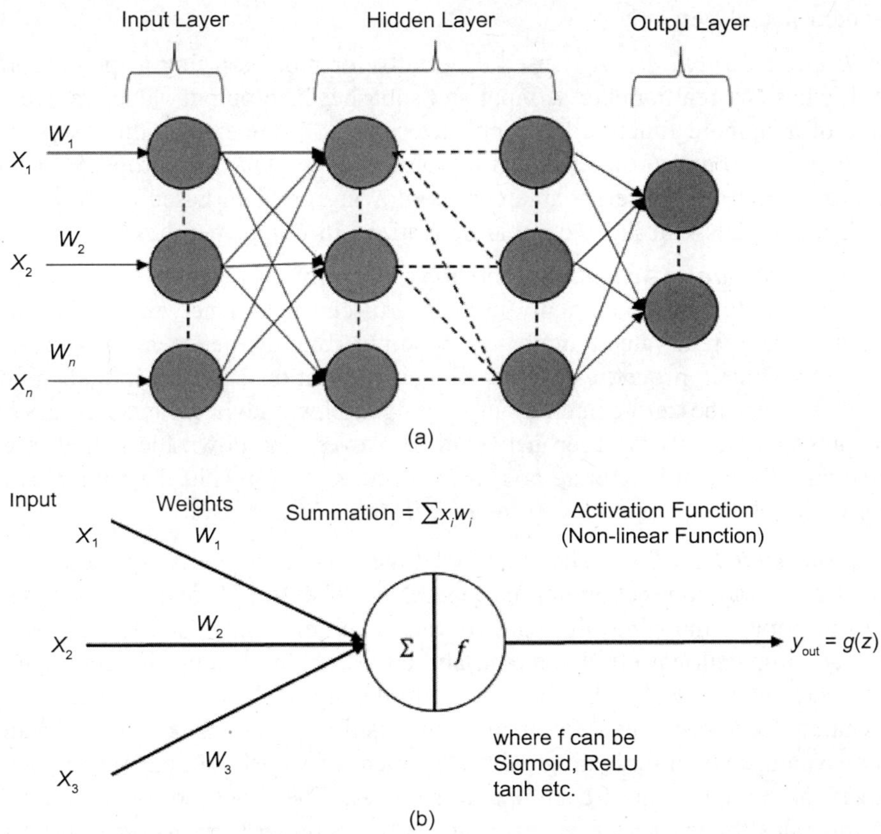


**FIGURE 4.4** Diagrammatic representation of ANN (a) with different layers and (b) Fundamental Structure of single neuron structure in ANN.

## 4.7 DIFFERENT TYPES OF ACTIVATION FUNCTIONS

The intricate calculations inside neural networks are powered by mathematical formulas called activation functions. By introducing non-linearity, they enable the network to learn and simulate intricate correlations between different data points. Activation functions are of utmost importance as they introduce not only non-linearity but also provide valuable contribution in output. Moreover, these functions possess the capability to significantly impact the network's ability to acquire intricate patterns and relationships embedded within the data.

***Step Function:*** In ANNs, the step function also known as Heaviside step function or the binary step function is used to provide the network with non-linearity. The step function is a discontinuous function that outputs a binary value based on the input.

The step function has some limitations:

1. It is not differentiable at $x = 0$, which can make gradient-based learning methods (like backpropagation) challenging.
2. It does not provide a smooth transition between the two output values.

Due to these limitations, following mentioned activation functions are more commonly used in modern neural networks:

***Sigmoid Activation Function:*** It is used especially for models trying to predict probabilities as outputs. It takes any real number as input and squashes it to output values ranging from 0 to 1. The curve of a sigmoid function has a characteristic "S" shape, smoothly mapping negative inputs to values near 0 and positive inputs to values near 1. One key property of the sigmoid is that it has a smooth and differentiable curve, allowing gradient-based optimization methods to work well for models that have sigmoid activations in output neurons.

***Hyperbolic Tangent (tanh) Activation Function:*** The hyperbolic tangent or tanh is another sigmoidal activation function commonly used in artificial neural networks. Like the standard sigmoid, it maps any real-valued input to an output ranging between –1 and 1. The tanh activation enjoys similar properties to the sigmoid activation such as smooth gradients that avoid oscillations, but the zero-centered output range helps alleviate vanishing gradient issues during backpropagation in some deep networks. However, one downside is that large positive and negative outputs can still saturate at 1 and –1 limits. As a result, the tanh activation helps model both positively and negatively correlated features in data well.

***Rectified Linear Unit (ReLU):*** The Rectified Linear Unit, or ReLU for short, has become a very popular activation function for use in ANN. The ReLU applies a simple threshold operation to its inputs, mapping all negative values to zero and maintaining positive values unchanged. Its computational efficiency and ability to enable training of deep neural network stacks has fuelled widespread ReLU adoption. Unlike sigmoid or tanh activations, the ReLU does not saturate at upper limits for increasing positive input values. Its utilisation proves particularly advantageous in mitigating the predicament of vanishing gradients, a challenge that often hampers the optimisation of deep neural networks. The proposed transformation function effectively mitigates the impact of negative values by mapping them to zero, while preserving the integrity of positive values.

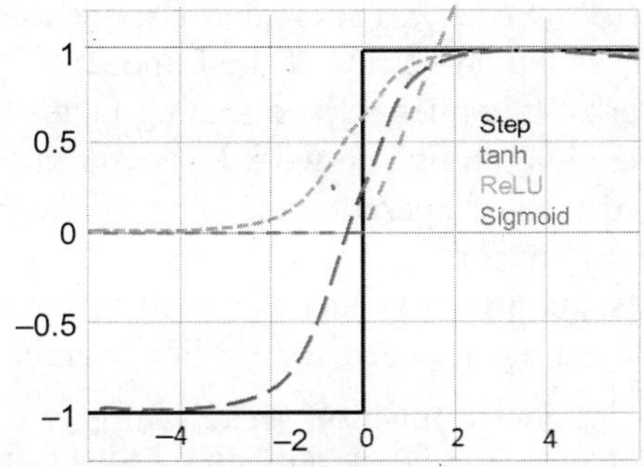


**FIGURE 4.5** Different Activation Functions.

***Leaky ReLU:*** The Leaky ReLU activation function aims to improve on some limitations of the popular ReLU used in many neural networks. Like the standard ReLU, Leaky ReLU maps all positive input values directly to the output. However, instead of mapping negative inputs strictly to zero, a small negative slope is maintained for negatives. This leaky slope helps prevent dying ReLU units that can occur when neurons only output 0 despite having significant negative inputs. By having a small negative slope rather than hard zero cutoff, gradients can continue to flow backwards during training even when inputs to the Leaky ReLU unit become totally negative. This alleviates vanishing gradient problems and can accelerate training and improve model generalization.

***Parametric ReLU (PReLU):*** This is another variant of the ReLU activation that aims to improve model fitting performance. Unlike the leaky ReLU which has a predefined negative slope value, the PReLU makes the leakiness coefficient into a learnable parameter. This introduces additional adaptability for the model to tune the slope dynamically during training, rather than fixing it as a hyperparameter initially. This augmentation empowers the model with an increased ability to adapt and improve its overall capacity. By learning the optimal leakiness, PReLU activations can regulate their sensitivity in a more customized way tailored to the intricate dependencies in the data. This helps models achieve lower error rates. Moreover, unlike a predefined leaky ReLU slope which uniformly applies to all negative inputs, the PReLU can capture subtleties in the data trends through its trained model parameters.

***Exponential Linear Unit (ELU):*** This function aims to provide improved discovering characteristics compared to the widely used ReLU and its variants. The key distinction is that negative inputs are mapped using an exponential function rather than being zeroed out or just applying a linear leakiness. Using an exponential mapping rather than hard cut-offs or linear leaks allows effects of negative inputs to diminish smoothly but still retain enough influence, enabling backpropagated gradients to flow robustly. Moreover, the exponential curve grows much slower than linear leak functions, providing regularization effects against oversaturation. This balanced behaviour for negative values coupled with direct identity mapping for positives makes the ELU suitable for deep networks where stabilization during training is vital. By dampening negative activations exponentially, ELUs avoid biases shifting toward positive distributions as commonly happens for ReLU-based models, allowing more balanced and nuanced mappings from inputs to outputs across a wide range of real-world problems.

***Scaled Exponential Linear Unit (SELU):*** The Scaled Exponential Linear Unit or SELU is an activation function that enhances the properties of the Exponential Linear Unit (ELU) to enable self-normalizing neural networks. It applies a fixed scaling factor to the ELU output in order to continuously normalize propagation through network layers during training. This helps networks automatically converge towards robust operating regions. SELU models tend to achieve solid convergence with relatively basic hyperparameter tuning while sustaining strong self-regulation and generalization capabilities. Its primary objective is to foster convergence in a remarkably efficient manner, all while obviating the need for explicit weight normalisation techniques.

***Swish Activation Function:*** The Swish function seeks to improve neural network performance through an elegantly simple design. Standard activations like ReLU, sigmoid, and tanh apply predefined fixed transformations to map neuron inputs to outputs. In contrast, Swish adaptively modulates its own activation in proportion to the input, essentially learning to reconfigure itself automatically based on dynamic context. Swish activations can learn specialized behaviours catered to the specific distributional properties of inputs passing through each neuron. Small inputs modulate minimally while large inputs modulate maximally. Moreover, the gating ensures smooth gradients during backpropagation which aids training. Overall, the data-driven automatic gating grants Swish activations superior representational capabilities relative to static activations, enabling enhanced nonlinear modeling, faster convergence, and state-of-the-art results across challenging deep neural network architectures and applications.

***Softmax Activation Function (for multiclass classification):*** The softmax activation function is commonly used in the output layer of neural network classifiers to convert logit values into normalized probability scores representing class membership likelihoods. While other activations like sigmoid or tanh squash real-valued outputs into fixed ranges like [–1, 1] or [0, 1], softmax ensures the sum totals of outputs sums precisely to 1, facilitating interpretation as a categorical probability distribution.

***Softplus Activation Function:*** The softplus activation function is a smooth approximation to the rectified linear unit (ReLU) which compresses real number inputs to strictly positive outputs. While ReLU clamps all negative values to zero, softplus allows a smooth, differentiable transition for negatives that asymptotically approach zero. Unlike ReLUs which have a non-differentiable breakpoint at $x = 0$, the softplus gradient stays continuous everywhere. This smoothness allows networks utilizing softplus to be trained without concerns over dying neurons or discretized breaks for negative inputs. However, softplus is more computationally expensive and converges slower than ReLU due to permitting graduated negative activations.

***Gaussian Activation Function:*** The Gaussian Activation Function, commonly known as the Gaussian or Radial basis function (RBF), exhibits a distinctive bell-shaped curve that defines its characteristics. The algorithm exhibits a propensity to assign augmented magnitudes to inputs in close proximity to the origin, while progressively attenuating the magnitudes as inputs deviate from the central point. The utilisation of this activation function proves to be highly advantageous when it comes to effectively representing radial symmetry or accurately capturing intricate patterns that are centred around specific data points.

The Gaussian activation function is adept at assigning elevated magnitudes to input values that are in close proximity to zero, thereby facilitating the capture of intricate patterns that are centred around distinct data points.

**TABLE 4.6** Activation functions

| *Activation Function* | *Mathematical Expression* | *Brief Description* |
|---|---|---|
| *Unit step* | $f(x)=\begin{cases}0, & \text{if } x<0\\ 1, & \text{if } x\geq 0\end{cases}$ | Outputs 1 if input is greater than or equal to 0, otherwise outputs 0. |
| *Sigmoid* | $f(x)=\dfrac{1}{1+e^{-x}}$ | Squashes input values to a range between 0 and 1, with an S-shaped curve. |
| *Hyperbolic Tangent (tanh)* | $f(x)=\tanh(x)=\dfrac{e^{x}-e^{-x}}{e^{x}+e^{-x}}$ | Similar to sigmoid, but squashes input values to a range between –1 and 1. |
| *Rectified Linear Unit (ReLU)* | $f(x) = \max(0, x)$ | Outputs the input if it's positive, otherwise outputs 0. Helps alleviate the vanishing gradient problem. |
| *Leaky ReLU* | $f(x)=\begin{cases}x, & \text{if } x>0\\ \alpha x, & \text{otherwise}\end{cases}$ <br> where $\alpha$ is a small positive slope for negative value.. | Similar to ReLU, but allows a small negative slope for negative inputs, helping to prevent "dead" neurons. |
| *Parametric ReLU (PReLU)* | $f(x)=\begin{cases}x, & \text{if } x>0\\ \alpha x, & \text{otherwise}\end{cases}$ <br> where $\alpha$ is a learnable parameter | Leaky ReLU with a learnable parameter for the negative slope, allowing the model to adapt the activation function during training. |
| *Exponential Linear Unit (ELU)* | $f(x)=\begin{cases}\lambda x & , \text{ if } x>0\\ \lambda\alpha(e^{x}-1), & \text{otherwise}\end{cases}$ <br> Where $\alpha$ is a positive constant. | Similar to ReLU, but has a smooth transition for negative inputs, which helps the model learn faster and achieve better performance. |
| *Scaled Exponential Linear Unit (SELU)* | $f(x)=\begin{cases}\lambda x, & \text{if } x>0\\ \lambda\alpha(e^{x}-1), & \text{otherwise}\end{cases}$ <br> $\lambda$ and $\alpha$ are constants | ELU with a scaling factor that helps normalize the outputs, making the model more robust to perturbations in the input. |
| *Swish* | $f(x) = x\cdot\sigma(\beta x)$ <br> where, $\sigma$ is the sigmoid function and $\beta$ is a positive constant. | A smooth, non-monotonic activation function that multiplies the input by the sigmoid of the input. It has shown improved performance compared to ReLU in some cases. |
| *Softmax* | $f(x_i)=\dfrac{e^{x_i}}{\sum_{j-1}^{n} ex_j}$ | Converts a vector of real numbers into a probability distribution, often used for multi-class classification problems. |

(*Contd.*)

| *Activation Function* | *Mathematical Expression* | *Brief Description* |
|---|---|---|
| *Softplus* | $f(x) = \ln(1 + e_x)$ | A smooth approximation of the ReLU function, defined as $\ln(1 + e^x)$. It is differentiable everywhere and can help prevent dead neurons. |
| *Gaussian* | $g(x) = \exp^{\left(\frac{-(x-\mu)^2}{2\sigma^2}\right)}$ Where, exp is the natural exponential function, $\mu$ is the mean or center of the Gaussian distribution and $\sigma^2$ is the variance or spread of the Gaussian distribution | Applies a Gaussian function to the input, which can be useful in some specific applications like radial basis function networks. |
| *Sinusoidal* | $f(x) = \sin(x)$ | Uses sine functions as activation function, which can be useful in capturing periodic patterns in data. Often used in neural networks dealing with time series or audio data. |
| *RReLU (Randomized Leaky ReLU)* | $f(x) = \begin{cases} x, & \text{if } x > 0 \\ \alpha x, & \text{otherwise} \end{cases}$ | Similar to Leaky ReLU, slope randomized during training. |
| *Bent Identity* | $f(x) = \frac{\sqrt{x^2+1}-1}{2} + x$ | Close to linear, with a slight bend. |
| *Hard Sigmoid* | $f(x) = \max\left(0, \min\left(1, \frac{x+1}{2}\right)\right)$ | Faster approximation of sigmoid. |
| *Hard Tanh* | $f(x) = \max(-1, \min(1, x))$ | Faster approximation of Tanh. |
| *Identity* | $f(x) = x$ | Direct pass-through, output equals input. |
| *ArcTan* | $\arctan(x) = \tan^{-1} x = \int_0^x \frac{1}{t^2} dt$ | Maps values to the range $(-\pi/2, \pi/2)$. |
| *ISRLU (Inverse Square Root Linear Unit)* | $ISRLU(x) = x \cdot \left(\frac{1}{\sqrt{1+\alpha x^2}}\right)$ | Combines linear and square-root components. |

## 4.8 TYPES OF LOSS FUNCTIONS

In NN, a loss function serves as a metric that evaluates the network's performance. The network's primary task is to generate predictions, while the loss function quantifies the difference between these predictions and the correct answers. During training, the network aims to reduce this score by adjusting its internal settings, such as weights and biases. When the score is lower, it indicates that the network has a higher level of accuracy in making predictions. If the predictions are wrong, the loss function gives a high score. The neural network uses this loss score to get better. By minimizing the loss, the neural network updates itself to make its predictions more aligned with the real answers.

The choice of loss function has significant impacts on the learning dynamics and predictive capabilities of the trained ANN model. Loss functions themselves can be categorized based on several key criteria. The most fundamental distinction is based on the type of machine learning problems—regression versus classification. Regression problems involve predicting a continuous numerical target variable. Classification problems require assigning instances among discrete categories or classes. Cross-entropy loss and Hinge loss are more suited for classification tasks.

Another way to classify loss functions is based on how the ANN output activations are interpreted as representing class probabilities versus not.

### 4.8.1 Mean Absolute Error (MAE) or L1 Loss

ANNs produce a continuous output that is compared to the ground truth target variable to compute a loss value that quantifies prediction accuracy. For regression related tasks where the outputs are real-valued numbers, MAE provides a robust yet simple loss function for ANNs. It calculates the absolute differences between each ANN predicted output ($\hat{y}$) and actual target ($y$). Averaging these absolute differences gives the mean absolute error or L1 loss. Mathematically, MAE loss for an ANN is represented as:

$$MAE = \left(\frac{1}{n}\right) * \Sigma \,|\, y - \hat{y} \,| \tag{4.11}$$

Where $n$ is the number of samples. Taking absolute difference makes MAE loss more resilient to outliers as compared to squared error losses. This linear loss function gives straightforward interpretability into how close the ANN's predictions are to the desired values, on average.

### 4.8.2 Mean Squared Error (MSE) or L2 Loss

This is the most widely utilized loss function, especially for training models and neural networks. As the name suggests, it calculates the average of the squared differences between each predicted value ($\hat{y}$) from the model and the actual true target value ($y$). Mathematically, MSE loss is represented as,

$$MSE = \left(\frac{1}{n}\right) * \Sigma(y - \hat{y})^2 \tag{4.12}$$

Where $n$ is the total number of observations. By squaring the errors before summation, MSE amplifies the influence of larger individual errors.

This quadratic nature makes MSE sensitive to outliers. However, the simple formulation also provides clear interpretability about expected model performance. Since squares accumulate faster than linear terms, reducing MSE guides the learning algorithm more aggressively towards the optimal parameters.

### 4.8.3 Huber Loss

The Huber loss is an interesting alternative for regression problems in machine learning and neural networks for MAE and MSE. As the name suggests, it combines both MSE and MAE into a smooth hybrid loss function. Concretely, Huber loss behaves like MSE for relatively small prediction errors—thereby quadratically penalizing smaller deviations to prioritize modelling accuracy. But for larger errors beyond a threshold 'delta', Huber loss switches character and takes on a linear MAE form instead. This makes it robust to outliers. By not heavily punishing substantial errors, model stability is retained. The 'delta' hyperparameter defines the frontier between the MSE region and MAE region for this smooth transition.

Mathematically, this yields a flexible piecewise function definition for Huber loss,

$$L_\delta = \begin{pmatrix} \frac{1}{2}(y-\hat{y})^2 & \text{if} |y-\hat{y}| \leq \delta \\ \delta\left((y-\hat{y})-\frac{1}{2}\right) & \text{otherwise} \end{pmatrix} \tag{4.13}$$

### 4.8.4 Cross Entropy Loss

For an ANN classifier making probabilistic predictions over target classes, cross entropy loss measures the divergence between the ANN's predicted class probabilities and the true distribution of labels. It aggregates the difference between probability outputs from the ANN (after SoftMax layer) and original one-hot encoded categories.
Mathematically, cross entropy loss for an ANN is:

$$CELoss = -\sum p(x) * \log(q(x)) \tag{4.14}$$

Here $p(x)$ is the true distribution and $q(x)$ is ANN's predicted probabilities. By heavily weighing confident false predictions, cross entropy focuses the ANN on instances it is uncertain about. This enables efficient exploration of misclassified cases.

### 4.8.5 Categorical Cross Entropy Loss

For an ANN making probabilistic predictions across multiple target classes, the categorical cross entropy loss measures divergence between the ANN's predicted class probabilities and the true distribution of labels. It aggregates the differences between the SoftMax output layer activations and the one-hot encoded categories averaged over the classes.

Mathematically, categorical cross entropy loss for an ANN classifier is given by:

$$CCE = -\sum Cp(c)\log(q(c)) \tag{4.15}$$

Where $p(c)$ is the true probability distribution and $q(c)$ is the ANN probability estimates over classes $C$. By amplifying confident false predictions, it directs the ANN to focus learning on uncertain and misclassified cases through informative signal gradients.

In summary, categorical cross entropy loss facilitates training reliable ANN models for multiclass classification by directing probability-based predictions reflective of ground truth distributions.

### 4.8.6 Binary Cross Entropy (BCE) Loss/Log Loss

Binary cross entropy loss applies to binary classification contexts where the output categories are labelled as 0 or 1. It measures the divergence between two probability distributions—the predictions from the neural network and the ground truth distribution. By heavily penalizing confident false predictions, it encourages the model to make probabilistic predictions that closely align with the actual distribution of labels. Binary cross entropy loss is an important metric that play crucial role in ANN to evaluate the accuracy of binary classification. Mathematically,

$$BCE = -(p(x) * \log(q(x)) + (1 - p(x)) * \log(1 - q(x))) \tag{4.16}$$

Where:

$p(x)$:

- $p(x)$ represents the true probability distribution of the target variable.
- For binary classification, $p(x)$ takes value 0 or 1 based on ground truth labels.
- $q(x)$:
- $q(x)$ is the probability prediction made by the machine learning model for the positive class.
- Values range from 0 to 1, with 1 meaning 100% probability prediction.

$p(x) * \log(q(x))$:

- Penalizes the model if it predicts low probability ($q(x)$) but actual label was 1 (as per $p(x)$).
- Contribution is higher for more incorrect confidence.

$(1 - p(x))$ *Symbol* $\log(1 - q(x))$:

- Similarly, penalizes the model if it predicts high probability ($q(x)$) but actual label was 0.
- Increases loss for more incorrectly confident predictions.

The negative sign flips the loss to a positive quantity. Overall, BCE nudges model probability predictions to align with actual label distribution.

### 4.8.7 Hinge Loss

Hinge loss introduces a marginal gap or distance between the class decision boundaries. It penalizes predictions that lie within the margin while exonerating those outside it. Unlike MSE, outliers do not heavily influence hinge loss due to the linear region. This enables robust classification.

In an ANN classifier, hinge loss introduces a margin that ensures the correct class score exceeds incorrect class scores by a minimum value. Rather than probabilities, it focuses on margin-based classification.

Mathematically for an input with true label $y$, ANN prediction score $s$ for that class, and maximum score *s_max* across other classes, the hinge loss is given by,

$$Hing\ Loss = \max(0, 1 - (y * s - s_{\max})) \tag{4.17}$$

### 4.8.8 Kullback-Leibler (KL) Divergence

In an ANN, KL divergence loss measures how much the predicted class probability distribution from the ANN diverges from the actual original probability distribution based on the true labels. Mathematically, KL divergence loss is:

$$KL(P \parallel Q) = \Sigma c P(c) \log(P(c)/Q(c)) \tag{4.18}$$

Where, *P(c)* = true probability distribution over target classes *c* (the ground truth), *Q(c)* = probability distribution predicted by the ANN over classes *c*. *P(c)/Q(c)* = element-wise division of true and predicted probabilities. *log(P(c)/Q(c))* = amplifies the differences in probabilities and Σ = sums the result over all classes. The higher the divergence, the more loss, providing feedback to tune the ANN's predictions.

## 4.9 FEEDFORWARD NEURAL NETWORK

The feedforward neural network (FNN) architecture consists mainly of an input layer, one or more hidden layers, and an output layer, all connected sequentially in a feedforward topology without any recursion or feedback loops. Within the input layer, the features are injected and made to propagate to the first hidden layer via weighted connections, where each node computes a weighted sum of its inputs and passes it through an activation function like sigmoid or ReLU to induce non-linearity. These proceeds feedforward as the transformed representations from antecedent layers get pooled and reinterpreted by successive layers in the chain of functional transformations. Stacking multiple hidden layers in depth enables learning hierarchical abstract features at various levels amenable for the final desired output representation. The parameters including connection weights and node biases span across the layered architecture and get updated based on error backpropagated from output layer to input layer using gradient descent. As data flows feedforward, predictions emerge at the output layer by incremental tuning of distributed parameters to accurately model the mappings between inputs and targets using sufficient training examples. The modular architecture with chained parametric transformations empowers universal approximation by coordinated learning across layers.

### 4.9.1 Working of FNN

**Input Data:** The input data such as an image, text etc. is fed into the input layer of the neural network.

**Weighted Sum:** Weighted sums of input connections from nodes in the preceding layer are computed by each node in the output layer and hidden layers. The weights modulate the signal strengths being passed.

**Activation Function:** This introduces non-linearity to enable modelling complex relationships by transforming the summed input. Common activation functions are ReLU, sigmoid, and tanh.

**Forward Propagation:** The transformed input serves as input to the next layer, repeating the computation down the network propagated forward to final output.

**Prediction:** The output layer activations produce the resulting prediction—a classification or regressed value depending on the task.

### 4.9.2 Components of FNN

FNN represents a pivotal archetype of ANN, adept at processing data in a unidirectional fashion. Its simplicity and versatility render it an optimal choice for an array of tasks, including but not limited to classification, regression, and pattern recognition. A comprehensive exposition of the architectural framework of FNN is as follows:

**Input Layer:** It receives real-world data like text corpus, image pixels, sensor readings, stock prices etc that are to be processed, just like our human senses detect sights, sounds, smells from the environment. The number of input layer nodes define the dimensions of input features being funnelled into subsequent transformations.

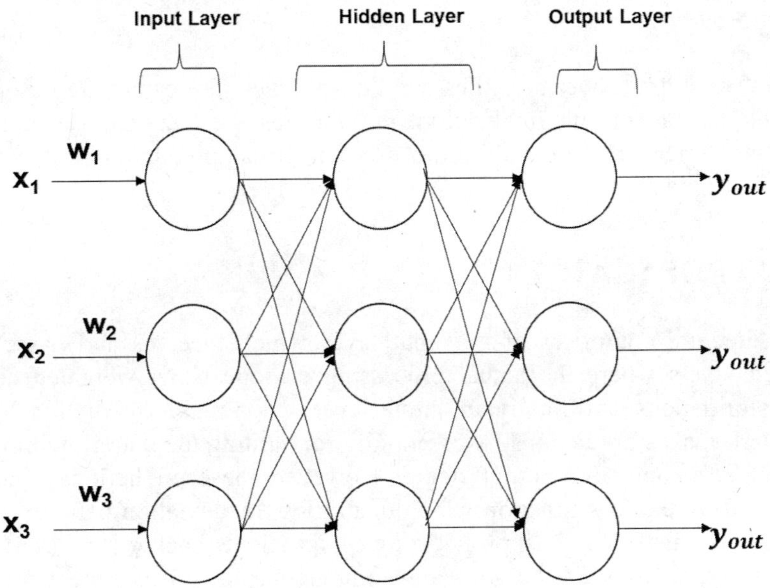


**FIGURE 4.6** Feed Forward Neural Network with different layers

**Hidden Layers:** All of the layers that exist between both input and output layers are known as hidden or concealed layers.

They take the data from input, process it, generate representations, identify features and patterns in transformation stages through the depth of the network. Just like parts of our brain draw inferences.

The hidden layers contain interconnected processing units called neurons or nodes that perform mathematical transformations on weighted sums of inputs via activation functions to enable identification of statistical patterns between inputs and target variables. Multiple hidden layers allow formation of hierarchical abstract features with increasing complexity, enabling modelling of intricate relationships. The depth contributes significantly to modelling capacity.

***Activation Function:*** This function adds the non-linearity in feedforward neural network thereby improving the ability to approximate the complicated functional association that may be inherently non-linear in nature. These transform aggregated input signals enabling nonlinear mixing of input variables.

***Weight and Bias:*** Adjustable parameters on the connections and nodes enable personalized tuning of signals to improve processing over many examples during training, similar to strengthening of neuron connections in the brain. The interconnections between each layer have adjustable

weights assigned to them, which get tuned and optimized during network training based on backpropagated gradients to minimize loss. In addition, bias terms associated with each hidden and output layer neuron enable regulation of activations supporting faster learning.
All the neurons are interconnected by direct links pertaining to their corresponding weights whose details may be represented via matrix (W) as mentioned below:

$$W = \begin{bmatrix} w_{11} & \cdots & w_{1m} \\ \vdots & \ddots & \vdots \\ w_{n1} & \cdots & w_{nm} \end{bmatrix} \tag{4.19}$$

***Output Layer:*** The output layer compiles and consolidates the features representation patterns identified by hidden layers into final output possibilities – either likelihoods associated with classification categories or regressed values for numerical prediction problems to fulfil the desired functional objective.

## 4.10 BACKPROPAGATION

The ANN architecture comprises of an input layer which receives and passes on data, one or more hidden layers where the actual processing is done using weighted connections and activation transformations, and finally an output layer which makes predictions for the problem task. The network makes predictions by essentially forwarding the data flow through this chain of integrated input-computation-output stages. However, these predictions need improvement and tuning guided by the loss function which quantifies the deviation between predictions and true targets. This is enabled by backpropagating the gradients backwards through the network. Specifically, local gradients of the loss are computed using chain rule with respect to all parameters—the weights and biases across connections between nodes and layers.

This gradient signal gets recursively propagated back towards the input layer via applications of chain rule through each intermediate hidden layer. By successively calculating gradients layer-by-layer, the gradient information paths all the way back even reaching first layer parameters. Finally, these compiled loss gradients with respect to all parameters are used to update the weights and biases in the descent direction to minimize loss and better train the network using gradient descent optimization.

The key objective of backpropagation is to optimize the weights and biases parameters of an ANN by minimizing a loss function that quantifies the difference between model predictions and true targets. This optimization is achieved by employing gradient descent. The gradients provide the direction of steepest rate of change of loss. Additional optimization algorithms like RMSprop and Adam adaptively control stepping to accelerate training by balancing out gradient noise across updates.

### 4.10.1 Operative Steps in Backpropagation

The learning in NN works by first making predictions using the current settings, seeing how far those predictions are from the actual targets, and then tweaking its parameters to get better. This tweaking requires knowing which parameters are more responsible for the errors and need more correcting. Backpropagation does this by splitting the whole network into layers, and looking at how each layer's computations specifically contribute to overall errors based on chain rule from calculus.

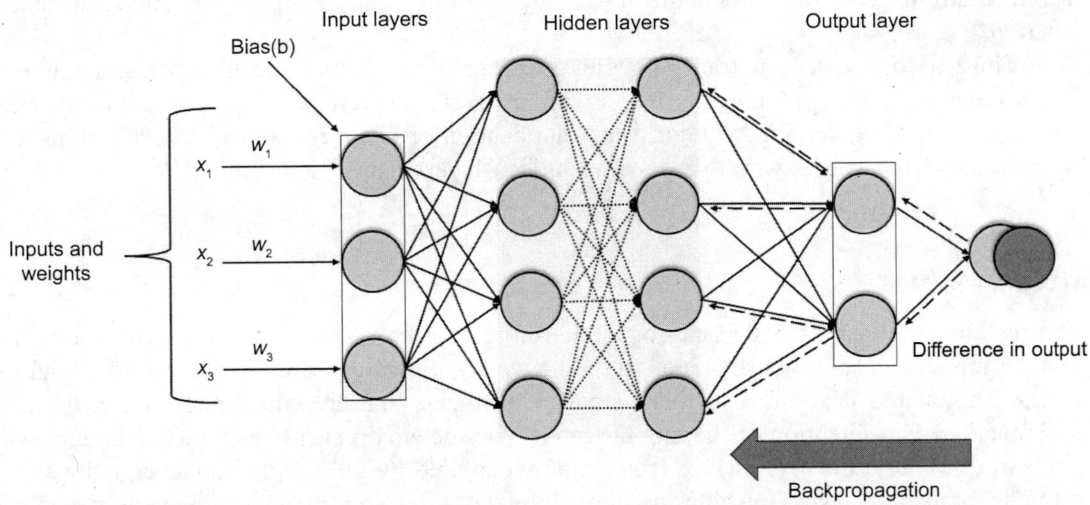


**FIGURE 4.7** Backpropagation in ANN (difference in desired output so backpropagation).

### *Output Layer Error Calculation*

The backpropagation learning strategy in NN works by first quantifying the errors in predictions from the network's final output layer and then tracing back those errors layer-by-layer incrementally to identify adjustments needed across parameters distributed over the depth. Specifically, the output layer error quantification assigns responsibility by multiplying two terms—first directly compares overall network errors with output layer activations using calculus chain rule, second checks the local activation curve changes. By clubbing, the interconnected effects get cleanly disentangled into attribution fractions more relevant for this layer.

Mathematically, the error delta at output layer L denoted by $\delta L$, gets computed as the Hadamard product or element-wise multiplication of the loss gradient ∇C with present layer activations, and the derivative of activation function □' w.r.t weighted input $zL$. Intuitively, this neatly disentangles the interconnected influences utilizing calculus's chain rule. By tying both components, impact of parameters on loss gets accurately attributed. This modular separation of node-wise functional tuning from holistic loss landscape allows granular dissection of credit assignment across layers. The error signals hence produced kickstart the layered unwinding passage towards initial layers to institute optimized learning across the neural architecture.

$$\delta L = \nabla C \odot \sigma'(zL) \tag{4.20}$$

### *Error Backpropagation to Hidden Layers*

In order to direct layer-by-layer improvements, backpropagation primarily entails incrementally assigning the total network defects across all hidden levels in the model. This depends on carefully removing the combined distortions from the output side all the way to the hidden block's beginning. To be more precise, the posterior hidden layer mistakes are quantified and offer inputs for adjusting the significance of the prior module. Relevance fractions are parsed incrementally closer to the beginning layers by carefully factorising impacts at each paused junction.

Thus, second equation transports this error gradient further towards preceding hidden layers recursively by applying the derivatives involved, dissecting loss contribution layer-by-layer till the first hidden unit via consistent application of chain rule. It recursively transports error signals from later layers to preceding hidden layers using chain rule.

$$\delta l = ((wl+1)T\delta l+1) \odot \sigma'(zL) \tag{4.21}$$

### Weight Update

The fundamental idea behind backpropagation is to use the error signals that flow backwards to determine the proper modifications to the network weights that are dispersed throughout the layers. This makes it possible to make small adjustments that are aimed at lowering the total loss function. This intention of shaping the model parameters proportionately in accordance with gradient descent on the loss surface is essentially captured by the weight update equations. The formulas basically suggest pushing the intrinsic node biases and inter-layer synaptic weights in the opposite direction of gradients, with learning rate-moderated steepness.

The third set of equations essentially capture the parameter update rules that rely on the calculated gradients to nudge weights and biases. The following equations are helpful to get the insights on gradients of loss functions:

$$\Delta wl = \eta \delta l al - 1 \tag{4.22}$$

$$\Delta bl = \eta \delta l \tag{4.23}$$

### Activation Function Forward Pass

The sequencing of computations in neural networks relies on an orderly propagation of signals from input end to output side interspersed with isolated transformations at each intermediate halt. This singular directional data flow underpins predictions emergent at final layer. Specifically, the activation functions sprinkle key processing strides layer wise to inject non-linear mixes of inputs suitably recombined towards object targets. At each neuron, weighted amalgamation of prior stage signals undergoes mathematical reshaping via sigmoid, tanh or ReLU functions as exemplars, to compress or expand or threshold signals gliding forward. In effect, this introduces vital non-linear enablers for intrinsically curve-linear real-life relationships mapping between informational entities and target variables. Chaining such unit-level functional modification traces a guided forward passage for initial stimuli towards object match in closed-form differentiable path amenable for recursively fine-tuning weights through backward traversal. Thereby, forward propagation fulfils key data transforming roles to fulfil representational learning towards precise predictive modelling.

$$al = \sigma(zl) \tag{4.24}$$

Finally, the activation function equation transforms weighted input signals arriving at each node into output activations that get propagated onto the next layer along the forward pass, eventually culminating in predictions.

These four equations orchestrate the complex mechanistic computations involved in both accurately dispatching errors backwards and efficiently forwarding activations to minimize the loss function.

### 4.10.2 The Epochs

While an ANN is being trained, an epoch is one complete run of the training dataset. As the ANN optimization occurs in an iterative fashion by backpropagating loss gradients for parameter updates, iterating over batches of data samples; an epoch marks the completion of propagating through all training samples in the dataset once. Tracking key metrics like loss, accuracy per epoch allows gauging the ongoing progress in the learning of the ANN. Going through multiple epochs enables convergence of the weights and biases in the network as it sees all data points repeatedly across training cycles and gets chance to update gradients accordingly. Choosing appropriate number of epochs requires balancing trade-offs—too few limits effective learning while too many causes overfitting without generalizing to new data. Common practice is to halt training if validation loss stops improving with more epochs.

## 4.11 RADIAL BASIS FUNCTION NETWORKS (RBF)

Radial Basis Function Networks (RBF) are ANN that use radial basis functions as activation functions in the hidden layers. This differs from the simple threshold functions used in a common multilayer perceptron network. In an RBF network, the output layer is typically linear. The nodes in the hidden layer contain radial basis functions cantered at different points, effectively dividing up the input space in clusters. The output is then determined by the hidden layer responses to the inputs weighted by the output layer weights. This allows RBF network to model complex nonlinear functions by transforming the input space into a new space where the inputs can be classified or predicted with a linear model. A key advantage of RBF networks is that they can model complex functions using fewer neurons in the hidden layer than multilayer perceptron networks. Training involves determining suitable radial basis functions, choosing the centres and widths of these functions, and setting the output layer weights. Overall, RBF networks serve as powerful nonlinear function approximators while having relatively simple network architectures.

## 4.12 FROM ANN TO DEEP NEURAL NETWORKS

The field of artificial neural networks has undergone a remarkable evolution since its inception decades ago. Early ANNs, inspired by the structure and function of biological neurons, were relatively simple and shallow, typically consisting of an input layer, a hidden layer, and an output layer. These networks, while ground-breaking at the time, had limitations in their ability to model complex, non-linear relationships in data. However, as computational power increased and new training techniques were developed, researchers began to explore deeper architectures with multiple hidden layers. So, the DNNs come into picture.

The success of DNNs can be attributed to several key advancements, including the use of rectified linear units (ReLUs) as activation functions, which alleviate the vanishing gradient problem; the development of efficient training algorithms like backpropagation and stochastic gradient descent; and the availability of large-scale datasets and powerful hardware, such as

GPUs, for training. Today, deep learning has become the dominant paradigm in AI, with architectures like convolutional neural networks (CNNs), recurrent neural networks (RNNs), and transformers pushing the boundaries of what is possible with artificial intelligence. As we continue to refine and expand these architectures, the future of deep learning holds immense promise for tackling some of the world's most complex and pressing challenges.

## SUMMARY

Artificial neural networks are powerful machine learning techniques inspired by biological neural systems that excel at finding complex patterns in data for tasks like classification, regression, clustering, dimensionality reduction, and more. They consist of interconnected layers that sequentially transform input representations via a mathematical processing function that adaptively maps inputs to target outputs. The network is trained iteratively using optimization algorithms like backpropagation to minimize loss between predictions and true labels until it learns suitable feature relationships reflecting statistical regularities that enable generalizations to unseen data. Beyond multilayer perceptron, many intricate network architectures cater to specialized data types like convolutions for images, recurrent layers for sequential data, and hybrid combinations of methods tapping their complementary strengths. Key advantages include highly flexible nonlinear modelling capacity, robustness to noisy inputs, and self-learning capabilities that automatically extract intricate data representations without extensive feature engineering.

## WORKED OUT EXAMPLES

**EXAMPLE 4.1** A neural network is being trained on a dataset containing 50,000 samples. The batch size is set to 500. If the network is trained for 10 epochs, how many iterations (i.e., gradient updates) will be performed during the training process?

***Solution:*** We know,

**Step1:**

***Iterations per epoch:*** Divide the total number of samples (50,000) by the batch size (500): 50,000/500 = 100 iterations per epoch.

**Step2:**

**Total iterations:** Multiply the iterations per epoch (100) by the number of epochs (10): 100 ∗ 10 = 1000 total iterations.

Therefore, 1000 iterations (gradient updates) will be performed during the training process.

**EXAMPLE 4.2** A perceptron is trained to classify points in a 2D plane. The training dataset consists of four points: (1, 1) with label 1, (2, 2) with label 1, (–1, –1) with label 0, and (–2, –2) with label 0. The initial weights are $w_1 = 0.1$, $w_2 = 0.2$, and the bias weight is 0.3. The learning rate is 0.1. After one epoch of training, what are the updated weights?

***Solution:*** For each training point, calculate the weighted sum and update the weights if the prediction is incorrect.

Point (1, 1): Weighted sum = $(0.1 \times 1) + (0.2 \times 1) + 0.3 = 0.6 > 0$, prediction is 1 (correct).
Point (2, 2): Weighted sum = $(0.1 \times 2) + (0.2 \times 2) + 0.3 = 0.9 > 0$, prediction is 1 (correct).

Point (–1, –1): Weighted sum = (0.1 × –1) + (0.2 × –1) + 0.3 = 0, so prediction is 0 (correct).

Point (–2, –2): Weighted sum = (0.1 × –2) + (0.2 × –2) + 0.3 = –0.3 < 0, prediction is 0 (correct).

Since all predictions are correct, no weight updates are needed.

Updated weights: $w_1 = 0.1$, $w_2 = 0.2$, bias weight = 0.3.

**EXAMPLE 4.3** Consider a simple linear regression problem where we want to predict the output (*y*) based on a single input feature (*x*). We have a dataset of (*x*, *y*) pairs and want to find the optimal slope (weight) and intercept (bias) of the linear model using gradient descent optimization.

***Solution:***

```
import numpy as np
import matplotlib.pyplot as plt
np.random.seed(0)
X = np.random.uniform(0, 10, 100)
noise = np.random.normal(0, 1, 100)
y = 2*X + 3 + noise
def gradient_descent(X, y, learning_rate=0.01, epochs=100):
  w = 0
  b = 0
  for epoch in range(epochs):
    y_pred = w*X + b
    dw = (1/len(X)) * np.dot(X, (y_pred - y))
    db = (1/len(X)) * np.sum(y_pred - y)
    w -= learning_rate * dw
    b -= learning_rate * db
      return w, b
optimal_w, optimal_b = gradient_descent(X, y)
plt.scatter(X, y, label='Data Points')
plt.plot(X, optimal_w*X + optimal_b, color='red', label='Regression Line (Gradient Descent)')
plt.xlabel('Input (x)')
plt.ylabel('Output (y)')
plt.title('Linear Regression with Gradient Descent Optimization')
plt.legend()
plt.grid(True)
plt.show()
```

## EXERCISES

1. Consider a neural network with a single hidden layer containing 4 neurons. The inputs to these neurons are [2, –1, 0, 3], and their respective weights are [0.5, –0.3, 0.8, 1.2]. The hidden layer uses the Rectified Linear Unit (ReLU) activation function. Calculate the output of each neuron in the hidden layer.

2. Compute the output of the tanh activation function for the input values $x = [-2, -1, 0, 1, 2]$ wth plot.
3. Implement the backpropagation algorithm to update the weights of a neural network for a regression problem.
4. In a feedforward neural network, the input layer has 10 neurons, the hidden layer has 6 neurons, and the output layer has 1 neuron. If the input is a vector of size 10, how many weights are there in the network? (Assume bias terms are used in the hidden and output layers).
5. A McCulloch-Pitts network has three input neurons ($x_1$, $x_2$, $x_3$) and two output neurons ($y_1$, $y_2$). The weights for $y_1$ are ($w_{11} = 0.6$, $w_{12} = -0.2$, $w_{13} = 0.4$), and the weights for $y_2$ are ($w_{21} = 0.1$, $w_{22} = 0.7$, $w_{23} = -0.3$). The thresholds for both output neurons are 0.5. Determine the outputs of the network for the input values: $x_1 = 1$, $x_2 = 1$, and $x_3 = 0$.

## BIBLIOGRAPHY

Aggarwal, Charu C. (2023). *Neural Networks and Deep Learning—A Textbook*, Springer Cham, ISBN:978-3-031-29642-0.

Fausett, Laurene V. (2006). *Fundamentals of Neural Networks: Architectures, Algorithms and Applications*, Pearson, ISBN: 9788131700532.

Yegnanarayana, B. (2005). *Artificial Neural Network,* PHI Publication, ISBN: 9788194884897.

# Chapter 5

# Machine Learning

## 5.1 WHAT IS MACHINE LEARNING?

In order to comprehend the concept of machine learning (ML), it is crucial to have a clear understanding of the concept of learning and how machines learn. There have always been some common parameters under which humans and animals learn. These can be the environment to which they are adapted, the experience which is being gathered, behavioural changes according to situations, through observations on how others behave which can also related to transfer learning and through some cognitive aspects like perceptions, reasoning, or problem-solving. For both humans and animals, learning is a continuous process, and in general the more they learn, the less they tend to make mistakes.

ML has a different perspective where a mathematical formula is taken, applied to a collection of inputs and produces desired outputs. These formulas will also produce desired outputs for those inputs that come from a similar source or distribution. But is it learning? If the inputs are slightly slanted, it might give an output which is completely wrong. This is the fundamental difference between human or animal learning and machine learning. This makes the term "*machine learning*" not a kind of learning, but a global term that refers to the concept of building machines which are able to do things without being specifically programmed to do so.

### *Origin of Machine Learning*

Industrial revolutions have always bestowed human civilization with ease of doing work. From the steam engine in the first industrial revolution of 1765 to the internet and web in the fourth industrial revolution of 2000, machines have gone a very long way. Although, electronics had a major impact during the third industrial revolution in 1969, the idea of using machines to learn and behave like humans was almost two decades prior to it. In 1943, Walter Pitts, an American logician and Warren McCulloh, a computational neurologist published the first-ever mathematical model of a neural network for developing algorithms which can mimic the human brain. When the Turing test was developed in 1950 by Allen Turing, it became a fundamental basement to believe that a machine can actually demonstrate human intelligence. This led to the beginning of the era of Artificial Intelligence (AI), a term which was first coined in 1956 by John Macarthy, Marvin Minsky, Nathaniel Rochester and Claude Shannon. Ever since then, under the umbrella of AI, the concept of ML has been flourishing.

***Can Machines Think?***

The Turing test developed by Alan Turing 1950 was the answer to the fundamental question if machines can think like humans. This test was conducted in an interrogation room, where there was a computer program and a human subject, and they were hidden from a Judge. The Judge has a time frame to interact with both parties and if he fails to identify which is a computer program and which is human, then that computer program is considered to pass the Turing test and succeeded in demonstrating that it can think like humans. While there is no such machine so far to have passed this test, many claims have been made.

### 5.1.1 Principles of Machine Learning

The ML principles encompass the fundamental concepts, methodologies, and guidelines towards the development, application, and understanding of ML algorithms and systems. There may be many other principles which can contribute to a more detailed understanding of ML, but some of the significant ones are as follows:

***Quality of the Data and Exploratory Data Analysis (EDA):*** ML models are dependent on the data that is used to train, validate and test the model performance. It is always essential to have good quality data, and reliable data in modelling. The concept of "Garbage in, garbage out (GIGO)" or "Rubbish in, rubbish out (RIRO)" should be well avoided as the quality of the output is directly related to the nature of the input data. Further, the raw data is generally unstructured and needs to be cleaned and transformed through data preprocessing before actually feeding into the model for training. Exploratory data analysis or EDA covers all the aspects like cleaning, visualization, segmentation, correlation analysis etc. which contribute to better model building.

***Feature Engineering:*** Post-data preprocessing, it's pertinent to choose, extract, or construct the required features from raw data to improve model performance. Good and relevant features can greatly improve the prediction ability of the model. There are many feature selection methods like embedded, and wrapper, which have the potential to identify the relevant features for training.

***Model Selection and Evaluation:*** ML is known for solving complex problems and choosing the appropriate model that fits the problem is an important task. It primarily involves understanding different algorithms and selecting the one best that suits the data and task. Later, the evaluation metrics should be chosen to suit the specific problem, ensuring they are meaningful and insightful and justify the predictability of the model.

***Optimization:*** Through iterative model training, the optimization process yields an evaluation of the maximum and minimum functions. Getting precise results is one of the goals in machine learning. As we adjust the hyperparameters — such as learning rate, number of iterations, etc.— in each step of the optimization process, we compare the outcomes in each iteration until we reach the ideal outcomes. The objective of optimization is to build a precise, accurate model with a lower error rate. The optimization methods known as Gradient Descent and Stochastic Gradient Descent are extensively utilized and have gained significant popularity.

***Applicability Domain:*** The applicability domain helps in knowing the space within which the developed machine learning models can make their predictions more accurately. While this terminology is more common in chemistry and drug discovery research, it is an important principle in general ML. It also defines the dataset on which the model has been trained and validated and where needs to be applied.

***Generalization:*** It is important that the models developed should generalize well to new and unseen data. A significant drawback known as overfitting is observed when a model demonstrates high performance on training data but poorly on fresh or untested data. Regularization and cross-validation help combat overfitting and make promising ways for the generalization of a model.

***Interpretability or Explainability:*** There are often trade-offs between interpretability and model performance. Some models might offer higher accuracy but may be harder to interpret, while simpler models might be more interpretable but sacrifice accuracy. Both explainability and interpretability are important in making ML free from being only a black box where the users do not know what has been predicted, how has been predicted and why has been predicted.

***Continual Learning and Adaptability:*** The ability of models to adapt to changing data distributions and learn over time is an important aspect of developing ML models. Continual learning models can update themselves with new information and adapt to evolving scenarios. What was not predicted prior, may be well predicted later through continual learning.

***Reproducibility and Documentation:*** It is important to properly document the methodologies, code, and experiments that can enable reproducibility and verification by others to replicate, and extend the work. The concepts of FAIR (findability, accessibility, interoperability, and reusability) data principles and open-source data repositories play an important role in this concept. These principles guide the development, application, and ethical considerations of ML.

### 5.1.2 Supervised Learning

This learning encompasses the training of models using annotated data to enable accurate predictions and classifications. Supervised learning revolves around the utilisation of training data comprising input features alongside their corresponding output labels or target values. This training process involves the delicate adjustment of the model's internal parameters, with the ultimate objective of minimising the discrepancy between predicted outputs and their corresponding actual values. Supervised learning encompasses a diverse array of algorithms to solve complex problems for classification and regression. Among these algorithms, linear regression excels at modelling relationships between variables whereas logistic regression navigates the classification into binary outcomes. Other algorithms like decision trees, with their hierarchical structure, which offer an intuitive approach to decision-making, and support vector machines (SVM) leverage the power of hyperplanes to tackle both linear and non-linear classification problems.

Supervised learning may seem simple, but the volume and complexity of data points in contemporary applications pose a significant difficulty. These learning algorithms are required to handle billions of data points, each of which has the potential to have a significant number of features.

### *Semi-Supervised Learning*

This learning often uses a small amount of labelled and annotated data (creating supervised) and a big number of unlabelled training data (making unsupervised). Semi-supervised learning aims to achieve similar goals to supervised learning; the only difference is that a huge number of unlabelled examples may aid the learning algorithm in identifying or creating a reliable model. Semi-supervised learning encompasses a wide range of approaches, including generative, graph-based, and heuristic approaches.

### *Self-Supervised Learning*

Self-supervised learning uses raw, unlabelled data to train the models. These models do not rely on a large volume of labelled or annotated data but generate labels from unstructured inputs. There is a pre-training stage which is meant to create these annotations with the aim to iteratively achieve accurate ground truths and then into production. These learning methods find application in fields like natural Language processing (NLP) and computer vision, where the amount of training data is quite large. With self-supervised learning, with even fewer data which are annotated iteratively till accurate results are achieved, the process becomes efficient as well as cost-effective.

## 5.1.3 Unsupervised Learning

Unlike supervised learning, unsupervised learning entails the training of models on unannotated data in order to unearth latent patterns, intricate relationships, and underlying structures without the need for explicit guidance or supervision. Clustering, a widely employed methodology in the field of unsupervised learning, involves the grouping of data points according to their inherent similarities or spatial proximity. The utilisation of clustering techniques facilitates the discernment of inherent groupings or clusters within a given dataset, thereby providing valuable insights into the latent patterns within the data.

Dimensionality reduction is another crucial facet within unsupervised learning, as it endeavours to effectively decrease the number of input features while concurrently safeguarding the fundamental information. Such approaches are well established effective ways to reduce complexity in high-dimensional data, thereby facilitating the visualisation and analysis of patterns and relationships within the data. Principle Component Analysis (PCA), a linear transformation method, identifies the principal components that capture the maximum variance. Through the process of dimensionality reduction, the field of unsupervised learning offers a powerful means to streamline data visualisation, enhance computational efficiency, and eliminate superfluous or inconsequential features. These techniques play a pivotal role in unravelling patterns, extracting salient features, and identifying aberrations within unlabelled datasets.

## 5.1.4 Reinforcement Learning

Reinforcement learning is another prominent subfield within the vast field of machine learning, which centres its attention on training intelligent agents to adeptly navigate the intricate landscape of sequential decision-making. These agents, armed with the ability to learn from

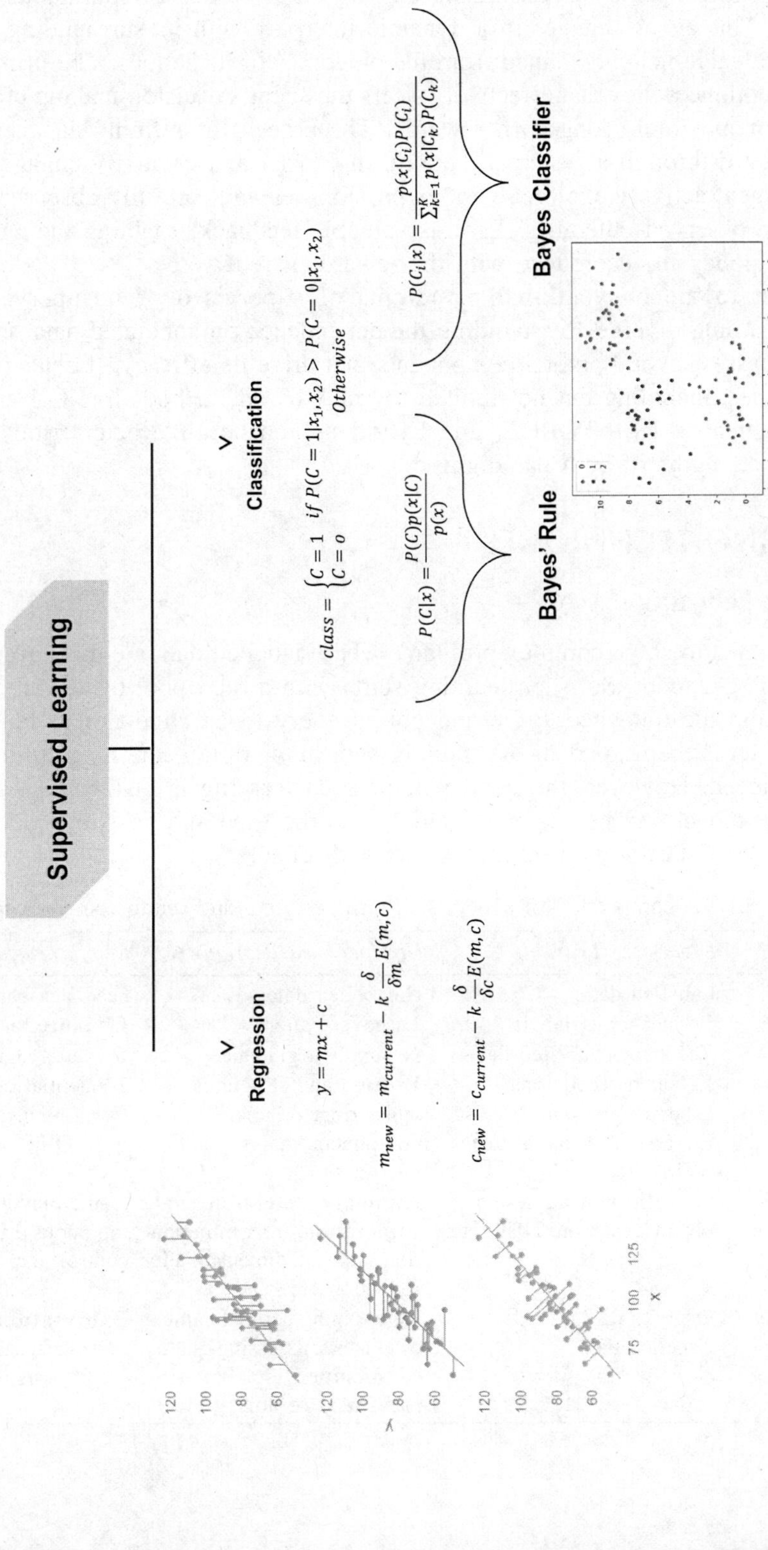


**FIGURE 5.1** A general overview of supervised learning.

the feedback provided by their environment, embark on a journey of continuous improvement and refinement. This agent engages in a dynamic interplay with its surrounding environment, leveraging the valuable insights gained from the outcomes of its actions. The primary objective is to acquire an optimal policy that effectively steers the agent's decision-making process towards the attainment of maximum long-term rewards. The process of refining an agent's policy is commonly achieved through a systematic approach of trial and error. By engaging in a series of actions, the agent actively explores various possibilities and carefully observes the resulting outcomes. These observed outcomes serve as valuable feedback, enabling the agent to update and enhance its policy in accordance with the rewards it receives.

In contrast to the conventional paradigms of supervised or unsupervised learning, reinforcement learning diverges by avoiding the dependence on annotated data. Reinforcement learning encompasses several pivotal components that drive its efficacy. It deals with a diverse array of techniques, including but not limited to value-based methods like Q-learning, policy-based methods such as REINFORCE, and hybrid approaches like actor-critic methods that amalgamate the strengths of both paradigms.

## 5.2 LEARNING TECHNIQUES

### 5.2.1 Active Learning

This learning is used to solve complex problems where labelled data are difficult to obtain, but unlabelled data is abundant. So, such learning starts with a mini pool of tagged data and then chooses a set from the untagged space and puts a query to an annotator (a human) to label the subset. This set is then a part of the training and this iteration continues till a considerable accuracy is achieved. However, the good part of such learning is that, with a smaller set, a robust predictive model can be designed. This saves the time and cost to annotate data, and further, the labelled data that is used are correct and reliable.

**TABLE 5.1** A comparison of supervised, unsupervised, and reinforcement learning

| *Aspect* | *Supervised Learning* | *Unsupervised Learning* | *Reinforcement Learning* |
|---|---|---|---|
| Training Data | Labelled data | Unlabelled data | Feedback-based interactions |
| Learning Objective | Predict target labels | Discover patterns | Optimize long-term rewards |
| Guidance | Teacher or labelled data | No explicit guidance | Rewards and penalties |
| Output | Labelled predictions | Patterns and structures | Sequential decision-making |
| Typical Algorithms | Linear regression, logistic regression, decision trees, SVM, etc. | Clustering, principal component analysis, auto encoders | Q-learning, policy gradient, deep Q-networks, etc |
| Common Applications | Classification, regression, object detection, NLP, etc. | Anomaly detection, data exploration, recommendation systems, dimensionality reduction etc. | Game playing, robotics, autonomous driving, inventory control, etc. |
| Key Challenge | Overfitting, Limited Labelled data | Determining optimal number of clusters, assessing quality of unsupervised results, robustness of noises, etc. | Exploration-exploitation trade-offs, sample efficiency, credit assignments etc. |

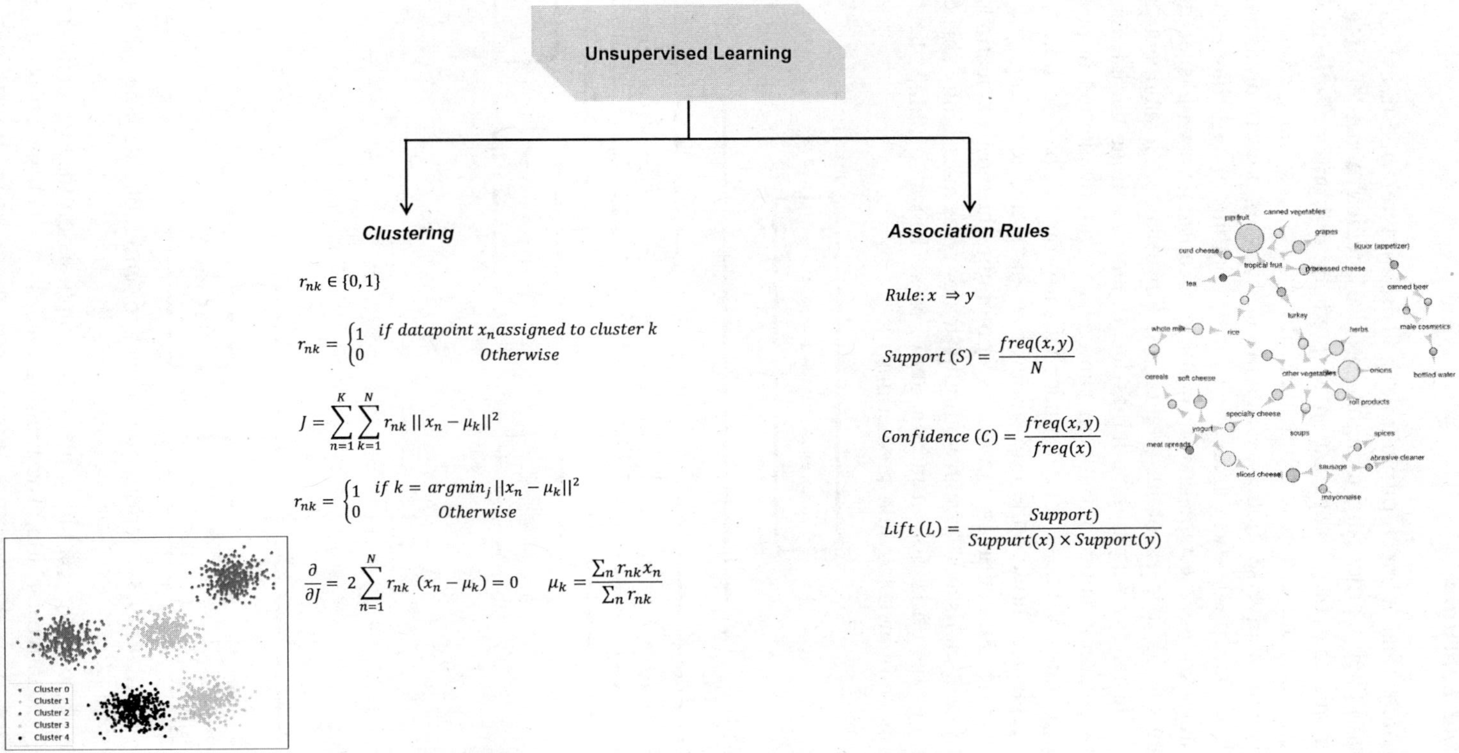


**FIGURE 5.2** A general overview of unsupervised learning.

### 5.2.2 Ensemble Learning

This learning technique has a bunch of multiple models, aptly referred to as elementary models or weak learners, thereby producing a highly precise predictive model. It is based on the fundamental principle that the amalgamation of predictions from multiple models can yield enhanced performance when contrasted with the utilization of a solitary model. By harnessing the collective wisdom of diverse models, ensemble learning empowers practitioners to unlock the full potential of their predictive capacity. By incorporating diverse modelling approaches, this type of learning exhibits the remarkable ability to encapsulate a wide spectrum of patterns, thereby enhancing the robustness of its predictions. Furthermore, it augments the process of generalization by effectively mitigating both bias and variance. Among these techniques, bagging and boosting have emerged as two prominent approaches, widely adopted in practice. Bagging involves training of multiple base models independently on various sections of the training data. This is accomplished through the utilization of sophisticated techniques such as bootstrap sampling. The ultimate prediction is derived by combining the prognostications of individual models, frequently accomplished through voting by majority or averaging. This concept is well demonstrated through the utilization of the Random Forest (RF) algorithm, wherein a collection of decision trees is combined to yield predictions.

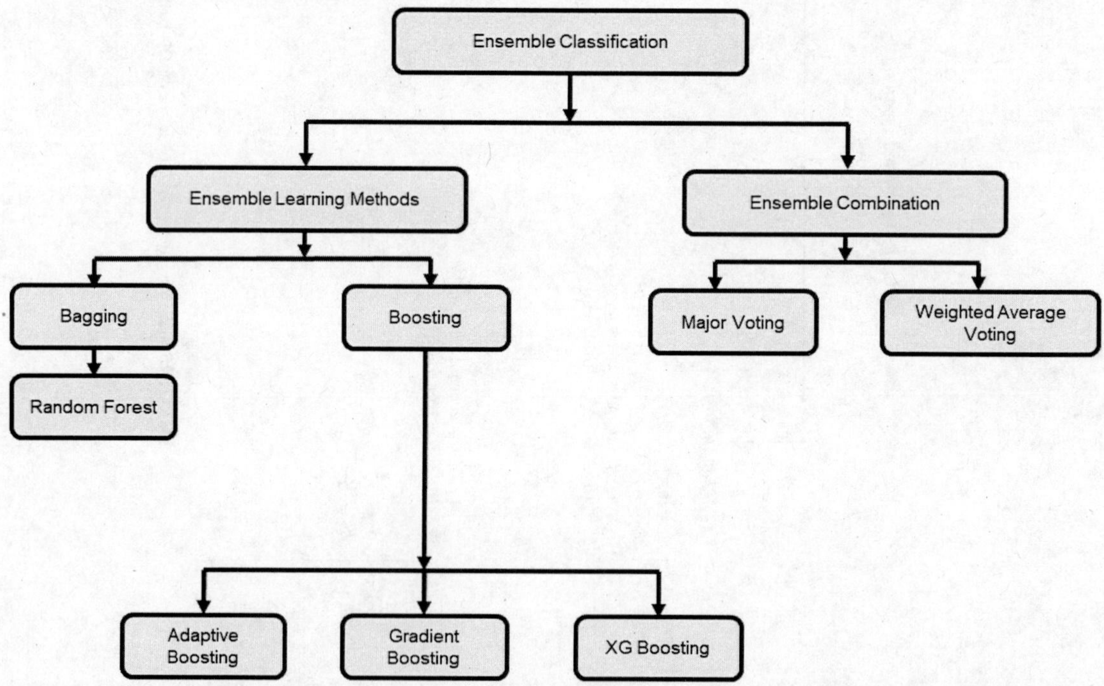


**FIGURE 5.3** Various components of ensemble learning.

In contrast, the boosting technique places its emphasis on the sequential training of base models in a highly adaptive fashion. The training process of each model is designed to rectify the errors committed by its predecessors, placing greater emphasis on instances that have been misclassified. Boosting algorithms like AdaBoost and Gradient Boosting Machines (GBM), exhibit a remarkable ability to progressively enhance the ensemble through iterative adjustments of the weights or parameters associated with the base models.

### 5.2.3 Interpretable Learning

Interpretable learning (IML) is one way to convince that machine learning is not a black box, but can be understood. Interpretability can be defined as the extent to which humans can understand without external help. Interpretable learning refers to machine learning which can be interpreted or the intermediate steps can be understood by humans without any additional tools. In general, simple models like linear regression, and decision trees are generally considered interpretable provided the number of inputs or number of nodes is less. But, in contrast, multiple or polynomial regression or decision trees with a large number of nodes may not be necessarily interpretable.

### 5.2.4 Explainable Learning

Both explainable learning (XAI) and interpretable learning are sometimes difficult to differentiate but where interpretable learning does not need any additional tools to understand a model, explainable learning is dependent on additional methods or tools to understand why a model predicts the way it predicts. Complex algorithms like random forest which is built with a large number of decision trees are not interpretable but are explainable. Methods like Partial Accumulated Local Effects (ALE), Partial Dependence Plot (PDP), and Local Surrogate (LIME) are used in explainable learning.

### 5.2.5 Deep Learning

Deep learning (DL) is dedicated to training complex neural networks to acquire knowledge and generate predictions based on vast amounts of data. Deep neural networks, also termed as deep learning frameworks, are characterised by their complex architecture comprising numerous layers of interconnected nodes, commonly referred to as neurons. The hierarchical architecture of the model facilitates the extraction of progressively more abstract representations from the input data. This enables the model to acquire a profound understanding of intricate patterns and interdependencies within the dataset. Artificial neural networks (ANN), which are modelled after the human brain, are capable of learning intricate patterns from vast volumes of data.

The discipline of deep learning is expanding quickly, and it will probably have a significant influence on how we live in the decades to come.

### 5.2.6 Transfer and Deep Transfer Learning

Transfer learning as the word suggests is a way in which the learning from one model to solve a problem is transferred to solve another task. This is very common in deep learning because they use multiple hidden layers such that the initial layers extract the features and pass them to later layers and so on till the final layer predicts some specific outcome. In general, deep

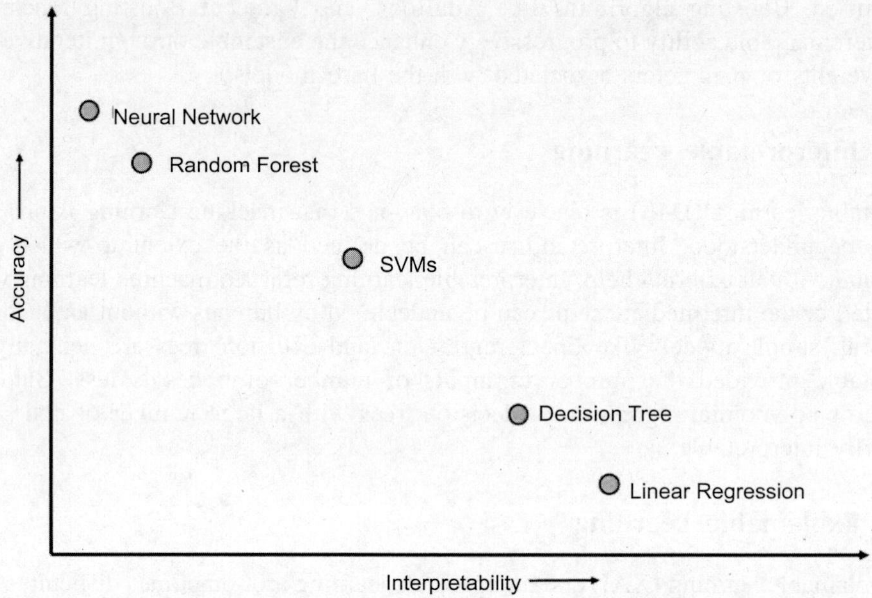


**FIGURE 5.4** A plot of accuracy versus interpretability shows that complex algorithms are more difficult to interpret than simpler ones.

learning models are dependent on a large amount of data also they consume quite good amount of time to reach a considerable accuracy. So, if such a model is being reused with transfer learning to solve a similar problem, a good amount of time is saved. DL models like AlexNet, and ResNet are quite popular in the context of transfer learning. While transfer learning can be implemented in any machine learning model, they are quite common with deep learning and are also called deep transfer learning.

## 5.3 ENGINEERING THE DATA

### 5.3.1 Data Cleaning

This is one of the most significant process to be carried out in any ML workflows, as it encompasses the indispensable task of meticulously refining and enhancing the quality of the data employed for model training. The primary objective of this approach is to discern and address a multitude of concerns within the dataset, thereby guaranteeing outcomes that are both precise and dependable. This entails the removal of the data set of mistakes and discrepancies. Typographical errors can be found and fixed; duplicate data can be deleted; and values that are missing can be filled in.

***Noisy Data***

The term "noisy data" pertains to the undesirable fluctuations or inaccuracies that manifest within the training dataset, thereby impeding the learning mechanism and compromising the efficacy of the model. These noises can be from a multitude of sources, encompassing data collection intricacies, measurement inaccuracies, or discrepancies in the labelling process. If a dataset has noisy data, it can negatively impact ML models' performance. These effects manifest in the form of misleading patterns or outliers, which can significantly compromise the accuracy of predictions and hinder the model's ability to generalise well.

### *Missing Data*

The phenomenon of missing data pertains to the conspicuous absence of values or information within a dataset, a circumstance that can manifest due to a multitude of factors including inadvertent errors during data collection, the presence of incomplete surveys, or unforeseen system failures. The management of missing data holds paramount importance in the field of machine learning, as it possesses the potential to significantly influence the training of models and consequently result in predictions that are biased or inaccurate.

In order to effectively handle the issue of missing data, a multitude of techniques can be employed. A widely employed strategy involves the elimination of instances or features that contain missing values, albeit this course of action may lead to the inadvertent loss of crucial information. Imputation methods serve as invaluable tools for estimating and filling in missing values through the application of sophisticated statistical techniques. These techniques encompass a range of approaches, including mean imputation, regression imputation, and more advanced methodologies like multiple imputation.

### *Duplicate or Redundant Data*

Duplicate or redundant data pertains to instances or records present within a dataset that exhibit either complete or near-perfect resemblance to one another. Duplicate occurrences can manifest as a result of various factors, consisting of inadvertent errors during data entry, technical malfunctions within the system, or complications arising from data integration procedures. The management of duplicate data holds paramount significance within the field of machine learning, as it possesses the potential to compromise the integrity of the dataset, introduce bias during model training, and ultimately impede the accuracy of predictions.

In order to effectively address the issue of duplicate data, a widely employed strategy entails the identification and subsequent elimination of duplicate instances by leveraging the values associated with specific features or attributes.

**TABLE 5.2** Representation of a noisy dataset

| *Values* | *Colour* | *Class* |
|---|---|---|
| Attribute Noise | | Class Noise |
| 0.25 | Red | Positive |
| 0.25 | Red | Negative |
| 0.98 | Green | Negative |
| 1.02 | Green | Positive |
| 2.06 | ? | No |

### 5.3.2 Dimensionality Reduction

Dimensionality reduction is a widely employed technique aimed at mitigating the detrimental effects of the curse of dimensionality, which arises when datasets possess a substantial number of features or variables. The primary objective of this approach is to effectively minimise the number of features, while simultaneously preserving the utmost pertinent information. Dimensionality reduction is a fundamental task in machine learning, aimed at extracting the most informative features from high-dimensional data. Among the plethora of techniques available, Principal Component Analysis (PCA), Linear Discriminant Analysis (LDA), and Generalized Discriminant Analysis (GDA) stand out as widely adopted approaches.

#### *Principal Component Analysis*

The fundamental goal of PCA is to devise a fresh coordinate system that is capable of accurately representing the most important differences present in the data. The path along which there is the greatest amount of variation in the data is mapped to the first principal component. By projecting the information onto these primary components, researchers are able to generate a representation with fewer dimensions while preserving the patterns and frameworks that were most significant in the initial data set.

The use of PCA can be advantageous in a variety of contexts. In the first place, it makes the complexity of high-dimensional data easier to understand and analyse, which in turn makes visualisation simpler. When we see the data in a space with fewer dimensions, we are able to obtain insights and recognise underlying patterns that may not have been obvious in the high-dimensional area in which the data was originally stored. Also, principal component analysis helps eliminate unnecessary repetition and background noise in the data, which paves the way for more effective and precise analysis. It assists in removing associated characteristics, which might ultimately lead to an improvement in the performance of future machine learning models. In conclusion, PCA might be useful for feature extraction due to the fact that its principal components can function as new relevant features for later analysis.

PCA has applications in many different fields, such as image and signal processing, data compression, feature extraction, and exploratory data analysis, to name a few. It enables enhanced analysis, visualisation, and decision-making by providing a strong tool for comprehending and expressing complex information in a manner that is more condensed and understandable.

#### *Linear Discriminant Analysis*

It is a technique used in either of the cases that is in dimensionality of data and also classifying it. The goal of LDA is to identify a linear combination of variables that simultaneously reduces the amount of variance that exists within each class while simultaneously increasing the amount of separation that exists between the various classes. LDA preserves the information that differentiates classes while simultaneously projecting the original data onto a space with less dimensions. LDA is especially helpful for classification problems since it minimises the dimensionality of the data while simultaneously maximising class separability. As a result, LDA may be used to change data in this manner.

The LDA accomplishes this objective by calculating the scatter matrices for both between-class and within-class variations. The between-class scatter is a statistical quantity that quantifies the variability between distinct classes, thereby providing an indication of the degree to which these classes are effectively segregated within the original feature space. The measure of within-class scatter quantifies the dispersion of data points within each class, thereby indicating the level of compactness exhibited by the class distributions. LDA subsequently endeavours to identify a projection that maximises the correlation between-class scatter to within-class scatter, thereby yielding the most favourable discriminant directions. The linear discriminants that emerge from the analysis, commonly referred to as canonical variables, offer novel feature values that effectively distinguish between different classes. The discriminants mentioned possess the potential to serve as input features for subsequent classification algorithms.

Reduction techniques prove to be highly advantageous in scenarios characterised by high-dimensional data, the presence of redundant or irrelevant features, or the affliction of noise. Dimensionality reduction techniques, such as feature selection or feature extraction, play a crucial role in enhancing computational efficiency, mitigating overfitting, and bolstering the model's capacity to discern significant patterns from the data.

#### *Generalized Discriminant Analysis*

Generalised Discriminant Analysis (GDA) emerges as a compelling advancement of LDA, aiming to surmount the constraints imposed by LDA's presumptions regarding equal class covariances or adherence to Gaussian distributions in scenarios where such assumptions are not upheld. GDA effectively mitigates the constraints imposed by these assumptions, thereby offering a versatile and adaptable structure for discriminatory analysis.

In the conventional framework of LDA, the underlying assumption is that the within-class scatter matrix remains constant across all classes. Nevertheless, it is imperative to acknowledge that in practical situations, this assumption may not necessarily remain valid. The GDA framework introduces the concept of accommodating distinct within-class scatter matrices, thereby enhancing the model's adaptability to the underlying class distributions. The inherent capability of machine learning algorithms to successfully deal with irregular connections among features as well as class labels enhances their robustness and applicability across a diverse array of data distributions.

The GDA algorithm effectively estimates the scatter matrices within each class as well as the scatter matrix between classes by using the training data at hand. The computational process involves the computation of the generalised eigenvalues and eigenvectors, which are subsequently utilised to ascertain the discriminant directions. The discriminant directions, in their essence, serve as a means to encapsulate the utmost discriminative information, rendering them invaluable for the purpose of classification tasks. GDA presents a multitude of advantages in comparison to LDA. This model effectively handles unequal class covariances. This becomes particularly advantageous in scenarios where the classes exhibit varying variances or covariances. Furthermore, this approach exhibits enhanced adaptability when confronted with datasets that deviate from Gaussian distributions and defy linear separability.

### 5.3.3 Data Transformation

In data transformation, the information is arranged into an organisation that is better suited for analysis and interpretation. This can be accomplished in two ways: by transforming categorical information into numerical information or by normalising the data. The concept of transformation in machine learning encompasses the intricate process of altering or converting the initial features or data representation with the aim of enhancing the efficacy of the model or fulfilling particular prerequisites. The process entails the utilisation of mathematical or statistical operations to optimise the quality of the data, standardise its distribution, or derive more significant representations from it.

Data transformation encompasses a plethora of techniques, including but not limited to normalisation, standardisation, logarithmic transformation, and feature scaling. Normalisation is an important measure in the data preprocessing pipeline, as it ensures that the data values are appropriately scaled within a specific range. Consequently, normalisation fosters a more balanced and equitable learning environment, enabling machine learning models to effectively discern patterns and make accurate predictions. Standardisation is a fundamental preprocessing technique in machine learning, plays a pivotal role in rescaling data to exhibit an average of '0' and a standard deviation (SD) of 1. By undertaking this transformative process, the aim is to render features comparable, thereby mitigating the undue influence of outliers.

Data transformation is an indispensable component within the ML pipeline, assuming a pivotal role in facilitating data augmentation, feature engineering, and normalisation.

### 5.3.4 Handling Imbalanced Data

ML often faces the problem of handling unbalanced data, which is characterised by large variations in the variety of observations between classes. Prejudiced models which conduct effectively on the vast majority class but badly for the minority class may result from this imbalance. In simple words, one class is underrepresented, while another class is overrepresented. Let us consider a scenario where you want to distinguish between two classes: "toxic" and "non-toxic" in a small molecule dataset. If 80% of the datapoints are toxic, and only 20% are non-toxic, then such a data set is imbalanced. In this case, the "toxic" class is overrepresented, while the "non-toxic" class is underrepresented. Because these datasets typically perform poorly in the minority class, machine learning algorithms may encounter difficulties when dealing with them. This is because the algorithms may become biased towards the majority class, as they optimize their performance based on overall accuracy. To deal with such imbalances in the dataset, methods like resampling, synthetic data generation, cost-sensitive learning and even ensemble methods are used.

***Resampling:*** In general, resampling of an imbalanced dataset is executed prior to the training of the prediction model and is generally seen as a data pre-processing step. Oversampling and undersampling are two ways which contribute to resampling. In case of oversampling, the number of instances in the minority class is increased by duplicating existing instances or generating synthetic data points. Undersampling on the other hand involves dropping the number of instances in the majority class. The instances may be randomly removed, as in random undersampling (RUS) or increased randomly to oversample (ROS). This is a quick and easy way to balance an imbalanced dataset and is therefore widely used. An important disadvantage of RUS is that samples that are useful for the learning process may be deleted. However, some advanced strategies aim at removing samples from overlapping regions such as NearMiss, Tomek Links or Edited Nearest-Neighbors (ENN). Sometimes, a hybrid of both oversampling and undersampling is also used to report the imbalanced dataset issue. Other than random sampling, a few widely used techniques for generating synthetic data are SMOTE (Synthetic Minority Over-sampling Technique), and ADASYN (Adaptive Synthetic Sampling) which create new data points by interpolating between existing minority class samples.

***Cost-Sensitive Learning:*** Cost-sensitive learning (CSL) takes the costs of prediction errors into consideration while training a machine learning model. It has a close relationship to imbalanced learning, which deals with classifying datasets that have a skewed distribution of classes. For binary classification, we have a matrix,

| | *Positive* | *Negative* |
|---|---|---|
| Positive | C (+, +) | C (–, +) |
| Negative | C (+, –) | C (–, –) |

Assuming that there is only cost for negative classification, from the cost matrix, the cost ratio can be defined as,

$$Cost\ Ratio = \frac{C(-,+)}{C(+,-)} \tag{5.1}$$

The sole objective of cost-sensitive learning is to develop a model having minimum misclassification which makes the total cost as,

$$Total\ Cost = C(-,+) \times FN + C(+,-) \times FP \tag{5.2}$$

Where *FN* is false negative and *FP* is false positive.

## 5.4 TESTING THE ALGORITHMS

### 5.4.1 Overfitting and Underfitting

These are two frequent problems that often arise in learning algorithm models, particularly in the setting of supervised learning. Overfitting happens when an algorithm for ML becomes excessively proficient at learning the training data, even capturing noise and random fluctuations. Consequently, the model exhibits remarkable performance on the training set of data, but its performance is not transferable to new, unobserved data. When a model is overly complicated in comparison to the quantity of training data available, overfitting frequently occurs. Rather than understanding the underlying patterns, the model effectively learns by heart the training set. High accuracy on training data but noticeably poorer performance on validation or test data are indicators of overfitting. In order to overcome overfitting, cross-validation is implemented. Another way is to use only the most relevant features to build the model. However, choosing the relevant features are again dependent on some machine learning algorithms. Regularization is another concept which add penalties or constraints to the model to prevent overfitting, like L1 or L2 regularization in linear models.

Balancing the model's complexity and ensuring it generalizes well to unseen data is the key to avoiding overfitting and underfitting. It's important to understand these concepts when developing ML models to create robust and accurate models that perform well on new or unseen data.

### 5.4.2 Train, Validation and Test Sets

A general pipeline of developing ML models involves the process of training, evaluating, and testing models with distinct datasets. Each set serves a specific purpose in developing and assessing the way a model performs.

***Data Splitting:*** A typical approach involves randomly splitting the available dataset into training, validation, and test sets. Common splits include 60–80% for training, 10–20% for validation, and 10–20% for testing, depending on the dataset size. This method is also popularly known as the hold-out method. Another way for splitting is using a time-based approach where the training set consists of earlier period data and a test set of later periods. Stratified sampling is another method which is used to split when the dataset is not even. Such a method splits the dataset in such a way that each class is proportionately distributed in each set.

The choice of how to split the dataset depends on various components, like dataset size, it's nature, the problem being solved, and the desired trade-off between computational cost and the accuracy of the performance estimation. Maintaining the separation between these sets is crucial for developing a model that generalizes well to new, unseen data.

***Training Set:*** The training set constitutes a portion of the entire collected data, which the model uses to learn patterns and relationships between input features and their corresponding output or target values. It is during this phase that the model's parameters (weights and biases) are adjusted iteratively by minimizing a chosen loss function, allowing the model to make predictions closer to the actual target values. The model learns the primary patterns, associations, and structures present in the data. Here the main objective is to tune model's performance on this specific data.

***Validation Set:*** In order to optimize the hyperparameters of the model and evaluate its training results, the validation set plays a crucial role. After training the model, its performance is evaluated using the validation set. This step helps in understanding the extent to which the model is generalizing to new or unseen data and how well it is performing under various hyperparameter settings. The primary aim is to prevent overfitting to the training data by altering the hyperparameters based on the performance with the independent validation set. This helps in ensuring that the model can generalize properly to new or unseen data.

***Test Set:*** The test set or hold-out test set is a separate subset of the dataset that is held out and not seen by the model during training or validation. It's used for evaluating the final performance of the trained model. The main objective is to recreate the performance of the model on completely novel and unfamiliar data in real-world scenarios. The performance of the model on the test set provides an unbiased estimation of its ability to generalize, as it serves as a representation of unseen data.

***External Set or Benchmark Set:*** An external or benchmark dataset is an entirely separate dataset for checking the execution of model in a more standardized or general setting. It serves as an independent reference or standard against which different models or methods can be compared or benchmarked. These sets generally represent real-world scenarios where the models developed can be deployed. It acts as a standard against which the performance of different models, algorithms, or techniques can be compared. Because this dataset is common and known within the field, it allows for fair comparisons across different approaches. In most cases these benchmark datasets are well-established and are widely recognized and used by the research community or industry to compare different methodologies or algorithms.

Using an external or benchmark dataset is crucial in the field of machine learning to ensure that the developed models are not just performing well on a specific subset of data but can also generalize to new, unseen data that represent real-world scenarios. It allows researchers, practitioners, and data scientists to validate the generalization ability and effectiveness of their models across various settings or applications.

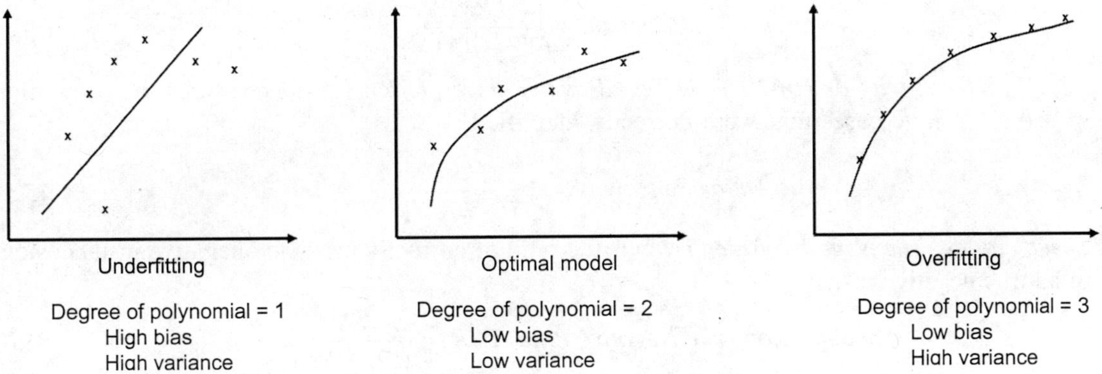


**FIGURE 5.5** A pictorial representation depicting bias and variance and their relation with model development.

### 5.4.3 Confusion Matrix

It describes how well a classification model performs. It allows visualization of the performance of an algorithm by showing how well it predicted the outcomes compared to the actual results.

The confusion matrix consists of four different values which are:

*True Positive (TP)* is the actual positive cases that are correctly identified. In other words, these are the cases where the actual result was positive and the model's prediction is same.

*True Negative (TN)* is the total false cases accurately forecasted. In simple words, these are the cases where the actual result was negative and the model's prediction was also negative.

*False Positive (FP) or Type I error*, is the sum of cases that in reality are false and are wrongly forecasted as positive.

*False Negative (FN) also termed as Type II error* indicates total positive instances predicted wrongly as negative.

### 5.4.4 Performance Metrics

In classification problem addressed by machine learning, the confusion matrix provides a comprehensive way to understand the effectiveness of the model and related errors it makes in predicting outcomes. Some of the common metrics used for analysing a classification model performance are as follows :

*Accuracy* or the ratio of correctly predicted instances to the total number of instances. Mathematically,

$$Accuracy = \frac{(TP + TN)}{(TP + TN + FP + FN)} \tag{5.3}$$

*Precision* or the ratio of true positive predictions out of the total positive predictions made by the model.

$$Precision = \frac{TP}{(TP + FP)} \tag{5.4}$$

*Recall or Sensitivity or Hit Rate or True Positive Rate (TPR)*: Recall measures the proportion of actual positive cases that were correctly identified.

$$Recallor\ Sensitivity = \frac{TP}{(TP + FN)} \tag{5.5}$$

*Specificity or True Negative Rate (TNR)* is the ratio of correctly predicted negative instances out of all true negative instances.

$$Specificity\ or\ True\ Negative\ Rate\ (TNR) = \frac{TN}{(TN + FP)} \tag{5.6}$$

*F1 Score* is a statistical measure used to assess the accuracy of a binary classification model and is given as:

$$F1Score = 2 * \frac{(Precision * Recall)}{(Precision + Recall)} \tag{5.7}$$

*Matthews Correlation Coefficient (MCC)* is a metric used to measure the quality of binary classifications, predominantly when dealing with imbalanced datasets. Mathematically,

$$MCC = \frac{TN * TP - FN * FP}{\sqrt{(TP + FP)(TP + FN)(TN + FP)(TN + FN)}} \tag{5.8}$$

*Cohen's Kappa Coefficient* is the measure of the agreement between predicted and real classifications, correcting for the possibility of the agreement occurring by chance. It is especially useful when there are imbalanced classes in the dataset.

$$K = \frac{(p_o - p_e)}{(1 - p_e)} \tag{5.9}$$

Where $p_o$: is the overall accuracy of the model and $p_e$: is the measure of agreement between the predictions of the model and actual class values.

*Jaccard Index* measures how similar is the predicted and true class labels. It can be mathematically represented as the ratio of the size of the common values in both sets and the size of the union of the two sets (predicted set and true labels set). However, it is commonly used in multi-class classification problems.

$$\textit{Jaccard's Similarity} = \frac{\textit{Number of observations in both sets}}{\textit{Number of observations in either set}} \tag{5.10}$$

Or, mathematically,

$$J(A,B) = \frac{|A \cap B|}{|A \cup B|} \tag{5.11}$$

Where $|A|$ and $|B|$ are the number of elements in sets $A$ and $B$ respectively, and $|A \cap B|$ and $|A \cup B|$ are the intersection and union of sets $A$ and $B$ respectively.

*Log Loss (Logarithmic Loss)* is used to quantify the accuracy of a classifier by penalizing the false classifications based on the confidence score of prediction.

$$L_{log}(y, p) = -(ylog(p) + (1-y)\log(1-p)) \tag{5.12}$$

Where $L$ is the log loss, $y$ is the actual label for the $i$th instance, $p$ is the predicted probability for the $i$th instance.

*Zero-one loss* is the simplest one as it measures the number of misclassifications made by the model. It assigns a value of 0 for correct classifications and 1 for incorrect classifications. For binary classifications,

$$L(y,\hat{y}) = \begin{Bmatrix} 1 & \text{if } y \neq \hat{y} \\ 0 & \text{if } y = \hat{y} \end{Bmatrix} \tag{5.13}$$

Where $y$ represents the true label (0 or 1) and represents the predicted label. Different metrics emphasize different aspects of classification model performance, such as the correlation among precision and recall, handling imbalanced data, or measuring overall accuracy.

Unlike classification problems, the performance of a regression model can be measured by various other parameters.

*Mean Absolute Error (MAE)* is the mean of the total amount of difference in the outcomes that were anticipated and those that were actually observed and is given as:

$$MAE = \frac{1}{n}\sum_{i=1}^{n} |x_i - y_i| \tag{5.14}$$

Where $x_i$ is the actual or observed value for the $i^{th}$ data point and $y_i$ is the corresponding predicted value for that data point.

*Mean Squared Error (MSE)* is the mean of the square of difference in the outcomes that were anticipated and those that were actually observed.

$$MSE = \frac{1}{n}\sum_{i}^{n} (x_i - y_i)^2 \tag{5.15}$$

Where $x_i$ is the actual or observed value for the $i$th data point and $y_i$ is the corresponding predicted value for that data point.

*Root Mean Squared Error (RMSE)* symbolizes the average of the quadratic discrepancies between the expected and actual values, expressed as a square root and is given as:

$$RMSE = \frac{1}{n}\sqrt{\sum_{i=1}^{n}(x_i - y_i)^2} \tag{5.16}$$

Where $x_i$ is the actual or observed value for the $i$th data point and $y_i$ is the corresponding predicted value for that data point.

*$R^2$ (R-squared)* indicates the quantity of the variance in the dependent variable which are predicted from the independent variable(s). A greater value of R-squared represents that the data fits the model significantly.

$$R^2 = 1 - \frac{SSR}{SST} \tag{5.17}$$

Where, $SSR$ = sum of squared residuals and $SST$ = total sum of squares.
Apart from these common metrics, there are several other parameters as discussed below:

*Mean Squared Logarithmic Error (MSLE)* which is similar to Mean Squared Error (MSE), but the logarithm of the predicted and actual values is used. It is useful when the target variable's range is large and you're interested in relative errors more than absolute errors.

*Mean Absolute Percentage Error (MAPE)* is a commonly used measure for predicting accuracy in statistics and forecasting. It expresses the average absolute error as a percentage of the actual values.

*Root Mean Squared Logarithmic Error (RMSLE)* is a logarithmic scale of measurement which quantifies the proportional discrepancy among real and projected outcomes. It assigns a higher value to undervalues compared to overestimates by quantifying the typical number of relative mistakes.

*Explained Variance Score* indicates the proportion of variance in the target variable that the model explains. It generally measures how well the model accounts for the variability in the data.

*Huber Loss* finally combines the characteristics of MSE and MAE by being less sensitive to outliers. It uses a delta parameter to provide a threshold, beyond which it switches to MAE.

Different metrics highlight different aspects of model performance, such as accuracy, precision, or robustness to outliers, and can be selected based on the needs of the given regression problem. These metrics help assess how well a regression model fits the data and how accurate its predictions are in terms of continuous numerical values.

Both regression and classification are supervised machine-learning problems. Performance analysis in clustering, which is unsupervised learning, involves evaluating and assessing the quality of the clusters generated by a clustering algorithm. The evaluation of clustering methods is more challenging and is often based on intrinsic and extrinsic methods. Intrinsic evaluation involves assessing the streak of the clusters relying on the data itself, without external references or ground truth labels. The primary aim is to assess the structure and coherence of the clusters formed by the algorithm. Some of the metrics for intrinsic evaluation are:

*Silhouette Score* measures degree of the similarity of an object within its own cluster (cohesion) in comparison with other clusters (separation). Its value ranges from –1 to 1, where higher values is proportional to better-defined clusters.

$$S(i) = \frac{(b(i) - a(i))}{max(b(i), a(i))} \tag{5.18}$$

Where, *S(i)* is the silhouette score for data point *i*, *a(i)* and *b(i)* are the mean distance from data point *i* to other data points within the same cluster and data points in a different cluster respectively.

*Davies-Bouldin Index (DBI)* helps to gain useful insights on the clusters' similarity and also helps to know the clusters that look alike to a great degree.

$$\text{DB}(C) = \frac{1}{k}\sum_{i=1}^{K} \max_{i \neq j} \frac{\Delta(c_i) + \Delta(c_j)}{\delta c(i, j)} \tag{5.19}$$

Where $\Delta(C_i)$ is the intra-cluster distance and $(C_i\ ,\ C_j)$ is the inter-cluster distance.

*Calinski-Harabasz Index (CHI)* computes the correlation of dispersion between and within the clusters. Higher values indicate better clustering.

$$CH = \frac{\frac{BCSS}{k-1}}{\frac{WCSS}{n-k}} = \frac{BCSS * (n-k)}{WCSS * (k-1)} \tag{5.20}$$

Where *BCSS* is between-cluster sum of squares, *WCSS* is within-cluster sum of squares, *k* is number of clusters, and *n* is number of observations.

*Dunn Index (DI)* is the measurement of the compactness of clusters and the separation between them. Higher values are better, indicating better-defined clusters.

$$DI = \frac{\min(\delta(Ci, Cj))}{\max(\Delta(Ci))} \tag{5.21}$$

Where, $\delta(C_i, C_j)$ represents the minimum intra-cluster distance between clusters $C_i$ and $C_j$, while $\Delta(C_i)$ is the diameter of cluster $C_i$.

*Gap Statistic* compares the clustering solution against a reference distribution of data points that are generated based on a random uniform distribution. The gap statistic measures the difference between the observed within-cluster dispersion and the expected dispersion in a random data set. Extrinsic evaluation involves assessing the performance of clustering algorithms by comparing their results with some external, known ground truth or reference information. Some of the common extrinsic evaluation metrics used in clustering are defined below.

*Adjusted Rand Index (ARI)* is the measure of similarity between two clusters, which considers all pairs of samples and counting pairs that are allocated in the same or different clusters in both the predicted and true cluster. ARI considers all possible pairs and corrects for chance. Its values range from –1 to 1, where 1 indicates perfect labelling agreement.

$$ARI = \frac{(Observed\ Rand\ Index - Expected\ Rand\ Index)}{\max(Expected\ Rand\ index)} \tag{5.22}$$

*Fowlkes-Mallows Index* measures the similarity between two clusters by considering the pairs of sample data and assigned data to the same or different clusters in both the predicted and actual clusters. Mathematically,

$$FM = \sqrt{PPV * TPR} = \sqrt{\frac{TP}{TP+FP} \cdot \frac{TP}{TP+FN}} \tag{5.23}$$

Extrinsic evaluation metrics are particularly useful when ground truth information or actual class labels are available. They measure how well the clusters align with the known labels or ground truth, providing insight into the accuracy of the clustering in line with the known structure of the data.

### 5.4.5 Receiver Operator Characteristics (ROC) Curve

It is a pictorial depiction that explains analytical ability for binary classification system across different cut-off values. The ROC curve is a common tool used to evaluate the performance of a classification model. It uses two parameters—True Positive Rate (TPR) and False Positive Rate (TPR).

*True Positive Rate (TPR) or Sensitivity* indicates how good the model is at correctly identifying positive instances. It's calculated as , where TP is True Positives and FN is False Negatives.

*False Positive Rate (FPR)* on the other hand measures the ratio and it indicates how often the model makes an incorrect prediction of the positive class when the actual class is negative. where FP is False Positives and TN is True Negatives.

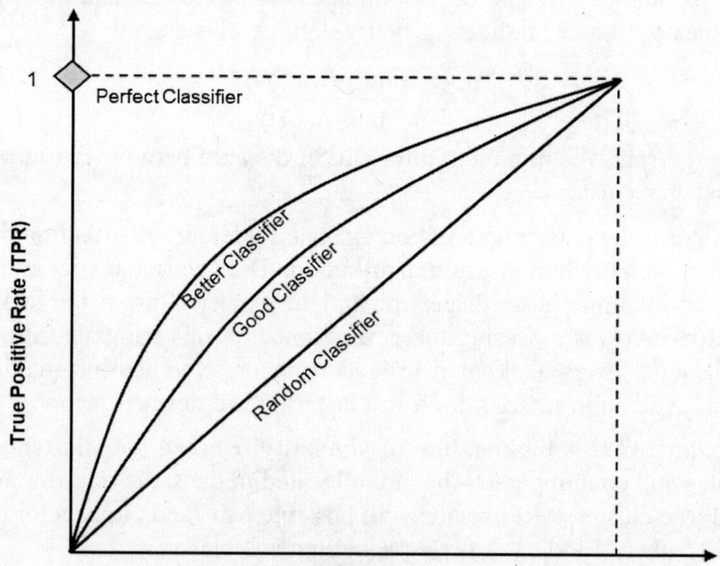


**FIGURE 5.6** Interpretations from a ROC-AUC curve in a classification problem.

The ROC curve is plotted with TPR on the y-axis and FPR on the x-axis. Each point on the ROC curve represents a different threshold used by the classifier to classify the instances. The curve portrays the balance among specificity and sensitivity across various thresholds. In the ROC curve, the top-left corner (0, 1) represents a perfect classifier that achieves 100% sensitivity (or no false negatives) and 100% specificity (or no false positives). The diagonal line (from bottom-left to top-right) represents a classifier that performs no better than random guessing (an AUC of 0.5). In this curve, single scalar value helps to know the efficiency of the classifier.

### 5.4.6 Test for Robustness

While ML models are developed taking into consideration of some domain-specific problems, they may however be implemented in extreme conditions often leading to breakdown. In such circumstances, it is necessary to test how robust the model has been built. A randomization test, also known as a permutation test, is a non-parametric statistical technique used for hypothesis testing, especially when the assumptions of classical parametric tests are not met or when the distribution of the data is not known. It works by assessing the distribution of a test statistic under a null hypothesis by repeatedly shuffling the data, effectively creating a null distribution of the test statistic.

Typically, "*Y Randomization Test*" is a type of randomization or permutation test that is specifically used for examining the relationship between a predictor variable in a statistical model. This test is widely used to check the robustness of machine learning models. This test generally involves the following steps:

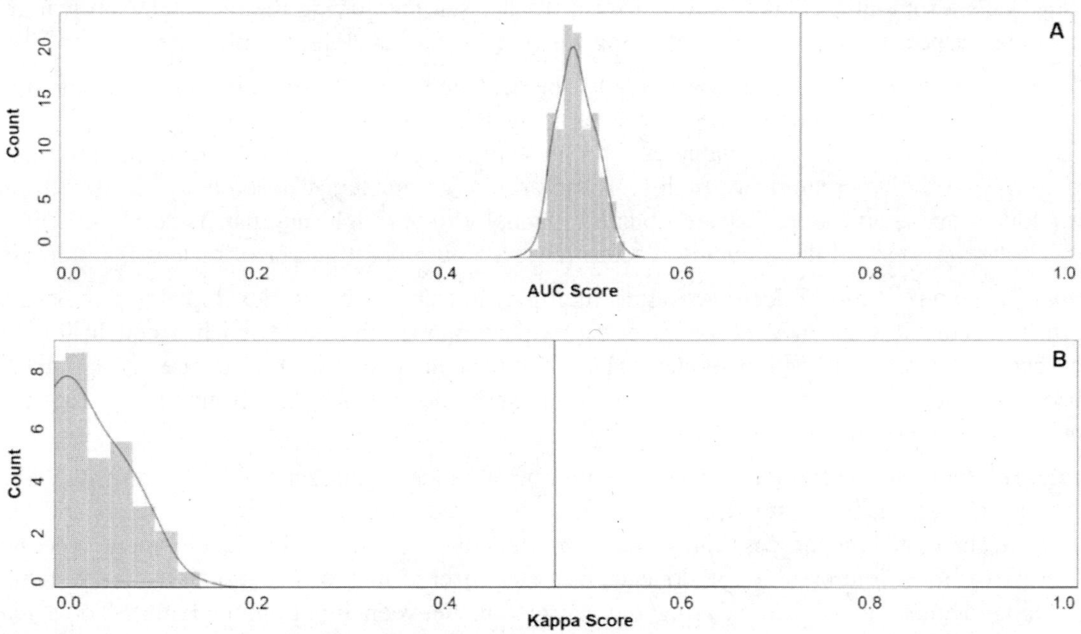


**FIGURE 5.7** A typical visual inspection of the Y-randomization test, which shows (A) the AUC score and (B) Kappa Score.

1. Observe the behaviour with the original data.
2. Randomly shuffle the observed data, effectively breaking any potential association or relationship between groups or conditions. This shuffling is done a large number of times (often thousands) to create a distribution of the test statistic under the null hypothesis.
3. Calculate the test statistic for shuffled data.
4. Compare the observed test statistic with the shuffled data.

If the model is robust, the test statistics with the shuffled data will be more extreme than the observed test statistics and vice versa.

Randomization tests provide a flexible and distribution-free approach to hypothesis testing, allowing researchers to test hypotheses without making strong assumptions about the data. They are especially useful in situations where parametric assumptions are not met or for testing in scenarios with complex, real-world data.

## 5.5 PIPELINE OF MACHINE LEARNING

From the principles and concepts of ML learnt in previous sections, a general pipeline can be fabricated. For any ML model developed for solving complex problems, these steps will be a part of the development pipeline.

***Data Preprocessing:*** The raw data which is collected to build the dataset has multiple issues like unstructured, missing values, redundant values, noise etc. Data processing enables us to make this unstructured data and also clean them so that they can be used for training and validating the models. From all the features which form the dataset, identifying the most relevant features is another aspect of the data preprocessing module in the development pipeline.

***Model Development:*** With the dataset ready, the next step in the pipeline is model development where the first step is to choose the most suitable models based on the complexity of the problem. The model is then trained and evaluated through steps like cross-validation and further improved or optimized by hyperparameter tuning. These are the parameters whose controls are with the developers and their values can be updated manually or through automated methods. This is an iterative process till the accuracy reaches the maximum point and error or loss is minimum.

***Model Evaluation and Selection:*** While multiple models are being developed, an important step is to compare the models using the same performance metric to reach a conclusion for the best and worst-performing models. Here, the benchmark or external dataset is applied to the best models and further scientific validation can be done. Once, this component is reached, the model is ready for deployment.

***Interpretation and Communication:*** Interpreting a model redirects the focus on "why this prediction was made" instead of "what was the prediction?" It helps to understand the entire decision-making process and is an important component of the development pipeline. Generally, model interpretation is done with model-specific methods (interpreting the weights) or model-agonist methods (analysing the correlation between input-output pairs). Tools like ELI5, LIME, SHapley Additive exPlanations (SHAP), and MLXTEND are frequently used for model interpretation and communication. The figure below demonstrates an overview of the development pipeline of the machine learning model.

## SUMMARY

The present chapter is dedicated to machine learning, its principles and concepts which offers a thorough and exhaustive examination of the fundamental views that serve as the foundation for the ever-evolving domain of machine learning. This comprehensive exposition embarks on a methodical journey to unveil the fundamental nature of machine learning, deftly explaining its primary classifications, learning types, how to evaluate, and various performance metrics to do so. By delving into the intricate concept of machine learning and its underlying mechanisms, this chapter empowers readers with a profound comprehension of the development pipeline by which machines acquire knowledge from data and finally deploy it for utilization.

## WORKED OUT EXAMPLES

**EXAMPLE 5.1** A classification model is trained and then tested with 100 samples dataset. The test results represented in the confusion matrix give $TP = 24$; $TN = 65$; $FP = 3$; and $FN = 8$. What is the accuracy of the model? Evaluate the recall and f-score?

***Solution:***

Given $TP = 24$; $TN = 65$; $FP = 3$; and $FN = 8$, $FP = 3$

We know that the accuracy is given as:

So,
$$Accuracy = \frac{(TP + TN)}{(TP + TN + FP + FN)}$$

Accuracy = 0.89 × 100 = 89%

Thus, we can say that the classification model has an accuracy of 89%.

**EXAMPLE 5.2** The model's predictive performance is encapsulated in the confusion matrix as below. Use the numpy library to evaluate the MCC. Also comment on its prediction:

| | | Predicted | |
|---|---|---|---|
| Actual | | Yes | No |
| | No | FP(5) | TN(375) |
| | Yes | TP(15) | FN(5) |

***Solution*:**

```
import numpy as np
from sklearn.metrics import matthews_corrcoef
actual = np.repeat([1, 0], repeats = [20, 380])
pred = np.repeat([1, 0, 1, 0], repeats = [15, 5, 5, 375])
matthews_corrcoef(actual, pred)
```

**Output:** 0.7368

So, the computed Matthews correlation coefficient is 0.7368. As this number approaches unity, it suggests the model exhibits satisfactory performance in forecasting players' likelihood of being drafted.

## EXERCISES

**1.** The table presented below displays the $x$ coordinates alongside their associated $y$ coordinates.

| $x$ | 9 | 11 | 13 | 15 | 17 |
|---|---|---|---|---|---|
| $y$ | 22 | 24 | 26 | 28 | 30 |

(a) Evaluate y = a x + b.

| | | Predicted | |
|---|---|---|---|
| | | *F* | *NF* |
| Actual | *F* | 10 | 5 |
| | *NF* | 20 | 965 |

(b) Find y if $x = 20$.

**2.** A telecom company has developed a classifier for detecting whether a cell phone network base station is faulty or not. The classifier is evaluated on a test set. Here is the confusion matrix. (In the table, *F* means faulty and *NF* not faulty.) Compute the accuracy of the classifier.

**3.** In a multinational company, you are working on a binary classification task to predict whether an email is spam (positive class) or not spam (negative class). After training your machine learning model, you obtain the following confusion matrix:

| | | Predicted | |
|---|---|---|---|
| | | Spam | Not Spam |
| Actual | Spam | 120 | 30 |
| | Not Spam | 15 | 335 |

Utilizing the data presented in the confusion matrix, quantify the model's effectiveness by determining its accuracy, precision, recall, and F1 score metrics.

**4.** Consider a dataset representing the spatial coordinates of cities on a map. The coordinates are given in (latitude, longitude) format. Extract the spatial separation between the given city pairs by applying the Euclidean distance:

1. City A (40.7128, –74.0060) and City B (34.0522, –118.2437)
2. City C (51.5074, –0.1278) and City D (35.6895, 139.6917)

**5.** Distinguish between the two types of learning, known as supervised and unsupervised. Illustration with examples.

6. Define dimensionality reduction and give some examples of its use. Give an illustration of a method for reducing the number of dimensions.
7. Write in brief a short note on the important ML libraries useful for analyzing ML models.
8. From a well-established company, you have a categorical feature containing missing values that you want to replace with predicted values. (**Hint:** Use Python)
9. Use the numpy to evaluate the RMSE, MAE and MSE for the following dataset:

| Actual | 8 | 6 | 4 | 2 |
|---|---|---|---|---|
| Predicted | 6 | 5 | 2 | 1 |

10. Using the Iris dataset, compute the variance ratio for the Linear Discriminant Analysis.

## BIBLIOGRAPHY

Géron, A. (2022). *Hands-on Machine Learning with Scikit-Learn*, Keras, and TensorFlow, O'Reilly Media, Inc.

Mitchell, T.M. (1997). *Machine Learning*, McGraw-Hill.

Mohri, M., Rostamizadeh, A., and Talwalkar, A. (2018). *Foundations of Machine Learning*, MIT Press.

Muller, A.C., and Guido, S. (2017). *Introduction to Machine Learning with Python*, O'Reilly.

Raschka, S., and Mirjalili, V. (2017). *Python Machine Learning*, second edition, Packt Publishing Ltd.

Richert, W. (2013). *Building Machine Learning Systems with Python*, Packt Publishing Ltd.

Sarkar, D., Bali, R., and Sharma, T. (2018). *Practical Machine Learning with Python*, Apress.

Shalev-Shwartz, S., and Ben-David, S. (2014). *Understanding Machine Learning: From Theory to Algorithms*, Cambridge University Press.

Swamynathan, M. (2019). *Mastering Machine Learning with Python in Six Steps*, Apress.

Usuelli, M. (2014). *R Machine Learning Essentials*, Packt Publishing Ltd.

Chapter 6

# Supervised and Unsupervised Learning

## 6.1 INTRODUCTION

Supervised learning is a type of machine learning (ML) which deals with training models to predict target outputs from input data or to learn the insights from labelled data. The term implies that the input data is associated with a known output, and this learning helps in making correct predictions and drawing conclusions from the available data. The primary goal of supervised learning is to construct a model, which possesses an exceptional property—the capacity to make accurate predictions for unknown data points. These models have become extremely popular due to their efficient implementation in various applications, comprising image classification, natural language processing, and speech recognition, among others. As an illustration of the supervised learning process, consider a case of solving a classification task, where the training data is comprised of images, which were labelled with the information that the picture was made of a dog or a cat. While training, the model analyzed the traits and patterns, which seemed to characterize the images and made the associations between these patterns and the accurate labels. Thus, the model gained an ability to classify the novel images, which it has never encountered before, as a picture of a dog or a cat. Apart from classification, other common supervised learning tasks are regression, where the algorithm predicts a numerical value and sequence learning.

In unsupervised learning, there is a set of data points but their labels are not known in the beginning. This is exactly the type of learning you will use in a situation like this, where we are letting our algorithm learn on its own to discover any patterns or relationships, without providing it with what actually represents and make sense. Unsupervised learning algorithms help in extracting patterns and valuable information from their inherent structure of the data. In the case of unsupervised learning, it is used to predict a model and make decisions based on features in order to reveal patterns or structures that can be found within the dataset. There are numerous applications for them in a variety of areas, including applications in different fields such as clustering, dimensionality reduction and anomaly detection. An algorithm might be fed with customer purchase data (without labels), The algorithm will detect similarities and differences in the customers to create a cluster of people who purchase similar products.

More examples for unsupervised learning include dimensionality reduction algorithms, which are used to locate essential variables and anomaly detection algorithms detecting irregular data points. Unsupervised learning may help technicians understand the data and sort through huge amounts of obscure or cost-prohibitive to label.

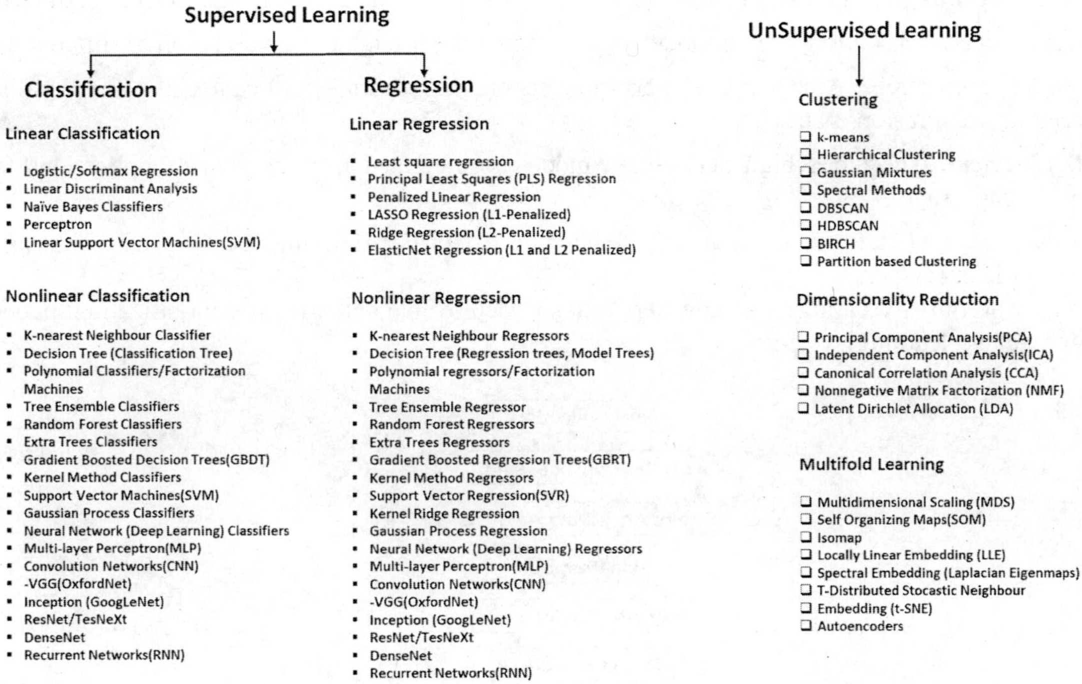


**FIGURE 6.1** Classification of Supervised and Unsupervised Learning.

## 6.2 CLASSIFICATION LEARNING STEPS

The process of classification learning encompasses a series of pivotal stages that are fundamental in constructing a precise and efficient classification model. The main steps involved in building a classification model in ML are:

***Data Collection:*** This is the preliminary step in gathering crucial labelled data containing the input features and output class labels from suitable sources pertinent to the problem. Real-world data is imperative for training robust models.

***Data Preprocessing:*** Before model training, the collected data is prepared by handling missing values, removing duplicate samples, transforming features for consistency, normalization etc. Quality data ensures quality models.

***Exploratory Data Analysis:*** Next, distributions, outliers, correlations and other statistics are analyzed to gain insights into data. Summary visualizations illuminate trends.

***Train-Test Split:*** Building and evaluating the model performance needs two different datasets—training set for the models to train and test set for evaluating the performance.

***Feature Engineering:*** Here, we construct additional informative features from existing ones to improve modeling.

***Model Selection:*** Choose appropriate classification algorithms like SVM, logistic regression etc. based on the data.

***Model Training:*** Train classification models on the training data to optimize model parameters.

***Hyperparameter Tuning:*** Tune model hyperparameters through cross validation to improve fit.

***Model Evaluation:*** Assess model performance on the separate test data using metrics like accuracy, confusion matrix etc.

***Deployment:*** The tuned high performing model is integrated into real-world applications for beneficial usage.

***Monitoring:*** Models are continuously tracked to detect deteriorating accuracy over time and retrain if necessary.

Carefully executing these key steps leads to deployable and effective classification models in machine learning projects.

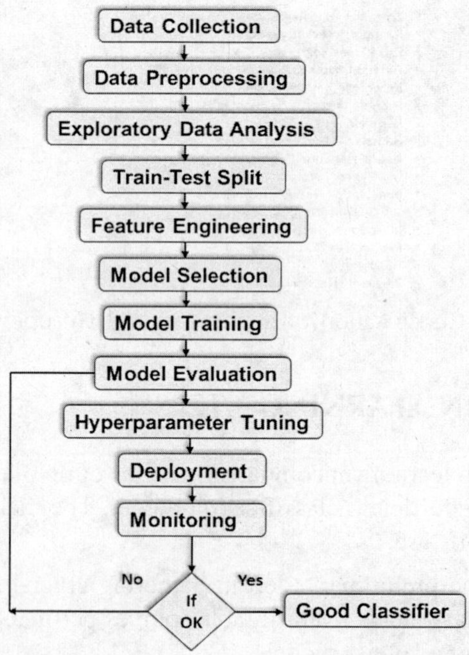


**FIGURE 6.2** Classification Learning Steps.

## 6.3 CLASSIFICATION ALGORITHMS

In the growing field of ML, numerous classification algorithms have gained significant traction and are extensively employed across diverse tasks. Described below are some of the common classification algorithms are described below:

### 6.3.1 Decision Trees

This can be used not only for classification but also for regression problems. They work by training a model until it can provide accurate answers to the value of your target variable based on simple decision rules made over data features. A decision tree (DT) is a flowchart-like structure in which each internal node represents a feature (or attributes), the branch of these trees represent outcome from this feature, the area where we can link an observation to its value for that attribute. The ability of DT to handle both numerical and categorical data, as well as the fact that they are simple to comprehend and explain, are all advantages which can be attributed to their use.

#### *Gini Index*

The index known as Gini is a statistical index that is frequently utilized to evaluate the degree of inequality or impurity present in a particular dataset. It is alternatively referred to as Gini impurity, serves as a quantifiable metric for assessing the degree of impurity or uncertainty present within a given dataset. On the basis of the distribution of classes within the node, the metric provides a quantitative representation of the probability of incorrectly categorizing a randomly selected element if that element were to be randomly assigned a label. In DT, the Gini index serves as a pivotal tool for assessing the efficacy of a given feature in dividing the dataset, thereby aiding in the identification of the optimal split at every node.

Gini index is used as a measure of homogeneity, or purity, at a given node or subset. It works by computing the probability that two randomly selected samples will be incorrectly labelled if labelled according to the distribution of class labels at that node. For example, a node containing 100 samples of which 80 are 'apples' and 20 are 'oranges' will have a lower Gini index than a 50-50 split, indicating greater homogeneity. The Gini index helps decision tree algorithms determine the optimal branching factor that results in the purest child nodes. The attribute with the lowest Gini index for its split provides the most homogeneous branches. By recursively splitting nodes using the Gini index, the decision tree can isolate the most informative features for prediction of the target variable. Using measures like Gini index prevents overfitting and enables more accurate classification and regression trees.
The Gini Index of dataset $D$ is given as follows:

$$gini(D) = 1 - \sum_{j=1}^{n} p_j^2 \tag{6.1}$$

Where $p_j$ is the relative frequency of class $j$ in $D$.

If a dataset $D$ split on $A$ into two subset $D1$ and $D2$, Gini index of $D$ defined as:

$$gini_A(D) = \frac{|D_1|}{|D|} gini(D1) + \frac{|D_2|}{|D|} gini(D2) \tag{6.2}$$

Reduction in impurity is given as:

$$\Delta gini(A) = gini(D) - gini_A(D) \tag{6.3}$$

### Entropy-based Approach

Entropy is a fundamental concept derived from the field of information theory, which serves as a metric for quantifying the degree of uncertainty or randomness present within a given dataset. In the field of decision trees, entropy serves as a measure to assess the lack of purity within a node, akin to the Gini index. The entropy-based approach is a methodology that aims to identify the optimal split that effectively minimises the ambiguity present in the child nodes.

The Entropy is given by the formula:

$$Entropy(S) = \sum_{i=1}^{c} (-p_i log_2 p_i) \tag{6.4}$$

Where $c$ is the number of different class labels and $p$ referes to the proportion of values falling into the i$^{th}$ class label.

Similar to the Gini index, the concept of entropy is utilised in machine learning algorithms. The entropy measure also exhibits a range from 0 to 1, wherein a value of 0 signifies a node that is entirely pure, while a value of 1 signifies the utmost level of impurity. When the decision tree is formed, algorithm endeavours to minimise entropy by selecting the feature that yields the most informative split. The difference between the two approaches may be well understood as follows,

***Computational Efficiency:*** The Gini index exhibits a slight advantage in terms of computational efficiency compared to entropy due to its reduced computational complexity, primarily stemming from the absence of logarithmic operations. With extensive datasets or intricate tree structures, the computational advantage offered by this phenomenon can prove to be quite substantial.

***Sensitivity to Class Imbalance:*** The Gini index exhibits a higher degree of sensitivity towards class imbalance in contrast to entropy. In scenarios characterised by imbalanced class distributions, it is worth noting that the Gini index has the potential to generate splits that exhibit a certain degree of bias, thereby displaying a preference towards the majority classes.

The precise nature of the issue being tackled dictates which method of decision tree development is going to be most effective. If noise is a primary problem, the Gini index is a potential solution that should be considered. If precision is of utmost importance, then using entropy can be the most appropriate strategy. Generally, the first node is termed as root node however the branches that follow the root node are termed as leaf nodes. Experimenting with both strategies to see which one is more effective for solving the particular issue at hand is a prudent plan of action in general.

### Information Gain

The degree to which a particular attribute or characteristic provides valuable insights in determining the target category we aim to predict is called information gain. The aim, when building a DT, is to split the training data on attributes that best separate the different classes. Information gain helps quantify which attributes provide the most purity in the resulting splits. Mathematically, information gain is based on the concept of entropy in information theory. Entropy measures the impurity of an arbitrary collection of examples. Information gain calculates the difference in entropy from before versus after the dataset is split on an attribute. It enables an attribute's ability to divide the training data efficiently to be assessed by the DT algorithm. The attribute with the highest information gain is selected as the splitting attribute at a given node in the tree. This splitting process recursively occurs on each branch to grow an optimal decision tree that successfully partitions the training examples using the fewest possible nodes. Information gain is extremely useful as it is simple to calculate and implement. The result is an interpretable tree that yields accurate models even when datasets have complex decision boundaries.

The information gain is expressed as:

$$Information\ gain\ (S, A) = Entropy(S_{bs}) - Entropy(S_{as}) \tag{6.5}$$

Where $S_a$ is the entropy after split and $S_b$ is the entropy before split such that,

$$Entropy\ (S_{as}) = \sum_{i=1}^{n} w_i\ Entropy\ (p_i) \tag{6.6}$$

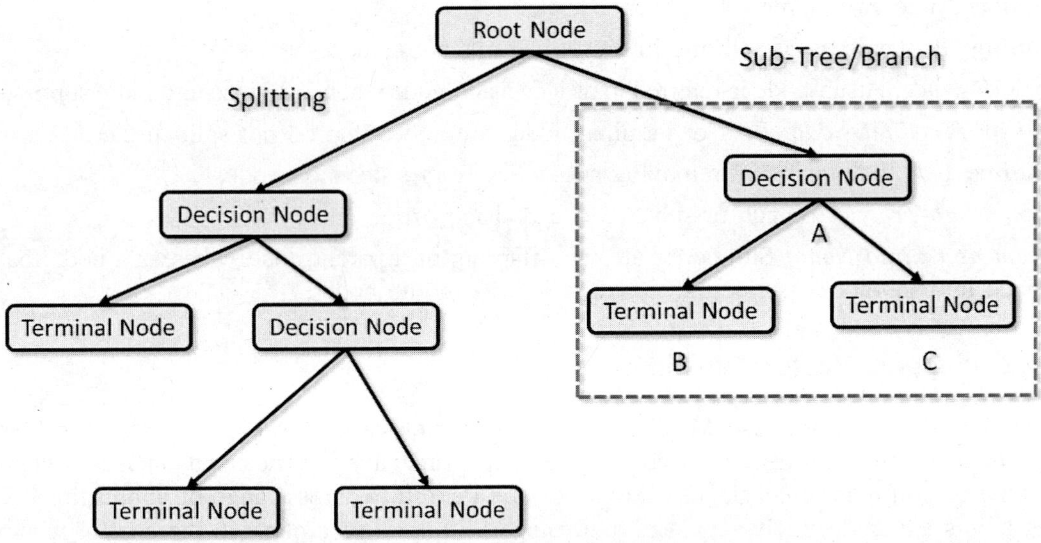


**FIGURE 6.3** Decision Tree with Sub tree and different nodes.

### *Types of Decision Trees*

There are several decision trees that may be employed. Following two are the main types– Categorical variable decision tree and Continuous variable decision tree.

***Categorical Variable Decision Tree:*** A categorical variable DT is a ML algorithm that is specifically designed to handle categorical variables as input features. Instead of using continuous variables to divide the data, this kind of algorithm for decision trees uses the outcomes of categorical variables. The decision tree in question is commonly referred to as a categorical variable-based decision tree, as it is designed to handle a target variable that falls within the categorical data type.

***Continuous Variable Decision Tree:*** This is specifically designed to handle continuous variables as input features. Unlike traditional decision trees that can only handle categorical variables, the continuous variable decision tree is capable of handling numerical data. This algorithm works by recursively partitioning the input space. This particular decision tree pertains to a dynamic goal variable that exhibits continuous fluctuations.

Some of the DT algorithms are:

(a) ID3 (an extension of D3) C4.5 (ID3's successor)
(b) CART (Classification And Regression Tree)
(c) CHAID (Chi-square Automatic Interaction Detection) for calculating classification trees, does multi-level splits.
(d) MARS (Multivariate Adaptive Regression Splines).

***Key Terminologies***

***Root Node:*** It is the first node which symbolises the entire population or sample that is then partitioned into two or more homogenous sets.

***Splitting:*** It is process of splitting in more than one sub-node.

***Decision Node:*** A sub-node is referred to as a decision node when it divides into more sub-nodes.

***Leaf or Terminal Node:*** Leaf or terminal nodes are nodes that do not split further.

***Pruning:*** It is the process of removing sub-nodes from a decision node.

***Branch/Sub-Tree:*** A branch or sub-tree is a division of the entire tree.

***Parent and Child Node:*** Sub-nodes are the offspring of a parent node, whereas a node that is divided into sub-nodes is referred to as the parents of sub-nodes.

### 6.3.2 Support Vector Machines

Support Vector Machines (SVM) are used widely for classification and regression problems. They belong to the class of supervised learning models and have significant advantages, including effectiveness in high dimensional data spaces and flexibility across range of applications. The data points are distinctively separated and categorised by a hyperplane in the area of features, illustrating the way SVMs operate.

The objective is to maximize the margin between the hyperplane and closest data points belonging to two classes, which are called support vectors. This makes SVM highly adept at handling more complex datasets as increasing the dimensionality helps in better separation and avoids overfitting. Kernels are functions used to effectively project lower dimensional data to higher dimensions, thereby increasing separability. The kernel and margin size are key parameters when optimizing SVM to fit a given dataset. SVM is particularly powerful because unlike other machine learning algorithms, it focuses more on instances close to hyperplane which contain the most information.

With tuning of parameters and integration of appropriate kernels, SVMs can model diverse data patterns for classification and regression with high accuracy and are integral to many machine learning applications.

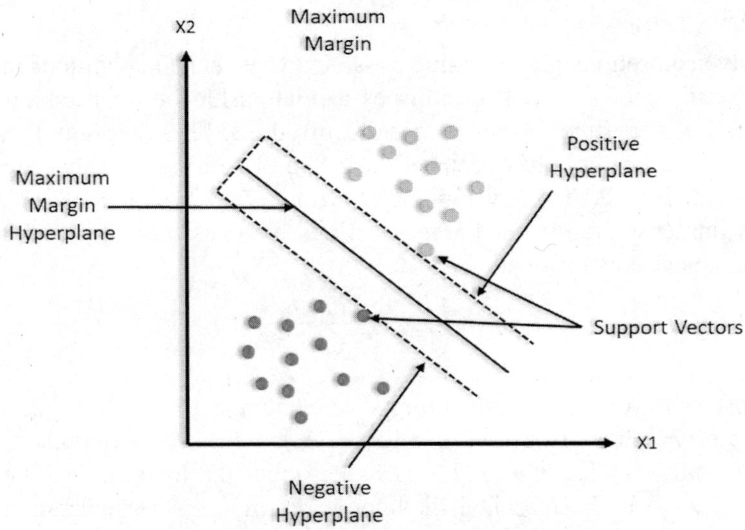


**FIGURE 6.4** SVM with Hyperplane.

### 6.3.3 Naïve Bayes

Naïve Bayes is an effective algorithm which is commonly used in a vast variety of classification and predictive modelling tasks. The idea behind the algorithm is its utilisation of Bayes' theorem and the principal assumption on the conditionally independence of features. In this case, since the assumption is "naive", the algorithm treats each of the feature as independent of the others if the class label is known. Although this condition may not hold in a real world, Naive Bayes classifiers have shown to work effectively in a lot of practical examples including, but not limited to, text categorisation, email spam detection, sentiment analysis and recommendation engines. It works because of its great simplicity in both model training and prediction making. The algorithm is capable of working with a comparatively low quantity of training data and has no problem with both continuous and discrete classes supporting it. Probably, the most attractive feature of Naive Bayes is the fact that it yields human easily read probabilities as an output.

Naive Bayes works by estimating the conditional probability of each possible output class given the input features. It assumes that each input feature contributes independently to the probability of a certain class, regardless of any possible correlations between features. While not always true in reality, this simplifying assumption allows the model to estimate these probabilistic contributions very efficiently. By multiplying those per-feature conditional probabilities together for a possible output class, the algorithm arrives at robust overall probability estimations for each class. The independent assumption greatly simplifies the necessary calculations, allowing for a straightforward implementation, faster training, and ease of interpretation without much loss of overall accuracy. With appropriate pre-processing and hyperparameter tuning, Naive Bayes can build high quality models that serve as a competitive baseline classifier and scale well to large datasets across text classification, sentiment analysis, spam filtering and many other application domains.

### *Bayes' Theorem*

Using previously acquired insight regarding possible event-related conditions the Bayes theorem calculates an event's probability. It establishes a relationship between conditional probability and likelihood. Let's assume event *X* has occurred. Bayes' theorem then calculates the probability of event *Y* given *A* has occurred, using information about the opposite conditional probability—the likelihood of *A* given *Y* along with overall probabilities of *X* and *Y*. Bayes' Theorem holds immense significance across various domains, notably machine learning, data science, and statistical conclusions.

$$P(X \mid Y) = \frac{P(Y \mid X)P(X)}{P(Y)} \tag{6.7}$$

$P(X|Y)$ is the posterior probability of hypothesis *X* given the evidence *Y*; $P(Y|X)$ is the likelihood, representing the probability of observing evidence *Y* given that the hypothesis *X* is true; $P(X)$ is the prior probability, indicating our initial belief about the hypothesis *X* before considering any evidence and $P(Y)$ is the marginal likelihood, serving as a normalization factor. It is the probability of observing evidence *Y* without conditioning on any specific hypothesis.

## 6.3.4 k-Nearest Neighbors (kNN)

This is a simple supervised ML algorithm used for both classification as well as regression tasks. It's regarded as being one of the most fundamental algorithms for machine learning because it relies on memorizing the training data sets and using similarity measures to classify new data points. kNN works by storing all training observations and their labels. When new unlabelled data is introduced, the algorithm finds the top *k* closest observations from the training data, where distance is calculated using metrics like Euclidean or Manhattan distance. The most frequent label or the average of the k-nearest neighbour labels is then assigned to the new unlabeled observation. The choice of *k* is critical-a small *k* risks overfitting but a large k risk smoothening out distinct class boundaries.

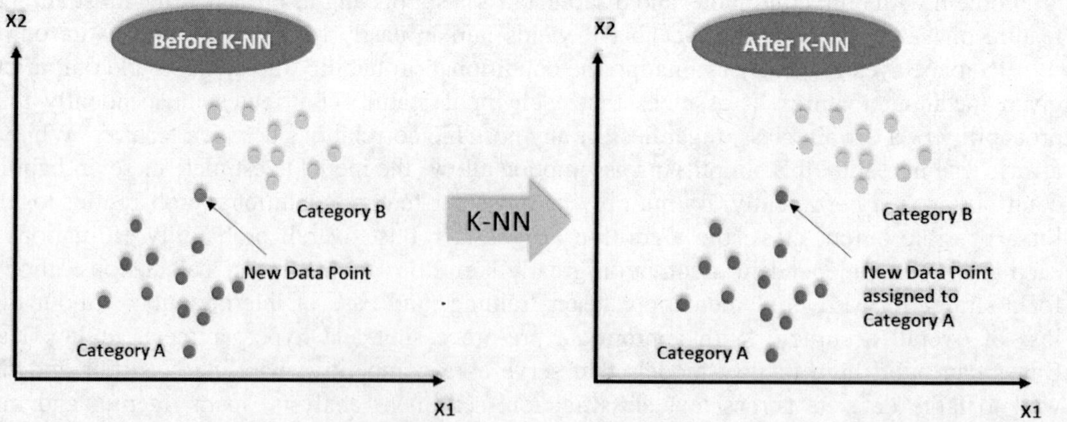


**FIGURE 6.5** KNN Algorithm.

The distance metric used also has a major effect on results. Key advantages of KNN include simplicity, low computational requirements during prediction, and often greater effectiveness when the training data is large. However, it is sensitive to noisy data and redundant features. Overall, KNN is easy to comprehend and adapts well to changing data, and serves as a fundamental machine learning algorithm for applications in object recognition, document classification and disease diagnosis.

### *Characteristics of kNN*

***Lazy Learning Algorithm:*** kNN is a sluggish algorithm due to the fact that it utilises all of the information for training while classifying so lacks a dedicated training phase.

***Non- Parametric Learning Algorithm:*** kNN is a not parametric learning algorithm as well because it makes no assumptions on the underlying data.

## 6.3.5 Random Forest

Widely adopted in data science, Random Forest (RF) is a supervised learning approach that leverages the power of numerous models to address classification and regression challenges. It functions by building a large number of decision trees during training and outputs the mode of the classes as classification for categorical targets or mean prediction for continuous targets. The "forest" it builds eliminates problems like overfitting and high variance that single decision trees often encounter.

During training, random forest uses bootstrap aggregating, or bagging, to randomly sample subsets of the data which helps improve the predictive accuracy and control overfitting. It further introduces randomness when splitting nodes in DT by limiting the candidate features that can be selected at each node.

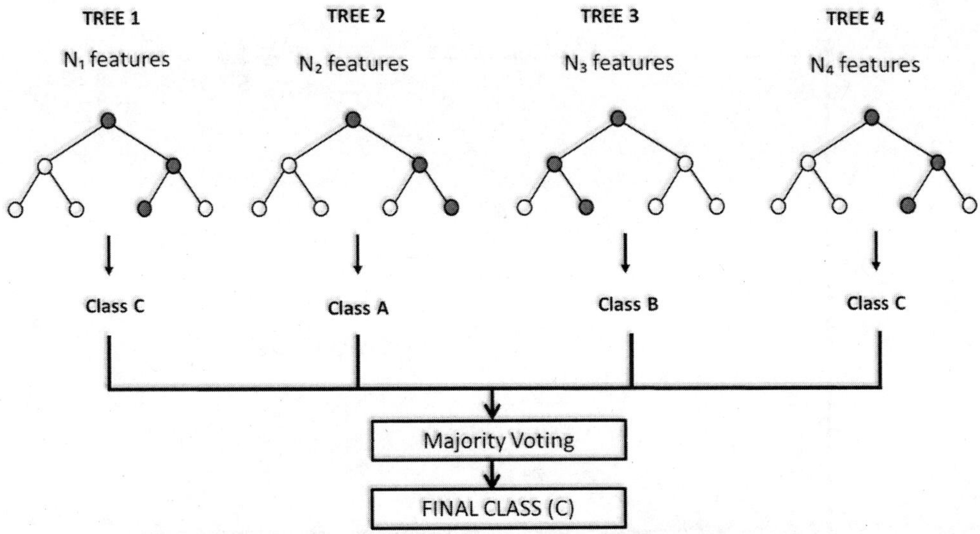


**FIGURE 6.6** A simple Random Forest model representation.

This decoration relates the forest trees making the algorithm very accurate. Key advantages are that it handles nonlinearity well, provides good accuracy results for many types of data, avoids overfitting issues, and is relatively robust to outliers and noise. It also determines feature importance and handles missing values implicitly. However, it can be slow to create and use for predictions and lacks interpretability compared to a single decision tree. Overall, this is a highly adaptable and efficient technique in the current state of research. Ensembles using random forests consistently rank as one of the most accurate modeling techniques.

### 6.3.6 Logistic Regression

A statistical method for anticipating binary results from data is called logistic regression. Using the logistic sigmoid function, logistic regression converts its output into a probability value that is limited between 0 and 1, as compared to linear regression, which produces continuous number values. This makes logistic regression well-suited for classifying observations into one of two possible discrete outcomes. This algorithm calculates the odds ratio for each input variable and determines a fitting logic function that can model the probabilities of binary outcomes in the data. Logistic regression can determine the percent influence each independent variable has on the dependent variable during classification. Key properties that make logistic regression powerful for analytics include easy implementation, low computational intensity, capacity to handle noisy data well, and no requirement for normal distribution in the feature variables. However, it is prone to overfitting with very high-dimensional data and cannot inherently handle multiclass problems. Logistic regression's advantages have ensured its place as a foundational and popular predictive modeling technique for probability-based classification tasks. It sees ubiquitous use across industries like healthcare, marketing, social sciences, and more.

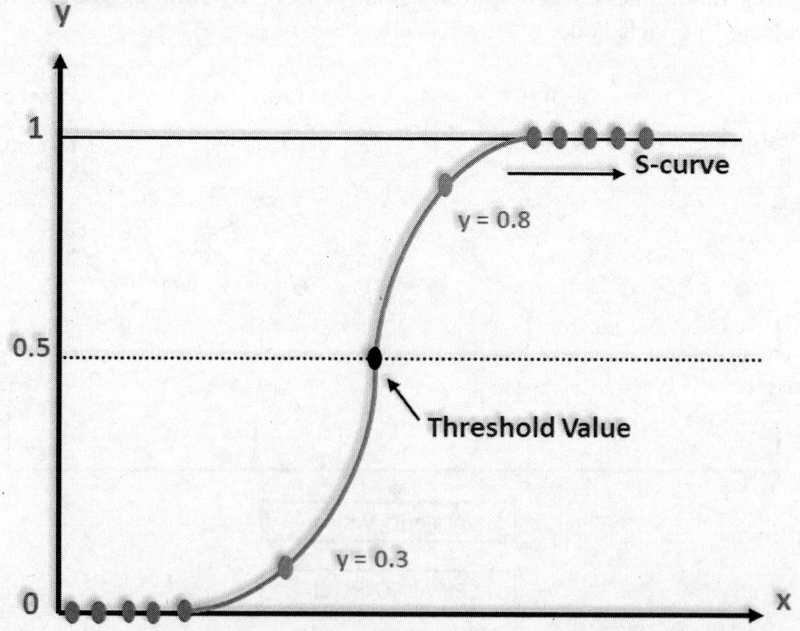


FIGURE 6.7 Representation of Logistic Regression.

## 6.4 REGRESSION ALGORITHMS

As the field of ML is expanding, numerous regression algorithms have gained significant popularity due to their efficacy in tackling diverse prediction tasks. Below are some concise explanations of several regression algorithms.

### 6.4.1 Linear Regression

Linear regression is one of the most powerful and widely-used statistical methods helping us not only investigate but also measure the relation between one dependent variable and one or more independent variables. The point is that the process of predicting the variables' levels and influences is a perfect measure to understand to what extent two variables are related to one another. In fact, the main purpose of linear regression is to find the best-fitting straight line that reduces the differences between the observed data points and the estimated values on the line. There are several assumptions that the process of linear regression states: linearity, independence of errors, homoscedasticity, and normality of errors. As soon as any of them is not met, the process of estimating the coefficients becomes inefficient and biased, and the outcomes are not accurate. The equation of the line of regression is conventionally denoted as,

$$y = b_0 + b_1x + \varepsilon \tag{6.8}$$

Where, $y$ is the dependent and $x$ is independent variable, $b_0$ is the $y$-intercept and $b_1$ is the slope and $\varepsilon$ is the error term.

#### *Multiple Linear Regression Model*

This is a powerful statistical tool that enables researchers to investigate the intricate relationships between a dependent variable and multiple independent variables. Rooted in the principles of mathematics and statistics, this technique has found applications in different fields of scientific disciplines, from economics and psychology to biology, environmental science etc. It is given as:

$$y = b_0 + b_1x_1 + b_2x_2 + \cdots + b_mx_m + \varepsilon \tag{6.9}$$

Where, $y$ is the dependent variable; $x_{1,}$ …, $x_m$ are independent variables ($p$ predictors); $b_m$ is the $y$-intercept and $\varepsilon$ is error term (unobserved factors affecting $y$).

Employing the values of two or more independent variables, multiple linear regression serves as a popular statistical method for predicting or clarifying the outcome of a dependent variable. In this context, it is essential to emphasize that multiple linear regression is based on certain assumptions, namely, linearity, independence, homoscedasticity, normality, and the lack of multicollinearity. If these assumptions are violated, the results of the data analysis can be biased or inefficient. For example, multicollinearity can make it extremely difficult to evaluate the individual effects of different independent variables. At the same time, if one knows of a potential relationship between a dependent variable and more than one independent variable, omitting any critical potential risk in the analysis might also result in biased conclusions. Overfitting can be another serious problem. In particular, if the number of independent variables is larger than the size of a sample, an analyst should expect that a model can perfectly fit the training data. Nevertheless, this model is unlikely to show similar results when applied to new data. In this case, professional analysts can use alternatives such as variable selection, principal component analysis, regularization, and cross-validation. In summary, it is necessary to say that multiple linear regression can be helpful for data analysis, provided that conditions attached to this method are met. However, this fact does not mean that this technique is flawless, and analysts should consider these assumptions and alternatives to put the results of the analysis in the proper context.

### 6.4.2 Polynomial Regression

This is a type of supervised learning algorithm that extends linear regression to model nonlinear relationships among the dependent variable and the independent variable(s) by introducing polynomial terms. It is given as,

$$y = b_0 + b_1 x + b_2 x^2 + b_3 x^3 + \cdots + b_n x^n \tag{6.10}$$

Where, $y$ is the dependent variable; $x$ is the independent variable; $b_0$ is the $y$-intercept (constant term); $b_1$, $b_2$, $b_3$, ..., $b_n$ are the coefficients of the polynomial terms $n$ is the polynomial degree.

The polynomial's degree affects the model's complexity. When a model gets too complicated for the available data, a higher degree may give rise to overfitting but also provide more versatility in detecting nonlinear trends. Here are some examples of polynomial regression equations for different degrees,

1. **Linear Regression (Degree 1):** $y = b_0 + b_1x$
2. **Quadratic Regression (Degree 2):** $y = b_0 + b_1x + b_2x^2$
3. **Cubic Regression (Degree 3):** $y = b_0 + b_1x + b_2x^2 + b_3x^3$
4. **Quartic Regression (Degree 4):** $y = b_0 + b_1x + b_2x^2 + b_3x^3 + b_4x^4$

The coefficients ($b_0$, $b_1$, $b_2$, ..., $b_n$) are estimated using optimization techniques, such as least squares or gradient descent. It finds applications in different domains, say for example in economics, engineering, and natural sciences, wherever nonlinear relationships between variables are common. It provides a flexible and interpretable way to model data.

The higher the degree of the polynomial ($n$), the complex is the model. In the context of ML, it is noteworthy to mention that when the value of $n$ is set to 1, it corresponds to the utilisation of Linear Regression. Similarly, when $n$ is assigned a value of 2, it signifies the application of Quadratic Regression. Furthermore, when $n$ is set to 3, it denotes the utilisation of Cubic Regression. This pattern continues, with each subsequent value of $n$ corresponding to the implementation of the respective regression technique. Larger values of $n$ helps the model to apprehend more intricate relationships, albeit at the expense of escalating the peril of overfitting the data.

### 6.4.3 Shrinkage Methods

#### *Ridge Regression*

Ridge Regression, a technique derived from linear regression, incorporates regularisation by introducing an additional term that imposes a penalty to the coefficients of the model. This term effectively mitigates the adverse effects of multicollinearity and overfitting, which can otherwise hinder the model's performance. Ridge regression is a highly advantageous technique in the context of handling datasets with a high number of dimensions and interrelated features. Ridge regression, commonly referred to as L2 regularisation, represents a refined adaptation of linear regression that effectively tackles the challenges posed by multicollinearity and overfitting. It is important to acknowledge that the presence of highly correlated input features can introduce a degree of sensitivity within the model. This sensitivity manifests as a heightened responsiveness to even minor fluctuations in the data, ultimately resulting in predictions that lack stability and reliability. Ridge regression incorporates a regularisation term into the cost function, thereby imposing a penalty on the coefficients of the model. This penalty effectively discourages the presence of excessively large weight values. The regularisation is governed by hyperparameter denoted by lambda ($\lambda$), that plays a pivotal role in striking a balance between effectively capturing the data patterns and constraining the magnitudes of the coefficients. Ridge regression, through the imposition of a penalty on large coefficients, effectively mitigates the influence of correlated features. This regularisation technique fosters the development of a model that is characterised by enhanced stability and robustness, thereby diminishing the susceptibility to overfitting. Consequently, Ridge Regression becomes better equipped to generalise well to novel, unseen data, rendering it a more suitable choice in such scenarios. The Ridge Regression equation is given as,

$$y = b_0 + b_1x_1 + b_2x_2 + \cdots + b_nx_n + \lambda\sum(b_i^2) \tag{6.11}$$

Where, $y$ is the predicted value of the target variable; $b_0$, $b_1$, $b_2,\ldots, b_n$ are the coefficients (weights) of the model; $x_1$, $x_2,\ldots,x_n$ are the input features; $\lambda$ is the regularization parameter, and is $\Sigma(b_i^2)$ the sum of the squares of the coefficients.

The regularisation parameter $\lambda$ is crucial hyperparameter which governs the magnitude of penalty term, thereby exerting control over the strength of regularisation. Increasing the regularisation parameter, $\lambda$, will lead to the attenuation of the coefficients, thereby facilitating the mitigation of overfitting. Ridge regression, a popular technique in the domain of ML, exhibits a remarkable capability to strike an optimal equilibrium between effectively fitting the data and mitigating the detrimental effects of overfitting. This unique characteristic renders it an invaluable tool in scenarios characterised by a high degree of correlation among input features or datasets boasting an extensive array of features.

### *Lasso Regression*

Lasso regression, a regularised variant of linear regression, distinguishes itself through the utilisation of a distinct penalty term. A vital process in machine learning is feature selection, which enables us to recognize the most important properties and ignore the ones that are not essential. In order to choose the most relevant features, this technique entails accurately pushing some coefficients to zero. By doing so, we can enhance the model's performance and ensure that only the most informative features are utilised for accurate predictions.

Lasso regression, also known as Least Absolute Shrinkage and Selection Operator, is a regression technique that incorporates L1 regularisation into the linear regression framework. This regularisation method is specifically designed to tackle multicollinearity issues and facilitate feature selection. Lasso regression adds a regularisation term to the cost function, just like ridge regression does. However, in contrast to ridge regression, lasso regression employs the absolute values of the coefficients rather than their squares as the penalty term. This phenomenon results in a sparsity-inducing characteristic, thereby causing certain coefficients to attain a value of precisely zero. Lasso regression, as a powerful ML technique, exhibits the remarkable capability of conducting automatic feature selection. This is achieved through its ability to effectively eliminate features that are deemed less significant or irrelevant to the model. With an extra regularisation component, the lasso regression equation is comparable to the linear regression equation,

$$y = b_0 + b_1x_1 + b_2x_2 + \cdots + b_nx_n + \lambda\sum(|\, b_i \,|) \tag{6.12}$$

Where, $y$ is the predicted value of the target variable; $b_0$, $b_1$, $b_2$, …, $b_n$ are the coefficients (weights) of the model; $x_1$, $x_2$, ..., $x_n$ are the input features; $\lambda$ is the regularization parameter, and $\Sigma(|b_i|)$ is the sum of the absolute values of the coefficients.

The regularisation parameter $\lambda$ governs the magnitude of the penalty term, exerting influence over the degree of regularisation applied. A higher value of $\lambda$ promotes sparsity in the coefficient vector, thereby facilitating feature selection by favouring a larger number of exactly zero coefficients that correspond to the most significant features for the model. Lasso regression is a powerful technique that proves to be highly advantageous in the field of machine learning, especially when confronted with datasets that possess a multitude of features, resulting in high-dimensionality. By effectively reducing the complexity of the model, lasso regression effectively addresses the prevalent issue of overfitting, thereby enhancing the model's generalisation capabilities.

Lasso regression is quite effective and has been shown to be flexible in a different field, including signal processing, finance, and genetics. Its significance lies in its ability to effectively extract vital features from extensive collections of variables, a task of utmost importance in these fields. The inherent capability of this tool to autonomously execute feature selection renders it an invaluable asset in constructing models that are both interpretable and efficient, all the while upholding the utmost predictive accuracy. However, it is imperative to meticulously select the optimal value for the regularisation parameter $\lambda$, as an excessively large value could potentially cause numerous coefficients to shrink to zero, thereby resulting in an excessively simplified model. In regression tasks that necessitate feature selection, lasso regression emerges as a formidable solution, offering a potent and efficient approach to tackle datasets with a high number of dimensions. By using its capabilities, one can effortlessly obtain models that are both sparse and easily interpretable, thereby enhancing the overall effectiveness of the regression process.

### *The Elastic Net*

This is a shrinkage and variable selection method for regression and classification problems. Ridge regression and lasso regression, two of the most popular approaches, are combined in this way. In particular, the L1 norm — which Lasso uses as the sum of absolute values — and the L2 norm — which Ridge uses as the sum of squares, combine linearly to form the Elastic net penalty. This hybrid constraint allows the elastic net to select variables like lasso, while still maintaining some strong coefficients like Ridge.

So, the L1 portion of the elastic net penalty generates sparsity in coefficient values - driving extraneous coefficients to zero and excluding inferior variables altogether. The L2 component, on the other hand, encourages grouping effects and stability in selection. The relative weights between the two can be easily tuned as well. As such, the elastic net often outperforms Lasso in terms of prediction accuracy in many real-world settings. It also maintains interpretability owing to the sparse solutions produced. As such, the elastic net provides an appealing combination of parsimony, coefficient stability, variable selection power and overall generalization ability. It has become an extremely useful tool for performing shrinkage and dimensionality reduction in modern machine learning pipelines dealing with wide datasets. Thus, it can be used to produce a shrinkage regression method with superior and customizable variable selection capabilities as well as predictive stability and accuracy.

## 6.5 BIAS-VARIANCE AND TRADEOFF

The bias-variance trade-off is a core concept in supervised learning for analyzing model generalization error. It refers to balancing two key properties of models that contribute to error—bias and variance. Bias represents the simplifying assumptions a model makes that can result in underfitting. Variance captures model sensitivity and tendency to overfit the training data. Mathematically, for any model, the expected test error can be expressed as the sum of three components—bias, variance and an irreducible error. High bias can cause high errors on the training data due to underfitting while high variance leads to large differences in model predictions on similar new data owing to overspecialization in capturing noise. An optimal model balances two extremes - it fits key patterns in data well without adjustments to noise or random fluctuations. The bias-variance decomposition provides insight on expected generalization capabilities. Various regularization techniques exploit this trade off-methods like early stopping, L1/L2 norms, dropout prevent overfitting by smoothing and stabilizing model behaviour for robust predictive performance on unseen data.

$$Total\ Error = Bias^2 + Variance + Irreducible\ Error \tag{6.13}$$

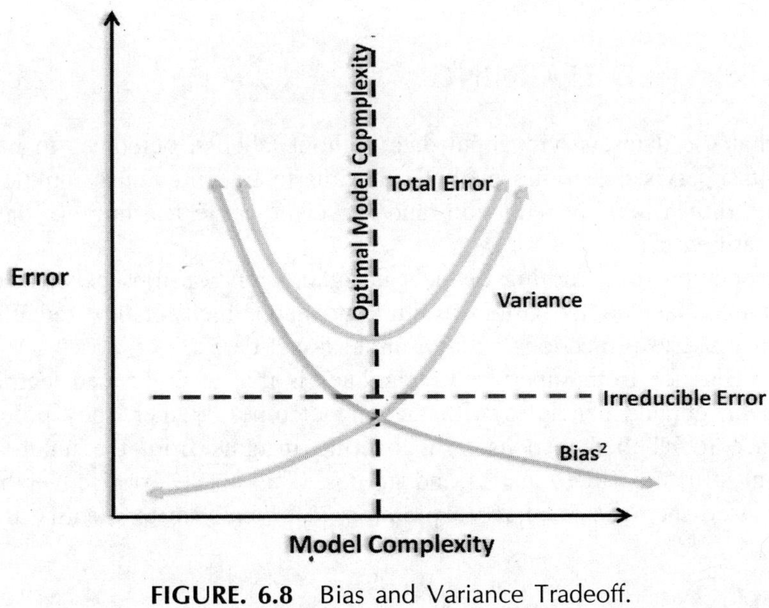


**FIGURE. 6.8** Bias and Variance Tradeoff.

*Low Bias:* Less presumptions regarding the target function's shape are made.

*High Bias:* Makes additional assumptions on the target function's shape.

*Low Variance:* Makes modest recommendations for modifications to the training dataset that will impact the target function estimation.

*High Variance:* Suggests making significant adjustments to the target function estimate in response to training dataset modifications.

Understanding this trade-off informs optimal model design for accurate real-world deployment across machine learning applications.

### No Free Lunch Theorem

A model is a simplified representation of the observations. In simple terms, the simplifications aim to remove unnecessary details that are unlikely to apply to new cases. To determine which data should be discarded and which data should be retained, certain assumptions need to be made. When using a linear model, it is assumed that the data follows a linear pattern. Any deviation from this line is considered to be noise and can be disregarded. In a well-known paper of 1996, David Wolpert showcased that when no assumptions are made about the data, there is no basis to favour one model over another. This concept is referred to as the No Free Lunch (NFL) theorem. For certain datasets, a linear model may be the most suitable choice, whereas for other datasets, a neural network may yield better results. No model can be guaranteed to work better from the start (hence the name of the theorem). To determine the most suitable model, it is necessary to evaluate all of them. In practice, when dealing with complex problems, it is not feasible to consider every possible scenario. Therefore, experts in ML make certain assumptions about the data and focus on evaluating selected few models that are considered reasonable. For instance, when dealing with straightforward tasks, you can assess linear models with different levels of regularisation. On the other hand, when tackling a more intricate problem, you can assess different neural networks.

## 6.6 UNSUPERVISED LEARNING

ML methods that use datasets with input data without labelled outcomes to make inferences are known as unsupervised learning methods. It aims to find previously unknown patterns in data. Clustering, dimensionality reduction, and association rule learning are the most popular unsupervised learning tasks.

While association rule learning extracts intriguing relationships between characteristics, clustering combines data points based on similarity and dimensionality reduction techniques like PCA identify useful projections of high-dimensional data.

The key difference from supervised techniques is that unsupervised learning algorithms are not trained on curated examples with known outcomes. Rather, they process input data without reference to labelled responses, uncovering insights from the unlabeled data itself through inherent structures like clusters and groups. This ability to discover hidden patterns makes unsupervised methods ideal for exploratory data analysis to identify trends, interpret complex data, and reduce dimensions for pre-processing before supervised techniques. From inferring segments of customer bases to grouping genes with similar expressions, unsupervised learning powers critical analysis across use cases involving massive, complex datasets in fields ranging from computer vision, finance, e-commerce and healthcare.

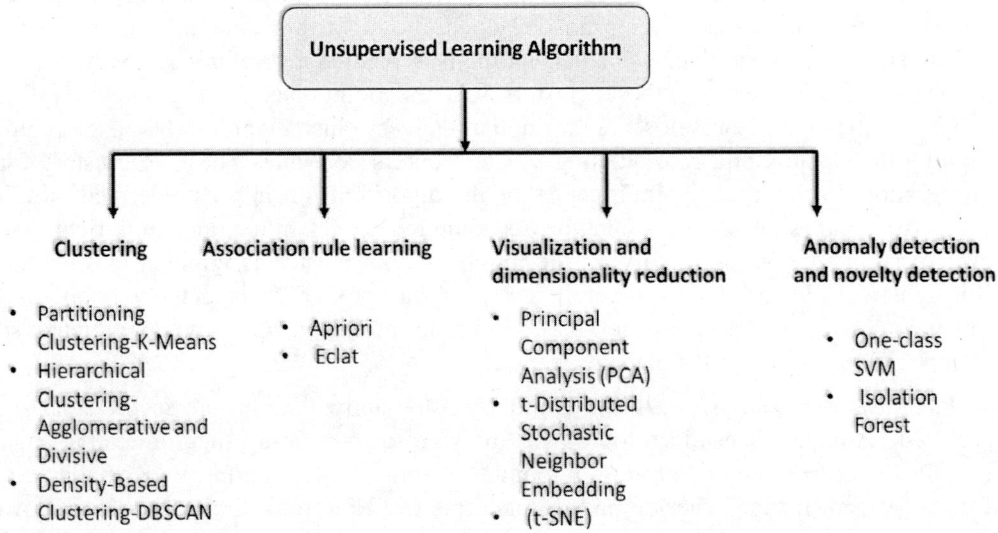


**FIGURE 6.9** Classification of Unsupervised Learning Algorithms.

## 6.6.1 Clustering

Clustering refers to the unsupervised learning task of identifying intrinsic groups or segments within data based on similarity. In order to ensure that items in one cluster are similar to each other and items in different clusters are dissimilar, it automatically divides a heterogeneous dataset into several more homogeneous clusters. Clustering algorithms achieve this by quantifying attributes of data points to measure similarities and differences between them. Many clustering algorithms exist; some of the more well-known ones are probability-based clustering such as Gaussian mixture models, density-based clustering such as DBSCAN and optics, hierarchical clustering, and partitioning techniques like k-means. Clustering powers widespread critical analysis by revealing natural structures and behavioural patterns in data. Key applications include customer segmentation for targeted marketing, grouping related documents like research papers or news articles, bioinformatics analysis by clustering genes or tissue types, and anomaly detection. The clusters identified can inform specialized analysis pertaining to the shared traits within that cluster. Clustering requires expertise to select suitable similarity measures for the data type and domain, choose an appropriate algorithm, determine the optimal number of clusters and interpret results. Unsupervised clustering analysis provides actionable insights from the unlabeled existing data to support improved decision-making.

### Partitioning Clustering Algorithms

***K-means:*** Unsupervised ML algorithms involving cluster analysis that are widely used include K-means. The method divides a given dataset into k unique, non-overlapping clusters according to the resemblance among data instances. It is a straightforward sequential clustering algorithm.

In order to have the ability to operate as centroid points later in the k-means algorithm, these points have to be initially determined. Hence, the algorithm randomly assigns points to k initial clusters, and after that, each data point is separated by reference to the Euclidean distance between the centre of these clusters and the point. Next, the average of them is calculated, and the obtained result serves for updating every cluster centre. This iterative process of assigning data points and recalculating cluster centers continues until the clusters formed at each iteration do not change significantly or the algorithm reaches a predefined number of iterations. Advantages of k-means include its simplicity, scalability, and empirical success. However, performance relies heavily on the initial random cluster assignment and works well only for spherical cluster shapes. Overall, k-means has proven to be hugely popular across domains including customer segmentation, text mining, bioinformatics, and spatial analysis for its efficient clustering of large unlabeled datasets.

***Hierarchical Cluster Analysis (HCA):*** Building a hierarchy of clusters is the goal of this unsupervised learning process in a top-down (divisive) or bottom-up (agglomerative) manner. It successively merges similar groups of points or splits larger groups into smaller clusters based on a defined linkage criterion and distance metric. Hierarchical clustering is a powerful technique that leverages a tree-like structure, commonly known as a dendrogram, to effectively organise data points into a hierarchical arrangement of nested clusters. The hierarchical clustering algorithm can be implemented using either the agglomerative approach, also known as bottom-up, or the divisive approach, also known as top-down. In the context of agglomerative clustering, the initial state involves each individual data point being treated as an independent cluster. Through a series of iterations, these clusters are gradually merged together based on their proximity to one another, ultimately causing a unified cluster to form, encompassing all data points. In the context of clustering algorithms, divisive clustering is a technique where the initial state involves all data points being grouped together in a single cluster. Subsequently, an iterative process takes place wherein these data points are partitioned into progressively smaller clusters. Until a stopping condition is satisfied, this recursive division keeps going, resulting in a hierarchical structure of clusters. Hierarchical clustering exhibits the advantageous characteristic of not necessitating the a priori specification of the number of clusters, thereby endowing it with enhanced flexibility.

***Agglomerative and Divisive Clustering:*** Agglomerative and divisive clustering are widely recognised as two fundamental methodologies in the domain of hierarchical clustering, a pivotal technique employed in the field of unsupervised learning to effectively amalgamate akin data points into cohesive clusters.

***Agglomerative Clustering:*** One popular machine learning technique is agglomerative clustering. Every data point is first viewed as a distinct cluster in this "bottom-up" methodology. These clusters are then progressively merged together based on their similarity. This iterative process continues till a stopping criterion is met, resulting in a hierarchical structure of clusters. In the initial stage of the clustering process, each individual data point is treated as an independent cluster. The algorithm employs an iterative process wherein it systematically merges the two clusters that exhibit the highest degree of similarity, ultimately culminating in the formation of a singular, comprehensive cluster encompassing all data points. The aforementioned procedure entails the generation of a hierarchical dendrogram, which exhibits a tree-like arrangement. This dendrogram is constructed by means of a sequence of merging operations, leading to the formation of distinct clusters. Agglomerative clustering, a widely used technique in machine learning, leverages distance measures such as Euclidean distance or similarity measures like correlation to effectively ascertain the proximity between clusters.

***Divisive Clustering:*** All data points are first assigned to a single cluster in a systematic manner known as "top-down" methodology or dividing clustering. Subsequently, these clusters are iteratively divided into smaller clusters based on their dissimilarity. The algorithm commences by initialising a solitary cluster encompassing all data points. Subsequently, it iteratively partitions the cluster into two smaller sub-clusters, employing dissimilarity criteria as the basis for division. The iterative procedure persists until every data point is assigned to its own distinct cluster. Divisive clustering, akin to agglomerative clustering, yields a dendrogram as well, albeit with a contrasting hierarchical construction from the apex downwards.

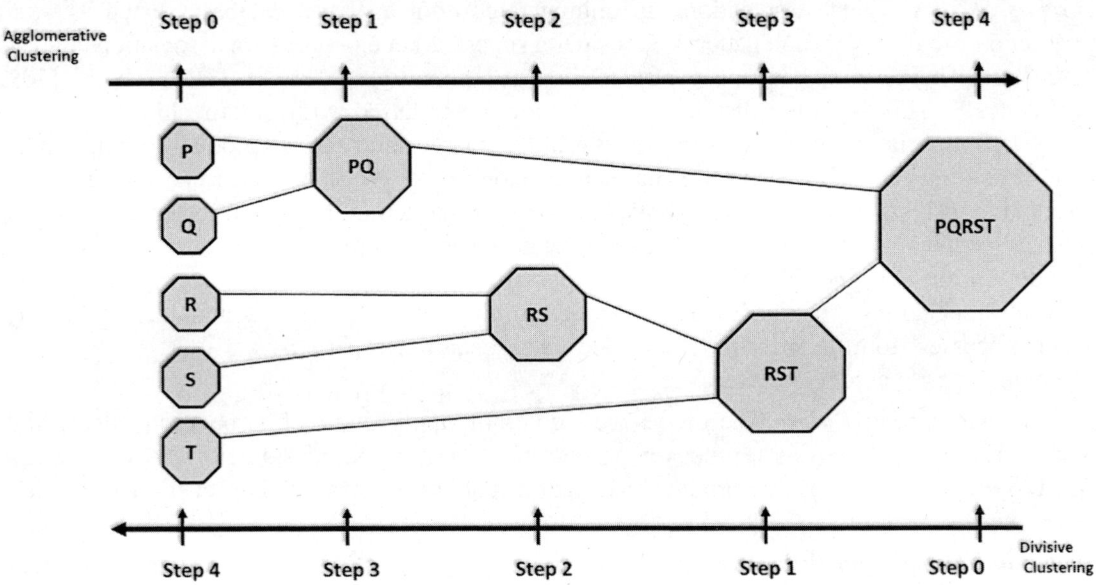


**FIGURE 6.10** Agglomerative and Divisive Clustering.

### Density-based Clustering

***Density-based Spatial Clustering of Applications with Noise (DBSCAN):*** Capable of grouping densely packed points according to spatial density, DBSCAN eliminates the need to specify the number of clusters in advance. The key idea is that points inside a cluster demonstrate higher local point density than points located in clusters boundaries or outside clusters. DBSCAN only requires two parameters—the maximum radius/neighbourhood distance (eps) and the minimum points required within that radius to form a cluster. It starts with labelling an arbitrary point and expands a cluster from that seed point if sufficient neighbours are within eps distance. DBSCAN keeps expanding clusters to higher density regions, marking low density areas between clusters as noise. Benefits include ability to discover arbitrary non-linearly separable clusters based on density connectivity and identify noise points not belonging to any clusters. Due to reliance on parameter eps based on data, applications of DBSCAN range from bioinformatics, anomaly detection in networks to geospatial and aircraft trajectory analysis, where domain information aids appropriate tuning. By distinguishing dense clusters separate from noise based on variable density, DBSCAN facilitates impactful analysis across domains involving heterogeneous clustered data distributions.

### 6.6.2 Association Rule

Association rule is an unsupervised learning method that discovers interesting associations and correlation relationships among items, events or attributes in large databases. It extracts rules that express probabilistic co-occurrence between data items in the form "IF Antecedent, THEN Consequent", without requiring any historical labels or supervision. Let us understand with an example, "*If a customer buys items A and B together, they are 70% likely to also purchase C*". A typical association rule mining algorithm analyzes databases, such as retail transactions, to discover such patterns. Consider a supermarket example—an association analysis on customer basket data can uncover rules like "IF {potato chips, salsa} THEN {beer} [70% confidence]". This signifies that beer is commonly purchased with potato chips and salsa. Uncovered associations can discover meaningful links between disparate products, demographic groups, and indicate subtle drivers of human decision processes. The retailer can leverage such associative insights to tailor store layouts, better target marketing offers and influence customer behaviours. Commonly used algorithms to generate association rules from database transactions include Apriori, FP Growth. Metrics like support, confidence help determine significant and relevant associations. Overall, association rules mining allows tapping actionable intelligence about processes from underneath database-level co-occurrence patterns.

The main types of association rules are:

***Product Association Rules:*** One of the most common applications of association rule mining is in market basket analysis to uncover product relationships like customers who buy item A also buy item B. Retailers use product association rules to get insights into customer purchase behaviour and patterns.

***Sequential Association Rules:*** These rules discover associations considering ordered sequences, like a customer who does activity A goes on to do activity B. They are temporal association rules useful for analyzing navigation trails, buying patterns over time etc.

***Spatial Association Rules:*** Associations considering spatial or location-based dimensions like a store region with products A, B will likely sell product C. Useful for store planning.

Additionally, there are other categorizations:

***Multidimensional Association Rules:*** Rules that consider additional dimensions like customer demographics on top of just products or items. For example, males aged 20-30 who buy A also buy B.

***Quantitative Association Rules:*** Rules involving numeric values of variables rather than just binary vectors. For example, customers who spend > $100 also buy premium products.

So, the most common application is in market basket analysis, association rules can also tap into sequential, spatial, multidimensional and numeric aspects underlying patterns in business databases, websites, diagnostic logs and more. The key focus is uncovering interesting conditional dependencies between co-occurring entities.

### *Apriori Algorithm*

The Apriori algorithm is one of the most popular and classical algorithms for association rule mining. It employs a "bottom up" approach to uncover frequent item sets and derive association rules between items in transactional databases. First, the minimum support threshold is set to identify frequent individual items based on their occurrence frequency. Then k-item sets are used to generate candidate $(k + 1)$—item sets in an iterative manner by pruning infrequent items and extending the length of item sets. This iterative approach prunes the search space at each pass by only exploring frequent candidates at each level. Frequent itemset lists of all lengths are used to generate rules filtered by confidence thresholds, and the algorithm ends when no more successful extensions can be found. For example, consider market basket database of items purchased by customers. Item milk has support 60% based on its occurrence frequency. Fix minimum support at 40% to filter items. Then find all frequent 2-itemsets from remaining items, say {milk, bread}, {milk, eggs} etc. Repeat to generate 3-itemsets then 4-itemsets and so on till no more frequent item sets are found. This network of frequent item sets is then mined to form rules like: IF {milk, bread} THEN {eggs} [70% confidence]. By iterating from small to large item sets, Apriori prunes ineffective candidates early on while discovering hidden associations in transaction data. Despite potential candidate explosions, it remains very widely used for uncovering association rules.

### *FP-Growth*

FP-growth stands for Frequent Pattern-growth, and it is an efficient and scalable data mining algorithm to identify frequent patterns in large datasets. As Jiawei Han, Jian Pei, and Yiwen Yin developed FP-growth in 2000, it has eventually become a popular and extensively employed algorithms for frequent itemset mining. It works differently from its predecessor, the Apriori algorithm, which generates candidate itemset in the first step, after which it tests their frequency. In turn, FP-growth utilizes an esoteric data structure, an FP-tree or Frequent Pattern Tree, to encode the input data in a compressed form. Therefore, the algorithm can identify frequent patterns at once without generating candidates. The algorithm performs in two steps: FP-tree and frequent itemset generation. In the initial step, the algorithm scans the dataset to identify frequent items in the input data. The items already ordered by their frequency are encoded in an FP-tree. The next transaction is then inserted into the tree, and if an item is inserted into a shared prefix path, nodes and path frequency are updated. In the second step, the algorithm recursively finds frequent patterns and grows pattern fragments in the FP-tree by evaluating different combinations of the input items. Thus, conditional pattern bases and conditional FP-trees for each frequent item set are constructed. The biggest advantage of using

FP-growth is that the algorithm generates frequent patterns without producing candidate item sets, which significantly reduces memory consumption, making the method faster and more cost-efficient.

After the initial FP-tree construction, the mining process divides the compressed database into a set of conditional databases, each associated with one frequent item. Recursively, FP-trees are built for each such conditional database. This recursive decomposition leads to discovery of all frequent item sets rooted at the given item efficiently, without needing candidate generations. For example, an FP-tree on customer transactions can recursively mine patterns for {milk}, {bread} etc. By avoiding costly candidate generations and database scans, FP-growth provides efficient and scalable mining. It utilizes sophisticated data structures and partitioning without compromising on performance. The frequent item sets are finally used to generate high-confidence association rules. Though complex, FP-trees enable efficient frequency counting and pattern fragmentation for mining massive databases. Hence, FP-growth recursively decomposes the mining problem into smaller conditional cases using a special compressed data structure to discover all frequent patterns and association rules efficiently.

### 6.6.3 Anomaly and Novelty Detection

#### *Anomaly Detection*

Analyzing patterns in data which deviate from expected behaviour is known as anomaly detection. When observations differ so significantly from one another that it raises questions about whether a distinct underlying process is responsible for them, they are referred to as outliers or anomalies. For example, in credit card transaction analysis, extremely large or unusual purchases may be flagged as potential frauds. Scientific datasets often contain anomalous sensor errors requiring cleaning before analysis. Anomaly detection finds applications in diverse domains like intrusion detection in cybersecurity, detecting defects and unwanted process dynamics in manufacturing chains, identifying suspicious behaviours and activities, fraud analysis etc. The objective is to discover anomalous items, events or observations which behave considerably differently from the majority of normal instances. Algorithms like density-based outlier estimation, proximity-based techniques and predictive methods can quantify deviations from norm using statistical metrics and distance computations. Care has to be taken to distinguish genuine anomalies from noise or changes in baseline behavioural patterns. Overall, anomaly detection delivers crucial insights by discovering deviant phenomena from massive datasets.

#### *One-Class SVM*

One-class SVM is an unsupervised algorithm used primarily for anomaly detection. Unlike binary classification SVM that separates two classes, one-class SVM models the normal behaviour to detect outliers that deviate from it. It is trained on normal data instances only without requiring target labels or abnormal examples during training stage. The method locates the optimum hyperplane, which serves as the decision boundary dividing the normal data points from the point of origin with the greatest margin, iteratively after mapping the input data into a high dimensional space of features. Data instances falling outside this decision boundary are then classified as anomalies during the testing stage. One-Class SVM is thus well-suited for applications with primarily normal data and scarce or no abnormal instances. The technique extends effectively to high dimensional spaces. One-class SVM also provides flexibility in defining tighter or wider set of normal behaviours as per application needs by tuning the kernel parameters. Low false positive rates can be achieved if normal behaviours demonstrate homogeneity. The ability to build models specific to target domain normally assists effective identification of exceptional or atypical novel instances across applications from intrusion or fraud detection to fault diagnosis.

### *Isolation Forests*

Isolation forests are an efficient unsupervised learning algorithm for anomaly detection that isolates anomalies instead of profiling normal data instances. It operates by recursively partitioning the data space through random splits until instances are isolated or anomalies are isolated faster than normal data. The core principle is that anomalies are few and different, so trees built on random splits will isolate those points faster using fewer partitions owing to their relative isolation in sparse regions. By contrast, normal points needing more partitions dwell around dense neighborhoods. Anomaly scores are calculated as the path lengths to isolate those points - anomalies have short average lengths. Benefits include fast training and testing, detecting global and local anomalies and model interpretability. Applications span fraud analytics, infrastructure monitoring, network intrusion detection etc. Isolation works well for low dimensional datasets with varying data distributions. Choice of coarseness for recursive partitioning and number of trees influence accuracy. Isolation forests exemplify how simple ideas can model inherent data characteristics effectively for useful anomaly interpretation across domains.

### *Novelty Detection*

Novelty detection refers to the identification of new, unobserved patterns in data that have not been seen during training. It requires models to be trained only on normal data instances first. Subsequently, significant deviations from learned baseline behaviours are flagged as novelties. For example, an aerospace system monitoring algorithm can characterize normal sensor data when functioning properly. New sensor readings diverging markedly from established normal trends get classified as novel sensor anomalies requiring investigation. Email spam detectors also utilize novelty detection by modeling legitimate email and alerting on unprecedented emerging spam patterns. Novelty detection has applications in temporal pattern recognition for time-series analysis, text topic detection, image classification etc. Techniques used include establishing boundaries around normal training data using proximity algorithms or neural networks to estimate densities. Classification models can also be semi-supervised trained only on normal instances. Inputs substantially differing from learned decision boundaries are then detected as novelties. Overall, the ability to recognize emerging novel patterns without needing prior abnormal samples broadens the scope of anomaly detection and allows identifying unfolding events of interest. The main types of novelty detection types are absolute novelty and relative novelty.

***Absolute Novelty:*** The notion of absolute novelty refers to completely new patterns detected in data that are fundamentally unprecedented compared to all prior knowledge during training. Unlike anomalies which deviate statistically but share some attributes with normal instances, absolutely novel examples have no prior representatives in the historical data. For instance, emergence of a new genre of songs substantially divergent from all existing training song types. Designing algorithms to recognize and identify patterns demonstrating absolute novelty poses unique research challenges. The exclusive availability of normal instances renders estimating likelihoods of unseen novel instances very difficult. In some cases, one class classifiers like autoencoders reconstructing only normal data can set thresholds on reconstruction errors to detect absolute novelties. But reconstruction is an imperfect proxy lacking semantic representability. A promising paradigm involves growing a vocabulary of normal pattern primitives first. For example, patterns with no predecessors during training.

**TABLE 6.1** Difference between Supervised and Unsupervised Learning

| *Supervised Learning* | *Unsupervised Learning* |
|---|---|
| This learning is used when we know how to classify a given data, or in other words classes or labels are available. | This learning is used when there is no idea about the class or label of a particular data. The model has to find pattern in data. |
| Labelled training data is needed. Model is built based on training data. | Any unknown and labelled data set is given to the model as input and records are grouped. |
| The model performance can be evaluated based on how many misclassifications have been done based on a comparison between predicted and actual values. | Difficult to measure whether the model did something useful or interesting. Homogeneity of records grouped together is the only measure. |
| There are two types of supervised learning problems: (a) Classification and (b) Regression | There are two types of unsupervised learning problems: (a) Clustering and (b) Association |
| Simplest one to understand. | More difficult to understand and implement than supervised learning. |
| Standard Algorithms are:<br>(1) Naïve Bayes<br>(2) k-nearest neighbour (kNN)<br>(3) Decision Tree<br>(4) Linear Regression<br>(5) Logistic Regression<br>(6) Support Vector Machine (SVM) etc. | Standard Algorithms are:<br>(1) k-means<br>(2) PCA (Principal Component Analysis)<br>(3) Self Organizing Map (SOM)<br>(4) Apriori algorithm<br>(5) DBSCAN etc. |
| Prone to overfitting if not properly regularized or validated. | Less prone to overfitting since it doesn't have explicit labels guiding the model. |
| Practical Applications include:<br>(1) Handwriting Recognition<br>(2) Stock market prediction<br>(3) Disease Prediction<br>(4) Fraud Detection, etc. | Practical Applications include:<br>(1) Market basket Analysis<br>(2) Recommender System<br>(3) Customer Segmentation, etc. |

***Relative Novelty:*** Relative novelty refers to the detection of test patterns exhibiting significant statistical drift or divergence from the distribution of training patterns even if not entirely alien. The key principle is quantifying the distance a given data point lies from the cluster of normal observations in a relative sense. For example, emergence of a genre of songs which blends some attributes from existing types but contains new elements like lyrics, instruments or composition styles distorting from established norms. Unlike absolute novelties which focus on binary presence or absence in the train corpus, relative novelties necessitate computing degrees of drift from expected baselines. Techniques often involve estimating multivariate densities not along individual variables but jointly considering correlations of normal points. At testing, comparisons using divergence measures like KL-divergence or Mahalanobis distance against these densities can highlight relative outliers. Binary decision boundaries prove restrictive. Instead, ranking novelty scores based on magnitude of departure from contours of existing patterns works better. Effectively, the algorithms learn a smooth topological representation of the normal class. Patterns exhibiting spikes in relative deviation signals from learned normal manifolds get flagged as relatively novel. Overall, factoring notion of degrees rather than discrete absolute judgments helps discovery of emerging new trends and topics.

## SUMMARY

Supervised learning employs labelled data to create models that can predict the outputs for new inputs. It is suitable for such tasks as classification and regression and is typically implemented with decision trees and neural networks as algorithms. Unsupervised learning, however, makes use of unlabeled data to find hidden patterns and structures. It is suitable for clustering and dimensionality reduction and is normally applied with k-means and PCA as methods. Thus, it can be concluded that a prediction task with data that has known outcomes should apply supervised learning, whereas unexplained data that needs to be divided into many groups with more of such data should use unsupervised learning.

## WORKED OUT EXAMPLES

**EXAMPLE 6.1** A binary classification dataset has 100 samples with 60 positive samples and 40 negative samples. A supervised classification model was trained on this dataset which predicted 55 positives and 35 negatives correctly in the test set. Determine the accuracy, precision, recall and F1-score of this classifier.

***Solution:*** Actual Positives = 60; Actual Negatives = 40; True Positives = 55; True Negatives = 35; False Positives = 35 – 5 = 5; False Negatives = 60 – 55 = 5

Accuracy = (TP + TN)/(Total) = (55 + 35)/100 = 90%

Precision = TP/(TP + FP)

= 55/(55+5) = 0.917

Recall = TP/Actual Positives

= 55/60 = 0.917

F1 score = 2 × (Recall × Precision)/(Recall + Precision)

= 2 × 0.917 × 0.917/(0.917 + 0.917) = 0.917

Therefore, the model has accuracy 90%, precision 91.7%, recall 91.7% and F1-score 91.7% This demonstrates an evaluation of classification predictive performance on key metrics like precision, recall, accuracy and F1 score.

**EXAMPLE 6.2** Consider a dataset with a feature A having 3 possible values a1, a2, a3. The feature entropy is calculated as 0.9. If the dataset is split on feature A and respective entropies are found to be 0.2, 0.5 and 0.1. What is the information gain by splitting on A?

***Solution:*** Feature A Entropy before split = 0.9. Feature A entropies after split: H(a1) = 0.2 H(a2) = 0.5 H(a3) = 0.1

Assuming uniform distribution, split proportions: P(a1) = P(a2) = P(a3) = 1/3

$$\text{Information gain} = \text{Initial entropy} - \text{Expected Entropy} = \text{Initial entropy} - \Sigma P(x) \times \text{Entropy}(x)$$
$$= 0.9 - ((1/3) \times 0.2 + (1/3) \times 0.5 + (1/3) \times 0.1)$$
$$= 0.9 - 0.3$$
$$= 0.6$$

Information gain from 0 to 1 indicates efficacy of selected attribute in increasing population purity post-split. Higher the value, the better suited that feature is in creating class homogeneous branches.

## EXERCISES

1. Develop a linear regression algorithm that estimates home values using the square footage of the property as the predictor variable (in square feet). Use the following data:

   Home sizes (in sq ft): [1000, 1500, 2000, 2500, 3000]

2. Suppose you have a dataset with 100 samples, and you want to build a polynomial regression model to predict the target variable. You split the dataset into a training set (80 samples) and a test set (20 samples). For training set, you train polynomial regression models of degrees 1, 2, 3, and 4.

   Calculate the efficiency on the test set. The details are given below:

   | *Degree* | *Training MSE* | *Test MSE* |
   |---|---|---|
   | 1 | 100 | 120 |
   | 2 | 60 | 80 |
   | 3 | 20 | 60 |
   | 4 | 5 | 100 |

   Analyze the bias-variance tradeoff in this scenario and determine which model degree strikes the best balance.

3. Perform k-means clustering on the following data points to group them into 3 clusters:

   Points: [(1, 2), (1.5, 1.8), (5, 8), (8, 8), (1, 0.6), (9, 11)]

4. Train an SVM regressor to predict the price of a house based on its size (in square feet) and the number of bedrooms. Use the following data:

| *Size (sq ft):* | *Number of bedrooms* | *Price* |
|---|---|---|
| 1000 | 2 | 300000 |
| 1200 | 2 | 350000 |
| 1500 | 3 | 450000 |
| 2000 | 4 | 550000 |
| 2500 | 5 | 700000 |

Also, predict the price of a house with a size of 1800 sq ft and 3 bedrooms and calculate the accuracy of the model.

**5.** Given a dataset with two classes, Class A and Class B, and their respective probabilities, calculate the Gini index for each attribute and determine the best attribute for splitting the data.Use Python to solve it.

| *Attribute* | *Class A* | *Class B* |
|---|---|---|
| X1 | 0.6 | 0.4 |
| X2 | 0.8 | 0.2 |
| X3 | 0.3 | 0.7 |

**6.** A decision tree classifier is trained on a dataset with 1000 samples and 5 features. The tree is constructed using the ID3 algorithm, which uses entropy as the impurity measure. The maximum depth of the tree is set to 4, and the minimum number of samples required to split an internal node is 10. The tree is built using binary splits.

(a) If the dataset is perfectly balanced, meaning that each class has an equal number of samples, what is the entropy of the dataset before any splitting occurs?

(b) Suppose that at a particular internal node, there are 100 samples, and the class distribution is as follows: 60 samples belong to class A, and 40 samples belong to class B. What is the entropy at this node?

(c) If the tree is grown to its maximum depth of 4, and each internal node makes a binary split that divides the samples equally, what is the maximum number of leaf nodes in the decision tree?

**7.** Determine the two linear regression equations (X as a function of Y, and Y as a function of X) using the provided dataset. In your calculations, use the actual means of X and Y as reference points for computing deviations.

| Price (₹) | 20 | 22 | 23 | 22 | 26 | 25 |
|---|---|---|---|---|---|---|
| Amount | 80 | 48 | 63 | 65 | 57 | 53 |

**8.** Develop a linear regression algorithm to forecast residential property values using input variables such as square footage, bedroom count, and neighborhood. Gauge the model's effectiveness by calculating performance indicators including mean absolute error, root mean square error, and R-squared. Examine whether the prerequisites for linear regression are satisfied, and implement suitable methods to correct any departures from these conditions.

9. Develop a naive Bayes classifier to classify news articles into different categories like politics, sports, tech etc. Compare its performance against SVM and logistic regression models. Check the multivariate Gaussian assumption.
10. A Random Forest classifier is trained on a dataset with 1000 samples and 10 features. The forest consists of 100 decision trees, each with a maximum depth of 5. During the training process, the algorithm uses bootstrap sampling with replacement to create subsets of the training data for each tree. The minimum number of samples required to split an internal node is set to 2, and the minimum number of samples required to be at a leaf node is 1. The Gini impurity is used as the splitting criterion.
    (a) What is the total number of nodes (internal nodes + leaf nodes) in a single decision tree of the Random Forest, assuming that each tree is grown to its maximum depth?
    (b) If the dataset is perfectly balanced, meaning that each class has an equal number of samples, what is the expected Gini impurity at the root node of each decision tree before any splitting occurs?
    (c) Suppose that for a single decision tree in the forest, the bootstrap sample used for training contains 800 unique samples. What is the probability that a specific sample from the original dataset is not included in the bootstrap sample for this tree? Assume that the bootstrap sampling is done with replacement.

## BIBLIOGRAPHY

Hastie, T., Tibshirani, R., and Friedman, J. (2009). *The Elements of Statistical Learning,* Springer.

Mitchell, T. M. (1997). *Machine Learning,* McGraw Hill.

Raschka, S., and Mirjalili, V. (2019). *Python Machine Learning*, Packt.

Shwartz, S. S., and Davis, S. B. (2014). *Understanding Machine Learning: From Theory to Algorithm,* Cambridge University Press.

Tang, P. N., Steibach, M., and Kumar, V. (2016). *Introduction to Data Mining,* Pearson.

# Chapter 7

# Deep Learning

## 7.1 INTRODUCTION

Deep learning (DL) is more about statistical machine learning where the primary concern is about how the data is represented. The foundation of deep learning comes from Artificial Neural Network (ANN) which has been discussed previously in chapter 4. The term *'deep'* has been coined because DL comprises of several complex mathematical equations which are in the form of layers, more complex is the equation, more are the number of layers making conventional neural networks (CNN) deeper and hence the concept of deep learning or deep neural networks is used.

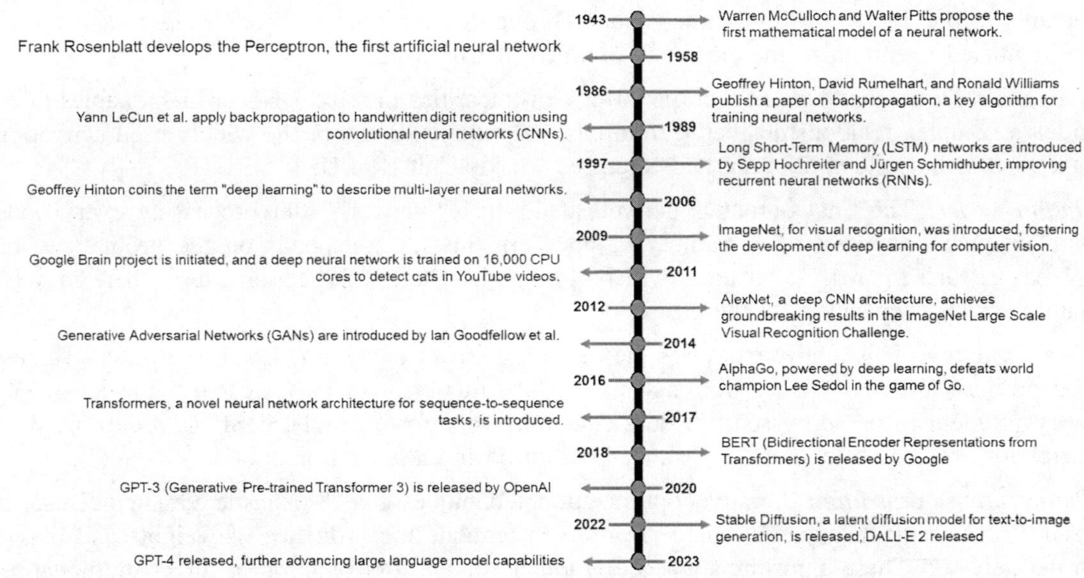


**FIGURE 7.1** Timeline for Deep Learning from 1943 to 2023.

### 7.1.1 Deep Neural Network Architecture

The Deep Neural Network (DNN) architecture is characterized by its layered structure, with each layer comprising a set of nodes or neurons which are interconnected to each other. The edges which connect these nodes transmit the input data from one layer to another. With the help of activation functions, the intricate relationships between inputs and outputs are analysed to produce the final outcome. The structure of a DNN may differ depending on the particular task, data complexity, and intended outcomes. These networks are customized by choosing the number of layers, neurons in each layer, selecting activation functions, and other hyperparameters. A comprehensive outlook at the DNN architecture can be depicted with various components.

***Input Layer:*** This is where the unprocessed information is fed to the system for processing. Each node in this layer represents one of the features of input data. The dimensionality of the input, defines the number of nodes in the layer.

***Hidden Layers:*** This layer is sandwiched between the input and output layer and are accountable for learning the complex pattern in the input data. The network's depth, defined by the quantity of hidden layers, enables the model to acquire tiered representations of the input information, encompassing both fundamental and sophisticated characteristics.

***Nodes or Neurons:*** Nodes, or neurons are the computational units that process information. As a course of action, each neuron in the hidden layers obtains inputs from the neurons in preceding layer, which are then multiplied with some weights, summed up and combined with a bias term, and finally passing the result through an activation function. This function introduces non-linearity, enabling the network to learn complex mappings.

***Weights and Biases:*** Each connection between the neurons contains weights and biases. The weights signify strength of the connections between the neurons whereas biases are supplementary features to provide flexibility to the mode. Throughout the training, both weights and biases are regulated to minimize the error and optimize the network.

***Activation Functions:*** These functions offer non-linearities into the DNN, which enables them to learn complex relationships between inputs and outputs. Some of the widely used activation functions include sigmoid, tanh, and Rectified Linear Unit (ReLU).

***Output Layer:*** The final output is derived at this layer network after processing every node with weights and biases. The number of nodes in this layer depends on the problem to be solved, as such for regression there will be one node whereas for classification there may be multiple nodes depending on the classes.

***Loss Function:*** This metric measures the disparity between forecasted and true output values. The primary objective during training is to reduce this error to its lowest feasible level. For every problem to be addressed, the loss functions vary for example, MSE is widely used in regression whereas categorical cross-entropy is used in classification.

***Optimization Algorithm:*** Iterative optimization techniques like Stochastic Gradient Descent (SGD) or its variants such as Adam are used to regulate the influence of weights and biases in the network. These algorithms use the gradients of the loss function to direct the updating process.

***Backpropagation:*** This learning procedure is employed in DNN. It computes the rate at which the error function changes with respect to the weights and biases, which then uses these calculations to adjust the parameters, disseminating the error in reverse through the network's layers.

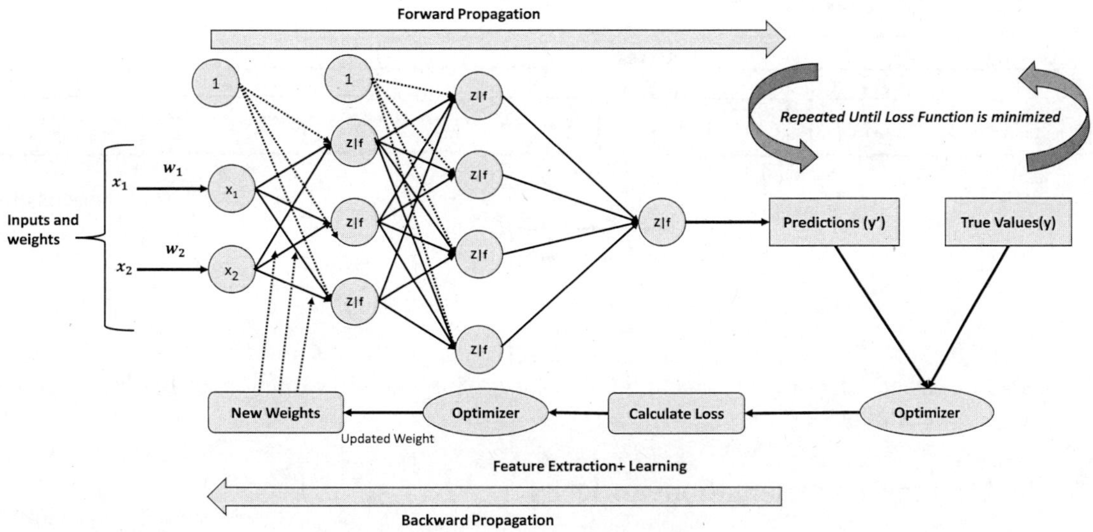


**FIGURE 7.2** Fundamental Deep Learning Architecture in (a) forward propagation and (b) backward propagation.

Based on the learning strategies (supervised or unsupervised), DNN architectures can be broadly classified into two broad categories. The first category comprises of CNNs that deals mainly the image categorization, RNNs which pertains to sequence tagging or temporal data prediction, and Feedforward Neural Networks (FFNNs) related to regression or classification challenges. These frameworks are calibrated using an error metric that quantifies the disparity between predicted results and actual labels. The network's parameters are fine-tuned via backpropagation to reduce this discrepancy.

The second category of DNN are designed to learn from unlabeled data, where no explicit target or output is provided. These architectures discover hidden patterns, structures, or representations in the data without any guidance or supervision. Autoencoders, which learn to compress and reconstruct the input data through an encoder-decoder structure, and Variational Autoencoders (VAEs), which learn a probabilistic latent representation of the data, Generative Adversarial Networks (GANs) that create realistic samples and a discriminator network to distinguish between real and generated samples are some of popular architectures under this category. Self-Organizing Maps (SOMs) and Deep Belief Networks (DBNs) are other such architectures that can learn hierarchical representations of the data.

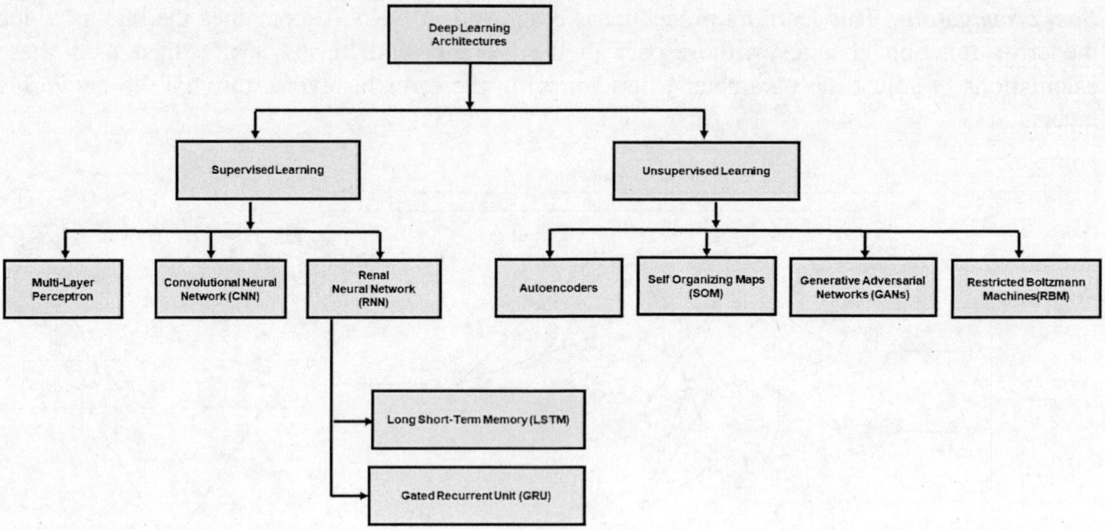


**FIGURE 7.3** Deep Learning Architecture based on (a) Supervised Learning and (b) Unsupervised Learning.

### 7.1.2 Learning Representations in DNN

Learning representations in a DNN refers to the process of capturing and encoding meaningful features or patterns from the input data in a hierarchical manner across the layers of the network. These representations are learned through the optimization process during training, where the model tunes its parameters to reduce the error between actual and predicted outputs. Some of the learning representations which are commonly available and used for DNN are discussed below.

***Hierarchical Feature Extraction:*** This is one of the fundamental aspects of DNN, where hierarchical features are automatically extracted from raw data. In this approach, the lower layers or early layers captures the basic low-level features like edge, corners, simple patterns, colours etc. As these information progresses towards the upper layers, they try to combine these extracted features to understand more complex patterns which are carried toward the top layers for getting more abstract and meaningful features. The semantic encodings are done at the top most level and finally passed to the output layer which is task-specific and delivers the predicted result.

***Mid-Level Representations:*** The mid-level representations are those features which are learned in the middle level layers of the DNN. They are essential for capturing complex and meaningful patterns in the data, often representing higher-level abstractions beyond simple edges and textures. As the learning progresses, the neurons in mid-level layers start responding to the combinations of lower-level features and forming more complex structures. These representations contribute in understanding the spatial relationships and compositional structures within the input data. The mid-level features are able to recognize patterns even if there is a small variation making the network robust and able to generalize. The mid-level features are involved in learning task-independent characteristics which promotes transfer learning like a bridge between the low-level features and high-level representations. This characteristic makes the mid-level representations valuable for tasks such as feature visualization, model interpretation, and understanding the internal representations of the DNN.

***High-Level Abstractions:*** High-Level abstractions summarize the rich, semantically meaningful representations that go beyond basic features. This enables the network to understand and process complex information for specific tasks. These features often capture compositional structures, making the network to distinguish the relationships between various components of the input data. These abstractions are invariant, which means that even in the presence of changes or alterations in the input, the network can still identify patterns and remain robust. Despite the network being a 'black box' i.e. lack of interpretability, efforts are made in the visualization techniques to understand the semantics of high-level features.

***Task-Specific Features:*** These features are from the top most layers of DNN comprising complex patterns and representations which are essential for a specific task. The decision-making components of the DNN heavily rely on the information that is embedded in these task-specific features. Similar to mid-level and high-level features, the task-specific features are also relevant in recognizing the patterns despite variations or transformation. How well these features are understood by the network is very important for overall prediction capability of the network. However, for these features, interpretation of the semantics at human level is still a challenge.

***Invariant Representations:*** There are situations in training DNN where the learning needs to be done in diverse conditions. In such case, the invariant representations help in extracting the meaningful features across the diverse conditions. These representations contribute in making the network more adaptive by ensuring that the learned features are not excessively sensitive to those variations which do not affect the underlying semantics of the data. The invariance representations in DNN are generally guided by the choice of specific layers. Invariant representation is not only limited to spatial but also active to temporal invariance in sequence data. This makes NLP recognize semantic patterns in sentences regardless of the order of words. Techniques like data augmentation, which introduces differences in the training data, assist in training the network to learn invariant features.

***Transfer Learning:*** The learned representations from one task can be transferred to another related task to use the knowledge that is encoded in them. This transfer of knowledge from the pre-trained models occurs through feature extraction such that low-level layers are used as fixed feature extractors, and high-level layers are fine-tuned for the target task. Transfer learning facilitates domain adaptation, enabling the model to adjust to different data distributions. It often involves adding task-specific layers to the pre-trained model, responsible for making predictions related to the target task. When the labelled data is very less, this approach is highly beneficial to overcome overfitting.

## 7.2 TRAINING DEEP NEURAL NETWORKS

Training DNN involves several important steps to optimize the model for a specific task. The process begins with data preparation, where input data is pre-processed and augmented followed by designing the model architecture by specifying the layers, activation functions, and connections. Using a suitable loss function, the difference between predicted and true values is measured, which also helps the optimizer to adjust model parameters and reduce this loss. The training process iterates through the dataset, performing forward and backward passes, updating the parameters, and assessing performance on validation data. One of the crucial steps in training is hyperparameter tuning, which involves adjustments to learning rate and regularization, for optimizing model performance. The learning procedure persists for a predetermined number of cycles, with intermittent assessment checks, until an ideal outcome is attained.

### 7.2.1 Activation Functions and Loss Functions

Activation functions are a crucial component that brings forward non-linearity. Some of the frequently used activation functions include ReLU, which returns the input value if it is positive and zero otherwise, and its variants such as Leaky ReLU and ELU (Exponential Linear Unit). Sigmoid and hyperbolic tangent (tanh) functions are also used, particularly in the output layers of binary classification tasks and in recurrent neural networks, respectively. Other activation functions have been proposed to address specific challenges in DL such as, Swish, defined as x · sigmoid(x), has shown improved performance in some DL tasks compared to ReLU. For problems involving classification into multiple categories, the Softmax function is frequently employed at the neural network's final layer. Its role is to convert the unprocessed outputs into a set of probabilities. These probabilities indicate how likely it is that the input belongs to each of the possible classes, aiding in determining the most probable classification. Activation functions like Scaled Exponential Linear Unit (SELU) and Gaussian Error Linear Unit (GELU) have been designed to help with normalization and stabilization of deep networks during training. The selection of an activation function is determined by the particular needs of the DL objective and the structure of the NN. The selection of error metrics in DNN establishes the model's goal, which is to be reduced during the learning phase. Loss functions quantify the variance between the actual and predicted outputs. The various activation functions and loss functions used in designing simple to complex NNs has been discussed in section 4.7 and 4.8 of Chapter 4.

**TABLE 7.1** Activation Functions used in Deep learning

| *Activation Function* | *Mathematical Expression* | *Brief Description* |
|---|---|---|
| GELU (Gaussian Error Linear Unit) | $GELU(x) = x * \varphi(x)$ Where, $\varphi(x) = \frac{1}{2}\left(1 + \text{erf}\left(\frac{x}{\sqrt{2}}\right)\right),$ | A smooth, non-linear function that uses the Gaussian cumulative distribution function. It introduces stochasticity while providing a deterministic output. |
| Smish | $f(x) = x * \tanh(ln(1 + sigmoid(x)))$ | A smooth variation of the Swish function (which is itself a variation on the Sigmoid). |
| Mish | $mish(x) = x * \tanh(softplus(x))$ where, $softplus(x) = \log(\exp(x) + 1)$ | A smooth, non-monotonic activation function that can sometimes outperform ReLU. |

| *Activation Function* | *Mathematical Expression* | *Brief Description* |
|---|---|---|
| Maxout | $f(x)=\max(w_1^T x+b_1+w_2^T x+b_2)$ where b is the bias, w is the weight | Takes the maximum output from a set of linear functions, creating piecewise linear segments. |
| Hard Hyperbolic Function | $f(x)=\begin{cases}-1 & \text{for } x<-1\\ x & \text{for } -1\le x\le 1\\ 1 & \text{for } x>1\end{cases}$ | A faster and computationally cheaper approximation of the hyperbolic tangent function. |
| RSigELU | $f(x)=\begin{cases}x\left(\frac{1}{1+e^{-x}}\right)\alpha+x, & \text{if } 1<x<\infty\\ x & \text{if } 0\le x\le 1\\ \alpha(e^x-1), & \text{if } -\infty<x<0\end{cases}$ | A regularized SigELU function improving gradient flow and avoiding vanishing gradients. |
| Soft Clipping | $f(x)=\frac{1}{a}\log\left(\frac{1+e^{ax}}{1+e^{a(x-1)}}\right)$ for $a>0$. | Smoothly limits the output range of a neuron, ensuring outputs and gradients stay within bounds. |
| Softsign | $\frac{x}{1+\lvert x\rvert}$ | A smooth approximation of the sign function, allowing for differentiation, unlike the standard sign function. |
| Softmax | $f(z_i)=\frac{\exp(z_i)}{\sum_j expz_j}$ | Mainly used in the output layer of neural networks for classification task. |
| ELiSH | $f(x)=\begin{cases}\frac{x}{1+e^{-x}}, & \text{if } x\ge 0\\ \frac{e^x-1}{1+e^{-x}}, & \text{if } x<0\end{cases}$ | Combines the benefits of ELU and Swish, with exponential behavior for negative inputs and a smooth transition near 0. |
| CRELU (Concatenated Rectified Linear Units) | *CReLU(x) = [ReLU(x), ReLU(–x)]* | Concatenates the ReLU activation with its negative counterpart, creating two output channels for each input channel. |
| RMAF (ReLU Memristor-like Activation Function | $RMAF(x)=\left[j\left(\frac{1}{\left(0.25\left(1+e^{-x}\right)+0.75\right)^p}\right)\right].\alpha x$ | Inspired by how memristors work. The goal of RMAF is to make neural networks more nonlinear while also having some of the same properties as memristors. |

## 7.2.2 Usage of Activation Functions in Hidden Layer

Activation functions are extremely important components in DL and are used in the hidden layers of neural networks for several important reasons. Some of the primary justifications for applying activation functions to the hidden layer neuron output can be as follows:

***Introducing Non-Linearity:*** The primary reason for using activation functions in hidden layers is to introduce non-linearity into the NN. A NN's capacity to learn and represent intricate, non-linear relationships in the data would be severely limited in the absence of activation functions, which would reduce it to a linear combination of its inputs. Activation functions allow the network to model non-linear decision boundaries and learn more intricate patterns.

***Enabling Complex Representations:*** The input data can be changed by hidden layers into a high-dimensional space where it is easier to separate the data by using non-linear activation functions. Each hidden layer can learn increasingly abstract and sophisticated representations of the input data, allowing the network to capture hierarchical features and intricate patterns. This capability is vital in processes like image analysis, where the system must acquire basic visual elements such as contours and material qualities in its initial phases, before progressing to more sophisticated concepts like individual entities and settings in its deeper layers.

***Preventing Exploding or Vanishing Gradients:*** Activation functions help in overcoming the problem of exploding or vanishing gradients during the training of deep neural networks. Some activation functions, such as the ReLU, have properties that allow gradients to flow more easily through the network, preventing the gradients from becoming too small (vanishing) or too large (exploding) during backpropagation. This facilitates effective learning and convergence of the network.

***Sparsity and Feature Selection:*** Sparsity refers to the situation where only a subset of neurons in a layer is activated for a given input. This can be beneficial as it allows the network to selectively focus on relevant features and ignore irrelevant ones, resulting in improved performance for representation learning and improved generalization.

***Controlling the Output Range:*** Activation functions can control the range of the output values of neurons in the hidden layers. For example, the sigmoid activation function squashes between the range 0 and 1, while the hyperbolic tangent (tanh) function maps the output between -1 and 1. Controlling the output range can be useful for regulating the training process and ensures that the activations do not become too large or too small. These reasons highlight the importance of activation functions in the hidden layers of NNs.

### 7.2.3 Usage of Activation Functions in Output Layer

The usage of activation functions in the output layer of a NN is also crucial, but the reasons may differ from those in the hidden layers. Here are some of the main reasons for using activation functions in the output layer.

***Mapping to Desired Output Range:*** These functions help in mapping the output of the NN to the desired range or format that suits the specific task. For example, in binary classification problems, the output layer uses sigmoid activation function to map the output probability in the range between 0 and 1, which represents the possibility that the input belongs to a specific class.

***Producing Probability Distributions:*** The output layer of multi-class classification tasks frequently employs the softmax activation function. The softmax function takes the outputs from the neurons and converts them into a probability distribution over the classes. This in turn generates class probabilities in the network, which depicts the likelihood of the input belonging to a specific class.

***Enabling Thresholding and Decision Making:*** Activation functions in the output layer can facilitate thresholding and decision making based on the output values. For instance, in binary classification, a threshold can be applied to the sigmoid output to make a binary decision (e.g., class 0 if the output probability < 0.5, and class 1 if the output probability > 0.5). Similarly, in multi-class classification, the class with the highest probability (as determined by the softmax output) is typically chosen as the predicted class.

***Ensuring Compatibility with Loss Functions:*** The choice of activation function in the output layer should be compatible with the loss function. For various kinds of operations, there are a variety of loss functions that are appropriate. As an illustration, for classification involving multiple categories, the categorical cross-entropy loss is frequently employed alongside softmax activation.

***Interpretation and Usability:*** Activation functions in the output layer can provide interpretable and usable outputs for downstream tasks or decision-making processes. For instance, the sigmoid function produces a probability value that can be easily interpreted as the likelihood of a particular event or class. The softmax function provides a probability distribution over classes, which can be useful for tasks like uncertainty estimation or confidence-based decision making.

The activation functions in the output layer provides the concluding transformation, converting the network's learned internal representations into the required output format. This process ensures that the network's predictions are both comprehensible and applicable to the particular task being addressed.

### 7.2.4 Optimization Techniques

Optimization techniques are used to ensure that DNNs converge to optimal sets of parameters by minimizing the loss function, aligning the model's predictions close to the true labels in the training data. Without effective optimization, the training process could deteriorate or result in suboptimal solutions, hindering the overall network's performance. Optimization techniques employ approaches like weight regularization, dropout, and early stopping to prevent the model from retaining noise or insignificant patterns in the training dataset, thereby fostering its ability to generalize to unseen examples.

***Stochastic Gradient Descent (SGD):*** SGD operates on mini-batches of data rather than the entire dataset. This permits for more frequent parameter updates and can lead to faster convergence during training. In executing SGD, the training dataset is divided into mini-batches ($m$) which can be adjusted based on convergence properties. During each cycle or epoch, SGD arbitrarily selects a small subset of data and calculates the variation rate of the error function relative to the model's parameters, based on the chosen examples, using the backpropagation method. After computing these gradients, SGD modifies the model's parameters in a direction that reduces the error function. The update is typically done by,

$$\theta_{t+1} = \theta_t - \alpha.\nabla L(\theta_t) \tag{7.1}$$

Here, $\theta_t$ = parameters of the model at iteration $t$, $\alpha$ = learning rate, and $\nabla L(\theta_t)$ = rate of change of the loss function relative to the model's parameters during the $t^{th}$ iteration of the optimization process.

***RMSprop (Root Mean Square Propagation):*** RMSprop was developed to overcome certain shortcomings of the conventional SGD method by adjusting the learning rate for individual parameters according to the scale of past gradients. This technique initializes a parameter $v$, which is a vector of the same length as the model parameters ($\theta$) and is used to maintain a moving average of the squared gradients. For every iteration t, RMSprop determines the rate of change of the error function in relation to the parameters ($\theta$) using backpropagation and then $v$ by,

$$v_t = \beta.v_{t-1} + (1-\beta).(\nabla L(\theta_t))^2 \tag{7.2}$$

Where, $\nabla L(\theta_t)$ = rate of change of the error function relative to the parameters at iteration $t$, $\beta$ = exponential decay rate and $v_{t-1}$ = moving average from the previous iteration. Finally, the parameters ($\theta$) is updated by,

$$\theta_{t+1} = \theta_t - \frac{\alpha}{\sqrt{\widehat{v_t}} + \varepsilon} \cdot \nabla L(\theta_t) \tag{7.3}$$

Where, $\alpha$ = learning rate, $\varepsilon$ = a small constant (typically on the order of $10^{-8}$) added to the denominator for numerical stability.

***Adam (Adaptive moment estimation):*** The Adam optimizer is a combination of the concepts of momentum and adaptive learning rates to achieve efficient and effective optimization. While executing, Adam initializes two moving average parameters $m$ and $v$ to zero vectors of the same length as the model parameters ($\theta$). These parameters estimate the first and second moments of the gradients. At every iteration (t), Adam computes the gradient using backpropagation and then updates the parameters $m$ and $v$ as:

$$\begin{aligned} m_t &= \beta_1 \cdot m_{t-1} + (1-\beta_1) \cdot \nabla L(\theta_t) \\ v_t &= \beta_2 \cdot v_{t-1} + (1-\beta_2).(\nabla L(\theta_t))^2 \end{aligned} \tag{7.4}$$

Where $\beta_1$ and $\beta_2$ = exponential decay rates for the moving averages $m$ and $v$. Finally, Adam updates the parameters ($\theta$) using,

$$\theta_{t+1} = \theta_t - \frac{\alpha}{\sqrt{\widehat{v_t}} + \varepsilon} \cdot \widehat{m_t} \tag{7.5}$$

Where, $\alpha$ = learning rate, $\widehat{m_t}$ and $\widehat{v_t}$ = bias-corrected estimates of first and second moments of gradients, respectively and $\varepsilon$ = a small constant (typically on the order of $10^{-8}$) added to the denominator for numerical stability.

***Adagrad (Adaptive gradient algorithm):*** Adagrad was designed to adaptively adjust the rate of learning. While executing, it initializes a parameter called $G$ as a vector of the same length as the model parameters ($\theta$). The loss function gradient at every iteration is mathematically given as:

$$G_t = G_{t-1} + (\nabla L(\theta_t))^2 \tag{7.6}$$

Where, $\nabla L(\theta_t)$ represents the rate of change of the error function in relation to the parameters at iteration $t$, $G_{t-1}$ is the sum of squared gradients from previous iteration $t-1$. Finally, Adagrad updates the parameters ($\theta$) using,

$$\theta_{t+1} = \theta_t - \frac{\alpha}{\sqrt{G_t} + \varepsilon} \cdot \nabla L(\theta_t) \tag{7.7}$$

Where, $\alpha$ = learning rate, $\varepsilon$ = a small constant (typically on the order of $10^{-8}$). To maintain numerical stability, a small constant value is included in the denominator.

***Adadelta:*** Adadelta is an improved version of Adagrad, specifically in regards to its decreasing learning rate over time. Adadelta modifies the learning rate by considering both past gradients and a rolling average of parameter adjustments. It is executed through initialization of two state variables of the same shape as the model parameters ($\theta$) to maintain exponential rolling averages of the squared gradients and squared parameter updates. Like other optimization techniques, Adadelta updates the parameters at each iteration $t$ using backpropagation as,

$$E[g^2]_t = \rho \cdot E[g^2]_{t-1} + (1-\rho)\cdot(\nabla L(\theta_t))^2 \tag{7.8}$$

Where, $\rho$ = decay rate hyperparameter which controls the weight of the earlier gradients. After this, the optimizer computes the parameter update and state variable as follows,

$$\Delta\theta_t = -\frac{\sqrt{E\left[\Delta\theta^2_{t+\varepsilon}\right]+\varepsilon}}{\sqrt{E\left[g_t^2\right]}+\varepsilon}\cdot\nabla L(\theta_t) \tag{7.9}$$

$$E[\Delta\theta^2]_t = \rho \cdot E[\Delta\theta^2]_{t-1} + (1-\rho)\cdot(\Delta\theta_t)^2 \tag{7.10}$$

Where, $E[\Delta(\theta^2)]_{t-1}$ = the exponential moving average of the squared parameter updates from the earlier iteration and $\varepsilon$ is a small constant (of order $10^{-8}$) added to the denominator for numerical stability. Finally, with all these new parameters, Adadelta updates $\Delta\theta_t$ by,

$$\Delta\theta_{t+1} = \theta_t + \Delta\theta_t \tag{7.11}$$

This optimizer is widely used for handling noisy gradients and variable learning rates effectively. As Adadelta does not require setting a global learning rate, it is more robust and easier to use in practice.

***AdaMax:*** This is a variant of the Adam optimizer designed to improve the stability factor. Unlike Adam which uses both mean and uncentered variance of the gradients, AdaMax only considers the mean and uses the maximum of the uncentered variance. During the execution, two variables $m$ (exponentially decaying average of the gradients) and $u$ (exponentially decaying average of the uncentered gradients) of the same length as the model parameters ($\theta$) are initialized. Thereafter in every iteration AdaMax first updates $m$ using,

$$m_t = \beta_1 \cdot m_{t-1} + (1-\beta_1).\nabla L(\theta_t) \tag{7.12}$$

Where, $\beta_1$ = exponential decay rate to controls the weight of the past gradients. Then, it updates the $u$ by,

$$u_t = \max(\beta_2 \cdot u_{t-1}, |\nabla L(\theta_t)| \tag{7.13}$$

Where, $\beta_2$ = a hyperparameter to control the weight of the past squared gradients and $|\nabla L(\theta_t)|$ = the element-wise absolute value of the gradient. Finally, the parameters ($\theta$) get updated by,

$$\theta_{t+1} = \theta_t - \frac{\alpha}{1-\beta_1^t}\cdot\frac{m}{u_t+\varepsilon} \tag{7.14}$$

Where, $\alpha$ = learning rate, $\beta_1$ = exponential decay rate for the first moment estimate and $\varepsilon$ = a constant ($10^{-8}$) incorporated with the denominator for numerical stability. Besides these optimizers, there are many others like Resilient Backpropagation (Rprop), Limited-memory

Broyden-Fletcher-Goldfarb-Shanno (L-BFGS), Lookahead Optimizer, Stochastic Weight Averaging (SWA), YellowFin, Proximal Gradient Descent, Fused Proximal Newton Method, Kronecker-factored Approximate Curvature (K-FAC) which can be used in DNN models. However, choosing the right optimizer depends on the characteristics of the problem, the dataset, and empirical performance on the task at hand.

## 7.3 TYPES OF DEEP NEURAL NETWORKS

DNN are in available in different architectures which stem from a combination of structural and design principles that cater to distinct data types and tasks. Each architecture exhibits unique traits, such as network topology, layer types, and connectivity patterns. The subtle variations in network structure, together with tailored approaches for different tasks, account for the wide-ranging applicability and high performance of DNNs.

### 7.3.1 CNN and RNN

Convolutional Neural Networks (CNN), is specifically crafted to analyze and interpret data that possesses a grid-like arrangement or structure such as images. These networks have proven to be highly effective in tasks like image recognition, classification, for their ability to understand spatial hierarchies of features without manual interventions. The fundamental components of CNNs are the convolutional layers, which utilize a sequence of trainable filters or kernels to process the input information. These filters capture various features present in the input, such as edges, textures, or patterns, by performing convolutions across the input image. The output of these convolution layer forms features maps, which are then passed through activation functions and pooling layers to extract relevant information and reduce dimensionality.

Recurrent Neural Networks (RNN) can memorize the internal state at each instant and use such a state to predict the next output. Unlike FFNN, RNNs which contain loops among their structure, possess the ability to manifest temporal dynamics and to capture dependencies over a specific time period. For instance, sequential learning is crucial when identifying consecutive words in a sentence or forward movement of time series. RNNs excel in these types of tasks by virtue of their memory system which enable them to recall previous inputs (hidden/memory states). This hidden state functions as a short-term memory mechanism during the course of the computation as it enables the network to persist with the information about the previous inputs and the consequent outputs are calculated. Contrary to FFN where each layer is separated both in parameters and functions, RNN use the same set of parameters for each time step. Through this parameter sharing, model gets to be more straightforward to understand, thus using the resources more efficiently, particularly for sequential data tasks. Both these deep neural networks have been explained in detail in subsequent chapter.

### 7.3.2 Generative Adversarial Networks

Generative Adversarial Networks (GAN), specifically consists of two types of NN, the generator and the discriminator that are trained competitively through a minimax game paradigm. The generator's network learns how to synthesize samples that are indistinguishable from real data when it takes a certain distribution as input while the discriminator's network destroys any notion that the samples came from the fake class. The synthesizing mechanism employs the adversarial training which aims to produce data samples that cannot be distinguished from real data.

### *GAN Architecture*

GAN is comprised of mainly two important types of neural networks – generator and discriminator.

***Generator:*** The generator network is responsible to generate synthetic data samples from random noise or a latent vector . It typically consists of multiple layers of fully connected layers and activation functions to produce the desired output.

***Discriminator:*** The discriminator network takes two types of data samples – genuine samples training set and synthetic samples from the generator to classify these samples as real or fake. Similar to the generator, the discriminator is composed of multiple layers of neural units with activation functions, followed by a binary classifier (e.g., sigmoid activation).

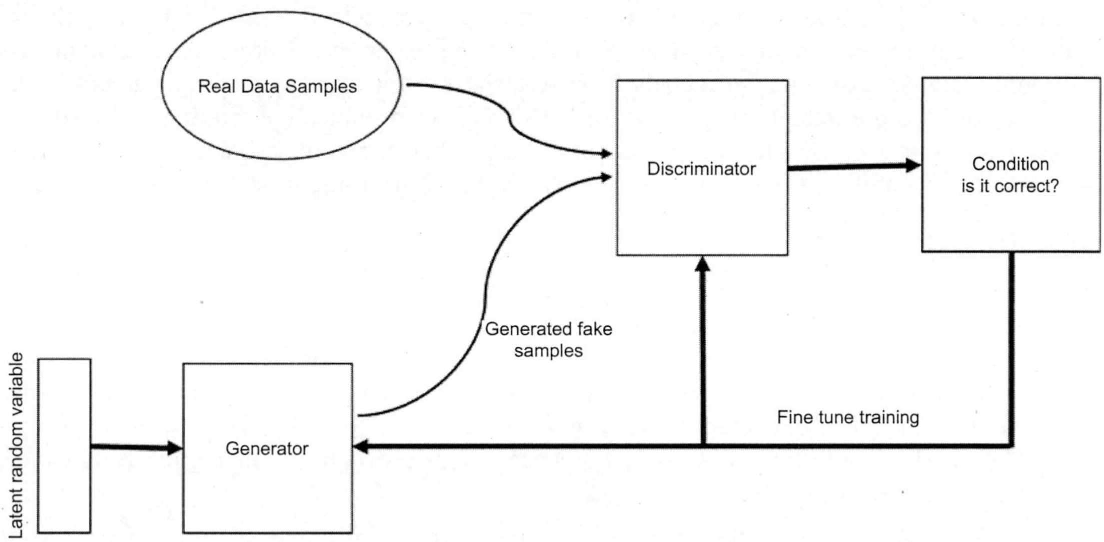


**FIGURE 7.4** The general architecture of GAN.

### *Training in GANs*

The training of GAN typically involves a minimax game between the generator and discriminator. The generator strives to craft artificial samples that can deceive the discriminator, aiming to mitigate the likelihood of its creations being spotted as fake. Meanwhile, the discriminator's objective is to sharpen its discernment, working to boost its proficiency in correctly flagging the generator's output as artificial while accurately recognizing genuine samples. As a result, the training process can be formulated independently for the generator and discriminator, each optimizing their respective objectives within the overall minimax framework.

***Generator Training:*** The generator generates fake samples using random noise or latent vectors as input. These samples are fed into the discriminator, and the resulting classification scores are used to update the generator's parameters.

The loss function for the generator is given by,

$$\mathcal{L}_{GAN}(G,D) = \mathbb{E}_{x\sim p_{\text{data}}(x)}[\log D(x)] + \mathbb{E}_{z\sim p_{\text{wols}}(z)}[\log(1 - D(G(z)))] \tag{7.15}$$

***Discriminator Training:*** The discriminator is trained on a combination of actual data from training set and synthetic samples from the generator from where it learns to distinguish between real and synthetic samples by maximizing the log-probability of correct classification. The loss function is given by,

$$\mathcal{L}_{\mathbb{D}}(D) = -\mathbb{E}_{\text{x}\sim p_{\text{data}}(\text{x})}[\log D(\text{x})] - \mathbb{E}_{\text{z}\sim p_{\text{noise}}(\text{z})}[\log(1 - D(G(\text{z})))] \tag{7.16}$$

The iterative adversarial training process persists until equilibrium is obtained. At this point, the generator creates samples that are highly realistic, and the discriminator is unable to consistently differentiate between genuine and generated samples.

### 7.3.3 Transfer Learning

Transfer learning bypasses the problem of training DL models for small sample problems with a limited number of labelled data, by utilizing the experience learnt from a similar task or domain. Rather than training models from scratch, transfer learning envisages how to fine-tune an available pre-trained model on a new task and so expedites the training and results in a better performance. This framework is appropriate when the new assignment has a smaller data set or it is similar to the assignment on which the pre-learning model was initially learnt.

#### *The Architecture*

In transfer learning, pre-trained models are deployed as feature extractors and the learned representations are reused in ensuring that the model can perform a new task. Generally, the pre-trained model may be a CNN or an RNN network which is primary model used. Lastly, the base model's last layers that estimate task-specific predictions are replaced or fine-tuned to convert the model to be suitable for the new task.

The transfer learning training procedure encompasses two phases: extracting features and adjusting parameters (fine tuning).

***Feature Extraction:*** During this phase, the initial model's parameters remain fixed, while exclusively the terminal layers (such as dense layers) are substituted or re-trained using the novel dataset. The pre-trained model acts as a feature extractor, and the extracted features are used to train a new classifier for the target task.

***Fine-tuning:*** Fine-tuning involves tuning the pre-trained model on the new dataset, often with a smaller learning rate which prevents catastrophic forgetting of previously learned features. This method enables the network to modify its parameters for the new objective while preserving crucial information acquired from the original model.

#### *Why transfer learning*

Transfer learning offers a wide range advantage over other DNN models.

***Reduced Training Time:*** Transfer learning, leveraging pre-trained models, substantially decreases the training duration and computational demands, since the network has previously acquired valuable feature representations from extensive datasets.

***Improved Performance:*** Employing transfer learning frequently results in enhanced performance on the intended task, particularly when the initial model was trained using a comprehensive and varied dataset. This approach enables the model to more effectively extrapolate to unseen data and rapidly acquire pertinent features.

***Robustness to Overfitting:*** Models trained on extensive datasets prior to transfer exhibit improved generalization capabilities when applied to novel information, mitigating the risk of overfitting. This advantage is particularly beneficial in situations where labelled data is scarce.

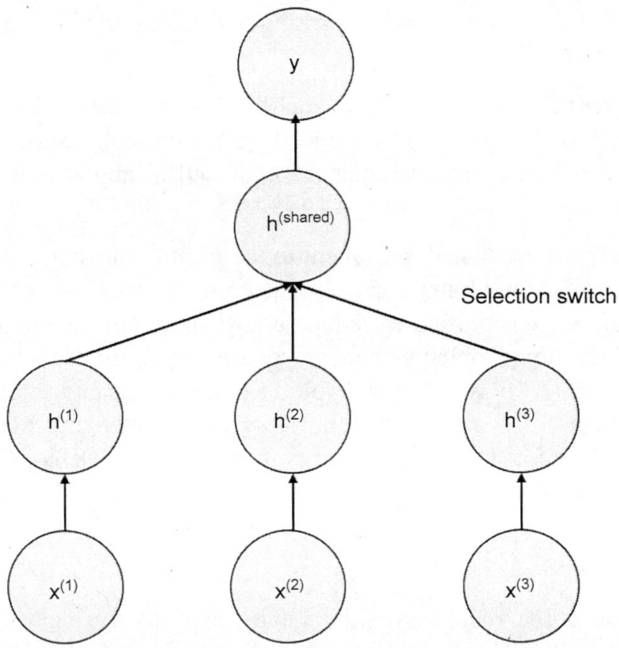


**FIGURE 7.5** Example architecture for multi-task or transfer learning when the output variable has the same semantics for all tasks while the input variable has a different meaning (and possibly even a different dimension) for each task (or, for example, each user), called and for three tasks. The lower levels (up to the selection switch) are task-specific, while the upper levels are shared. The lower levels learn to translate their task-specific input into a generic set of features.

### 7.3.4 Deep Belief Networks

Deep Belief Networks (DBN) are composed of multiple layers of stochastic units, including visible and hidden layers, arranged in a hierarchical fashion. They are generative models that can learn to extract meaningful features from unlabelled data and generate new samples that resemble the training data distribution. DBN merge the advantages of unsupervised learning techniques with the capability to represent sophisticated, multi-dimensional data patterns.

### *DBN Architecture*

The architecture of a DBN typically consists of input layer or visible units and the hidden layer:

***Input Layer (Visible Units):*** The input layer represents the observed variables or features of the data. Each visible unit corresponds to a feature in the input data.

***Hidden Layers:*** DBNs can have one or more hidden layers, each containing stochastic hidden units. These internal layers encode structured representations of the input, with deeper levels capturing progressively more abstract attributes.

### *Training in DBN*

The training process of DBN involves two major stages – greedy layer-wise pretraining and fine-tuning with back propagation.

***Greedy Layer-wise Pretraining:*** At this stage, each layer of the DBN is trained as a Restricted Boltzmann Machine (RBM) using unsupervised learning techniques such as contrastive divergence. This stage initializes the parameters of the DBN and learns a good initialization of the network weights.

***Fine-Tuning with Backpropagation:*** Subsequent to the pretraining stage, the entire Deep Belief Network undergoes optimization through supervised learning approaches, such as backpropagation. The network's parameters are modified to reduce a cost function, commonly employing cross-entropy loss for categorization problems or mean squared error for continuous prediction tasks.

The energy function ($E$) plays a crucial role in the learning and inference processes. The energy function is typically associated with the Restricted Boltzmann Machines (RBMs) that form the building blocks of a DBN. The energy function of a DBN with visible units and hidden units is mathematically defined as,

$$E(v,h) = -\sum_{i} a_i v_i - \sum_{j} b_j h_j - \sum_{i,j} v_i w_{ij} h_j \tag{7.17}$$

Where, $a_i$ and $b_j$ = biases of the visible and hidden units respectively, and $w_{ij}$ = weight connecting visible unit $i$ to hidden unit $j$. The joint probability distribution of the visible and hidden units follows the Boltzmann distribution,

$$P(v,h) = \frac{1}{Z} e^{-E(v,h)} \tag{7.18}$$

Where, $Z$ = normalization constant (partition function) ensuring that the distribution sums to one over all possible configurations of $v$ and $h$.

## 7.3.5 Long Short-Term Memory

The Long Short-Term Memory (LSTM) is a version of RNN which has been designed to get over the vanishing gradient problem in RNNs and capture long-term dependencies in sequential data effectively. LSTM networks are composed of memory cells and various gates that control the information flow such as the forget gate, input gate, output gate, and cell state. The architecture of LSTM enables it to selectively remember or forget information over varying time scales, making it well-suited for processing sequential data.

### *LSTM Architecture*

The fundamental structure of an LSTM unit comprises multiple essential elements.

***Cell State ($C_t$):*** This represents the internal memory of the cell and allows it to retain information over long sequences.

***Hidden State ($h_t$):*** Extracts pertinent data from the cell state to generate the output at each sequential point.

***Gates:*** LSTM networks incorporate four gating mechanisms –forget gate, input gate, output gate, and candidate cell gate.

***Forget Gate ($f_t$):*** This gating mechanism assesses which elements of the prior cell state ($C_{t-1}$) should be removed and which should be maintained. It takes input from the preceding hidden state ($h_{t-1}$) and the current input ($x_t$).

$$f_t = \sigma(W_f \cdot [h_{t-1}, x_t] + b_f) \tag{7.19}$$

***Input Gate ($i_t$):*** The flow of new information into the cell state is controlled by this gate. It decides which parts of the candidate values $\tilde{C}_t$ should be added to the cell state.

$$i_t = \sigma(W_i \cdot [h_{t-1}, x_t] + b_i) \tag{7.20}$$

***Output Gate ($o_t$):*** This gate regulates the output of cell based on current input and the updated cell state.

$$o_t = \sigma(W_o \cdot [h_{t-1}, x_t] + b_o) \tag{7.21}$$

$$h_t = o_t \cdot \tanh(C_t) \tag{7.22}$$

***Candidate Cell State ($\tilde{C}_t$):*** This is the new information which could be added to the cell state and is computed based on the current input ($x_t$) and previous hidden state ($h_{t-1}$).

$$\tilde{C}_t = \tanh\,(W_c \cdot [h_{t-1}, x_t] + b_c) \tag{7.23}$$

$$C_t = f_t \cdot C_{t-1} + i_t \cdot \tilde{C}_t \tag{7.24}$$

The above-mentioned gates and their associated operations regulate information transit within the LSTM unit, allowing it to capture and preserve extended temporal relationships in sequential information while circumventing the diminishing gradient issue typically faced by conventional RNNs.

## 7.3.6 Autoencoders

Autoencoders are typical NN architectures used for unsupervised learning of efficient data representations. Autoencoders function by condensing the input information into a reduced-dimension latent space depiction, then rebuilding the initial input from this compressed representation. Autoencoders have applications in dimensionality reduction, feature learning, and generative modelling.

### *The Architecture*

An autoencoder's structure generally comprises two primary elements—encoder and decoder.

***Encoder:*** The input data is processed by the encoder and transformed into a compact latent space representation. It consists of multiple layers of neurons, usually decreasing in size towards the bottleneck layer, which represents the compressed representation of the input data.

***Decoder:*** The decoder receives the condensed representation from the encoder and reconstructs it into the original input domain. Similar to encoder, it consists of multiple layers of neurons, usually increasing in size from the bottleneck layer back to the original input size.

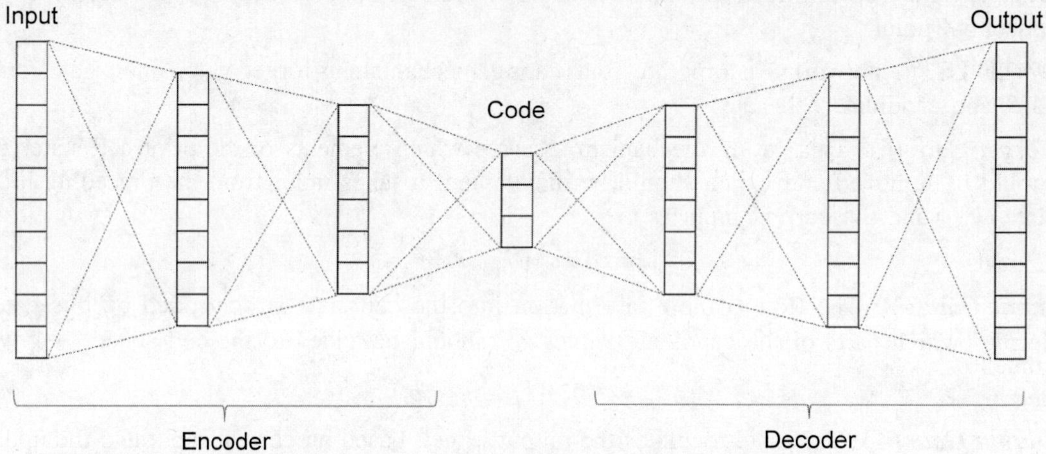


**FIGURE 7.6** General architecture of an autoencoder.

### *Computations in Autoencoders*

The computations in an autoencoder involves the activity of both encoder and decoder. The output of the encoder $h$ given the input $x$ is computed as,

$$h = f_{enc}(x) \tag{7.25}$$

Similarly, the output of the decoder $\hat{x}$ given the compressed representation $h$ is computed as,

$$\hat{x} = f_{dec}(h) \tag{7.26}$$

Where, $f_{enc}$ and $f_{dec}$ represent the encoder and decoder functions, respectively, $x$ represents the input data, $h$ represents the compressed representation (latent space) and $\hat{x}$ represents the reconstructed output.

## 7.3.7 Attention Mechanism

In DL, the attention mechanism allows models to selectively emphasize crucial aspects of input data by allocating different levels of significance to various components. This approach mirrors the human ability to concentrate on specific details while disregarding others. By establishing flexible, context-sensitive links between input and output elements, attention enables models to better manage intricate data relationships. As a result, performance is enhanced in applications such as language translation and image description generation, where the model's ability to identify and focus on key information is critical.

### *The Architecture*

The architecture of an attention mechanism typically involves three main components—the query, attention scores and context vector.

***Query, Key, and Value:*** The attention mechanism operates on three inputs: the query ($Q$), key ($K$), and value ($V$). These inputs are often derived from the hidden states of an encoder in sequence-to-sequence models. The query represents the current decoder hidden state, while the key and value represent the encoder hidden states.

***Attention Scores:*** The attention system determines important values that reflect the pertinence of individual encoder hidden states relative to the present decoder hidden state. These attention scores are typically calculated using a similarity function, such as dot product, scaled dot product, or multi-layer perceptron (MLP). The attention scores are calculated using a similarity function, such as dot product or scaled dot product, between the query ($Q$) and key ($K$) vectors.

$$Attention\,(Q,K) = softmax\left(\frac{QK^T}{\sqrt{d_k}}\right) \tag{7.27}$$

***Context Vector:*** The context vector is derived from the weighted average of encoder hidden states and weights determined by the attention scores. It represents the attended information from input sequence that is relevant for making predictions at the current time step. The context vector is computed as a weighted sum of the value ($V$) vectors, where the weights are determined by the attention scores.

$$\text{Context}(V, \text{Attention}) = \sum_i \text{Attention}_i \cdot V_i \tag{7.28}$$

Where, $V_i$ are the value vectors obtained from hidden states and $Attention_i$ are the attention weights, computed using softmax over the attention scores.

### 7.3.8 Transformer Models

Transformer models represent a ground-breaking architecture in the field of natural language processing (NLP) and have revolutionized various sequence modelling tasks such as machine translation, text generation, and language understanding. Transformers, presented by Vaswani and collaborators in their work "Attention is All You Need," (2017) have evolved into the prevailing standard for natural language processing tasks, thanks to their capacity to efficiently model distant dependencies using self-attention mechanisms.

#### *The Architecture*

The architecture of a transformer model consists of four key components like encoder, decoder, self-attention mechanism and positional encoding.

***Encoder:*** The encoder consists of multiple layers of self-attention mechanisms and FFNNs. It can process the input sequence and extract meaningful representations from it. Each layer in the encoder processes the input sequence independently in parallel for efficient computation.

***Decoder:*** The decoder generates the output sequence by leveraging the representations learned by the encoder. Structurally, the decoder mirrors the encoder with a notable difference. Throughout the decoding process, the decoder attends to the encoder's output, allowing it to produce the output sequence incrementally, one step at a time.

***Self-Attention Mechanism:*** The self-attention mechanism in transformer models facilitates the efficient capture of long-range dependencies throughout the input sequence. It computes attention scores between each position in the sequence and allows the model to focus on relevant information while making predictions. The attention scores are computed as a weighted sum of the query ($Q$), key ($K$), and value ($V$) vectors and dimension of key vectors ($d_k$).

$$Attention(Q, K, V) = softmax\left(\frac{QK^T}{\sqrt{d_k}}\right)V \tag{7.29}$$

In order to improve the model's proficiency in capturing different types of information, multi-head attention is used, where the self-attention mechanism is applied multiple times in parallel.

$$MultiHead(Q,K,V) = Concat(head_i,\ldots,\ head_h)W^O \tag{7.30}$$

Where, $head_i$ = Attention ($QW_i^Q$, $KW_i^K$, $VW_i^V$) and $W_i^Q, W_i^K, W_i^V$ represent the weight matrices for the $i^{th}$ attention head. The $W^O$ is an output projection matrix that projects the concatenated heads back to the model dimension.

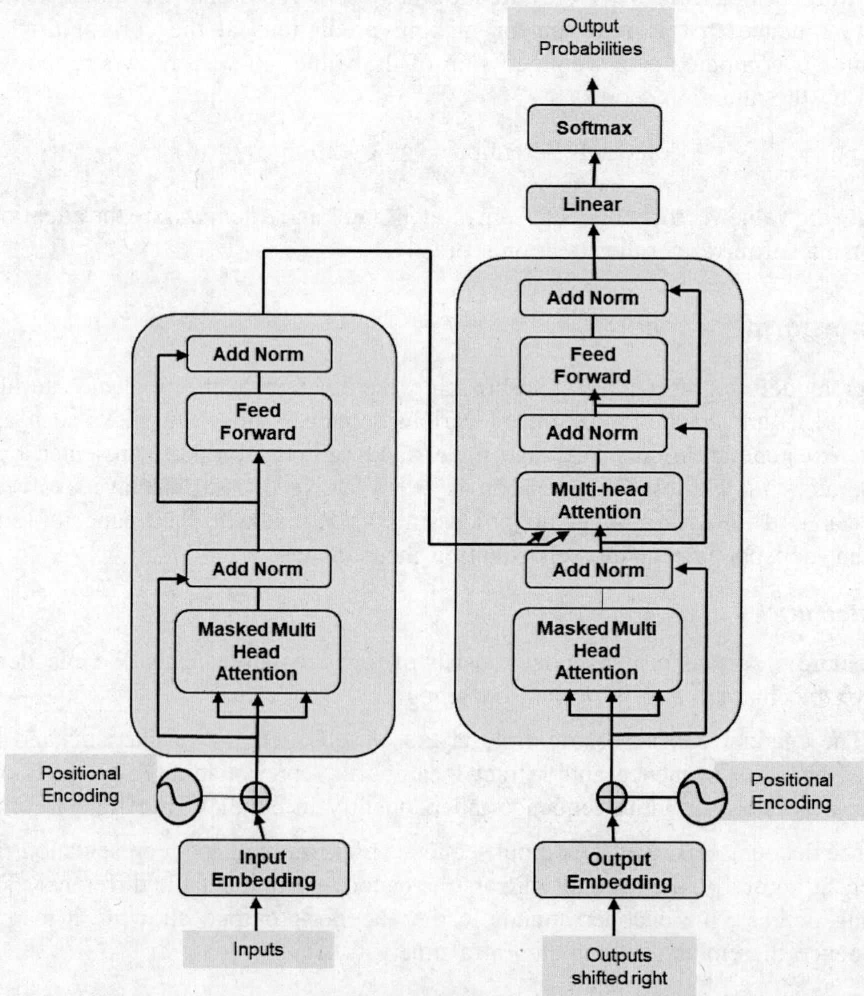


**FIGURE 7.7** The general architecture of the transformer model.

***Positional Encoding:*** As transformer models do not have a built-in mechanism to capture the sequential order of the input, positional encodings are appended to the input embeddings which assists the model to access information about the position of each token within the sequence. After self-attention, the representations are passed through position-wise feed-forward neural networks to capture non-linear interactions.

$$FFN(x) = ReLU(xW_1 + b_1)W_2 + b_2 \tag{7.31}$$

Where, $W_1$, $W_2$ represent the weight matrices for output transformations, $b_1$, $b_2$ represent bias terms.

For a wide range of sequence modeling tasks, transformer models have proven to be a highly capable architecture, demonstrating better performance and scalability in comparison to conventional recurrent neural networks. Transformers employ self-attention mechanisms and position-specific feed-forward networks to effectively model extensive contextual relationships within input sequences.

## 7.4 APPLICATIONS OF DEEP LEARNING

Deep learning has contributed in almost all the major areas of scientific research. Its capability to assimilate information from enormous datasets makes it exceptionally suitable for tackling intricate problems using the most practical methods. Some of those applications which are applicable in real time are discussed below. However, there are many others which are available in literatures, books, and other resources.

### 7.4.1 Computer Vision

Computer Vision (CV), an important field in Artificial Intelligence helps to understand the visual world. With the help of computer vision, computers can now "see" the world. It means getting visual data, pre-processing of that data to extract information like object detection and image classification, and using that information such as self-driving vehicles navigation, medical image analysis, and augmented reality. Advanced neural networks have significantly enhanced machine vision by boosting precision, expandability, and dependability, consequently enabling its application in diverse fields like autonomous vehicles, facial identification systems, and robotic technologies. Some of the real-life examples that exist among us using CV are:

***Self-Driving Cars:*** Using CV to navigate roads, recognize traffic signs and signals, detect objects and pedestrians, and avoid obstacles.

***Facial Recognition:*** Used in security systems, law enforcement, and social media (Google photos, Snapchat, Instagram) applications to identify individuals.

***Medical Imaging analysis:*** Assists doctors in diagnosing diseases by analysing X-rays, CT scans, and MRIs.

***Augmented Reality (AR):*** Overlays computer-generated visuals onto the real world, used in gaming (Microsoft Kinect), education, and product visualization.

***Virtual Reality (VR):*** Creates an immersive, simulated environment using computer vision to track user movement and interact with the virtual world.

***Agriculture:*** Drones equipped with computer vision assist in crop monitoring, disease detection, and yield prediction.

### 7.4.2 Natural Language Processing

Natural Language Processing (NLP) aims to equip computers with the ability to comprehend, decipher, and create human language in the most significant and practically relevant manner achievable. NLP includes a broad range of tasks, such as language understanding (e.g., sentiment analysis, named entity recognition), language generation (e.g., text summarization, machine translation), and language modelling (e.g., predicting the next word on the sentence). DL methods have greatly boosted NLP by developing sophisticated approaches to handle and comprehend natural language data. Some examples of NLP applications across various domains are:

***Virtual Assistants:*** AI-powered conversational interfaces, including Alexa, Siri, and Google's Assistant, leverage Natural Language Processing to interpret and address user requests and questions.

***Machine Translation:*** NLP powers machine translation systems such as Google Translate, Microsoft Translator, and DeepL, which can translate text between different languages.

***Sentiment Analysis:*** Text analysis algorithms evaluate content from platforms like social networks, consumer feedback, and news sources to ascertain the emotional tone conveyed in the text (positive, negative, or neutral).

***Text Classification:*** The process of sorting written documents into predetermined groups or classifications according to the subject matter or information they contain is known as text classification.

***Named Entity Recognition:*** NER is used in information extraction tasks, including entity linking, relationship extraction, and event detection.

***Text Summarization and Generation:*** Text summarization algorithms generate concise summaries of longer documents, articles, or texts while preserving the most important information and key points. Text generation models, like large language models (LLM) can generate coherent and contextually relevant text based on a given prompt or input.

***Information Retrieval and Text Mining:*** NLP techniques are used in information retrieval systems to search, index, and retrieve relevant documents or information from large text corpora.

### 7.4.3 Speech Recognition

Automatic speech recognition (ASR), also referred to as speech recognition or speech-to-text (STT), is a technology that allows computers to accurately identify spoken language and transcribe it into written text. Its process constitutes decoding the audio input that contains human speech and turning it into a written text that is suitable for digital processing, analysis, or presentation by computers or other devices. Speech recognition techniques which are based on the DL principles have been an enormous improvement, as they offer robust tools for dealing with complicated patterns hidden in audio data. Numerous real-world instances exemplify the practical implementation of deep learning-based speech recognition.

'Siri' by Apple, 'Alexa' by Amazon, Google Assistant, and 'Cortana' by Microsoft rely on DL for speech recognition, enabling them to comprehend and respond to user commands and inquiries. Search engines like Google employ DL algorithms for speech recognition in their voice search features, allowing users to verbally pose questions or initiate searches. Platforms like Otter.ai and Rev.com utilize deep learning-driven speech recognition for transcription services, accurately converting spoken words from audio and video recordings into written text.

***Voice-controlled Smart Home Devices uses:*** DL enabling users to seamlessly control these devices using voice commands, enhancing overall convenience and accessibility.

### 7.4.4 Healthcare

Advanced NNs have been applied across numerous areas in medicine, transforming multiple facets of health-related research, diagnostic processes, and therapeutic approaches. Extracting knowledge and practical insights from intricate, multi-dimensional, and diverse biomedical data presents a significant hurdle in revolutionizing healthcare. Some of the critical areas where deep leaning's contribution is worth mentioning are:

***Medical Imaging:*** DL excels in detecting abnormalities in CT scans, X-rays, and MRIs, and assists radiologists in diagnosing conditions like cancer, fractures, and neurological disorders. DL aids in scrutinizing histopathology slides, identifying disease-indicative patterns, and enhancing accuracy in cancer diagnosis.

***Drug Discovery and Development:*** DL predicts potential drug targets by analysing biological data, expediting the drug discovery process. Generative models assist in designing novel drug candidates by predicting molecular structures with desired properties.

***Electronic Health Records (EHR) and Clinical Data:*** DL models analyse patient data from EHRs, predicting disease risks, hospital readmissions, and treatment outcomes, enabling personalized healthcare interventions. DL enhances the extraction of valuable information from unstructured clinical notes and medical literature.

***Remote Patient Monitoring:*** DL analyses data from wearable devices, tracking patient vital signs, and detecting anomalies, facilitating timely interventions and personalized healthcare recommendations.

***Genomics and Personalized Medicine:*** DL aids in analysing extensive genomic datasets, identifying genetic variations, and comprehending their implications for personalized treatment plans. Models predict disease susceptibility based on genetic markers, enabling preventive measures and personalized treatment strategies.

***Telemedicine and Virtual Health Assistants:*** Telemedicine companies such as Teladoc, Amwell, and MDLIVE offer virtual consultations with doctors for a wide range of non-emergency medical issues. AI-powered virtual assistants like Babylon Health's app provide personalized health advice and symptom checkers to help individuals assess their symptoms and determine the need for seeking medical attention.

***Predictive Analytics for Disease Outbreaks:*** DL models analyse health data patterns, predicting and monitoring the spread of infectious diseases, aiding in early detection and containment.

### 7.4.5 Natural Sciences

The influence of deep learning on the natural sciences include progress in various fields such as Chemistry, Earth Sciences, Biology, and Physics. DL models are used in chemistry to develop novel materials with the necessary properties, forecast molecular attributes, and even optimize chemical reactions. Using the complex neural networks, the data generated from experiments and simulations can be easily interpreted and processed to decipher valuable insights of the large unexplored chemical space. The advancements in space technology has enabled to capture spatial images from various satellites and provide tera bytes of data in regular intervals. These data have benefitted earth sciences for interpretation of geological, geomorphological, seismic data interpretation, mineral exploration, climate data and for building predictive models for early warning. DL algorithms are employed in biological domains to examine genetic sequences, model and predict protein structures, and comprehend cellular processes on a never-before-seen scale. With physics-inspired networks, analysing experimental data, simulating quantum systems, and solving complex differential equations have become quite easy and reliable with DL.

**TABLE 7.2** Deep Learning Frameworks their typical use and target platform

| *Deep Learning Framework* | *Typical Use Cases* | *Target Platform* |
|---|---|---|
| *TensorFlow* | Image classification, natural language processing, reinforcement learning | Desktop, Cloud, Mobile, IoT |
| *PyTorch* | Research, rapid prototyping, dynamic computation graphs | Desktop, Cloud, Mobile |
| *Keras* | Rapid prototyping, beginners, easy-to-use API | Desktop, Cloud, Mobile, IoT |
| *MXNet* | Scalability, distributed training, production-ready models | Desktop, Cloud, Mobile, IoT |
| *Caffe* | Image classification, convolutional neural networks | Desktop, Cloud |
| *Theano* | Research, numerical computations | Desktop, Cloud |
| *CNTK* | Speech recognition, image recognition, language understanding | Desktop, Cloud, Mobile |

**TABLE 7.3** Deep Learning datasets for (a) Image, (b) Text, (c) Audio and (d) Time series

| *Data Type* | *Dataset Name* | *Brief Description* | *URLs* |
|---|---|---|---|
| Image | MNIST | Sketches of handwritten numbers for classification work | http://yann.lecun.com/exdb/mnist/ |
| | CIFAR-10 | Small pictures from a 10-class object recognition dataset | https://www.cs.toronto.edu/~kriz/cifar.html |
| | ImageNet | Thousands of object classes in a large set of images | ImageNet (image-net.org) |
| | COCO | The Common Objects in Context collection is used for identifying objects. | COCO - Common Objects in Context (cocodataset.org) |

| *Data Type* | *Dataset Name* | *Brief Description* | *URLs* |
|---|---|---|---|
| | Pascal VOC | The Visual Object Classes collection helps find objects. | http://host.robots.ox.ac.uk/pascal/VOC/ |
| | OpenImages | A large set of pictures that have been labelled for different uses | https://storage.googleapis.com/openimages/web/index.html |
| Text | IMDb Reviews | A set of movie reviews for sentiment analysis | Sentiment Analysis (stanford.edu) |
| | AG News | A dataset of news stories organised by class | https://www.kaggle.com/amananandrai/ag-news-classification-dataset |
| | Penn Treebank 3 | Tagged and processed text from the Wall Street Journal | https://catalog.ldc.upenn.edu/LDC99T42 |
| | Yelp Reviews | Explores a dataset for opinion mining and mood analysis that can help you learn NLP. | https://www.yelp.com/dataset |
| Audio | UrbanSound8K | Information and a classification system for studying urban sound | https://urbansounddataset.weebly.com/ |
| | Common Voice | An open source, multilingual collection of voices to train speech-enabled apps. | Common Voice (mozilla.org) |
| Time Series | ECG5000 | A collection of electrocardiograms for finding problems | https://www.kaggle.com/shayanfazeli/heartbeat |
| | Traffic Violations | Predict where taxi trips will end up by looking at their beginning partial paths. | https://www.kaggle.com/c/pkdd-15-predict-taxi-service-trajectory-i/data |
| | Energy Consumption | Collection of info on how much energy is used for predictive | Individual Household Electric Power Consumption - UCI Machine Learning Repository |

## SUMMARY

This chapter provides useful insights into the fundamental concepts of DL and its mathematical background. It provides a comprehensive explanation on the pivotal significance of activation functions, loss functions, and optimisation techniques in the intricate process of training deep neural networks. Some of the most common DL models are also explained to have an overview of their architecture and trainings. DL models have emerged as the vanguard of technological advancements, empowering intelligent automation and augmenting human-machine interactions across various domains such as image and speech recognition, NLP and autonomous decision-making. By presenting a detailed explanation on the fundamental tenets, practical implementations, and critical deliberations of DL, this chapter benefits the readers with the requisite expertise and resources to harness the potential of this revolutionary technology, thereby propelling the forthcoming surge of industrial advancement.

## WORKED OUT EXAMPLES

**EXAMPLE 7.1** Implement the Smish activation function in Python, where Smish($x$) = $x$ * tanh(ln(1 + sigmoid($x$))).

Given an input array $x$ = [–2, –1, 0, 1, 2], calculate the output of the SMISH activation function for each element in the array.

***Solution:***

```
import numpy as np
def sigmoid(x):
    return 1/(1 + np.exp(-x))
def smish(x):
    return x * np.tanh(np.log(1 + sigmoid(x)))
x = np.array([–2, –1, 0, 1, 2])
output = smish(x)
print("Input:", x)
print("Output:", output)
```

**EXAMPLE 7.2** Implement the Softsign activation function in Python. Given an input array $x$ = [3, 1, 0, 2, 4], calculate the output of the Softsign activation function for each element in the array.

***Solution:***

We know,

```
import numpy as np
def softsign(x):
    return x/(1 + np.abs(x))
x = np.array([–3, –1, 0, 2, 4])
output = softsign(x)
print("Input:", x)
print("Output:", output)
```

**EXAMPLE 7.3** Examine a neural architecture featuring one concealed layer composed of 5 processing units. Each neuron in the hidden layer uses the Mish activation function. You have been provided with the following inputs and weights:

Inputs: [2,–1,3,0,4][2,–1,3,0,4] Weights: [0.5,–0.3,0.2,0.7,–0.1][0.5,–0.3,0.2,0.7,–0.1]

Compute the activation values for each node in the intermediate layer, then determine the network's ultimate response at the output stage. Assume no bias terms are used in this network.

***Solution:***

```
import numpy as np
def mish(x):
    return x * tf.nn.tanh(tf.nn.softplus(x))
inputs = np.array([2, –1, 3, 0, 4])
```

```
weights = np.array([0.5, –0.3, 0.2, 0.7, –0.1])
hidden_outputs = mish(np.dot(inputs, weights))
final_output = np.sum(hidden_outputs)
print("Final output of the network:", final_output)
```

## EXERCISES

1. The GELU (Gaussian Error Linear Unit) activation function has become increasingly prevalent in contemporary deep learning frameworks, especially within transformer-based models. Provide a description of GELU, detail its computational method, and contrast its performance against the ReLU (Rectified Linear Unit) activation function. Furthermore, create a Python implementation of GELU, showcasing both its precise formulation and a widely-used approximation.
2. Examine an artificial neural architecture comprising one intermediate tier with 3 processing units. Each unit in this concealed stratum employs the activation function f(x) = x·tanh(ln(1+sigmoid(x)). The following data has been supplied:

   Input vector: [3, −1, 2] Weight vector: [0.5, −0.2, 0.3]

   Determine the activation value for each processing unit in the intermediate tier, then compute the ultimate output of the entire network. Assume the model operates without bias parameters.
3. Implement a deep neural network with 20 hidden layer and one output layer for a classification problem.
4. Three neurons are found in the output layer of a deep neural network, whereas twenty neurons are found in the input layer and thirty in the concealed layer. What number of weights are available in the neural network if the input data is a 20-sized vector? (Presume that the output and hidden layers contain terms associated with bias)
5. Take into consideration a neuron that makes use of the Swish activation function in a neural network. What is the neuron's output if it is determined that the weighted sum of its inputs is −1.5?

## BIBLIOGRAPHY


Aggarwal, C. C. (2018). *Neural Networks and Deep Learning: A Textbook*, Springer.

Goodfellow, I., Bengio, Y. and Courville, A. (2016). *Deep Learning*, MIT Press.

Krohn, J., Beyleveld, G. and Bassens, A. (2019). *Deep Learning Illustrated*, Addison-Wesley Professional.

Nielsen, M. (2015). *Neural Networks and Deep Learning: A Textbook*, Determination Press.

Trask, A. W. (2019). *Grokking Deep Learning*, Manning Publications.

Chapter 8

# CNN and RNN

## 8.1 INTRODUCTION

Convolution neural networks (CNN) and Recurrent neural networks (RNN) are specialized type of artificial neural network (ANN) which are designed to process specific types of data such as images. The 'convolution' operation in CNN is the most significant task that involves sliding a filter matrix over the input to produce activation maps that respond to trained visual patterns. RNN on the other hand are designed to handle sequential data by incorporating recurrent loops that contain feedback connections. With help of this internal memory, RNN are able to retain information from prior inputs and inform predictions at subsequent time steps. The prior hidden state is combined with the present input and passed through the recurrent loop to produce the updated hidden state. Simple RNNs suffer from vanishing and exploding gradients that inhibit learning long-term temporal dependencies. More complex gated RNNs such as Gated Recurrent Units (GRU) networks and Long Short-Term Memory (LSTM) introduce memory cells and gates to modulate information flow to better model longer sequences.

CNN and RNN has delivered very significant results on important image processing and sequential processing tasks including language translation, text generation, speech recognition, image captioning, predictive typing, time series forecasting, and video activity recognition among many other applications involving temporal data.

## 8.2 CONVOLUTIONAL NEURAL NETWORKS

CNNs are composed of a series of layers that apply convolutional filters to the input followed by some form of nonlinearity and pooling to gradually transform the data into higher-level representations. The architecture of a CNN is specially designed to process data which have grid-like topology, like 2D images. It consists of a series of convolutional layers combined with pooling layers, and followed by fully connected layers or dense layers. A convolutional layer employs a set of filters to the input in a way that each filter slides over the spatial dimensions of the input to detect patterns. These convolution layers extract hierarchical feature representations directly from the raw pixel inputs. Multiple filter maps are learned to activate different visual features in the images. After certain layers, pooling is performed, which serves to down sample the feature maps spatially to consolidate the activations and reduce computation. As the data progresses through successive convolutional and pooling layers, the features become more complex, encapsulating higher level patterns. Finally, after multiple stages of convolutional feature extraction, fully connected layers are added at the end which integrate all the features and make final classifications or predictions. Essentially, the convolutional base automates discovery of spatial hierarchies of features by learning filters scoped locally. This is stacked with fully connected layers that combine the convolutional outputs for downstream decision making.

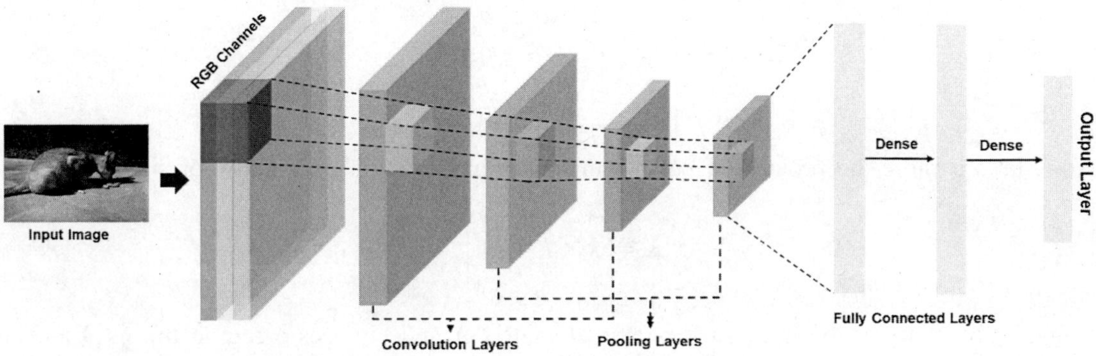


**FIGURE 8.1** A general overview of Convolution Neural Network with various layers.

### 8.2.1 Convolution in CNN

To fully understand CNNs, one must first comprehend the convolution operation. In a few simple cases, it's easier to see how it works. Within neural networks, convolution takes place first between tensors which are just n-dimensional matrix. With two tensors as input, the convolution operation (represented as '*') results into another tensor as the output. For example, let us try with two tensors, each with 3 × 3 dimensions. Using the following formula, the convolution process is carried out,

$$\begin{bmatrix} a_1 & a_2 & a_3 \\ a_4 & a_5 & a_6 \\ a_7 & a_8 & a_9 \end{bmatrix} * \begin{bmatrix} k_1 & k_2 & k_3 \\ k_4 & k_5 & k_6 \\ k_7 & k_8 & k_9 \end{bmatrix} = \sum_{i=1}^{9}(a_i k_i) \tag{8.1}$$

Simply multiplying each element $a_i$ by its corresponding element $k_i$ yields the output in this instance. This formula could be expressed as follows using a double sum in a more common matrix formalism,

$$\begin{bmatrix} a_{11} & a_{12} & a_{13} \\ a_{21} & a_{22} & a_{23} \\ a_{31} & a_{32} & a_{33} \end{bmatrix} * \begin{bmatrix} k_{11} & k_{12} & k_{13} \\ k_{21} & k_{22} & k_{23} \\ k_{31} & k_{32} & k_{33} \end{bmatrix} = \Sigma_{i=1}^{3} \Sigma_{j=1}^{3} (a_{ij} k_{ij}) \tag{8.2}$$

From equation 8.1 it can be easily interpreted how each element in one tensor is multiplied with the corresponding element in the second tensor (i.e., the element in the same position), and the resulting values are then added to obtain the final outcome.

Convolution is typically performed between a tensor, denoted as $A$, and a kernel $K$. Usually, kernels are smaller, like 3 × 3 or 5 × 5, while the input tensors A are generally larger. When dealing with matrices of different dimensions, applying convolution can be a bit tricky. The process involves carefully aligning the matrices and performing element-wise multiplication. This allows to extract relevant features and patterns from the data. However, it is important to note that the dimensions of the resulting output will be different from the original matrices which makes it crucial to handle the discrepancy appropriately to ensure accurate results. Let us take a matrix $A$ that has dimension of 4 × 4 to better understand the concept,

$$\begin{bmatrix} a_1 & a_2 & a_3 & a_4 \\ a_5 & a_6 & a_7 & a_8 \\ a_9 & a_{10} & a_{11} & a_{12} \\ a_{13} & a_{14} & a_{15} & a_{16} \end{bmatrix} \tag{8.3}$$

Now, let's explore the process of performing convolution using a kernel $K$ of size 3 × 3,

$$K = \begin{bmatrix} k_1 & k_2 & k_3 \\ k_4 & k_5 & k_6 \\ k_7 & k_8 & k_9 \end{bmatrix} \tag{8.4}$$

Convolution starts at the upper-left corner of matrix $A$ and chooses a region that is 3 × 3 in size. For example, in matrix $A$, this upper-left corner matrix can be represented as $A_1$ such that,

$$A_1 = \begin{bmatrix} a_1 & a_2 & a_3 \\ a_5 & a_6 & a_7 \\ a_9 & a_{10} & a_{11} \end{bmatrix}$$

Which are the bold elements in $A$,

$$A = \begin{bmatrix} \mathbf{a_1} & \mathbf{a_2} & \mathbf{a_3} & a_4 \\ \mathbf{a_5} & \mathbf{a_6} & \mathbf{a_7} & a_8 \\ \mathbf{a_9} & \mathbf{a_{10}} & \mathbf{a_{11}} & a_{12} \\ a_{13} & a_{14} & a_{15} & a_{16} \end{bmatrix} \tag{8.5}$$

Thus, the convolutions between this smaller matrix $A_1$ and $K$, yielding (we will use $B_1$ to signify the result),

$$B_1 = A_1 * K = a_1k_1 + a_2k_2 + a_3k_3 + k_4a_5 + k_5a_5 + k_6a_7 + k_7a_9 + k_8a_{10} + k_9a_{11} \tag{8.6}$$

The chosen 3 × 3 area in matrix A then moves by one column to the right, and the next elements indicated in boldface as below are chosen to obtain another sub matrix $A_2$.

$$A = \begin{bmatrix} a_1 & \mathbf{a_2} & \mathbf{a_3} & \mathbf{a_4} \\ a_5 & \mathbf{a_6} & \mathbf{a_7} & \mathbf{a_8} \\ a_9 & \mathbf{a_{10}} & \mathbf{a_{11}} & \mathbf{a_{12}} \\ a_{13} & a_{14} & a_{15} & a_{16} \end{bmatrix} \quad A_2 = \begin{bmatrix} a_2 & a_3 & a_4 \\ a_6 & a_7 & a_8 \\ a_{10} & a_{11} & a_{12} \end{bmatrix} \tag{8.7}$$

Again, convolution of the smaller matrix $A_2$ and $K$ are carried out as,

$$B_2 = A_2 * K = a_2k_1 + a_3k_2 + a_4k_3 + a_6k_4 + a_7k_5 + a_8k_6 + a_{10}k_7 + a_{11}k_8 + a_{12}k_9 \tag{8.8}$$

At the next step, we must move it one row down and begin over from the left side. The following area chosen would be

$$A_3 = \begin{bmatrix} a_5 & a_6 & a_7 \\ a_9 & a_{10} & a_{11} \\ a_{13} & a_{14} & a_{15} \end{bmatrix} \tag{8.9}$$

Once more, convolution with K is carried out to obtain $B_3$ such that,

$$B_3 = A_3 * K = a_5k_1 + a_6k_2 + a_7k_3 + a_9k_4 + a_{10}k_5 + a_{11}k_6 + a_{13}k_7 + a_{14}k_8 + a_{15}k_9 \tag{8.10}$$

Finally, the last sub matrix $A_4$ is chosen in similar fashion and the convolution is repeated to obtain $B_4$.

$$A_4 = \begin{bmatrix} a_6 & a_7 & a_8 \\ a_{10} & a_{11} & a_{12} \\ a_{14} & a_{15} & a_{16} \end{bmatrix} \tag{8.11}$$

and the outcome will be obtained via convolution

$$B_4 = A_4 * K = a_6k_1 + a_7k_2 + a_8k_3 + a_{10}k_4 + a_{11}k_5 + a_{12}k_6 + a_{14}k_7 + a_{15}k_8 + a_{16}k_9 \tag{8.12}$$

Through these initial convolution operations, a new tensor B is generated such that,

$$B = \begin{bmatrix} B_1 & B_2 \\ B_3 & B_4 \end{bmatrix} \tag{8.13}$$

If tensor $A$ is larger, the procedure remains the same and but the resultant B tensor will just be larger. It is necessary for us to address one more minor point before continuing, and that is the idea of stride ($s$). The 3 × 3 region was always moved one row down and one column to the right in the previous procedure. A common way to represent stride is the number of rows and columns, as in the above example, a shift of two columns to the right and two rows down would be indicated by the formula stride $s = 2$. Further, the size of the selected sub-matrix from the input should match the kernel's dimensions. If the kernel is of size 5 × 5, the area to be chosen as sub-matrix from the input should also be 5 × 5. In general, $n_K \times n_K$ area in input matrix is chosen every time if the kernel is of size $n_K$ x $n_K$. This results in formation of a simple definition of convolution with stride ($s$) as a procedure that receives a tensor A with dimensions $n_A \times n_A$ and a kernel K with dimensions $n_K \times n_K$, to produce an output matrix B with dimensions $n_B \times n_B$ such that,

$$n_B = \left\lfloor \frac{n_A - n_K}{S} + 1 \right\rfloor \tag{8.14}$$

Considering A as the input tensor and K as kernel, the generalised procedure to produce the new tensor B is,

$$B_{ij} = (A * K)_{ij} = \sum_{f=0}^{n_k-1} \sum_{h=0}^{n_k-1} A_{i+f,j+h} K_{i+f,j+h} \tag{8.15}$$

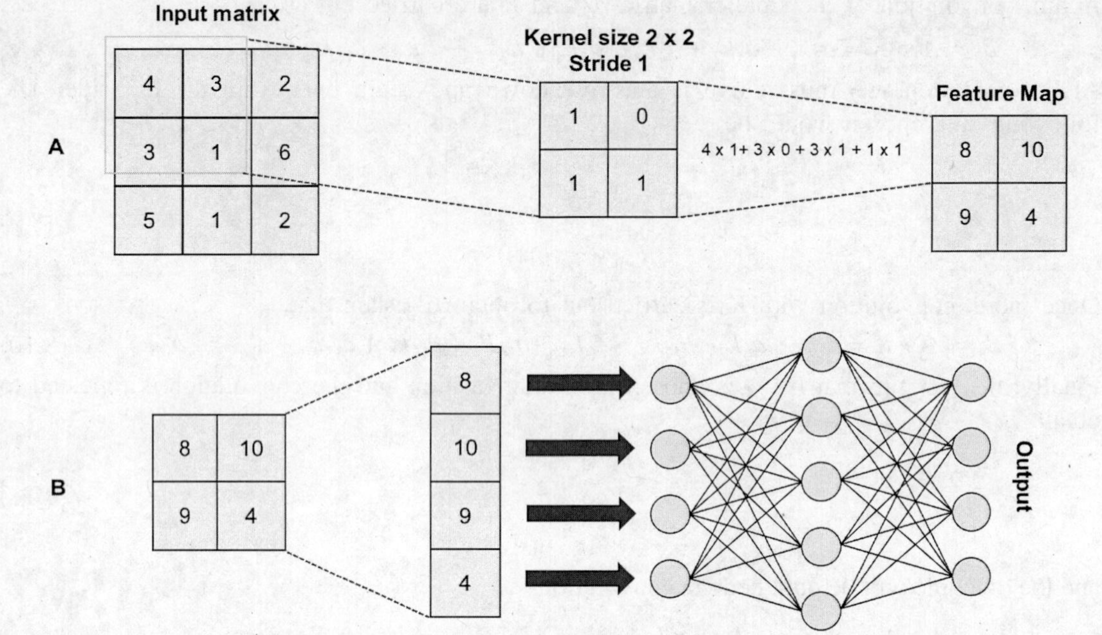


FIGURE 8.2 (A) The convolutional operation in CNN to extract the feature maps from the input data with kernel size 2 × 2 and stride = 1. (B) Flattened feature map towards as input to the fully connected layers for output.

## 8.2.2 Pooling

The second crucial procedure for CNNs is pooling. Comparing this procedure to convolution, it is far simpler to understand. To comprehend it, let us take a closer look at a real-world example and the concept of max pooling and use the same 4 × 4 input $A$ as in 8.3.

In order to execute max pooling, a $n_K \times n_K$ region must be defined, as for convolution such that $n_K = 2$. The objective is to choose a $n_K \times n_K$ region from the matrix $A$, starting at the top-left corner i.e. consider the components in matrix $A$ that are boldfaced,

$$A = \begin{bmatrix} \mathbf{a_1} & \mathbf{a_2} & a_3 & a_4 \\ \mathbf{a_5} & \mathbf{a_6} & a_7 & a_8 \\ a_9 & a_{10} & a_{11} & a_{12} \\ a_{13} & a_{14} & a_{15} & a_{16} \end{bmatrix}$$

The max pooling procedure chooses the maximum value from the items chosen, $a_1$, $a_2$, $a_5$, and $a_6$, producing a result that we will denote with $C_1$

$$C_1 = max_{i=1,2,5,6}\ a_i \tag{8.16}$$

In order to choose the items shown in boldface, we must now move our 2 × 2 window to the right by two columns, which are usually the same number of columns as the selected region.

$$A = \begin{bmatrix} a_1 & a_2 & \mathbf{a_3} & \mathbf{a_4} \\ a_5 & a_6 & \mathbf{a_7} & \mathbf{a_8} \\ a_9 & a_{10} & a_{11} & a_{12} \\ a_{13} & a_{14} & a_{15} & a_{16} \end{bmatrix}$$

or, alternatively, the reduced matrix

$$\begin{bmatrix} a_3 & a_4 \\ a_7 & a_8 \end{bmatrix} \tag{8.17}$$

The maximum value will then be chosen using the max-pooling process, producing a result that we will denote with $C_2$

$$C_2 = max_{i=3,4,7,8}\ a_i \tag{8.18}$$

As we can no longer move the 2 × 2 region to the right, we move it two rows down and begin the procedure over from the left side of $A$. This time, we choose the parts that are bolded, find the maximum, and name it $C_3$. It looks like this:

$$A = \begin{bmatrix} a_1 & a_2 & a_3 & a_4 \\ a_5 & a_6 & a_7 & a_8 \\ \mathbf{a_9} & \mathbf{a_{10}} & a_{11} & a_{12} \\ \mathbf{a_{13}} & \mathbf{a_{14}} & a_{15} & a_{16} \end{bmatrix} \tag{8.19}$$

In this context, the meaning of stride is the same as it was discussed earlier in the convolution debate. It is just how many rows or columns you shift your region in while choosing the pieces. Lastly, we choose the final area, measuring 2 × 2, located in the lowermost portion of A's bottom, and choose the components $a_{11}$, $a_{12}$, $a_{15}$, and $a_{16}$. After obtaining the maximum, it is designated as $C_4$. *A* final output tensor *C* using the values is acquired from this process,

$$C = \begin{bmatrix} C_1 & C_2 \\ C_3 & C_4 \end{bmatrix} \tag{8.20}$$

In the above example, $s = 2$. In essence, this operation returns a new matrix $C$ whose dimensions are determined by the same formula as in equation.

### 8.2.3 Max Pooling

CNNs which are employed for tasks like object detection and picture classification, depend heavily on max pooling. It is mostly used for feature extraction and downsampling.

***Downsampling:*** By minimising the spatial dimensions (height and breadth) of the data, max pooling lowers the computational cost and improves the network's ability to handle the data. The process is to choose the maximum value within each window as you move a fixed-size window typically 2 × 2 across the input feature map. Only the most noticeable elements of the original data are retained in the reduced form of the output that is produced.

***Feature Extraction:*** Max pooling highlights the most well-defined and robust features in the surrounding area by choosing the highest possible value. Tasks like object recognition, where it's critical to recognise important edges, corners, and other visible features, benefit greatly from this. The network is also made more resilient to minute changes in the data by max pooling, which adds a degree of invariance to tiny translations and rotations in the input. However, there are other ways of pooling too apart from max pooling as depicted in the figure below.

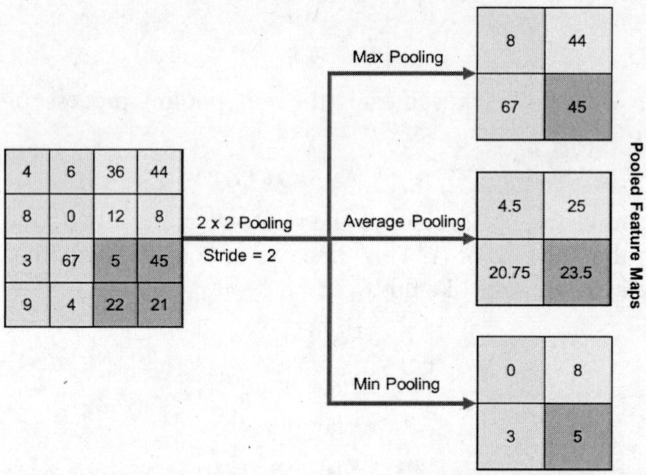


**FIGURE 8.3** Depiction of different ways of executing pooling operations in CNN, i.e. max pooling, average pooling and min pooling. However, max pooling is commonly used to derive feature maps.

## 8.3 OPTIMIZATION AND REGULARIZATION ALGORITHMS

Optimization and regularization algorithms are often used to ensure that DNNs converge to optimal sets of parameters by minimizing the loss function without overfitting. Optimization algorithms have been discussed in detail in section 7.2.5 of Chapter 7, hence here the regularization algorithms are explained for better comprehension.

### *L1/L2 Regularization*

Regularization techniques are often used in training CNNs to prevent overfitting by adding an additional parameter to the loss function that penalizes model complexity. L1 and L2 regularization are most common forms of regularization. L1 regularization adds the sum of the absolute values of the CNN parameters multiplied by a coefficient to the loss. This encourages sparsity in the parameter values, effectively forcing weights toward zero. In CNN filters, L1 regularization automatically prunes redundant or non-informative features maps to compress the model. In contrast, L2 regularization adds the sum of squared parameter values, multiplied by a coefficient. This causes a smoothing effect by reducing extreme parameter fluctuations. For CNNs, L2 regularization helps control outlier activations and encourages model robustness.

The coefficients for both L1 and L2 regularization control the model compression-robustness trade-offs. A larger value prevents overfitting but leads to high bias, while a small value enables potential overfitting. The choice of which to use and strength to apply depends on the CNN architecture and dataset. Often a combined L1 + L2 regularization works best to balance sparsity and smoothing. Additionally, applying regularization only to certain layers in the CNN can enable specificity in preventing overfitting while retaining representational capacity.

### *Dropout*

Dropout is a common regularization technique in CNNs that prevents overfitting by randomly dropping out neurons during training. In standard neural nets, dropout randomly removes a percentage of hidden units from the network on each training iteration. In CNNs, dropout is normally applied after convolutional layers before fully connected layers. On any pass, individual nodes in these layers are either retained with probability $p$ or dropped out with probability $1 - p$ based on samples from a Bernoulli distribution. Typically, $p$ is set between 0.5 to 0.8.

Dropout has several beneficial regularizing effects for CNNs. By preventing complex co-adaptations of features on each training iteration, it adds noise and forces layers to learn more robust representations that can withstand random removal of peers. The threat of disruption also encourages redundancy. Dropped out neurons don't contribute to training loss for that iteration, allowing other features to compensate. This ensemble-like effect retains diversity across the representation space. During inference the full CNN is used, benefiting from multiple specializations across neurons. Adding dropout before final layers also acts as model averaging to address overfitting. Inserting dropout at different points in the CNN and tuning p per layer allows customization of regularization needs.

### *Batch Normalization*

Batch normalization is a technique that enables much faster and stable training of deep CNNs. Normalization addresses the issue of internal covariate shift—as parameters in earlier layers change during training, the distribution of inputs to later layers keeps changing. This slows down training and requires delicate parameter initialization and low learning rates. Batch normalization solves this by explicitly fixing means and variances of layer inputs. Specifically, in CNNs, batch normalization is inserted after convolution layers and before activations. Each activation gets normalized to have 0 mean and unit variance within a minibatch. The model then learns to separate a fine transform parameters to restore representation power of the layer. By fixing the first two input moments, normalization allows high learning rates, makes training faster, and reduces need for dropout. However, there is a trade-off between normalization and losing identity-preserving information in representations. Various refinements like layer normalization, group normalization and batch renormalization have been proposed.

**TABLE 8.1** Insights into various algorithms used in CNN optimization and regularizations

| *Type* | *Algorithm* | *Mathematical Formula* |
|---|---|---|
| Optimization | Stochastic Gradient Descent | $x_{k+1} = x_k - t_k \Delta f(x_k)^i$ |
| | Momentum | $V(t) = \gamma V(t-1) + \alpha . \nabla J(\theta)$ |
| | Nesterov Accelerated Gradient (NAG) | $V(t) = \gamma V(t-1) + \alpha . \nabla J\big(\theta - \gamma V(t-1)\big)$ |
| | AdaGrad | $\theta_{t+1,i} = \theta_{t,i} - \frac{\eta}{\sqrt{G_{t,ii} + \varepsilon}} \cdot g_{t,i}$ |
| | RMSProp | $E_t = \gamma E_{t-1} + (1-\gamma) g_t^{\,2}$ |
| | Adam | $\theta_{t+1} = \theta_t - \frac{\eta}{\sqrt{\hat{v} + \varepsilon}} \hat{m}_t$ |
| Regularization | L1 Regularization (Lasso Regression) | $\text{Cost} = \frac{1}{n} \sum_{i=1}^{n} (y_i - \hat{y}_i)^2 + \lambda \sum_{i=1}^{m} \lvert w_i \rvert$ |
| | L2 Regularization (Ridge Regression) | $\text{Cost} = \frac{1}{n} \sum_{i=1}^{n} (y_i - \hat{y}_i)^2 + \lambda \sum_{i=1}^{m} w_i^2$ |
| | Dropout | $E_R = \frac{1}{2}\left(t - \sum_{i=1}^{n} p_i w_i I_i\right)^2 + \sum_{i=1}^{n} p_i (1 - p_i)\, w_i^2 I_i^2$ |
| | Batch Normalization | $y = \frac{\gamma}{\sqrt{V_{ar_x} + \varepsilon}} x + \left(\beta + \frac{\gamma E_x}{\sqrt{V_{ar_x} + \varepsilon}}\right)$, where<br>$E_x = \frac{1}{m} \sum_{i=1}^{j} \mu_B^{(i)}$ and<br>$V_{ar_x} = \left(\frac{m}{m-1}\right) \frac{1}{m} \sum^{j} \sigma_B^{2(i)}$ |

## 8.4 COMMON MATHEMATICAL INTERPRETATIONS IN CNNs

### *Convolutional Layer Output Size*

The convolutional layer output size refers to the spatial dimensions (width and height) of the output volume after passing an input through a convolutional layer in CNN. It is computed with three key parameters—the input dimension, convolutional filter size, and convolution strides. Additionally, padding may also be used to provide space between the borders of the input volume and where the filters are applied.

The formula to compute the output width ($W_{out}$) of a convolutional layer is,

$$W_{out} = \frac{W - F + 2P}{S} + 1 \tag{8.21}$$

Where, $W_{out}$ is output width, $W$ is input width, $F$ is filter or kernel spatial size, $P$ is padding size (zeroes added to borders) and $S$ is stride (displacement applied to filters). Knowing the output size formula allows configuring the convolutional layers appropriately to match dimensions as needed in designing the CNN architecture.

### *Number of Parameters in Convolution Layer*

The number of parameters in a convolutional layer denotes the total quantity of learnable weights and biases present in that layer. It determines the parameter capacity and representational power of a conv layer.

$$P = F * K^2 * C_{in} \tag{8.22}$$

Where, $P$ represents parameters, $F$ is number of filters, $K$ is Filter size ($K \times K$) and $C_{in}$ number of input channels.

### *Computational Cost of Convolution Layer*

The computational cost of a convolutional layer depends on the number of mathematical operations it performs during the forward propagation of a single input to compute the output. Specifically, it counts the multiply-accumulate operations.

$$M = F * K^2 * C_{in} * W_{out} * H_{out} \tag{8.23}$$

Where, $M$ is floating point operations, $F$ is number of filters, $K$ is Filter size, $C_{in}$ is number of input channels and product of $W_{out}$ and $H_{out}$ represents output of spatial size.

### *Pooling Layer Output Size*

The pooling layer output size represents the spatial dimensions (width and height) of the feature map output from a pooling layer in a CNN. It is determined based on two key parameters—input feature map size into the pooling layer and the pooling window size and stride. The mathematical formula to calculate the output width ($W_{out}$) after passing an input through a pooling layer is,

$$W_{out} = \frac{W - F}{S} + 1 \tag{8.24}$$

Where, $F$ is pooling filter size and $S$ is stride.

### *Dense Layer Parameters*

The dense layer parameters are the total number of learnable weights and biases present in a fully connected (dense) layer of a CNN. It is computed as,

$$P = (C_{in} * W * H) * C_{out} + C_{out} \tag{8.25}$$

Where, P is total number of parameters (weights + biases), $C_{in}$ is number of channels (depth) of the input volume into the dense layer, $W$ is width of the input volume, $H$ is height of the input volume and $C_{out}$ is number of neurons (nodes) in the dense layer.

### *Receptive Field Size*

The receptive field size is another important concept in CNNs which refers to the region in the input image that a particular CNN neuron is looking at or is receptive to. The formula to calculate the receptive field size is,

$$RF = ((K - 1) * S) + F \tag{8.26}$$

Where $RF$ is total receptive field size, $K$ is spatial size of the convolutional filter (kernel size), $S$ is stride of the convolutional filters and F is spatial size of the pooling filter.

## 8.5 SOME WIDELY USED CNNs

CNNs are widely used for image classification and recognition. The simplest models generally consist of convolutional layers, pooling layers, and fully connected layers, however, with the complexity of the problem, the architectures keep changing. Some of the widely used CNN models are LeNet-5, Alexnet-5, VGGNet, GoogLeNet, Resnet and few more.

***LeNet-5:*** LeNet-5 was a one of the pioneers in deep neural networks for image classification developed by Yann LeCun in the 1990s. Built specifically for distinguishing handwritten and machine-printed characters, the LeNet architecture marked one of the very early applications of convolutional neural networks. LeNet-5 takes a 28 × 28 image as input which passes through a set of alternating convolutions and subsampling layers designed to extract increasing abstract feature representations while reducing spatial dimensions. The LeNet-5 architecture consists of two sets of convolutional and average pooling layers which are followed by a flattening convolutional output layer connected to a multilayer perceptron with one hidden layer. Nonlinearity comes from a *tanh* activation unit. Despite having only 60,000 parameters, modest by today's standards, LeNet achieved excellent accuracy at recognizing MNIST digit classification challenges. The network demonstrated how backpropagation could be used to train multilayer convolutional networks directly from pixels to classify images.

***AlexNet-5:*** AlexNet was developed in 2012 by Alex Krizhevsky, Ilya Sutskever and Geoff Hinton, and marked a breakthrough in computer vision through its deep CNN design. The architecture of AlexNet model is comprised of 8 layers—5 convolutional layers for hierarchical feature extraction, along with 3 fully connected layers for high-level reasoning. Trained with a large as 60 million parameters and 650,000 neurons, AlexNet had considerably larger depth and complexity compared to prior CNNs like LeNet. AlexNet uses GPU accelerators during training, allowing it to exploit data parallelism by running backpropagation across multiple GPUs simultaneously. This reduced training times from weeks to days. Powered by its deep architecture and scalable GPU-accelerated training pipeline, AlexNet achieved unprecedented accuracy on the 2012 ImageNet LSVRC competition with a top-5 error rate of 15.3%.

This breakthrough performance for computer vision tasks proved the viability of training very deep convolutional models for visual recognition problems.

***VGGNet:*** VGGNet was developed in 2014 by researchers at Oxford's Visual Geometry Group (VGG), pushed the depth limits of CNNs by using significantly more layers than AlexNet. The core insight behind VGGNet was using consecutive 3 × 3 convolutional layers with very small receptive fields instead of larger 7 × 7 or 5 × 5 sized filters. Stacking these tiny convolution layers, VGG-16 contained 16 weight layers and achieved impressive accuracy on ImageNet with lower complexity. VGG also showed that neural network depth plays a crucial role in accuracy. With VGG-19, they used 19 weight layers, which gave a further boost. To enable training such deep CNNs, VGGNet used fractions of convolutional feature maps rather than huge fully connected layers, along with augmentations like dropout. The uniformity of using tiny 3 × 3 conv layers repeatedly made VGG models easy to tweak by adding or removing layers. VGGNet convincingly demonstrated that outstanding performance could be achieved by using only 3 × 3 convolutions in a homogeneous architecture while scaling up depth and using fractionally stride layers with dropout to regularize training.

***GoogLeNet:*** The GoogLeNet model developed by researchers at Google in 2014 employed a unique architectural building block design called the Inception module. These modules used convolutions of multiple sizes – 1 × 1, 3 × 3, and 5 × 5 filters in parallel within the same layer, concatenated alongside max pooling operations. This allowed each layer to leverage multi-scale feature extraction simultaneously. By stacking a series of these Inception modules, the overall network could achieve increased depth and complexity without blowing up parameters or computations compared to similarly sized sequential convnets. GoogLeNet also employed average pooling before classification, auxiliary classifiers on intermediate layers to regularize learning, and aggressive factorization within Inception modules to limit model size. The result was a 22 layers deep CNN that achieved record breaking accuracy on ImageNet classification with 4 million parameters—a considerable reduction compared to previous VGG models. Beyond this clever module design balancing depth and width, GoogleNet showed how branching within a CNN can effectively extract richer, multi-resolution information from input feature maps in tandem. Its power and computational efficiency made Inception a widely adopted building block in numerous computer vision architectures since its inception.

***ResNet:*** The ResNet architecture, introduced in 2015, tackled a key challenge of training extremely deep convolutional networks—that of declining accuracy beyond a certain depth due to gradient vanishing/exploding. ResNets addressed this through a novel Residual Learning building block. These residual blocks enable shortcuts directly across convolutional layers by introducing identity skip connections that bypass the main layers. This allows gradients to flow directly through these shortcut connections during backpropagation, which makes it easier to optimize very deep networks.

Additionally, ResNet used batch normalization right after each convolution, before activation, in order to stabilize layer inputs which further eased training. This allowed residual networks to eventually scale up to over 1000 layers while still maintaining compelling performance. Key achievements included exceeding human-level accuracy on ImageNet classification and winning multiple computer vision challenges. Beyond engineering innovations like shortcut connections and batch normalization, ResNet convincingly showed that neural network depth plays a crucial role in advancing machine perception capabilities. Practically all modern convolutional networks today build on principles introduced in ResNet, typically using residual learning schemes in some form to accelerate training of very deep models for computer vision.

***DenseNet:*** The DenseNet architecture was introduced in 2017 and focused on more tightly connecting all the layers directly to improve information flow within CNN. DenseNets contain dense blocks which iteratively concatenate inputs from all preceding layers as inputs to current layers. This allows later layers to reuse features from multiple previous layers leading to implicit deep supervision and feature propagation benefits. Such dense connectivity patterns help ease vanishing-gradient problems, reinforce feature propagation, feature reuse, and significantly reduce the number of parameters. By densely combining previous layers as cumulative inputs to subsequent layers, DenseNets facilitate reuse of features and implicitly deepen supervision. Alongside optimizations like bottleneck layers and compression to improve model scaling, DenseNets achieved significant results on benchmarks like ImageNet with fewer parameters and faster training than prevailing methods.

***Mobilenet:*** MobileNets are a class of CNNs designed specifically for efficient deployment on mobile and embedded devices with significant resource constraints. A key aspect of their efficient design is the use of depth wise separable convolutions as the primary building block. This dramatically reduce computation and model size by factorizing a standard convolution into a depth wise convolution performed over each input channel separately, followed by a 1 × 1 pointwise convolution to combine channel outputs.

Additional techniques like network width multipliers and input resolution adjustments allow finding the right balance between model size, compute requirements and accuracy for any given application constraints. Despite having an extremely lightweight architecture in the 4-6 million parameter range, MobileNets have achieved impressive image classification results competitive with models 10 to 20 times larger. The architectural innovations that underpin training compact yet accurate MobileNets have been tremendously impactful for the viability of deep learning across a wide range mobility-constrained platform—from mobile phones, embedded electronics to Internet of Things devices.

**TABLE 8.2** Overview of some of the widely used CNNs architectures

| *CNN Architecture* | *Layers* | *Parameters* |
|---|---|---|
| LeNet-5 | 7(5 Convolution + 2 FC) | 60 thousand |
| AlexNet-5 | 8(5 Convolution + 3 Fully Connected) | 60 million |
| VGGNet | 16–19(13–16 convolution + 3 FC) | 134 million |
| GoogLeNet | 22 Convolution layers, 9 Inception modules | 4 million |
| ResNet | 50 in ResNet-50, 101 in ResNet-101, 152 in ResNet-152 | 25.6 million in ResNet-50, 44.5 million in ResNet-101, 60.2 million in ResNet-152. |
| DenseNet | 117 Convolution layers, 3 Transition layers and 1 Classification layer | 27.2 million |
| Mobilenet | 53 layers including the initial convolutional layer and the following residual bottleneck layers | 3.4 million |

## 8.6 RECURRENT NEURAL NETWORKS

Recurrent neural networks (RNNs) were designed for processing sequential data such as time series or texts or spatial data. Their key characteristic is the presence of feedback connections that link previous outputs back into the network to influence predictions for later time steps. This allows RNNs to exhibit dynamic temporal behaviour and use contextual information from the input history. The overall RNN architecture processes sequences by iterating through input tokens one timestep at a time while maintaining an internal hidden state that gets updated based on new inputs and previous hidden states.

At each timestep the RNN takes the latest input and preceding hidden state as inputs to the recurrence formula to generate the new hidden state. This hidden state captures historical context information to inform the processing of new inputs as they arrive in the sequence. The updated hidden state gets fed as input to an output layer to make a prediction at that timestep, while also being fed back into the recurrent loop as the new starting hidden state for the next inputs in the sequence.

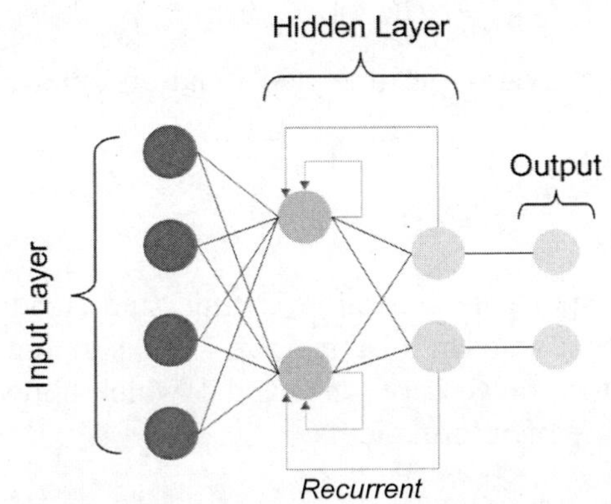


**FIGURE 8.4** An overview of Recurrent Neural Network depicting back propagation to hidden layers.

So, this closed loop architecture with context being passed along a chain of updates allows RNNs to naturally handle variable length sequential data for use cases ranging from time series forecasting to language translation.

## 8.6.1 Key Terminologies in RNN

***Number of Parameters:*** This refers to the total quantity of learnable weights and biases present in the model which influences its modelling capacity and complexity and can be computed by,

$$\text{Number of Parameters} = (D_i \times D_h) + (D_h \times D_h) + (D_h \times D_o) + D_h + D_o \tag{8.27}$$

Where, $D_i$ is input dimension, $D_h$ is hidden layer dimension and $D_o$ is output layer dimension.

***Computational Cost per Timestep:*** This term refers to the number of mathematical operations (multiply-add) performed by the model during the forward pass propagation of a single input to calculate the output. It can be computed by,

$$n_i * n_h + n_h * n_h + n_h * n_o \tag{8.28}$$

Where the cost of input-to-hidden is $n_i * n_h$, hidden-to-hidden is $n_h * n_h$ and hidden-to-output is $n_h * n_o$.

***LSTM Gates:*** LSTM gates are key components which addresses the vanishing gradient problem in basic RNNs. The LSTM gates govern how information dynamically flows through the timesteps. The three main gates are represented as,

***Input Gate (i)***

$$i_t = \sigma(W_i * [h_{t-1}, x_t] + b_i) \tag{8.29}$$

Where, $i_t$ is input gate activation at time step $t$; $\sigma$ represents sigmoid activation function (ranging between 0 and 1); $W_i$ is the weight matrix for the input gate; $[h_{t-1}, x_t]$ represents the concatenation of the previous hidden state ($h_{t-1}$) and the current input ($x_t$) and $b_i$ is the bias vector for the input gate allowing an additional learnable offset.

***Forget Gate (f)***

$$f_t = \sigma(W_f * [h_{t-1}, x_t] + b_f) \tag{8.30}$$

Where, $f_t$ is the forget gate activation at time step $t$ and all other parameters as same as input gate.

***Output Gate (o)***

$$O_t = \sigma(W_o * [h_{t-1}, x_t] + b_o) \tag{8.31}$$

Where, $O_t$ represents the output gate activation at time step $t$ and all others are the common parameters of input and forget gate. In all three gates, the sigmoid activation function is used to squash the input values to a range between 0 and 1 which allows the gates to act as "soft" switches, controlling the flow of information.

### 8.6.2 Some Widely Used RNNs

#### *Vanilla RNN*

Vanilla RNN are the simplest type of recurrent network architecture which consist of a recurrent hidden state where each activation depends on that of preceding time steps. They contain a single recurrent hidden layer whose hidden state output is fed back into the same layer as input for the next step. This creates an information loop that allows the network to remember and preserve information across a sequence. They include an internal loop that allows information to persist in the network's hidden state. The hidden state encodes knowledge of all inputs seen previously at any given timestep. This memory allows vanilla RNNs to develop complex temporal dynamics and model long range sequential dependencies. However, in practice vanilla RNNs suffer from issues like exploding and vanishing gradients that make it hard to learn long-term patterns. Variations like LSTMs and GRUs overcome some of these limitations via gated architectures better suited to capture long-range dependencies. But the basic formulation of RNN recurrence remains at the heart of all such sequential modelling networks in machine learning.

#### *Long Short-Term Memory (LSTM)*

Long Short-Term Memory networks are suited for learning long-term dependencies within sequential data. LSTMs incorporate a specialized gating mechanism in their recurring memory cell that regulates information flow and enables the networks to preserve and selectively pass context over longer spans of input sequences. This capability addresses a core issue with vanilla RNNs—that of vanishing and exploding gradients over time that inhibit learning correlations over larger time lags. Each LSTM unit or cell contains a cell state vector storing contextual representations necessary for such long-range modelling. A set of learnable gates—the forget gate, input gate and output gate are responsible for operations on this longer-term memory. The forget gates output (a value between 0 and 1) for each cell state component controls its retention or forgetting whereas input gates regulate incoming cell updates. The output gates determine components of the cell state to output. Combining all, LSTM gates enable selective storage, update and retrieval of long-term knowledge. Chained LSTM units pass updated memory cell contents from one processing step to the next, allowing information persistence over extended time intervals. This functionality allows LSTMs to effectively preserve context and model intricate long-term temporal dynamics within sequence data. So, these addresses the problem of long-term dependencies and gradients in vanilla RNNs. These use gates and an internal cell state to store information over longer sequences and are very commonly used. The key elements which comprises the LSTM architecture are:

***Cell State:*** This is the memory of the LSTM cell which runs straight down the entire LSTM chain, carrying relevant information.

***Forget Gate:*** It decides what information should be removed or kept from the cell state.

***Input Gate:*** It determines which values from the input will be updated in the cell state. It has a sigmoid layer for importance filters and tanh layer for creating candidate values.

***Output Gate:*** It determines which parts of the cell state will be output. Output is based on cell state filtered by the output gate.

***Hidden State:*** It carries output information from the LSTM cell to the next cell in the chain or final neural network layers.

The LSTM has explicit memory capabilities due to the cell state component. Chaining LSTM units enables selectively passing relevant context down the sequence chain via cell and hidden states. This architecture lets LSTMs retain and access longer term temporal dependencies.

### *Gated Recurrent Unit (GRU)*

Gated Recurrent Units or GRUs are another gating mechanism-based variant of RNN, and similar to LSTMs, they are also used for processing sequential data while retaining long-range dependencies. They were formulated to be a simpler alternative to LSTMs with fewer parameters, yet competitive predictive capabilities. GRUs contain two main gates – a reset gate and update gate which allows adaptive control of how information flows along recurrent connections to subsequent time steps.

The reset gate in a GRU layer is responsible for selectively allowing parts of the previous hidden state and influence the current hidden state. Whereas, the update gate determines what quantity of the candidate activation should be transferred to the next state. A larger update gate value indicates more information passed along the sequence chain while the reset gate disregards non-salient portions of earlier states dynamically based on current inputs. By combining the previous hidden representation and element-wise weighted candidate activation using these dual gates over timesteps, GRUs can better model complex temporal relationships as signals propagate down recurrent connections. While GRUs lack an isolated memory component as in

LSTMs, their cell state nonetheless integrates useful history from potentially long input sequences to make predictions informed by wider context at each timestep. With fewer parameters and operations per gating, GRUs can offer computational advantages and often achieve comparable performance to LSTMs on sequence modelling tasks.

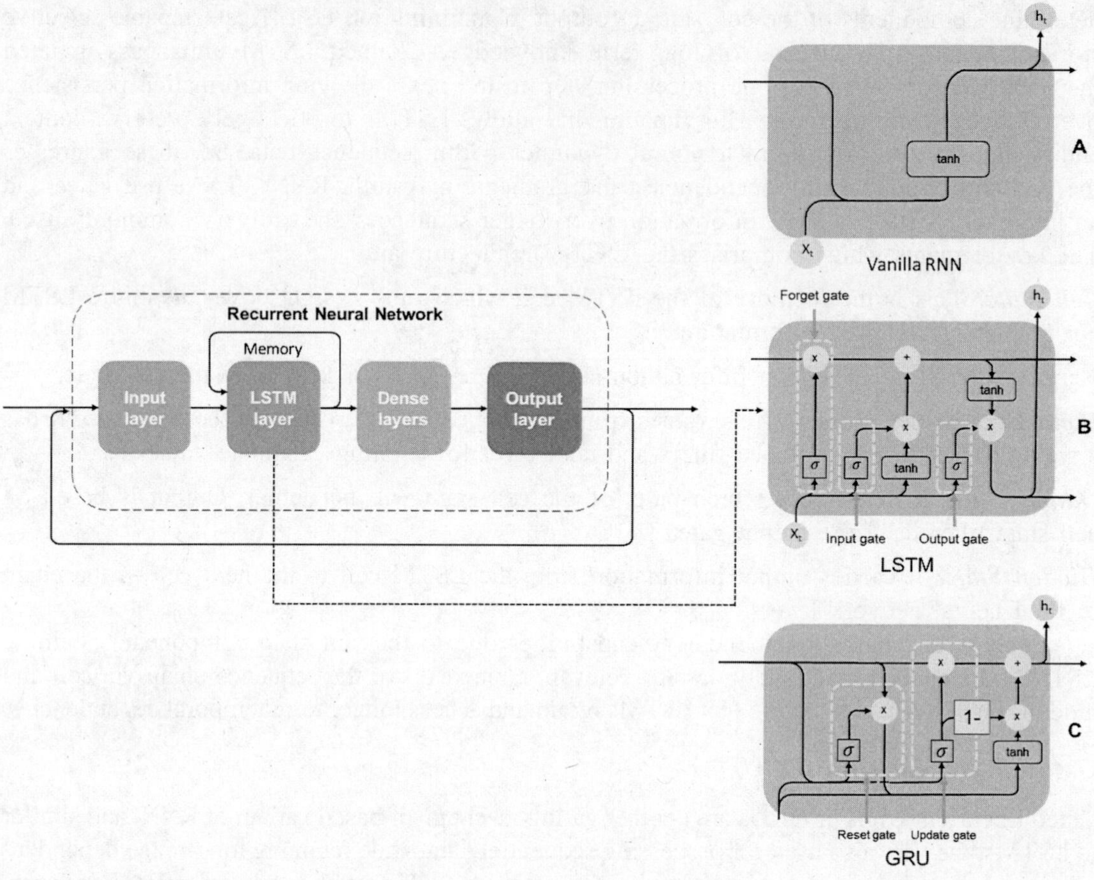


**FIGURE 8.5** Representations of RNN networks with some widely used models (A) Vanilla RNN (B) LSTM and (C) GRU.

**TABLE 8.3** A detailed comparison among RNNs, LSTM, GRU and Transformer

| *Features* | *RNNs* | *LSTM* | *GRU* | *Transformer* |
|---|---|---|---|---|
| Overview | Recurrent Neural Network that processes sequential data by maintaining a hidden state. | Long Short-Term Memory, a type of RNN that addresses the vanishing gradient problem | Gated Recurrent Unit, a simplified variant of LSTM with fewer parameters | Employs self-attention mechanisms to directly understand relationships between elements in a sequence, without recurrence. |

| *Features* | *RNNs* | *LSTM* | *GRU* | *Transformer* |
|---|---|---|---|---|
| Key Characteristics | Recurrent connections, hidden state | Memory cell with forget, input, output gates | Has two gates: Update and reset gates, simpler structure | Multi-head self-attention layers, encoder-decoder structure, positional encoding |
| Model Variants | Vanilla, Bi-directional RNN, Deep RNN, GRU-RNN | Peephole LSTM, Coupled Input and Forget Gate LSTM (CIFG), Deep stacked LSTM | Minimal Gated Unit (MGU), various attention-based GRUs | BERT, GPT Series, T5, variations with different attention types |
| Data Requirements | Moderate (can overfit on smaller datasets). | Moderate to large (better with more data to handle long-term dependencies). | Moderate to large (similar to LSTM) | Very large datasets for optimal performance. |
| Computational Cost | Moderate. | High. | Moderate to high (lower than LSTM). | Very High. |
| Training | Gradient vanishing/ exploding issues during backpropagation can impede training on long sequences. | Addresses vanishing gradient problem better than RNNs, but still faces challenges with very long sequences. | Generally faster convergence due to fewer parameters and simpler structure, but may struggle with very long sequences. | Self-attention mechanisms enable efficient training on very long sequences, but require large amounts of data. |
| Training Time | Longer training time due to sequential processing and vanishing gradient problem. | Longer training time compared to GRU and Transformer due to more complex structure. | Shorter training time compared to LSTM and RNN due to simpler structure. | Can be faster to train due to highly parallelizable nature, but may require more data. |
| Parallelization | Limited parallelization due to sequential nature, hindering training speed. | Limited parallelization compared to GRU and Transformer. | Allows for more parallelization than LSTM due to simpler architecture. | Highly parallelizable computation, enabling faster training on hardware with multiple cores or GPUs. |
| Memory Usage | Linearly increases with sequence length due to recurrent connections. | Linearly increases with sequence length, but can maintain long-term dependencies more effectively. | More memory efficient compared to LSTM due to fewer parameters. | Memory efficient due to parallelization and self-attention mechanisms. |

(*Contd.*)

| *Features* | *RNNs* | *LSTM* | *GRU* | *Transformer* |
|---|---|---|---|---|
| Utility | Speech recognition, language translation, time series forecasting. | Machine translation, text generation, sentiment analysis, handwriting recognition, video captioning. | Similar applications to LSTM, potentially faster with slightly less accuracy in some cases. | Machine translation, language modeling, text summarization, question answering, excels in many NLP tasks. |
| Advantages | Handles sequential data, temporal dependencies. | Handles long-term dependencies effectively, mitigates vanishing/ exploding gradients. | Faster training compared to LSTM, potentially less computationally expensive. | Efficient for long sequences, parallelizable, better performance on many NLP tasks. |
| Disadvantages | Vanishing/ exploding gradients, especially for longer sequences. | More computationally intensive and Complex structure, computationally expensive. | Less powerful memory compared to LSTM. | Requires very large datasets for optimal training, can be computationally intensive. |

### 8.6.3 Bidirectional RNNs

Bidirectional RNNs (BiRNNs) are an extension of traditional RNNs that enable the network to learn from both past and present context within input sequences. This is achieved by simultaneously training two separate recurrent networks on the same sequence - one processing the sequence in chronological order and another in reverse order. BiRNNs consists of forward and backward RNNs layers with independent sets of recurrent weights applied to the sequence in opposing time directions. The forward layer trains on the input sequence as it is, while the backward layer trains on a reversed copy, allowing the networks to preserve both past and future information at every timestep. This dual processing allows encoding of the full context around each point in the sequence as it flows through the dual recurrence flows. The outputs from the forward and backward passes are typically combined via concatenation or summation to give the final output layer access to synthesized bidirectional context. Intuitively, this bilateral context exposure allows BiRNNs to learn implicit relationships within sequential data more effectively than single-direction RNNs alone. Bidirectional architectures are commonly employed to boost performance across applications involving natural language processing, handwriting recognition, speech recognition, and other temporal sequence modelling tasks.

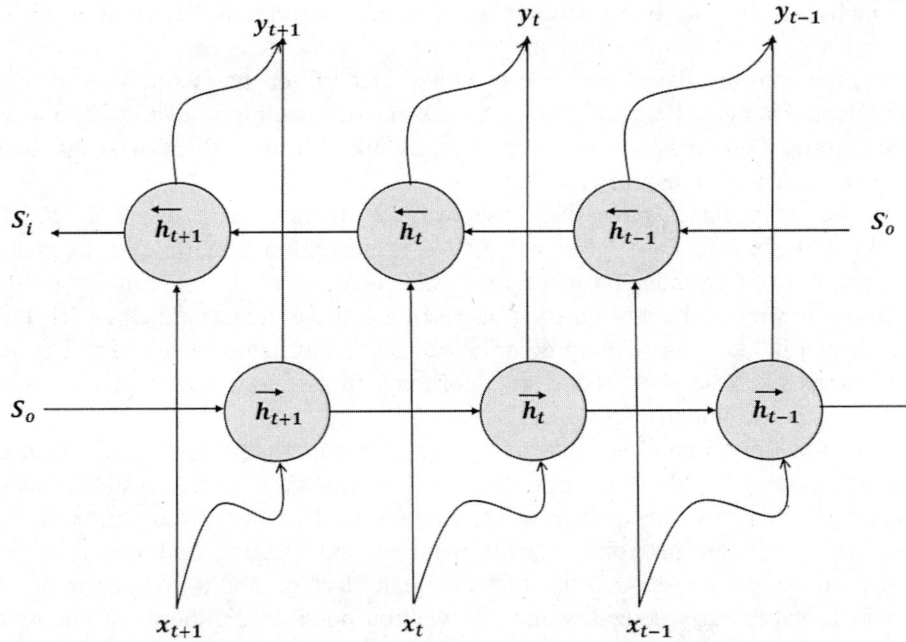


**FIGURE 8.6** Generic representation of Bi-directional RNNs.

## 8.7 CNN AND RNN IN HEALTHCARE: A CASE STUDY

The human liver, which is the largest internal organ (around 1.5 kg in adults) plays a vital role in regulating many essential physiological processes. The liver is located in the upper abdominal cavity just below the diaphragm and performs over 500 critical functions related to digestion, immunity, metabolism, detoxification, nutrient storage and blood clotting regulation. Given its central role in regulating essential chemicals, metabolizing substances, and filtering the blood, liver disease can be very serious. Some of the critical liver diseases commonly seen in human population includes Tumours, Cancer, fibrosis and Non-Alcoholic Fatty Liver Disease (NAFLD).

Liver tumours develop when normal liver cells grow abnormally and uncontrollably to form abnormal mass growths within the organ. Primary liver tumours originate in the liver itself. This includes hepatocellular carcinomas (HCC) stemming from hepatocytes, and cholangiocarcinoma originating in bile duct cells. Risk factors are cirrhosis, chronic inflammation, and some genetic conditions. Diagnosis incorporates imaging, blood tests and biopsies. Liver cancer refers to malignant tumours originating in the liver's cells and HCC which starts in the main liver cell type called hepatocytes are quite predominant. HCC accounts for 75-85% of primary liver cancers. Imaging tests like CT scans and MRIs examine tumours while biopsies confirm malignancy. Liver fibrosis refers to the buildup of scar tissue in the liver resulting from chronic damage and inflammation. It stems largely from non-alcoholic fatty liver disease (NAFLD), viral hepatitis infections, alcohol abuse, autoimmune disorders, or metabolic conditions. When the liver is injured repeatedly over years by these causes, excessive extracellular matrix proteins and collagen fibres accumulate as part of the healing response. NAFLD is the build-up of excess fat in liver cells that is not caused by alcohol consumption. It ranges from simple fatty liver, which by itself causes no damage, to non-alcoholic steatohepatitis (NASH) where severe inflammation can scar liver tissue and eventually lead to cirrhosis similar to that caused by long–term alcohol abuse. Diagnosis of NAFLD and determining severity into steatosis, NASH-induced fibrosis or cirrhosis relies on imaging like ultrasound, MRI scans and liver enzyme tests plus invasive biopsy for confirmation.

Whereas medical sciences have their own way of treating these diseases, the role of neural networks and specifically CNNs and RNNs is exceptional in tumour segmentation, cancer prediction, fibrosis grading, fat assessment and many more. In most of these diseases, imaging is a common way of diagnosing liver diseases, but these images are also a large source of dataset which can be used to develop complex models using neural networks. The various ways or applications of these state-of-the-art algorithms in different stages of these diseases have been depicted in the underlying table.

Neural networks are so good at interpreting complex patterns from a variety of datasets, they have become essential tools in the diagnosis of liver disease. These models are excellent at feature learning; they can gather pertinent information on their own from unprocessed data, including demographics about patients, medical histories, and imaging findings. They provide excellent prediction accuracy by taking use of their flexibility and ability to capture non-linear interactions, which makes early detection and intervention possible. Furthermore, the precision of risk assessment and treatment planning is improved by their capacity to customize forecasts based on unique patient profiles. They are also essential research instruments that aid in the identification of new biomarkers and treatment targets. All things considered, neural networks in general and algorithms like CNNs/RNNs in particular are essential for the prediction of liver illness because they use machine learning to evaluate complicated medical data and provide priceless information for prognosis, diagnosis, and individualized patient care.

## SUMMARY

CNNs and RNNs represent two leading neural network architectures driving major advances in areas like computer vision and natural language processing. This chapter first introduces CNN, explaining how they use kernels and convolutional layers for hierarchical feature extraction from pixel inputs. Key concepts covered include local receptor fields, weight sharing, pooling layers, and shift invariance. The transformational impact of increasingly deep CNNs across image classification, object detection, segmentation, and other vision tasks is explored. Strengths like automatic feature learning as well as challenges like opacity and data dependence are discussed. The later part of the chapter covers RNNs, describing how they model variable length sequence data through cyclical connections passing state across time steps. LSTM networks and GRUs overcome issues like vanishing gradients and have made exceptional contributions in areas like translation, speech processing, and time series analysis. A case study is also discussed towards the end to show the large contribution of CNNs/RNNs in diagnosing critical liver diseases leading to cancer.

## WORKED OUT EXAMPLES

**EXAMPLE 8.1** A researcher is designing a CNN model for classifying images in the CIFAR-10 dataset which has the dimensions 32 × 32 × 3. If each input image passes through the following – a convolutional layer with kernel size of 5 × 5 and a stride of 1; a max pooling layer with a filter size of 2 × 2 and a stride of 2, what are the dimensions of the output feature map after the max pool layer?

***Solution:*** Given, input image dimensions: 32 × 32 × 3

Convolution layer:

Kernel size: 5 × 5
Stride: 1

Output dimensions of convolution layer is:

Width: 32 – 5 + 1 = 28
Height: 32 – 5 + 1 = 28
Channels remain same at 3

Max pooling layer

Filter Size: 2 × 2
Stride: 2

Output dimensions after max pool are:

Width: 28/2 = 14 (integer division rounding down)
Height: 28/2 = 14
Channels stay at 3

Therefore, the output feature map dimensions after the CNN convolutional and max pooling layers = 14 × 14 × 3

**EXAMPLE 8.2** A bidirectional RNN model is designed where the input sequence has a maximum length of 50 timesteps. If there are two RNN layers, one processing the sequence forwards and the other backwards, both with 128 hidden units, what is the total parameter size of the bidirectional model?

***Solution:***

*Given,*

Input sequence max length = 50 timesteps

There are two RNN layers (forward and backward)

Each RNN layer has 128 hidden units

So, parameters per layer is: $(\text{input}_{\text{features}} + \text{hidden}_{\text{units}}) \times \text{hidden}_{\text{units}}$

As only previous hidden state is input we take input as 128

Therefore, parameters per layer = (128 + 128) × 128 = 256 × 128 = 32,768

There are two such bidirectional layers

So total parameters = 2 × 32,768 = 65,536

Therefore, the total number of parameters in the full bidirectional RNN model is 65,536

**EXAMPLE 8.3** An RNN processes sequences with a maximum length of 50-time steps. If each time step processes an input vector of size 100 and the hidden state vector is size 200, how many multiply-add operations are needed per sequence?

***Solution:***

Given,

Maximum sequence length: 50-time steps

Input vector size: 100

Hidden state vector size: 200

To calculate the number of multiply-add operations per sequence, we need to consider the matrix multiplication operation between the input vector and weight matrix, and between the previous hidden state vector and another weight matrix.

**Step 1:** Calculate the number of multiply-add operations for the input vector multiplication. Number of operations = (Input vector size) × (Hidden state vector size) × (Sequence length) Number of operations = 100 × 200 × 50 = 1,000,000

**Step 2:** Calculate the number of multiply-add operations for the hidden state vector multiplication. Number of operations = (Hidden state vector size)$^2$ × (Sequence length) Number of operations = $200^2 \times 50 = 2{,}000{,}000$

**Step 3:** Add the operations from both steps to get the total number of multiply-add operations per sequence.

Total operations = Operations for input vector multiplication + Operations for hidden state vector multiplication

Total operations = 1,000,000 + 2,000,000 = 3,000,000

Therefore, for an RNN with a maximum sequence length of 50-time steps, an input vector size of 100, and a hidden state vector size of 200, the number of multiply-add operations needed per sequence is 3,000,000.

## EXERCISES

1. A colour image of size 224 × 224 × 3 passes through a convolutional layer with stride 2 and padding 1 followed by maxpool layer with kernel size 3 and stride 2. Find total compression from input to output of both layers.
2. If you have an input image of size 128 × 128 × 3 and you apply a convolutional layer with 20 filters of size 5 × 5 × 3 with a stride of 1 and no padding, what will be the depth of the output feature maps?
3. A 20-layer CNN model has the following architecture: First 10 layers have 256 filters each of 3 × 3 kernel Next 5 layers have 512 filters each of 3 × 3 kernel Last 5 layers have 512 filters each of 1 × 1 kernel Image input size if 84 × 84, find total parameters.
4. Video frames of 50 × 50 × 3 are input to 3D CNN filter of size 5 × 5 × 5, stride 2. What is the output dimension?

5. An input image of dimension 224 × 224 × 64 passes through a convolutional layer with 128 filters of kernel size 5 × 5 and stride 2 followed by a maxpool layer of size 3 × 3 and stride 3. What is the output dimension?

## BIBLIOGRAPHY


Aggarwal, C. C. (2018). *Neural Networks and Deep Learning* (Vol. 10, No. 978, p. 3), Springer.

Goodfellow, I., Bengio, Y. and Courville, A. (2016). *Deep Learning*, MIT Press.

Michelucci, U. (2018). *Applied Deep Learning. A Case-Based Approach to Understanding Deep Neural Networks,* Apress.

Michelucci, U. (2019). *Advanced Applied Deep Learning: Convolutional Neural Networks and Object Detection*, Apress.

Venkatesan, R. and Li, B. (2017). *Convolutional Neural Networks in Visual Computing: A Concise Guide,* CRC Press.

Chapter 9

# Pattern Recognition and Feature Recognition

## 9.1 INTRODUCTION

Pattern Recognition is a key area in computer science that focuses on developing algorithms capable of identifying and interpreting repetitive patterns or behaviors in data. This technology is invaluable for a wide array of applications including anomaly detection, image classification and speech recognition. By leveraging advanced algorithms, computers can effectively analyze and understand complex datasets, leading to enhanced decision-making and problem-solving capabilities. These sophisticated algorithms employ methodologies from machine learning, neural networks, and statistical techniques to recognize intricate patterns, thus enabling applications ranging from medical diagnostics to security surveillance.

Pattern recognition helps in various fields including data mining, document detection, speech recognition, Bioinformatics, remote sensing and computer assisted diagnosis.

In statistical terms, pattern recognition often involves drawing general conclusions from specific observations, using an empirical and nonparametric approach. This process is similar to classification engineering where the primary goal is classifying the data based on observed variables.

The quality of features is assessed by their effectiveness in distinguishing between different classes. Similar feature values are grouped together within the same class samples. To enhance classification accuracy, features are mapped to a feature space and subsequently analyzed by a classifier. Classification methods are broadly categorized into statistical techniques, which focus on quantitative attributes like length and texture, and structural (or syntactic) techniques, which address qualitative features and the structural relationships within objects. A third category, cognitive methods, combines elements of both approaches, utilizing techniques including neural networks and genetic algorithms to further refine pattern recognition capabilities.

## 9.2 CLASSIFICATION SYSTEM

### 9.2.1 The Classification Process

The process begins with a sensing stage where a microphone or camera captures the signal. This is followed by a pre-processing step, which prepares the image for segmentation—a critical phase for effective analysis. During pre-processing, issues such as missing data and outliers are addressed to ensure data integrity. Segmentation then divides the image into meaningful regions including foreground (the objects of interest) and the background (remaining areas). Segmentation can be performed using two primary approaches: Region based methods which detect similarities within regions and the boundary-based methods that identify and connect the edges to delineate the boundaries of these regions. Post-processing of the segmented image is often employed for feature extraction, which further refines the analysis by highlighting relevant characteristics of the identified regions. Figure 9.1 depicts a fundamental classification system without feedback loops among different stages.

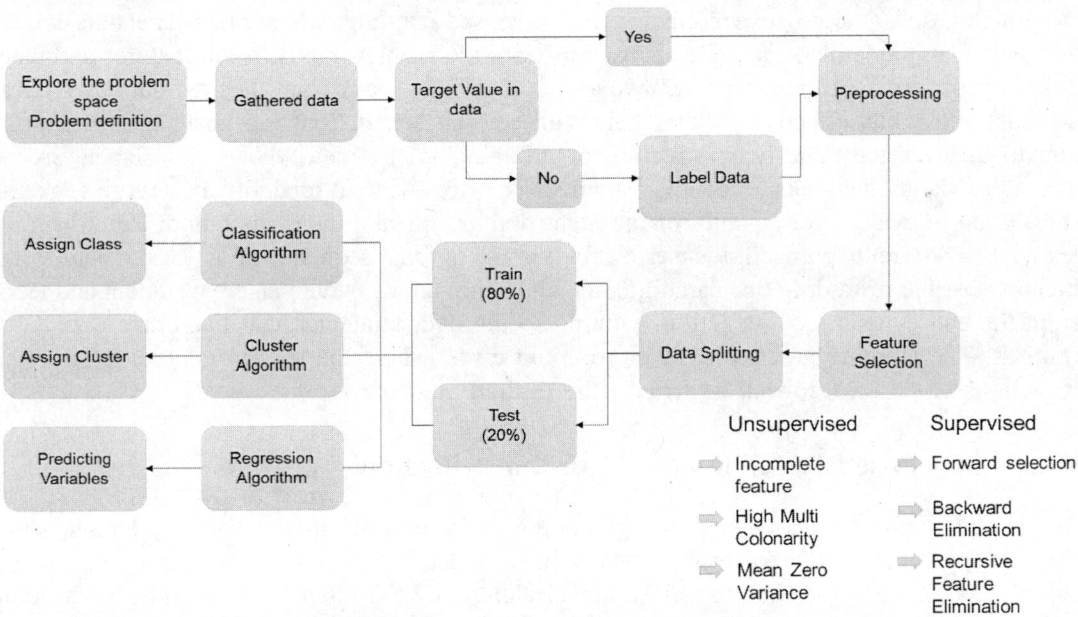


**FIGURE 9.1** A basic classification system.

### 9.2.2 Features

The next step in the classification process is feature extraction, which involves identifying and quantifying unique properties of objects that are consistent within a class but distinct between different classes. Features can be continuous, such as measurements of length or area, or categorical, like department names or object labels. They encapsulate various attributes of objects, including structural and shape characteristics, such as size, aspect ratio, and circularity, often derived from histograms or texture analyses. The aim of the classification is to assign objects to respective classes based on these features. A critical challenge is selecting the most effective features and determining how many to measure. Measuring too many features increases the dimensionality of the feature space, which can complicate the classification process and lead to issues such as overfitting. Feature selection techniques are employed to address this by identifying most relevant features that enhance classification accuracy and reducing complexity.

Classification is typically performed using a training set of labeled objects, where each object is represented as a feature vector in the vector space. A classifier is built based on the training data which defines a decision boundary/hyperplane that separates different classes. The classifier learns from the examples to accurately assign new, unseen objects to the appropriate class based on their feature vectors.

### 9.2.3 Training and Learning

Effective training and testing of a classification system are crucial for achieving accurate results. The primary objective is to identify features that minimize variations within classes while maximizing differences between classes. In supervised learning, where class labels are known, a dataset with predefined categories is used to learn the relationship between features and labels is known as "training the classifier," where the algorithm learn from labelled data to generate a model and it can effectively classify new unseen dataset. In contrast, unsupervised learning aim to uncover the underlying structure or grouping in the data whose class labels are not available. The model seeks to identify patterns or clusters without predefined categories, making it essential to evaluate the quality of the identified groups and their separation. Reinforcement learning, a different approach, focuses on finding the optimal sequence of actions to achieve the highest possible reward. In this paradigm, the algorithm interacts with an environment and learns from the consequences of its actions, aiming to discover strategies that maximize cumulative rewards. The learning process involves trial and error, where the system continuously refines its actions based on feedback to achieve the desired outcome.

### 9.2.4 Supervised Learning and Algorithm Selection

Supervised learning employs empirical reasoning to derive rules from a training dataset, which are then applied to new instances (test sets) using a selected or developed classifier algorithm. In this method, a dataset is used to train a model along with the input features and known output labels. The goal of the algorithm is to learn the relationships and underlying pattern among the features and label them during training methods. After the model is trained, it is applied on a new or unseen data to make predictions. Figure 9.2 illustrates a basic representation of this process, showing how supervised learning involves training a classifier on labelled data and then using it to classify new examples.

Selecting the appropriate learning algorithm is an important step in developing an effective classification model. The chosen algorithm must be applied to the training set and evaluated to ensure its reliability before deployment. Prediction accuracy is the common measurement to validate the developed model and it can be assessed using several techniques:

***1. Train-Test Set Split:*** This technique entails partitioning the dataset into two segments: a training set and a test set, commonly employing a 3:1 ratio. The classifier undergoes training with the training set and is subsequently assessed using the test set. This methodology offers a fundamental estimation of the model's efficacy when applied to novel, previously unobserved data.

***2. Cross-Validation:*** Cross-Validation (CV) involves partitioning the training dataset into several equally sized subsets, referred to as folds. The classifier is trained on a selection of these folds, while one-fold is reserved for testing purposes. This procedure is iterated for each fold, allowing for the calculation of the average error across all iterations. This methodology enhances the reliability of performance estimation by utilizing various subsets for both training and evaluation.

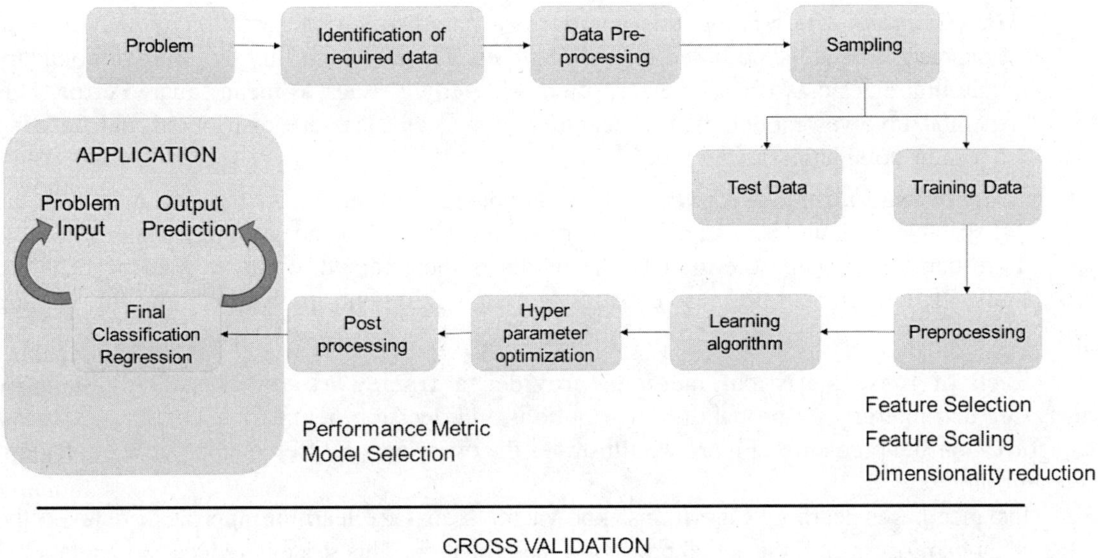


**FIGURE 9.2** A pictorial representation of classification process. Once we identified the problem, collection of required data is the preliminary step. The second step is data preprocessing technique including handling of missing data, feature selection and feature extraction methods. The data is further divided as training and testing set. The training data will be used to train the algorithm whereas the testing data will be used evaluate the model. If the model produces satisfactory results in cross validation stage it will be considered as the final model.

***3. Leave-One-Out Validation:*** It is a CV method in which every instance within the dataset is considered as a test set at a time while other instances are collectively considered as the training set. Such an approach yields a thorough assessment of the classifier's error, as it evaluates the model against each distinct data point, thereby offering an extensive perspective on its performance.

These techniques help gauge the accuracy and reliability of the classifier, ensuring that the chosen algorithm performs well on new, unseen data.

## 9.2.5 Classification Approaches

There are several distinct approaches to classification, each employing different methodologies to categorize data into predefined classes:

1. ***Statistical Methods:*** These methods rely on probability models to classify objects based on features extracted from input data. They involve determining the probability

distribution of each object to establish decision boundaries between classes. Classification is performed by comparing these distributions to user-defined criteria or algorithmically derived boundaries. For instance, Bayesian networks, a prominent statistical machine learning algorithm, use prior probabilities to compute posterior probabilities, aiding in classification.

2. ***Discriminant Analysis:*** In this approach, a parametric representation of the decision boundary is established based on training data. The aim is to find the optimal boundary that minimizes classification error, often using criteria such as mean squared error. This method involves modeling how features from each class are distributed and defining decision boundaries accordingly.
3. ***Maximum Entropy Methods:*** These methods are grounded in the principle that the distribution should be as uniform as possible. Using labeled training data, constraints are derived to shape the model. The model is then trained to ensure that the resulting distribution aligns with these constraints, maximizing entropy while fitting the training data.

Each of these statistical methods provides a framework for classifying data by analyzing and interpreting probability distributions and decision boundaries, enabling effective categorization and prediction. Figure 9.3 illustrates the overview of different approaches in pattern recognition.

Instance based learning algorithms, known for their lazy learning approach, delayed the generalization process until the actual process of classification. This strategy reduces computational demands during the training phase but increases the computational load during classification. The nearest neighbor algorithm exemplifies this method, offering a straightforward approach to instance-based learning. It operates by comparing the features of new instances with those in the training set to find the closest match, thus determining the classification based on proximity.

***Rule-based Classifiers, Syntactic Methods, and Decision Methods:*** These non-metric approaches classify patterns by posing a series of questions. This method is more intuitive for categorical data where responses are typically binary (e.g., "true/false" or "yes/no"). The subsequent question relies on the previous question. However, this approach can also be adapted for quantitative data. In the decision tree structure, where nodes represent decision points connected in a hierarchical manner until reaching terminal nodes that indicate the final classification.

***Neural Networks (NNs) Support Vector Machines (SVMs):*** These cognitive approaches are inspired by the human brain's structure and functionality. Neural networks, akin to the brain's network of neurons, excel in modeling complex non-linear relationships between inputs and outputs through serial training processes. SVMs, on the other hand, hypothesize training examples as points in a "*d-dimensional space*", with a hyperplane (of dimension d-1) used to separate these points. The objective is to arrange this hyperplane in a manner that maximizes the separation between the various classes on either side, thereby improving the accuracy of classification.

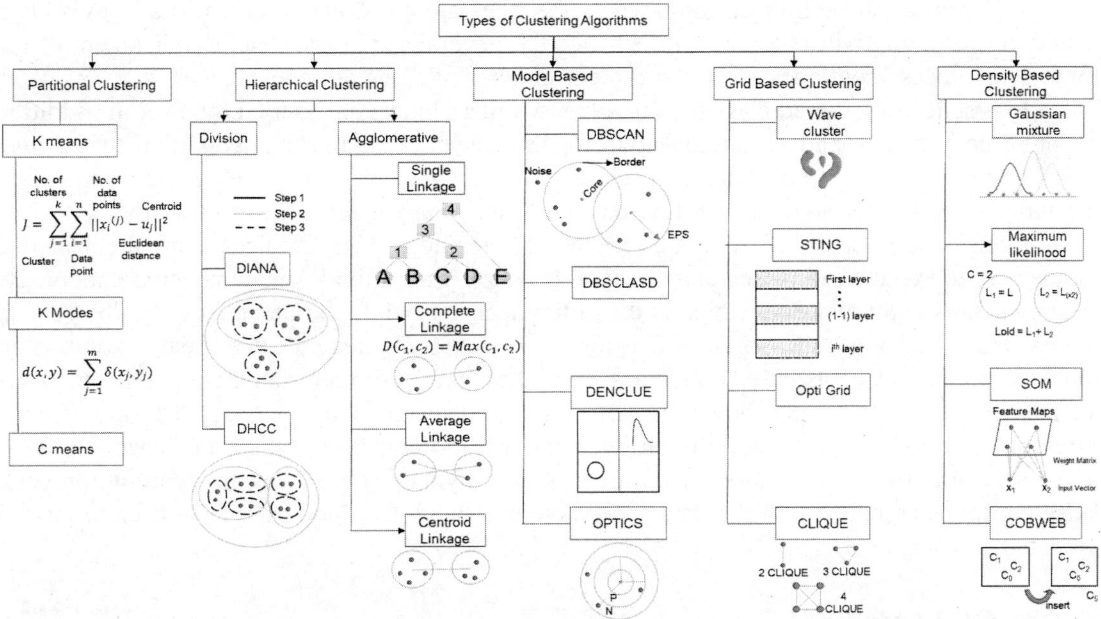


**FIGURE 9.3** Different approaches in pattern recognition. Partitional clustering, hierarchical clustering, model-based clustering, grid-based clustering and density-based clustering are the four major classifications in clustering algorithms.

## 9.3 NONMETRIC METHODS

When dealing with nonmetric data, attributes are treated as features. For example, consider a fruit characterized by attributes such as texture, color, taste, and size, represented as {(texture=rough), (color=black), (taste=salty), (size=small)}. Similarly, a DNA segment might be represented as "GTACCGGATT". These types of data are well suited to rule based classifiers, decision trees, and syntactic methods that can handle categorical data very effectively. These methods work by evaluating each feature against predefined criteria or decision rules, making them particularly adept at classifying nonmetric data where numerical measurement is not applicable.

### 9.3.1 Rule-based Classifier

The development of classifiers based on rules proves to be particularly advantageous when addressing issues that demonstrate overarching relationships rather than merely straightforward examples. These rules can be obtained from a decision tree, where each route from the root node to a leaf node signifies a rule articulated in the format of an **IF...THEN** statement. In situations where multiple leaves within a node are assigned to the same class, the different paths can be combined using "OR" logical function.

Rules can also be directly derived from input data using a rule-based approach. Unlike decision trees, which use a breadth-first approach to generate all possible paths simultaneously, rule-based methods typically employ a depth-first search. The aim of this approach is to minimize the specific criterion such as entropy, where the rules are constructed incrementally by adding conditions. Pruning will take place to enhance the generalisation after the establishment of the rule. This process continues until a sufficient number of rules are created.

In practice, rule-based classifiers involve two main loops: an external loop for the addition of one rule at a time and an internal loop for incrementally adding one condition to the rule. Both loops follow a greedy approach, aiming for practical efficiency rather than optimality. Pruning is applied throughout to refine the rules and improve their generalizability.

Decision tree approach serves as a classification tool which utilizes a hierarchical tree framework to execute supervised classification by employing a divide-and-conquer methodology. The tree starts at a root node, which is the initial decision point, and branches out into decision nodes. Each decision node poses a question about a specific feature of the data, resulting in binary or multi-way splits based on the answers. These branches represent the possible outcomes of the questions. During the processing of data, the decision tree is navigated to a leaf node from the root node, at this point the ultimate classification or category is established. Unlike a fixed structure, the configuration of the tree evolves dynamically during the learning process, adapting to the complexity of the data and problem at hand. Decision trees have been discussed in detail in Chapter 6.

### 9.3.2 Other Methods

Strings in languages, whether English words or DNA sequences like "TACGAATCCGCA" (A = adenine, G = guanine, C = cytosine and T = thymine respectively), are discrete sequences of nominal elements. These sequences can vary in length and present challenges in measuring similarity. For example, determining if a substring appears within a string often involves shifting characters and comparing their arrangement. Edit distance is one method to calculate the similarity or dissimilarity between two strings. It is helpful by implementing multiple basic operations including substitution, insertion, deletion to convert one string to another string.

Character arrangements often adhere to specific structural guidelines, known as grammar. For instance, legitimate phone numbers, which include area codes and local numbers, follow a defined format. Grammar can enforce such constraints and improve accuracy by providing structural rules. Optical Character Recognition (OCR) systems that interpret mathematical equations from scanned images exemplify this approach. They use predefined "slots" to match a limited set of symbols, guided by grammatical constraints.

In natural language processing, sentences are constructed based on grammatical rules. The goal of pattern recognition here is to determine whether a given sentence adheres to these rules, a process known as parsing. Various parsing techniques, including those based on finite-state machines, are employed to handle different types of grammatical models and structures.

## 9.4 SUPERVISED LEARNING

### 9.4.1 Parametric and Non-Parametric Learning

Parametric statistical classification methods leverage probability distributions, mean, and standard deviation to effectively represent different classes. Techniques such as Bayes' decision rule and discriminant analysis fall into this category. While parametric methods might experience slower training times, they offer efficiency in classifying test data once the model is trained. In contrast, non-parametric methods are particularly useful when the underlying probability distribution of the data is unknown. These methods do not assume a specific form for the distribution and instead focus on calculating density functions or identifying decision boundaries directly from the training data. An exemplary illustration of a non-parametric approach is the K-nearest neighbor (KNN) algorithm, which categorizes data points by identifying the predominant class among their closest neighbors. This method proves to be particularly effective in situations where the data distribution is intricate or poorly defined.

### 9.4.2 Supervised Pattern Detection—Bayes Decision Theory

#### *Gaussian Naïve Bayes*

The Gaussian Naive Bayes classifier represents a specific adaptation of the Naive Bayes classifier, tailored to manage continuous numerical features by presuming that these features adhere to a Gaussian (normal) distribution for each class. This variant capitalizes on the observation that numerous real-world datasets, particularly those with continuous attributes, can be accurately represented through the assumptions of normal distribution.
In the Gaussian Naive Bayes classifier, the key steps involve:

***1. Assumption of Normality:*** For each class, the features are assumed to be normally distributed. This implies that within each class, the distribution of a feature can be described by its mean μ and variance.

***2. Calculation of Probabilities:*** Given a data point with continuous features, the classifier computes the likelihood of the features belonging to each class using the probability density function of the normal distribution. For a feature $x_i$ in class $y$, the probability density function is given by:

$$\frac{1}{\sqrt{2\pi\sigma_y^2}}\exp\left(-\frac{(x_i-\mu_y)^2}{2\sigma_y^2}\right) \tag{9.1}$$

where $\nu$ and $\sigma$ represents the mean and variance of the feature in class $y$, respectively.

***3. Classification:*** The posterior probability associated with each class was calculated by employing Bayes' theorem and also it subsequently assigned the data point to the class that exhibits the highest posterior probability. This process entails evaluating the likelihood of the feature values being observed for each class and integrating this with the prior probability of the respective class.

The Gaussian Naive Bayes classifier is particularly useful in scenarios where the feature distributions are approximately normal, and it can handle continuous data effectively by modelling each feature with its own Gaussian distribution. Despite its simplicity, this approach can perform well in various practical applications where the assumptions hold reasonably well.

### *Multinomial Naïve Bayes Classifier*

This is a variant with the Naive Bayes family and is particularly effective for classification of texts that involve discrete features, such as the frequency of word occurrences. In contrast to the Gaussian Naive Bayes, which presumes that continuous features adhere to a normal distribution, the Multinomial Naive Bayes employs a multinomial distribution to model discrete features. This methodology manages word counts in documents by assessing the likelihood of feature occurrences for each class and integrating this with the prior probability of the class to generate predictions. Naive Bayes classifier is popular because of its robustness and adaptability; however, it operates under the premise of feature independence, a condition that may not always be applicable in practical scenarios. When features are interdependent—such as when certain words tend to co-occur—the classifier's accuracy may suffer. While the independence assumption streamlines the model and enhances its efficiency, it can compromise accuracy if it does not correspond well with the actual data. Therefore, while the Naive Bayes classifier is a formidable and useful tool, particularly for large datasets, it is crucial to acknowledge its limitations and explore alternative strategies or improvements when addressing feature interdependencies.

## 9.5 FEATURE SELECTION AND EXTRACTION

The intricacy of classification applications is greatly affected by the overall number of features, the quantity of training samples, and the feature space dimensionality. As the dimensionality rises, the volume of training data necessary also escalates, a phenomenon commonly known as the "curse of dimensionality." To address computational complexity, it is essential to choose a minimal yet adequate set of features. Eliminating superfluous features can aid in lowering computational expenses and improving data analysis. Nevertheless, an increase in the number of features may result in overfitting, where the model excels on training data but falters on new, unseen data. Effective dimensionality reduction techniques can be utilized to counteract this issue.

Feature selection and feature extraction are the popular dimensionality reduction techniques. Feature selection focuses on identifying a subset of the most relevant features from the initial dataset. Calculating inter and intra class distances and subset selection are common techniques which are involved in feature selection. This can be applied in supervised and unsupervised learning methods. Conversely, PCA and LDA are feature extraction techniques that seek to convert the original features into a lower dimensional representation while preserving the most critical information. Both PCA and LDA utilize linear projection methods to facilitate this reduction, thereby enhancing the efficiency and effectiveness of the classification process.

### 9.5.1 Feature Selection

#### *Interclass Distance and Intraclass Distance*

Instinctively, a small interclass distance and considerable intraclass distance can be considered as a signature class.

***Subset Selection:*** The objective of the feature selection is to determine the minimal subsets of features to optimize the accuracy of the model. Given that there are $2^d$ possible subsets for d features, assessing all subsets is not feasible when d is large. Consequently, heuristic approaches such as forward selection and backward selection are frequently employed.

***Forward Selection:*** The process commences with a null set of features, progressively incorporating one feature at a time. At each iteration, the feature that most effectively diminishes a selected error metric is included in the subset. This procedure persists until the addition of further features ceases to enhance the model's performance.

***Backward Selection:*** Starts with all available features and systematically removes them one by one. The model's performance is evaluated after each removal, and the process continues until the removal of any additional feature which significantly increases the error.
Both methods aim to find an optimal subset of features by balancing complexity and accuracy, thus improving the model's efficiency and effectiveness.

### 9.5.2 Feature Extraction

The primary objective of projection methods for dimensionality reduction is to identify a new $k(<d)$-dimensional space derived from the original d-dimensional space. The classification error probabilities from both original d-dimensional space and the reduced k-dimensional space is calculated and compared to get the efficacy of these projection methods. Ideally, when employing a Bayes decision rule, the classification error should remain stable across both dimensions, signifying that the dimensionality reduction process has successfully retained the critical information necessary for accurate classification. PCA and LDA are recognized as the two standard techniques utilized in feature extraction. These methods have been discussed in detail in Chapter 5.

## 9.6 UNSUPERVISED LEARNING

### 9.6.1 Clustering

The class labels are unknown in the unsupervised learning and thus the data are allowed to cluster themselves based on different algorithms to understand their natural cluster pattern. The data is divided into different meaningful classes or clusters in cluster analysis.
The cluster analysis is helpful in different domains,

In Biology, one can find a group of genes/proteins with similar functions.

In Medicine, different variants can be identified in diseases.

In Business, customers can be grouped for marketing activities.

In Imaging, segmentation of images to other regions or compressing image or video data (i.e., vector quantization).

Each cluster will have objects similar to each other and different from other clusters. The objects in each cluster are similar within the cluster and differ from those in other clusters

This process is effectively implemented by calculating different (dis)similarity measures, referred to as proximity measures (i.e., a power norm, such as the $L_1$ norm (city-block distance or the Manhattan distance), given by $|x_1 - y_1| + |x_2 - y_2|$; the $L_2$ norm (the Euclidean distance) given by $\sqrt{(x_1 - y_1)^2 + (x_2 - y_2)^2}$ ; or the $L_\infty$ norm (the Chebyshev or chess-board distance), given by max $\{x_1 - y_1, x_2 - y_2\}$. Defining the criterion which needs to be optimized is the next step after the selection of similarity measure (Figure 9.4).

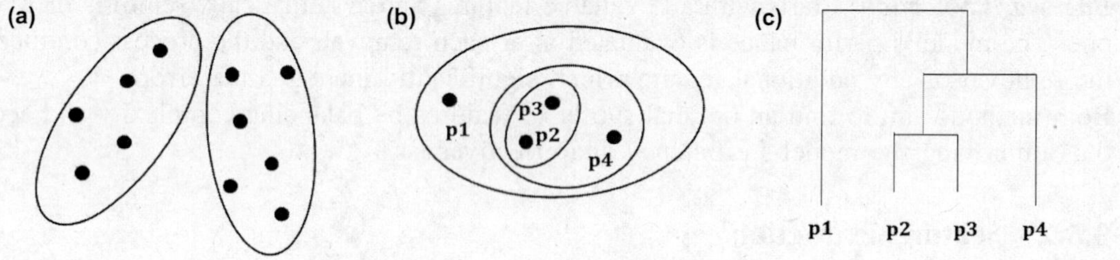


FIGURE 9.4 Different types of representation including (a) partitional clustering; (b) hierarchical clustering and (c) dendrogram.

Partitional or hierarchical are the two methods of clustering. In partitional clustering, the data is segmented into distinct, non-overlapping subsets, with each data point belonging to precisely one subset. Conversely, hierarchical clustering involves nested clusters, which are typically illustrated using a hierarchical tree or dendrogram.

### 9.6.2 k-Means Clustering

In this method similar type of prototype objects are clustered together. The newly acquired data sample will be allocated to the closest prototype, thereby it forms a cluster. The algorithm trains the data in an iterative manner to adjust to the prototype placing:

(i) Define the prototypes by randomly selecting $k$ objects from the training set
(ii) Form a cluster by assigning nearest objects to the clusters
(iii) Update the new prototype based on the centroid of the clusters
(iv) Return to step (ii) and repeat the process until convergence

The algorithm can be classified as a form of "generalized expectation-maximization (EM)" due to its inclusion of both an "assignment step" and an "update step." It is important to note that k-means clustering may not achieve convergence to the global optimum, as it operates as a heuristic algorithm. The outcomes are particularly sensitive when applied to small datasets, while it performs effectively with larger datasets containing approximately 200 to 100,000 observations. To reduce error, it is advisable to execute this algorithm multiple times with varying initial conditions (Figure 9.5).

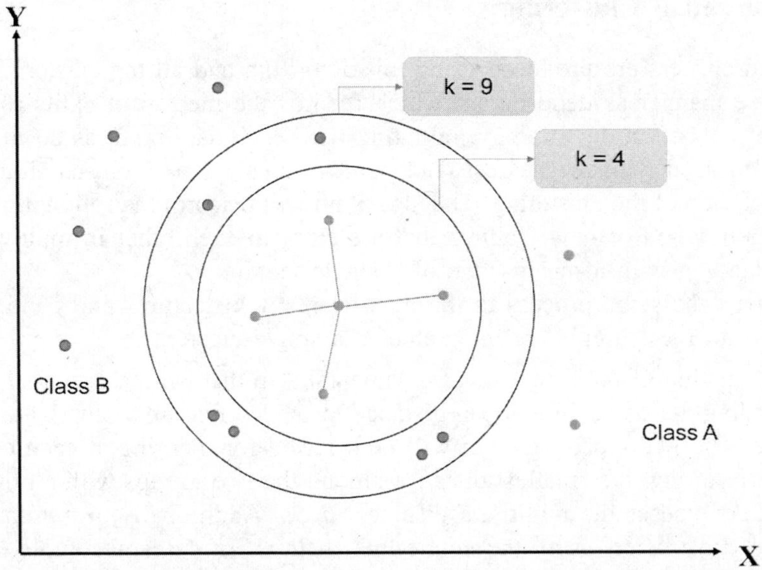


**FIGURE. 9.5** The image represents with $k = 5$, the test points can be labelled with the class of black points.

The clustering algorithm can be characterized as a greedy approach, wherein n samples are divided into $k$ clusters with the aim of minimizing the objective function. Sum of squared errors (SSE) is defined by the aggregation of the squared distances from each data point to the respective cluster. For each individual data point, the error is estimated calculating the distance between each point and distance from the nearest centroid and subsequently we can calculate the total of the squared errors.

$$SSE = \sum_{i=1}^{K} \sum_{x \in C_i} dist(c_i, x)^2 \tag{9.2}$$

In the above equation, $c_i$ = centroid of the ith cluster, dist = Euclidean distance.

The algorithm operates with a consistent value of $k$, yet employs different initial prototypes for two separate $k$-means computations. The optimal cluster is determined by identifying the lowest value of the SSE.

The algorithm's complexity is expressed as,

$$O(n \times k \times I \times d) \tag{9.3}$$

where

$n$ = the number of data points,
$k$ = the number of clusters,
$I$ = the number of iterations, and
$d$ = the number of features.

Standardization, normalization and division of loosely formed clusters are a few of pre-post-processing techniques to mitigate the influence of outliers.

### 9.6.3 Hierarchical Clustering

A set of nested clusters are produced using this algorithm and all the clusters are organized in hierarchical tree manner as dendrogram which records the merges or splits as sequence. This method employs a bottom-up strategy, initiating with each data point as an individual cluster, which is then merged with the nearest data point to create a new cluster. Larger clusters are obtained at each step of the clustering. The algorithm will perform the following tasks including:

(a) Identification of new features that are close to each other in multivariate space
(b) Replace it with a mean value of a single feature
(c) Repeat the same process to the next nearest two features and continue this process until all the features are integrated in a single cluster.

The computation of proximity is a fundamental step that can be executed through various methods, including the use of Euclidean distance, provided that all features are standardized to the same scale. The two closest groups will be selected for merging at each criterion. In case of single link clustering, the smallest distance among the two groups with all the possible pairs of elements is denoted as the minimum distance ($d_{min}$). Additionally, a minimal spanning tree (MST) will be constructed using the single-link method. In case of complete link clustering the maximum distance($d_{max}$) is calculated that represents the maximum distance between all possible pairs. The Complete-linkage clustering identifies compact clusters with relatively uniform diameters, resulting in a hierarchical structure known as a dendrogram.

## SUMMARY

In summary, this chapter has navigated the multifaceted landscape of classification and pattern recognition, delving into both supervised and unsupervised learning paradigms. We began by outlining the fundamental concepts and processes underlying classification, from feature extraction and training to the selection of appropriate algorithms. The exploration of nonmetric methods highlighted the significance of decision trees, rule-based classifiers, and other techniques. Statistical pattern recognition was addressed through the lens of probability theory and various classifiers, such as the Naïve Bayes models. Moving forward, the chapter examined supervised learning with a focus on parametric and non-parametric methods, including the nuances of Gaussian and multinomial Naïve Bayes. Nonparametric approaches, such as k-Nearest Neighbors and neural networks, were discussed alongside advanced techniques like kernel machines. The importance of feature extraction and selection was emphasized with methods like Principal Component Analysis and Linear Discriminant Analysis. Finally, we covered unsupervised learning, highlighting clustering techniques such as k-Means and hierarchical clustering. Collectively, these topics provide a comprehensive overview of the principles and methods used in pattern recognition, equipping readers with a solid foundation to apply these techniques in various practical scenarios.

## WORKED OUT EXAMPLES

**EXAMPLE 9.1** Devise a simple classifier that can properly classify all the four patterns and also How is a fifth adult of weight 76 kg classified using this classifier?

| *Weight (kg)* | *Class label* |
|---|---|
| 50 | Unhealthy |
| 60 | Healthy |
| 70 | Healthy |
| 80 | Unhealthy |

***Solution:***

```
def classify_weight(weight):
  if weight < 55:
  return "Underweight"
  elif 55 <= weight < 75:
  return "Normal weight"
  elif 75 <= weight < 90:
  return "Overweight"
  else:
  return "Obese"
patterns = [50, 65, 80, 95]
for weight in patterns:
  print(f"Weight: {weight} kg - Classification: {classify_weight(weight)}")
new_adult_weight = 76
print(f"\nNew adult weight: {new_adult_weight} kg - Classification: {classify_weight(new_
adult_weight)}")
```

**EXAMPLE 9.2** Three binary nodes, $M_1$, $M_2$, and $M_3$, split examples into (0, 6), (1, 5), and (3, 3), respectively. For each node, calculate its entropy, Gini impurity, and classification error.

***Solution:***

$M_1$: $P(C_0) = 0$ , $P(C_1) = 6/6 = 1$

Entropy $H(M_1) = -( 1 * \log_2(1) + 0 * \log_2(0) ) = 0$

Gini impurity $= 1 - ( 1^2 + 0^2) = 0$

Classification error $= 1 - \max(0 , 1) = 1 - 1 = 0$

$M_2$: $P(C_0) = 1/6$ , $P(C_1) = 5/6$

Entropy $H(M_2) = - ( 1/6 \times \log_2(1/6) + 5/6 \times \log_2(5/6) ) = 0.65$

Gini impurity $= 1 - ( 1/6^2 + 5/6^2) = 0.28$

Classification error $= 1 - \max(1/6 , 5/6 ) = 1 - 5/6 = 0.166$

$M_3$: $P(C_0) = 3/6 = 1/2$, $P(C_1) = 3/6 = 1/2$

Entropy $H(M_3) = - ( 0.5\log_2(0.5) + 0.5 * \log_2(0.5)) = 1$

Gini impurity $= 1 - (0.5^2 + 0.5^2) = 0.5$

Classification error $= 1 - \max(0.5, 0.5) = 1 - 0.5 = 0.5$

**EXAMPLE 9.3** The following data is collected from a supermarket. Which among the available three features (cost, volume and color) is the best classifier?

| *Item no.* | *Cost ($)* | *Volume ($cm^3$)* | *Color* | *Class label* |
|---|---|---|---|---|
| 1 | 20 | 6 | Blue | Inexpensive |
| 2 | 50 | 8 | Blue | Inexpensive |
| 3 | 90 | 10 | Blue | Inexpensive |
| 4 | 100 | 20 | Red | Expensive |
| 5 | 160 | 25 | Red | Expensive |
| 6 | 180 | 30 | Red | Expensive |

***Solution:*** First, the feature "Cost" is the best classifier because it classifies every item that is equal to or more than $100 as "expensive" and items that cost less than that amount as "inexpensive". The relationship between "cost" and "class label" is clearer than that of the two other feature because for example, if the item 7 would be pink this classifier cannot work well.

## EXERCISES

1. In a game show (Monty Hall's Let's Make a Deal) there are three closed doors. Behind one of these doors is a car, and behind the other two are goats. The contestant picks a door, and Monty opens one of the remaining doors to reveal a goat. The contestant is then given the option to switch doors. Is it to their advantage to do so? Think about it for a while. (This problem has attracted a lot of coverage, and it has been said that no other statistical problem comes so close to fooling all of the people all of the time!)
2. Three coins are tossed simultaneously. What is the probability of them showing two heads?
3. Explain the following terms (1) a patter n, (2) a class, (3) a classifier, (4) feature space, (5) a decision rule, and (6) a decision boundary.
4. The following data obtained from questionnaire survey based on two attributes (acid durability and strength) to classify whether a special paper tissue is good or not. Acid durability = 3 and strength = 7

| *X1 = Acid Durability (Seconds)* | *X2 = Strength (kg/square meter)* | *Y = Classification* |
|---|---|---|
| 7 | 6 | Bad |
| 6 | 3 | Bad |
| 2 | 3 | Good |
| 2 | 3 | Good |

## BIBLIOGRAPHY

Bishop, C. (2006). *Pattern Recognition and Machine Learning (Information Science and Statistics)*, Springer, ISBN-10: 0-387-31073-8.

Duda, R. O., Hart, P. E., and Stork, D. G. (2001). *Pattern Classification*, Wiley Publications, ISBN-10: 9788126511167.

H. Witten, H. and Frank, E. (2008). *Data Mining: Practical Machine Learning Tools and Techniques,* 2nd Edition, Elsevier, ISBN: 0-12-088407-0.

Marques, J. P. (2012). *Pattern Recognition Concepts, Methods and Applications*, Springer, ISBN: 978-3-540-42297-6.

Mitchell, T. M. (2017). *Machine Learning*, Hill Education (1st edition), ISBN-10: 1259096955.

Chapter 10

# Natural Language Processing

## 10.1 WHY NATURAL LANGUAGE PROCESSING?

Language is one of the finest ways to communicate as it helps in understanding both nature and intelligence. Natural Language Processing (NLP) is an interdisciplinary area that is derived from the convergence of Linguistics, Computer Science, and Artificial Intelligence (AI). It signifies the advancement in our capacity to establish a connection between human language and computational comprehension. NLP has become an integral part of today's digital existence, infusing various aspects of our lives. It encompasses a wide range of applications, including machine translation services that effectively break down language barriers and sentiment analysis tools that adeptly decipher the underlying emotional nuances within textual content.

NLP is also interchangeably used with computational linguistics wherein the 'linguistics' is the head of the phrase with an adjectival modifier 'computational'. This term signifies another important aspect that mere use of computers may not help modelling languages, it also requires the expertise of a linguist or language expert. These models should be simple and elegant yet detailed and precise so that it can be employed to real life data or languages which people use. Thus, language processing has turned as a confluence of different areas such as Linguistics, Statistics, Mathematics, AI, Cognitive Sciences along with Logic and Psychology. However, Machine Learning (ML) and Pattern Recognition and classification methods have become the mainstream areas. There are three major concerns in NLP—(a) Natural Language Understanding (NLU), (b) Natural Language Acquisition (NLA), and (c) Natural Language Generation (NLG). The terms producer, one who produces the language in form of speech or text and comprehender, one who listens or reads the text can be used to understand the concepts of NLP. As such, NLU refers to models of the comprehenders with which the meanings of the intentions encoded in language are understood. NLG on the other hand refers to the models of producers which explains how language can be generated to express the meaning and intensions. Finally, there are NLA, which are also the models of the comprehenders to explain how the languages can be acquired, refined for perfection as they undergo analysis. The aim of all these concepts is to build perfect mathematical models for language processing through computations.

## 10.2 PHASES OF NLP

NLP involves a series of phases or tasks which aims at processing and understanding human language. These phases are often interconnected, and the output of one phase may serve as input to another. However, they can vary to some extent depending on the specific NLP task or application.

***Text Preprocessing:*** This phase involves tasks for cleaning and equip the text data for further analysis. These tasks can be tokenization (or splitting text into words or sentences), stop words removal (or remove the common words that lack significant meaning), stemming or lemmatization (reducing words to their root form), and also managing special characters.

***Lexical Analysis:*** Also known as tokenization, this phase involves splitting the text into specific tokens, which could be words, or phrases, or any other meaningful units. This phase helps to comprehend the structure of the text and identifying the fundamental units or meaning.

***Syntactic Analysis:*** This phase focuses on analyzing the structure of sentences and how words relate to each other grammatically. It involves tasks such as parsing, which identifies the syntactic structure of sentences and assigns a grammatical label to each word (e.g., noun, verb, adjective), and part-of-speech (POS) tagging i.e. assigning specific POS to each word in the text.

***Semantic Analysis:*** Semantic analysis helps to understand the meaning of the text beyond its syntactic structure. This phase involves tasks such as named entity recognition (identifying and categorizing named entities in text), word sense disambiguation (or finding correct meaning of a word based on its context), and semantic role labeling (identifying the roles such as subject, predicate in the text).

***Discourse Analysis:*** Discourse analysis focuses on understanding the structure and flow of larger units of text, such as paragraphs, conversations, or documents. Tasks in this phase may include coreference resolution (identifying when different words or phrases refer to the same entity), discourse parsing (analyzing the relationships between sentences or segments of text), and sentiment analysis (unravelling the sentiment in the text).

***Pragmatic Analysis:*** Pragmatic analysis considers the context in which language is used and aims to understand the intentions, implications, and effects of communication. This phase involves tasks such as speech recognition (identifying the intended action or purpose behind a statement) and conversational analysis (analyzing patterns and structures in dialogues or conversations).

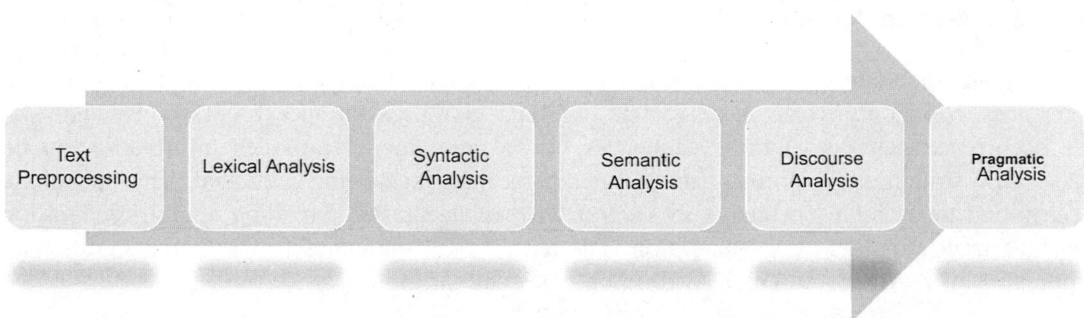


**FIGURE 10.1** Various phases in Natural Language Processing.

## 10.3 PREPROCESSING IN NLP

The progression from unprocessed text to valuable insights in NLP is guided by a series of meticulous preprocessing procedures. During the initial phase, unstructured textual data is subjected to a series of refinement and transformation steps. These steps are essential for preparing the data in a structured format that is amenable to further analysis using sophisticated machine learning techniques.

### 10.3.1 Tokenization and Segmentation

Tokenization is a fundamental process in NLP that involves segmentation of text into discrete units known as tokens such as individual words, phrases, or characters, depending on the requirements of the task under consideration. By splitting down the text into these atomic units, tokenization serves as a crucial step in various language-related applications, such as machine translation, text classification, sentiment analysis, virtual assistants, and information retrieval. As an example, consider the sentence, "Natural Language Processing is fascinating!" which can be effectively tokenized by segmenting it into individual words, resulting in the following tokens: ["Natural", "Language", "Processing", "is", "fascinating", "!"]. Tokenization is not limited to dividing text into individual words. It can also be employed in a more nuanced manner, wherein text is further disintegrated into subword units.

Segmentation is another crucial step in NLP that surpasses the mere tokenization process by discerning more substantial linguistic units within a given language. This step involves the identification and isolation of phrases, clauses, or even entire sentences, enabling a deeper insights and interpretation of the text. In English language, the process of segmentation encompasses the identification of various linguistic units, such as noun phrases exemplified by "the big brown dog" or clauses as demonstrated by "while it was raining." In languages such as Chinese, the process of segmentation assumes high importance due to the absence of explicit word delimiters. Consequently, the identification and delineation of significant linguistic units, commonly known as characters or morphemes, becomes indispensable. Segmentation encompasses the intricate procedure of partitioning a given text into its fundamental units, namely sentences. This fundamental task involves the identification and isolation of individual sentences within a given text corpus.

### 10.3.2 N-gram Model

The n-gram model involves statistical language model that controls the frequency of item sequences, commonly words or characters, within a given text or speech corpus. By analysing the occurrence patterns of these sequences, the n-gram model provides information on the underlying structure and probabilistic nature of the language being modelled. This model has been found to be highly effective in several NLP related tasks, including speech recognition, machine translation, and text generation. The term "n" in the context of n-grams signifies the cardinality of the items contained within each sequential unit.

***Unigram (n = 1):*** considers one item at a time, typically a single word.

***Bigram (n = 2):*** considers sequences of two items, usually adjacent words.

***Trigram (n = 3):*** considers sequences of three items, often adjacent words.

N-grams contributes in estimating the conditional probability of a word or item, based on the previous $n$–1 words. Mathematically, the probability of a word "W" in a set of words can be represented by,

$$p(W) = p(w_n \mid w_1, w_2, \ldots w_n) \tag{10.1}$$

Here the chain rule of probability is used to make the entire calculations which can be generalized by,

$$P(X_1, X_2, X_3, \ldots, X_n) = P(X_1)P(X_2 \mid X_1)P(X_3 \mid X_1, X_2), \ldots, P(X_n \mid X_1, X_2, \ldots, X_n) \tag{10.2}$$

$$P(w_1 w_2 w_3 .. w_n) = \prod_i P(w_i \mid w_1 w_2 .. w_n) \tag{10.3}$$

These models exhibit a remarkable ability to capture both syntactic and semantic characteristics of a language, despite their apparent simplicity. Despite their utility, these models are not without any limitations. Long-range dependencies pose a significant challenge for these models, as they exhibit limitations in capturing contextual information that extends beyond the immediate vicinity of the current position within a given sequence. This phenomenon is also commonly referred to as the "sparse data problem." The performance of n-gram models have even surpassed sophisticated models like Recurrent Neural Networks (RNNs) and Transformer models in several NLP applications.

### 10.3.3 Stemming and Lemmatization

During preprocessing and normalising of textual data, stemming and lemmatization are extensively used. Both of these techniques share the common objective of reducing words to their fundamental forms, though employing distinct methodologies to achieve this goal.

Stemming, a fundamental technique in NLP, encompasses a rule-based approach aimed at extracting the root form, or stem, of words by eliminating any attached prefixes or suffixes. This process facilitates the consolidation of related word forms, enabling more efficient analysis and comprehension of textual data. The resultant stem may not invariably conform to the lexical standards of a valid word, yet it encapsulates the fundamental essence and semantic significance of the original word.

Porter Stemmer, Snowball Stemmer, and Lancaster Stemmer are some of the widely used stemming algorithms in NLP tasks such as text classification, information retrieval, and sentiment analysis. Stemming proves to be highly advantageous in domains that prioritise efficiency, such as information retrieval or text classification tasks. However, it is important to note that the generated output may not consistently yield valid or semantically coherent words.

Lemmatization, in contrast to stemming is a highly advanced procedure with an objective to effectively reduce words to their fundamental or root form, commonly referred to as the lemma. This process is carried out with the utmost care to ensure that the resultant word remains within the confines of the given language and retains its intended semantic significance. Lemmatization surpasses stemming in terms of accuracy due to its consideration of contextual and grammatical factors associated with words. In order to map words to their base form, a common approach employed in NLP is the utilisation of dictionaries and morphological analysis techniques.

**TABLE 10.1** Comparison between stemming and lemmatization

| *Feature* | *Stemming* | *Lemmatization* |
|---|---|---|
| Accuracy | Less accurate | More accurate |
| Speed | Faster | Slower |
| Complexity | Less complex | More complex |
| Applications | Corpus analysis, text classification, information retrieval | Machine translation, information extraction |

Based on the particular application, either stemming or lemmatization is preferable. Stemming is an excellent option if speed is required whereas lemmatization is a superior option if precision is crucial.

**TABLE 10.2** Some examples of stemming and lemmatization

| *Word* | *Stemmed* | *Lemmatized* |
|---|---|---|
| better | bet | better |
| running | run | run |
| saw | saw | see |
| cats | cat | cat |
| talked | talk | talk |

### 10.3.4 Cleaning

Cleaning is an initial step in the preparation of unrefined textual data for subsequent analysis or modelling endeavours. Textual data, frequently obtained from diverse sources, can be abundant with noise, inconsistencies, and extraneous details. Text cleaning refers to the crucial process of detecting and resolving irregularities within textual data, thereby converting unprocessed text into a more polished and uniform format. The improvement in data quality not only amplifies its overall efficacy but also streamlines the efficiency of subsequent NLP tasks. By eliminating noise, inconsistencies, and irrelevant information, text cleaning improves the data quality and reliability, thereby enhancing the performance of ML models.

Some of the important steps in text cleaning includes noise reduction, case changing, tokenization, stop words removal, stemming and lemmatization.

### 10.3.5 Bag of Words

It is one of the fundamental concepts in NLP also known as BoW and holds significant importance among the various preparatory steps. The BoW methodology represents a pivotal technique in facilitating the transformation of unprocessed textual data into a quantitative representation. This approach involves the representation of textual data as a non-sequential assemblage, commonly referred to as a "bag," wherein the emphasis is placed on the individual words themselves, rather than their grammatical structure or sequential arrangement. This approach enables the facilitation of quantitative analysis and empowers algorithms to effectively operate on textual data. There are some key steps in implementing BoW.

***Tokenization:*** The initial phase of executing the BoW methodology involves tokenization, a process that entails the segmentation of text into discrete units known as tokens, which typically correspond to individual words. The aforementioned procedure entails the elimination of punctuation marks and the subsequent division of the text into a comprehensive array of individual words.

***Vocabulary Creation:*** The subsequent phase entails the development of a lexicon or compendium comprising exclusive lexical units found within the corpus. In computational linguistics, a distinctive identifier or index is allocated to every individual word, serving as a means to represent the word in a numerical format.

***Vectorization:*** Vectorization is the process of converting each document in the corpus into a numerical vector. The frequency of each word in a document is measured and populated in the corresponding entry in a vector.

Fundamentally, BoW is one way to extract features from some text through modelling. Let us consider a simple corpus of text C such that,

$$C = I\begin{cases}\text{It was the best time of life}\\ \text{It was worst time of life}\\ \text{It is a life of being wise}\\ \text{It is a life of being stupid}\end{cases}$$

A unique vocabulary list from this corpus C will be,

'It', 'was', 'the', 'best', 'time', 'of', 'life', 'worst', 'is', 'a', 'being', 'wise', 'stupid'

If each of these unique vocabular is marked as '1' for present and '0' for absent on the corpus, then they can be represented as set of 13 characters such that,

Line 1 of C = [1, 1, 1, 1, 1, 1, 1, 0, 0, 0, 0, 0, 0]
Line 2 of C = [1, 1, 0, 0, 1, 1, 1, 1, 0, 0, 0, 0, 0]
Line 3 of C = [1, 0, 0, 0, 0, 1, 1, 0, 1, 1, 1, 1, 0]
Line 4 of C = [1, 0, 0, 0, 0, 1, 1, 0, 1, 1, 1, 0, 1]

One notable constraint pertains to the disregard of word order within a given document. The issue at hand can pose a significant challenge for tasks that necessitate a comprehensive grasp of word sequencing, such as the field of machine translation. One additional constraint pertains to the BoW model's failure to incorporate contextual information associated with words. The aforementioned issue can pose a challenge in tasks that necessitate the comprehension of lexical semantics, such as sentiment analysis.

Although the BoW model possesses certain limitations, it remains an influential and versatile tool applicable to a wide range of NLP endeavours such as document classification, spam filtering, sentiment analysis, named entity recognition etc.

### 10.3.6 Vector Space Model: TF and IDF

The vector space model comprises of two pivotal steps—Term Frequency (TF) and Inverse Document Frequency (IDF) which play a vital role in the process of extracting meaningful insights from textual data. By comprehending the workings of TF and IDF, one can unlock the potential for enhanced information retrieval and document ranking.

### *Term Frequency (TF): Capturing Word Frequency*

Computing TF helps to quantitatively assess the frequency of a specific terminology (or a 'word') within a given document. This helps to quantify the importance of a term in a document by considering its frequency relative to the total number of words in that document. The information gained from these metrics are of immense value in comprehending the significance of words within distinct contextual frameworks. The key steps in for using TF are stated below:

***Tokenization and Vocabulary Creation:*** These are the same steps as mentioned in BoW which builds individual tokens and generate a vocabulary or dictionary of original terms.

***Calculating TF:*** Count the frequency of the words that appears in each document in the corpus.

***Normalization:*** In order to account for the inherent variations in document length, it is imperative to normalise the term frequency. This normalisation process ensures that the impact of term frequency is accurately represented across documents, regardless of their respective lengths. The process of achieving this is commonly accomplished by dividing the raw term frequency by the total terms count present in the document. Mathematically, for a term T, the term frequency (TF) can be computed by,

$$TF(T) = \frac{\text{No. of times T occurs in the article}}{\text{Total no. of terms in the article}} \tag{10.4}$$

### *Inverse Document Frequency (IDF): Assessing Word Importance*

IDF serves as a valuable complement to TF such that, while TF measures the frequency of a term within a specific document, IDF focuses on assessing the significance of a term across the whole corpus. IDF consider the fact that certain terms may appear frequently in individual documents but may not possess substantial importance in the broader context of the corpus. Mathematically, for a term T, the inverse document frequency (IDF) can be computed by,

$$IDF(T) = \log\left(\frac{\text{No. of documents in the corpus}}{\text{No. of documents in the corpus containing T}}\right) \tag{10.5}$$

TF-IDF quantifies the rarity or commonality of a term by considering its frequency within a specific document in relation to its occurrence across multiple documents. This metric serves as a valuable tool in information retrieval and text mining tasks, enabling the identification of terms that carry substantial discriminative power and distinguishing characteristics within a given dataset. TF and IDF are fundamental elements in NLP that quantifies the importance of terms within a given document or corpus. TF-IDF provides a powerful mechanism for determining the significance of terms in a collection of texts. The TF-IDF score is calculated by the following equation,

$$w_{ij} = TF_{ij} \times \log\left(\frac{M}{df_j}\right) \tag{10.6}$$

Where, $TF_{ij}$ is the frequency of the term $T_j$ occurs in document $D_i$ and $df_j$ is the total number of documents which contains $T_j$. This approach is widely employed in several NLP tasks, such as information retrieval, text classification, document clustering, etc. and enhance the accuracy and effectiveness of ML models.

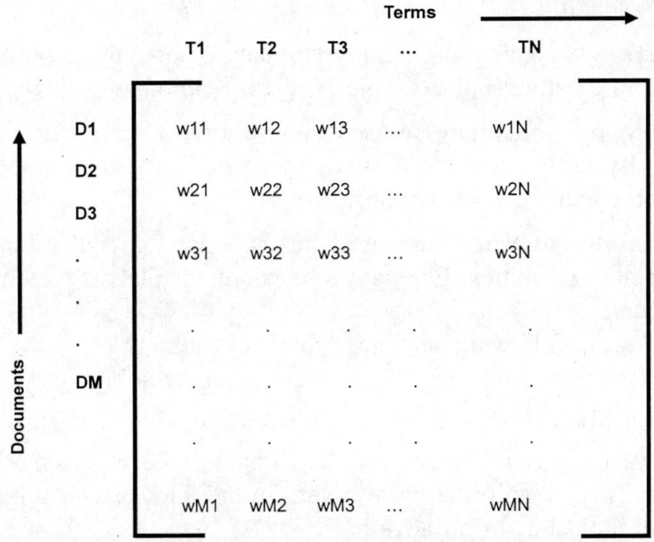


**FIGURE 10.2** Representative structure of document—term matrix.

### 10.3.7 POS Tagging

POS tagging is an essential computational linguistic task that involves the assignment of a specific grammatical category, known as a Part-Of-Speech (POS), to each word within a given document. This process relies on the analysis of contextual signs and lexical definitions to accurately determine the appropriate classification for each word. The categories encompass a wide range of linguistic elements, such as nouns, verbs, adjectives, adverbs, pronouns, prepositions, conjunctions, and various others. The task of POS tagging is commonly accomplished through the utilisation of sophisticated algorithms and models, such as Hidden Markov Models (HMMs) or neural network-based methodologies.

| **CC** Coordinating conjunction | **CD** Cardinal number | **DT** Determiner |
|---|---|---|
| **EX** Existential there | **FW** Foreign word | **IN** Preposition or subordinating conjunction |
| **JJ** Adjective | **JJR** Adjective, comparative | **JJS** Adjective, superlative |
| **LS** List item marker | **MD** Modal | **NN** Noun, singular or mass |
| **NNS** Noun, plural | **NNP** Proper noun, singular | **NNPS** Proper noun, plural |
| **PDT** Predeterminer | **POS** Possessive ending | **PRP** Personal pronoun |
| **PRP$** Possessive pronoun | **RB** Adverb | **RBR** Adverb, comparative |
| **RBS** Adverb, superlative | **RP** Particle | **SYM** Symbol |
| **TO** to | **UH** Interjection | **VB** Verb, base form |
| **VBD** Verb, past tense | **VBG** Verb, gerund or present particle | **VBN** Verb, past particle |
| **VBP** Verb, non-3rd person singular present | **VBZ** Verb, 3rd person singular present | **WDT** Wh-determiner |
| **WP** Wh-pronoun | **WP$** Possessive wh-pronoun | **WRB** Wh-adverb |

**FIGURE 10.3** Tags used in Part-of-Speech (POS) tagger.

### *Significance of POS Tagging*

***Understanding Syntax:*** POS tagging offers important details about the grammatical organisation of sentences. It assists in locating subjects, objects, verbs, and other syntax-related components.

***Ambiguity Removal:*** Many words may be used in a variety of ways (for instance, "lead" can be a verb or a noun). By designating the most likely section of speech based on context, POS tagging aids in disambiguating such situations.

***Extraction of Information:*** POS tags are used in extraction of vital information from text, including recognising named entities (like names of people or places) or sentences that follow a certain syntactic pattern.

For example, take the following sentence "She runs quickly."

The outcome after tokenization and POS tagging can resemble this:

[ ('She', 'PRP'), ('runs', 'VBZ'), ('quickly', 'RB')]

In the given context, the abbreviation 'PRP' denotes the representation of a personal pronoun, 'VBZ' signifies the manifestation of a verb in the third person singular present tense, and 'RB' serves as an indicator for an adverb.

## 10.3.8 Named Entity Recognition

NER is one of the fundamental tasks in NLP which involves the identification and classification of named entities within textual data and assigning them to predefined categories. These categories comprise of a wide range of entities, such as person names, organisations, locations, quantities, monetary values, and many more. The main objective of NER is to effectively extract and organise structured information from unstructured textual data, ultimately transforming it into a format that can be easily interpreted and processed by ML algorithms.

Development of NER tools use two prominent methodologies that have emerged–rule-based and statistical learning-based approaches.

***Rule-based NER:*** Rule-based NER systems employ a precisely designed collection of rules to effectively detect and classify named entities. These systems rely on a predetermined set of guidelines, meticulously crafted by human experts, to accurately identify and categorise entities of interest within textual data. The formulation of these rules is commonly rooted in the examination of the syntactic and semantic attributes inherent in words. Rule-based NER systems exhibit commendable speed and accuracy, making them a popular choice in various applications. However, their maintenance and adaptability to novel domains can pose significant challenges.

***Statistical Learning Based NER:*** Statistical Learning-based NER systems leverage sophisticated mathematical models to acquire the ability to discern and classify named entities. The algorithms utilised in this context have undergone training on a meticulously annotated corpus of text, wherein named entities have been identified and labelled manually. Statistical learning based NER systems frequently exhibit superior accuracy compared to their rule-based counterparts. However, these ML models may incur trade-offs in terms of computational speed and training complexity. There are numerous applications of NER which have proven it as a very important component in NLP. Some of them include information extraction, machine translation, question answering, biomedical text mining and many more.

### 10.3.9 Syntax Parsing

Syntax parsing also referred to as syntactic analysis or parsing, is an essential procedure within NLP. It encompasses the meticulous examination of the grammatical arrangement of sentences, with the aim of comprehending their underlying syntax. It is employed to ascertain the hierarchical associations among words within a given sentence, thereby discerning key constituents such as subjects, objects, verbs, and their corresponding dependencies. The comprehension of sentence meaning is contingent upon this process, as it facilitates the establishment of a systematic representation delineating the intricate interplay between words. Syntax parsing serves as a fundamental component in a multitude of NLP applications, encompassing machine translation, sentiment analysis, and question-answering systems. By enabling a more profound and intricate comprehension of language, syntax parsing plays a pivotal role in enhancing the capabilities of these NLP applications.

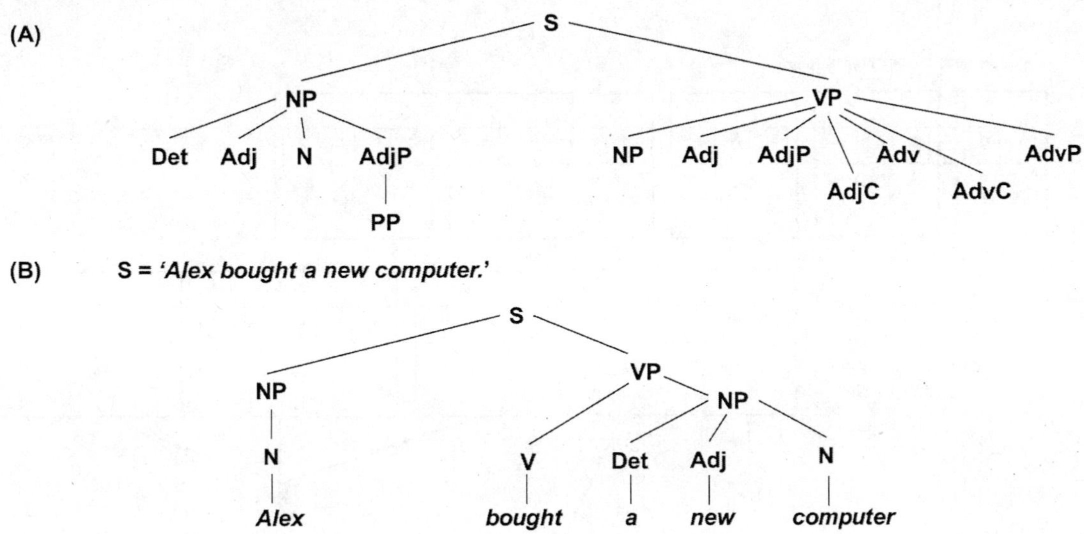


**FIGURE 10.4** (A) Syntax tree used in NLP and (B) example of forming a syntax tree.

Efficient syntax parsing is contingent upon the utilisation of sophisticated algorithms and techniques, encompassing a spectrum that spans from rule-based systems to cutting-edge statistical and machine learning models. These methodologies consider the contextual and grammatical aspects of sentences, enabling precise analysis even in intricate linguistic structures.

### 10.3.10 Chunking and Chinking

Chunking is a fundamental NLP task that entails the identification and extraction of concise phrases, commonly referred to as "chunks," from sentences. This process relies on the utilisation of POS tags to accurately identify and isolate these chunks. The constituent elements of these chunks typically comprise noun phrases, verb phrases, and other constituents. In the given example, "*The cat chased the mouse*" the application of chunking would effectively discern the constituent components, namely the noun phrase "*the cat*" and the verb phrase "*chased the mouse*." The simplification of sentence structure while preserving vital linguistic information is a pivotal undertaking in various tasks such as information extraction, NER, and shallow parsing.

In contrast, chinking refers to the systematic procedure of selectively excluding particular components from the chunks that have been identified through the process of chunking. This method offers a means to effectively eliminate extraneous components from segments, while simultaneously retaining the essential linguistic data. In the given sentence "*She purchased a visually appealing dress*" the application of a chinking rule can be employed to exclude the determiner "*a*" from the noun phrase, thereby yielding the chunk "*visually appealing dress.*" This methodology proves to be highly advantageous in the process of enhancing segmented data for the purpose of conducting more accurate and detailed analysis. The combined utilisation of chunking and chinking techniques plays a pivotal role in the development of well-organized textual representations, thereby facilitating enhanced and precise processing across a wide range of NLP applications.

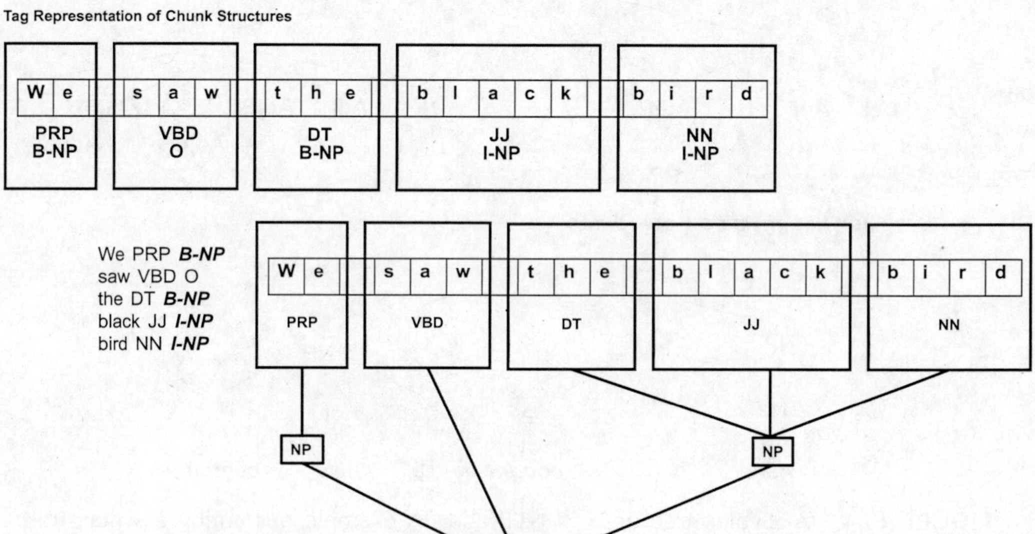


**FIGURE 10.5** The processes of chunking and chinking of a sentence(s) in NLP.

## 10.4 TEXT REPRESENTATION AND WORD EMBEDDING

Text representation and word embedding enables machines to comprehend and analyse textual data. Text representation is a crucial step in the field of ML, as it involves converting unstructured raw text data into a structured numerical format that can be effectively processed and analysed by computational algorithms. This transformation enables the application of various mathematical and statistical techniques to extract meaningful insights and patterns from textual data. By representing text in a numerical format, ML models can use the power of mathematical methods such as BoW and TF-IDF, thereby facilitating the processing and analysis of linguistic information by ML algorithms.

Word embedding represents a highly advanced approach that effectively maps words onto continuous vectors within a multi-dimensional space, thereby capturing and encapsulating intricate semantic relationships. Word2Vec and GloVe, two prominent methodologies in the field of NLP, have revolutionised the way we comprehend word semantics and contextual relationships. By generating word embeddings, these approaches enable a more sophisticated comprehension of word meanings, thereby improving the efficacy of several NLP applications such as sentiment analysis, machine translation, and information retrieval. In contrast to conventional sparse representations, which treats each term as an independent entity, word embeddings employ a novel approach by mapping words onto a continuous space according to their semantic similarities.

### 10.4.1 Matrix Factorization

Matrix decomposition, also known as matrix factorization, is a fundamental technique that entails the process of breaking down a complex matrix into its constituent parts, thereby enabling a more interpretable representation. By decomposing a matrix, it is aimed to extract underlying patterns, structures, or features that may be obscured within the original data. This process facilitates enhanced understanding and analysis of the data, leading to improved interpretability and potentially enabling more effective decision-making. This technique holds immense value for a variety of tasks, most notably collaborative filtering within recommendation systems, sentiment analysis, and topic modelling. Through the process of decomposing large matrices into lower-dimensional representations, an array of hidden patterns and intricate relationships within the data can be unveiled.

In numerous practical NLP applications, the data often exhibits high dimensionality and sparsity, thereby posing computational challenges when attempting direct processing. Matrix factorization is a powerful technique that effectively addresses the aforementioned concern by diminishing the dimensionality of the data. This process not only renders the data more tractable but also ensures that the crucial information is retained.

### 10.4.2 Word2vec, Text2vec, Glove, Paragraph2vec

#### *Word2Vec: Unlocking Word Representations*

The Word2Vec algorithm has fundamentally transformed the way we conceptualise and comprehend words. The model acquires distributed representations of words by leveraging the power of continuous vector spaces. Word2Vec adeptly captures the intricate semantic relationships between words by leveraging the ability to predict words within a given context window. This innovative approach enables a nuanced analysis of language, unveiling deeper insights into the underlying meaning and connections between words. The ability to capture semantic relationships with such precision empowers applications like sentiment analysis, document clustering, and recommendation systems, revolutionising the way we comprehend and interact with textual data.

***Text2Vec: Document-Level Embeddings***

Text2Vec is an innovative extension of the widely acclaimed Word2Vec model, designed to generate embeddings not just for individual words, but for entire documents. By using deep learning techniques, Text2Vec revolutionizes the field of NLP by enabling the representation of textual data at a higher level of granularity. Text2Vec offers a novel approach to document analysis by transcending the conventional treatment of documents as mere assemblages of isolated words. Instead, it empowers users to obtain a comprehensive and condensed representation of entire text segments.

***GloVe: Capturing Co-Occurrence Statistics***

GloVe, short for Global Vectors for Word Representation seamlessly integrates global matrix factorization with local context window techniques. By fusing these two approaches, GloVe achieves remarkable results in the realm of word representation. Word embeddings are generated through the efficient capture of co-occurrence statistics of words within extensive corpora. GloVe, offers highly significant word embeddings that hold immense value across a diverse spectrum of NLP applications.

***Paragraph2Vec: Embeddings for Document-Level Context***

Paragraph2Vec, also referred to as Doc2Vec, is an advanced technique that expands upon the principles of Word2Vec in order to produce embeddings for complete documents. In contrast to the approach taken by Text2Vec, which views documents as mere aggregations of individual words, the Paragraph2Vec methodology regards them as cohesive and uninterrupted textual entities. This particular approach offers a comprehensive and refined comprehension of semantics at the document level, thereby enabling the seamless execution of tasks such as document classification and information retrieval.

### 10.4.3 Words Similarity

The notion of word similarity is a foundational concept for quantifying the proximity or correlation between a pair of words. The computation of word similarity encompasses a range of techniques that leverage advanced methodologies, including distributional semantics and lexical resources such as WordNet. These methods enable the analysis of the contextual usage of words and the extraction of structured information pertaining to word relationships.

### 10.4.4 Continuous Bag of Words

The Continuous Bag of Words (CBOW) algorithm is a widely recognised and influential technique that focuses on the utilisation of word embeddings. The main objective CBOW is to acquire highly informative and compact vector representations of words within a continuous vector space. The CBOW model operates by taking a set of context words that surround a specific target word as input and then predicts the most likely target word based on this context. This approach is particularly effective in tasks such as word embeddings and language modelling, where understanding the relationships between words is crucial. With help of the contextual information provided through extensive corpora for training, the CBOW model adeptly captures the intricate semantic relationships that exist between words, thereby facilitating a sophisticated comprehension of language.

## 10.5 DOCUMENT CLASSIFICATION

Document classification is employed to assign documents to predetermined classes or categories, based on the content within the documents themselves. This process plays a crucial role in various applications, enabling efficient organization, retrieval, and analysis of large textual data. The typical procedure entails a two-fold methodology—initial feature extraction, wherein pertinent information is extracted from the documents, often leveraging techniques like TF-IDF or word embeddings, followed by the utilization of a classification algorithm, such as a Support Vector Machine (SVM) or Random Forest (RF) or a deep learning model, to assign a class label to each document. The successful task of document classification necessitates the utilization of a synergistic approach encompassing meticulous feature selection, judicious algorithm selection, and a meticulously curated training dataset. Document classification exhibits a large set of practical applications that span across various domains.

### 10.5.1 Classification Techniques

Classification techniques help in accomplishment of several tasks such as sentiment analysis, spam detection, and document categorization etc. Feature engineering is a crucial step in classification where the most relevant features are selected and extracted for determining the efficacy of the classification models. Methods such as BoW, TF-IDF, and word embeddings are important for text data representation and enabling ML algorithms to efficiently process textual information. In addition, effectively managing imbalanced datasets and implementing strategies such as resampling or leveraging specialised algorithms tailored for imbalanced data are crucial in attaining precise classification outcomes.

### 10.5.2 Model Evaluation in Classification

Model evaluation is done to assess the performance and efficacy of NLP models. This process entails a meticulous analysis of the model's ability to generalize effectively to novel, unseen data. There are number of evaluation metrics to assess the efficacy of ML models such as accuracy, precision, recall, and F1-score that offer valuable quantitative insights into the performance of such models. These metrics are reliable indicators of the model's ability to accurately classify and predict linguistic patterns and phenomena, facilitating a comprehensive evaluation of its overall effectiveness.

## 10.6 DOCUMENT CLUSTERING

Document clustering is the process of categorising and grouping documents that exhibit similarities in their content. By using the intrinsic characteristics of the documents, this technique enables the identification and organisation of related textual data. The standard procedure entails transforming textual documents into numerical vectors through methodologies such as TF-IDF or word embeddings. Subsequently, clustering algorithms such as K-means, hierarchical clustering, or Latent Dirichlet Allocation (LDA) are employed to effectively categorise these vectors into coherent clusters. The successful implementation of document clustering necessitates a meticulous curation of features, judicious choice of similarity metrics, and a profound comprehension of the intrinsic data characteristics.

### 10.6.1 Clustering Techniques

Clustering techniques facilitates the automated categorization of extensive textual datasets into coherent and significant clusters. These techniques are of utmost importance in various tasks such as document categorization, topic modelling, and information retrieval. The TF-IDF technique is a common practice to represent documents as numerical vectors. Once the documents are converted into numerical vectors, clustering algorithms are used to group the documents into clusters. The successful application of clustering techniques relies heavily on the careful consideration and implementation of effective feature selection, distance metrics, and cluster validation methods. These three components have crucial role in ensuring the accuracy and reliability of the clustering results. Similar to classification, feature selection is also a critical step in the clustering process as it involves identifying and selecting the most relevant and informative features from the dataset. By carefully choosing the appropriate features, the clustering algorithm can focus on the essential characteristics of the data, leading to more meaningful and accurate clusters. Distance metrics, on the other hand, serve as a fundamental measure of similarity or dissimilarity. It is crucial to emphasise that the selection of a clustering algorithm and the identification of suitable features play a vital role in determining the efficacy and accuracy of clustering results.

### 10.6.2 Model Evaluation in Clustering

Unlike classification, in clustering methods, the assessment of cluster quality is done through the utilisation of metrics such as the Silhouette score or Davies-Bouldin index yields significant insights into the efficacy of the clustering procedure. As in most cases the ground truth is unknown due to unlabelled dataset, these metrics helps to understand how well and relevantly the clusters have been formed. In the pursuit of attaining optimal performance, it is imperative to acknowledge the crucial role played by techniques such as hyperparameter tuning.

## 10.7 TOPIC MODELLING

Topic modelling empowers to unveil the concealed and underlying themes that saturate a corpus of textual documents. The utilisation of topic modelling techniques offers a systematic approach to comprehending the principal themes or subjects that are prevalent within an extensive collection of textual data. In addition, it is of utmost importance to underscore the significance of ensuring the interpretability of the topics generated by these models. Topic modelling also undergo the preprocessing steps like stemming, lemmatization, and stop word removal for improving the overall quality of outcomes. By reducing words to their root forms through stemming or lemmatization, and eliminating commonly used but insignificant words via stop word removal, the noise in the data is minimised. Consequently, the resulting topic models are more refined, coherent, and representative of the underlying themes within the corpus.

### 10.7.1 Latent Dirichlet Allocation (LDA)

LDA stands as a fundamental technique facilitating the unearthing of concealed topics residing within a corpus of textual documents. The fundamental principle of this technique is predicated on the notion that every document within a given corpus can be viewed as a combination of a limited set of topics. Furthermore, it suggests that each individual word present in a document can be attributed to one of these aforementioned topics. LDA uses probabilistic modelling to effectively reveal the hidden topics that exist within a corpus of documents, along with their respective distributions across the entire collection. It is of utmost importance to underscore the significance of enhancing the interpretability of the topics produced by LDA. The construction of a meticulously designed LDA model is expected to produce topics that exhibit a high degree of coherence and semantic significance.

### 10.7.2 Probabilistic Latent Semantic Indexing (PLSI)

The PLSI technique is a seminal technique which is specifically designed to tackle the intricate obstacles posed by high-dimensional text data. The proposed approach is founded upon a sophisticated probabilistic framework that effectively captures the intricate process of word generation within documents. This framework uses the concept of latent topics, which are hidden thematic structures that underlie the textual content. In contrast to conventional approaches such as Latent Semantic Indexing (LSI), PLSI offers a more refined and intricate portrayal of the intricate connections that exist between words and documents. The utilisation of a probabilistic approach offers a highly adaptable and articulate framework for capturing the inherent structure of extensive text corpora.

### 10.7.3 Variations of Topic Modelling

Topic modelling variations encompass a range of extensions and alternative methodologies that deviate from conventional topic modelling techniques, such as LDA, and PLSI. The main objective of these variations is to augment the capabilities and effectively tackle specific challenges associated with the extraction of latent topics from textual data. There exist several noteworthy variations in the field of topic modelling, each designed to address specific challenges and enhance the modelling capabilities. One such variation is Dynamic Topic Modelling (DTM), which introduces the ability to capture temporal changes in topics over time. By incorporating time as a factor, DTM enables the identification of topic evolution and shifts in documents over different time periods. Another notable variation is Correlated Topic Modelling (CTM), which extends LDA by allowing topics to be correlated. Further, Non-negative Matrix Factorization (NMF) and Hierarchical Dirichlet Process (HDP) are alternative methodologies that offer distinct viewpoints on the task of topic modelling.

## 10.8 TEXT GENERATION

Text generation is dedicated to the creation of coherent and contextually appropriate textual content. ML utilises a diverse range of techniques to achieve its objectives. These techniques encompass rule-based systems, Markov models, and, more recently, cutting-edge approaches such as Recurrent Neural Networks (RNNs) and Generative Adversarial Networks (GANs). The field of text generation has witnessed significant advancements in recent times, exemplified by the remarkable prowess of techniques such as Generative Pre-trained Transformer 3 (GPT-3). These models have showcased their ability to generate text that is not only highly coherent but also contextually relevant, thereby pushing the boundaries of what is achievable in this domain.

### 10.8.1 Text-to-data Generation

Text-to-data generation involves converting unstructured text into structured data that can be used for data analysis, ML, and knowledge extraction. This process typically includes a well-defined set of steps, some of which have been stated below.

***Data Collection:*** Gathering raw text data from reliable sources such as articles, documents, social media posts, or any other text-based content.

***Text Preprocessing:*** Cleaning the text data by removing irrelevant characters, special characters, tokenization and stop word removal.

***Entity Recognition:*** Identify and extract entities (such as names, locations, dates, organizations) from the text with NER.

***Feature Engineering:*** Extract the most relevant features from the text that can be used as input for ML models. These features could include word embeddings, TF-IDF, or any other numerical representations of the text.

***Data Structuring:*** Organize the extracted information into a structured format, such as a table or a graph, depending on the specific requirements of your application.

***Model Training:*** Train ML models for specific tasks, such as sentiment analysis, classification, or clustering, using the structured data generated from the text.

***Evaluation and Refinement:*** Evaluate the performance of the models using appropriate metrics and then refine the text-to-data generation pipeline based on the evaluation results.

### 10.8.2 Text-to-text Generation

Text-to-text generation involves building models that can generate human-like text in context of a given input. This is a versatile method and can be applied to various tasks, including text summarization, language translation, image captioning, and more. Some of the wisely used models for text-to-text generation are explained below:

***Sequence-to-Sequence (Seq2Seq) Models:*** These are fundamental architecture for text-to-text tasks which consist of an encoder-decoder framework, where the encoder processes the input text into a fixed-size context vector, and the decoder generates the output text based on this context vector. This architecture is commonly used for tasks like machine translation and summarization.

***Transformer Models:*** Some of the popular transformer-based architectures are BERT (Bidirectional Encoder Representations from Transformers) and GPT (Generative Pre-trained Transformer) which are designed for autoregressive text generation. It predicts the next word in a sequence given the context of the previous words.

***Conditional Generation:*** Here, the model generates text based on a given prompt or condition. For example, prompting a model with the beginning of a sentence and asking it to complete the rest.

***Text Summarization:*** Abstractive or extractive summarization involves generating a concise and coherent summary of a given document. Seq2Seq models, transformer-based models, and reinforcement learning approaches have been applied to text summarization tasks.

***Language Translation:*** Translate text from one language to another using Seq2Seq models or transformer-based models. Attention mechanisms in transformers help the model focus on relevant parts of the input sentence during translation.

***Data-to-text Generation:*** Generate natural language descriptions from structured data which can be applied in areas such as report generation from databases or creating textual descriptions from tabular data.

***Fine-tuning and Transfer Learning:*** Pre-trained models, especially transformer-based models, can be fine-tuned on specific tasks to adapt them to particular domains or datasets.

### 10.8.3 Dialogue

Dialogue involves understanding and generating human-like conversations. Dialogue systems aim to enable machines to interact with users in a natural and contextually relevant manner. Some of the key aspects of dialogue in NLP are as follows:

***Dialogue Understanding:*** This involves understanding the intention of the user for the dialogue through entity recognition and contextual understanding.

***Dialogue State Tracking:*** Keep track of the state of the conversation, including user and system actions, to maintain context and coherence. This is crucial for maintaining a meaningful and relevant conversation over multiple turns.

***NER in Dialogue:*** Identify and extract named entities (such as names, places, dates) mentioned in the conversation. This information is valuable for understanding and responding appropriately to user queries.

***Slot Filling:*** Identify specific slots or parameters in a user's request and fill them with relevant information. For example, in a restaurant reservation system, slots could include the date, time, and number of guests.

***Intent-based Responses:*** Generate responses based on the identified intent and context. The system should provide relevant and coherent replies that address the user's queries or requests.

***Contextual Embeddings:*** Utilize embeddings and representations that capture the contextual information in the dialogue. Transformer-based models like BERT and GPT have been quite successful in capturing contextual nuances.

***Reinforcement Learning in Dialogue:*** Applying reinforcement learning techniques to train dialogue systems. Reward models can be used to improve the system's responses over time based on user feedback.

***Generative Dialogue Models:*** Use generative models, such as GPT, to generate human-like responses in a conversational setting. These models are trained on large amounts of data to capture the diversity and complexity of natural language.

## 10.9 NLP WITH R AND PYTHON

R and Python have several libraries and packages for NLP that facilitate various tasks, including text processing, sentiment analysis, part-of-speech tagging, and more. These libraries and packages can be implemented with GUIs like Jupyter Notebook or R Studio. A comprehensive detail on the various packages and libraries available in both R and Python for NLP tasks has been provided below.

**TABLE 10.3** List of popular libraries in R and Python used for various tasks in NLP

| *NLP Task* | *R Libraries (purposes)* | *Python Libraries (purposes)* |
|---|---|---|
| Text Mining and Preprocessing | tm (cleaning, transformation) quateda (cleaning, text data analysis) text (mining, visualization) udpipe (tokenization, POS) textstem (stemming) lsa (semantic analysis) tokenizers (tokenization) openNLP (POS, chunking) slam (mining) | nltk (comprehensive NLP library) spaCy (tokenization, POS, NER) TextBlob (tokenization, POS) Gensim (topic modelling, similarity analysis) scikit-learn (comprehensive package) re (regular expression pattern matching) |
| Sentiment and Semantic Analysis | sentimentr (sentiment analysis) textTinyR (mining, analysis) textreg (regression analysis) RTextTools (text classification) textcat (categorization and classification) tm.plugin.sentiment (sentimient analysis) lexicon (sentiment analysis) topicmodels (topic modelling) lsa (semantic analysis) | VADER sentiment analysis (sentiment analysis) transformers (access GPT) Word2Vec (word embedding, sentiment analysis) |
| Web Mining and Scraping | tm.plugin.webmining (web mining) rvest (web scrapping) httr (web scrapping) RSelenium (web mining) ScrapyR (web scraping) XML and XML2 (parsing XML data) | requests (handling HTTP requests) beautifulsoup4 (HTML, XML parsing) selenium (web scrapping) scrapy (web scrapping) LXML (XML parsing) XPath and CSS Selectors (element selection from HTML/XML) |
| General NLP | NLP (POS, NER) spacyr (interface to spaCy) koRpus (linguistic analysis) udunits2 (numeric data handling) tm.plugin.dc (distributed computing) | scikit-learn (Comprehensive package) nltk (comprehensive NLP library) |

| NLP Task | R Libraries (purposes) | Python Libraries (purposes) |
|---|---|---|
| Machine Learning | scikit-learn (Comprehensive package) RWeka (interface to Weka) textreg (regression analysis) caretEnsemble (ensemble models rpart (recursive partitioning) xgboost (XGBoost) e1071 (SVM) randomForest (Random Forest) naivebayes (Naïve Bayes) glm (Logistic Regression) neuralnet (Neural Networks) | scikit-learn (Comprehensive package) tensorflow (deep learning TensorFlow) torch (deep learning PyTorch) |
| Classification and Clustering | RTextTools (text classification) caret (text classification) text2vec (text vectorization) tm.plugin.snowball (text classification) stats (k-means, hierarchical clustering) dbscan (DBSCAN, OPTICS) Mclust (Gaussian mixture model) apcluster (affinity propagation) kernlab (spectral clustering) | scikit-learn (Comprehensive package) nltk (comprehensive NLP library) spaCy (tokenization, POS, NER) transformers (access GPT) Gensim (topic modelling, similarity analysis scipy (k-means) |
| Visualization | wordcloud (word freqeuncy) ggplot2 (data visualization) tm.plugin.tags (tag cloud generation) wordcloud2 (interactive word cloud) corpus (text visualization) plotly (text visualization) syuzhet (sentiment analysis visualization) | matplotlib (general purpose plotting) seaborn (data visualization) plotly (interactive plotting) wordcloud (generating word cloud) tensorflow (embedded visualzation) |

There are many other sets of packages and libraries in R and Python which can be used for many other NLP tasks which are readily available as open source.

## SUMMARY

NLP represents a vibrant and ever-evolving domain situated at the convergence of linguistics, computer science, and AI. The primary objective of this field is to build machines with the capability to comprehend, interpret, and produce human language in a manner that is filled with significance and contextual appropriateness. This is a comprehensive field that encompasses a diverse array of tasks aimed at understanding and processing human language. In this chapter we have provided a comprehensive overview of what is NLP, how it can be applied and where it can be applied. Some of the widely used packages in R and Python for executing NLP tasks has also been shown, however, there are many other open-source packages too which can be used to address complex problems in NLP.

## WORKED OUT EXAMPLES

**EXAMPLE 10.1** A research article comprising of 6000 words contains the word 'parsing' 30 times. While investigating 5000 similar articles, it was found that 'parsing' was present in 300 articles. What is the TF-IDF for the term 'parsing'?

***Solution:*** The term frequency (TF) is calculated as follows:

$$TF = 30/6000 = 0.005$$

Out of 5,000 documents, the term "parsing," appeared in 300 documents, thus the inverse document frequency can be calculated as,

$$IDF = \log 5000/300 = 1.22$$

Now, we can calculate the TF-IDF score by multiplying these two numbers:

$$TF\text{-}IDF = TF \times IDF = 0.005 \times 1.22 = 0.0061$$

**EXAMPLE 10.2** Take the following sentence for character tokenization, word tokenization, sentence tokenization and n-gram tokenization.

"I hate boring lectures."

***Solution:***

```
install.packages('tm')
library(tm)
text <- (c("I hate boring lectures."))
Install.packages('tokenizers')
library(tokenizers)
tokenize_characters(text)
tokenize_words(text)
tokenize_sentences(text)
tokenize_ngrams(text, n = 2)
```

**EXAMPLE 10.3** Example of stemming and lemmatization using python.

***Solution:***

```
Stemming
import nltk
from nltk.stem import RegexpStemmer
Reg_stemmer = RegexpStemmer()
Reg_stemmer.stem('ingeat')
Lemmatization
import nltk
from nltk.stem import WordNetLemmatizer
lemmatizer = WordNetLemmatizer()
lemmatizer.lemmatize('books')
```

## EXERCISES

1. Given the following sentence: *Albert Einstein was born in Ulm, Germany in 1879.* Perform the POS tagging.
2. Consider the sentence: *The 5 biggest countries by population in 2017 are China, India, United States, Indonesia, and Brazil.* Identify and remove the stop words.
3. Calculate the edit distance between the following two sentences:

   *Italy is widely known for being the birthplace of opera*
   *The birthplace of opera is known as Italy*

First, write the formulation of the edit distance from a dynamic programming perspective. Then, show the execution of the algorithm systematically on a table (matrix). In addition to finding the edit distance, determine the operations necessary for converting one sentence to the other (and explain how you identify these operations).

4. A dataset containing 20 categories with around 11500 observations for training and 7300 observations for testing has been extracted. Design a document classification model and analyse its efficiency. Also, enable the model to predict category of new unknown data by user using R.
5. Using the "Associated Press dataset" containing 2246 news articles from the First Text Retrieval Conference, design LDA based model for topic modeling in R.

## BIBLIOGRAPHY

Indurkhya, N. and Damerau, F. J. (Eds.) (2010). *Handbook of Natural Language Processing* (Vol. 2), CRC Press.

Kibble, R. (2013). *Introduction to Natural Language Processing,* University of London.

Manning, C. and Schutze, H. (1999). *Foundations of Statistical Natural Language Processing,* MIT Press.

Martin, J. H. (2009). *Speech and Language Processing: An Introduction to Natural Language Processing, Computational Linguistics, and Speech Recognition*, Pearson/Prentice Hall.

Murthy, K. N. (2006). *Natural Language Processing: An Information Access Perspective*, Ess Ess Publications for Sarada Ranganathan Endowment for Library Science.

Chapter 11

# Metaheuristic Algorithm

## 11.1 FUNDAMENTALS OF OPTIMIZATION

Optimization is a fundamental concept across diverse fields, including Mathematics, Engineering, Natural Sciences, Computer Science, and more. It involves finding the best solution among a set of possible solutions to a given problem. This "*best solution*" is typically defined based on certain criteria or objectives, which can vary depending on the context of the problem. Primarily there are two types of optimizations—unconstrained and constrained. In case of unconstrained optimizations, the primary aim is to find the maximum/minimum of a function without any restrictions or in other words, there is no constraints that defines the function. However, for constrained optimizations, there are limits such as equality (*e.g.* $f(x) = 0$) or inequality (*e.g.* $f(x) \geq 0$) and the aim is to find optimal solutions that satisfy these constraints. Optimization process is based on some fundamental concepts such as objective functions, decision variables, constraints, and a few others.

***Objective Function:*** This is the main function that needs to be minimized or maximized representing the goal of the optimization problem. In minimization problems, the objective function is represented as $f(x)$ where $x$ denotes the decision variables whereas, in maximization problems, the objective function is often denoted as $g(x)$ or $h(x)$. The objective function can be linear, nonlinear, convex, concave, or a combination of these.

***Decision Variables:*** This consists of a set of variables that can be adjusted or controlled to influence the objective function. The values of these variables are what we seek to optimize. They are generally represented by $x_1$, $x_2$, …., $x_n$. These variables can be continuous (such as real numbers), discrete (such as integers), or binary (0 or 1).

***Constraints:*** Constraints are restrictions or limitations on the values that the decision variables can take. They can be equality constraints (where certain expressions must be equal) or inequality constraints (where certain expressions must be less than or greater than certain values). Constraints can be linear or nonlinear, and they define the feasible region of the optimization problem.

***Feasible Region or Space:*** This is the space constituting all possible values of the decision variables after satisfying the constraints. It represents the space within which the optimization process can search for the optimal solution.

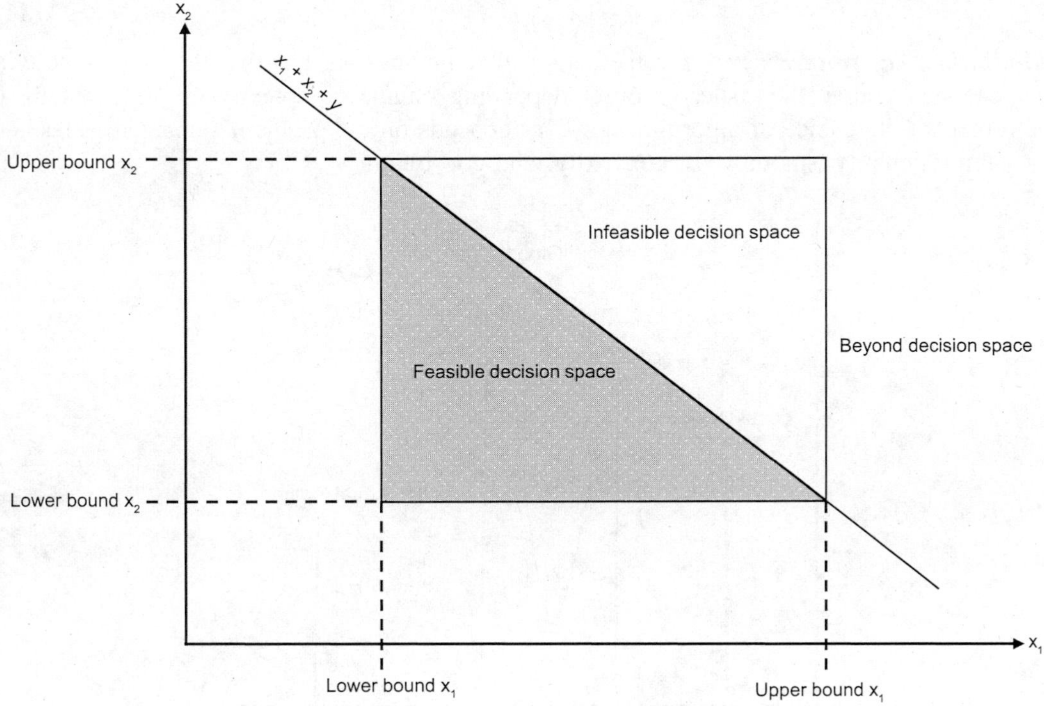


**FIGURE 11.1** Decision space for a bounded 2D optimization problem.

***Optimal Solution:*** A solution which may be a single value or combination of values for decision variables that can minimize/maximize the objective function by satisfying all the constraints is considered as the optimal solution. In case of minimization problems, this solution depicts the lowest objective function value whereas for maximization problems, it is the highest value of objective function.

***Local and Global Optima:*** A local optimum is a solution that is optimal within a certain neighbourhood but may not be the best possible solution globally whereas global optimum is the best possible solution across entire feasible solutions space. Different optimization algorithms may converge to local or global optima depending on their characteristics. In case of one-dimensional optimization problems, a decision variable, say $X^*$ will be accepted as the local optima for maximization if,

$$f(x^*) \geq f(x), X^* - \varepsilon \leq X \leq X^* + \varepsilon \tag{11.1}$$

If the problem is a minimization problem, then the equation becomes,

$$(x^*) \leq f(x), X^* - \varepsilon \leq X \leq X^* + \varepsilon \tag{11.2}$$

Similarly, for a one-dimensional optimization problem, $X^*$ will be considered as the global optima if,

$$f(X^*) \geq f(X) \tag{11.3}$$

$$f(X) \leq f(X) \tag{11.4}$$

***Optimization Algorithms:*** These are methods and techniques used to find the optimal solution. They can be iterative, heuristic, or exact depending on the complexity of the problem and requirements. The choice of algorithm however depends on the problem's characteristics, such as its dimensionality, smoothness, convexity, and constraints.

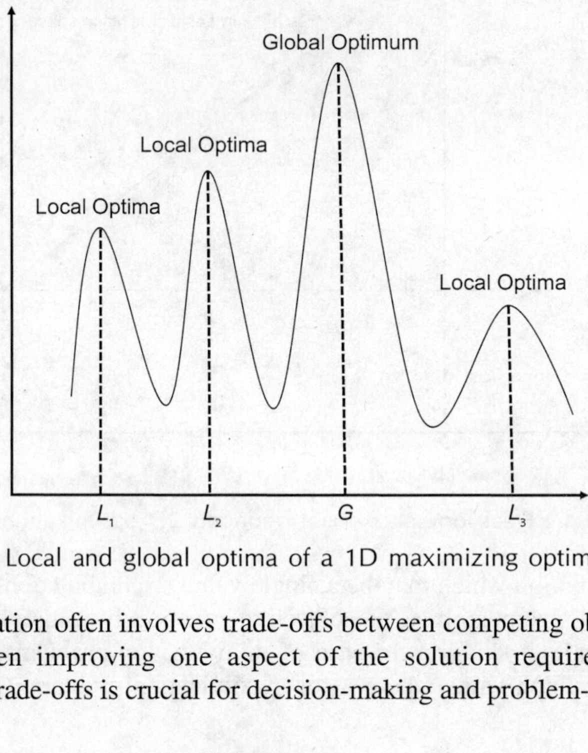


**FIGURE 11.2** Local and global optima of a 1D maximizing optimization problem.

***Trade-Offs:*** Optimization often involves trade-offs between competing objectives or constraints. Trade-offs arise when improving one aspect of the solution requires sacrificing another. Understanding these trade-offs is crucial for decision-making and problem-solving in optimization.

## 11.2 METAHEURISTIC ALGORITHMS

While solving optimization problems, all the possible solutions build the decision space, the challenge is to find the best among all of them. One of the ways to reach the solution is trial-and-error method which can be executed through random sampling or sampling grid. In case of sampling grid, the idea is to evaluate each possible solution and choose the best. When the sample space is small, sampling gird method can be a feasible solution, but when the sample space turns large, time turns to be a constraint. In contrast, random sampling involves selecting samples at random from the decision space. The set of potential solutions is randomly selected, their objective functions are assessed, and the best option among those selected is referred to as the optimum. It is crucial to explore the whole decision space in both situations, which is a drawback of employing these approaches in terms of wasting computational power.

Metaheuristic algorithms are implemented for problems that are difficult to solve or cannot be solved at all using any techniques. In such cases, one feasible way is to find the near-optimal solutions. These algorithms may be computationally intensive, but in absence of an exact solution, a near-optimal solution is quite adequate. Metaheuristic algorithms are generally problem independent and are applied over a diverse range of problems across multiple domains. Some of the key components of metaheuristic algorithms are a set of initial data, state, iterations, decision and state variables, objective and fitness function, and a final state.

***Initial Data:*** All metaheuristic algorithms start with an initial data which can be either generated randomly or through some calculations. These data also include the parameters of the algorithm used which can be adjusted to calibrate for solving the problem.

***Initial State:*** This is an initial set of variables with which the algorithm starts looking for an optimal solution.

***Iterations:*** While searching for solutions, a set of steps need to be performed repeatedly to generate new solutions. The iteration stops when a possible or near optimal solution is obtained.

***Decision Variables:*** These are all the values that are computed while executing a metaheuristic algorithm and are considered as solutions for the optimization problem.

***State Variables:*** The state variables are dependent on the decision variables i.e. as decision variable changes, the values of state variables also change.

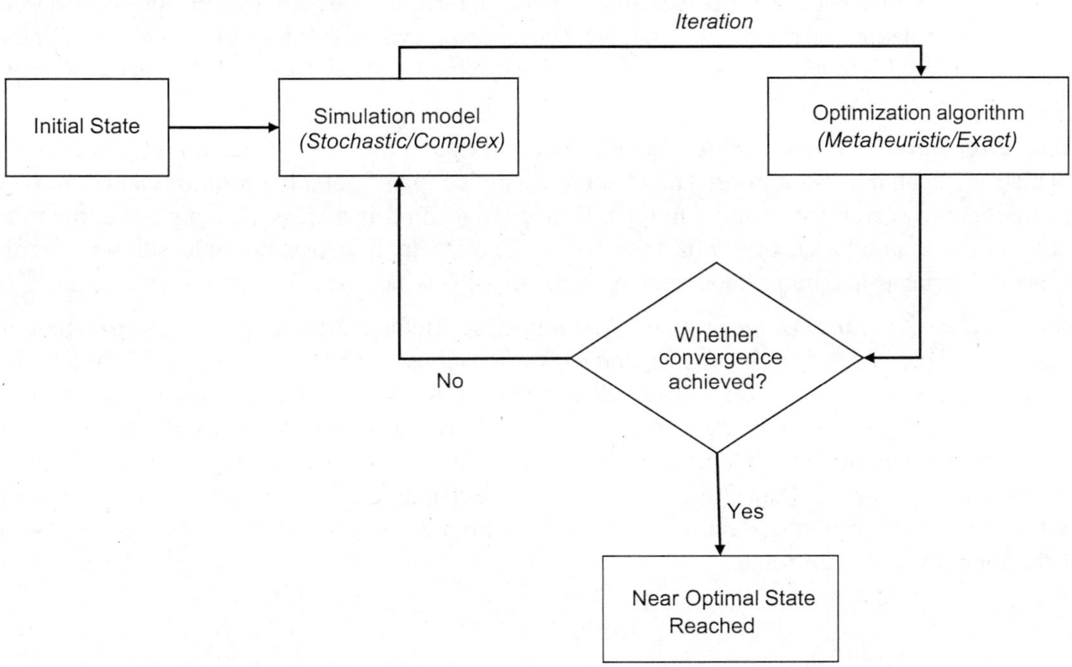


**FIGURE 11.3** Fundamental components of metaheuristic algorithms.

***Objective Function:*** The objective function determines the optimality of a solution as it is applied to the entire decision space of the problem.

***Constraints:*** Constraints are another set of parameters which are calculated to delimit the feasible decision space. Constraints are evaluated after the objective function and state variables, and if they are satisfied, the solution is accepted as a feasible solution, otherwise not.

***Fitness Function:*** Often, the objective function may be transformed by using some penalties to avoid the violations of the constraints. These transformed functions are the fitness function.

***Termination Criteria:*** This is the stopping criteria of the algorithm which can be based on the factors like: (a) iterations, (b) tuning of the threshold value of solution, and (c) the run time of the algorithm.

***Final State:*** On satisfaction of the termination criterion, execution of the algorithm stops and final/optimal solution(s) are generated as final state.

## 11.3 CLASSIFYING METAHEURISTIC ALGORITHMS

Metaheuristic algorithms can be classified into different types such as nature-inspired or non-nature-inspired, population-based or single-search based, and memory-based or memory-less. Although these classes are well defined, at time it is difficult to differentiate which algorithm belongs to which class, and in many cases, they overlap with one another.

***Nature-Inspired Versus Non-Nature-Inspired:*** Nature-inspired algorithms are the ones which are related to some natural processes like genetic algorithm, particle swarm optimization etc. Whereas, non-nature inspired do not have a necessary origin from natural processes, rather they use artificial intelligence aspects like memory. Simulated annealing, Tabu search, Genetic Programming are some examples.

***Population-Based Versus Single Search-Based:*** Population-based algorithms operate on a population of candidate solutions. They maintain a collection of potential solutions and iteratively update them to search for better solutions. Genetic algorithm is a classic example. On the other hand, single search-based algorithms iteratively operate to find one possible solution for the problem. Variable neighbourhood search, iterated local search are few examples.

***Memory-Based Versus Memory Less:*** Memory-based metaheuristic algorithms use memory structures to guide the search process and make decisions during optimization. They also use historical information to make current decisions. Algorithms like Ant colony optimization, memetic search, tabu search are some memory-based algorithms. Memoryless metaheuristic algorithms or memoryless optimization techniques, do not rely on storing information about past solutions or search trajectories. They make decisions exclusively based on the present state of the search process. Random search, Hill climbing, and simulated annealing are some of the memory-less algorithms.

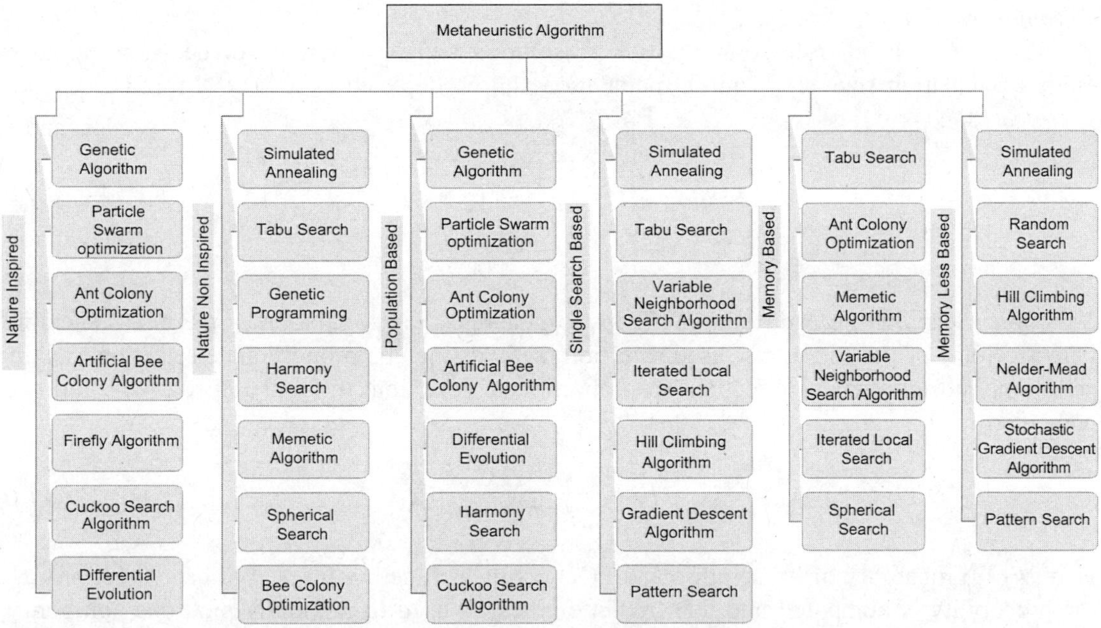


**FIGURE 11.4** Classification of metaheuristic algorithms.

## 11.4 METAHEURISTIC ALGORITHMS—OPTIMIZATION

### 11.4.1 Genetic Algorithm

Genetic Algorithm (GA) is considered among the best early evolutionary algorithms which was proposed by Holland (1975) and later popularized by Goldberg (1989). This algorithm is based on the fundamental principle of '*survival of the fittest*', and embody the essence of natural selection to progressively refine and enhance solutions through iterative evolution. GA starts by creating an initial population of potential solutions that are encoded as chromosomes, mirroring the concept of genetic material. Thereafter, a combination of selection, crossover, and mutation operators are employed to emulate the fundamental processes of reproduction, genetic recombination, and mutation. Through a series of iterative processes, the selection of individuals with superior fitness, as determined by the problem's objective function, becomes increasingly probable. This phenomenon results in the dissemination of solutions of superior quality throughout the system. The iterative process of population refinement contributes to effectively explore the entire solution space, crossing local optima, and converging towards optimal or near-optimal solutions. The steps involved in implementing GA is described below in details.

***Initial Population:*** A solution in GA is called a chromosome which consists of a series of genes which are actually the decision variables.

*Chromosome (X) = ($x_1$, $x_2$, $x_3$, .. ,$x_N$)*

Here, $X$ = a possible solution; $x_i$ = $i^{th}$ solution and $N$ = number of decision variables. With a population size M, an initial population can be depicted as a M × N matrix,

$$Population = \begin{bmatrix} X_1 \\ X_2 \\ \vdots \\ X_N \end{bmatrix} = \begin{bmatrix} x_{1,1} & \cdots & x_{N,1} \\ \vdots & \ddots & \vdots \\ x_{M,1} & \cdots & X_{M,N} \end{bmatrix} \tag{11.5}$$

***Selection:*** Selection procedure in GA helps to generate new population or the next generation parents. Some of the commonly used selection methods include proportionate selection, ranking selection, and tournament selection. In proportionate selection, the probability of a solution is computed by,

$$P_k = \frac{F(X_k)}{\sum_{j=1}^{m} F(X_j)} \tag{11.6}$$

Here, $P_k$ = probability of $k^{th}$ solution and F(X) = fitness function for X. For each solution first, the probability is computed and then roulette wheel is used to randomly pick one solution.

In ranking selection method, the possible solutions are first ranked based on their fitness function. A probability is then assigned to each solution using a linear function,

$$P_k = U - (S_k - 1) \times Z \tag{11.7}$$

$$S_k = Rank(X_k) \tag{11.8}$$

$$\sum_{j=1}^{M} P_j = 1 \tag{11.9}$$

$$U = \frac{Z(M-1)}{2} + \frac{1}{M} \tag{11.10}$$

Where, $S_k$ = rank of $k^{th}$ solution in the population and the best solution is defined by $S_k$ = *1*. $Z$ = any user defined value and M = population size.

In tournament selection method, the solutions are randomly selected such that the probability of each solution to be selected is identical. In every iteration, the best solution is considered as parent and it is repeated until all parents are selected.

***Crossover:*** Crossover operator is used between the parents to generate new population of offsprings. To build a new population, this operator retains certain decision variables from one parent and some from the other. The crossovers can occur at a single point or two points or uniformly over the parents and these points are randomly chosen between [1, N] where N is the size of decision space.

***Mutation:*** During mutation, some of the genes of the new population is randomly substituted with new values while keeping others intact. The mutation probability (PM) quantifies the likelihood of an individual gene being mutated. The *Rand(0, 1)* function is used by the mutation operator on each decision variable in the new population such that if the computed random value is greater than PM value, then the decision variable is mutated, otherwise not.

***Termination Criteria:*** In order to stop the execution of GA algorithm and converge, termination criteria such as number of iterations or improvement in objective function or runtime are used.

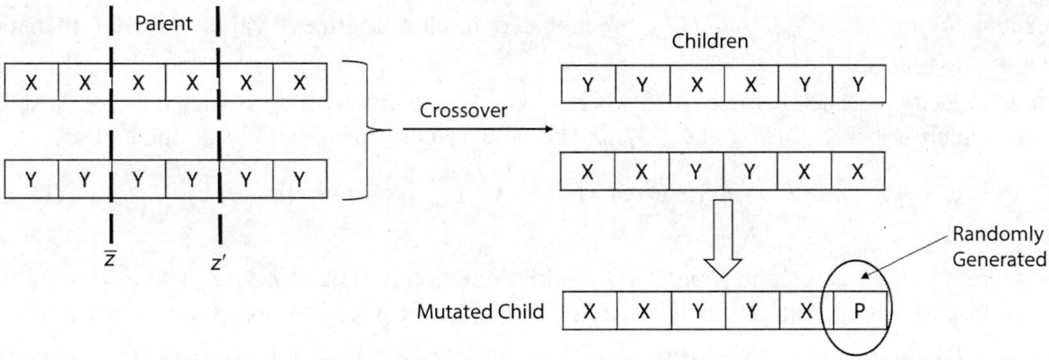


**FIGURE 11.5** Two-points crossover and mutation operations in Genetic Algorithm.

## 11.4.2 Particle Swarm Optimization

Particle Swarm Optimization (PSO) represents a nature-inspired metaheuristic algorithm that adeptly encapsulates the essence of social dynamics, thereby facilitating the resolution of complex optimisation problems. Inspired by the remarkable collective behaviour exhibited by flocking birds and schooling fish, PSO elegantly leverages the fundamental principles of cooperation and information exchange to deftly navigate intricate solution spaces. PSO is an inventive algorithm that binds the power of a population of particles to explore and exploit potential solutions within a given search space. Each particle's position elegantly corresponds to a specific point in this vast search space, thereby encapsulating the essence of the problem at hand. The particles in this iterative process dynamically adapt their positions by using both their individual experiences and the collective experiences of their neighbouring particles. Their ultimate objective is to effectively identify the optimal or near-optimal solutions. The steps involved in implementing PSO are described below.

***Initial State:*** Each solution in PSO is designated as particle and their positions denotes the decision space in an N-dimensional optimization problem.

$$\text{Particle (X)} = (x_1, x_2, x_3, \ldots, x_N)$$

Like GA, PSO also starts by building a matrix of particles of size M x N such that,

$$Population = \begin{bmatrix} X_1 \\ X_2 \\ \cdot \\ \cdot \\ X_N \end{bmatrix} = \begin{bmatrix} x_{1,1} & \cdots & x_{N,1} \\ \vdots & \ddots & \vdots \\ x_{M,1} & \cdots & X_{M,N} \end{bmatrix} \tag{11.11}$$

***Local and Global Best Positions:*** To achieve the optimal position, each particle explores through the decision space using parameters $P_{best}$ *and* $G_{best.}$ The $P_{best}$ is the best positions in the particle's history while $G_{best}$ represents the best position in swarm's histories. They are mathematically represented by,

$$P_{best_i} = (p_{i,\,j},\, p_{i,\,2},\, p_{i,\,3},\, \ldots,\, p_{i,\,N}),\ i = 1, 2, \ldots, M \tag{11.12}$$

$$G_{best} = (g_1,\, g_2,\, g_3,\, \ldots,\, g_N),\ for\ all\ i \tag{11.13}$$

In each iteration, the $P_{best}$ and $G_{best}$ are updated if current fitness value is better than the previous $P_{best}$.

***Particle Velocity:*** As each particle in PSO is in motion, a velocity term is associated in optimization process which is based on $P_{best}$ and $G_{best}$. The new velocity of a particle is updated as,

$$v_{i,j}^{(new)} = \omega \times v_{i,j} + c_1 \times Rand \times (p_{i,j} - x_{i,j}) + c_2 \times Rand \times (g_i - x_{i,j}) \tag{11.14}$$

$i = 1, 2, \ldots, M, j = 1, 2, \ldots, N$

Here, $\omega$ = inertia weight; *Rand()* = a random function in range [0, 1]; $c_1$ and $c_2$ = cognitive and social parameters that commands the shift of $P_{best}$ and $G_{best}$ towards the optimal point.

***Updating Positions:*** The new positions of the particles are updated based on the velocities such that,

$$x_{i,j}^{(new)} = x_{i,j} + v_{i,j}^{(new)}, i = 1,2,.., M\ and\ j = 1,2,\ldots,N \tag{11.15}$$

***Termination Criterion:*** In order to stop the execution of PSO algorithm and converge, termination criteria such as number of iterations or improvement in objective function or runtime are used.

### 11.4.3 Ant Colony Optimization

Ant Colony Optimisation (ACO) algorithm draws inspiration from the remarkable foraging behaviour exhibited by ants in order to effectively tackle complex optimisation problems. The underlying principle of this concept lies in the intricate communication system employed by ants, wherein they utilise pheromone trails to effectively navigate between their nest and sources of sustenance. ACO algorithms emulate the intricate workings of nature by leveraging the power of probabilistic decision-making and the dynamic updating of artificial pheromone trails. These algorithms ingeniously construct solutions by intelligently navigating the search process, drawing inspiration from the behaviour of ants in their quest for optimal paths.

As time progresses, ACO gradually converges towards optimal or near-optimal solutions. One of the fundamental principles that underlies ACO is its remarkable capacity to keep a delicate equilibrium between exploration, or the discovery of novel paths, and exploitation, which entails the concentration of efforts on paths that exhibit higher levels of pheromones. This unique characteristic empowers ants to effectively navigate through the search space in their quest for optimal solutions.

***Initial State:*** The initial state in ACO comprises decision variables which represents the path of an ant in an N-dimensional space. These variables are selected from a set of values ($V_i$) where,

$$V_i = \{v_{i,1},\ v_{i,2},\ v_{i,3},\ \ldots,\ v_{i,m}, \ldots,\ v_{i,M}\}\ \text{and}\ i = 1,2,\ \ldots,\ N \tag{11.16}$$

Here, $V_i$ = set of values for $i^{th}$ decision variable; $v_{i,m}$ = $m^{th}$ possible value of the $i^{th}$ decision variable, and $M$ = total possible values for $i^{th}$ decision variable.

In ACO, a solution is depicted as a graph with a specific pathway connecting the decision variables. Each decision variable in the graph is represented by a layer and the number of nodes in that layer indicates the number of discrete possible values for that particular decision variable.

***Allocate Pheromones:*** Unlike previous optimization algorithms, ACO generates new population by allocating a concentration of pheromone to each decision variable based on the fitness function. If the solution is more fit, the concentration is higher and vice-versa. Consider a pheromone concentration matrix $C_i$, such that,

$$C_i = \{c_{i,1}, c_{i,2}, c_{i,3}, ..., c_{i,d}, ..., c_{i,Di}\} \text{ where } i = 1, 2, ..., N \tag{11.17}$$

Initially, all these elements are assigned zero and during the algorithmic search they are updated. These updates enhance the convergence of good decision variable's values. Mathematically, the pheromone concentration for $d^{th}$ possible value of the $i^{th}$ decision variable can be updated by,

$$c_{i,d}^{\text{new}} = (1-\rho)\times c_{i,d} + \sum_{j=1}^{N} \Delta c_{i,d}^{(j)} \tag{11.18}$$

Where, $d = 1,2, .., D_i$ and $i = 1, 2, ..., N$; $\rho$ = evaporation rate and $\Delta c_{i,d}^{(j)}$ = quantity of pheromone placed in $d^{th}$ possible value of $i^{th}$ decision variable by the $j^{th}$ ant, which is nothing but the fitness value of $j^{th}$ solution.

$$\Delta c_{i,d}^{(j)} = \begin{cases} \dfrac{Q}{F_x} & \text{if } x_{i,j} = v_{i,d} \\ 0 & \text{otherwise} \end{cases} \tag{11.19}$$

$j = 1, 2, \ldots, M$; $i = 1, 2, \ldots, N$; $d = 1, 2, ..., D_i$
Where, $Q$ = a constant and $F(X_j)$ = fitness value of $j^{th}$ solution.

***Generate New States:*** ACO generates new states using stochastic methods based on the concentration of pheromone, each decision variable $i$ is assigned a probability value $P_{i,d}$ computed as,

$$P_{i,d} = \frac{\left[(c_{i,d})^{\alpha} \times (\eta_{i,d})^{\beta}\right]}{\Sigma_{k=1}^{d_i}\left[(c_{i,k})^{\alpha} \times (\eta_{i,k})^{\beta}\right]}, d = 1,2,...,D_i, i = 1,2,...,N \tag{11.20}$$

Where, $\eta_{i,d}$ is the heuristic value of $i^{th}$ decision variable for the $d^{th}$ possible value and $\alpha$ and $\beta$ are control parameters for the relative importance of pheromone with respect to the heuristic information. The new values of decision variables are randomly selected based on probabilities. A cumulative probability of all the possible values is then computed and compared with a random number between [0, 1]. This comparison helps to decide whether to add a new value to the population or not.

***Termination Criteria:*** In order to stop the execution of ACO algorithm and converge, termination criteria such as number of iterations or improvement in objective function or runtime are used.

### 11.4.4 Simulated Annealing

Simulated Annealing (SA) is a probabilistic optimisation technique that draws inspiration from the annealing process observed in metallurgy. It was developed in 1983 by Kirkpatrick et al. who demonstrated how a SA model proposed by Metropolis et al. in 1953 for solids can be used to solve optimization problems. Annealing is a metallurgy process which involves the gradual heating and subsequent controlled cooling of a material, ultimately leading it to attain a state of minimal energy. Similar approach is used by SA to tackle optimisation challenges, emulating the cooling process of a system and enabling it to traverse the solution landscape in search of the most favourable configuration.

SA optimisation procedure commences by establishing an initial solution. Subsequently, a series of candidate solutions is generated by means of random perturbations. The algorithm exhibits a propensity to embrace novel solutions that surpass the existing one, with a heightened likelihood during the initial stages of the optimisation process. As the optimisation progresses, the acceptance probability gradually diminishes, effectively simulating the cooling process. The utilisation of a probabilistic approach in SA enables the algorithm to effectively navigate away from local optima. By intermittently accepting suboptimal solutions, SA avoids becoming ensnared within suboptimal regions of the solution space.

***Initial Population:*** The initial population in SA generated optimization problem corresponds to a state of $N$ decision variables in an $N$-dimensional space of a $1 \times N$ array depicting arrangement of atoms of a substance such that,

$$\text{State} = (X_1, X_2, X_3, \ldots, X_N)$$

Where, $x_i = i^{th}$ decision variable of the solution $X$. These decision variables can be continuous values, discrete values or even floating numbers.

***Generating New State:*** A new state is generated from the current state using various deterministic and stochastic approaches. A very simple method is random walk where a small random value is generated between and added to the old value to obtain a new decision variable. However, these new values are evaluated with an acceptance function prior to consideration as a new state or population.

***Acceptance Function:*** The acceptance function is the deciding factor for newly generated solution ($X^{new}$) to replace the current solution ($X$). The acceptance or rejection of the new solution is dependent on the fitness function ($F(X)$) in a way that if the new value of F(X) is better than the earlier ones, the new solution will substitute the older ones, else not. The old solution is retained and assigned a probability ($P(X, X^{new})$) which is based on the difference ($\Delta$) between the current and old fitness values. In case of minimization problem, acceptance of new solution depends on the acceptance probabilistic function such that,

$$P(X, X^{new}) = \begin{Bmatrix} 1 \; if \; F(X^{new}) < F(X) \\ e^{\frac{-\Delta F}{\lambda}} \; Otherwise \end{Bmatrix} \tag{11.21}$$

$$\Delta F = | F(X^{new}) - F(X) | \tag{11.22}$$

***Thermal Equilibrium:*** Thermal equilibrium in SA model depends on the amount of neighbourhood movements that occurs at a particular temperature. Conventionally, it follows the Boltzmann distribution and at every instance of temperature $\lambda$, a new set of states are first generated and then accepted/discarded before the temperature reduces. The acceptance function validates these new states. The number of new states to be generated is user defined as parameter $\beta$, such that thermal equilibrium state is satisfied only when a predefined number $\beta$ is generated and validated.

***Temperature Reduction:*** Temperature ($\lambda$) is an important factor for generation of new states and convergence is SA. When the algorithm starts, the value of $\lambda$ is relatively high to avoid premature local optimum, and gradually reduces with the growth of the algorithm. Mathematically, with $t$ number of iterations,

$$\lim_{t \to +\infty} \lambda_t = 0, t > 0 \tag{11.23}$$

***Termination:*** In order to stop the execution of SA algorithm and converge, termination criteria such as number of iterations or improvement in objective function or runtime are used.

### 11.4.5 Gradient Descent

Gradient Descent (GD) is a popular optimization algorithm used in minimization problem which iteratively moves in the direction same as steepest descent of the function. The term 'gradient' depicts first order derivative (slope of the curve) and 'descent' is moving to lower points, which describes the fundamental working of this algorithm. During the execution of the algorithm, it iteratively calculates the next point that has to be reached by using the gradient at the current position, and subtracting it from the parameter value ($p_n$) by scaling it with a learning rate ($l$) such that,

$$p_{n+1} = p_n - l\nabla f(p_n) \tag{11.24}$$

Where, $\nabla f(p_n)$ = gradient of expected loss function.

***Initialization:*** The GD algorithm initiates with a preliminary guess ($x_0$) which is randomly chosen or with help of some heuristic function. The main objective is to minimize the objective function ($f(p)$), where $p$ represents the decision variables of the optimization problem.

***Gradient Computation:*** In every iteration $n$, the gradient of the objective function ($f(p)$) is computed at the point $p_n$. The gradient provides the direction of steepest ascent, indicating the direction in which the function increases most rapidly from the current point. Based on this value, the current value is updated using eqn. 11.22. The learning rate is typically chosen as a small positive value and it determines the size of the steps taken in gradient direction. It is responsible for preventing overshoot from the minimum as well as hanging around it. Techniques like learning rate schedules, momentum, and adaptive learning rate methods like Adam or RMSprop are generally used to adjust the learning rate dynamically.

***Termination Criteria:*** GD iteratively updates the current point ($p_n$) till a stopping criterion is fulfilled. Some common termination criteria include number of iterations, achieving a sufficiently small gradient norm, or satisfying a desired tolerance level for the objective function. When the GD algorithm terminates, it signifies that the algorithm has converge to a local minimum.

There are many other metaheuristic algorithms which are implemented for optimization purposes such as Artificial Bee Colony, Firefly algorithm, Differential evolution, Genetic programming and many more. Literature provides comprehensive detail of these algorithms and their utility in different fields.

**TABLE 11.1** Various characteristics of the metaheuristic algorithms for optimization

| *General Terminology* | *GA* | *PSO* | *ACO* | *SA* | *GD* |
|---|---|---|---|---|---|
| Decision variable | Gene of chromosome | Particle's position in each dimension | Track of ant | Atom position | Gradient position |
| Solution | Chromosome | Particle's position | Ant | State of substance | Position |
| Initial Solution | Random chromosome | Random Particle | Random ant | Random position | Random position |
| Old Solution | Parent | Old position of particle | Old ant | Current state of substance | Current position |
| New Solution | Offspring | New position of particle | New ant | New state of substance | New position |
| Best solution | Elite | Leader of particles | – | – | – |
| Fitness function | Quality of chromosome | Distance—particle to food | Pheromone | Energy of substance | Gradient of loss function |
| Selection | Surviving parent | – | – | Acceptance function | – |
| Generate new solutions | Genetic operators | Flying in specific direction and velocity | Stochastic mechanism | Atom movements | Slope movement |

GA: Genetic Algorithm; PSO: Particle Swarm Optimization; ACO: Ant Colony Optimization; SA: Simulated Annealing; GD: Gradient Descent

## 11.5 METAHEURISTIC ALGORITHMS—SEARCHING

### 11.5.1 Pattern Search

Pattern search (PS) is a version of direct search method which is used to solve diverse numerical problems using simple strategies. Each trial solution in PS is compared with the previous best solution, which turns as a basis for the next trial solution. PS can converge pretty fast and reach a near optimal solution. PS begins with a random point $P_1$ which is considered as the base point after which a second point $P_2$ is again randomly chosen. Both these points $P_1$ and $P_2$ are compared and if the second point is better than the previous one, the base point gets replaced. This process iterates till either one of the termination conditions is satisfied or the algorithm is considered to have converged.

***Initial State:*** PS starts with an initial population of randomly generated decision variables which can be continuous or discrete depending on the optimization problem.

$$X = (x_1, x_2, x_3, \ldots, x_N)$$

***New Trial Solutions:*** PS generates new trial solutions around the first base points in two ways–exploratory move and pattern move. During exploratory move, one of the coordinate's value is changed, and its corresponding effect on the fitness value is assessed. If the new fitness value is better than the earlier one, the move is considered to be successful, else a failure. Through exploratory move, new solutions can be generated using two patterns–generalized pattern search (GPS) and mesh adaptive direct search (MADS). To generate new solutions, PS first computes the fitness function (from GPS or MADS) and then assesses them with the best fitness value among them. Among these newly generated solutions, if at least one of them has higher fitness value, the search point is then substituted by this new point. In general, a successful exploratory move is always tailed by pattern move to progress the search in the probable direction of improvement. The new trial solution is given by,

$$\mathrm{X}^{(new)} = \mathrm{X}' + \alpha(X - X') \tag{11.25}$$

Where, $X'$ and $X$ = previous and current base points respectively and $\alpha$ = accelerating factor.

***Update:*** In the quest of generating new trial solutions, when the search point is updated with a new point, expansion coefficient is applied and new solutions are generated such that the new mesh size (μ) larger as compared to previous one and is reset to the initial value as,

$$\mu^{(new)} = \mu^{\circ} \tag{11.26}$$

On the other hand, if exploratory move fails to generate better solutions, then the mesh size is reduced to a smaller value using the contraction coefficient such that,

$$\mu^{(new)} = \mu - \delta \tag{11.27}$$

Where, $\delta$ = decreasing step of mesh size.

***Termination Criteria:*** One of the most common termination conditions in PS is mesh size where a sufficiently smaller mesh size ensures that near optimum has been reached, and final termination can be executed. Other termination criteria can be the number of iterations, running time, and improved solution in consecutive iterations.

### 11.5.2 Local Search

Local search (LS) is a special case of GA where the initial population consists of one combination. Then the entire search space is explored iteratively by updating the combinations and moving to next neighbouring combination.

***Initial State:*** In LS, the initial combination which is either randomly generated or through greedy approach. However, if it is a hybrid of other metaheuristic algorithm like GA or ACO, then some search processes may be executed to arrive at the initial combination.

***Neighbourhood Function:*** The neighbourhood function *f(S)* plays an important role in finding solutions in LS. It defines a set of combinations *n(s)* which are obtained from different transformation operations like altering the value of single variable or substituting the values of two variables in a way that each transformation results into a new neighbourhood of varying sizes. But, for this transformation to occur, there should be dedicated paths to reach out the optimal combination from the base.

***Choosing Neighbours:*** In every iteration of LS, it has to choose a combination *s'* around the proximity of current combination *s* for substitution. These combinations are chosen by greedy strategies like best improvement or first improvement. In best improvement strategy, the entire neighbourhood is scanned and the best, which improves the objective function, is selected. Whereas, in first improvement strategy, the very first neighbourhood which boosts the objective function is selected. However, during this search there is a chance of reaching the local optima and all the combinations have only deteriorate the objective function leading to deadlock. Under such situations, alternative strategies like random walks, tabu search, SA can be used.

***Termination:*** Like all other metaheuristic algorithms, LS also need a termination criterion to be satisfied to both stop as well as converge. In general, these criteria can be number of iterations, stagnation, improved objective function, and run time.

### 11.5.3 Tabu Search

An extended version of LS is Tabu search (TS) where the solutions are designated in an N-dimensional space where N is number of decision variables. Travelling in TS from the searching point (or old solution), to a neighbouring point (or new solution) in called a move. During a move, the current searching point is considered as the local best and other neighbouring points are being searched for (except the one marked as tabu). In contrast to other algorithms, TS replaces the initial searching point with the best neighbouring point, even if it is poorer, and marks the current searching point as a tabu. This process repeats till a termination criterion is arrived at and the best point reached is marked as the best solution during the search. All the recently explored points are recorded in the tabu list which helps the algorithm to effectively mitigate the risk of arriving at a deadlock and rather foster a dynamic and expansive search across the uncharted territories of the solution space.

***Initial State:*** The initial decision space in TS consists of points which are feasible solution of the specific optimization problem. A single solution in TS can be represented as,

$$\mathrm{X} = (\mathrm{x}_1, \mathrm{x}_2, \mathrm{x}_3, \ldots., \mathrm{x}_\mathrm{N})$$

***Neighbourhood:*** The neighbourhood in TS has all the feasible solutions in proximity such that the decision variable is replaced by its immediate next values in a sorted list of discrete values. In an N-dimensional space, if the searching point is designated as $X = (x_1, x_2, x_3, \ldots., x_N)$, then number of neighbourhood solutions are 2N and can be represented as a large matrix of new solutions. In this large search space, a new solution can be searched by,

$$X^{(\mathrm{new})} = \mathrm{X} \pm (\varepsilon \cdot e_{1\times N}) \tag{11.28}$$

Where, $X^{(\mathrm{new})}$ = neighbour of *X*; *e* = direction vector comprising 0s and 1s and $\varepsilon$ = the discrete space.

***Tabu List:*** Tabu list is a deterministic approach that allows shift to the poorest neighbouring solutions if the improved solution is absent. There is a possibility that the TS algorithm might encounter a deadlock in reaching any optimal solution. In such case, the tabu list is used to break the cycle. There are different ways of maintaining a tabu list, one way is to record the visited solutions and other is to memorise the performed transformations to avoid reverse transformation. The second way is more preferable.

***Updating Tabu List:*** A user-defined parameter tabu tenure represented as $\delta$ is used in TS to record the iteration counts during which tabu lists are saved. If the list is full and a new solution has to be added, then the oldest solution is deleted.

***Memory:*** Attributive memories which stores the attributes of solutions is widely used in TS. Frequency and recency based are two prevalent approaches for such memories. Frequency based approach records the number of times a solution is visited whereas recency based keeps a track of the solutions parameters that have recently changed. Recency based tabu list is easy to save as well as access.

***Termination Criteria:*** In order to stop the execution of TS algorithm and converge, termination criteria such as number of iterations or improvement in objective function or runtime are used.

### 11.5.4 Harmony Search Algorithm

Harmony Search (HS) algorithm draws inspiration from the intricate art of musicians improvising melodies. By emulating the harmonious interplay of musical notes, HS algorithm endeavours to provide optimal solutions in a manner reminiscent of nature's own creative processes. The metaheuristic algorithm under consideration effectively replicates the intricate process of harmony creation by skilfully converting musical concepts into powerful optimisation strategies. This unique capability empowers the algorithm to diligently explore a wide range of problem domains, ultimately leading to the discovery of optimal or near-optimal solutions.

In HS, each harmony is considered as a solution and the corresponding pitch determines the desirability, it being a decision variable. While generating new solutions in HS, a new harmony, if it is better than the old ones, will be considered for replacement. In general, several random harmonies will be generated as initial solutions which are first memorized ant then their fitness values are calculated. A sorted list of solutions prepared based on the fitness values leads to determine the worst solution. Thus, there will be only two possible cases – if the newly generated solution is better than the ones currently in the memory, it is replaced, else the memory stays unaltered. This is repeated until the termination criteria are satisfied and optimal solutions are arrived.

***Initial State:*** The initial state of HS consists of harmony's pitches as the decision variables of decision space. It is represented by an array of size $1 \times N$ such that,

$$\text{Harmony} = X = (x_1, x_2, x_3, \ldots, x_N)$$

The initial population is generated randomly in the form of a M x N matrix, where M = size of harmony memory and N = number of decision variables such that each value in this matrix is a discrete value.

***Generating New Harmonies:*** Generating new solutions is also known as improvising the harmony in HS. Although HS is a population-based optimization algorithm, it generates only one solution in every iteration. However, there are three main strategies for improvisation—memory strategy, random selection and adjustment pitch.

In the first strategy, decision variables are chosen from the already stored data such that any one of the memorised solutions for each decision variable is chosen and a new solution is assigned such that,

$$x' = x_{j,i}, i = 1,2,..,N \text{ and } j = Irnd(1,m) \tag{11.29}$$

Where, $x_{j,i}$ = $i^{th}$ decision variable of $j^{th}$ solution in the memory and *Irnd()* = function ot generate integer random number. This is quite similar to the crossover operation in GA where previous solutions are combined to generate a new solution.

In the second strategy, decision variables are assigned values which are not in the memory. So, first the memory strategy is employed to generate a new solution and then one or more decision variables are probabilistically selected to replace with random values. This strategy uses a user-defined parameter called harmony memory considering rate (HMCR) that ranges from 0 to 1 which is compared with a random number ranging 0 to 1. If this randomly selected value is larger than HCMR then there is a replacement, otherwise not.

$$x' = v_{i,d}, \text{and } d = Irnd(1, D_i) \tag{11.30}$$

$x'$ will be considered as a new solution if,

$$x' = \begin{cases} x_{j,i} & \text{if } Rand \le \delta \\ v_{i,d} & \text{if } Rand \ge \delta \end{cases} \quad i = 1,2,\ldots, N \tag{11.31}$$

$$j = Irnd(1, M) \text{ and } d = Irnd(1, D_i) \tag{11.32}$$

Where, *Rand()* = random number generator between values 0 and 1 and $\delta$ = HMCR.

The third strategy, improves the newly generated solutions obtained from the memory strategy and then decide whether the pitch should be tuned or not. This procedure uses a separate user defined parameter called pitch adjustment parameter (PAR) which also ranges from 0 to 1 as in case of HCMR. The same approach is then used to update the decision variable as in random selection strategy, however here PAR is compared with the randomly generated value.

$$x' = \begin{cases} v_{i,d+1} & \text{if } Rand > 0.5 \\ v_{i,d-1} & \text{if } Rand \le 0.5 \end{cases} \tag{11.33}$$

Here, the present value of pitch is replaced based on the satisfiable condition with the neighbouring values i.e. $v_{j,d+1}$ or $v_{j,d-1}$.

***Updating Memory:*** In HS, selection of a new solution for update depends on whether the fitness value is improved than the worst solutions currently stored in HM.

***Termination Criteria:*** In order to stop the execution of TS algorithm and converge, termination criteria such as number of iterations or improvement in objective function or runtime are used.

**TABLE 11.2** Various characteristics of the metaheuristic algorithms for searching

| *General Terminology* | *PS* | *LS* | *TS* | *HS* |
|---|---|---|---|---|
| Decision variable | Coordinate of points | Candidate | Position of point | Pitch |
| Solution | Point | Combination | Point | Harmony |
| Initial Solution | Random point | Initial combination | Random point | Random harmony |
| Old Solution | Base point | Current combination | Searching point | Memorised harmony |
| New Solution | Trial point | Neighbour combination | Neighbour point | New harmony |
| Best solution | Base point | – | Best point | – |
| Fitness function | Desirability | Neighbourhood function | Desirability | Aesthetic criteria |
| Selection | Compare trial and base point | Choice of neighbourhood | Tabu list | Update memory |
| Generate new solutions | Exloratory and pattern move | Generate combinations | Movement | Improvisation |

PS: Pattern Search; LS: Local Search; TS: Tabu Search; HS: Harmony Search

## 11.6 APPLICATIONS OF METAHEURISTIC ALGORITHMS

Due to their effectiveness in solving challenging optimisation issues, metaheuristic algorithms have found use in a variety of areas and domains. Some of the noteworthy applications are as follows.

### 11.6.1 Engineering and Design Optimization

Metaheuristic algorithms have many different applications, but engineering and design optimisation stands out. The effectiveness, dependability, and performance of numerous engineering systems and designs are significantly improved, thanks to these algorithms.

***Structural Design:*** Buildings, bridges, and dams are only a few examples of the structures whose designs are optimised using metaheuristics. They support the discovery of combinations that satisfy safety requirements, reduce material use, and enhance structural integrity.

***Aerospace and Automotive Design:*** Vehicle designs, propulsion systems, and component layouts are all optimised via metaheuristics. While taking into account elements like weight, aerodynamics, and fuel efficiency, they allow engineers to attain desired performance characteristics.

***Mechanical Component Design:*** Designing mechanical parts like springs, bearings, and gears is made easier by these algorithms. They guarantee that components can endure operating stress and that they fulfil particular functional criteria.

***Electrical and Electronic Circuit Design:*** Electrical circuits may be designed with improved performance, less interference, and less power consumption by using metaheuristics to tweak their layout and parameters.

***Manufacturing Process Optimization:*** Manufacturing procedures like welding, casting, and machining are all improved by metaheuristics. They aid in the optimisation of production parameters for increased effectiveness and decreased faults.

***Material Selection:*** Through the optimisation of material characteristics in accordance with particular design restrictions and performance demands, these algorithms help with the selection of materials for engineering applications.

***Energy Systems Optimization:*** In power grids and renewable energy installations, metaheuristics are used to optimise the energy distribution, load management, and control systems.

***Chemical Process Design:*** Metaheuristics are used in the chemical industry to maximise production, reduce waste, and increase efficiency of chemical reactions, material synthesis, and separation processes.

***Environmental Engineering:*** By using these algorithms, environmental systems for managing water resources, controlling air quality, and treating waste may be designed to have the least possible negative environmental effects.

***Urban Planning and Traffic Management:*** Urban planning and traffic control are two areas where metaheuristic algorithms are specifically applied. The utilisation of metaheuristic algorithms presents a promising avenue for the creation of highly efficient and populace-centric public transportation networks. It is possible to design transportation systems that not only optimise resource allocation but also cater to the diverse requirements of the population. Metaheuristic algorithms also present a promising avenue for optimising land use planning, with the overarching goal of minimising traffic congestion and enhancing the overall efficiency of transportation systems. By harnessing the power of these advanced computational techniques, planners can devise strategies that effectively allocate land resources, taking into account various factors such as population density, infrastructure availability, and transportation demand. In traffic management, offering a promising avenue to tackle the pervasive issue of traffic congestion. By using these sophisticated algorithms, we can effectively optimise traffic signals and intelligently route vehicles, thereby alleviating the burden of congested road networks. Further, these algorithms also plays a major role in making avenue for the creation of smart cities that embody efficiency, sustainability, and liveability. Metaheuristic algorithms, which are inspired by natural phenomena and biological processes, offer a versatile and powerful toolset for tackling the complex challenges associated with urban design.

### 11.6.2 Resource Allocation and Scheduling

Metaheuristic algorithms for resource allocation and scheduling have several specialised applications, some of which are as described below.

***Cloud Computing:*** In cloud computing systems, resource distribution may be done using metaheuristic algorithms. They can be used, for instance, to decide how many virtual machines to supply for a specific workload and where on real servers to put them.

***Big Data Analytics:*** Resource allocation for large data analytics projects may be done using metaheuristic algorithms. They may be used, for instance, to decide on the best distribution of the data across these processors and the best number of processors to utilise for a certain activity.

***Distributed Computing:*** In the realm of distributed computing, the utilisation of metaheuristic algorithms emerges as a promising approach for the allocation of resources. These algorithms, rooted in the field of artificial intelligence and optimisation, offer a powerful means to tackle the complex task of resource allocation in distributed computing environments. By leveraging their inherent ability to explore and exploit search spaces, metaheuristic algorithms provide an effective solution to optimise the allocation. Machine learning algorithms have remarkable ability to ascertain the most suitable quantity of computers required for a specific task, along with the most efficient approach to allocate the workload across these computational units.

***Machine Learning:*** Resources can be distributed for machine learning tasks using metaheuristic algorithms. They may be used, for instance, to figure out the best strategy to divide the training data across several computers and the best number of training iterations to utilise for a particular model.

### 11.6.3 Other Areas

Using heuristics and stochastic elements, metaheuristic algorithms can efficiently navigate complex problem landscapes, even when traditional optimisation techniques fall short. Their versatility and robustness make them a valuable tool in the domains of data mining and machine learning due to their ability to effectively address intricate problems that involve multiple constraints.

***Image and Signal Processing:*** Metaheuristic algorithms demonstrate exceptional prowess in various tasks, particularly in the domain of image restoration. Using their advanced capabilities, they possess the ability to intelligently reconstruct degraded images by effectively recovering lost details while simultaneously mitigating the adverse effects of noise. In addition, it is worth noting that metaheuristics hold significant importance in the domain of image segmentation. This technique enables the division of images into coherent regions, thereby facilitating subsequent analysis. Its applications extend to various fields such as medical image segmentation, object tracking, and scene comprehension. In addition to their primary functions, these algorithms possess the capability to optimise the feature selection and extraction processes. This optimisation empowers the algorithms to perform pattern recognition and image classification tasks with enhanced efficiency and effectiveness.

In signal processing, metaheuristics demonstrate exceptional utilization in various tasks, particularly in the domain of signal denoising. These algorithms excel at improving the quality of audio, video, or sensor-generated data by efficiently mitigating undesired noise while maintaining the integrity of the underlying signal. Additionally, they are also important in machine learning (ML) applications in optimisation of filter design, enhancement of accurate frequency analysis and modulation. This is crucial particularly in applications such as audio compression and wireless communication, where precise filtering is imperative for optimal performance. Metaheuristic algorithms are also effective in achieving optimal performance for filters, transforms, and modulation schemes. The integration of metaheuristic algorithms with image and signal processing offers a powerful arsenal for tackling complex optimisation problems, enhancing the precision and reliability of data analysis, manipulation, and interpretation in various domains. These domains encompass a wide range of applications, including medical imaging, multimedia, telecommunications, and more.

***Financial Optimization:*** The utilisation of metaheuristic algorithms in financial optimisation serves as a testament to their remarkable efficacy in tackling complex challenges within the domain of finance. The utilisation of nature-inspired principles in these algorithms presents highly efficient solutions for the optimisation of portfolios, management of risks, and development of trading strategies. In portfolio optimisation, metaheuristics facilitates the discovery of the most optimal asset allocation strategy that effectively balances the delicate equilibrium between risk and return. These sophisticated algorithms serve as invaluable tools in navigating the intricate and multifaceted terrain of diverse investment options and the various constraints that accompany them.

Metaheuristics have proven to be highly advantageous in the domain of algorithmic trading, showcasing their ability to generate efficient trading strategies that leverage market trends and exploit lucrative opportunities. These algorithms use advanced optimisation techniques to fine-tune trading parameters and decision rules, empowering automated systems to execute trades with utmost efficiency and capitalise on momentary market opportunities. Furthermore, ML algorithms have emerged as indispensable tools in the realm of finance, particularly in the domains of option pricing, derivative valuation, and asset-liability management. The utilisation of metaheuristic algorithms in financial optimisation has revolutionised the way institutions and individuals approach the complexity of contemporary finance.

***Transportation and Logistics:*** The utilisation of metaheuristic algorithms in the field of transportation and logistics has a profound and revolutionary effect on enhancing the optimisation of intricate operations within this domain. In areas like route optimisation, metaheuristics demonstrate their prowess by effectively discerning the optimal paths for vehicles, thereby minimising travel time, distance, or costs. The utilisation of these algorithms holds significant value in sectors such as delivery services, public transportation, and freight management. Furthermore, it is worth noting that metaheuristics have demonstrated exceptional performance in the domain of vehicle scheduling. Specifically, they have shown great efficacy in efficiently managing complex timetables for fleets of vehicles, all the while considering various constraints that include driver shifts, vehicle capacities, and time-sensitive deliveries.

Metaheuristic algorithms have proven to be highly advantageous in the domains of warehousing and inventory management. These algorithms offer the capability to optimise storage allocation, order picking routes, and replenishment strategies, thereby enhancing overall operational efficiency. By using the capacity of metaheuristics, organisations can achieve optimal utilisation of their warehousing facilities, streamline order fulfilment processes, and implement effective replenishment plans. This ultimately leads to enhanced productivity, decrease in cost, and better customer satisfaction. By optimising storage expenses and reducing order fulfilment duration, these advanced algorithms significantly improve the overall operational efficiency of supply chain systems. In the realm of facility location optimisation, it is imperative to acknowledge the pivotal role that metaheuristics play. These powerful algorithms serve as invaluable tools in aiding strategic decision-making processes pertaining to the most advantageous positioning of distribution centres, warehouses, and production facilities. The aforementioned factors contribute to the optimisation of transportation expenses, the reduction of delivery durations, and the improvement of customer satisfaction. The convergence of metaheuristics and transportation/

logistics entails the intricate management of resource allocation, route planning, and strategic decision-making, thereby enhancing operational efficiency and cost-effectiveness in this dynamic and indispensable domain.

## SUMMARY

This chapter provides a thorough examination of these intelligent optimisation methods that are based on natural laws and skilled at resolving challenging issues in a variety of fields. The chapter opens with a concise introduction that lays the groundwork for comprehending the relevance and essence of metaheuristics. Following that, it digs further into the fundamental definitions, categories, and traits of these algorithms, illuminating their variety and flexibility. The fundamental principles, benefits, and potential applications of nature-inspired metaheuristics including Genetic Algorithms, Particle Swarm Optimisation, Ant Colony Optimisation, and Simulated Annealing are carefully examined. The chapter methodically reveals how they operate, demonstrating how they can explore complex optimisation environments and find the best answers. Highlighted applications of these algorithms include engineering, image processing, transportation, and logistics, demonstrating their adaptability in solving realistic problems.

## WORKED OUT EXAMPLES

**EXAMPLE 11.1** Rosenbrock function is a common test problem for gradient-based optimization algorithms. Use gradient descent algorithm in Python to optimize this function.

***Solution:***

```
import numpy as np
learning_rate = 0.001
num_iterations = 1000
initial_point = np.array([0.5, 0.5])
def rosenbrock(x, y):
    return (1 – x)**2 + 100 * (y – x**2)**2
def gradient_rosenbrock(x, y):
    dx = –2 * (1 – x) – 400 * x * (y - x**2)
    dy = 200 * (y – x**2)
    return np.array([dx, dy])
def gradient_descent():
    current_point = initial_point
    for _ in range(num_iterations):
    gradient = gradient_rosenbrock(current_point[0], current_point[1])
    current_point -= learning_rate * gradient
    return current_point, rosenbrock(current_point[0], current_point[1])
best_point, best_value = gradient_descent()
```

**EXAMPLE 11.2** One of the benchmark problems for optimization algorithms is the Sphere Function denoted by $f(x)=\sum_{i=1}^{n} x_i^2$. Implement the Harmony Search algorithm to optimize the sphere function.

***Solution:***

```
import numpy as np
num_harmonies = 50
harmony_memory_size = 10
iterations = 1000
harmony_memory_consideration_rate = 0.95
par_rate = 0.6
bw = 0.01
def sphere(x):
    return np.sum(np.square(x))
harmony_memory = [np.random.uniform(-5, 5, size=2) for _ in range(harmony_memory_size)]
for _ in range(iterations):
    new_harmony = np.random.uniform(-5, 5, size=2)
    for i in range(2):
    if np.random.rand() < harmony_memory_consideration_rate:
    new_harmony[i] = harmony_memory[np.random.randint(harmony_memory_size)][i]
    for i in range(2):
    if np.random.rand() < par_rate:
    new_harmony[i] += np.random.uniform(-bw, bw)
    for i in range(harmony_memory_size):
    if sphere(new_harmony) < sphere(harmony_memory[i]):
    harmony_memory[i] = new_harmony
best_solution = min(harmony_memory, key=sphere)
```

**EXAMPLE 11.3** A very well-known problem in combinatorial optimization is the Eight Queens Problem. Placing eight chess queens on an 8 × 8 chessboard with no two queens posing a threat to one another is the primary objective. Use Pattern Search to optimize the Eight Queen problem.

***Solution:***

```
import random
initial_queens = [random.randint(0, 7) for _ in range(8)]
num_iterations = 1000
step_size = 1
def objective_function(queens):
    num_attacks = 0
    for i in range(len(queens)):
    for j in range(i+1, len(queens)):
    if queens[i] == queens[j] or abs(i - j) == abs(queens[i] - queens[j]):
    num_attacks += 1
    return 28 - num_attacks
```

```
def generate_neighbor(queens):
    neighbor = queens.copy()
    col = random.randint(0, 7)
    row = random.randint(0, 7)
    neighbor[col] = row
    return neighbor
def pattern_search():
    current_queens = initial_queens
    current_value = objective_function(current_queens)
    for _ in range(num_iterations):
    neighbor = generate_neighbor(current_queens)
    neighbor_value = objective_function(neighbor)
    if neighbor_value > current_value:
    current_queens = neighbor
    current_value = neighbor_value
    return current_queens, current_value
best_queens, best_value = pattern_search()
```

## EXERCISES

1. Given an undirected graph, the objective is to allot colours to vertices in a way that no two adjacent vertices share common colour, using as few colours as possible. Write the python program to solve this problem using genetic algorithm.
2. Consider a Boolean formula *BF*. Find if there exists an assignment of truth values to the variables that makes *BF* true. Write the python program to solve this problem using PSO.
3. Given a set of passengers with demands, and a fleet of vehicles, the aim is to search a set of routes for these vehicles to serve all passengers while minimizing total distance travelled or total cost. Write a program to optimize the problem using pattern search.
4. Consider a set of items with different sizes and a fixed number of bins, the objective is to pack the items into the bins in a way that the number of bins used is minimum. Use Ant Colony Optimization algorithm to solve this problem in python.
5. Find maximum cliques in a given graph by iteratively exploring the space of possible cliques and accepting moves that increase the size of the clique using simulated annealing algorithm in python.

## BIBLIOGRAPHY


Bozorg-Haddad, O., Solgi, M. and Loáiciga, H. A. (2017). *Metaheuristic and Evolutionary Algorithms for Engineering Optimization*, John Wiley & Sons.

Glover, F. and Laguna, M. (1997). *Tabu Search*, Kluwer Academic.

Goldberg, D. E. (1989). *Genetic Algorithms in Search, Optimization and Machine Learning*, Addison-Wesely.

Michalewicz, Z. (1996). *Genetic Algorithms + Data Structures = Evolution Programs*, Springer.

Petrowski, J. D. A. and Taillard, P. S. E. (2006). *Metaheuristics for Hard Optimization*, Springer.

Chapter 12

# AI in Natural Sciences

## 12.1 INTRODUCTION

Artificial intelligence (AI) has a major impact across many fields of natural science research and its intersections with other domains. In areas like biology, chemistry, and environmental sciences, which are the core subjects of natural sciences, AI is used to analyze massive datasets, model complex systems, and accelerate the discovery of new knowledge. For example, AI techniques help scientists to predict protein structures, design new drugs and materials, map ecosystems, track climate change patterns, and many more.

The experts firmly believe that AI will become an indispensable tool for nearly all-natural sciences research. It allows scientists to uncover insights from huge volumes of data that would be impossible for humans to process manually. AI also has the potential to automate certain experimental and testing procedures in areas like genetics and drug development. However, there are still challenges in AI that can truly mimic advanced human skills like creativity and strategic thinking. Natural science research will likely involve collaboration between AI systems and human scientists, each bringing complementary strengths to scientific discovery.

## 12.2 DIFFERENT PARADIGMS OF SCIENCE

### *Empirical Paradigm*

This is the first paradigm of science. Direct observation of the natural world is emphasized as the major means of information acquisition in the Empirical Paradigm of Science. Under this paradigm, scientists prioritize their senses or tools to collect evidence to minimize the impact of prior hypotheses and maintain objectivity. They concentrate on precisely characterizing and classifying things while looking for trends in what they see. They may make speculative assumptions or generalizations based on these patterns through inductive reasoning. However, establishing a solid base of objective observations upon which theories and explanations for the future can be constructed is the main objective of the Empirical Paradigm.

### *Theoretical Paradigm*

This is the second paradigm of science. The development of fundamental laws and explanatory models replaces the emphasis on direct observation in the theoretical paradigm of science. This paradigm acknowledges that the underlying mechanisms controlling the natural world are not always apparent through observation alone. Science aims to develop hypotheses, which are logical, cogent explanations for events that are seen. These theories aim to determine causal linkages and frequently entail mathematical formulations. Testability is a fundamental component of this paradigm: a well-crafted theory produces predictions that may be confirmed or refuted by means of experiments or more observation. With the advent of the Theoretical Paradigm, science has made a significant step forward by actively attempting to explain why phenomena occur rather than only describing their appearance.

### *Computational Paradigm*

This is the third paradigm of science. The Computational Paradigm of Science has emerged with the development of powerful computers. Focusing on problems that are too complex or impossible to solve using conventional analytical equations, it uses sophisticated computations and computer simulations. According to this paradigm, scientists build computational models that simulate certain features of the actual world. With the help of these models, they may conduct "virtual" experiments, altering the variables and tracking the results. This is very useful for chaotic systems (like weather forecasting), systems with an excessive number of interacting components (like protein folding), or scenarios where conducting tests in the actual world would be expensive or risky. Researchers may now address issues that were previously unsolvable because to the Computational Paradigm, which has completely changed the way that research is done.

### *Data-Intensive/e-Science Paradigm*

This is the fourth paradigm of science. The explosion of data in the modern world has led to a substantial shift known as the Data-Intensive/e-Science Paradigm. It is distinguished by the extensive gathering and examination of scientific data made feasible by advancements in technology such as distributed computing, the internet, and potent sensors. In this paradigm, scientists mine massive datasets for patterns, correlations, and insights that may be hidden from view by conventional techniques using sophisticated tools and algorithms. In order to solve complicated problems, scientists and computational professionals frequently collaborate across different academic disciplines. The Data-Intensive paradigm enhances theoretical and experimental methods in scientific discovery by emphasizing the ability to derive information from the massive amount of data at one's disposal.

### *"AI for Science" or Fifth Paradigm*

This is the fifth paradigm of science. The field known as "AI for Science" or Fifth Paradigm is a rapidly developing area that involves the seamless integration of Artificial Intelligence (AI) and machine learning (ML) methods into the realm of scientific exploration. Within this framework, AI serves as a valuable instrument for researchers, extending its capabilities beyond mere data management. AI algorithms have the capability to expedite intricate simulations, uncover concealed patterns in vast datasets, and provide recommendations for innovative experiments or assist in the creation of new materials. The objective is to establish a genuine collaboration between human scientists and AI systems, capitalizing on their unique strengths. This approach can potentially transform our understanding of the world, possibly resulting in significant discoveries in various fields such as drug development and fundamental physics.

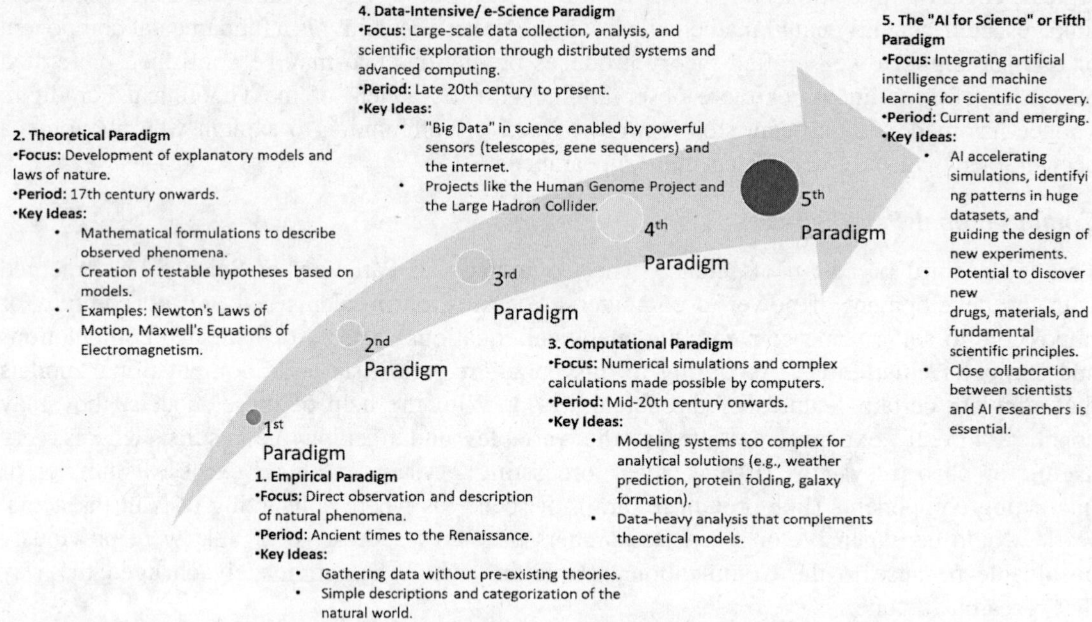


**FIGURE 12.1** Different Paradigms of science.

## 12.3 AI IN PHYSICAL SCIENCE

### 12.3.1 Physics-Informed Neural Networks (PINN)

Physics-Informed Neural Networks (PINN) are a class of neural networks that incorporate physics principles and governing equations directly to the loss function and architecture of the network. This enables the neural network to learn the behavior and properties of physical systems while respecting the underlying scientific constraints that determine that behavior. Specifically, the loss function of a PINN has two key components—a data-fitting loss that regresses model predictions to match observations and data examples, as well as a physics-informed loss that penalizes violations of encoded physics laws. By jointly optimizing these two loss components, PINN can effectively learn the spatial fields, dynamics, and parameters of complex physical systems using relatively little data, compensating for the lack of data by leveraging expertise encoded into the physics constraints.

Researchers have demonstrated promising results applying PINN to problems in domains as diverse as fluid mechanics, molecular dynamics, cosmology, and more. Key advantages of this approach include accurate solutions from limited noisy sensor data, as well as the ability to infer hard-to-measure system states from easy-to-collect data paired with scientific first principles. Going forward, scaling PINN to 3D systems, enhancing stability, improving uncertainty quantification, and expanding the complexity of encoded physics remain active innovation areas. Overall, PINN represents an exciting synergy between scientific computation and deep learning for tackling modeling challenges spanning the physical and natural sciences. By fusing data and first principles within a neural network framework, PINN offers a new paradigm for leveraging laws of physics to inform data-driven learning and inference.

***Some key principles of physics-informed learning:***

1. ***Encoding Expert Knowledge:*** At the core of physics-informed learning is encoding domain expertise and scientific principles into the ML model. This could include fundamental laws (e.g. conservation of energy), governing equations (e.g. Navier-Stokes equations), symmetries, or relational inductive biases.
2. ***Mixed Training Objectives:*** Along with standard data-driven loss functions (e.g., MSE loss), physics-informed learning utilizes physics losses that measure violate expert domain knowledge constraints. Minimizing a combination of physics and data losses enables models to match data patterns while satisfying scientific laws.
3. ***Inferring Unseen Quantities:*** An important capability enabled is inferring difficult-to-measure quantities from easy-to-collect data via domain knowledge. For example, inferring 3D flow fields from sparse 2D measurements using fluid equations. This allows expanding model applicability.
4. ***Extrapolation Beyond Data:*** By heavily leveraging structured scientific knowledge, models can plausibly extrapolate and make predictions substantially beyond the scope of the original training data, a key limitation of pure data-driven approaches.
5. ***Uncertainty Quantification:*** Quantifying predictive uncertainty and reliability is critical for applying learned models to real-world systems. Some physics-informed learning methods can produce well-calibrated uncertainty estimates grounded in the reliability of model assumptions.

Thus, physics-informed ML aims to synergistically combine scientific theory and data to produce models that are accurate, robust, interpretable, and capable of generalization across physical regimes. Fusing the strengths of human scientific understanding and neural architectures offers an exciting path for tackling complex modeling problems with reliability guarantees.

**TABLE 12.1** Libraries for Physics-informed Machine Learning

| *Software* | *Purpose* | *Language* | *Backend* |
|---|---|---|---|
| DeepXDE | Solver | Python | TensorFlow |
| SimNet | Solver | Python | TensorFlow |
| PyDEns | Solver | Python | TensorFlow |
| NeuroDiffEq | Solver | Python | PyTorch |
| NeuralPDE | Solver | Julia | Julia |
| SciANN | Wrapper | Python | TensorFlow |
| ADCME | Wrapper | Julia | TensorFlow |
| GPyTorch | Wrapper | Python | PyTorch |

***Limitations of PINN***

Even though physics-informed learning is applied in various applications, more advancements are indispensable for multiphysics problems. For instance, the literature refers to the "F-principle" or "spectral bias" as the difficulties fully connected neural networks have learning high-frequency functions.

Further research determined training convergence rates as a function of target frequency and conclusively demonstrated the presence of frequency bias in DNNs. Furthermore, high-frequency features in the target solution typically led to steep gradients, which makes it difficult for PINN models to penalise the PDE residuals appropriately. Consequently, networks may fail to train for multiscale issues due to their difficulty learning high-frequency components. The problem of learning high-frequency components requires the development of novel methods to support network learning, such as multiscale DNN, domain decomposition, and Fourier features. On the other hand, it might be computationally costly to learn multi-physics concurrently. One possible solution to this problem would be to master each branch of physics independently before combining them. When applying the DeepM&M method to the electro-convection and hypersonic problems, multiple DeepONets were first trained independently for each field. They then used supervised learning based on extra data to learn the coupled solutions through either a serial or parallel DeepM&M architecture. Using the fine-scale simulation data limited to narrow domains, it is also feasible to understand the physics at a coarse scale.

### 12.3.2 Application in Fluid Mechanics

Turbulence, a flow regime marked by erratic, time-dependent variations in pressure and velocity, has long been a source of concern in fluid dynamics. In recent years, there has been a notable surge in the application of data-driven approaches, leading to the development of novel modelling tools for intricate turbulent flows. ANNs have been used to forecast the instantaneous velocity vector field in turbulent wake flows and turbulent channel flows as examples of how machine learning has been applied to model turbulence. The widespread acceptance of ML techniques, particularly deep learning (DL), as a viable approach to addressing intricate fluid flow issues is reinforced by the availability of excellent open-source data sets released by scholars. Currently, a lot of work is being done to employ ML algorithms to increase the accuracy of Reynolds-averaged Navier-Stokes (RANS) models, which have been quantified and had uncertainties reduced using Gaussian Processes (GPs).

### 12.3.3 High Energy Physics Quantum Machine Learning

The branch that deals with building blocks of matter and the physical laws is known as High-energy physics. Historically, theoretical models have provided major advances in understanding, while experiments at particle colliders validate the latest theories. Increasingly, though, ML is playing a role in both understanding the large volumes of data from particle detectors and assisting theorists. On the experimental side, DL algorithms are used for pattern recognition and signal/background discrimination. They also help analyse the huge quantities of simulation data needed to design detectors and interpret results. From a theoretical perspective, quantum machine learning holds promise for significant breakthroughs. Quantum computing leverages quantum mechanical phenomena like superposition and entanglement for exponential speedups. Quantum machine learning algorithms built on quantum computers can probe theoretical models of quantum chromodynamics and other high energy physics frameworks. They potentially uncover new particles, forces, and other exotic physical manifestations that classical techniques may miss. High energy physics exists at the cutting edge of understanding the deepest laws of nature. Quantum machine learning's ability to probe how enormous high-dimensional spaces can provide the next major leap ahead.

Quantum computers perform computations using different quantum mechanical phenomena (i.e. superposition and entanglement). Quantum computers use quantum bits (referred as qubits) that can be 0, 1 or superposition of both simultaneously. The advantage of qubits is, it allows store more information. This ability of qubits to encode more information allows quantum computers to solve certain problems much faster than classical computers, especially problems related to simulation, optimization, and machine learning. Some examples include chemical simulation, financial modeling, traffic optimization, and AI. However, quantum computing is still in its early stages. Quantum computers are very fragile and susceptible to errors and decoherence (loss of quantum properties). Current quantum computers only have less than 100 qubits while thousands of logical qubits are likely needed for most practical applications. Major tech companies like IBM, Google, Microsoft, Intel, and startups like Rigetti and IonQ are working hard to develop practical, large-scale quantum computers. Key areas of focus are developing better qubits through materials science and engineering, error correction schemes, and quantum algorithms.

## 12.4 AI IN MATERIALS SCIENCE

The materials science community within higher education, national laboratories, and industries has benefited from and contributed to the advancement of sophisticated quantitative methodologies. Recently, AI-ML techniques have emerged as pivotal elements in data-driven approaches to materials science. These techniques have enabled various materials science and engineering domains to discern predictive patterns within the interrelationships of structure, property, and function. The ongoing evolution of computing capabilities, software, and algorithms, coupled with a substantial increase in data derived from experiments and simulations, has fostered a robust synergy between materials science and data science. It remains challenging to ascertain which aspect has experienced greater growth over the past decade: the volume of data generated by increasingly intricate simulations and experiments, or the advancement of AI/ML algorithms designed to analyze this data. Moreover, significant progress has been made in integrating materials research with data sciences, leading to a more cohesive relationship between the two fields.

Data-driven strategies are employed in these so-called active learning paradigms to direct subsequent trials, frequently in an iterative, closed-loop fashion. Navigating material space in a high throughput, efficient, and regulated manner is made possible by such autonomous materials discovery paradigms.

AI is rapidly advancing materials discovery and development. Rather than relying solely on time-consuming trial-and-error experimental approaches, AI allows properties of new compounds to be predicted by applying ML algorithms to large materials databases. Models can accurately identify completely novel materials compositions or structures that exhibit target attributes like electrical conductivity, magnetism, phase transition temperatures, oxidative resistance, and more. This accelerates the exploration and optimization of materials for specialized applications across industries.

Additionally, AI is optimizing materials manufacturing techniques. By comprehensively modeling the impacts of processing methods and parameters on material qualities, the most efficient pathways can be simulated before even attempting production. AI agents can even autonomously run experiments now—intelligently choosing reagents to mix or conditions to test to produce a material with desired qualities efficiently. Rather than incremental tuning, AI allows enormous material parameter spaces to be mapped, illuminating production breakthroughs. The capacities of AI systems to generate new knowledge via big data outmatch what humans can achieve manually. Experts forecast that AI techniques will support the discovery and optimized manufacture of over 90% of new products and advanced materials innovations across sectors like electronics, energy, transportation, healthcare, and construction over the next decade. This undoubtedly marks the advent of an intelligence revolution in material science.

**Materials Discovery & Design:**

✓AI can predict the properties of hypothetical materials before they are even synthesized. By analyzing massive datasets of known materials, AI models learn patterns and relationships. This allows them to suggest new compounds with tailored properties (e.g., stronger, lighter, more conductive).

**Property Prediction:**

✓Instead of time-consuming experimental testing, AI can predict crucial properties of materials like strength, conductivity, stability, and band gaps. This helps researchers screen and prioritize materials for specific applications.

**Optimizing Synthesis: .**

✓AI assists in finding the best lab procedures for creating materials. It can analyze past experiments, suggest changes to parameters, and even control laboratory equipment autonomously to achieve the desired results more efficiently

**Analyzing Complex Data: .**

✓AI is adept at handling data from characterization techniques like X-ray diffraction, microscopy, and spectroscopy. It can extract valuable insights, identify phases, and detect subtle defects that might be missed by humans

**Scientific Literature Analysis:**

✓AI can process vast amounts of research papers, helping researchers keep up with the latest advancements, find relevant studies, and identify potential knowledge gaps.

**FIGURE 12.2** Key Areas of AI Impact in Materials Science.

Many open-source ML tools are available to help with the use of ML in materials science. SchNet, for instance, is a DL framework for molecular materials that has been specially created to use continuous filter convolution layers to simulate atomic systems. Machine learning software called DScribe can potentially revolutionise feature transformation for atomic material simulations.

Matminer is an open-source program built on Python that uses a data-driven approach to evaluate and forecast material properties. A powerful open-source Python Materials Genomics package called Pymatgen is available for material analysis. It can provide the first calculations and setup needed for high-throughput materials science computation. Using random feature graphs, Thompson sampling, first-order Cholesky updates, and automatic hyperparameter adjustment, COMBO creates an efficient Bayesian optimisation strategy available as an open-source Python module. One can get COMBO from the following website: https://github.com/tsudalab/combo. AFLOW-ML makes an open RESTful API with direct access to constantly updated algorithms possible. These algorithms may be seamlessly incorporated into any process, including electronic retrieval and mechanical or thermal performance prediction. Together with the packages already mentioned, the open-source framework that consists of TensorFlow, Pytorch, Keras, Scikit-Learn etc., can help speed up creating models from scratch and increase productivity. For instance, machine learning, feature selection, and model evaluation are employed in Scikit-Learn, a Python library-based program, to forecast the thermal stability of perovskite materials.

## 12.5 AI IN CHEMICAL SCIENCE

Several modeling and simulation codes available today are either public or private. Open-source software (OSS) has contributed significantly to scientific advancement while closed-source softwares is developed by businesses for financial gain. The Open-Source Software (OSS) ideology encourages the sharing of code or tools and, consequently, the knowledge of computer science and nature that is included in the code. OSS enables researchers to critically study the code, comprehend its mathematical formulations, parameters, and assumptions as well as the logic of the process, and alter it as needed. Although commercial usage may still be limited, free and open-source software (FOSS), a subtype of open-source software (OSS), still requires licencing models that offer a legal foundation for the code's free distribution, use, and development.

There has been a noticeable increase in the number of research publications published that discuss ML and public interest, indicating the growth of this discipline. Sharing ML algorithms and their trained models for open source brings three main advantages to the field: (1) creating common interfaces, (2) allowing for experimentation, and (3) fostering a sense of community.

### 12.5.1 Exploring the Relationship between Quantum Mechanics and Density Functional Theory

Quantum Mechanics (QM), Density Functional Theory (DFT), and Machine Learning (ML) intersect in various ways. Using QM/DFT calculations to generate accurate data for training and validating a model is crucial. High accuracy achieved through QM is balanced by the significant computational resources required. After creating these datasets, there is a great chance to train machine learning models faster to calculate wave-function-based observables like orbital energies and polarizability.

### 12.5.2 Strengthening DFT Functionals with AI

Density Functional Theory (DFT) is one of the most widely used computational methods for studying chemical systems, however, approximations in its functionals can lead to accuracy issues for certain properties. An emerging machine learning approach to improve DFT focuses on modeling these functional inaccuracies. Large datasets of higher-level benchmark calculations done for representative chemical systems are used to train models that effectively learn the systematic errors of a functional. These models then act as corrections when that functional is applied to new systems, considerably improving results. Examples of such machine learning-corrected functionals include GMTKN55-correlated, DP-DFT, and B3MLYP-D4. They use model structures ranging from simple linear fits to complex neural networks. Accessibility of vast computational power and chemical data has fuelled rapid innovation in this subfield. ML-improved functionals attain benchmark-level accuracy at just a fraction of the computational expense, unlocking a new paradigm in computational chemistry. Chemical insights provided by future chemically-interpretable ML models will be invaluable across drug design, materials development, spectroscopic studies, and more by elevating the precision of the most widely accessible computational method for modeling molecular systems.

**TABLE 12.2** Computational Chemistry Focused ML Tools for Improving DFT Functionals

| *Software* | *link* | *license* | *public data* | *public model* |
|---|---|---|---|---|
| *PROPhet* | https://github.com/biklooost/PROPhet | GPL-3.0 | N | N |
| *DeepKS* | https://github.com/deepmodeling/deepks-kit | LGPL-3.0 | Y | N |
| *NeuralXC* | semodi/neuralxc: Implementation of a machine learned density functional (github.com) | BSD-3-Clause | Y | Y |
| NNFunctional | https://github.com/ml-electron-project/NNfunctional | MIT | Y | Y |
| DQC | https://github.com/diffqc/dqc | Apache-2.0 | Y | N |
| JAX-DFT | google-research/jax_dft at master · google-research/google-research (github.com) | Apache-2.0 | Y | Y |
| Cider | https://github.com/mir-group/CiderPress | MIT | Y | N |
| SyFES | Code for "evolving symbolic density functionals" (zenodo.org) | CC-BY-4.0 | Y | N |

### 12.5.3 Molecular Mechanics Force Fields

All Molecular Mechanics (MM)-based techniques rely heavily on their force fields, whose state-of-the-art parameter optimization is being sought using ML. Newtonian equations provide an explicit definition for MM potentials. These equations can be classified into two categories: bonded components, such as bonds, angles, and torsion, and nonbonded components, such as partial atomic charges and Lennard-Jones. The ML algorithms' isolated goals among these are frequently the nonbonded parameters. However, ML that models the potential energy surface can completely replace the force field equation's functional form, allowing MD simulations to continue.

For use in materials research, the force field precursors for metal-organic frameworks (FFP4MOF) tool was created. It can forecast nonbonded parameters for systems including metal. The two GitHub repositories contain molecules-specific (ammonium perchlorate, pentafluoroethane, and difluoromethane) examples of how multiobjective surrogate-assisted Gaussian process regression and support vector machine workflows can be used to optimise Lennard-Jones parameters. Similarly, PREMSO employs a global evolutionary optimisation technique augmented by presampling and surrogate assistance, allowing characteristics at various sizes (e.g., bulk-phase and single-molecule observables) to be used. GNN is used to predict nonbonded characteristics based on QM target data, including atom type prediction, which was also recently released. Using a GNN to sense chemical surroundings and then forecast bonded and nonbonded parameters, the remarkable Extensible Surrogate Potential Optimised by Message-passing Algorithms (espaloma) comes from the Codera lab. Several research groups have developed ML approaches for predicting partial atomic charges (PACs). The Atom-Path-Descriptor (APD) trains random forest and extreme gradient boosting models for PAC prediction by focusing on tiny molecules using a novel atomic descriptor.

**TABLE 12.3** Computational Chemistry focused ML Tools for Force Field Parameter Determination

| *Software* | *link* | *license* | *public data* | *public model* |
|---|---|---|---|---|
| FFP4MOF | https://github.com/korolewadim/ffp4mof | MIT | Y | Y |
| PREMSO | https://github.com/maxm89/PREMSO-2022 | GPL-3.0 | Y | N |
| GNN Parametrized Forcefields | https://github.com/rinikerlab/GNNParametrizedFF | MIT | Y | Y |
| espaloma1 | https://github.com/choderalab/espaloma | MIT | Y | Y |

### 12.5.4 Synthesis and Chemical Reactions

ML is transforming the field of chemical synthesis by helping automate the search for optimized routes to produce desired compounds. Rather than manually exploring possible sequences of reagents and reactions, ML algorithms can learn from reaction datasets and published synthetic pathways to predict optimal combinations to synthesize a target molecule. Models can suggest new one-pot reactions, incompatible functional groups to avoid, byproduct predictions, and solvent/catalyst recommendations. Another active area uses generative ML to design novel reactions by learning key patterns and constraints. In terms of optimization, neural networks analyze prior conditions (temperature, duration, concentrations etc.) across reaction types to suggest optimized parameters for maximum yield and purity. Some platforms even employ robotic experimentation guided by *in silico* ML predictions to try reactions and refine models iteratively. With capacities far exceeding human chemical intuition, ML promises to drastically accelerate the discovery of new chemical transformations while enhancing efficiencies - saving costs, resources, and waste. Experts envision a future where ML drives automated synthesis planning and experimentation for chemicals, advanced materials, and potentially new pharmaceuticals.

## 12.6 AI IN BIOLOGICAL SCIENCE

AI profoundly impacts biological research across multiple fronts from DNA sequencing to microscopic imaging and drug discovery. Advanced AI techniques like machine and deep learning allow researchers to rapidly analyze massive genomics datasets to uncover mutations implicated in cancer, predict the 3D folding of protein structures from sequences, and even design novel proteins with desired functions. Beyond sequencing, AI enables automation and augmentation of other biomedical workflows as well. Algorithms can now process and discern complex patterns in cellular imagery that elude human vision, powering rapid disease screening and identifying morphological changes over time. Robotic automation guided by computer vision facilitates high-throughput manipulation of samples, while ML radically accelerates pharmaceutical developers' ability to identify viable new drug candidates or combinations by screening billions of compounds.

Also, seamless integration of AI across the workflow from hypotheses to experimental design, data collection, and analysis will likely become the norm in biology. Rather than brute force approaches, AI agents will strategically determine informative subsequent experiments to refine models and achieve targets most efficiently. Beyond bench applications, AI personalization of medicine, diagnostics and wearable monitoring will transform how findings get translated to improve human health outcomes. With capacities far beyond what any lone researcher can achieve, AI's role in biological research is projected to grow exponentially and become integral across disciplines from bioinformatics to evolutionary biology to medicine—providing an indispensable toolkit illuminating life's mysteries.

The field of biology has led to groundbreaking advancements in various areas. AI algorithms are adept at processing and analyzing vast amounts of biological data including medical images, genomic sequences and protein structures, etc. This enables researchers to identify complex patterns, uncover disease-causing mutations, and predict protein interactions crucial for drug development. Moreover, AI is driving the development of personalized medicine, where algorithms tailor treatments based on an individual's genetic makeup and medical history. AI-powered tools facilitate the design of novel drugs, targeting specific molecules involved in disease processes. Furthermore, AI's image analysis capabilities are revolutionizing microscopy and diagnostics, allowing for faster and more accurate identification of cells, tissues, and disease biomarkers. The integration of AI into biology is accelerating discoveries and leading to a deeper understanding of biological processes, ultimately paving the way for improved healthcare and potential cures for complex diseases.

### 12.6.1 Molecular Docking

Molecular docking is modeling and simulating how a ligand, typically a small molecule/drug candidate, binds to a target protein receptor or enzyme. It aims to predict the binding mode and affinity. Docking is used extensively in structure-based drug design as a computational method to screen large libraries of potential drugs and predict which are likely to bind a protein target in therapeutically relevant ways.

Some key aspects relating docking to biology:

- Target proteins are central components of biological pathways, so docking reveals potential ways to modulate biomolecular function and biology using drug molecules.
- The docking process considers conformational flexibility and geometric complementarity between the small molecule and binding pocket in the target protein's 3D structure. This structure-function relationship is central in biology.
- Scoring functions used to predict ligand binding affinity rely heavily on modeling biochemical interactions like hydrogen bonding and hydrophobic effects which govern bio-molecular interactions and structural biology.
- Results provide insights into fundamental biomolecular recognition and binding mechanisms between a drug-like small molecule and receptor protein target within a biological system.

So, molecular docking firmly resides within computational structural biology and is a bio-chemically aware simulation technique used to predict and model ligand-receptor binding interactions underlying pharmacological modulation of biological systems.

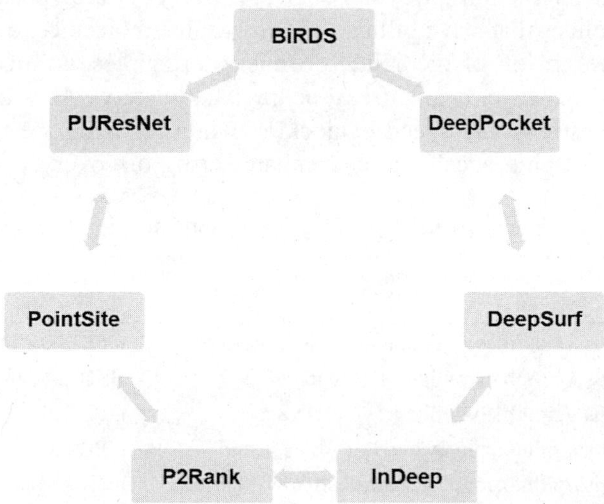


**FIGURE 12.3** Machine Learning Tools for Estimating Potential Protein Binding Pockets.

Protein-ligand interactions are fundamental to pharmacological modulation of targets, making their accurate modeling and prediction vital in drug discovery. ML advances this by going beyond simple docking scores to provide richer learned insights into binding interactions. Specialized ML tools can reveal per-atom contributions to overall affinity and highlight pharmacophore features that drive potency. SVM and neural net models have been trained on large structural interaction fingerprints to predict affinity changes from protein mutations seen across genotypes. Other creative approaches employ generative ML to propose structural modifications predicted to improve affinity. Tools like Machine Learning for Interaction Fingerprints (MLIF) and DeepChem are shining light on molecular determinants of target selectivity too. On the protein side as well, ML can find sequence motifs and rare mutations associated with ligand subtype preference. Instead of just binding scores, ML infuses predictions with chemical interpretability, capturing nuances affecting potency. This provides invaluable guidance as medicinal chemists work to optimize hits - a process still demanding human logic, creativity, and scientific insight. In time collaborative frameworks between ML tools and human experts may dominate drug optimization.

### 12.6.2 Docking and Virtual Screening Tools and Machine Learning Scoring Functions

Molecular docking is crucial *in silico* methods in drug discovery, predicting how drug candidates bind to receptors by modeling their fit and scoring affinity. ML advances docking by producing more predictive and chemically insightful scoring functions. Traditionally, docking uses physics-based or empirical scoring, but these often lack accuracy. By training ML models on large binding affinity data sets, improved scoring functions are being developed that outperform traditional techniques. Prominent examples include RF-Score, AlphaScore, and Pafnucy which exhibit enhanced binding affinity and hit-rate prediction. ML functions better account for intricate biochemical interactions. Beyond scoring, ML tools are speeding up structure-based virtual screening pipelines that sieve billions of purchasable molecules to identify good prospects using learned comprehension of medicinal chemistry principles. AutoDock Vina's integration with ML allows fast exhaustive grid-free docking. Ultimately ML shows immense potential to strengthen the robustness and speed of docking while reducing the need for CPU-intensive physics calculations, helping accelerate and enhance drug discovery.

**TABLE 12.4** Docking and Virtual Screening Tools and Machine Learning Scoring Functions

| *Software* | *link* | *license* | *public data* | *public model* |
|---|---|---|---|---|
| ΔvinaXGB | https://github.com/jenniening/deltaVinaXGB | GPL-3.0 | Y | Y |
| AEScore | https://github.com/bigginlab/aescore | BSD-3-Clause | Y | Y |
| ET-Score | https://github.com/miladrayka/ET_Score | GPL-3.0 | Y | Y |
| ΔLinF9XGB | https://github.com/cyangNYU/delta_LinF9_XGB | GPL-3.0 | Y | Y |
| PharmRF | https://github.com/Prasanth-Kumar87/PharmRF | unavailable | Y | Y |
| *GB-Score* | https://github.com/miladrayka/GB_Score | AGPL-3.0 | Y | Y |
| *AnnapuRNA* | https://github.com/filipspl/AnnapuRNA | GPL-3.0 | Y | Y |
| DeepBSP | https://github.com/BaoJingxiao/DeepBSP | GPL-3.0 | Y | Y |
| *NNforDocking* | https://github.com/mksmd/NNforDocking | MIT | Y | N |

### 12.6.3 Protein-Protein Interactions and Machine Learning

Protein-Protein Interactions (PPIs) are fundamental to nearly all biological processes. Machine learning tools provide new ways to model these intricate biomolecular relationships and gain insights into folding and binding dynamics. For example, deep convolutional neural networks can now predict binding interfaces between proteins with high accuracy solely using sequence data.

Other techniques like Random Forest have also shown promise in extracting PPI patterns from knowledge graphs. On the protein folding front, advanced ML architectures like AlphaFold have achieved incredible breakthroughs predicting 3D protein structures from amino acid sequences by learning from large public databases. Beyond modeling interactions and conformations, data-derived machine learning models can also infer functional aspects like disordered regions or allosteric communication pathways transmitting signals between distant protein sites upon binding. Compared to physics-based simulation, machine learning approaches are faster and can uncover hidden relationships in large protein dataset troves that humans cannot. As databases are continuously growing, integration of ML techniques promises to reveal principles governing protein interaction networks, evolutionary dynamics, and the blueprints encoding protein structure-function relationships.

**TABLE 12.5** ML Tools for Exploring Protein–Protein Interactions and Protein Folding

| *Software* | *link* | *license* | *public data* | *public model* |
|---|---|---|---|---|
| masif | https://github.com/LPDI-EPFL/masif | Apache-2.0 | Y | Y |
| DOVE | https://github.com/kiharalab/DOVE | GPL-3.0 | Y | Y |
| iScore | https://github.com/DeepRank/iScore | Apache-2.0 | Y | Y |
| DeepRank2 | https://github.com/DeepRank/deeprank | Apache-2.0 | Y | Y |
| DeepRank-GNN | https://github.com/DeepRank/DeepRank-GNN | Apache-2.0 | Y | Y |
| AlphaFold and AlphaFold2 | https://github.com/deepmind/alphafold | Apache-2.0 | Y | Y |
| RoseTTAFold | https://github.com/RosettaCommons/RoseTTAFold | MIT | Y | Y |
| DMPfold | https://github.com/psipred/DMPfold2 | GPL-3.0 | Y | Y |

## 12.7 AI IN EARTH SCIENCE

AI is advancing earth sciences by enabling the rapid analysis of massive, multifaceted environmental data troves that would be impossible for humans to study manually. ML and neural networks are being applied across climate modeling, weather prediction, seismology, ecology, hydrology, and more to uncover hidden patterns and insights that can improve scientific understanding as well as practical forecasting capabilities. For instance, AI can simulate complex climate phenomena, predict storms and extreme weather, automatically classify vegetation in satellite images, pick out seismic signals, track species movements, and map changes in ice sheets over time. This is achieved by training models on large labeled datasets from sensors, radars, traps and other monitoring infrastructure. The algorithms can capture subtle correlations and nonlinear trends that reflect earth system dynamics in order to project likely scenarios or emergent events. As observational earth data accumulates exponentially, AI will become integral to keeping pace, enhancing the discovery power of environmental research, accelerating predictions, and informing resilience initiatives in the face of growing climate change impacts in the 21st century.

Some of the major applications of AI in earth sciences:

1. ***Weather Forecasting:*** AI models analyze massive datasets from satellites, radars, and sensors to generate highly accurate weather predictions and climate projections. Techniques like machine learning and neural networks can detect complex and nonlinear patterns to model atmospheric dynamics.
2. ***Earth Observation:*** AI significantly enhances remote sensing satellite and aerial imagery analysis. Algorithms automate the detection of features like vegetation, water bodies, land use patterns, flood-damaged areas, snow cover, etc. This generates insights about environmental changes.
3. ***Climate Modeling:*** AI reduces uncertainties around climate phenomena like precipitation variability, extreme weather events, ozone levels etc. by drawing predictive insights from correlations in historical climate data. Models also simulate future scenarios to guide mitigation policies.
4. ***Seismology:*** ML algorithms can pick out weak natural and induced earthquake signals from substantial background noise. They also crunch seismic data to advance earthquake early warning systems and assess future seismic hazards.
5. ***Ecosystem Monitoring:*** Computer vision techniques allow tracking of plant phenology, animal migration and behaviours, population counts etc. through camera traps and drone magery to assess ecosystem health over time.

Hence, AI & ML elevate earth science to new levels by amplifying analytical capabilities and knowledge discovery across various earth sphere domains through continually improving computational techniques.

## SUMMARY

AI is being used increasingly to help scientists across all fields of the natural sciences such as biology, chemistry, physics, and earth science. By using ML and DL, we can find complex patterns in huge amounts of data much faster than humans can, AI can reveal new discoveries and facts about the natural world. For example, AI programs can predict the best new medicines by studying chemical structures, figure out the effects of climate change by analyzing earth data, simulate advanced materials, and even run science experiments to test ideas. They devise creative new solutions and plans that human scientists may not consider. In many cases, AI works side-by-side with human researchers, complementing their intelligence. Together, humans and intelligent machines can advance discoveries faster than either could alone. As scientific instruments and projects generate more and more data every year, AI will become a boon for humanity. It gives scientists a very powerful tool to help unravel mysteries about nature more completely and rapidly than past human efforts allowed. With AI, the future of making new findings in every branch of science, from outer space to tiny cells, seems tremendously promising.

## WORKED OUT EXAMPLES

**EXAMPLE 12.1** A research institute is developing a BERT-like transformer model to automatically classify medical research papers into relevant subspecialties based on their abstracts. The model has 8 layers, each with 8 attention heads and a hidden size of 512.

(a) If the model uses a vocabulary size of 50,000 and supports sequences up to 512 tokens, calculate the total number of parameters in the model.

(b) The model is trained on 100,000 research paper abstracts. If each abstract is on average 250 tokens long, and the training uses a batch size of 64 with gradient accumulation over 2 steps, how many weight updates will occur during one epoch?

(c) After initial training, the model achieves an accuracy of 85% on a held-out test set. However, it performs poorly on papers from emerging interdisciplinary fields. Propose a strategy to improve the model's performance on these new categories, and explain how you would measure its effectiveness.

***Solution:***

(a) Calculating the total number of parameters in the model:

1. Embedding layers:

   Token embeddings: $50{,}000 \times 512 = 25{,}600{,}000$

   Positional embeddings: $512 \times 512 = 262{,}144$

2. Each transformer layer:

   Self-attention:

   - Query, Key, Value matrices: $3 \times (512 \times 512) = 786{,}432$
   - Output projection: $512 \times 512 = 262{,}144$

   Feed-forward network:

   - First layer: $512 \times (512 \times 4) = 1{,}048{,}576$
   - Second layer: $(512 \times 4) \times 512 = 1{,}048{,}576$

   Layer normalization: $2 \times (512 \times 2) = 2{,}048$

   Total per layer: $786{,}432 + 262{,}144 + 1{,}048{,}576 + 1{,}048{,}576 + 2{,}048 = 3{,}147{,}776$

   For 8 layers: $8 \times 3{,}147{,}776 = 25{,}182{,}208$

3. Output layer:

   Linear layer: $512 \times 50{,}000 = 25{,}600{,}000$

   Total parameters: $25{,}600{,}000 + 262{,}144 + 25{,}182{,}208 + 25{,}600{,}000 = 76{,}644{,}352$

The model has approximately 76.6 million parameters.

(b) Calculating weight updates during one epoch:

1. Total tokens in the dataset: $100{,}000 \times 250 = 25{,}000{,}000$ tokens
2. Tokens per batch: $64 \times 250 = 16{,}000$ tokens
3. Effective batch size with gradient accumulation: $64 \times 2 = 128$
4. Tokens processed per weight update: $128 \times 250 = 32{,}000$ tokens
5. Number of weight updates per epoch: $25{,}000{,}000/32{,}000 = 781.25$

So, there will be around 781 weight updates during one epoch.

**EXAMPLE 12.2** You're using a neural network to predict the band gap of semiconductors based on their crystal structure. Your model takes as input a 3D voxel grid representation of the crystal (32×32×32 voxels) and outputs a single value (the band gap in eV). If you use a 3D convolutional neural network with the following architecture:

Input layer (32×32×32×1)
3D Conv layer (16 filters, 3×3×3 kernel, stride 1)
MaxPooling3D layer (2×2×2 pool size)
3D Conv layer (32 filters, 3×3×3 kernel, stride 1)
MaxPooling3D layer (2×2×2 pool size)
Flatten layer
Dense layer (64 neurons)
Output layer (1 neuron)

How many trainable parameters does this model have?

***Solution:***

```
import tensorflow as tf
from tensorflow.keras import layers, models
def create_model():
    model = models.Sequential([
        layers.Input(shape=(32, 32, 32, 1)),
        layers.Conv3D(16, (3, 3, 3), activation='relu', padding='same'),
        layers.MaxPooling3D((2, 2, 2)),
        layers.Conv3D(32, (3, 3, 3), activation='relu', padding='same'),
        layers.MaxPooling3D((2, 2, 2)),
        layers.Flatten(),
        layers.Dense(64, activation='relu'),
        layers.Dense(1)
    ])
    return model
model = create_model()
model.summary()
total_params = sum([tf.keras.backend.count_params(w) for w in model.trainable_weights])
print(f"Total trainable parameters: {total_params}")
```

## EXERCISES

1. Design a Convolutional Neural Network (CNN) to classify particle types (electrons, pions, and muons) based on simulated Large Hadron Collider (LHC) calorimeter data. Your tasks:

Implement the given create_dataset function to generate 12,000 20 × 20 pixel images with overlapping particle signatures.
Create and train a simple CNN for 5 epochs, with reasonable accuracy.
Evaluate the model using accuracy, confusion matrix, and classification report.
Visualize results, including training curves and sample predictions.

2. A brachytherapy treatment uses Ir-192 seeds. The initial dose rate at Point A (2 cm from the source center) is 120 cGy/hr. Calculate: a) The dose rate at Point B, located 4 cm from the source center b) The total dose delivered to Point A over 50 hours, accounting for decay (Ir-192 half-life = 74 days)

3. A team is developing a Graph Neural Network (GNN) for 3D dose prediction in radiotherapy. The model takes as input a graph representation of the patient's anatomy, where each node represents a voxel and edges connect neighboring voxels. The GNN has 3 graph convolutional layers with 64, 128, and 256 filters respectively, followed by a global pooling layer and a fully connected layer for final dose prediction. Find:
   (a) If each voxel node has 5 input features (e.g., density, organ label) and is connected to its 6 nearest neighbors, calculate the number of parameters in the first graph convolutional layer.
   (b) The model is trained on a dataset of 500 treatment plans, each containing approximately 100,000 voxels. If the training uses a batch size of 1 (due to memory constraints) and runs for 100 epochs, estimate the total number of voxels processed during the entire training.

4. Scientists are training a machine learning model to predict the concentration of particulate matter (PM2.5) in the air based on various meteorological factors (temperature, humidity, wind speed, etc.). They are using a dataset containing 1000 samples.
   The dataset is split into a training set (800 samples) and a testing set (200 samples).
   The model achieves a Mean Squared Error (MSE) of 9 on the training set and an MSE of 16 on the testing set.
   What can you infer about the model's performance and potential issues?

5. A research team is developing a Convolutional Neural Network (CNN) to classify radiotherapy treatment plans into different complexity levels. The input to the CNN is a 2D dose distribution map of size 128×128 pixels. The CNN architecture consists of three convolutional layers (with 32, 64, and 128 filters respectively, all using 3x3 kernels), each followed by a max pooling layer, and then two fully connected layers of 256 and 64 neurons, with a final softmax layer for 4-class classification.
   (a) Calculate the number of trainable parameters in the first and last convolutional layers of this CNN.
   (b) The team uses categorical cross-entropy as the loss function and the Adam optimizer for training. Write out the categorical cross-entropy loss function and explain why it's suitable for this multi-class classification task.
   (c) During training, the team observes that the model quickly achieves 100% accuracy on the training set but performs poorly on the validation set. Identify three potential causes of this behaviour and suggest solutions for each.

## BIBLIOGRAPHY

Bonnet, F., Mazari, J., Cinnella, P., and Gallinari, P. (2022). AirfRANS: High Fidelity Computational Fluid Dynamics Dataset for Approximating Reynolds-Averaged Navier–Stokes Solutions, *Advances in Neural Information Processing Systems*, 35, 23463–23478, arXiv.

Gardner, J., Pleiss, G., Weinberger, K. Q., Bindel, D., and Wilson, A. G. (2018). Gpytorch: Blackbox matrix-matrix gaussian process inference with GPU acceleration, *Advances in Neural Information Processing Systems*, 31, ACM Digital Library.

Hennigh, O., Narasimhan, S., Nabian, M. A., Subramaniam, A., Tangsali, K., Fang, Z., and Choudhry, S. (2021, June). NVIDIA SimNet™: An AI-accelerated multi-physics simulation framework. In *International conference on computational science* (pp. 447–461), Springer International Publishing.

Jin, D., Guo, D., Ho, T. Y., Harrison, A. P., Xiao, J., Tseng, C. K. and Lu, L. (2021). DeepTarget: Gross tumor and clinical target volume segmentation in esophageal cancer radiotherapy, *Medical Image Analysis*, 68, 101909, Elsevier.

McConkey, R., Yee, E., and Lien, F. S. (2021). A curated dataset for data-driven turbulence modelling, *Scientific Data*, 8(1), 255, Springer Nature.

Chapter 13

# AI in Cheminformatics and Bioinformatics

## 13.1 INTRODUCTION

Cheminformatics (also known as chemoinformatics) and Bioinformatics play crucial roles in the field of drug discovery and biological research. Cheminformatics covers the utilisation of advanced computational techniques to investigate and comprehend the multifaceted dimension of chemical structures, properties, and interactions. Cheminformatics strives to discover the underlying patterns and principles governing the behavior of molecules, thereby enabling the design of novel compounds with enhanced efficacy and safety profiles. However, the field of Bioinformatics encompasses the intricate examination and elucidation of biological information, encompassing the domains of genomics, transcriptomics, and proteomics, with the ultimate objective of comprehending the underlying mechanisms governing biological processes and the manifestation of diseases.

## 13.2 FUNDAMENTALS OF CHEMINFORMATICS

Cheminformatics utilizes computational techniques and methods to analyze, store, and share chemical data. Some core areas of Cheminformatics include chemical structure representation and storage, chemical databases and search methods, quantitative structure-activity relationships (QSAR), chemical data mining and machine learning (ML). The key goals of Cheminformatics include organizing data on chemical compounds and reactions, predicting biological activities and chemical properties of new drug candidates, identifying quantitative patterns and structure-activity trends, and gaining insights for drug design and discovery pipelines. Overall, Cheminformatics aims to derive knowledge from chemical information using algorithms, tools, and databases playing an integral role in diverse fields like drug development, material sciences, biochemistry and more by revealing relationships between chemical structures and their activities.

### 13.2.1 Chemical Structure Representations

Representing chemical structures in digital formats is essential for Cheminformatics. Common chemical structure representations include SMILES (simplified molecular-input line-entry system) strings, InChI (International Chemical Identifier) codes, and molecular connection tables. SMILES use a simple ASCII format to encode molecular structures as strings that can be parsed and interpreted by algorithms. InChIs are alphanumeric strings representing chemical structures in a standardized, computable way for databases. Connection tables store information on atoms, bond types, ring systems and branches in molecules using matrix formats. Molecular graphics programs can convert these digital formats into 2D and 3D structures. These chemical structure representations enable efficient storage, sharing, analysis and search of compound libraries in Cheminformatics. They allow quantitative structure comparisons, property predictions, and structure-activity analyses using specialized algorithms and molecular descriptors calculated from the structural data. There are different types of file format available including SMILES, InChIKey, MOL, SDF, etc. Molecular fingerprints are another representation to analyse the similarities of the molecule quickly. Some of the examples of SMILES notation are represented in Table 13.1. A detailed molecular representation of different forms is shown in Figure 13.1.

**TABLE 13.1** Examples of a few molecules with SMILES notation

| *Molecules* | *SMILES Notations* | *Chemical formulas* | *Chemical structures* |
|---|---|---|---|
| Methane | C | $CH_4$ | 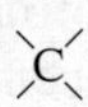 |
| Ethene | C=C | $H_2C{=}CH_2$ |  |
| Benzene | c1ccccc1 | $C_6H_6$ (aromatic ring) | 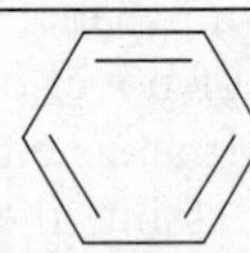 |
| Acetone | CC(=O)C | $CH_3COCH_3$ | 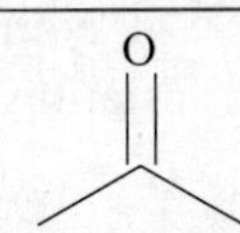 |
| Acetylsalicylic Acid (Aspirin) | CC(=O)OC1=CC=CC=C1C(=O)O | $C_9H_8O_4$ | 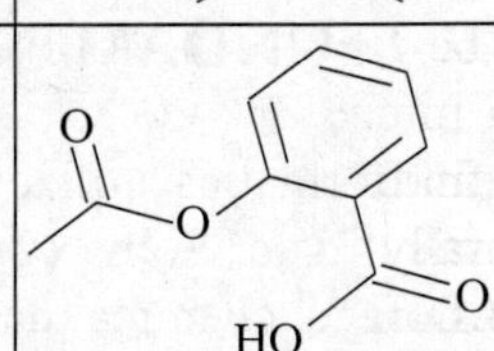 |
| Caffeine | CN1C=NC2=C1C(=O)N(C(=O)N2C)C | $C_{27}H_{46}O$ | 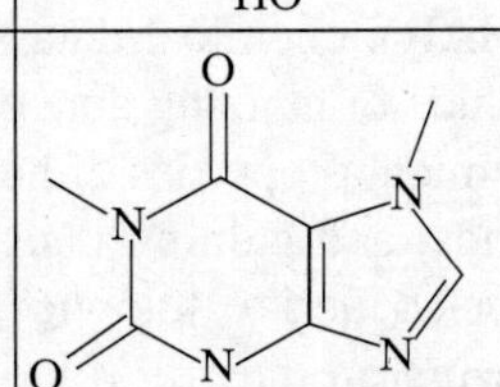 |

| *Molecules* | *SMILES Notations* | *Chemical formulas* | *Chemical structures* |
|---|---|---|---|
| Penicillin G | CC1(C(N2C(S1)C(C2=O)NC(=O)CC3=CC=CC=C3)C(=O)O)C | $C_{16}H_{20}N_2O_4S$ | 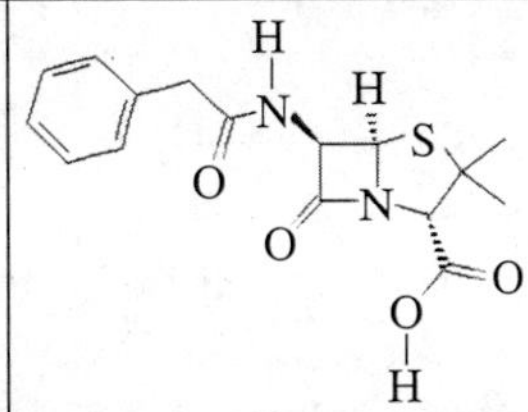 |
| Taxol (Paclitaxel) | CC1=C2C(C(=O)C3(C(CC4C(C3C(C(C2(C)C)(CC1OC(=O)C(C(C5=CC=CC=C5)NC(=O)C6=CC=CC=C6)O)O)OC(=O)C7=CC=CC=C7)(CO4)OC(=O)C)O)C)OC(=O)C | $C_{43}H_{53}NO_{14}$ | 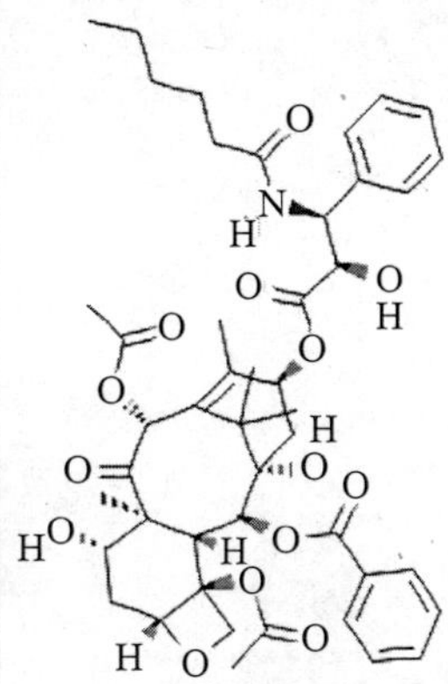 |

## 13.2.2 Chemical Databases and Data Sources

Chemical databases are used in Cheminformatics to store and retrieve chemical molecules along with specific information. Using these databases, one can analyse enormous chemical datasets or search for particular chemicals. Chemical databases hold enormous volumes of information about small molecules including their structures, biological activity, physiochemical properties, etc. Managing and utilising these databases is crucial to the training of models. Target prediction can be facilitated by these databases through information retrieval, knowledge discovery, and data mining. These databases help with finding patterns in data, discovering new knowledge, and finding specific information for making predictions. There are specific databases that contain naturally occurring compounds. These databases, such as LOTUS, COCONUT, SuperNatural-III, OSADHI, and NEIMPDB, etc. are useful sources of information apart from the well-known publicly available databases for Cheminformatics and Bioinformatics like Pubchem, PDB etc.

## 13.2.3 Machine Learning Based QSAR/QSPR

QSAR/QSPR models are invaluable computational approaches that establish a mathematical correlation between chemical structure and biological activity or physicochemical properties respectively. Chemical structures are encoded into molecular descriptors such as molecular weight, LogP, polar surface area, fingerprint-based structural bit strings and several topological, their quantum-mechanical and physicochemical descriptors and moreover Cheminformatics is the core concept.

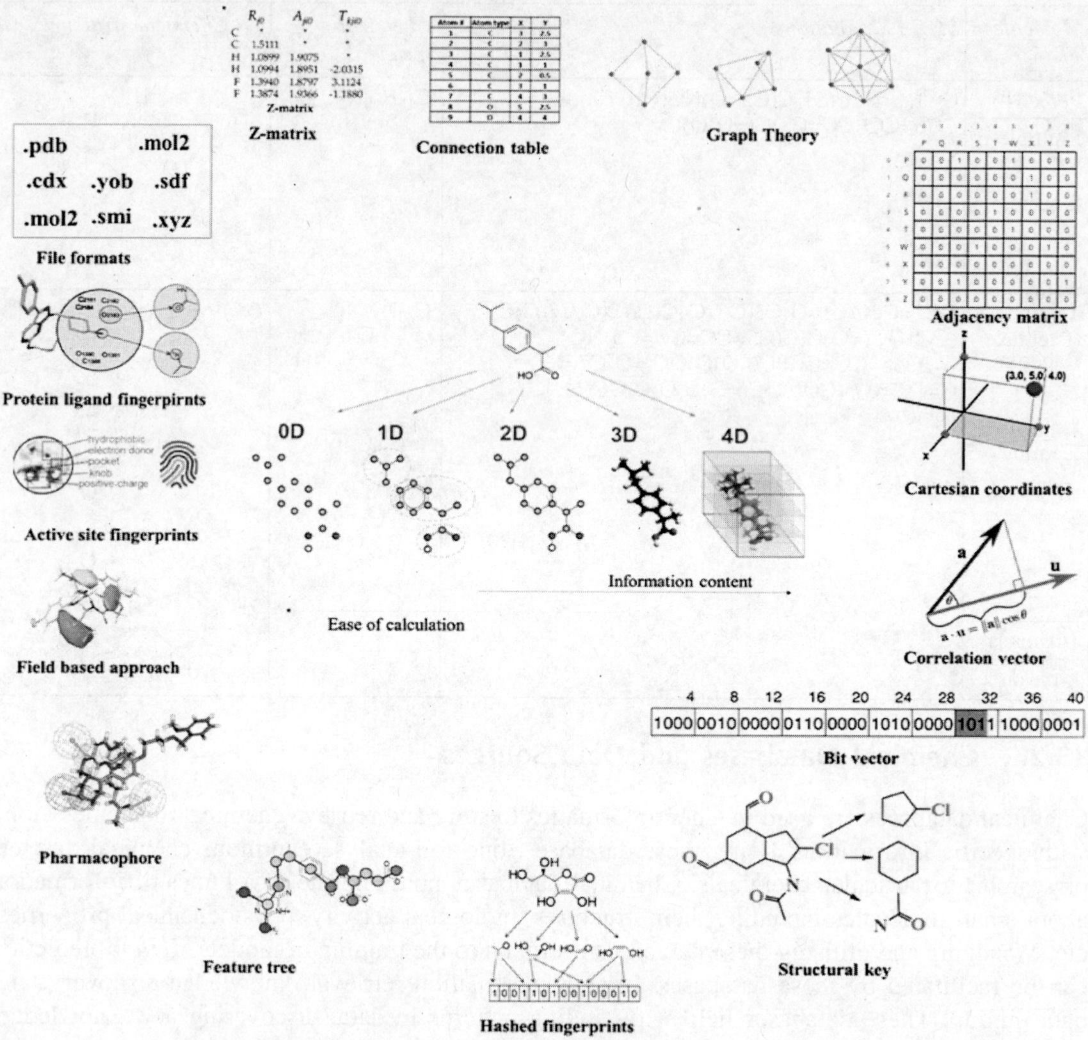


FIGURE 13.1 A detailed molecular representation in different form.

Advanced statistical methods and ML algorithms then build predictive models correlating these structural descriptors to measured experimental endpoints. These *in silico* models enable prediction of the activity or property for new chemical entities solely from their structural features. When integrated into Cheminformatics pipelines and database screening workflows, QSAR/QSPR models significantly accelerate hit/lead identification, library prioritization and enrichment, molecular optimization cycles and de-novo molecular design in drug discovery programs through structure-based extrapolations. With the help of AI/ML advancement, the traditional QSAR model have become more advanced with latest regression techniques. Table 13.2 shows the summary of ML methods for QSAR.

**TABLE 13.2** Summary of machine learning methods for QSAR

| *Methods* | *Descriptions* |
|---|---|
| ***Supervised learning*** | |
| Multiple regression analysis | An analysis using statistics to determine the correlations between one or more independent and dependent variables. |
| k-nearest neighbour | Instance-based learning is a type of machine learning where we classify an object based on the majority rule of its k closest neighbours. In this case, k represents a whole number. |
| Naive bayes | A probabilistic method that predicts membership by assuming feature independence, using probability prior and Bayes' rule. |
| Random forest | This is a classification method that uses a combination of many decision trees and a rule that selects the most common prediction among the trees. |
| Neural network and deep learning | An approach to model-based learning that uses layers of interconnected neurons—input, several hidden layers (for deep learning), and output layers—to gain knowledge from input data. |
| Support vector machine | A statistical technique that uses a nonlinear kernel to map data into high-dimensional space and find the lowest dimensions hyperplane that maximises the data separation. Maximising the space between hyperplanes, or support vectors, is how this is accomplished. |
| ***Unsupervised learning*** | |
| k-means clustering | A technique for classifying data into k groups by reducing the distances between groups within the centre of each group. |
| Hierarchical clustering | An approach to classification that creates a hierarchical structure of clusters using either divisive or agglomerative clustering, such as dividing a large cluster into smaller ones, or by merging smaller clusters. |
| Principal component analysis | A statistical technique that creates new independent variables known as principle components from a set of associated data using an orthogonal strategy. |

### 13.2.4 Molecular Similarity

In cheminformatics and related fields (including medicinal chemistry and drug discovery), molecular similarity is one of the most widely applied concepts. Virtual screening, similarity hunting, properties prediction, synthesis design, molecular diversity analysis, and virtual screening are among the numerous applications of this technique. There are different types of coefficients of similarity which are discussed below.

***Tanimoto Coefficient:*** The Tanimoto coefficient ($T_c$) is a widely used similarity measure in Cheminformatics to quantify the degree of similarity between two binary molecular fingerprints. It calculates the ratio between the number of common set bits over the combined uncommon and common set bits in the fingerprints of two chemical compounds or molecules.
Tanimoto similarity can be calculated by,

$$T_C = \frac{N_{ab}}{N_a + N_b - N_{ab}} \tag{13.1}$$

Where, $N_{ab}$ = number of set/ON bits (1's) that are present in BOTH fingerprints A and B. This gives us the number of common features. $N_a$ = number of set bits in fingerprint A. This gives us the count of distinct features just in fingerprint A. $N_b$ = number of set bits in fingerprint B. This gives us the count of distinct features just in fingerprint B. $N_a + N_b - N_{ab}$ = Total number of distinct features in both fingerprints combined (union bits).

The Tanimoto coefficient generates values from 0 to 1, with 0 corresponding to completely dissimilar fingerprints and 1 corresponding to identical fingerprints. A higher Tanimoto score indicates more similarity between two molecules. It is widely used due to its simplicity, interpretability, and is an efficient means to screen large chemical libraries to find similar compounds.

***Dice Coefficient:*** The Dice coefficient (Dc) is a statistical measure used in Cheminformatics to quantify the degree of similarity between two molecular fingerprints. Mathematically, it is represented as follow,

$$D_C = \frac{2N_{ab}}{N_a + N_b} \tag{13.2}$$

Where, $N_{ab}$ = no. of bits set in BOTH fingerprints A and B (number of features common between the two fingerprints). $N_a$ = no. of set bits in fingerprint A (no. of features unique to fingerprint A) and $N_b$ = no. of set bits in fingerprint B (no. of features unique to fingerprint B).

The denominator contains the sum of sizes of the two fingerprint bit vectors. The numerator doubles the number of bits in common between the two fingerprints.

By dividing, we get a metric that gives the ratio of bits in common to the average fingerprint size. This ratio is converted into a decimal value between 0 and 1, with 0 meaning completely dissimilar and 1 meaning identical fingerprints.

The Dice coefficient is very similar to the Tanimoto coefficient but differs slightly in the denominator calculation. It remains a very useful measurement for rapidly assessing molecular similarity for virtual screening.

***Carbo Index:*** The Carbo index is a similarity metric used in Cheminformatics to quantify the structural similarity between two molecules or compounds based on the features or fragments they have in common. Mathematically,

$$Carbo\ Index\ (CI) = \frac{N_c}{\sqrt{N_a * N_b}} * 100 \tag{13.3}$$

Where, $N_c$ = number of fragments or features which are common between the two molecules, $N_a$ = total number of fragments or features in molecule A and $N_b$ = total number of fragments or features in molecule B.

The Carbo index directly uses the number of shared features between two molecular structures to quantify their similarity. It accounts for differences in total features by normalizing using the geometric mean of total features in each structure.

Multiplying the fraction by 100 converts the value into an intuitive 0-100% range output, where 0% indicates absolutely no similarity and 100% indicates identical molecules.

The major advantage of Carbo index is its simple interpretation in terms of common features as an easily understood percentage score. It remains invariant to inconsistent molecular fragmentation schemes. Lower sensitivity makes it more suitable for diverse library comparisons.

***Tversky Coefficient:*** The Tversky coefficient is an asymmetric similarity metric used to compare two sets of binary features or molecular fingerprints in Cheminformatics applications. It is a generalization of the Tanimoto coefficient. Mathematically,

$$Tversky\ Coefficient\ (T_c) = \frac{N_a b}{N_{ab} + \alpha N_a + \beta N_b} \tag{13.4}$$

Where, $N_{ab}$ = number of feature bits set in both fingerprints (common bits), $N_a$ = number of bits set in fingerprint A (bits unique to A), $N_b$ = number of bits set in fingerprint B (bits unique to B) and $\alpha$ and $\beta$ are adjustable bias parameters. By changing $\alpha$ and $\beta$ asymmetry is introduced into the similarity measure. For example, setting $\alpha = \beta = 1$ reduces the Tversky coefficient to the Tanimoto coefficient which treats the fingerprints equivalently. Values closer to 0 indicate dissimilar fingerprints while values nearing 1 signal highly similar fingerprints. Tuning $\alpha$ and $\beta$ allow controlling relative significance of uniqueness in each fingerprint.

***Russell-Rao Coefficient:*** The Russell-Rao coefficient is a similarity measure used in Cheminformatics to quantify the degree of similarity between two binary molecular fingerprints. It uses the number of common feature bits normalized by the total possible feature combinations. Mathematically,

$$Russell - Rao\ Coefficient = \frac{N_{ab}}{N_a * N_b} \tag{13.5}$$

Where, $N_{ab}$ = number of ON or set bits common between fingerprints A and B, $N_a$ = total number of set bits in fingerprint A, $N_b$ = total number of set bits in fingerprint B and $N_a * N_b$ = total possible number of bit pairs between the two fingerprints. The formula divides the actual common bits by the maximum possible number of bit combinations between two fingerprints if all bits matched. This generates values from 0 to 1. Zero indicates no similarity while 1 shows maximum similarity. The Russell-Rao coefficient penalizes all differences strongly making it more sensitive to small deviations than Tanimoto or Dice coefficients. This can be useful for some similarity focused virtual screening tasks.

***Kulczynski Coefficient:*** The Kulczynski coefficient is a similarity metric used in Cheminformatics to compare chemical structures represented as binary molecular fingerprints. It incorporates features unique to each fingerprint along with common features between them. Mathematically,

$$Kulczynski\ Coefficient\ (Kc) = \frac{1}{2}\left(\frac{N_{ab}}{N_a} + \frac{N_{ab}}{N_b}\right) \tag{13.6}$$

Where, $N_{ab}$ = number of bits set in BOTH fingerprints A and B (common features), $N_a$ = number of bits set in fingerprint A (unique to A) and $N_b$ = number of bits set in fingerprint B (unique to B). It takes the average of two asymmetric similarity measures—one biased towards fingerprint A and one biased towards B. This means fingerprints with many unique features will still match well if they share even a small set of common features. Useful when comparing diverse or heterogeneous datasets. The Kulczynski coefficient generates values from 0 (completely dissimilar) to 1 (identical fingerprints). Values closer to 1 indicate greater overlap and molecular similarity.

***McConnaughey Coefficient:*** The McConnaughey coefficient is a similarity measure used to compare binary molecular fingerprints in Cheminformatics. It accounts for the relative proportion of bits set in each fingerprint when quantifying structural similarity. Mathematically,

$$McConnaughey\ Coefficient\ (MCc) = \frac{N_{ab}}{N_a} * \frac{N_{ab}}{N_b} \tag{13.7}$$

Where, $N_{ab}$ = number of ON bits common in both fingerprints A and B, $N_a$ = total ON bits present in A, $N_b$ = total ON bits present in B, $N_{ab}/N_a$ = proportion of bits in A that match bits in B, $N_{ab}/N_b$ = proportion of bits in B that match bits in A. By taking the product of these proportions, the coefficient generates a score sensitive to differences in the relative fingerprint sizes.

Values range from 0 (completely dissimilar) to 1 (identical). Scores near 1 indicate higher molecular similarity. The McConnaughey coefficient provides a simple statistic to assess overlap between fingerprints adjusted for population-size differences. This can aid similarity analysis in highly skewed datasets.

***Baroni-Urbani-Buser (BUB) Coefficient:*** The Baroni-Urbani-Buser coefficient is a similarity measure used for comparing binary molecular fingerprints in Cheminformatics applications. It builds upon the Jaccard index to provide increased sensitivity. Mathematically,

$$BUB\ Coefficient = \frac{N_{ab} - E_{ab}}{N_a + N_b - N_{ab}} \tag{13.8}$$

Where, $N_{ab}$ = number of feature bits set in BOTH fingerprints (common bits), $N_a$ = number of bits set in fingerprint A, $N_b$ = Number of bits set in fingerprint B and $E_{ab}$ = expected number of common bits by chance. $E_{ab}$ adds statistical rigor accounting for random chance matches, making the final coefficient more sensitive at quantifying true structural similarity. The BUB coefficient subtracts the expected chance matches from the observed common bits. The result is normalized by dividing by maximum possible unique bits. Output values also range from 0 (dissimilar) to 1 (identical fingerprints). Values near 1 represent higher molecular similarity.

### 13.2.5 Molecular Descriptors

Molecular descriptors are fundamental to quantitative representation, analysis, and modelling of small molecules in Cheminformatics and Bioinformatics techniques. Numerous structural characteristics of compounds are encoded in numerical vectors by the hundreds of molecular descriptors that have been produced, enabling the use of statistical and machine learning methods. By mapping molecule topology, shape, physicochemical behaviours, and other properties into mathematical representations that can be used by algorithms, descriptors convert abstract chemical space into useful knowledge. This knowledge helps in lead optimisation, property modelling, library screening, and systematic categorization, etc. A fundamental procedure in Cheminformatics is the computation of relevant descriptors and the creation of QSAR/QSPR models. Compound design is guided by models that predict the behaviour of synthesized molecules based on the relationship between descriptors and biological activities or physical qualities. Thus, rather than depending exclusively on expensive and time-consuming experimental methods, the scope and scale of rational *in silico* screening and optimisation are increased by developments in molecular descriptors and Chemoinformatic modelling.

In order to obtain structure-activity insights, interpretable modelling of chemical space is the second essential component. The molecular characteristics underlying certain methods of action, toxicity, and other aspects are clarified by descriptors. Comprehending these associations subsequently facilitates customised design—scaffold-hopping, incorporating advantageous substructures, eliminating hazardous compounds, and so forth. Descriptor models thus turn vast chemical space into information that can be mapped and used. As new modelling techniques and descriptors give up new opportunities for small molecule analytics, particularly when combined with contemporary ML, their development and implementation remain an active research topic. Chemical structure can still be informationally encoded and statistically related to an increasing number of target attributes, but more reliable and understandable. Cheminformatics and Bioinformatics approaches combined with chemical descriptors provide a potent platform for data-driven materials engineering, chemical safety evaluation, and expedited, logical medication development.

### 13.2.6 Calculation of Descriptors from 2D Structure

#### *Simple Counts*

One way to describe molecules in a simple manner is by counting certain features such as hydrogen bond acceptors, hydrogen bond donors, aromatic/aliphatic rings, molecular weight and rotatable bonds. We can easily determine how often they appear by analysing a 2D table of connections between atoms in the molecule. Further, the presence of such smaller parts in larger molecules can be analysed in detail.

#### *Physicochemical Properties*

Drug action and transport are significantly influenced by various physicochemical properties. For example, how firmly a molecule binds to a protein as well as how easily it can cross a cell membrane can be represented as hydrophobicity. The logarithm of the value of the coefficient of partition (log P) among n-octanol and water is the most widely used model for hydrophobicity. Low logP values, which result from low hydrophilicities, lead to ineffective absorption or penetration. The logP value $< 5.0$ can be considered as acceptable range of a molecule to be properly absorbed.

The value of a compound containing a substituent X is equivalent to the log P of the parent compound as determined by the initial method of estimating log P, which utilized an additive approach. Based on experimental data, the substituent constants, $\pi_X$, were computed in the following way as:

$$\pi_X = \log P_X - \log P_H \tag{13.9}$$

Numerous alternative techniques have been put out to estimate log P. A few of these rely on disassembling the molecule into smaller parts. The partition coefficient of a molecule is represented as the sum of the fragment values and the number of correction factors and this gives an account for interaction between the fragments including intramolecular hydrogen bonding. As proposed by Rekker,

$$logP = \sum_{i=1}^{n} a_i f_i + \sum_{j=1}^{m} b_j F_j \tag{13.10}$$

As an alternative to fragment-based techniques, atom-based methods are often used by adding the contributions from each individual atom and log P is determined using these approaches.

$$log\,P = \sum n_i a_i \tag{13.11}$$

The formula for molar refractivity is,

$$MR = \frac{n^2 - 1}{n^2 + 2} \cdot \frac{MW}{d} \tag{13.12}$$

Wiener Index is the calculated distance among the number of bonds between every pair of atoms and adding up the distances, $D_{ij}$, and is given as:

$$W = \frac{1}{2} \sum_{i=1}^{N} \sum_{j=1}^{N} D_{ij} \tag{13.13}$$

For every bond in the molecule, the branching index is equal to the total of the bond connectivity such that,

$$Branching\,Index = \sum_{bonds} \frac{1}{\sqrt{\delta_i \delta_j}} \tag{13.14}$$

As a result, for atom *i*, the simple delta value is provided by,

$$\delta_i = \sigma_i - h_i \tag{13.15}$$

The $\delta$ for atom *i*, in the valence delta value for atom i, is,

$$\delta_i^v = Z_i^v - h_i \tag{13.16}$$

As a result, $-CH_3$ and $-CH_2$ are distinguished by the simple delta value. Although $-CH_3$ and $-NH_2$ have the same simple delta values, they differ in their valence delta values, which allows for the differentiation of the two groups using this descriptor. The valence delta expression has been modified to look like this for elements in the periodic table other than fluorine.

$$\delta_i^v = \frac{Z_i^v - h_i}{Z_i - Z_i^v - 1} \tag{13.17}$$

where $Z_i$ is the atomic number.

Sequential indices are represented by calculating the atomic delta values over bond routes of varying lengths are added up to form the chi molecular connectivity indices. Consequently, the total of all the atoms in a molecule (i.e., pathways of length zero) equals the zero$^{th}$ order chi index ($^0X$):

$$^0X = \sum_{bonds} \frac{1}{\sqrt{\delta_i \delta_j}};$$

$$^0X^v = \sum_{atoms} \frac{1}{\sqrt{\delta_i}} \tag{13.18}$$

The first-order chi index is known as a summation over bonds.Thus, when simple delta values are employed, the first-order chi index is the same as Randic's branching index,

$$^1X = \sum_{bonds} \frac{1}{\sqrt{\delta_i \delta_j}};$$

$$^1X^v = \sum_{bonds} \frac{1}{\sqrt{\delta_i^v \delta_j^v}} \tag{13.19}$$

### Kappa Shape Indices

The kappa form indices compare a molecule to the "extreme shapes" that are feasible for a given number of atoms in order to describe different characteristics of molecular shape. Similar to the indices of molecular connection, there exist shape indices with different orders, such as first, second, etc. A count across single bond fragments is a component of the first-order shape index.

The definition of the first-order kappa index is:

$$^1K = 2\,^1P_{max}\,^1P_{min}/(^1P)^2 \tag{13.20}$$

The formula for calculating the shape index is as follows: number of bonds in the linear molecule; $^1P_{min}$ = number of edges (or pathways of length one) in the completely connected graph and $^1P$ = number of bonds in the molecule. With all atom pairs being connected, $^1P_{max}$ for a molecule with A atoms is equal to A(A–1)/2 and $^1P_{min}$ equals (A–1). Thus, $^1K$ turns into,

$$^1k = A(A-1)^2/(^1P)^2$$

$$^2k = (A-1)(A-2)^2/(^2P)^2$$

$$\alpha_i = \frac{r_i}{r_{Csp^3}} - 1 \tag{13.21}$$

For every non-$sp^3$ hybridised carbon, the atom count A is therefore modified (whether it's by a rise or a fall). The following formula is used to get the kappa-alpha indices,

$$1k\alpha = \frac{(A+\alpha)(A+\alpha-1)^2}{(1P+\alpha)2} \tag{13.22}$$

$$2k\alpha = \frac{(A+\alpha-1)(A+\alpha-2)^2}{(2P+\alpha)2} \tag{13.23}$$

for every atom in the molecule, where $\alpha$ is the total of the $\alpha_i$.

### Electrotopological State Indices

The electrotopological state indices (ETSI) was proposed by Hall et al. in 1991 and it has emerged as a valuable tool. Unlike traditional approaches that consider entire molecules as a unit of analysis, ETSI takes into account individual atoms, including hydrogen atoms if desired. By focusing on atom-level characteristics, ETSI offers a more granular perspective, enabling a deeper understanding of molecular properties and facilitating various applications in the field. The intrinsic state of an atom, $I_i$, on the first row of the periodic table determines its properties.

$$I_i = \frac{\delta_i^v + 1}{\delta_i} \tag{13.24}$$

Thus, the electrical and topological properties of atoms are encoded in the intrinsic state. The number of bonds that exist between atom *i* and each of the remaining atoms, *j*, is used to incorporate the impact of its relations to the other atoms. A perturbation $I_{ij}$ is defined as follows if the path size is $r_{ij}$:

$$\Delta I_{i,j} = \sum_j \frac{I_i - I_j}{r_{ij}{}^2} \tag{13.25}$$

The total of $\Delta I_{ij}$ and $I_i$ determines an atom's electrotopological state, or E-state. By determining the mean-square value across all atoms, atomic E-states can be integrated into a whole-molecule description. Additionally, bitstring or vector representations can be created. Since there are only a limited number of possible I values, each distinct I value that can exist in a molecule can have its corresponding bit set to produce a bitstring representation.

## 13.3 OPEN SOURCE CHEMINFORMATICS TOOLS

There are many open source Cheminformatics tools publicly available. These tools help in calculating different molecular properties in less time for the given set of molecules. The popular Cheminformatics tools and short description are given below.

### 13.3.1 RDKit

The RDKit is a prominent open-source toolkit for Cheminformatics, offers a comprehensive suite of tools and functionalities to facilitate the manipulation and analysis of chemical information. It encompasses a diverse array of capabilities, such as molecular structure representation, substructure searching, molecular similarity assessment, and numerous others. By leveraging the RDKit, researchers and practitioners in the field of Cheminformatics can effectively tackle a broad spectrum of challenges.

RDKit provides extensive machine learning capabilities for building predictive models on chemical data through its integrated RDKit.ML package. This allows developers to leverage the robust Cheminformatics and feature extraction toolkits offered by RDKit while seamlessly training and validating models on the generated molecular fingerprints and descriptors.

Key functionalities supplied by the RDKit.ML package include data sampling methods like diversity picking and scaffold splitting to create train/test sets, automated feature vectorization utilizing RDKit's rich descriptors, integration with Python's scikit-learn toolkit to construct models like Random Forest and Support Vector Machines, model performance evaluation modules for k-fold cross-validation and accuracy measurement, data preprocessing tools for handling missing values and outliers, model export functionality to the standard and deep integration with Jupyter notebooks for visual analysis.

### 13.3.2 Open Babel

Open Babel is a software tool that can understand and work with different types of chemical information. This tool can convert different types of chemical file formats, perform calculations to determine molecular properties, and assist with making changes to molecules. Moreover, it empowers users with the ability to perform molecular descriptor calculations, thereby enabling comprehensive analysis and characterization of chemical structures. Additionally, it offers robust support for molecular manipulation, empowering researchers to efficiently modify and manipulate molecular entities.

### 13.3.3 ChemPy

ChemPy is an open-source Python library providing a specialized toolkit for computational chemistry and cheminformatics applications. It offers capabilities to model, analyze, transform, simulate and visualize chemical structures and systems. Core functionality includes APIs for chemical database access, molecular structure diagram generation, QSAR analysis, chemical ontology interfaces, spectroscopy data parsing, and visualization of chemical graphs.

ChemPy builds on top of cheminformatics C/C++ libraries to provide an interoperable Python framework encoding domain knowledge and patterns through abstractions. This allows rapid development of materials informatics and chemical modelling software by supplying essential building blocks for typical tasks like predicting chemical properties, generating molecular descriptors, applying ML on chemical data, interfacing public/private databases, and processing spectroscopy outputs.

## 13.4 MACHINE LEARNING TOOLS FOR CHEMINFORMATICS

### 13.4.1 ChemSuite

The creation of the stand-alone application "ChemSuite" which is useful for Cheminformatics computations and ML model construction, is described. Because of its many functionalities, it is generally accepted in a variety of sectors. A tool for optimising molecules incorporates a force field, like UFF. More than ten different types of fingerprints and 1D, 2D, and 3D descriptors can be calculated with the use of packages like RDKit, PyDPI, and PaDEL. To normalise descriptor values, two techniques are available: Z-Score and MinMax Scaler. A variety of descriptor selection and ML techniques are available for the building of models. It lets the user modify the software for other scientific uses or add their own algorithm. It is compatible with all main systems, offers an intuitive graphical user interface, and is open source. It includes many algorithms for training the models. The programme includes machine learning techniques like Random Forest and Support Vector Machine, among others.

### 13.4.2 MoleculeNet

MoleculeNet is a platform that collects various public datasets, defines standards for evaluation, and provides reliable open-source implementations of different molecular featurization and learning algorithms. These algorithms are available as part of the DeepChem, an open-source library. Learnable representations in molecular machine learning have proven to be highly effective, as demonstrated by the impressive performance showcased in the MoleculeNet benchmarks. Nevertheless, there are a few important things to consider with regards to this outcome. Complex tasks and imbalanced classification pose challenges for learnable representations when data is scarce. When dealing with quantum mechanical and biophysical datasets, it is crucial to prioritise the use of physics-aware featurization over the selection of a specific learning algorithm.

### 13.4.3 ChemML

The goal of ChemML, an open suite of programmes for informatics and ML, is to facilitate and promote the data-driven research paradigm that is now taking shape in the fields of materials science and chemistry. ChemML enables users to carry out a variety of data science tasks and run machine learning algorithms tailored to the context of chemicals and materials. In order to make the application of modern data science a feasible and broadly accessible concept in the larger chemistry and materials community, key criteria include automation, general-purpose utility, adaptability, and user-friendliness.

### 13.4.4 Application of AI in Cheminformatics

AI is transforming Cheminformatics across diverse domains beyond traditional drug discovery, offering new possibilities for innovation. In material sciences, ML models guide the development of molecules with specific mechanical properties, photovoltaic efficiency or corrosion resistance that can lead to new polymers, nanoparticles or quantum dots. For environmental challenges, AI predicts biodegradation pathways and rates of chemicals, models reaction mechanisms and designs greener synthetic routes. Companies employ AI algorithms to determine compound combinations with desired textures, fragrance or preservative effects for cosmetics and personal care products. In food sciences, AI enables high-throughput virtual screening for flavour and taste enhancers, model's molecular changes during storage to improve shelf life and even creates new natural product formulations. With capacities for broad chemical data analysis and molecular optimization, the applications of AI in Cheminformatics span from pharmaceuticals to food, materials to environmental safety—supporting discoveries that enhance health, lifestyle and sustainability.

## 13.5 BIOINFORMATICS

Bioinformatics includes a wide range of disciplines, all aimed at discovering the mysteries hidden information within biological data. Through the development of advanced methods and cutting-edge software tools, researchers in this field are able to gain deep insights into the complexities of life. Applying principles from computer science, statistics, mathematics, and engineering, experts in the field analyse vast amounts of biological and biochemical data.

The field of Bioinformatics has been greatly impacted by the AI. It has proven to be a powerful tool in addressing key challenges, such as understanding gene function and disease association through genomic variation maps. Additionally, AI has been instrumental in reconstructing complex molecular signalling pathways by integrating data from various sources, including transcripts, proteins, and metabolites. It has also played a significant role in expediting the development of novel human creativity and oversight continue to play a crucial role, but the integration of AI has become a vital tool for Bioinformaticians.

### 13.5.1 Sequence Analysis

#### *First Generation of Sequencing*

The first generation of DNA sequencing technology is based on the chain termination method developed by Frederick Sanger and colleagues in 1977. This approach used dideoxynucleotides (ddNTPs) to randomly terminate DNA fragment elongation mediated by DNA polymerase, resulting in strands of varying lengths. Fluorescently labelled ddNTPs enabled separation of these fragments by size using gel or capillary electrophoresis. The sequence was determined based on the order of detected fluorescent signals. Early Sanger sequencing allowed 96 samples to be processed in parallel, determining several hundred bases per sample with each 2-hour run. This meant that substantial sections had to be sequenced individually and computationally assembled to decode full genomes over a period of years due to its low throughput and high cost. While limited, Sanger sequencing formed the fundamental basis for later generations of technology by proving the principle that DNA sequence information could be derived through biochemical techniques. Incremental improvements brought down Sanger sequencing time to 15 minutes per run, reducing costs and increasing throughput, but new approaches were ultimately needed to achieve rapid and economical genome scale analyses. Still, Sanger sequencing maintains usefulness today for smaller-scale, targeted sequencing applications requiring very high accuracy.

#### *Second Generation of Sequencing or Next Generation Sequencing (NGS)*

The second generation of DNA sequencing, also known as Next Generation Sequencing (NGS), emerged in the mid-2000s and enabled massively parallel high throughput analysis capabilities. Major platforms leveraged new approaches like pyrosequencing (454 Life Sciences), sequencing by synthesis utilizing reversible dye terminators (Illumina), ion semiconductor sequencing (Ion Torrent), and sequencing by ligation (SOLiD). These helps to overcome limitations in throughput and expense of classic Sanger sequencing, with some trade off in read lengths and accuracy initially. Second generation sequencing allowed vastly increased number of sequencing reactions in parallel, generating hundreds of megabases to gigabases per run, rather than kilobases. This new capacity opened capabilities like sequencing entire human exomes and genomes cost effectively in days rather than years. Additional innovations later on pushed read lengths to several hundred bases while improving accuracy to exceed 99.9%. The high throughput of second-generation DNA sequencing fuelled advances across research and clinical genomics, enabling previously impossible scales of investigation in fields ranging from oncology to microbiology to plant genetics and more. Ongoing improvements to NGS platforms today continue to drive new findings across the life sciences.

#### *Third Generation of Sequencing*

The 2010s saw the advent of third generation sequencing methods, seeking to overcome remaining challenges like short read lengths that complicated genome assembly. Major platforms include Pacific Biosciences (PacBio) Single Molecule Real-Time (SMRT) sequencing and Oxford Nanopore Technologies (ONT) nanopore-based sequencing. These leverage direct observation of single DNA molecules during synthesis, enabling read lengths in the tens of thousands to hundreds of thousands of bases. Long reads facilitate complete genome mapping, identification

of structural variants, and full-length transcript sequencing without need for assembly. Additional innovations enhance throughput and scalability using microfluidics and nanoscale sensing. For example, small, portable, real-time devices like the ONT MinION generate huge data, demonstrating potential for rapid point-of-care genome analysis. Hybrid sequencing combines second and third gen strengths—high accuracy short reads plus long read for scaffolding. Costs continue decreasing, positioning third generation sequencing for greater integration into clinical workflows. Future directions also include Fourth Gen techniques focused on portability, speed, and wide accessibility. Incremental advances across the sequencing technology landscape continue to fuel genetic investigation and expand practical application.
Key features of third generation sequencing include,

- Extremely high throughput—can sequence entire genomes (rather than just small sections) in a single rapid run
- Faster speed—run times are generally 2 hours or less, versus days or weeks for older (Sanger) sequencing methods
- Lower cost—cost per base or per genome sequenced is a fraction of older methods
- High scalability—massive parallelization allows sequencing of hundreds or thousands of samples at a time
- Longer read lengths—many third gen methods allow read lengths in the 10-100+ kb range, improving genome contiguity.

### *Fourth Generation of DNA Sequencing*

The fourth generation of DNA sequencing remains on the frontier of research and development, seeking to build upon previous generations to make rapid genome analysis widely accessible. Key goals include sequences generated in minutes, massive cost reductions enabling a "$100 genome", and capability suitable for point-of-care clinical use. Emerging techniques utilize novel strategies for single molecule detection, including physical principles like tunnelling currents, graphene-based sensors, or biological nanopores. Microfluidic lab-on-a-chip devices may integrate sample preparation, biochemical reactions, and analysis, minimizing external instrumentation. Quantum computing holds prospects for revolutionizing sequence alignment and genome assembly will likely play pivotal roles in analysis pipelines as well. Achieving the ambitions of fourth generation sequencing will demand convergence of advances across fields from nanotechnology to computing.

### *RNA Sequencing*

RNA sequencing has rapidly become a key technology for transcriptome analysis, revealing the presence and quantity of RNA in biological samples. The latest RNA sequencing methods provide extremely high-throughput capabilities for understanding RNA expression and regulation on a genome-wide scale. Leading platforms such as Illumina's NovaSeq can generate hundreds of gigabases of RNA-seq data per run. In addition to sequencing established coding transcripts, new techniques allow analysis of non-coding RNAs, splice variants, fusion transcripts, and targeted subsets of sequences. Latest RNA-seq methods also incorporate unique molecular identifiers (UMIs) to mitigate amplification bias. Single-cell RNA sequencing (scRNA-seq) is a rapidly growing approach to study transcriptomics at the individual cell level, uncovering new cell types and regulatory dynamics. Key innovations in scRNA-seq enable massively parallel analysis of hundreds of thousands of cells. Long-read RNA sequencing can also analyze full-length isoforms and splice patterns. Ongoing RNA-seq developments continue to drive understanding of the transcriptome and its critical functions in biological systems.

Isoform-level analysis clarifies alternative splicing variants—insertions and deletions within RNA transcripts are also detectable revealing mutations. Sequence homology searches can match non-coding RNAs to known families like tRNAs, rRNAs enabling downstream structure and functional predictions. The nucleotide order in RNA can adopt complex secondary structures like hairpins and internal loops based on minimum free energy considerations; secondary structure predictions thus complement sequence alignment approaches. For coding RNAs, sequence composition metrics can reflect selection pressures at codon sites and analyses extended to predict likely protein products. By interfacing RNA sequence data with epigenomic information and protein-RNA interaction studies, models of post-transcriptional gene regulation can be sharpened.

### *Protein Sequencing*

Protein sequence analysis is fundamental to deciphering structure-function relationships. Primary analysis involves searching protein databases to identify homologs and conserved domains based on sequence similarity. Multiple sequence alignments illuminate sequence conservation levels and phylogenetic relationships. Predictive algorithms can also determine secondary structures like alpha helix and beta sheets as well as intrinsically disordered regions within sequences. Surface accessibility predictions clarify interaction interfaces and functional sites like catalytic pockets and post-translational modification locations. Sequence-based methods aid tertiary structure modelling and protein design endeavours. With proteomic advances, comparing sequences between physiological and disease states now facilitates biomarker discovery. Quantitative analysis examining amino acid frequencies highlights compositional biases and interrelationships providing evolutionary insights. *De novo* peptide sequencing parses tandem mass spectrometry data to unravel proteins lacking representation in databases. Taken together, these sequence analysis approaches transform one-dimensional protein sequences into multidimensional functional, structural and evolutionary characterizations powering precision medicine and protein engineering breakthroughs.

### *Structural Biology*

Structural biology continues to progress at a rapid pace as new technique and technological innovations enable the field to visualize biomolecular structures at unprecedented resolution. One area of prime importance is cryo-electron microscopy (cryo-EM), which can now generate near atomic-resolution snapshots of protein complexes and dynamics in their native states without the need for crystallization. Powerful new cryo-EM microscopes, direct electron detectors, and computational image processing have led to a resolution revolution. Another key advancement is integrative modelling which combines data from multiple structural biology techniques to create highly accurate multi-scale models of huge macromolecular machines like the ribosome. X-ray free electron lasers have also begun to enable glimpse into the early events of biomolecular function one femtosecond at a time. On the horizon, new methods like high-speed atomic force microscopy, 3D genome mapping tools, and micro electron diffraction hold promise to further expand the boundaries of structural biology into new territories of space and time. Fuelled by this methodological progress, recent insights have explored areas ranging from protein synthesis to viral entry to CRISPR-Cas function and beyond. The synergy of technological and computational innovation with incisive scientific questions continues to drive structural biology forward.

### 13.5.2 Biological Network Analysis

Graphs in the field of biomedical research have the ability to depict the connections that exist among various biological entities, including but not limited to proteins, genes, small molecules, metabolites, ligands, diseases, drugs, and even database records. Certain biological networks are designed to represent the workings of molecular interactions that are specific to cells and tissues, operating at a level of cellular organization that spans from individual cells to an entire organ. The different types of biological networks are:

1. Protein-Protein Interaction (PPIs) Networks
2. Sequence Similarity Networks (SSNs)
3. Gene Regulatory Networks
4. Signal Transduction Networks
5. Metabolic Networks
6. Gene Co-expression Networks
7. Expression Quantitative Trait Loci (eQTL) Network
8. lncRNA–Protein Interaction Networks

### 13.5.3 Biological Pathway Analysis

Pathway analysis encompasses a range of widely utilized tools in life sciences research, aimed at interpreting high-throughput biological data. The methodology underlying these tools involves the collection and application of knowledge related to biomolecular functions, in conjunction with statistical testing and various algorithms. Although these tools are extensively used, the foundational principles and overall context of pathway analysis may not be completely grasped, which can result in the misinterpretation of analytical outcomes.

The processes of making predictions through network analysis and employing Gene Set Enrichment Analysis (GSEA) are fundamentally interconnected. Gene sets can be transformed into networks, and conversely, networks can be reconfigured into gene sets. For instance, a network can be established by linking genes that are regulated by the same microRNAs, share numerous Gene Ontology terms, or co-occur in various pathways. Additionally, networks can be utilized to formulate gene sets. As an example, we have developed a gene set comprising all genes that encode proteins within the human interactome, which interact with a minimum of 50 other proteins. This gene set serves as a valuable resource library for the gene set enrichment analysis tool, Lists2Networks. The directed graphs produced, which illustrate kinase-substrate interactions and transcription factor-target interactions, were subsequently converted into gene set libraries to facilitate gene set enrichment analysis.

### 13.5.4 Omics Sciences

Incorporation of omics sciences in Bioinformatics has enabled to study the biological molecules on a large scale. Omics sciences encompass various fields such as genomics, transcriptomics, proteomics, and metabolomics. Genomics is the study of an organism's complete set of Deoxyribonucleic acid (DNA), which includes both genes and non-coding regions. The study of RNA molecules including messenger RNA (mRNA), microRNA (miRNA), and long non-coding RNA (lncRNA) are known as transcriptomics. The study of proteins, their structure, functions and interactions, identification and quantification of proteins are known as Proteomics including analysis of their post-translational modifications. Metabolomics examines the whole set of metabolites, available in a biological system for identification and quantification of metabolites, as well as the exploration of metabolic pathways.

## 13.6 MACHINE LEARNING TOOLS FOR BIOINFORMATICS

### 13.6.1 Prop3D

Biomolecular sequence, structure, function, dynamics, and evolution have complex interactions, and contemporary methods like deep learning are transforming our understanding of these relationships. Machine learning has a long history in structural Bioinformatics.

There exist three main ways in which Prop3D and the corresponding Prop3D-20sf dataset can be widely useful. To begin with, the Prop3D workflow code is adaptable and may be implemented on different cloud computing platforms. Scalability is primarily attained by distributing the output to HDF5 files over HSDS. A second useful resource is the linked Prop3D-20sf dataset, which offers a manually created and optimised collection of protein domains for 20 popular CATH families. This pre-calculated resource can be very helpful in streamlining the construction and repeatable application of ML workflows. Lastly, the creation of Prop3D-20sf explicitly accounts for the mystery of "data leakage," which arises from the evolutionary interactions between proteins, when building datasets and data-splits.

### 13.6.2 Brain Predictability toolbox (BPt)

The Brain Predictability toolbox (BPt) represents an extensive suite of ML instruments designed to manage a wide range of data types. These instruments are adept at processing tabulated data, including variables derived from brain studies, psychiatric assessments, behavioral observations, and physiological measurements, in addition to neuroimaging-specific data such as brain volumes and surface measurements. This toolkit is particularly effective for investigating a variety of ML inquiries within the neuroimaging domain, especially when dealing with large datasets involving human participants.

### 13.6.3 CheckM2

CheckM2 is a powerful tool that utilises machine learning to quickly and accurately evaluate the quality of microbial genomes. It is designed to be efficient and capable of handling large amounts of data.

The recovery rate of microbial genomes from metagenomic data has significantly improved due to advancements in sequencing technologies and Bioinformatics tools. Evaluating the quality of metagenome-assembled genomes (MAGs) is an essential step prior to conducting further analysis. CheckM2 is an enhanced approach for predicting the quality of genomes in metagenome-assembled genomes (MAGs) through the utilisation of machine learning techniques. Through the use of synthetic and experimental data, we have shown that CheckM2 surpasses current tools in terms of both accuracy and computational speed. Furthermore, the database of CheckM2 can be easily and quickly updated with new reference genomes of excellent quality, even for taxa that are only represented by a single genome. CheckM2 is highly reliable in assessing the quality of genomes for MAGs from newly discovered lineages, including those with smaller genome sizes such as Patescibacteria and the DPANN superphylum. CheckM2 offers precise predictions on the quality of genomes in bacterial and archaeal lineages. This helps to enhance confidence in drawing biological conclusions from MAGs.

## 13.7 BIOINFORMATICS DATABASES

The growth of large-scale biological data resources offers an ideal environment to apply cutting-edge artificial intelligence approaches for knowledge discovery in Bioinformatics. Numerous open-access public databases like SwissProt, GenBank, PDB, KEGG, OMIM and PubChem now contain an enormous wealth of gene sequences, protein structures, chemical compounds, biomolecular binding data, metabolic pathways, molecular interaction networks and genotype-phenotype maps. When integrated, these diverse structural, functional and relational data can provide comprehensive insights into the intricate workings of biological systems.

Leveraging such rich information resources can enable AI algorithms like deep neural networks to derive meaningful biological patterns difficult to uncover with traditional methods. Annotation databases also provide the extensive labelled datasets critical for supervised training of predictive AI models in domains spanning across Cheminformatics, quantitative structure-activity modeling, protein structure prediction, biomarker discovery, and even drug synthesis pathway optimization. As modern databases continue to aggregate multi-modal omics data spanning genomics, transcriptomics, proteomics and metabolomics; there is an exciting future ahead for AI-powered bioscience applications built atop massive and growing data foundations provided by advanced Bioinformatics databases.

## 13.8 OPEN-SOURCE SOFTWARE IN BIOINFORMATICS

Bioconda is one of the repository that contains more than 10,000 Bioinformatics software packages. Bioconda is a vital community resource that makes it simpler to begin data analysis using standard Bioinformatics workflows by managing difficult components such as dependencies, builds, and testing for thousands of programmes. Biopython is another essential open-source Python toolkit for computational biology and Bioinformatics. It provides a broad set of reusable modules for common Bioinformatics. Biojava is a Java library to process the biological data. Bioperl contains Perl modules for Bioinformatics application development.

## SUMMARY

Cheminformatics and Bioinformatics have been transformed by the emergence of AI and ML, allowing large-scale data-driven discoveries that were impossible earlier. In Cheminformatics, algorithms like deep neural networks and reinforcement learning are used to explore immense chemical spaces to generate promising new drug-like small molecules with desired pharmaceutical properties *in silico*. Meanwhile, Bioinformatics applies ML on vast repositories containing DNA, RNA, protein, interaction and phenotype data to construct models that can predict disease risks, protein structures, precision medicine targets and more based on patterns incomprehensible to humans. Together, they accelerate the digital transformations of the life science industry. The augmented intelligence of mathematical models sifting valuable needles from inconceivable data haystacks has become indispensable to understand health, disease and accelerate biotherapeutics development.

## WORKED OUT EXAMPLES

**EXAMPLE 13.1** Write a Python script to convert a chemical structure from SMILES notation to InChI format using RDKit.

***Solution:***

```
from rdkit import Chem
def smiles_to_inchi(smiles):
    mol = Chem.MolFromSmiles(smiles)
    if mol is not None:
        inchi = Chem.MolToInchi(mol)
        return inchi
    else:
        return “Invalid SMILES input.”
smiles_input = “CC(=O)Oc1ccccc1C(=O)O”
inchi_output = smiles_to_inchi(smiles_input)
print(“Input SMILES:”, smiles_input)
print(“Output InChI:”, inchi_output)
```

**EXAMPLE 13.2** Implement a simple linear regression model to predict the boiling point of compounds based on their molecular descriptors. The sample data can be accessed for alkanes in https://ics.uci.edu/~baldig/learning/alkanes/. Calculate the 2D descriptors using RDKit. The labels are available in the data.

***Solution:***

```
import pandas as pd
import numpy as np
from sklearn.model_selection import train_test_split
from sklearn.linear_model import LinearRegression
from sklearn.metrics import mean_squared_error
data = pd.read_csv(‘molecular_descriptors.csv’)
```

```
X = data.drop('BoilingPoint', axis=1)
y = data['BoilingPoint']
X_train, X_test, y_train, y_test = train_test_split(X, y, test_size=0.2, random_state=42)
model = LinearRegression()
model.fit(X_train, y_train)
y_pred = model.predict(X_test)
mse = mean_squared_error(y_test, y_pred)
print("Mean Squared Error:", mse)
new_molecular_descriptors = pd.DataFrame({'Descriptor1': [value1], 'Descriptor2': [value2], ...})
predicted_boiling_point = model.predict(new_molecular_descriptors)
print("Predicted Boiling Point:", predicted_boiling_point)
```

**EXAMPLE 13.3** Consider the following is the molecular fingerprints for two molecules.
Molecule 1 = [1, 0, 1, 1, 0, 1, 0, 0, 1]
Molecule 2 = [1, 1, 0, 1, 0, 1, 1, 0, 0]
Calculate the Tanimoto similarity of these compounds.

***Solution:***
Let's calculate the Tanimoto similarity:

Tanimoto Similarity = (Number of shared 1s)/(Total number of 1s in either molecule – Number of shared 1s)

Count shared 1s (intersection): 3 (positions 1, 4, and 6)

Count total 1s: 5 (Molecule1) + 5 (Molecule2) – 3 (shared) = 7

Tanimoto = 3/7 ≈ 0.429

So the Tanimoto Similarity is 0.429

## EXERCISES

1. Download five molecules from PubChem and generate 3D conformers using RDkit.
2. Retrieve the chemical properties of a specific compound from the PubChem and ChEMBL database and compare the different properties.
3. Convert the small molecules file format from one to another using OpenBabel.
4. Download any publicly available dataset of small molecules with their solubility. Calculate 2D descriptors of those molecules using RDkit or Modred and train a neural network model with the descriptors.
5. Download any sequence from NCBI gene database and write a perl script to calculate GC content of that DNA sequence.
6. Download Vitamin D Receptor sequence for different organisms viz., human, rat and perform multiple sequence alignment using ClustalX and ClustalW and compare the results.
7. Download protein-protein interaction data from the STRING database and analyze the network properties (i.e., degree, betweeness centrality, closeness centrality) in Cytoscape.
8. Calculate the centrality measures of nodes in a biological network using igraph in R.

9. Identify a set of disease related genes from DisGenNET and visualize the metabolic pathways associated with these genes using KEGG Mapper.
10. Analyze the potential biases in machine learning models trained on biomedical data.

## BIBLIOGRAPHY

Gallo, K., Kemmler, E., Goede, A., Becker, F., Dunkel, M., Preissner, R. and Banerjee, P. (2023). SuperNatural 3.0—a database of natural products and natural product-based derivatives, *Nucleic Acids Research*, 51(D1), D654-D659, Oxford University Press.

Kiewhuo, K., Gogoi, D., Mahanta, H. J., Rawal, R. K., Das, D., Vaikundamani, S. and Sastry, G. N. (2023). OSADHI–An online structural and analytics-based database for herbs of India, *Computational Biology and Chemistry*, *102*, 107799, Elsevier.

Kiewhuo, K., Gogoi, D., Mahanta, H. J., Rawal, R. K., Das, D. and Sastry, G. N. (2022). North East India medicinal plants database (NEI-MPDB), *Computational Biology and Chemistry*, *100,* 107728, Elsevier.

Kim, Sunghwan, Paul A. Thiessen, Evan E. Bolton, Jie Chen, Gang Fu, Asta Gindulyte, Lianyi Han et al. (2016). PubChem Substance and Compound Databases, *Nucleic Acids Research*, 44, D1 (2016): D1202-D1213., Oxford University Press.

Rutz, A., Sorokina, M., Galgonek, J., Mietchen, D., Willighagen, E., Gaudry, A., and Allard, P. M. (2022). The LOTUS initiative for open knowledge management in natural products research, *Elife*, *11*, e70780, eLife Sciences Publications Ltd.

Sorokina, M., Merseburger, P., Rajan, K., Yirik, M. A., & Steinbeck, C. (2021). COCONUT online: collection of open natural products database, *Journal of Cheminformatics*, 13(1), 1–13, BioMed Central Ltd, Springer Nature.

Chapter 14

# AI in Healthcare, Medicine and Pharmacy

## 14.1 INTRODUCTION

Artificial Intelligence (AI) systems, capable of self-learning through the analysis of complex algorithms, have significantly impacted various fields of medicine. AI has transformed risk evaluation, diagnosis, and work processes in the field of medicine, leading to personalized medicine rather than relying on algorithmic methods. AI enhances diagnostic accuracy, streamlines clinical operations, and effectively monitoring therapies and patients or disease outcomes. The AI began with a focus on creating machines capable of decision-making and inference.The timeline of AI interventions in healthcare and medicine is illustrated in Figure 14.1, and the benefits of integrating AI into modern medical practice are detailed in Table 14.1.

## 14.2 AI IN DISEASE DIAGNOSIS

AI holds promising applications in disease analysis, treatment planning, and patient well-being. This section highlights AI applications in disease diagnosis, presenting novel methodologies and technologies based on a comprehensive literature review. The demand on healthcare systems is increasing significantly due to the growing human population. AI is increasingly used in classifying patients according to the severity of their conditions. By analysing extensive Electronic Health Record (EHR) and data from examinations and tests, AI can identify patterns and predict disease onset more accurately than traditional diagnostic or treatment methods. Early disease prediction facilitated by AI enables timely intervention, improves monitoring, and enhances treatment efficacy. Advanced DL algorithms are now instrumental in extracting and interpreting valuable information from large datasets. AI's impact is particularly notable in cancer biology and neurobiology, where it is used to analyze and interpret complex biological data. In AI applications for disease diagnosis, obtaining a relevant and well-defined dataset for supervised learning is crucial. The quality of the user inputs and data clusters are the two major components for the development of effective AI models. Key applications of AI in diagnostics include the classification of dermatological conditions and the detection of atrial fibrillation.

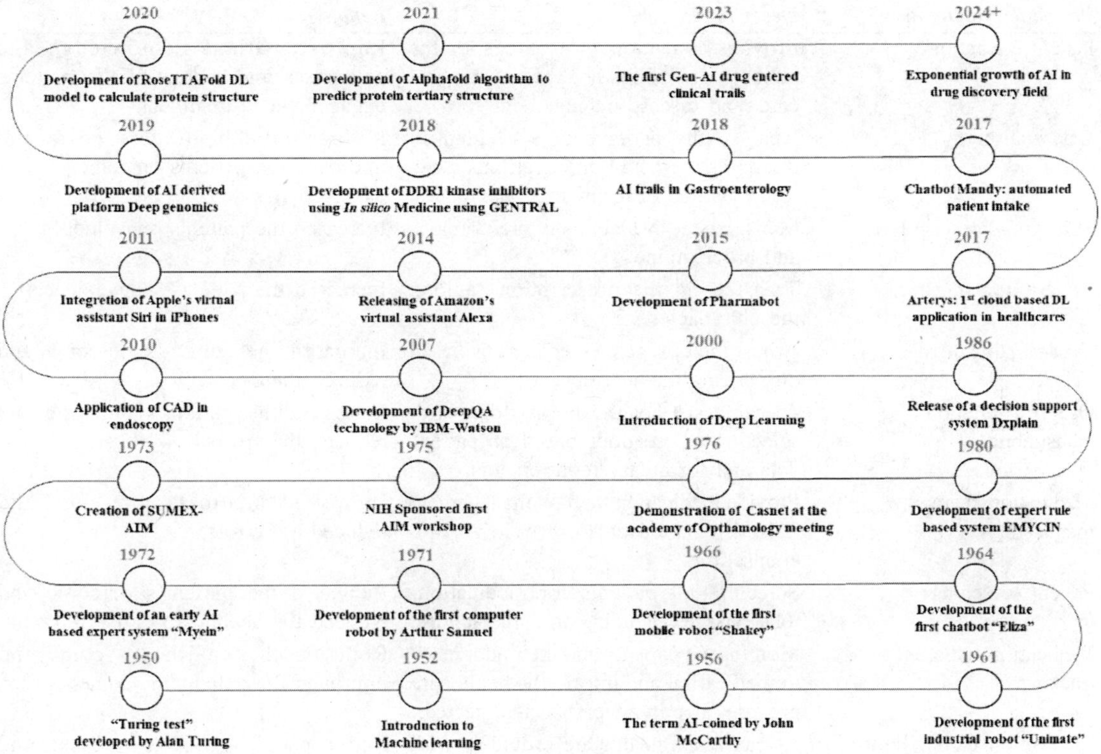


**FIGURE 14.1** Illustration of timeline in AI development in medicine.

**TABLE 14.1** Benefits of integration of AI in modern medical practice system

| *Pharmacy applications* | *Description* | *Benefits* |
|---|---|---|
| Reminders on medication | AI personalized reminders to the patients including time of administration and dosage level. | Reduced the risk of missing doses and improved the adherence of medication. |
| Drug interactions | Screening of potential drug—drug interactions and provide alternative combinations. | Reduced the adverse drug reactions risks and improve the patients safety. |
| Patients-doctor communication | Addressing the patient's questions and providing personalized support. | Personalized care and improved patient satisfaction. |
| Monitoring adverse drug reaction | Identifying the adverse drug reactions and provide alternative healthcare. | Reduced the healthcare costs and improved the patient's safety. |
| Personalized medication management | Managing the patients medication routines including frequency, dosage and time of administration | Reduced the risk of missing doses and improved the adherence of medication. |
| Integration of EHR | Real-time update on medication based on patients HER. | Reduced the medication errors and improved the medical care. |
| Chronic disease management | Personalized medication management system for chronic diseases patients including hypertension and diabetes, etc. | Reduced the healthcare costs and improved the patient's outcome. |

(*Contd.*)

| *Pharmacy applications* | *Description* | *Benefits* |
|---|---|---|
| Patient education | Provide educational resources to the patients, including healthcare, medical care, and disease management. | Improve patient's knowledge and awareness and increased the patients engagement in treatment. |
| Data analytics | Analyse the patients data to identify trends, patterns in medications, drug reactions and drug interactions. | Reduced the healthcare costs and improved the patients outcome. |
| Managing prescription refill | Managing the availability of prescriptions and order online. | Increased the patients convenience. |
| Prescription transfer | Transferring the prescriptions among the pharmacies. | Increased the patient's convenience. |
| Dosage adjustment | Adjust the dosage of medications based on patients medical data. | Increased the patient's outcome and reduced the errors. |
| Drug formulation adjustment | AI can assist healthcare providers with selecting medications based on patient data and formulary requirements. | Increased the patient's outcome and reduced the errors. |
| Medication therapy management | Provide medication therapy management including medication reviews and counselling. | Improved medical adherence and reduced the errors. |
| Patient screening | Screening of patients for medication-related issues including drug interactions. | Increased the patient's outcome and reduced the healthcare costs. |
| Medication adherence tracking | Monitor the patients and their adherence to medication and inform the healthcare provides if non-adherence is detected. | Reduced the healthcare costs and improved the patients outcome. |
| Medication reconciliation | AI can assist healthcare providers with reconciling medication lists between different care settings. | Reduced medication care risks and improved the patients outcome. |
| Telemedicine support | AI can provide telemedicine support, including virtual medication reviews and consultations. | Improved patients convenience and increased access to care. |
| Patient-centred care | AI can provide personalized medication management and support, tailored to each patient's unique needs. | Improved the patients satisfaction and patients engagement. |
| Patient triage | AI can assist healthcare providers with triaging patients based on their medication-related needs. | Increased the patient's outcome and reduced the healthcare costs. |

A holistic approach to medical diagnosis involves integrating various ML methods with DL networks. Techniques such as Support Vector Machines (SVM), Random Forests (RF), nearest neighbour algorithms, decision trees, logistic regression, and naïve Bayes classifiers are employed to enhance diagnostic accuracy. Predictive modeling has also contributed significantly to the early detection of Parkinson's disease. For lung disease diagnosis, rib segmentation algorithms have been used to analyze chest X-ray images. Recent advancements include a multi-scale network for pneumonia patient X-rays, which utilizes unpaired sample augmentation to improve feature extraction and outperforms traditional rib segmentation methods. Additionally, AI has shown effectiveness in classifying cardiac arrhythmias by analyzing electrocardiogram signals. Optimized genetic algorithms combined with SVM have also been successfully used for diagnosing tuberculosis. These advancements underscore the growing role of AI in improving diagnostic processes and patient outcomes across various medical fields.

## 14.3 AI IN PERSONALIZED TREATMENT AND DIGITAL THERAPY

AI has the capability to extract meaningful relationships from raw datasets, which can be leveraged for disease diagnosis and treatment. Emerging techniques in ML and DL are effective across various medical fields, addressing complex diagnostic and therapeutic challenges. A systematic approach to data collection and analysis, particularly with high-dimensional datasets, is crucial for solving intricate clinical problems. Advanced algorithms can process and interpret these complex data sets to uncover insights that may not be immediately apparent.

Healthcare professionals can harness the power of evolutionary computing, Artificial Neural Networks (ANNs), fuzzy expert systems and hybrid intelligent systems to manage and analyze data more effectively. These technologies provide advanced tools for developing predictive models, optimizing treatment plans, and improving overall patient care. A simple learning protocol from data to personalized medicine is depicted in Figure 14.2.

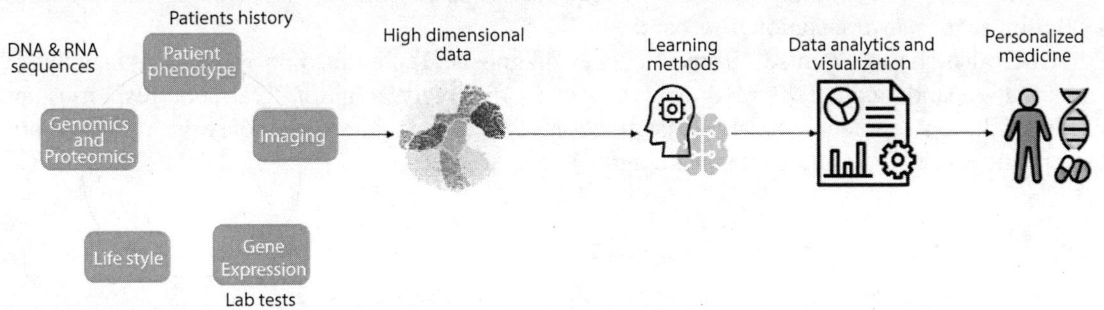


**FIGURE 14.2** A simple learning protocol from acquisition of data to personalized medicine.

## 14.4 AI IN RADIOTHERAPY

Automated treatment planning represents a significant advancement in radiotherapy, offering substantial improvements in plan quality, consistency, and error reduction. This technology is categorized into three main areas within the treatment workflow: automation in implementing multiple rules, modelling based clinical reasoning and prior clinical knowledge, and multi-criteria optimization. Automated treatment planning systems utilize sophisticated algorithms to analyze patient anatomy and physiology, replicating the reasoning processes typically used in manual treatment planning. These systems integrate clinical guidelines into a streamlined, automated process, enhancing efficiency and precision. The use of 3D dose distribution models and spatial dose assessments has demonstrated high accuracy in treatment planning. Radiomics, which involves in extracting and analysing a large number of imaging biomarkers, provides detailed information about tumors. This approach is effectively useful in the treatment prediction and individual patients' toxicity prediction and subsequently refining the personalization and effectiveness of radiation therapy.

## 14.5 AI IN CANCER

AI holds promise applications in cancer diagnosis and treatment. For example, multilayer perceptron neural networks have demonstrated their ability to accurately predict lymphoma subtypes using gene expression profiles. AI-driven methods can efficiently classify these subtypes with high precision. In the case of diffuse large B-cell lymphoma (DLBCL), DL techniques leverage genetic and transcriptional data from RNA sequencing (RNA-Seq) on next-generation sequencing (NGS) platforms to perform cell-of-origin (COO) classification. This aids in developing efficient, reproducible, and cost-effective assays for clinical applications.

In colorectal cancer (CRC), AI technologies are employed to analyze malignancy and predict *H. pylori* infection. AI can detect disease progression through blood tests and endoscopic imaging with high efficiency. Similarly, in lung cancer, AI facilitates early detection and supports pathologists by automating tasks such as carcinoma foci segmentation, lymph node metastasis detection, tumor cell counting, and mutation predictions. However, there is a need for more user-friendly tools that do not require extensive computational expertise to address AI's limitations in translational research.

AI also shows promise in breast cancer diagnosis. Techniques powered by AI, including quantitative and qualitative MRI analysis, can effectively monitor treatment responses and assist in lesion segmentation and classification. These applications demonstrate AI's potential to enhance efficiency and in cancer diagnosis and treatment.

## 14.6 AI IN CHRONIC DISEASES

Computer-based therapies utilize various programming techniques and technologies to enhance behavioural and cognitive interventions. These therapies often incorporate tools such as joysticks and multiple-choice questions to assess and improve cognitive functions. One of the recent advancements in this field is intelligent computer-assisted instruction, which leverages AI technologies like natural language understanding and expert systems to provide interactive learning experiences.

AI has also proven valuable in monitoring chronic disease patients through virtual medical assistants. These assistants offer regular check-ups and support via mobile applications, often using text messages for virtual consulting. This approach helps in managing chronic conditions more effectively by providing continuous, personalized guidance. In addition to patient monitoring, AI systems can offer nutritional recommendations based on an individual's gut microbiome and overall gut health. These systems analyze data to suggest diet adjustments that can improve health outcomes. ML technologies, including clinical decision support systems are increasingly used to predict long-term outcomes in chronic disease management. For example, ML models can forecast HbA1c responses in Type 2 diabetes patients following insulin initiation, aiding in personalized treatment planning and management.

## 14.7 AI IN CLINICAL TRIALS

Clinical trials are often referred to as the "*valley of death*" in the drug discovery process due to the significant investment and the high rate of attrition. Despite substantial financial resources and lengthy timeframes, only a small fraction of bioactive compounds ultimately receive approval from the U.S. Food and Drug Administration (FDA). Major challenges contributing to this high attrition rate include insufficient participant enrolment, adverse side effects, and inconsistent data. The economic burden on sponsor companies is particularly severe if clinical trial failures occur in later stages, such as Phase II and IV. Pharmaceutical companies may factor the costs of failed trials into the pricing of successful drugs due to the substantial financial losses that come with late-stage failures. Clinical trials involve a complex array of processes, including trial design, patient recruitment, site selection, monitoring, and data collection and analysis. Each of these stages requires meticulous planning and execution to mitigate risks and improve the likelihood of trial success.

## 14.8 CLINICAL TRIAL DESIGN, PATIENT IDENTIFICATION, RECRUITMENT AND ENROLMENT

AI can significantly enhance various aspects of clinical trials, including trial design, patient selection, and the management of population heterogeneity. Key benefits include:

1. ***Improving Trial Design:*** AI can optimize trial design by identifying the most effective strategies and reducing the duration of the design phase. Bayesian nonparametric models (BNMs) have emerged as influential tools in this area. These models use an infinite-dimensional parameter set with a finite subset of parameters, which helps to minimize clustering and streamline trial design.
2. ***Patient Selection:*** AI can refine patient selection by reducing population heterogeneity through better prognostic and predictive enrichment. This ensures that the selected patient cohorts are more homogeneous, which enhances the accuracy and reliability of trial outcomes.
3. ***Bayesian Nonparametric Models (BNMs):*** BNMs, including Dirichlet process mixture models and Markov Chain Monte Carlo (MCMC) techniques, are increasingly used in clinical trial design. These models offer flexibility and robustness in handling complex data structures and uncertainties. They are applied in various areas such as trial design optimization, dose selection, and the design of modified toxicity probability intervals (mTPI).

Overall, the integration of AI and BNMs into clinical trials can lead to more efficient design processes, better patient stratification, and more accurate assessments of treatment efficacy and safety.

### 14.8.1 Trials Monitoring, Patient Adherence and Endpoint Detection

Monitoring trial participants presents a significant challenge in clinical trials, but AI-enabled wearable devices offer a promising solution. These devices can continuously collect data on various physiological parameters, providing real-time insights into participant health and treatment effects. Risk-Based Monitoring (RBM) is a modern, AI-enabled approach that offers an effective and cost-efficient alternative to traditional monitoring systems. By leveraging predictive analytics and data visualization, AI-assisted smart monitoring enhances data quality checks and improves trial site performance. This approach helps in identifying potential issues earlier, allowing for timely interventions and reducing overall trial costs. Additionally, AI has significantly improved medical image-based endpoint and disease detection. AI-enabled systems can process and analyze medical images faster and more accurately than manual methods, making them both cost-effective and efficient. Overall, the integration of AI into clinical trials is transforming traditional practices, making them safer, faster, and more cost-effective. AI technologies streamline monitoring processes, enhance data accuracy, and facilitate more effective disease detection and management.

## 14.9 AI IN FORECASTING EPIDEMICS AND PANDEMICS

Pandemics can impose significant socio-economic burdens, with historical outbreaks such as the Black Death, Spanish flu, Cholera, Influenza, and COVID-19 highlighting their global impact. Effective early detection and management of these diseases are crucial for reducing strain on health, economic, social, and political systems. Disease surveillance plays a key role in this process, and AI is increasingly being leveraged to enhance these efforts.

AI is transforming disease surveillance and response. The utilization of resources and the effectiveness of health interventions are enhanced by these technologies. Despite the complexities involved in developing epidemiological models, AI has proven beneficial in various aspects of pandemic management, including detection, prevention, response, and recovery.

Followings are few examples where AI technologies are used in different pandemics,

- **Influenza:** Predicting influenza outbreaks is challenging due to variable epidemic peaks and periodic fluctuations. The Self Adaptive AI Model (SAAIM) has demonstrated significant accuracy in predicting these outbreaks.
- **Ebola:** Predicting Ebola outbreaks in African countries remains complex. Techniques such as hybrid neural networks and dynamic neural network forecast models, developed in 2015, have shown reliability in the early phases of the epidemic.
- **Zika Virus:** In the Zika project, mobile applications monitored mosquito populations, while AI models assisted in early detection.
- **HIV/AIDS:** ML has been utilized to identify potential candidates for pre-exposure prophylaxis (PrEP), enhancing HIV prevention efforts.
- **Dengue:** Support Vector Regression models have effectively predicted dengue outbreaks in China with minimal errors.

- **Tuberculosis (TB):** Artificial Neural Networks (ANNs) have been employed for the rapid diagnosis of TB, with a DL model achieving 97.94% sensitivity in detection.
- **COVID-19:** The COVID-19 pandemic has seen the application of various AI techniques, including Deep Learning Composite Monte Carlo (CMC) models combined with fuzzy rules for decision-making and prediction. Statistical DL systems, such as Autoregressive Integrated Moving Average (ARIMA), Multilayer Perceptron (MLP), Feed-Forward Neural Networks (FNN), and Long Short-Term Memory (LSTM) networks, have been incorporated to generate valuable predictive data.

Overall, AI technologies offer substantial improvements in the prediction and management of pandemics and epidemics, providing crucial insights that enhance preparedness and response strategies.

## 14.10 MEDICAL COMPUTER VISION

The medical and scientific fields have seen significant advancements with the rise of digital data capture. Computer vision, which encompasses object detection, localization, and classification, plays a critical role in this development. Figure 14.3 illustrates how computer vision models, utilizing large datasets, acquire advanced pattern-recognition capabilities. This technology has gained traction, with numerous companies receiving U.S. FDA and European CE approvals for medical imaging AI, leading to the emergence of sustainable commercial markets.

### 14.10.1 Applications in Medicine

1. **Cardiology:** In cardiology, computer vision and DL models are transforming clinical diagnosis and screening. Echocardiograms, a key source of cardiac imaging, benefit from DL algorithms that classify images and assess conditions such as hypertrophic cardiomyopathy, pulmonary arterial hypertension, and cardiac amyloid. EchoNet, a prominent DL model, excels in recognizing cardiac structures, estimating heart function, and predicting systemic phenotypes in a machine-readable format.
2. **Dermatology:** In dermatology, CNNs are utilized to differentiate malignant skin lesions from benign ones. These models have advanced diagnostic accuracy and efficiency in lesion classification.
3. **Ophthalmology:** Computer vision aids in diagnosing and managing eye conditions through fundus imaging and optical coherence tomography. AI-based personal therapy leverages high-resolution retinal imaging to extract detailed, personalized data from a single photograph. Google has developed a DL algorithm specifically for detecting diabetic retinopathy using retinal fundus photographs, which contributes to a continually improving healthcare system.
4. **Pathology:** Computer vision is also used for lesion-specific differential diagnostics, identifying concerning lesions among many benign ones, and tracking lesion growth. This capability enhances diagnostic precision and patient management.

Overall, computer vision and DL technologies offer transformative potential across various medical fields by improving diagnostic accuracy, personalizing treatment, and advancing clinical research. A sample DL architecture to develop model from EHR and medical images is depicted in Figure 14.3.

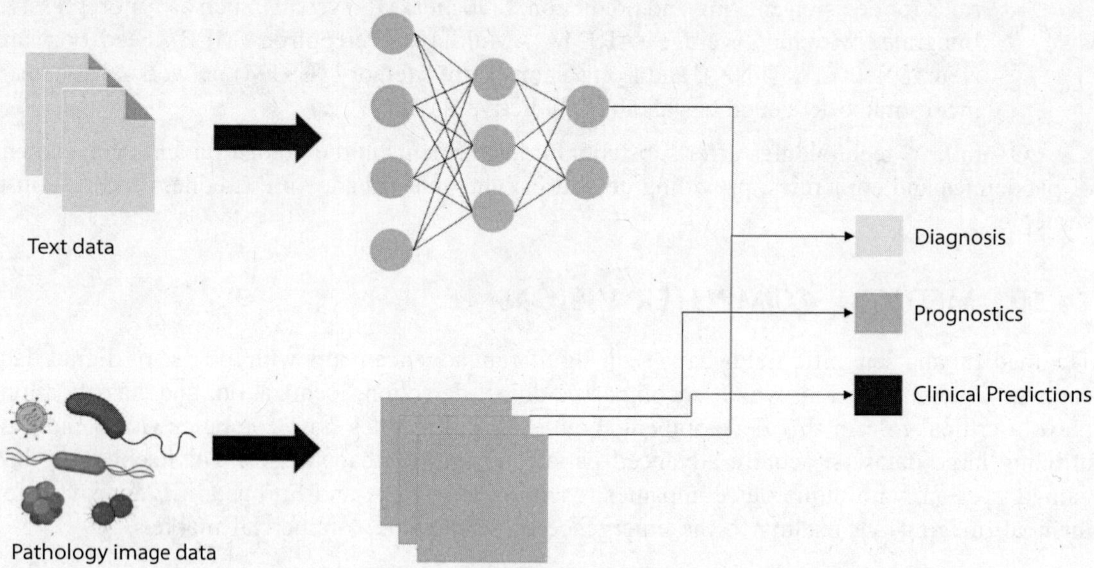


FIGURE 14.3 A sample DL Architecture totally from text data and image data. The text data will be passed through CNN and image data will be passed through CNN. The output can be used in disease diagnosis, disease prognostics and clinical predictions.

## 14.11 AI APPLICATIONS IN PHARMACY SYSTEM

AI is revolutionizing the pharmacy sector by offering personalized and real-time support to both healthcare providers and patients through advanced technologies like NLP and ML algorithms. These technologies allow AI systems to effectively understand and respond to patient queries and requests, significantly enhancing medication management and clinical decision-making. AI streamlines and automates various aspects of the pharmacy system, including drug development, patient monitoring, and clinical decision-making. AI leverages extensive data analysis to offer valuable insights that enhance patient outcomes, boost efficiency, and lower healthcare expenses. Additionally, AI plays a crucial role in identifying potential adverse drug reactions, drug interactions, and safety concerns, contributing to better patient safety. Overall, the implementation of AI in pharmacy promises to transform healthcare by making it more personalized, effective, and efficient, as illustrated in Figure 14.4 and detailed in Table 14.2.

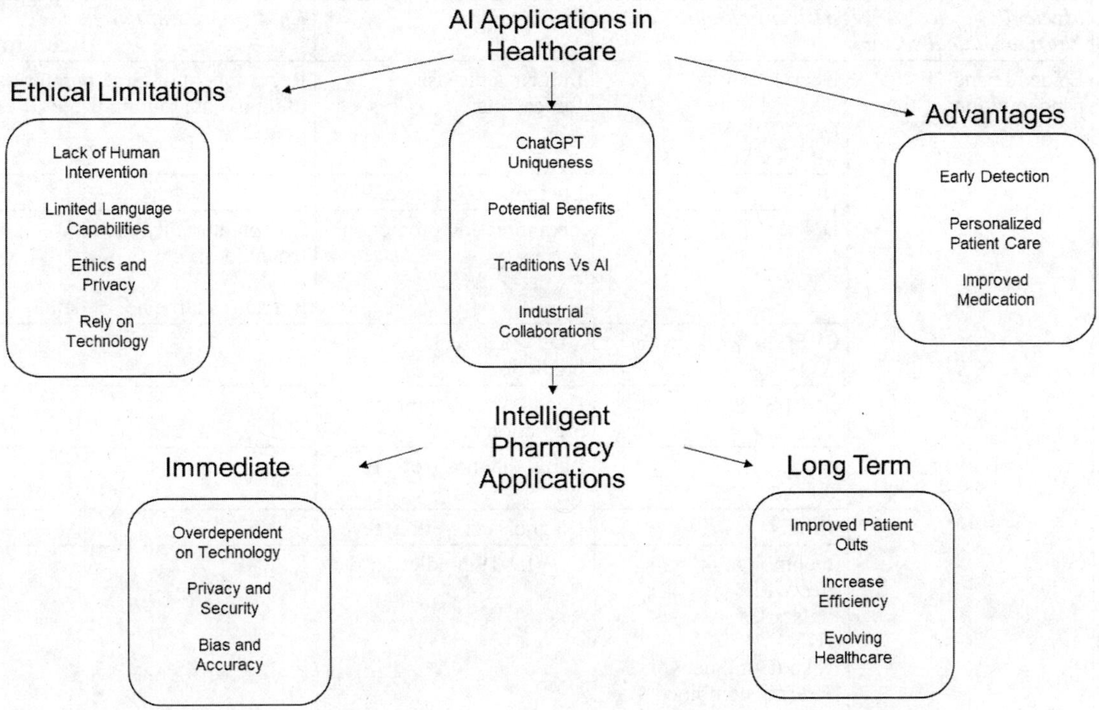


**FIGURE 14.4** Understanding Potentials and Limitations of AI in Pharmacy.

**TABLE. 14.2** Potential and limitations of AI applications in healthcare and pharmaceutical research

| *Medical/ Pharmaceutical sector* | *AI technologies* | *Applications* | *Challenges/ limitations* |
|---|---|---|---|
| Disease diagnosis | Deep neural network<br>Supervised/ unsupervised learning | Cancer<br>Retinopathy<br>Dementia<br>Dermatology related diseases | Required more data compared to traditional ML algorithms<br>Computationally expensive<br>As it is complicated it takes more time. |
| Personalized medicine and digital therapy | ANN<br>Evolutionary computing<br>Automated treatment planning | Clinical image analysis<br>Clinical data interpretation<br>Administration of Anesthesia and vasodilator | Dependency of hardware.<br><br>Determination of appropriate network structure.<br><br>Lack of optimum results due to multiple values. |
| | Radiomics | Radiotherapy<br>Toxicity prediction/ outcomes of radiation therapy | |
| | VR medical assistants.<br>Case based reasoning vector regression technique | Tracking chronic diseases | |
| | Computer-assisted instruction system.<br>Clinical support intelligent system. | Diabetes management | |

(*Contd.*)

| ***Medical/ Pharmaceutical sector*** | ***AI technologies*** | ***Applications*** | ***Challenges/ limitations*** |
|---|---|---|---|
| Epidemic and pandemic forecasting | Deep learning<br>SAAIM<br>MSDII-FFNN<br>ML-AMM | Influenza disease forecasting | Requirement of large number of input data to train the model. |
| | HNN | Ebola infection prediction | |
| | DNN | Zika infection prediction | Computationally expensive techniques.<br><br>It requires large no. of data. |
| | RVFL networks with WOA | VDPV outbreak prediction | |
| | BNM SVR | Dengue virus outbreak prediction | |
| | ANN, CNN<br>TB-AI | Rapid diagnosis of TB | |
| | MPNN | Diagnosis of yellow fever | |
| | in combination with Fuzzy rule<br>PNN + CF<br>CNN<br>Deep neural networks<br>Enterpol combined with bigdata | COVID-19 prediction | |
| | ARIMA | COVID-19 dynamic pattern analysis. | Poor performance while using in long term.<br>Difficult in prediction.<br>Less explainable than .<br>exponential smoothing. |
| | MLP | | Difficult to interpretation<br>Time consuming.<br>Depends on the quality of the training data. |
| | FNN | | Requires multiple hidden layers.<br>Complicated while using in colored images. |

AI: artificial intelligence; ANN: artificial neural networks; BNMs: Bayesian nonparametric models (BNMs); CT: clinical trial; mTPI: modified toxicity probability interval; MCMC: Markov Chain Monte Carlo; OCR: optical character recognition; NLP: natural language processing; RBM: risk-based monitoring; MSDII-FFNN: machine learning feed-forward propagation neural network model; ML-AMM: machine learning anonymized mobility map; SAAIM: self-adaptive AI model; HNN: hybrid neural network; DNN: dynamic neural network; RVFL: random vector functional link; WOA: whale optimization algorithm; SVR: support vector regression; CNN: convolutional neural network; TB-AI: tuberculosis-AI; MPNN: multilayer perceptron neural network classifiers; CMC: composite Monte Carlo; PNN + CF: polynomial neural network with corrective feedback; ARIMA: autoRegressive integrated moving average; MLP: multilayer perceptron; FNN: feed-forward neural network; LSTM: long short-term memory networks.

## 14.12 IoT IMPLEMENTATION IN MEDICAL FIELD

### 14.12.1 Telemedicine and Remote Patient Monitoring

The medical field has witnessed remarkable progress with the advent of the Internet of Things (IoT), particularly in the areas of remote patient monitoring and telemedicine.

Healthcare providers can remotely monitor the patients and provide medical services using these groundbreaking innovations. The advent of IoT devices has revolutionised the healthcare industry, particularly in patient monitoring. These cutting-edge technologies, including wearable sensors remotely connected with health monitors, have empowered healthcare providers with the ability to remotely track and analyse patients' various health metrics in real-time including vital signs and activity levels. In the field of healthcare, telemedicine platforms have emerged as a transformative solution, harnessing the power of the IoT to facilitate secure and seamless video consultations. This innovative approach empowers patients to effortlessly access medical advice and treatment from their own homes. The significance of this aspect has been particularly pronounced amidst the unprecedented COVID-19 pandemic, effectively mitigating superfluous contact and burden on healthcare infrastructures.

### 14.12.2 Smart Wearables and Implantable Devices

The convergence of smart wearable's and implantable IoT devices has ushered in a paradigm shift in the field of patient care. This ground-breaking integration has paved the way for unprecedented advancements in healthcare. Wearable devices have emerged as a prominent technological advancement, encompassing a wide array of devices such as smart watches and specialised health trackers. These devices have the remarkable capability to incessantly monitor vital parameters including heart rate, blood pressure, glucose levels, and record electrocardiogram (ECG) readings. These cutting-edge devices offer invaluable insights into the dynamic health trends of patients, thereby enabling the development and implementation of highly personalised treatment plans. Implantable IoT devices have brought about a new age of advanced medical technology. This remarkable development has revolutionised patient care, bolstering both safety and quality of life. Implantable IoT devices, such as pacemakers, have traditionally served as life-saving interventions for individuals with cardiac conditions. However, recent technological advancements have transformed these devices into sophisticated instruments that offer far more than just basic functionality. With the integration of IoT capabilities, pacemakers can now be remotely monitored and adjusted, providing healthcare professionals with real-time insights into a patient's cardiac health. The feature of remote monitoring enables the early detection of potential issues and also allows for timely intervention, reducing the risk of life-threatening complications. Similarly, insulin pumps, which are crucial for individuals with diabetes, have also undergone significant enhancements through IoT integration. These gadgets now have the capability to send data to healthcare providers, allowing them to monitor a patient's glucose levels and insulin needs closely.

### 14.12.3 IoT-enabled Drug Delivery Systems

The IoT has emerged as a force in revolutionising drug delivery systems. IoT has paved the way for unprecedented advancements in this critical domain by seamlessly integrating smart devices and advanced connectivity. The convergence of cutting-edge technologies has enabled the development of intelligent drug delivery systems that offer enhanced precision, efficiency, and patient-centricity. With the help of IoT support, healthcare professionals efficiently monitored the medication administration, treatment outcomes, and patient safety through real-time monitoring, data analytics, and remote-control capabilities. Smart inhalers is a prime example of cutting-edge technology in the field of respiratory medicine, are ingeniously designed with state-of-the-art sensors that meticulously monitor the utilisation of medication and offer invaluable insights into the efficacy of inhalation techniques. By seamlessly integrating these advanced sensors, these inhalers revolutionise the way patients manage their respiratory conditions, empowering them with real-time feedback and optimising their treatment outcomes. Healthcare providers can now ensure accurate medication administration to patients and improve treatment outcomes for common respiratory conditions like asthma and Chronic Obstructive Pulmonary Disease (COPD) by utilizing an advanced ML system.

### 14.12.4 Hospital Asset and Inventory Management

The implementation of IoT technology has revolutionised hospital operations by introducing efficient asset and inventory management solutions. Integration of RFID (Radio Frequency Identification) tags and IoT sensors has revolutionised the healthcare industry by enabling the efficient tracking of medical equipment. These advanced technologies work in tandem to monitor the precise location and real-time status of crucial medical assets, thereby guaranteeing their availability at the precise moment they are required. RFID tags, utilising electromagnetic fields, wirelessly transmit unique identification codes to IoT sensors, which are strategically placed throughout healthcare facilities. These sensors capture and relay the transmitted data to a centralised system, where it is processed and analysed. By leveraging this interconnected network, healthcare providers gain invaluable insights into the whereabouts and condition of medical equipment, ensuring that they are readily accessible when needed.

### 14.12.5 Predictive Analytics and Preventive Care

The convergence of IoT generated data, sophisticated analytics, and AI has revolutionised the healthcare industry by endowing healthcare providers with unprecedented predictive capabilities. Through the seamless integration of these cutting-edge technologies, healthcare professionals are empowered to harness the vast amounts of data generated by IoT devices, enabling them to gain valuable insights and make informed decisions. IoT-generated data serves as the foundation for this transformative paradigm, as it encompasses the vast array of information collected from interconnected devices within the healthcare ecosystem. By leveraging the wealth of information, healthcare professionals can effectively identify and address potential health concerns before they manifest into more serious conditions. Consequently, the integration of these algorithms into healthcare systems holds immense promise for enhancing patient outcomes and promoting proactive healthcare practises. The paradigm shift towards a proactive approach to healthcare, emphasising preventive care over reactive treatment, holds immense promise in enhancing patient outcomes and curbing healthcare expenditure over an extended period.

### 14.12.6 Enhanced Security and Privacy Measures

In light of the inherent sensitivity of healthcare data, the integration of IoT technologies in the medical domain has necessitated a paramount focus on ensuring robust security measures and safeguarding privacy. Cutting-edge encryption methodologies, revolutionary blockchain technology, and rigorous access control mechanisms are being strategically implemented to fortify the security of sensitive patient data. In the field of healthcare, it is of utmost importance to prioritise adherence to regulatory frameworks, such as the Health Insurance Portability and Accountability Act (HIPAA), in order to guarantee the secure and confidential handling of patient data. The advent of IoT technology in the medical domain has undeniably inaugurated a transformative epoch of healthcare that is centred on patients and driven by data.

## 14.13 TYPES OF SENSORS USED IN MIOT

The Medical Internet of Things (MIoT) encompasses a wide range of interconnected devices that leverage an array of sophisticated sensors to gather and analyse crucial health-related information. The sensors have been meticulously engineered to monitor a wide range of physiological parameters, detect any anomalies that may arise, and furnish healthcare professionals with invaluable insights. In the field of MIoT, a plethora of sensors are employed to facilitate the seamless integration of data-driven intelligence. Let us delve into a comprehensive exploration of the most prevalent sensor types utilised in this field:

### 14.13.1 Heart Rate Monitors

One essential element of the MIoT is the heart rate monitor, which is made to count the heartbeats. Wearable technology such as smartwatches, chest straps, and clothes may all incorporate these sensors. Healthcare providers may monitor cardiovascular health, identify anomalies, and adjust treatment programmes with the help of the heart rate monitor that records continuous heart rate data.

### 14.13.2 Blood Pressure Sensors

Sustaining cardiovascular health requires the use of blood pressure monitors. These sensors provide vital information about a patient's circulatory system by measuring both the systolic and diastolic blood pressure. Blood pressure monitoring in healthcare settings can be conventionally utilised or incorporated into wearable devices or smart patches.

### 14.13.3 Glucose Monitors

It is critical to continuously check blood glucose levels among diabetic patients. A vital component of the MIoT, glucose monitors let users track their blood sugar levels in real time. These sensors provide vital information for the treatment of diabetes and are present in devices such as continuous glucose monitoring (CGM) systems.

### 14.13.4 Temperature Sensors

When it comes to keeping an eye on a patient's body temperature, temperature sensors are essential. They have a number of uses, such as identifying fever, keeping an eye on body temperature during operations, and making sure medical facilities have the best possible atmosphere.

### 14.13.5 Oxygen Saturation ($SpO_2$) Sensors

$SpO_2$ sensors, also known as pulse oximeters, are medical devices designed to quantitatively assess the oxygen saturation level in a patient's blood. By utilising a non-invasive method, these sensors provide valuable insights into the oxygen-carrying capacity of haemoglobin molecules within the bloodstream. This information is crucial for healthcare professionals to monitor and evaluate a patient's respiratory function, enabling them to make informed clinical decisions. Pulse oximeters frequently incorporate these devices, thereby furnishing indispensable insights into respiratory functionality. The utilisation of these sensors is of utmost importance in the field of patient monitoring, particularly in cases where individuals are afflicted with respiratory ailments or are undergoing surgical procedures.

### 14.13.6 Motion Sensors

Motion sensors, also known as motion detectors, are electronic devices that are designed to detect and measure movement in a given area. They are widely used in various applications, including the monitoring of physical activity levels. These sensors operate based on different principles, such as infrared, ultrasonic, or microwave technology. Infrared motion sensors, for instance, work by detecting changes in heat patterns within their range. When a person or object moves within the sensor's range it detects their movement and record. Wearable devices have emerged as valuable tools in the field of healthcare, offering the ability to monitor and assess various aspects of a patient's well-being. Among their many applications, these devices have proven particularly effective in tracking mobility, posture, and even detecting falls, with a special focus on the elderly or individuals who are at a higher risk of experiencing such incidents. By leveraging advanced sensor technologies and sophisticated algorithms, wearable devices enable healthcare professionals to gather real-time data and gain valuable insights into patients' movements and physical conditions. This information can be instrumental in enhancing patient care, facilitating early intervention, and ultimately improving overall health outcomes. The implementation of these sensors is important in safeguarding the safety and overall welfare of patients.

### 14.13.7 Electrocardiography (ECG) Sensors

Electrocardiography (ECG) sensors are instrumental in capturing and monitoring the intricate electrical impulses generated by the cardiac muscle. ML algorithms play an essential role in the field of cardiac arrhythmia detection and monitoring, offering unparalleled value in assessing and comprehending the holistic state of the heart. By leveraging these sophisticated computational models, healthcare professionals gain invaluable insights into the intricate dynamics of cardiac rhythm irregularities, enabling them to effectively diagnose and manage such conditions. Furthermore, these algorithms empower clinicians to glean comprehensive information about the overall health of the heart, thereby enhancing the quality of patient care and promoting proactive interventions. ECG sensors are frequently incorporated into a variety of wearable devices as well as specialised monitoring equipment.

### 14.13.8 Respiration Rate Sensors

Respiration rate sensors are utilised to quantify the frequency of breaths per minute. Pulmonary function tests (PFTs) play a crucial role in assessing a patient's respiratory well-being and serve as valuable tools for monitoring various conditions, such as sleep apnea or respiratory distress. These tests offer vital insights into the functioning of the respiratory system, enabling healthcare professionals to evaluate lung capacity, airflow, and overall pulmonary health. By leveraging PFTs, clinicians can gather essential data to aid in diagnosis, treatment planning, and ongoing management of respiratory disorders.

### 14.13.9 Weight Sensors

Weight sensors help in the field of body weight measurement. These sophisticated devices are designed to accurately quantify the weight of an individual. By leveraging cutting-edge technology, weight sensors provide precise and reliable readings, enabling individuals to monitor their weight with utmost precision. With their ability to capture even the slightest fluctuations in body weight, weight sensors empower users to track their progress and make informed decisions regarding their health. Weight monitoring is a crucial aspect of health management as it can serve as a valuable indicator for detecting and tracking various health conditions. The integration of these sensors into smart scales or other weight-monitoring devices is feasible.

### 14.13.10 Environmental Sensors

In healthcare settings, the monitoring of environmental factors such as air quality, humidity, and temperature is facilitated through the utilisation of advanced sensor technologies. These sensors play a crucial role in ensuring the maintenance of optimal environmental conditions, which are of paramount importance for the well-being and safety of patients and healthcare professionals alike. Machine learning algorithms have become indispensable tools in healthcare, playing a pivotal role in maintaining high standards of patient care and well-being through continuous collection and analysis of relevant data.

The integration of these sensors into MIoT devices facilitates the seamless and uninterrupted monitoring of various parameters. This integration empowers the early identification and detection of anomalies, thereby enabling timely intervention and preventive measures. Furthermore, the utilisation of these sensors in MIoT devices paves the way for personalised healthcare solutions, tailoring medical interventions and treatments to the specific needs and requirements of individual patients. ML algorithms play a pivotal role in the field of MIoT, serving as the bedrock upon which this transformative technology is built. By harnessing the power of these algorithms, healthcare professionals gain access to a wealth of invaluable data, empowering them to make well-informed decisions and ultimately enhance patient outcomes.

## 14.14 AI IN MEDICINE

AI and ML are rapidly being adopted and integrated across nearly every area of healthcare. From clinical diagnosis, to drug development, to personalized patient treatment plans. AI promises to revolutionize how medical care is delivered. According to a recent report, investment in healthcare AI is predicted to grow over forty percent per year over the next half decade.

One major area where AI excels is in analyzing vast sets of complex medical data—from radiology images to genomic sequences to Electronic Health Technology (EHT). Algorithms can unlock insights that enable more accurate diagnoses of disease earlier, as well as better understand complex conditions based on subtle patterns within data. This also fuels discovery of new treatment methods tailored to a specific patient's condition and needs. Further, AI shows remarkable potential in assisting surgeons, speeding up drug development, and serving as virtual nursing assistants for patients. Adoption of healthcare AI during the past decade has already saved lives by detecting cancer earlier and matching patients with the treatments most likely to be effective based on their genetics and lifestyle. As researchers address remaining challenges surrounding patient privacy and biases in algorithms, the coming AI revolution aims to make preventative, evidence-based and personalized medicine a reality. With further development, AI may become a ubiquitous tool used by doctors, hospitals, pharmaceutical companies and insurers to provide better preventative care, diagnosis and treatment to patients around the world.

One of the first randomised controlled trials using AI-supported mammography was published in The Lancet Oncology. It showed a cancer detection rate that was comparable to unassisted reading and a screen-reading effort that was almost reduced. AI has accelerated advancements in molecular medicine, infectious disease research, and field-deployable diagnostic systems. However, the use of generative AI in medicine is still mostly hypothetical. Clinical research could be accelerated by automating the synthesis of evidence and the selection of *de novo* therapeutic candidates. Healthcare professionals may have more time to meet patients if AI-enabled medical note production reduces administrative workload. Large language models (LLMs) are being creatively applied in low- and middle-income countries through programmes like the Global Grand Challenges of the Bill & Melinda Gates Foundation.

Generative AI is difficult to apply to heterogeneous data. Evaluating the appropriateness and generalizability of many models is difficult due to their black box character. Big language models have the tendency to conjure up imaginary sources or produce errors that people would find easy to overlook. Patient privacy may be jeopardised if personal data is transferred to technological companies without sufficient regulation. One very important issue is health equity. For example, algorithms trained on healthcare statistics that show bias in healthcare spending made racial gaps in access to care worse in the United States. The majority of health data originate from wealthy nations, which may skew models and exacerbate historical unfairness and discrimination when applied in other contexts. A patient's trust could be damaged by any of these problems.

### 14.14.1 Cardiology

In cardiology AI was initially used in the early diagnosis of atrial fibrillation. The smartphone app Kardia, developed by AliveCor, was approved by the FDA in 2014 to enable atrial fibrillation detection and ECG monitoring. Atrial fibrillation is more difficult to detect through routine care in ambulatory patients compared to using Kardia for remote ECG monitoring, according to the current REHEARSE-AF research. The Apple Watch 4 has capable of record ECG and diagnosing fibrillation and it connects to the smartphone to record periodically and this has been approved by the FDA. There have been several criticisms of wearable and portable ECG technologies discussed, pointing out drawbacks including false positive rates resulting from movement artefacts and obstacles to wearable technology adoption among older patients who are more likely to experience atrial fibrillation. AI has outperformed conventional scales in predicting the risk of cardiovascular illness, including acute coronary syndrome and heart failure in EHR. It has been noted in recent thorough evaluations that the sample size utilised in a study report can affect the outcomes.

### 14.14.2 Endocrinology

Diabetic patients can monitor real-time interstitial glucose levels and receive information on the blood glucose rate. The Guardian glucose monitoring system, which pairs with a smartphone, was approved by the FDA by Medtronic. In 2018, Sugar I.Q system was developed by IBM Watson to monitor hypoglycemia episodes. While patients who receive continuous blood glucose monitoring can improve their blood glucose control and lessen the stigma attached to hypoglycemic episodes, a study on patients' experiences with glucose monitoring found that participants felt both personally inadequate to control their blood glucose levels and confident in the notifications.

### 14.14.3 Gastroenterology

AI is enormously used in gastroenterology to interpret endoscopy images and ultrasound to identify anomalous structures such as colonic polyps, gastroenterologists employed CNN among other deep learning models. Additionally, esophageal cancer survival, gastrointestinal bleeding, inflammatory bowel disease, metastasis in colorectal cancer and esophageal squamous cell carcinoma have all been predicted using ANN. These networks have also been used to diagnose atrophic gastritis and gastroesophageal reflux disease.

Some key ways AI is being used in medicine and healthcare:

- **Diagnostics:** AI systems can be trained on medical images, lab results, patient histories and other data to diagnose diseases, detect tumors, and interpret scans with high accuracy and consistency. This can assist doctors in making faster, more accurate diagnoses.
- **Treatment recommendations:** AI algorithms can analyze patient data and the latest medical research to suggest personalized treatment plans. This can help doctors select the best medications and therapies for each patient.
- **Drug development:** ML can screen potential lead compounds and predict how effective they may be based on their chemical structure. This accelerates the drug discovery and approval process.
- **Virtual nursing assistants:** AI chatbots and avatars can help patients track their symptoms, medication intake, and more between doctor visits. They can provide reminders, education, and 24/7 support.
- **Surgery and robotics:** AI is enabling more precise surgical robots that can automate repetitive tasks and improve the accuracy of tissue manipulation. This leads to better outcomes in less time.
- **Epidemiology:** The ability of AI systems to find patterns in huge population data sets aids researchers in understanding disease outbreaks, transmission patterns, risk factors, and more.
- **Personalized medicine:** The ultimate goal is to leverage AI and advanced analytics to customize disease prevention plans, diagnoses, and treatment for each individual patient. This is the promise of precision medicine powered by AI.

### 14.14.4 AI and Personalised Medicine

The ultimate promise of AI in healthcare is highly personalized medical treatment tailored to each individual patient's unique biology, lifestyle, and condition. AI tools allow physicians to analyze vast datasets including genomics, medical imaging data, electronic health records, and more to understand each person's disease risks, diagnose diseases earlier and more accurately, predict optimal treatment plans, and monitor patient progress. For example, AI can scan radiology images and detect tumors otherwise invisible to the human eye, unlocking an early diagnosis. ML can model how a tumor is likely to respond to various chemotherapies based on its rate of growth and genomic profile in order to match each patient to their optimal drug protocol. Researchers are also working on intelligent algorithms that can synthesize all of a patient's medical data with the latest scientific studies to generate personalized prevention plans for staying healthy. The benefit is superior outcomes and quality of life for patients. In future, AI aims to power truly personalized, precision medicine at scale—by putting tailored treatments for each patient at clinician's fingertips.

## 14.15 AI IN PHARMACY

AI and automation are bringing major changes to the pharmacy sector. One area noticing significant disruption is in the management of prescription. Robotic dispensing systems equipped with computer vision can automatically read paper prescriptions and enter details into the system. AI checks help ensure the correct drug, dosage, and patient information gets logged. Automated systems then fill prescriptions via robotic arms, freeing up pharmacists from this routine task. AI verification does a final analysis before medications are dispensed to catch any errors. This improves dispensing accuracy while allowing pharmacists to focus more attention on direct patient care.

AI innovations are also enhancing patient safety when it comes to drug recommendations. Sophisticated ML algorithms can analyze a patient's condition, medications, genetics, and biomarkers to predict drug interactions or contraindications. This allows pharmacists to better advise on appropriate therapies for each individual. NLP can mine clinical notes and patient history in electronic health records to further inform prescription decisions. AI-driven robotic assistants can help manage and package medications for patients, customizing dose dispensing based on their health needs.

### 14.15.1 AI-driven Pharmaceutical Functionality

A revolutionary age in medication research and development is being led by AI-driven pharmaceutical functionality. This cutting-edge method transforms the pharmaceutical pipeline at every level by utilising the power of sophisticated machine learning algorithms and data analytics. AI sorts through massive biological datasets to find possible drug targets with previously unheard-of precision, speeding up the process of target discovery. In order to speed up the discovery of lead compounds for additional research, Virtual Screening uses AI models to mimic interactions between medicinal compounds and target proteins. Using optimised chemical structures, *de novo* therapeutic design creates completely new therapeutic candidates with improved effectiveness and safety profiles, marking a major leap in drug development. Personalised medicine is about to take off because of AI's precision in drug administration, which guarantees creative delivery methods and effective dosage tactics. Conversely, AI-guided production process optimisation is reviving the drug manufacturing industry and offering lower costs and better product quality.

AI also has a greater impact on the more subtle facets of pharmaceutical development. AI algorithms are used in medication profiling and optimisation to optimise drug compositions and maximise therapeutic potential. Precision at the microscale is promised by the incorporation of AI into microfabrication technology, opening the door to the development of complex drug delivery systems. Furthermore, AI in Nano safety is essential for identifying and reducing any dangers related to nanoparticles, protecting people and the environment at the same time. With far-reaching effects on healthcare and medical advancement, the integration of AI with pharmaceutical functions represents a significant advancement towards more effective, safe, and efficient drug discovery and distribution.

### 14.15.2 AI Applications in Pharma Companies

#### *Johnson & Johnson*

Johnson & Johnson is an early pioneer within the pharmaceutical industry in leveraging AI and ML across drug development and commercialization efforts. J&J has partnered with startups like BenevolentAI to utilize its advanced computational platforms to predict drug combinations and possible new treatments. In 2022, J&J has actively been involved in over 50 partnerships and collaborations with AI-focused biotech startups to accelerate innovation. This includes deals with companies like Atomwise and Exscientia to utilize AI for novel drug discovery. One particular partnership helped identify a preclinical drug candidate for treating immune disorders in just 12 months—a process that traditionally takes over 4 years through conventional research.

Additionally, J&J has implemented AI more broadly into its consumer health, medical device technologies and global supply chain processes. Its partnership with Aetion utilizes real-world data and AI-based analytics to generate evidence regarding drug performance and patient outcomes. J&J also launched its own personalized health solutions platform, called Human Data Science Initiative, which connects various health data sources to respond to patient needs. According to J&J's CTO, implementing AI has delivered over $650 million in incremental value through improved supply chain monitoring, predictive distribution and inventory optimization. As one of the biggest pharmaceutical players, J&J plans to continue maximizing AI adoption to enhance patients' lives while reducing costs.

#### *Pfizer*

Pfizer has emerged as one of the leading pharmaceutical companies at the forefront of harnessing AI across their drug discovery and vaccine development pipelines. It has actively entered over two dozen partnerships with AI startups since 2020 to analyze complex immunology datasets and accelerate clinical decision-making. One of their key collaboration efforts led to the development of a vaccine candidate for the prevention of Clostridioides difficile infection in just 9 months—a significant improvement over traditional 3–4 year vaccine timelines.

Additionally, Pfizer is leveraging predictive analytics and deep learning to optimize its supply chain operations. This has enabled intelligent demand forecasting, inventory tracking, and serialization to address counterfeit products or quality control issues. As an example, Pfizer utilizes IBM's Watson AI to gather insights from unstructured data for better supply chain visibility and responsiveness across over 150 global markets. Through large real-world data simulations, Pfizer can model epidemic spread and healthcare system capacity to dynamically adapt production capacities and distribution for drugs as well as vaccines during a pandemic scenario. Such innovations showcase how AI is transforming pharmaceutical protocols radically. With advanced analytics and strategic partnerships, Pfizer aims to completely reimagine conventional pharmacy norms to improve patient outcomes.

#### *Novartis*

Novartis has been strategically ramping up investments in AI over the last 5 years, with plans to continue expanding its AI capabilities. It has collaborated with Microsoft to build an AI innovation lab that focuses on leveraging big data and ML models to transform drug discovery and development processes. One key achievement has been the use of AI to analyze heart disease patient records, helping identify a promising new gene target for treating cardiovascular conditions which Novartis has now started testing further.

In addition, Novartis uses AI-based advanced analytics across their global manufacturing operations which generate huge volumes of data every day. By connecting all this data and identifying root causes for deviations via AI algorithms, Novartis managed to reduce batch failure rates by up to 50% in the last two years across critical drug production lines. The company also managed to increase productivity in their labs and research facilities by automating tedious processes. As one example, an AI robot in their Boston facility successfully performed over 10,000 independent experiments on human cell samples to advance immuno-oncology research. Such innovations demonstrate how AI interventions are supporting Novartis in enhancing quality control and bringing drugs to market faster. Going forward, Novartis plans to continue collaborating globally with academia and partners to keep expanding the AI possibilities across the patient solution spectrum.

### *GSK*

GSK has focused extensively on leveraging AI and ML over the past few years to modernize and strengthen their pharmaceutical research and manufacturing capabilities. A major research focus area is to apply NLP to extract insights from scientific texts and medical journals to identify new potential drug targets and biomarkers. One such effort is they analyzed over 2 million research papers to find connections between specific proteins and over 200 diseases, enabling GSK scientists to zero in on high-potential areas faster.

Additionally, GSK has implemented intelligent automation and predictive analytics algorithms across their global vaccine manufacturing plants and distribution centers. By tapping into the IoT data from equipment sensors as well as historical trends, GSK optimized batch production scheduling and inventory management processes. As one example, their Canadian facility managed to increase vaccine batch production by over 20% within 12 months by using AI planning of equipment usage and personnel shifts. Their control systems can now forecast demand surges and supply constraints as well and adapt production rates automatically. Such innovations demonstrate how GSK is leveraging AI to strengthen pharmaceutical operations and public health outreach globally. Going forward, GSK aims to utilize AI-powered software as a service model to collaborate seamlessly with healthcare partners and patients.

### *Merk and co.*

Merck is utilizing AI to improve different parts of its drug business. One main area is speeding up the early science of finding possible new medicines. Merck scientists are teaming up with AI startups and tech companies to analyze huge amounts of genetic data. This helps them spot patterns and clues to diseases faster. In one case, Merck discovered a potential autoimmune drug in half the normal time with AI tools.

The other major use of AI is in manufacturing and testing Merck's drugs. Its factories are using smart robots, sensors, and advanced computing to improve quality control. Additionally, Merck is applying AI to study patient health records and find the right candidates quicker for clinical trials. For example, an AI system helped a cancer drug trial enrol participants 30%

faster than usual. Between acquiring AI startups, hiring data scientists, and strategic partnerships, Merck has dedicated over $2 billion to adopt more AI technology in all areas of pharmacy as a key innovation focus.

## SUMMARY

The application of AI and ML in the healthcare and pharmaceutical sectors is vast and transformative, with smart hospitals and healthcare facilities increasingly integrating these technologies alongside big data to shape the future of medicine. AI and ML have significantly accelerated drug development, reducing both the time and cost involved in bringing new drugs to market. Advanced neural networks and DL methods have established AI's critical role in disease diagnosis, enabling effective correlation of unstructured medical data with learned insights to predict outcomes and guide treatment strategies. AI technologies, such as intelligent computer-assisted instruction (ICAI) systems, case-based reasoning, vector regression techniques, and clinical decision support systems, are pivotal in developing personalized treatment methods and optimizing chronic disease management.

Moreover, Radiomics enhances personalized treatment by predicting outcomes and toxicity for individual patients undergoing radiation therapy, while high-resolution retinal imaging provides detailed insights into eye health. In clinical trials research, AI improves trial design and dose selection, thereby reducing both the duration and cost associated with drug development. Amid the ongoing COVID-19 pandemic, AI has demonstrated its value in detection, prevention, response, and recovery, with deep learning proving particularly effective in tracking epidemics. Other AI technologies, including neural networks, adaptive mixture models (AMM), and support vector regression (SVR), contribute to predicting and managing pandemics. As AI technologies continue to evolve, their advantages are expected to outweigh their limitations, opening up numerous opportunities in healthcare and pharmaceutical research. These advancements are poised to be game-changers in the field, paving the way for more efficient and effective healthcare solutions.

## WORKED OUT EXAMPLES

**EXAMPLE 14.1** Download the diabetes dataset from Kaggle (https://www.kaggle.com/code/melikedilekci/diabetes-dataset-for-beginners/input). Implement logistic regression model to calculate the risk score for diabetes based on given health metrics (e.g., BMI, blood sugar levels).

***Solution:***

```
import pandas as pd
import numpy as np
from sklearn.model_selection import train_test_split
from sklearn.linear_model import LogisticRegression
from sklearn.preprocessing import StandardScaler
from sklearn.metrics import accuracy_score, confusion_matrix, classification_report
df = pd.read_csv('diabetes_dataset.csv')
```

```
df.fillna(df.mean(), inplace=True)
X = df[['Pregnencies', 'Glucose', 'BloodPressure','SkinThickness','Insulin','BMI', '
DiabetesPedigreeFunction', 'Age']]
y = df['Outcome']
scaler = StandardScaler()
X = scaler.fit_transform(X)
X_train, X_test, y_train, y_test = train_test_split(X, y, test_size=0.2, random_state=42)
model = LogisticRegression()
model.fit(X_train, y_train)
y_pred_proba = model.predict_proba(X_test)[:, 1]
y_pred = model.predict(X_test)
accuracy = accuracy_score(y_test, y_pred)
conf_matrix = confusion_matrix(y_test, y_pred)
class_report = classification_report(y_test, y_pred)
print("Accuracy:", accuracy)
print("Confusion Matrix:\n", conf_matrix)
print("Classification Report:\n", class_report)
print("Risk Scores for the first 10 test samples:", y_pred_proba[:10])
```

**EXAMPLE 14.2** Write a Python script to clean and preprocess a dataset of electronic health records (EHRs) by handling missing values and normalizing data.

***Solution:***

```
import pandas as pd
from sklearn.preprocessing import StandardScaler
df = pd.read_csv('ehr_dataset.csv')
df.fillna(df.mean(), inplace=True)
numerical_cols = df.select_dtypes(include=['float64', 'int64']).columns
scaler = StandardScaler()
df[numerical_cols] = scaler.fit_transform(df[numerical_cols])
df.to_csv('cleaned_ehr_dataset.csv', index=False)
print("Data cleaning and normalization complete. The cleaned dataset is saved as 'cleaned_
ehr_dataset.csv'.")
```

**EXAMPLE 14.3** Download DrugBank dataset CSV from https://go.drugbank.com/releases/latest#structures. Perform Principal Component Analysis (PCA) on the dataset to reduce its dimensionality. Identify the top 3 principal components and explain the variance explained by each component.

***Solution:***

```
import pandas as pd
from sklearn.preprocessing import StandardScaler
from sklearn.decomposition import PCA
import matplotlib.pyplot as plt
file_path = 'path_to_your_drugbank_dataset.csv'
data = pd.read_csv(file_path)
```

```
data = data.dropna()
scaler = StandardScaler()
data_scaled = scaler.fit_transform(data)
pca = PCA(n_components=3)
principal_components = pca.fit_transform(data_scaled)
pc_df = pd.DataFrame(data=principal_components, columns=['PC1', 'PC2', 'PC3'])
explained_variance = pca.explained_variance_ratio_
print(f'Explained variance by PC1: {explained_variance[0]:.2f}')
print(f'Explained variance by PC2: {explained_variance[1]:.2f}')
print(f'Explained variance by PC3: {explained_variance[2]:.2f}')
plt.figure(figsize=(8, 6))
plt.scatter(pc_df['PC1'], pc_df['PC2'], alpha=0.5)
plt.xlabel('Principal Component 1')
plt.ylabel('Principal Component 2')
plt.title('PCA of DrugBank Dataset')
plt.show()
```

## EXERCISES

1. Write a script to diagnose heart disease from patient data using a support vector machine (SVM).
2. Using logistic regression develop a predictive model to assess the risk of stroke in patients using historical health data.
3. Using If-Else conditions in Python to write a simple rule-based expert system to provide clinical decision support for managing hypertension.
4. Perform a comparative analysis of different machine learning algorithms on a healthcare dataset.

   **Hint:** Compare algorithms like SVM, random forest, and logistic regression using cross-validation.
5. Write a script to train a deep learning model using CNN to detect anomalies in CT scan images.
6. Develop a simple recurrent neural network (RNN) to predict the progression of Parkinson's disease based on patient movement data.

   **Hint:** Use LSTM cells in your RNN.
7. Implement a named entity recognition (NER) model to extract medical terms from unstructured EHR data.

   **Hint:** Use spaCy or NLTK.
8. Analyze a dataset of genetic information and drug response rates to find correlations using Pearson correlation-coefficient method.

**9.** Predicting Patient Risk of Diabetes Using Decision Trees.

| *Age* | *BMI* | *Blood Pressure* | *Glucose level* | *Diabetes risk* |
|---|---|---|---|---|
| 45 | 22.0 | 80 | 120 | 1 |
| 30 | 27.5 | 70 | 140 | 1 |
| 50 | 25.0 | 85 | 110 | 0 |
| 40 | 23.5 | 75 | 130 | 0 |
| 35 | 30.3 | 80 | 150 | 1 |
| 60 | 29.0 | 90 | 160 | 0 |

**10.** Apply logistic regression model to predict the heart disease risk for the following data.

| *Age* | *Cholesterol* | *Max. heart rate* | *Exercise induced agina* | *Heart disease risk* |
|---|---|---|---|---|
| 55 | 220 | 150 | 1 | 1 |
| 60 | 250 | 120 | 0 | 0 |
| 45 | 180 | 160 | 1 | 1 |
| 50 | 200 | 140 | 0 | 0 |
| 40 | 230 | 170 | 1 | 1 |
| 70 | 240 | 130 | 0 | 0 |

## BIBLIOGRAPHY

Bohlmann, A., Mostafa, J. and Kumar, M. (2021). Machine learning and medication adherence: scoping review, *JMIRx Med*, *2*(4), e26993, JMIR Publication.

Butow, P. and Hoque, E. (2020). Using artificial intelligence to analyse and teach communication in healthcare, *The breast*, *50*, 49–55, Elsevier.

Kassem, L. M., Alhabib, B., Alzunaydi, K. and Farooqui, M. (2021). Understanding patient needs regarding adverse drug reaction reporting smartphone applications: a qualitative insight from Saudi Arabia, *International Journal of Environmental Research and Public Health*, *18*(8), 3862, MPDI.

Singh, N. and Varshney, U. (2020). IT-based reminders for medication adherence: systematic review, taxonomy, framework and research directions, *European Journal of Information Systems*, *29*(1), 84–108, Taylor and Francis.

Zhang, Q., Li, S., Chen, F., Zeng, R., and Tong, R. (2022). Targeted delivery strategy: A beneficial partner for emerging senotherapy, *Biomedicine and Pharmacotherapy*, *155*, 113737, Elsevier.

Chapter 15

# AI in Drug Discovery

## 15.1 INTRODUCTION

Drug discovery is a time-consuming and complex endeavour that involves considerable risks, taking roughly 10 to 15 years and around \$2.8 billion to bring a new drug to market. Approximately 80% to 90% of drug candidates fail at various stages. The process begins with identifying a disease or condition that lacks effective treatments, with a focus on targeting specific proteins or genes linked to the condition for potential therapeutic intervention. Researchers then identify and optimize lead compounds that interact with the target to improve their effectiveness, selectivity, and pharmacokinetic properties while reducing potential side effects. These optimized compounds are rigorously tested in laboratories and animal models to assess their safety, efficacy, and toxicity. The process continues with human clinical trials—Phase I, II, and III where the drug is tested on larger groups of people to determine its safety, effectiveness, and proper dosage.

Traditional drug discovery methods face numerous challenges, including low success rates at various stages, unpredictable outcomes regarding efficacy and safety, and the complexity of biological interactions in the human body. These methods often rely on trial-and-error, which leads to inefficiencies and delays. Additionally, traditional approaches may not fully account for individual differences in patient responses, resulting in suboptimal treatment outcomes. As a result, biotech and pharmaceutical companies are increasingly exploring Artificial Intelligence (AI) to improve productivity and ensure the long-term success of drug discovery. AI is proving to be crucial in revolutionizing drug development by streamlining research, cutting costs, and enhancing overall efficiency.

## 15.2 ROLE OF AI IN DRUG DISCOVERY

The AI is significantly shaped by foundational concepts from cheminformatics and machine learning (ML). The application of ML to develop quantitative structure-activity relationship (QSAR) models and predict toxicity has a long-standing history. Recently, the growth of big data, improvements in Graphical Processing Unit (GPU) acceleration, new algorithm developments, cloud computing, advanced data analytics, and refined AI toolkits have driven these methodologies forward.

A new dimension to the drug discovery and development process has been introduced by AI technologies from target identification to preclinical studies. Choosing the right target is crucial, as inadequate efficacy is a major reason for failures in Phase II clinical trials. AI can substantially aid in target selection by processing large volumes of complex data, including various ~omics datasets. This capability allows for the discovery of connections between diseases and potential targets, a deeper understanding of disease-target interactions, and helps identify targets closely associated with specific diseases. For example, TargetDB, a public database that integrates target data and uses ML-based classification algorithms to evaluate and prioritize drug targets, offering insights into target and ligand development.

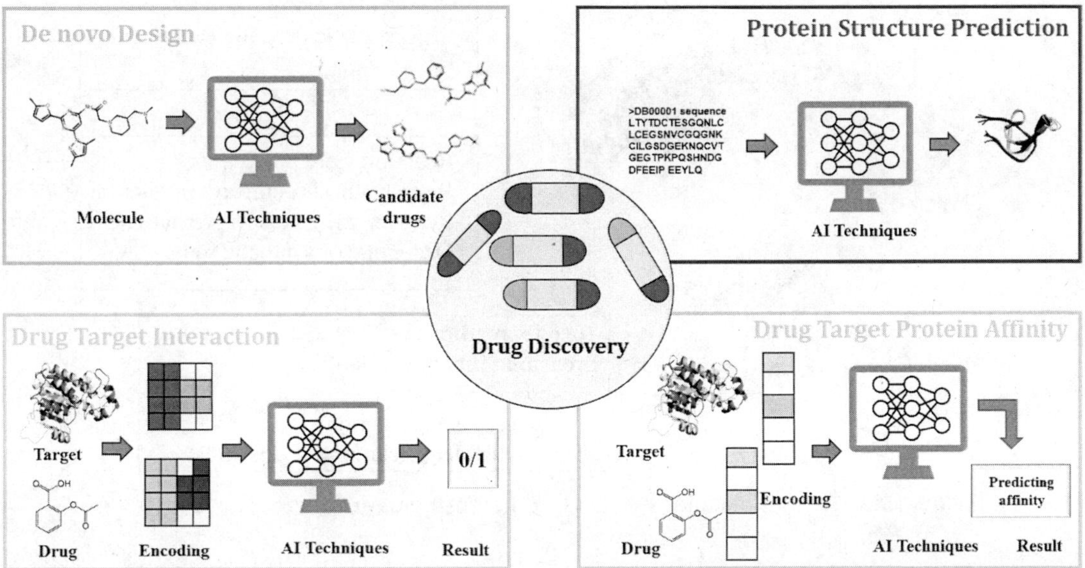


**FIGURE 15.1** Different applications of AI in computational drug discovery.

Once a drug target is validated, the next step is to find high-quality hits that can effectively bind and modulate the target. AI-driven methods can possibly improve virtual screening (VS) performance, making the process more cost-effective and efficient. These approaches help prioritize a subset of compounds for further testing, enabling the discovery of novel hits against previously identified targets. The ongoing efforts in ML algorithms continue to enhance drug discovery and it eventually speeds-up the research. Different AI applications in drug discovery and applications of AI in different drug discovery processes are shown in Figure 15.1 and Figure 15.2.

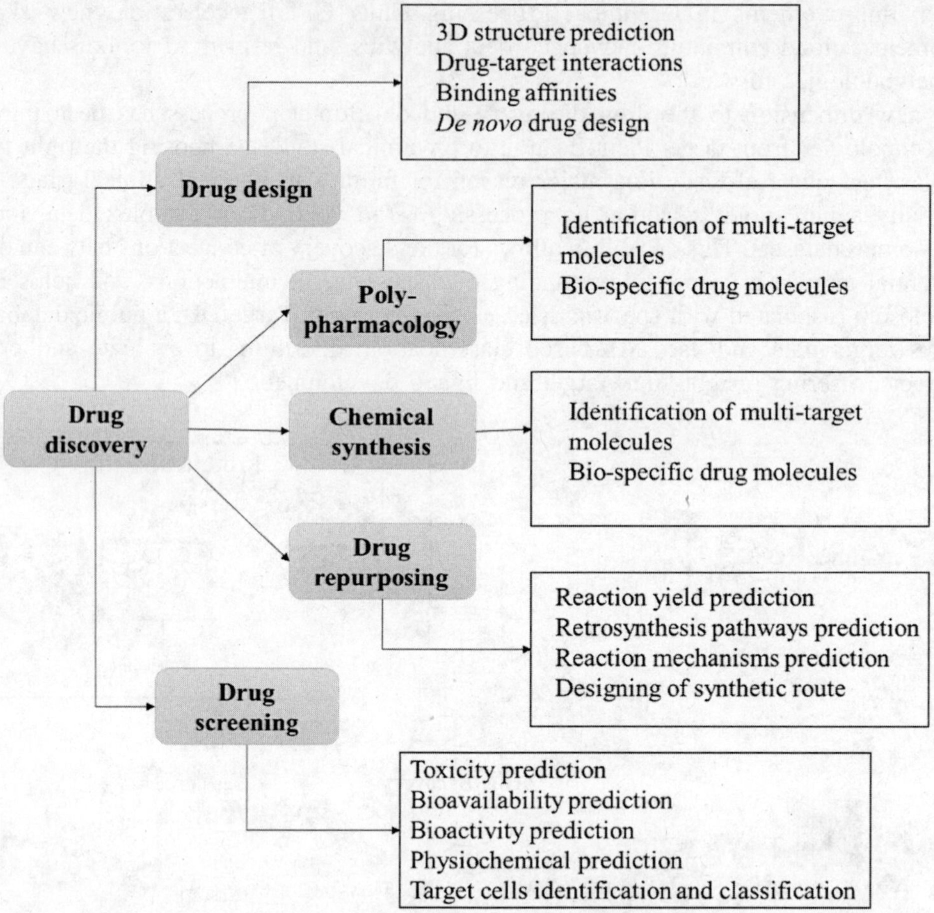


**FIGURE 15.2** The applications of AI in different fields in drug discovery process.

### 15.2.1 Machine Learning in Drug Discovery

ML involves algorithms to analyze processed data, uncover patterns, and make predictions about new data sets. This procedure, referred to as training, entails substantial volumes of data into algorithms, enabling the system to autonomously acquire the ability to execute tasks instead of adhering to predetermined directives established by a developer. The training data quality and quantity is the major factor to the effectiveness of these algorithms. The larger and more comprehensive data sets are important for the development of reliable model.

Supervised and unsupervised learning are the two major approaches in ML. Labelled data are used to train models in supervised learning, which can then predict the new values or classify new data based on past observations. This method involves understanding the relationship between input and output data to make accurate predictions. In contrast, unsupervised learning is used for exploratory data analysis. It involves clustering data without predefined labels, allowing users to identify patterns and groupings in the data. This method helps to uncover hidden structures or relationships within the data.

In drug development, the first step involves identifying a drug target and formulating a therapeutic hypothesis. This process, known as target identification and prioritization, uses existing evidence and hypotheses to focus research efforts. Although target validation is ultimately confirmed through clinical trials, early-stage screening and validation are crucial for efficient research focus. With the advancement of modern biology, large-scale datasets are becoming increasingly available, including human genetic information and disease profiling through transcriptomics, proteomics, and metabolomics. These datasets, often stored in public databases, provide new opportunities for early target identification and validation. However, analyzing such complex datasets requires sophisticated analytical methods to produce reliable models for predicting potential targets. ML is increasingly employed to meet these needs.

ML techniques can analyze large datasets to determine causal relationships between potential targets and diseases. For example, decision tree-based meta-classifiers use protein-protein network topology, metabolic interactions, and tissue expression data to predict druggable targets. Additionally, support vector machine (SVM) classifiers have been used on genomics datasets to distinguish between druggable and non-druggable targets in different types of cancers including pancreatic-, breast-, and ovarian- cancer.

### 15.2.2 Deep Learning in Drug Discovery

Deep Neural Networks (DNNs) are extensively used across various areas of drug discovery, including *de novo* molecular design, bioactivity prediction, molecule synthesis forecasting, and biological image analysis. The power of DNNs stems from their versatile architectures:

1. **Convolutional Neural Networks (CNNs):** These networks feature layers that are connected in a hierarchical fashion, with each layer processing data from the previous one. Image and speech recognition tasks can be effectively performed using CNN due to their ability in capturing spatial hierarchies in data.
2. **Graph Neural Networks (GNNs):** GNNs are designed to handle graphs or networks form of data. They are particularly useful for analyzing and predicting properties of data represented in network form.
3. **Recurrent Neural Networks (RNNs):** It consists of interconnected neural network modules arranged in a sequence, allowing them to process sequential data and capture temporal dependencies. A subtype of RNNs known as Long Short-Term Memory (LSTM) networks are adept at learning long-term dependencies in sequential data.
4. **Fully Connected Feedforward Networks:** These networks connect each input neuron to every neuron in the subsequent layer, and they have a well-defined gradient that can be computed through backpropagation. They are particularly effective in scenarios with abundance features relative to the number of samples, such as gene expression analysis.
5. **Deep Autoencoder Neural Networks (DAENs):** DAENs are unsupervised learning models that aim to map input data to output data while reducing dimensionality. They focus on preserving important features while discarding irrelevant ones.
6. **Generative Adversarial Networks (GANs):** A generator and a discriminator are the two available networks in GANs. New data samples are created by the generator and

the discriminator evaluates those samples. This adversarial process helps improve the quality of generated data.

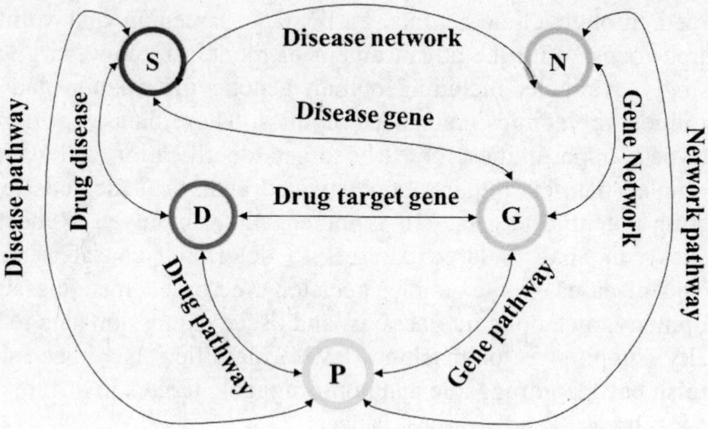


FIGURE 15.3 Representation of knowledge graph of drugs, diseases, their targets, pathways, genes and gene variants.

Deep learning (DL) methodologies are increasingly applied in drug discovery tasks (i.e., small molecules design and optimization, target identification and validation, biomarker discovery, computational pathology, etc.). Figure 15.3 shows the representation of knowledge graph integrating different biological information.

## 15.3 DATA MINING AND ANALYSIS

Data mining involves uncovering patterns or trends within large datasets, a process that is vital in pharmaceutical research. This era of drug discovery heavily relies on data from various sources, including high-throughput screening, combinatorial chemistry, and advanced instruments. The rapid expansion of such data highlights the need to extract valuable information efficiently. The process of discovering hidden, valuable insights in data is known as knowledge discovery.

Data mining typically includes six key tasks:

1. **Anomaly Detection:** Identifying unusual data points or errors.
2. **Association Rule Learning:** Discovering relationships between variables.
3. **Clustering:** Grouping similar data points to find patterns or structures.
4. **Classification:** Generalizing known data to categorize new data.
5. **Regression:** Modeling data to minimize prediction errors.
6. **Summarization:** Generating visual representations and reports.

In cheminformatics, common data mining techniques include descriptor calculations, structural similarity matrices, and classification algorithms. The effectiveness of data mining depends significantly on the selection of descriptors, which should meet four criteria: relevance to bioactivity, informativeness, independence, and ease of extraction. Research shows that

2D descriptors are often more effective than 3D descriptors. Pattern recognition is a core technology in data mining, with regression analysis and classification as primary techniques. Other common techniques include Markush structures, fingerprints, 3D pharmacophores, decision trees, hierarchical clustering, non-hierarchical clustering, and self-organizing maps (SOMs). Similarity or distance metrics are used to compare patterns, and classification algorithms help in developing methods to efficiently retrieve data.

Data mining algorithms can be categorized into hierarchical and partitional types. Hierarchical algorithms arrange objects in a tree-like structure, while partitional algorithms are better suited for non-parametric data but struggle with large datasets. Decision trees, such as Recursive Partitioning (RP), can process large datasets (e.g., 2,000,000 compounds) quickly but may generate multiple solutions, which can be a drawback.

The surge in biomedical data - from fundamental disease research to clinical trials presents significant analytical challenges despite the wealth of information. AI has been extensively used in addressing these challenges by revealing patterns and relationships within complex data networks. AI significantly aids in identifying biomarkers and targets, prioritizing indications, designing drug-like molecules, predicting drug-target interactions, forecasting pharmacokinetics, and planning clinical trials.

## 15.4 DRUG TARGET IDENTIFICATION

The identification of disease mechanisms and drug targets constitutes a fundamental aspect of the early stages of drug discovery, significantly contributing to the subsequent phases of drug development. Historically, target identification is a time-consuming process often conducted in academic environments, taking several years to complete. However, the emergence of AI has transformed this process by harnessing its ability to analyze extensive datasets and intricate biological networks. Target identification involves finding biological molecules or cellular pathways that drugs can interact with to produce therapeutic effects. This process is generally approached through experimental, multiomic, and computational methods. Combining these approaches can generate novel therapeutic hypotheses during the exploratory phase, thus improving our understanding of complex diseases.

Multiomic data provide a holistic view of molecular interactions, encompassing static genomic data as well as dynamic expression and metabolic profiles. Genomics, a foundational discipline in omics, focuses on genetic variants within DNA. Numerous links between genetic variants and diseases (or) traits are studied by analysing large scale genome-wide association studies (GWAS). These studies are helpful for the development of transformative therapies in different disease treatments including cystic fibrosis (i.e., CFTR mutations targeting drugs), inflammatory bowel disease treatment by targeting IL23A gene. Recent GWAS data meta-analyses uncovered new genetic loci that are associated with various diseases pave way to drug repurposing. AI's capability to analyze and interpret complex biomedical data networks enables the detection of patterns and relationships that might evade human researchers, potentially leading to more effective treatment strategies. AI has made remarkable progress in various areas, including the identification of biomarkers and targets, prioritization of indications, design of molecules with drug-like properties, prediction of pharmacokinetics, analysis of interactions between drugs and targets, as well as the structuring of clinical trials. AI-generated drugs are starting to enter clinical trials. Some of the AI designed molecules are GS-0976, EXS-21546, INS018_055 for non-alcoholic steatohepatitis, solid tumors and for idiopathic pulmonary fibrosis respectively. Among these molecules INS018_055 is the first drug that could produce positive results in Phase I clinical trial.

## 15.5 COMPOUND SCREENING AND DESIGN

Generative *de novo* design using deep neural networks (DNNs) helps to create novel molecules with specific attributes, such as high potency, optimal drug metabolism and pharmacokinetics (DMPK) profiles, and feasible synthetic pathways. Traditional computational approaches to *de novo* design have used methodologies like incremental "growing" of compounds or rule-based synthetic strategies. In contrast, modern generative models often leverage SMILES (Simplified Molecular Input Line Entry System) notations, which are text-based representations of molecules that convey chemical structures in a format similar to natural language processing (NLP). This analogy is due to DNNs proven effectiveness in NLP tasks, where they learn patterns and generate text based on linguistic rules. While one-dimensional SMILES strings are commonly used in *de novo* design, molecular graph representations offer another promising approach. Molecular graphs capture the relationships between atoms and bonds in a way that reflects the structure of the molecules more directly, potentially enhancing the effectiveness of generative models in predicting novel compounds.

### *Molecular Property Diagnostic Suite (MPDS)*

MPDS is our in-house Galaxy based open-source drug discovery platform which follows the FAIR data principles and is termed as the Molecular Property Diagnostic Suite (https://mpds.neist.res.in/). The aim of the MPDS is to integerate cheminformatics and bioinformatics tools along with disease specific information. The users can access drug targets, genes, etc. of a specific disease and they can perform drug discovery calculations. The available tools and modules are classified as diseases dependent and diseases independent web-portals under the umbrella of MPDS. MPDS has various disease specific web portals that are operational for diseases like for Tuberculosis we have $MPDS^{TB}$, for Diabetes Mellitus, we have $MPDS^{DM}$ and and for COVID-19, we have MPDSCOVID-19. The other portals in pipeline are Non-alcoholic fatty liver disease ($MPDS^{NAFLD}$), Metabolic Disorder ($MPDS^{MD}$), $MPDS^{ML}$, $MPDS^{BL}$ etc.

### *Molecular Property Diagnostic Suite—Compound Library ($MPDS^{CL}$)—A Structure-based Classification System for Chemical Space*

The $MPDS^{CL}$ (compound library) is an important web-portal that is available for the users with several novel features information about small molecules can be obtained and it also helps in small molecules discovery in general and drug discovery research in particular. The $MPDS^{CL}$ is a state-of-the-art attempt that is primarily focused on the structural classification of the molecules that were curated from the publicly available 42 different databases.

The $MPDS^{CL}$ has structurally well-defined classification of small molecules into 56 classes. Each classes has several clusters where 250000 is considered as cut-off. The molecular weight of all the molecules are calculated and all the molecules are arranged in the ascending order and each cluster is segregated, such that each contain 250000 molecules. Overall, the MPDS$^{CL}$ has 56 classes and 625 clusters. Each molecule is assigned with a unique number "class_number-cluster_number-molecule_number" and this is named as MPDS Aadhar ID and each molecule has MPDS Aadhar card. The MPDS Aadhar card contains the information about the molecule. The users can perform multi-layer search in MPDS$^{CL}$ including MPDS Aadhar ID search, exact structure search, sub-structure search, molecular properties based search and fingerprint based search. The MPDS Aadhar card is represented in Figure 15.4.

**Molecular Property Diagnostic Suite - AadharID**

**MPDS AadharID No.: 18-01-000124**

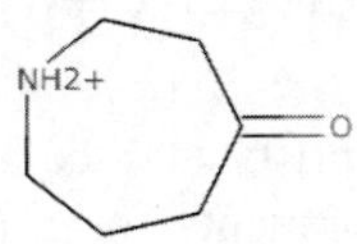


**Molecular Formula:**
$C_6H_{12}NO$

**IUPAC Name:**
4-oxoazepan-1-ium

**Canonical SMILES:** O=C1CC[NH2+]CCC1

**InChIKey:** GMHPWGYTSXHHPI-UHFFFAOYSA-O

**Fingerprint:**
00000000000000000010000000000000000000000000000000000000000

**Molecular Properties:**

| | | | |
|---|---|---|---|
| Mol. Wt. | 114.166 | LogP | 0.08 |
| HBD | 1 | LogS | 0.456 |
| HBA | 1 | pKa | pKa1: 19.13; pKa2: NULL; pKa3: 8.7; pKa4: -8.07 |
| Molar refractivity | 43.34 | Polar surface area | 33.68 |
| Heavy atoms count | 3,5,1 | Aromatic Rings count | 0 |
| Rotatable bonds | 0 | Polarizability | 12.76 |

**FIGURE 15.4** A sample MPDS Aadhar card shows the structure of a molecule with the MPDS Aadhar ID and other properties.

## 15.6 PREDICTIVE MODELING AND OPTIMIZATION

The application of AI in medicinal chemistry has significantly transformed the safety and efficacy of the drug compounds. Traditional drug discovery methods are often time-consuming and laborious. AI techniques, including ML, offer a solution by analyzing large datasets to reveal patterns and trends that might be overlooked by human researchers. This approach facilitates the faster identification of promising bioactive compounds with potentially fewer side effects compared to traditional methods. For instance, DL algorithms, trained on datasets of known drug compounds and their biological activities, can accurately predict the effects of novel compounds. Likewise, ML algorithms, which have been trained on extensive databases of both toxic and non-toxic compounds, enhance the ability to predict and reduce potential toxicity in new drug candidates.

AI also plays a crucial role in identifying drug-drug interactions, which occur when multiple medications are taken together, potentially leading to altered effects or adverse reactions. AI-driven methods analyze large datasets of known drug interactions to detect patterns and forecast interactions between new drug combinations. Additionally, AI supports personalized medicine based on individual patient characteristics by customizing treatment plans, such as genetic profiles and responses to medications, thus reducing the risk of adverse drug interactions. These advancements illustrate the potential of AI to improve the forecasting of drug effectiveness and safety, thereby facilitating the creation of more potent and safer pharmaceuticals while accelerating the research process in drug discovery.

## 15.7 COLLABORATION BETWEEN AI AND TRADITIONAL METHODS

The collaboration between pharmaceutical scientists and data scientists paves the way for the development of effective and innovative treatments for a range of diseases. By working together, these professionals can design advanced ML algorithms and robust models that identify potential drug candidates, significantly speeding up the drug discovery process. The synergy between these two fields enhances the accuracy and effectiveness of clinical trial research. Additionally, AI algorithms are proficient in analyzing clinical trial data, which assists in detecting potential adverse side effects. This capability provides pharmaceutical companies with a deeper understanding, enabling them to make better-informed decisions regarding drug candidate selection and thus hastening the introduction of new treatments.

AI's role extends to analyzing large population datasets to uncover trends and patterns, which can aid in predicting how well drug candidates will perform in specific patient populations. This approach enables the customization of treatments to better meet individual patient needs. An illustrative example of such collaboration is the partnership between Merck and Numerate, where AI-based methods are being applied to medicinal chemistry. As the field grows, more collaborations are likely to emerge, significantly impacting drug development and improving patient outcomes.

Despite its promise, AI in drug discovery encounters several significant challenges. A primary issue is the requirement for large, high-quality datasets to train AI models effectively. Inadequate or low-quality data can lead to inaccurate and unreliable predictions. Additionally, ethical concerns regarding fairness and bias must be addressed; if the data used to train ML algorithms is biased or unrepresentative, it can result in skewed predictions. Ensuring the ethical application of AI and addressing these issues are essential.

Strategies such as data augmentation and explainable AI (XAI) are valuable to tackle these challenges. Data augmentation involves creating synthetic data to complement existing datasets, enhancing both the diversity and quantity of training data, and thereby improving the accuracy of AI and ML models. XAI techniques aim to make AI predictions more transparent and understandable, helping to address concerns about fairness and bias and providing insights into the reasoning behind predictions.

It is crucial to understand that AI cannot replace traditional experimental methods or the expertise of human researchers. AI offers predictions based on the data it processes, but these predictions need to be validated and interpreted by researchers. The drug discovery process can be effective where AI is combined with traditional experimental methods. The drug discovery can be accelerated and effective medications can be designed when there is a cross-talk between human expertise with AI predictive capabilities. Table 15.1 illustrates a list of small molecules that are in clinical trials where it is initially identified through AI methods.

**TABLE 15.1** Illustration of list of small molecules that are in clinical trails where it is initially identified through AI methods

| *Company* | *Indication* | *Compound* | *Development Status* | *Trial Number* |
|---|---|---|---|---|
| Insilico Medicine | Idiopathic pulmonary fibrosis | INS018_055 | Phase II | NCT05938920, CTR20230776 |
| | COVID-19 | ISM3312 | Phase I | CTR20230768 |
| | BRCA-mutant cancer | ISM3091 | Phase I | NCT05932862 |
| Nimbus Therapeutics | Nonalcoholic steatohepatitis | NDI-010976/GS-0976 | Phase II | NCT02856555<br>NCT03987074<br>NCT02891408<br>NCT02876796 |
| BenevolentAI | Atopic dermatitis | BEN-2293 | Phase II | NCT04737304 |
| Pharos iBio | Acute myeloid leukemia<br>Ovarian cancer<br>Triple-negative breast cancer<br>Radiation sensitizer | PHI-101 | Phase I | NCT04842370<br>NCT04678102 |
| Schrödinger | Non-Hodgkin's lymphoma | SGR-1505 | Phase I | NCT05544019 |
| Exscientia | Solid tumors | EXS-21546 | Phase I | NCT04727138 |
| | Obsessive compulsive disorder | DSP-1181 | Phase I | - |
| | Alzheimer's disease | DSP-0038 | Phase I | - |
| | Inflammatory diseases | EXS4318 | Phase I/II | - |
| Valo Health | Post-myocardial infarction<br>Acute kidney injury | OPL-0301 | Phase II | NCT05327855 |
| | Diabetic retinopathy<br>Diabetic complications | OPL-0301 | Phase II | NCT05393284 |
| Pharos iBio | Acute myeloid leukemia<br>Ovarian cancer<br>Triple-negative breast cancer<br>Radiation sensitizer | PHI-101 | Phase I | NCT04842370<br>NCT04678102 |
| Recursion Pharmaceuticals | Cerebral cavernous malformation | REC-994 | Phase II | NCT05085561 |
| | Neurofibromatosis type 2 | REC-2282 | Phase II/III | NCT05130866 |
| | Familial adenomatous polyposis | REC-4881 | Phase II | NCT05552755 |

(*Contd.*)

| *Company* | *Indication* | *Compound* | *Development Status* | *Trial Number* |
|---|---|---|---|---|
| Relay Therapeutics | Solid tumors | RLY-1971/RG-6433 | Phase I | NCT04252339 |
| | FGFR2-driven cancers<br>Intrahepatic cholangiocarcinoma<br>Advanced solid tumors | RLY-4008 | Phase I/iI | NCT04526106 |
| | Solid tumors | RLY-2608 | Phase I | NCT05216432 |
| Structure Therapeutics | Type 2 diabetes<br>Obesity | GSBR-1290 | Phase I | NCT05762471 |
| | Pulmonary arterial hypertension<br>Idiopathic pulmonary fibrosis | ANPA-0073 | Phase I | ACTRN12621000644864 |

## 15.8 CHALLENGES AND ETHICAL CONSIDERATIONS

The ethical implications of using AI in the pharmaceutical industry are crucial and must be carefully considered. One significant concern is the potential impact of AI on individual health and well-being, including its influence on drug development, clinical trial selection, and drug marketing strategies. Bias within AI algorithms constitute a critical challenge, as it can create disparities in accessing medical treatments and result in unjustified treatment of particular demographic groups, which may contravene the foundational principles of equality and justice. Another concern is the potential for job displacement due to automation. The introduction of AI could lead to significant changes in workforce dynamics, necessitating careful planning and support for affected workers to mitigate negative impacts.

The protection of data privacy and security represents a significant concern. Medical records encompass sensitive personal information, and there exists a potential threat that such data may be accessed or exploited improperly. This could lead to serious repercussions for individuals and adversely affect the reputations of the organizations involved. Therefore, it is essential to handle sensitive medical data with the highest standards of privacy and comply with relevant regulations.

To ethically integrate AI into the pharmaceutical industry, several measures should be considered:

1. **Diverse and Representative Data:** AI systems should be trained on comprehensive and varied datasets to minimize bias and ensure that predictions and recommendations are equitable across different demographic groups.
2. **Regular Reviews and Audits:** Ongoing evaluations of AI systems are necessary to identify and address any biases or inaccuracies. This process ensures that AI tools remain fair and effective over time.
3. **Robust Data Privacy Protocols:** Implement stringent measures for protecting sensitive data, including encryption, access controls, and compliance along with data protection regulations.

By addressing these ethical concerns, the pharmaceutical industry can leverage AI responsibly and effectively, enhancing drug discovery and development while safeguarding individual rights and promoting fairness.

## 15.9 CASE STUDIES AND SUCCESS STORIES

Several case studies have demonstrated the impact of AI in drug discovery. For instance, in a recent study AI was used to identify novel compounds for cancer therapy. Researchers successfully identified new compounds with significant therapeutic potential by training DL algorithm on a large data set that consists of bioactive molecules with cancer biological activities. This shows the power of AI in discovering new drug candidates.

Another notable case study involves the use of ML to discover small molecule MEK22 inhibitors, a challenging target in cancer treatment. The algorithm successfully identified novel inhibitors, showcasing AI's capability to address complex drug discovery problems. Similarly, AI has played a crucial role in discovering new inhibitors for beta-secretase (BACE1), a protein linked to Alzheimer's disease, using ML techniques to uncover promising therapeutic agents. AI has also made significant strides in antibiotic discovery. An innovative ML approach sifted through over 100 million molecules to identify potent antibiotics, including one effective against a broad range of bacteria including tuberculosis and drug-resistant strains.

In the context of COVID-19, AI has been a valuable tool for identifying potential therapeutic agents. Machine learning algorithms have analyzed extensive datasets of compounds to find those with the highest potential for combating the virus, often identifying promising candidates much faster than traditional methods.

These examples underscore the potential of AI to accelerate drug discovery and facilitate the development of more effective treatments across a variety of diseases. AI-based methodologies continue to advance the field, demonstrating their ability to transform and expedite the drug discovery process.

## 15.10 AI POWERED PLATFORMS AND TOOLS USED IN DRUG DISCOVERY

The integration of AI with drug discovery has become a pivotal advancement, streamlining the process and improving outcomes significantly. Atomwise, a trailblazing organization in this field, exemplifies the transformative impact of AI. By utilizing sophisticated DL models for virtual screening, Atomwise can analyse chemical compounds against drug targets with remarkable precision. Their platform leverages extensive datasets and advanced machine learning techniques to predict compound binding affinities, enabling researchers to efficiently identify lead molecules with high potential for success.

IBM's Watson for drug discovery also represents a major leap forward. Employing NLP, Watson extracts valuable insights from a wide range of resources including scientific literature, patents, and clinical trial reports. This ability to analyze vast amounts of textual data helps researchers uncover promising targets, understand biological pathways, and identify potential drug candidates, significantly speeding up the early stages of drug discovery while reducing resource expenditure.

Similarly, BenevolentAI's platform integrates ML algorithms to analyze diverse biological and chemical data sources, generating hypotheses for novel drug targets and pathways. This innovative approach supports the development of new therapeutic strategies, advancing pharmaceutical research and development.

Insilico Medicine showcases the potential of deep generative models in drug discovery. By pushing the boundaries of traditional drug design, Insilico Medicine creates novel drug-like compounds and explores new avenues in pharmaceutical development. Their platform, Chemistry42, utilizes advanced ML techniques such as GANs and reinforcement learning, to design highly refined molecular structures with specific therapeutic properties.

AI-powered tools have revolutionized lead optimization as well, accelerating the process and introducing data-driven methodologies for drug design. These advancements enhance the efficiency of drug development and also contribute to the creation of safer and more effective therapeutics. Overall, the impact of AI in drug discovery has led to transformative changes, enabling faster development and improved outcomes across a wide range of medical conditions. AI enabled tools and platforms used in drug discovery is shown in Table 15.2.

**TABLE 15.2** Examples of AI enabled tools and platforms used in drug discovery

| *Platform* | *Brief Description* | *URLs* |
|---|---|---|
| AlphaFold | Prediction of proteins 3D structure using deep learning | AlphaFold Protein Structure Database |
| DeepChem | Multilayer Perceptron Model for the candidate selection in drug discovery. | https://deepchem.io/ |
| Chemputer | Synthesis of organic molecules using Monte Carlo tree search including Deep Neural Network. | https://winter.group.shef.ac.uk/chemputer/ |
| DeepTox | Chemical toxicity prediction using deep learning. | https://www.bioinf.jku.at/research/DeepTox/ |
| DeepNeuralNetQSAR | Predicting molecular activity of compounds. | https://github.com/Merck/DeepNeuralNet-QSAR |
| MoleculeNet | Machine learning methods for molecule properties prediction | https://moleculenet.org/ |
| Hit Dexter | Prediction of molecules that may have activity in biochemical assays using CNN and ANN. | https://nerdd.univie.ac.at/hitdexter3/ |
| DeltaVina | Prediction of protein-ligand binding affinities. | https://github.com/chengwang88/deltavina |
| Neural graph fingerprint | Molecules property prediction using CNN. | https://github.com/HIPS/neural-fingerprint |
| AIDDISON | Identification of drug-like candidates. | AIDDISON™, AI-powered drug discovery software \| Merck (merckgroup.com) |
| PandaOmics | Target discovery based on Omics data. | https://insilico.com/pandaomics |
| Chemistry42 | AI platform molecular design and optimization. | https://insilico.com/chemistry42 |
| DockAI | Screening of several billion of commercially available molecules. | https://iktos.ai/dockai-2/ |
| Spaya | Identifying the best synthetic routes of the compounds | https://iktos.ai/spaya/ |
| Inclinico | Prediction of clinical trials probability of success platform. | https://insilico.com/inclinico |

## 15.11 TOP PHARMACEUTICAL COMPANIES AND THEIR ASSOCIATION WITH AI

The transformative impact of AI on drug discovery and development has been notably embraced by leading pharmaceutical companies, who are leveraging AI to enhance various stages of the drug development process. Here's a closer look at how some of these companies are utilizing AI to revolutionize the industry:

1. **Novartis:**
    - **Partnership with IBM Watson Health:** Novartis has strategically partnered with IBM Watson Health to utilize AI for critical tasks such as target identification, validation, and clinical trial matching. This collaboration aims to harness AI's capabilities to streamline drug discovery and development processes, improving efficiency and effectiveness.
2. **Pfizer:**
    - **Collaboration with IBM Watson:** Pfizer has also teamed up with IBM Watson to advance its drug discovery efforts. By employing AI, Pfizer seeks to revolutionize target identification, a crucial step in developing new drugs, thus expediting the overall drug discovery pipeline.
3. **Roche:**
    - **Alliances with AI Startups and Research Institutions:** Roche has formed strategic alliances with AI startups and esteemed research institutions. AI is used to optimize various drug discovery stages, from target identification to lead optimization, enhancing Roche's ability to develop new therapeutics efficiently.
4. **Sanofi:**
    - **Investment in AI-Enabled Platforms:** Sanofi's investment in AI-enabled drug discovery platforms demonstrates its commitment to leveraging AI to enhance research and development capabilities. By applying advanced ML algorithms and data analytics, Sanofi aims to accelerate the discovery and development of novel therapeutic compounds.
5. **Merck:**
    - **Collaborative Alliances with AI startups:** Merck has been at the forefront of integrating AI into pharmaceutical research. Through collaborations with cutting-edge AI startups and research organizations, Merck is pioneering new applications of AI in drug discovery, focusing on improving the efficiency of lead optimization and drug development.
6. **GlaxoSmithKline (GSK):**
    - **Partnerships for AI integration:** GSK has strategically partnered with AI enterprises and research institutions to advance its drug discovery efforts. The company effectively employs AI techniques for target identification, validation, and lead optimization, demonstrating its commitment to incorporating advanced technology into its drug development processes.

These examples illustrate how leading pharmaceutical companies are proactively harnessing the power of AI to enhance their drug discovery efforts. By leveraging AI, these organizations aim to accelerate the development of new therapeutics, improve the accuracy of drug discovery processes, and ultimately create safer and more effective medications. Through strategic collaborations and investments in AI technology, these companies are driving innovation in the pharmaceutical industry and addressing unmet medical needs with greater efficiency and precision. Table 15.3 exhibits the successful collaboration between pharmaceutical companies and AI providers.

**TABLE 15.3** Outcome of collaboration between AI providers and pharmaceutical companies

| *AI provider* | *Pharmaceutical company* | *Project information* |
|---|---|---|
| IBM Watson Health Cambridge | Novartis | Real time breast cancer patients monitor system. |
| | Pfizer | Discovery of immuno-oncology medication. |
| Microsoft | Novartis | AI innovation lab creation to support medical research and commercialization process. |
| Owkin | Roche | Development of clinical testing AI platform. |
| Numerate | Takeda | AI enabled drug design for onclogy. |
| | Servier | Mimic the drug development for conditions of the CNS, cancer and the digestive system. |
| XtalPi | Pfizer | Integration of quantum mechanics and ML techniques for the target identification. |
| Exscientia | Sanofi | AI enabled lead refinement process for different diseases including obsessive-convulsive disorder. |
| | Merck and BenevolentAI | Identification of new drug candidates in the fields of oncology, neurology and immunology. |
| Atomwise | Lilly<br>Bridge Biotherapeutics | AI enabled structural modelling. |
| Sensyne Health | Bayer | Generation of AI schemes to improve the clinical trials. |
| BenevolentAI | Janssen | Development of AI-enabled Judgement Augmented Cognition Systems (JACS) for developing new drugs. |
| | AstraZeneca | Development of new clinical leads for Chronic renal disease. |
| Insilico Medicine | Pfizer | Identification of drug targets using data mining. |
| ConcertAI | Pfizer | Improvised clinical trails study design. |
| Johnson & Johnson | Pfizer | Collaborative research in the field of AI in drug discovery research for the identification of new targets and diseases. |
| Google Quantum AI | Boehringer Ingelheim | Leveraging quantum computing to accelerate the drug discovery process. |
| Insilico Medicine | Boehringer Ingelheim | AI research for identification of potential drug targets. |
| Exscientia | BMS | AI based immune-modulating candidate design. |
| Exscientia | GSK | AI powered treatment for COPD. |
| J&J Lung Cancer Initiative | Optellum | AI powered clinical decision support platform for early lung cancer treatment. |
| Mateon Therapeutics | Pointer data | Treatment for different cancers. |

## 15.12 CUTTING-EDGE APPLICATIONS OF AI IN DRUG DISCOVERY

In this section the successful application of AI in drug discovery has been explained in detail.

### 15.12.1 Drug Development

AI significantly speeds up target identification by leveraging ML algorithms to analyze extensive datasets. These algorithms facilitate the examination of large-scale genomic data related to diseases, aid in identifying potential drug targets, and predict the effectiveness of small molecules. NLP trained on vast collections of scientific literature, plays a key role in uncovering potential drug targets and identifying genetic biomarkers for disease prognosis and diagnosis. AI have also been used in predicting binding affinities between targets and small molecules, enhancing the drug discovery process. Additionally, AI can guide the design of new molecules by utilizing knowledge of protein target structures and comparing features from virtual libraries, thereby accelerating lead discovery. Furthermore, AI's analysis of preclinical data, such as gene expression profiles, enables predictions about safety and efficacy, which helps to shorten the preclinical trial phase.

### 15.12.2 Designing of Effective Drugs

AI can significantly enhance the lead optimization process by analyzing the pharmacological properties of small molecules based on their chemical structures. ML algorithms can develop predictive models to estimate various biological, chemical, and pharmacological characteristics, such as bioavailability, solubility, and toxicity. These models facilitate the creation of novel molecules with well-defined properties. AI also plays a crucial role in reducing the reliance on animal studies by predicting the safety and efficacy of lead compounds. Additionally, AI aids in designing more selective drugs with fewer side effects. For example, AI can identify specific proteins or disease associated molecular pathways, enabling the design of targeted drugs that address these specific targets and pathways. This approach helps to minimize off-target effects, thereby enhancing the overall safety and efficacy of the drugs.

### 15.12.3 Designing of Better Clinical Trials

AI can significantly enhance the design and execution of clinical trials by improving efficacy and accuracy. One major challenge in clinical trials is patient recruitment, which AI can address by analysing electronic health records (EHR) to develop precise inclusion and exclusion criteria. This improves the likelihood of successful trial outcomes. AI can also analyse patient data to identify subgroups that respond to specific treatments, optimizing trial size and statistical power to detect differences in treatment effects. During the trials, AI facilitates real-time patient monitoring through wearable devices equipped with AI algorithms, tracking vital signs and other health parameters. This enables adjustments to trial protocols to enhance patient safety. Additionally, AI plays a crucial role in analysing clinical trial data, contributing to more informed and effective decision-making.

### 15.12.4 Bioactivity Prediction

AI can analyze vast datasets using advanced machine learning algorithms to predict the biological activities of drugs. One highly effective method is QSAR modeling, which establishes the correlation between small molecules and their biological activities based on known data, including molecular properties and structural features. Another powerful technique is molecular docking, which predicts how well a molecule binds to a target protein. AI enhances these processes by optimizing the chemical structure of compounds, thereby improving their binding affinity and overall biological activity.

### 15.12.5 Quality Assurance

AI can play a crucial role in ensuring that drugs meet quality standards. It can efficiently analyze images of drug samples to detect defects such as contamination, discoloration, and improper packaging, thus significantly reducing the time and costs associated with manual inspection. This enhances the accuracy and consistency of the quality control process. Additionally, AI can support the maintenance of manufacturing equipment by predicting potential failures, enabling proactive maintenance, and minimizing downtime. This boosts the efficiency and reliability of the manufacturing process while reducing the risk of errors and defects. Furthermore, AI aids in fraud detection within drug production and distribution by analyzing sales and distribution data to identify unusual patterns or trends that may indicate fraudulent activity. This helps manage and prevent the distribution of counterfeit or substandard drugs effectively.

### 15.12.6 Drug Repurposing

AI significantly enhances computational drug repurposing by analyzing extensive datasets related to diseases, drugs, pathways, and omics data to uncover patterns and relationships. These insights can predict which existing drugs might be effective for treating new diseases. Additionally, AI examines complex interactions among drugs, targets, pathways, and diseases, revealing new therapeutic opportunities through a process known as "*network pharmacology*". By leveraging AI algorithms to analyze large-scale molecular interactions, researchers can identify novel drug targets or combinations with potential efficacy against various diseases. AI also facilitates the discovery of new drug combinations for repurposing by analyzing comprehensive drug and patient datasets to pinpoint promising combinations. Furthermore, AI can predict the synergistic effects of different drug combinations, identifying those with significant therapeutic potential.

### 15.12.7 Drug Combination Analysis

Drug combinations are a powerful strategy for addressing complex diseases such as cancer by targeting multiple pathways simultaneously. AI plays a crucial role in this analysis by predicting the synergistic effects of different drug combinations, which can be particularly effective in treating such multifaceted conditions. Additionally, AI can analyse the genetic and molecular profiles of individual patients and helps in developing personalized medicine. This allows for the identification of biomarkers that predict how patients will respond to various drug combinations. AI also helps in detecting drug-resistant pathways, providing insights into alternative drug combinations that may be effective. This capability ensures that patients who have developed resistance to certain treatments can be offered alternative therapeutic options.

### 15.12.8 Patient Stratification

Patient stratification involves grouping patients with similar characteristics or disease profiles to tailor treatment more effectively. AI enhances this process by analyzing large datasets to identify patterns and associations that might be missed using traditional methods. By examining comprehensive patient data, AI can uncover potential biomarkers that predict how different patients will respond to specific treatments or how diseases might progress. This stratification is crucial for optimizing clinical trial design by identifying appropriate patient subgroups, thereby improving the likelihood of successful drug development. Additionally, AI helps healthcare providers customize treatments based on individual patients' genetic, molecular, and imaging characteristics, leading to more personalized and effective healthcare solutions.

### 15.12.9 Post-Market Drug Safety Monitoring

Post-market drug safety monitoring aims to identify rare or unexpected side effects once a drug is in the market. AI plays a crucial role in this process by analyzing extensive patient datasets to detect potential adverse events related to a drug or its combinations. AI can provide effective surveillance of drug safety by integrating real-time data from various sources such as social media, electronic health records, and other health data repositories. This allows for early identification of potential safety issues and enhances the ability to monitor risks associated with specific patient characteristics and other factors. Additionally, AI can predict side effects related to drug-drug interactions by recognizing patterns and relationships between different drugs, thereby improving the overall safety profile of medications.

## SUMMARY

This chapter provides a comprehensive exploration of the transformative impact AI has had on the pharmaceutical industry. This detailed analysis highlights how AI-powered methodologies have revolutionized various stages of drug discovery, significantly enhancing both the efficiency and outcomes of the process.

In the initial phase of drug discovery, AI algorithms play a crucial role in identifying and validating disease targets. By sifting through extensive biological datasets, these advanced computational tools can pinpoint key genes, proteins, and pathways associated with specific diseases. The precision of ML models accelerates this early stage of research, providing researchers with highly accurate targets for therapeutic intervention.

During lead optimization, AI's contributions are equally transformative. The technology improves predictive modelling capabilities, refining potential drug candidates and optimizing their pharmacological properties. AI's computational prowess and sophisticated algorithms enhance the likelihood of success in subsequent development stages. Moreover, AI-powered screening methods prioritize the most promising compounds, saving considerable time and resources. The chapter also emphasizes AI's role in exploring traditionally "undruggable" targets. Through its comprehensive approach, the chapter illustrates how AI methodologies facilitate the investigation and targeting of challenging biological entities, expanding the scope of drug discovery beyond previously achievable limits.

## WORKED OUT EXAMPLES

**EXAMPLE 15.1** Collect the SMILES of the following drug molecules from drug bank (https://go.drugbank.com/) and calculate the molecular weight using Rdkit and analyze the distribution of molecular weights using Python and visualize the results using Matplotlib.
Drugs: Penicillin, Insulin, Morphine, Aspirin, Salvarsan, Atrovastin, Losartan, Clopidogrel, Glimepiride, Metformin

***Solution:***

```
import pandas as pd
import matplotlib.pyplot as plt
from rdkit import Chem
smiles_dict = {
    'Penicillin': 'CC1([C@@H](N2[C@H](S1)[C@@H](C2=O)NC(=O)Cc3ccccc3)C(=O)O)C',
    'Insulin': 'CCC(C)C1CCC2C3CCC4=CC(=O)CCC4C3C(CC2(C)C1(C)CCCC(C(=O)O)
    NC(=O)C(CCCNC(N)=[NH2+])N)O',
    'Morphine': 'CN1CCC23[C@@H]4[C@H]1CC5=C2C(=C(C=C5)O)OC3=C(C4)C',
    'Aspirin': 'CC(=O)OC1=CC=CC=C1C(=O)O',
    'Salvarsan': 'C1=CC(=CC=C1C2=C(C(=O)C3=CC=CC=C3N2)O)[N+](=O)[O-]',
    'Atrovastin': 'CC(C)C[C@H](C)C(=O)N1CCC[C@H]1C(=O)N[C@@H](CC2=CC=CC=C2)
    C(=O)O',
    'Losartan': 'C[C@H]1CC[C@@H](CC1)N1C2=CC=CC=C2NC1=O',
    'Clopidogrel': 'CCOC(=O)C1=CC=C(C=C1)S(=O)(=O)N1CCN(CC1)
    C1=NC2=CC=CC=C2S1',
    'Glimepiride': 'C1CC(=O)NC(=S)S1',
    'Metformin': 'CN(C)C(=N)N'
}
molecular_weights = []
for drug, smiles in smiles_dict.items():
    mol = Chem.MolFromSmiles(smiles)
    if mol:
    mw = Chem.Descriptors.MolWt(mol)
    molecular_weights.append(mw)
    else:
    print(f'Error: Could not process SMILES for {drug}")
plt.figure(figsize=(10, 6))
plt.hist(molecular_weights, bins=10, color='skyblue', edgecolor='black', alpha=0.7)
plt.xlabel('Molecular Weight')
```

```
plt.ylabel('Frequency')
plt.title('Distribution of Molecular Weights')
plt.grid(True)
plt.show()
```

**EXAMPLE 15.2** Calculate the molecular fingerprint similarity between two compounds using a Python library such as RDKit or Cheminformatics.

***Solution:***

```
from rdkit import Chem
from rdkit.Chem import AllChem
from rdkit.DataStructs import TanimotoSimilarity
smiles1 = 'CCO'
smiles2 = 'CCN'
mol1 = Chem.MolFromSmiles(smiles1)
mol2 = Chem.MolFromSmiles(smiles2)
fp1 = AllChem.GetMorganFingerprintAsBitVect(mol1, 2, nBits=1024)
fp2 = AllChem.GetMorganFingerprintAsBitVect(mol2, 2, nBits=1024)
similarity = TanimotoSimilarity(fp1, fp2)
print(f"Molecular fingerprint similarity between the compounds: {similarity}")
```

**EXAMPLE 15.3** Utilize CheMBL API and SQL queries to extract information from a relational database containing compound screening data, such as $IC_{50}$ values for different compounds against a specific target.

***Solution:***

```
import requests
target_id = 'CHEMBL203'
response = requests.get(url)
if response.status_code == 200:
    data = response.json()
    compound_ic50_data = [(item['molecule_chembl_id'], item['standard_value']) for item in data]
    for compound_id, ic50_value in compound_ic50_data:
    print(f"Compound ID: {compound_id}, IC50 Value: {ic50_value}")
else:
    print(f"Error: Unable to fetch data from ChEMBL API. Status code: {response.status_code}")
```

## EXERCISES

1. Collect the list of publications using keyword "Drug discovery" in Pubmed (https://pubmed.ncbi.nlm.nih.gov/). Analyze temporal trends using time series analysis techiques using Autoregressive integrated moving average (ARIMA) model.
2. Download any sequence from NCBI database. Perform sequence similarity and sequence identity analysis using BLAST. Identify the top hits and do homology modelling using SWISS-MODEL.

3. Download a list of drug like compounds from ChEMBL or Binding databases and calculate the descriptors using RDKit. Perform k-means clustering to group the molecules based on different descriptors.
4. Download a list of drug like compounds from ChEMBL or Binding databases and calculate the RDKit fingerprints. Apply principal component analysis (PCA) to reduce the dimensionality and visualize the results.
5. Create an interactive visualization dashboard using Plotly or Dash to explore the structure-activity relationships of compounds in a drug discovery dataset.
6. Download biomedical literature from pubmed and apply NLP techniques to extract the information about the drug targets, mechanisms of action and therapeutic indications.
7. Implement k-fold cross-validation to evaluate the performance of a machine learning model for predicting drug-target interactions.
8. Build an ensemble model combining multiple machine learning algorithms (e.g., random forest, gradient boosting) to improve the prediction accuracy of compound activities.
9. Apply graph algorithms (e.g., shortest path, centrality measures) to analyze the connectivity patterns in a chemical similarity network of drug compounds.
10. Conduct a statistical analysis to compare the efficacy of drug combinations versus single treatments using a dataset of experimental results.

## BIBLIOGRAPHY

Baum, Z. J., Yu, X., Ayala, P. Y., Zhao, Y., Watkins, S. P., and Zhou, Q. (2021). Artificial Intelligence in Chemistry: Current Trends and Future Directions, *Journal of Chemical Information and Modeling*, 61(7), 3197–3212, American Chemical Society (ACS).

Chen, W., Liu, X., Zhang, S. and Chen, S. (2023). Artificial intelligence for drug discovery: Resources, methods, and applications, *Molecular Therapy Nucleic Acids,* 31: 691–702, Cell Press.

Pun, F. W., Ozerov, I. V., and Zhanvoronkov, A. (2023). AI powered therapeutic target discovery, *Trends in Pharmacological Sciences*, 44(9), 561–572, Cell Press.

Sadybekov, A. V., and Kartich, V. (2023). Computational approaches streamlining drug discovery, *Nature*, 616, 673–685, Springer Nature.

Vijayan, R. S. K., Kihlberg, J., Cross, J. B. and Poongavanam, V. (2022). Enhancing preclinical drug discovery with artificial intelligence, *Drug Discovery Today*, 27(4), 967–984, Elsevier.

Chapter 16

# AI for Environment and Climate Change

## 16.1 DEFINING SUSTAINABILITY

Sustainability relates to the capacity to preserve or endure over the long term while reducing adverse effects on the environment, society, and economy. It involves addressing current needs without compromising the capacity of future generations to address their own. Sustainability has been defined in different ways by many pioneers as well as organizations working in these areas.

> *Sustainability is a state of dynamic balance between people and the planet, where the use of resources, the direction of investments, the orientation of technological development, and institutional change are all in harmony and enhance both current and future potential to meet human needs and aspirations.*
>
> —International Union for Conservation of Nature (IUCN).

> *Sustainable development is development that meets the needs of the present without compromising the ability of future generations to meet their own needs.*
>
> —Brundtland Commission, 1987.

The main pillars of sustainability are:

***Environmental Sustainability:*** It involves using resources in such a way that can minimize harming the natural environment like reducing carbon emissions, conserving biodiversity, protecting ecosystems, and using renewable resources.

***Social Sustainability:*** The focus is on maintaining and enhancing the well-being of individuals and communities involving considerations of social equity, justice, human rights, and community development.

***Economic Sustainability:*** It is all about using resources efficiently and creating economic systems that provide long-term benefits without causing negative impacts. It includes responsible business practices, fair trade, and the promotion of economic systems that do not deplete resources or exploit labour.

The Brundtland commission report of 1987 was used in foundation of the principles of Sustainable Development Goals (SDGs) formed by United Nations in 2015, as the agenda for

2030 sustainability development. Interestingly, for most of these SDGs, the impact of Artificial Intelligence (AI) is remarkable. Goals like sustainable agriculture, good health, clean water and sanitation, clean energy, climate actions, are some of these which are going to have huge interventions of AI.

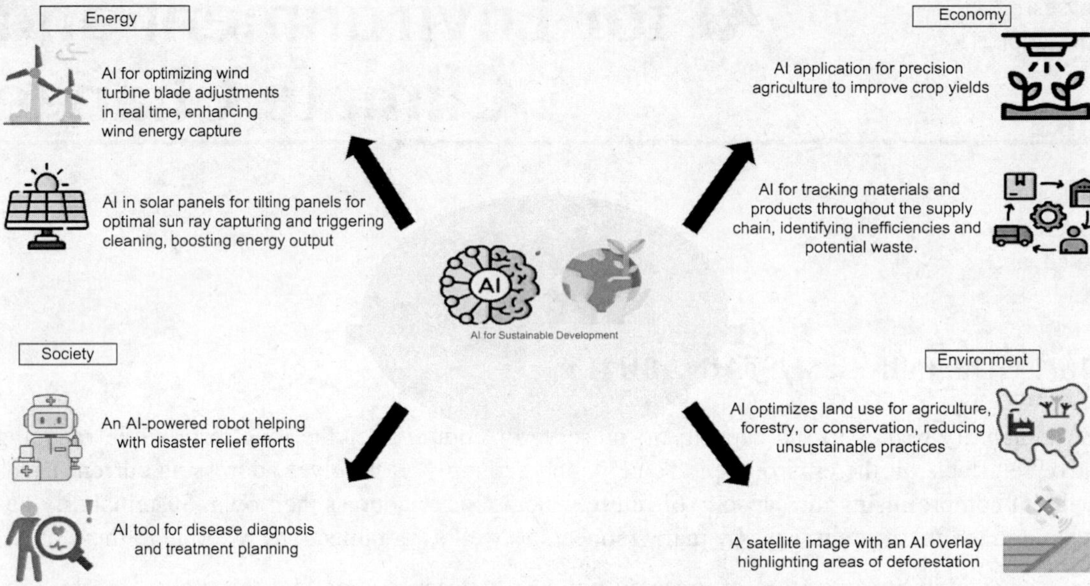


**FIGURE 16.1** Role of Artificial Intelligence in sustainable development of energy, economy, society and environment.

Environment and climate change are important components in the pursuit of sustainability. The interconnection between these factors underscores the importance of addressing environmental issues to achieve sustainable development. Some major aspects where they can contribute to sustainability are:

***Resource Availability:*** The environment provides essential resources such as clean water, air, and fertile soil, which are fundamental for human well-being. Preserving these resources is crucial for sustainability.

***Climate Stability:*** Stable climate conditions are essential for sustainable development. Climate change, resulting from human activities, poses significant challenges to ecosystems, agriculture, water resources, and human societies.

***Water Resources:*** Climate change affects precipitation patterns and water availability. Sustainable water management practices are crucial for ensuring a reliable and equitable supply of water for agriculture, industry, and human consumption.

***Renewable Energy:*** To combat climate change, one of the major steps is switching to sustainable energy sources, like solar, wind, and hydropower. This will play an important role in reducing greenhouse gas emissions and diminishing the impacts of climate change.

***Air Quality:*** Environmental factors, including air quality, have direct impacts on human health. Reducing air pollution and addressing climate change contribute to improved public health and well-being.

***Natural Disaster:*** Sustainable development involves building resilience to natural disasters, which are often exacerbated by climate change. This includes implementing strategies for disaster preparedness, response, and recovery.

***Greenhouse Gas Emissions:*** Climate change is also driven by the collection of greenhouse gases in the atmosphere. Sustainable development requires efforts to mitigate emissions through the adoption of clean energy, energy efficiency, and conservation measures.

## 16.2 ROLE OF AI IN ENVIRONMENT

The utilisation of AI has emerged as a major concern in tackling environmental issues and overcoming the adverse effects of climate change. This comprises of a wide range of factors, such as the assessment of air and water quality, monitoring soil quality, deforestation rates, and evaluating greenhouse gas emissions. Through advanced ML algorithms, these systems can analyse vast amounts of data, including satellite imagery and sensor data, to solve complex problems by identifying patterns. Air, water and soil are the three abiotic factors of habitat and make large contribution in addressing sustainability. Studying the role of AI and ML in solving complex problems associated with these three factors can help in understanding the potential applications in the entire environment.

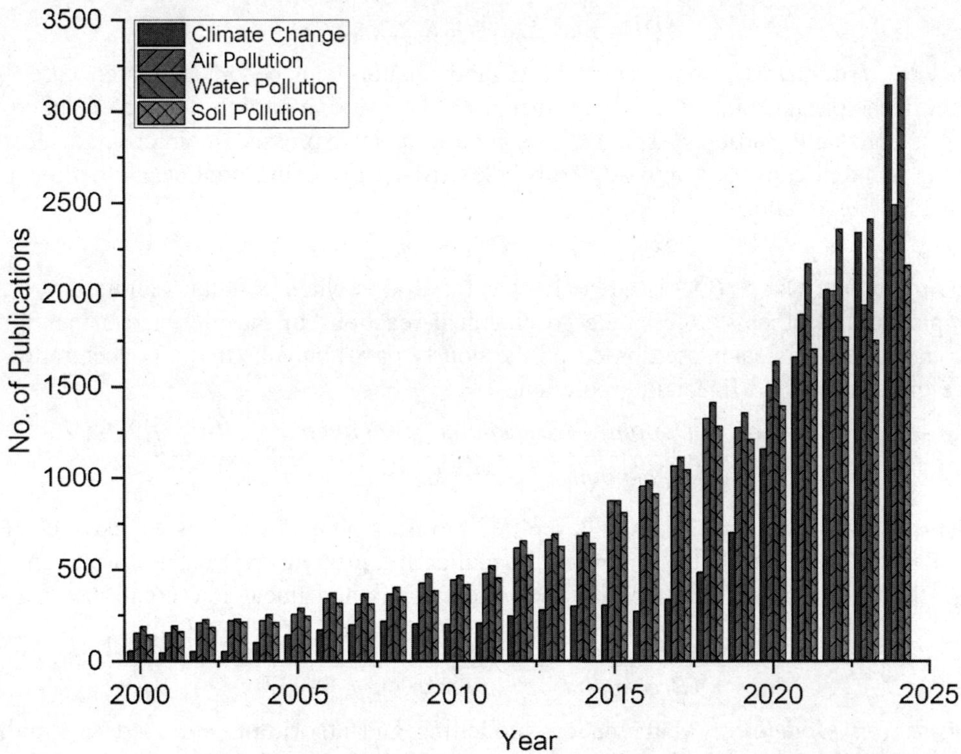


**FIGURE 16.2** Number of publications using AI for mitigating and assessment of Air, Water and Soil quality in last 25 years.

### 16.2.1 The Air Factor

Air is an influencing factor in various ecological, biological and climatic processes. Understanding and managing air quality is necessary for preserving the environmental balance and safeguarding the health and well-being of ecosystems and human populations. Air quality refers to the condition or cleanliness of the air in our environment, specifically the presence of pollutants and their concentrations. It is a measure of how the composition of the air, particularly in the lower atmosphere, may affect human health, the well-being of ecosystems, and the overall quality of life. The quality of air is commonly assessed using a set of specific metrics that measure the concentration of various air pollutants. This includes particulate matter, ground-level-ozone, nitrogen dioxide emission, sulphur dioxide emission, presence of carbon monoxide, volatile organic compounds, exposure to lead and finally the air quality index (AQI). These metrics are often monitored using a network of air quality monitoring stations strategically placed in urban, suburban, and industrial areas. Real-time data from these stations, as well as satellite observations, are used to assess and report air quality levels. Each of these parameters is a measurable metric with well-defined mathematical formula and modelling.

***Air Quality Index (AQI):*** It is a composite index which considers multiple pollutants each of which involves converting to a sub-indices (SI) and then selecting the highest among them. These sub-indices are computed based on the concentrations of pollutant and their corresponding breakpoints are defined by air quality standards.

$$AQI = max(SI_1, SI_2, SI_3, ..., SI_n) \tag{16.1}$$

***Particulate Matter (PM) Conversion:*** Particulate matters can be differentiated based on the diameter of the particles i.e. $\leq$ 2.5 micrometers ($PM_{2.5}$) as fine particles and $\leq$ 10 micrometers ($PM_{10}$) as inhalable particles. The PM concentration is expressed in micrograms per cubic meter ($\mu g/m^3$) and converted into AQI sub index ($SI_{PM}$) involving nonlinear functions specific to each PM size fraction,

$$SI_{PM} = f_{PM}(PM_{2.5}) + f_{PM}(PM_{10}) \tag{16.2}$$

***Ozone Sub Index:*** Ozone ($O_3$) is a reactive gas that forms when pollutants emitted by vehicles, power plants, and other sources undergo chemical reactions in the presence of sunlight. The $O_3$ sub-index ($SI_{O_3}$) is calculated based on the hourly or 8-hour maximum concentration which involve breakpoints and linear interpolation,

$$SI_{O_3} = \frac{(Concentration_{O_3} - Breakpoint_{low}) \times (Index_{High} - Index_{low})}{(Breakpoint_{High} - Breakpoint_{low} + Index_{Low})} \tag{16.3}$$

***Nitrogen Dioxide Sub Index:*** $NO_2$ is emitted from combustion processes like vehicles and power plants which contributes to particulate matter and ground-level ozone formation. Similar to $SI_{O3}$, the sub index of $NO_2$ also involves breakpoints and linear interpolation,

$$SI_{NO_2} = \frac{(Concentration_{NO_2} - Breakpoint_{low}) \times (Index_{High} - Index_{low})}{(Breakpoint_{High} - Breakpoint_{low} + Index_{Low})} \tag{16.4}$$

***Air Dispersion Modelling:*** Mathematical modelling and algorithms are used to simulate the transport and dispersion of air pollutants in the atmosphere. These models help assess the concentration and distribution of pollutants released from various sources. There are many ways to model them but one of the commonly used models is Gaussian dispersion model, which is based on the Gaussian distribution of pollutant concentrations downwind from a source. This ground-level concentration (C) of a pollutant at a distance x downwind from a continuous point source can be estimated using the Gaussian formula,

$$C(x, y) = \frac{Q \cdot \exp\left(-\frac{x^2+y^2}{(2\sigma^2)}\right)}{2\pi u\sigma} \tag{16.5}$$

Where, $Q$ is the emission rate of the pollutant from the source, $x$ is the downwind distance from the source, $y$ is the crosswind distance from the centre line of the plume, $\sigma$ is the standard deviation of the pollutant distribution (a measure of the plume spread) and u is the wind speed perpendicular to the pollutant plume.

It is noteworthy that these specific formulas may vary based on the air quality standards and methodologies used by different countries or regions. Typically, special software is used for getting these data.

### 16.2.2 AI Interventions for Air

AI and ML techniques are increasingly being applied to air quality data to analyse patterns, predict pollutant concentrations, and enhance decision-making in environmental management. Some of the important air quality parameters which have been used for ML modelling have been discussed earlier on which the following applications are based.

***Air Quality Index (AQI) Prediction:*** The historical air quality data, information from meteorological centres, and other relevant features have been used to predict the probable AQI values. Classical regression models, such as linear regression or more sophisticated models like support vector regression or neural networks, can be used to learn complex relationships between these input features and AQI.

***Particulate Matter (PM) Prediction:*** ML models have been developed for predicting PM concentrations using diverse factors like meteorological variations, traffic patterns, and industrial activities. The modelling involved feature engineering by time series features, considering lags, and incorporating spatial information. Some of the widely used algorithms are Random Forest (RF), Decision Trees (DT), Gradient Boosting, CatBoost and Neural network, which have achieved a very high accuracy levels, up to 99%, for predicting $PM_{2.5}$ readings.

***Predicting Ozone ($O_3$) and Nitrogen Dioxide ($NO_2$):*** Forecasting or early prediction of ozone and nitrogen dioxide concentration is another important area where ML based modelling have largely contributed. Algorithms like Artificial Neural Networks, Decision Trees, SVMs have been widely used to predict the concentrations of $O_3$ and $NO_2$ using meteorological data.

***Air Dispersion Modelling and Anomaly Detection:*** The real time data generated from the sensors and meteorological stations are used as features for prediction of air pollutant dispersion from specific sources. ML assisted dispersion modelling which uses metaheuristic algorithms too for optimal output are widely in practice now a days. ML models, particularly unsupervised learning algorithms, have also been applied for anomaly detection in air quality data. These models learn the normal patterns of pollutant concentrations and can identify deviations that may indicate unusual events or pollution sources.

***Optimizing Environmental Monitoring Networks for Early Warning Systems:*** With so many multi location monitoring stations, it is important to consider spatial correlations and variabilities in pollutant concentrations for accurate predictions as well as ensure more efficient and effective monitoring strategies. Further, the advanced ML models can also contribute to the development of early warning systems by analysing real-time data and weather forecasts, to predict the likelihood of elevated pollutant levels and issue warnings.

### 16.2.3 The Water Factor

Water is fundamental to sustainable development and is necessary for ecological health, socioeconomic growth, and human life. It is essential for raising population productivity, well-being, and health while lowering the worldwide burden of disease. It is essential to the creation and maintenance of numerous human advantages and services. Being the vital connection between the environment, human society, and the climate system, water is also essential for adapting to climate change. The quality of water is assessed by a variety of parameters that measure different physical, chemical, and biological characteristics of water. These parameters provide insights into the overall health and suitability of water for various purposes, such as drinking, recreation, and supporting aquatic ecosystems.

***Physical Parameters:*** Temperature and turbidity are two prominent physical parameters of water. Temperature measures how warm and cold the water is and it influences different chemical and biological processes in aquatic ecosystems. Turbidity on the other hand refers to the obscureness of the water triggered by suspended particles. A high turbidity can affect light penetration and aquatic plant growth.

***Chemical Parameters:*** There are large number of chemical parameters for water such as pH, conductivity, total dissolved solids (TDS), suspended solids, dissolved oxygen (DO), and a few more. The pH scale measures acidity or alkalinity of water which affects the minerals, solubility. DO depicts the amount of oxygen that is dissolved in water which is extremely essential for survival of organisms and also it defines the water quality. The salinity of water defines the ability of water to conduct current which is also known as conductivity. The TDS measures the concentration of dissolved substances in water like salts, minerals, or organic matters.

***Biological Parameters:*** The biological parameters in water redirects towards bacterial indicators, macroinvertebrates and algae. The contamination of water is primarily due to presence of fecal matter or harmful pathogens is indicated by these bacterial indicators (such as E. coli). Macroinvertebrates in water refer to the presence and diversity of aquatic insects, crustaceans, and other invertebrates that indicate the overall health of a water body. The type and abundance of algae can provide understandings into nutrient levels and water quality.

***Heavy Metals:*** The heavy metals correspond to compounds like Lead, Mercury, Cadmium, Copper and Zinc. Elevated levels of heavy metals can be hazardous to aquatic life and human health as they can bioaccumulate in the food chain.

***Organic Contaminants, Hormones and Pharmaceuticals:*** The influence of industries majorly chemical and pharmaceuticals to the quality of water is quite high. Pesticides, herbicides, estrogens, antibiotics which are primarily due to human activities can contaminate the water causing adverse effects to aquatic ecosystems and human health. In some cases, presence of protozoa can cause waterborne diseases which make access and monitoring of water quality extremely crucial.

### 16.2.4 Assessing the Water Quality

While assessing the water quality, several parameters are computed. The results from these parameters can serve as data for modelling using AI – ML techniques to make high quality predictions.

***Water Quality Index (WQI):*** WQI is a composite index which combines multiple water quality parameters into a single value. Computing WQI typically involve normalizing individual parameter values, assigning weights, and aggregating them. WQI can be computed as,

$$WQI = \left(w_1 \times \frac{I_1}{S_1}\right) + \left(w_2 \times \frac{I_2}{S_2}\right) + \cdots + \left(w_n \times \frac{I_n}{S_n}\right) \tag{16.6}$$

Where, $w_i$ is the weight assigned to parameter i, $I_i$ is the sub-index for parameter $i$, and $S_i$ is the standard value for the parameter $i$, such that $i \in 1$ to $n$.

***Hardness of Water:*** It refers to the concentration of specific minerals like calcium and magnesium ions, dissolved in water in form of calcium carbonate ($CaCO_3$) and magnesium carbonate ($MgCO_3$). The hardness of water is commonly expressed in terms of milligrams of calcium carbonate per Litre (mg/L) or parts per million (ppm).

$$Hardness = \left(\frac{Vol.\,of\ EDTA\ solution\,(mL) \times Normality\ of\ EDTA\ solution\,(N) \times 1000}{Vol.\,of\ water\ sample\,(mL) \times Equivalent\ weight\ of\ CaCO_3}\right) \tag{16.7}$$

Based on these standard range of hardness, water are termed as soft water (0–60 mg/L (or ppm)), moderately hard water (61–120 mg/L (or ppm)), hard water (121–180 mg/L (or ppm)) and very hard water (>180 mg/L (or ppm)).

***Chlorine Dosage:*** Chlorine dosage refers to the amount of chlorine added to water for the purpose of disinfection and water treatment to kill or inactivate harmful microorganisms, such as bacteria and viruses, and to prevent the spread of waterborne diseases. The appropriate dosage of chlorine depends on factors such as water quality, water contamination level, and desired level of disinfection and is mathematically defined as,

$$Dosage = \left(\frac{Desired\ concentration \times Vol.\,of\ water\ treated}{Concnetration\ of\ available\ Chlorine}\right) \tag{16.8}$$

***Dissolved Oxygen:*** Dissolved oxygen (DO) is an important parameter in water quality assessment, which represents the amount of oxygen dissolved in water. It is essential for the survival of aquatic organisms including fish, as they rely on dissolved oxygen for respiration. The concentration of dissolved oxygen in water is influenced by variety of factors like temperature, atmospheric pressure, salinity, and biological activity.

$$\%DO\ saturation = \left(\frac{Measured\ DO}{DO\ at\ saturation}\right) \times 100 \tag{16.9}$$

***Biochemical and Chemical Oxygen Demand (BOD, COD):*** Biochemical Oxygen Demand (BOD) depicts the amount of dissolved oxygen that is required by microorganisms to decompose organic matter in water. It is an important parameter to assess the level of organic pollution and the potential for water quality degradation in aquatic ecosystems. BOD is often used in environmental monitoring and wastewater treatment to evaluate the impact of organic pollutants on water bodies.

$$BOD = Initial\ DO - Final\ DO \tag{16.10}$$

**Chemical Oxygen Demand (COD)** on the other hand measures the amount of oxygen required to chemically oxidize organic and inorganic substances in water. It is used to assess the level of pollution and presence of organic and oxidizable inorganic substances in water samples. COD is commonly employed in environmental monitoring, wastewater treatment, and assessing the impact of industrial and agricultural activities on water quality.

$$COD = \frac{Vol.\ of\ Oxygen\ consumed}{Volume\ of\ sample} \times Dilution\ factor \tag{16.11}$$

***pH Adjustment:*** pH adjustment is a process in which the acidity or alkalinity of a solution, typically water, is modified to achieve a desired pH level. The pH scale ranges from 0 to 14, with values <7 being acidic, =7 being neutral, and >7 being alkaline (basic). It is a common practice in industries, environmental applications, and water treatment processes to meet specific requirements or standards.

$$Amount\ of\ Acid/Base\ to\ add = Buffer\ Capacity \times Target\ pH\ Change \tag{16.12}$$

***Total Nitrogen and Phosphorus:*** Nitrogen and phosphorus are crucial nutrients for the growth and development of plants and organisms in aquatic ecosystems. However, excessive levels of these nutrients in water bodies can lead to nutrient pollution, causing various environmental issues, such as algal bloom, oxygen depletion, and deterioration of water quality. Monitoring and managing nitrogen and phosphorus content are crucial for maintaining a balanced and healthy aquatic environment.

$$Total\ Nitrogen = \sum Nitrate\ Nitrogen, Nitrite\ Nitrogen, Ammonium\ Nitrogen \tag{16.13}$$

$$Total\ Phosphorus = \sum Orthophosphate\ Phosphorus, Organic\ Phosphorus \tag{16.14}$$

### 16.2.5 AI Interventions in Water

AI – ML techniques can be applied to water quality data to model complex relationships, predict pollutant concentrations, detect anomalies, and support decision-making processes.

***Water Quality Prediction:*** A large number of water parameters are being computed after regular intervals, ML models can be trained using these historical water quality data, including parameters such as temperature, pH, DO, TDS and nutrient levels, to predict the concentration of specific pollutants. Regression models, ensemble methods, or deep learning architectures may be used for accurate predictions.

***Algal Bloom Prediction:*** Water quality parameters like nutrient levels, temperature, and turbidity can be the relevant features for building ML models to analyze water quality data and predict the likelihood of algal blooms. Early detection can help implement preventive measures.

***Water Quality Index (WQI) Modelling:*** A vital parameter which need predictive modelling is for calculating the water quality index (WQI). These models can consider multiple water quality parameters and their interactions to generate an overall index value.

***Dissolved Oxygen Prediction:*** Assessing the dissolved oxygen can make critical contribution in monitoring the health of aquatic ecosystems. ML based models can predict dissolved oxygen levels in water bodies based on factors such as temperature, pH, and nutrient concentrations.

***Identification of Pollution Sources:*** The spatial and temporal patterns in water quality parameters can be analysed using the complex AI ML algorithms to identify potential pollution sources. This is a crucial information for targeted environmental management and pollution control.

***Impact of Climate Change:*** Time series-based prediction using complex ML algorithms can be deployed to analyse long-term water quality data in conjunction with climate data for assessing the impact of climate change on water quality parameters. This can assist in adaptive management strategies.

Integration of AI–ML with water quality monitoring parameters enhances the efficiency of data analysis, provides early warning systems, and supports evidence-based decision-making for water resource management and environmental protection. However, it's crucial to safeguard the quality and robustness of training data and consider interpretability and transparency in model outputs.

### 16.2.6 The Soil Factor

The role of soil is pivotal in promoting environmental sustainability through its multifaceted contributions to ecological processes. Nutrient cycling is one of the key functions which acts as a reservoir for essential elements like nitrogen and phosphorus critical for plant growth and overall ecosystem productivity. As a natural filter, soil aids in water purification by removing impurities from rainwater, mitigating the risk of pollution in groundwater and surface water bodies. Soil also serves as a significant storehouse of carbon, contributing to carbon sequestration and helping mitigate climate change. It holds cultural and societal significance, serving as the foundation for agriculture, influencing human settlement patterns, and supporting livelihoods. Sustainable soil management practices are integral to achieving global sustainability goals and ensuring the overall health of the planet.

Soil quality is assessed using various parameters that reflect the physical, chemical, and biological characteristics of the soil. These parameters provide insights into the soil's ability to assist plant growth, preserve nutrient cycles, and contribute to overall ecosystem health.

***Physical parameters:*** The physical parameters for measuring soil quality includes texture, structure, porosity and bulk density. The comparative proportions of sand, silt, and clay particles in the soil which impacts water retention, drainage, and aeration is referred as soil texture. Structure depicts the arrangement of soil particles into aggregates which promotes root growth and water movement. Porosity is the amount of open space between soil particles which affects water infiltration and drainage whereas bulk density gives measure to the mass of soil per unit volume, depicting information on soil compaction.

***Chemical Parameters:*** Major chemical parameters for soil quality assessment consists of pH, cation exchange capacity (CEC), electrical conductivity (EC) and the nutrients level. The acidity or alkalinity of the soil is measured by pH which influences nutrient availability and microbial activity. CEC indicates the soil's ability to hold and transfer essential cations to the plant roots. While, EC measures the soil's capacity to conduct electricity, providing an indication of salt content. The nutrient levels assess the concentrations of essential nutrients in the soil is crucial for the growth of plants.

***Organic and Biological Parameters:*** The organic matter refers to the 'Soil organic carbon (SOC)' which represents the amount of carbon stored in the soil. It improves the soil structure, water-holding capacity, and nutrient availability. Whereas, the biological parameters refer to microbial biomass and earthworm activity. Microbial biomass measures the abundance and action of microorganisms in the soil playing a crucial role in nutrient cycling and soil health. Earthworms and their activity contribute to soil structure and nutrient cycling. Monitoring their presence and activity is an indicator of soil health.

***Water Holding Capacity and Infiltration:*** The water holding capacity of soil is its ability to retain water and make it available for plant roots. It is a crucial soil property that influences plant growth, irrigation requirements, and overall water management in agricultural and natural ecosystems. It is generally measured by field capacity and wilting point. Field capacity is the highest amount of water that soil can hold against gravity after draining away of excess water. Wilting point is the level of moisture at which plants can no longer extract water from the soil. Water infiltration rate measures the rate at which water can penetrate the soil surface, influencing drainage and moisture availability for plants.

There are many other parameters for assessing soil quality but these parameters collectively provide a comprehensive understanding and its suitability for various agricultural, ecological, and environmental purposes. Monitoring these parameters helps in sustainable land management and conservation practices.

### 16.2.7 Assessing the Soil Quality

Soil quality assessment is essential for understanding its health, fertility, and ability to support plant growth. This involves evaluating various physical, chemical, and biological properties which have been discussed in previous section. The data which are generated during this assessment can serve as healthy dataset for building machine learning based predictive models.

***pH Calculation:*** The pH of the soil is computed based on the concentration of hydrogen ions ($H^+$). and, typically pH meter or litmus paper is used as a measuring device.

$$pH = -log_{10}(H^+) \tag{16.15}$$

***Cation Exchange Capacity (CEC):*** CEC is calculated based on the amounts of exchangeable cations in the soil. It is expressed as the total amount of cations that a soil can hold, typically measured in milliequivalents per 100 grams of soil (meq/100g) or centimoles of positive charge per kilogram of soil (cmolc/kg).

$$CEC = \sum exchangeble\ cations\ (meq/100\ g) \tag{16.16}$$

***Soil Organic Carbon (SOC):*** SOC is often measured using the Walkley-Black method which involves measuring the amount of carbon present in a soil sample and often expressed as a percentage of the soil's total weight or mass.

$$Organic\ Carbon(\%) = \left(\frac{Vol.\ of\ Potassium\ Dichromate}{Vol.\ of\ soil\ sample}\right) \times Conversion\ factor \times 100 \quad (16.17)$$

***Bulk Density Calculation:*** Bulk density (BD) a measure of the mass of soil per unit volume and is commonly used in soil science and is calculated as the mass of soil/unit volume. It is expressed in units such as grams per cubic centimetre (g/cm³) or kilograms per cubic meter (kg/m³).

$$Bulk\ density\ (BD) = \frac{Mass\ of\ Oven\ dry\ soil}{Vol.\ of\ soil\ core(cm^3)}\ or\ \frac{M}{V_t} \quad (16.18)$$

***Soil Water Content:*** Soil water content is calculated as the difference in weight before and after drying a soil sample (generally in percentage). Understanding soil water content is crucial for irrigation management, crop water requirements, and assessing the water-holding capacity of soils. Different soil types have varying water-holding capacities, and optimal soil moisture levels depend on the specific needs of crops and the surrounding ecosystem. Soil water content is also a key factor in studies related to water movement in soils, groundwater recharge, and hydrological modelling.

$$Water\ content\ (\%) = \left(\frac{Initial\ weight - dry\ weight}{dry\ weight}\right) \times 100 \quad (16.19)$$

***Electrical Conductivity (EC):*** EC is commonly used to assess the salinity or concentration of salt in the soil. The electrical conductivity of soil solution is influenced by the presence of dissolved ions, particularly salts and is often measured in soil saturation extract with deciSiemens per meter (dS/m) as unit. Considering I as current and V as voltage, the EC for soil is measured by,

$$EC = \frac{I}{V} \quad (16.20)$$

### 16.2.8 AI Interventions in Soil

AI is revolutionizing soil management by offering advanced tools and techniques to improve agricultural practices. Through precision agriculture, AI uses data from various sources, including satellites and sensors, to create detailed soil maps and optimize resource application. Smart irrigation systems use AI based algorithms to modify watering schedules based on real-time soil moisture data, which reduces water usage and improves efficiency. AI-driven technologies also play a crucial role in disease detection, analysing images to identify early signs of crop issues and enabling timely interventions. Farmers benefit from predictive modelling that anticipates soil behaviour and crop growth, guiding decisions on optimal planting times and soil conservation strategies. Recommendation systems utilize diverse datasets to provide personalized advice on crop rotations, nutrient management, and pest control. Moreover, AI contributes to modelling soil carbon sequestration and automates soil sampling processes, allowing for more comprehensive analysis. As AI continues to advance, its role in soil management promises increased sustainability, productivity, and environmental stewardship in agriculture. Some of the general areas where AI-ML has contributed largely for soil are discussed below.

***Soil Classification and Mapping:*** Models using ML, particularly supervised learning algorithms, can analyse soil data, including texture, pH, and nutrient levels, to classify and map different soil types. This is useful for precision agriculture and land use planning. ML based techniques, such as kriging or ML-based geo statistics, can predict soil properties across a geographic area based on limited soil samples. This aids in generating high-resolution soil maps for better land management.

***Crop Yield and Optimum Fertilizer Utilization:*** Based on the soil quality parameters, weather data and other relevant features, ML models can predict the crop yield. Regression models or ensemble methods can learn the relationships between soil characteristics and crop productivity. Further, to improve the yield, ML models can be developed to predict the optimum use of fertilizer based on soil nutrient levels and crop requirements. These models can recommend precise fertilizer dosages to improve nutrient use efficiency and reduce environmental impacts.

***Soil Health Assessment:*** This is one of the most significant areas where AI ML has contributed. By considering a combination of physical, chemical, and biological parameters ML models can be built to capture the complex interactions within the soil ecosystem. This in return can help to get early warning on soil degradation. Unsupervised learning algorithms have been used for anomaly detection to identify early signs of soil degradation. These models learn the normal patterns of soil parameters and can detect deviations that may indicate declining soil health. By analysing the soil properties, land cover, and precipitation data, possibility of erosion risk can also be predicted. Besides, these the nutrient levels, moisture, type and vegetation favourable can be predicted through ML modelling.

***Site-Specific Irrigation Management:*** The ML models can easily analyse the soil water content, texture, and climate data to optimize irrigation scheduling. This helps in site-specific irrigation management, water conservation and efficient crop water usage. Such models can assess the suitability of land for specific crops or land uses by considering various soil quality parameters. This supports informed decision-making in land-use planning and agricultural development. It is also possible to identify soil constraints, such as compaction or salinity, by analyzing relevant parameters. This information guides targeted interventions to address specific soil challenges.

***Carbon Sequestration Modelling:*** Carbon sequestration modelling use mathematical and computational models to simulate and predict the processes of carbon capture and storage in ecosystems, particularly in soils and vegetation. This is crucial for understanding how different land management practices impact the sequestration of carbon, a key component in mitigating climate change. ML models can predict soil organic carbon sequestration rates based on land management practices, climate data, soil characteristics and understanding the soil carbon dynamics.

**TABLE 16.1** List of AI infused tools for Air, Water and Soil quality assessment

| *Air Quality* | | *Water Quality* | | *Soil Quality* | |
|---|---|---|---|---|---|
| *Tool* | *Description* | *Tool* | *Description* | *Tool* | *Description* |
| BreezoMeter | Satellite data, weather patterns, and traffic emissions | Aquasend | Based on water quality sensors | Teralytic | Uses wireless sensors to measure various soil parameters |
| AirSense | Sensor technology with ML algorithms | BlueBox | Real time data in marine environment | Farm Dog | Data from field observations, including soil conditions |
| AtmoTube | Real time air quality data | WatrHub | Water infrastructure and water quality data | EarthScout | Oil sensors to monitor soil conditions such as moisture levels, temperature, and nutrient content |
| AirVisual | Satellite data, ground-based monitoring, weather patterns | SmartBall | Monitor water pipeline conditions | CropX | Combines soil sensors with AI algorithms to assess soil moisture levels and nutrient content |
| Aclima | Sensor and mobile networking | NOMAD | Water Nitrate levels | Agrosmart | Soil sensors, satellite imagery, and weather data |
| Hawa Dawa | Satellite imagery, traffic, and weather | Ayyeka Wavelet | Sensors and machine learning algorithms | Granular | Analyse farm data, including soil information |
| AirQo | Low-cost sensor networks and AI algorithms | WatrLiink | Detect leaks, assess water quality, and optimize distribution | Agworld | Integrates AI for analysing various data, including soil information |
| AirNode | Pollutants, including nitrogen dioxide and particulate matter | ArcticShark | Sensors to measure parameters such as turbidity, conductivity, and dissolved oxygen | PrecisionHawk | Drone-based solutions |
| Wynd Plus | Real-time air quality data | Pani Energy | Analyses data from water treatment plants | FarmBeats | Employs AI and IoT technologies for agriculture |
| Airly | Network of sensors to measure pollutants | PhytoOracle | Sensors to monitor parameters like heavy metals | Topsoil Mapper | Sensor technology and AI algorithms to analyse soil conditions, moisture levels, and organic matter content |
| Aeroqual | Pollutants, and AI algorithms | Rivertrace AI | Measure oil content and other pollutants in shipballast water | FieldX | AI for soil health analysis |
| CityAir | Stationary and mobile sensors | BlueIOT | Sensors to measure parameters such as turbidity, conductivity, and dissolved oxygen | Decipher | Analyse soil data from various sources, including satellite imagery |
| uHoo | Indoor pollutants | Apana | Monitors water usage patterns, identifies leaks, and optimizes water efficiency | Agrible | Utilizes AI to process data from various sources, including soil conditions, weather, and satellite imagery |
| AirBeam | Particulate matter levels | WaterLens | Sensors to monitor parameters like heavy metals | Sencrop | Integrates soil sensors and weather stations |
| Vayyar | 3D imaging sensors | WatEner | Wastewater treatment plants | Gamaya | Combines hyperspectral imaging from drones with AI for precision agriculture |

## 16.3 CLIMATE CHANGE: AI INTERVENTION

Climate change is today a global problem and needs urgent attention as the worst is likely to take place in near future. Addressing this problem involves mitigation of carbon emission as well as adaptation to its effects. AI seems to provide solutions for addressing the questions surrounding climate change, where the major challenge is data. While Green-house gases (GHGs) have been monitored for decades, the data has remained difficult to parse, analyse, and use productively. A comprehensive study of the climate change not only needs to collect data but also understand them and their correlations. The complex algorithms of ML have contributed to replace the conventional statistical approaches used in climate modelling and predictions. Some of the other crucial areas where AI has made tremendous interventions are discussed below.

### 16.3.1 Greenhouse Gases Emission Monitoring

Greenhouse gas (GHG) emission monitoring using Artificial Intelligence (AI) involves the application of advanced technologies to analyse, model, and manage emissions from various sources. AI can enhance the accuracy, efficiency, and scalability of GHG monitoring, providing valuable insights for climate change mitigation efforts. AI algorithms analyse remote sensing data and satellite imagery to detect and quantify GHG emissions, enabling monitoring of large geographical areas and diverse sources like industrial facilities, deforestation, and agriculture. Emission inventory models developed using AI consider multiple variables, simulating and predicting GHG emissions over time. Real-time monitoring through sensor networks and Internet of Things (IoT) devices allows for prompt intervention and adjustment of emissions reduction strategies. Natural Language Processing (NLP) is employed to analyse textual data, such as environmental reports, to extract information on GHG emissions. AI, particularly computer vision techniques, identifies and locates specific emission sources, aiding in compliance monitoring. ML algorithms are trained for anomaly detection, identifying abnormal patterns in emission data for rapid response. Predictive analytics use historical data to forecast future emission trends, assisting in proactive emissions reduction strategies. AI-powered carbon footprint calculators provide personalized recommendations for reducing carbon emissions. Blockchain technology, coupled with AI, enhances transparency and traceability in emission tracking, particularly in carbon markets and emissions trading. AI-driven optimization models evaluate the effectiveness of different policy interventions and emission reduction strategies, contributing to more informed decision-making in climate change mitigation.

### 16.3.2 Electricity and Grid Managements

Electricity is one of the largest contributors towards GHGs. The power sector is comprised of many phases—generation, transmission, distribution and consumption, and each of these phases has intervention of AI. AI is working towards optimizing the intricate dynamics of electrical grids, ensuring real-time adjustments to power flow, voltage regulation, and overall stability. It enables predictive maintenance by analysing sensory data, allowing timely interventions to prevent disruptions and minimize downtime. AI-powered energy forecasting uses past data and weather patterns to estimate supply and demand for energy, allowing utilities to effectively allocate resources and plan for periods of peak demand. The technology optimizes demand response programs, predicting consumer demand patterns and adjusting electricity consumption in real-time for improved grid management. Additionally, AI enhances grid resilience by quickly identifying and isolating faults, ensuring uninterrupted service. Its integration with the IoT devices in smart grids enhances grid visibility and supports decentralized energy generation. AI is also a key player in cybersecurity for the electricity sector, detecting and preventing cyber threats to ensure the security of critical infrastructure. Moreover, AI optimizes energy storage systems, supports grid planning and expansion by analysing demographic and economic trends, and monitors power quality parameters to maintain a stable and high-quality power supply. Overall, the integration of AI is steering the electricity sector toward more adaptive, resilient, and sustainable energy systems.

### 16.3.3 Renewable Energy

Renewable or clean energy is one way to transform the energy landscape and mitigating the impacts of climate change. AI-driven smart grids dynamically oversee the grid's amalgamation of renewable energy sources, like hydro, solar and wind energy. Real-time modifications for increased stability and better overall energy management are guaranteed by this improvement. Utilizing historical data and weather patterns, predictive analytics can contribute to improved resource allocation, less reliance on fossil fuels, and the advancement of a sustainable energy mix.

AI systems examine data from panels and turbines in wind and solar farms to maximize efficiency. The enhancement of energy yield and operational efficiency is facilitated by predictive maintenance and fault detection. It helps energy storage systems by optimizing cycles of charging and discharging, so assuring a consistent and dependable energy supply and excess renewable energy storage during peak hours of generation. In addition to maintaining grid frequency, AI also plays the role of grid balancing, renewable energy generation prediction, and real-time adjustment. This helps to provide a steady and dependable power source. Furthermore, AI technologies, including machine learning, evaluate and forecast patterns of energy consumption, optimizing energy use in buildings, industries, and other sectors, so raising total energy efficiency.

AI is one reason to speed up the process of finding novel materials for photovoltaics, improving solar cell efficiency and advancing solar energy technology. It is used in climate modelling to forecast extreme weather events, analyse the impact of climate change, and assist with adaptation plans. AI integration in the renewable energy space is speeding up the shift to a low-carbon, sustainable energy future while also improving the efficiency and dependability of current technology.

### 16.3.4 NLP and Climate Change

NLP has a crucial function in climate change research and communication, facilitating computers' ability to comprehend, interpret, and generate human language. Across various applications, NLP contributes significantly to advancing our understanding and tackling the problems brought on by climate change. In text mining and analysis, NLP techniques sift through extensive textual data from scientific literature, climate reports, and news articles. This enables researchers to identify trends, patterns, and critical information relevant to climate change. Additionally, NLP algorithms are employed to automatically summarize lengthy climate documents, distilling key information for accessibility. Sentiment analysis in climate change discussions leverages NLP to gauge public opinion and attitudes. By analysing social media, news articles, and public forums, sentiment analysis provides insights into how people see and respond to climate-related information. Information extraction from unstructured text is another application of NLP. This involves extracting specific pieces of information related to greenhouse gas emissions, climate events, or policy initiatives, contributing to comprehensive datasets for analysis.

NLP assists in climate risk assessment by analysing textual data related to weather patterns and extreme events. This information is invaluable for policymakers and organizations in planning adaptation strategies. Automated fact-checking, powered by NLP algorithms, helps verify the accuracy of climate change information, contributing to combating misinformation and ensuring the dissemination of reliable data. Enhanced search capabilities related to climate change are achieved through NLP, improving researchers' ability to find relevant literature, reports, and datasets efficiently.

### 16.3.5 Digital Data and Infrastructure

For AI algorithms to function properly, a multitude of additional technologies, inputs, and procedures must be in place. These encompass everything from unprocessed data to big data platforms and processing methods, computational infrastructure, and a variety of more specialized digital infrastructure. The recent achievements of AI applications are due as much to basic advancements in AI as they are to developments in large data processing and computation. While advances in computation and data processing have made AI more powerful overall, a lack of domain-specific technology and inputs is a major barrier preventing AI from being applied more specifically to climate change.

The core element of the input stack used by AI algorithms is data. For AI algorithms, data is the source of learning. They generate predictions, evaluate their performance, and find correlations between variables using the data that is given to them. The quality of the training data improves the algorithm's performance. Each application-specific set of processes is traversed by data. It can be generated, assembled, merged with other data, saved, cleaned, and tagged to train an AI system. On rare occasions, it can also be deleted and shared. Many, if not all, of these activities within the climate-relevant sectors (energy, transportation, land-use, industry, and buildings) need to be better supported in order to enable AI applications. AI can identify significant information in large volumes of unstructured data, often by scaling up annotations that humans could perform more laboriously. AI can search through large databases of corporate financial reports for information on climate change, identify metropolitan areas vulnerable to coastal flooding, and analyse satellite pictures to detect deforestation.

### 16.3.6 Combating Climate Change in the Mountains

Forecasting and modelling of the climate, specifically for mountainous regions is one of the important application of AI. Snowpack dynamics, temperature gradients, and other complicated data unique to mountainous areas may all be processed by AI-powered algorithms. Estimates of changes in precipitation patterns, the time of snowmelt, and glacier retreat may now be made with greater accuracy. Both the local community and downstream regions that depend on mountain-fed rivers need to be able to anticipate and plan for changes in water supply, which is made possible by these insights. AI has also emerged as a pivotal tool in the development of automated systems dedicated to monitoring glacier movement and ice loss. It is now possible to extract valuable insights from satellite imagery, remote sensing data, and other sources, utilise for the purpose of monitoring and assessing alterations in the well-being of glaciers, as well as for prognosticating the trajectory of glaciers in light of the prevailing climate change scenario.

## 16.4 THE BARRIERS

Despite having immense potentials in environment and climate change, AI has many barriers in its way. They are data, computing power, cost and the people.

***Data:*** All the AI models are dependent on the data, primarily the amount of data from where the patterns have to be extracted. However, data availability remains as a threshold which makes the AI tools of limited value. Most of the significant data which are collected from real time systems lack accessibility. In such cases, the developers and experts have to struggle in conceiving AI applications as well as deployment of the developed tools. Also, the data which has been acquired needs to be standardized as all the data are collected from diverse sources making them unstructured. Thus, having a benchmark dataset which can be readily applied to train, test and validate the AI models still remain unavailable forming a large barrier.

***Computing Power:*** Data handling and mapping needs high computation power to run and simulate the models. With the exponential growth in across all application areas, the demand of computation power also increases. The physical systems (CPUs, GPUs) need to be accessed remotely for handling real time data and analysis. The computational infrastructure once built need to be monitored and maintained regularly which needs manpower. Numerous electrical components, such as servers, networking devices, and temperature control equipment, make up computational infrastructure. Every component is prone to progressive deterioration, necessitating redundant design and a well-managed repair process. As demand for AI grows, maintenance of individual components may involve upgrading compute infrastructure capabilities and switching to processors with lower energy requirements.

***Cost:*** Cost is the primary barrier that penetrates and increases the above discussed barriers i.e., data and computing power. The acquisition of funding is necessary for the purchase and maintenance of equipment, hiring skilled manpower, processing, transfer, and storage of data, as well as digitize it for wide range AI applications in climatic use-cases. Institutions looking to attract highly talented personnel for climate applications must have adequate financing to remain competitive in the recruitment market, given the high demand for AI-developer skills. Experts in climate application are also in high demand; however, bringing these two groups of people together may be hampered by insufficient funding. Cost is the main barrier to accessing computation for institutions, regardless of whether they decide to purchase their own infrastructure or contract with outside suppliers for processing. AI development and application may come to a complete halt in the absence of sufficient funding or access to computing power.

***The People:*** How much AI will succeed depends on the developers, users and evaluators. A combination of specialized knowledge and abilities is needed to develop AI, including a solid foundation in computer science and software engineering as well as a strong command of statistics and information theory. The dependence on such specialized skill sets, like in any other highly technical profession, prevents AI from being developed and used to its full potential. Additionally, non-climate-focused organizations like technology, banking, and media corporations have a strong demand for AI engineers, creating intense rivalry to draw and keep these workers.

The mitigation of climate change cannot be handled by AI developers alone. Multidisciplinary expertise is required where AI developers work in collaboration with specialists in atmospheric chemistry, physics, materials science, engineering, finance, and even political science if they are to have an impact on mitigating climate change. When groups of talented people get a basic understanding of each other's fields, such collaborations are sparked but with lack of organizational structures that support joint efforts, such collaborations may be hampered. Any individual who uses decisions on AI results can be considered an AI user, that can be a chemist investigating new materials, economists assessing the effects of policies, pilots choosing their flight routes, and many more professions. Applications will differ in what kind of training is required to communicate with AI systems.

## SUMMARY

The chapter investigates into the key role that AI plays in reshaping strategies for environmental preservation and climate change mitigation. The fundamental pillars of environment – air, water and soil are explored in detail along with the various parameters for their assessment. It offers a thorough examination of the transformative impact AI has on these domains, illuminating the profound changes it brings to our approach. AI has proven to be an incredibly versatile tool, showcasing its prowess in various domains ranging from precision agriculture to wildlife conservation. Its ability to optimise resource utilisation, predict environmental trends, and aid in disaster response is truly remarkable. Some of the key areas in air, water and soil quality assessment where AI has intervened has been provided along with some of the well-established AI infused tools and their brief description.

Furthermore, this chapter emphasises the crucial role of AI in addressing the global challenge of climate change. The profound impact of advanced machine learning algorithms on climate modelling cannot be overstated, as they have emerged as a powerful tool for improving the accuracy of future climate projections. By harnessing the capabilities of these cutting-edge algorithms, climate scientists are now able to obtain more precise and reliable insights into the complex dynamics of our planet's climate system. This newfound ability to enhance climate modelling is paving the way for a deeper understanding of the intricate interplay between various environmental factors, ultimately enabling us to make robust decisions and develop effective policies to overcome the adverse effects of climate change. In addition, the chapter underscores the imperative nature of fostering interdisciplinary collaboration among climate scientists, environmental experts, and AI specialists and also some of the barriers in using AI for this complex domain.

## WORKED OUT EXAMPLES

**EXAMPLE 16.1** The concentrations of $PM_{2.5}$ and ozone ($O_3$) in a certain city are measured to be 60 μg/m³ and 70 ppb (parts per billion), respectively. Calculate the Air Quality Index (AQI) for both pollutants and determine the overall AQI for the city.

***Solution:***

To calculate the AQI for $PM_{2.5}$ and ozone, we first need to determine the AQI values for each pollutant separately and then take the higher of the two as the overall AQI.

For $PM_{2.5}$:

$$AQI_{PM2.5} = (AQI_{high} - AQI_{low})/(Conc_{high} - Conc_{low}) \times (Concentration - Conc_{low}) + AQI_{low}$$

From the AQI table for $PM_{2.5}$:

$$AQI_{low} = 51$$
$$AQI_{high} = 100$$
$$Conc_{low} = 15.5\ \mu g/m^3$$
$$Conc_{high} = 40.4\ \mu g/m^3$$

Substituting the values: $AQI_{PM2.5} = (100 - 51)/(40.4 - 15.5) * (60 - 15.5) + 51 \approx 138.57$

For ozone:

$$AQI_{O_3} = (AQI_{high} - AQI_{low})/(Conc_{high} - Conc_{low}) * (Concentration - Conc_{low}) + AQI_{low}$$

From the AQI table for ozone:

$$AQI_{low} = 101$$
$$AQI_{high} = 150$$
$$Conc_{low} = 55\ ppb$$
$$Conc_{high} = 70\ ppb$$

Plugging in the values: $AQI_{O_3} = (150 - 101)/(70 - 55) \times (70 - 55) + 101 = 150$

Now, compare both AQI values and take the higher one:

Overall AQI = max $(AQI_{PM2.5}, AQI_{O_3})$ = max (138.57, 150) $\approx$ 150

So, the overall Air Quality Index (AQI) for the city based on these measurements is approximately 150.

**EXAMPLE 16.2** A water sample contains $10^{-3}$ M $MgSO_4$. What is the hardness of this sample (in ppm) expressed as $CaCO_3$, given molar mass of $MgSO_4$ is 120.37g/mol.

***Solution:***

The hardness of water is measured in ppm (parts per million) in terms $CaCO_3$.

Which signifies $nCaCO_3 = nMgSO_4$ ppm

i.e., 1000 mL has $10^{-3}$ mols of $MgSO_4$

Thus, grams of $CaCO_3$ in 1000 mL = $10^{-3} \times 100$ grams

Grams of $CaCO_3$ in 1 mL = $10^{-3} \times 100/1000$ grams

Hence, hardness = $(10^{-3} \times 100/1000) \times 106 = 100$ ppm.

**EXAMPLE 16.3** What will be the BOD (Five-days) of a 10% diluted sample if $DO_i$ =6.7 mg/l, $DO_f$ = 2 mg/l and consumption of oxygen in blank = 0.5 mg/l?

***Solution:***

Given,

DO initial ($DO_i$) = 6.7 mg/litre

DO final ($DO_f$) = 2 mg/litre

And $DO_{blank}$ = 0.5 mg/litre with dilution = 10%

Five days BOD ($BOD_5$) = $[DO_i - DO_f - DO_{blank}] \times$ Dilution factor

$$BOD_5 = [6.7 - 2 - 0.5] \times \frac{100}{\%Dilution}$$

$$BOD_5 = [6.7 - 2 - 0.5] \times \frac{100}{10} = 42 \text{ mg/litre}$$

## EXERCISES

1. The concentrations of $PM_{10}$ and nitrogen dioxide ($NO_2$) in a certain area are measured to be 120 µg/m³ and 90 ppb (parts per billion), respectively. Calculate the Air Quality Index (AQI) for both pollutants and determine the overall AQI for the area.
2. The concentration of nitrogen dioxide ($NO_2$) in a city is measured to be 120 parts per billion (ppb). Calculate the sub-index for $NO_2$ in the Air Quality Index (AQI) for this concentration.
   Use standard AQI breakpoints for $NO_2$.
3. If the 8-hour maximum concentration of ozone ($O_3$) is 90 ppb, what is the corresponding sub-index ($SI_{O_3}$) value according to the air quality index (AQI) scale?
4. If a soil has a CEC of 40 meq/100 g, then how many grams of $Na^+$ will be required to saturate the CEC? (Given atomic weight of $Na^+$ = 23)
5. A hard water sample contains 1 mg/L and 3 mg/L of $CaCl_2$ and $MgCl_2$. Determine the hardness of this water sample (expressed in $CaCO_3$) per 106 parts of water.

## BIBLIOGRAPHY

Hassanien, A. E. and Darwish, A. (Eds.) (2023). *The Power of Data: Driving Climate Change with Data Science and Artificial Intelligence Innovations (Vol. 118)*, Springer Nature.

Kleine Deters, J., Zalakeviciute, R., Gonzalez, M. and Rybarczyk, Y. (2017). Modeling PM 2.5 urban pollution using machine learning and selected meteorological parameters, *Journal of Electrical and Computer Engineering*, 2017, Wiley.

Kottur, S. V., and Mantha, S. S. (2015). An integrated model using Artificial Neural Network (ANN) and Kriging for forecasting air pollutants using meteorological data, *International Journal of Advanced Research in Computer and Communication Engineering*, 4(1), 146–152, Tejass Publishers.

Liu, H., Li, Q., Yu, D. and Gu, Y. (2019). Air quality index and air pollutant concentration prediction based on machine learning algorithms, *Applied Sciences*, 9(19), 4069, MPDI.

Mani, G., and Viswanadhapalli, J. K. (2022). Prediction and forecasting of air quality index in Chennai using regression and ARIMA time series models, *Journal of Engineering Research*, 10(2A), 179–194, Elsevier.

# Further Readings


Abati, D., Nieto, M. and Cricri, F. (2020). *Deep learning for audio, image and video analysis: A practical handbook.* Apress.

Adam, C. (2010). *Essential mathematics and statistics for forensic science.* Wiley-Blackwell.

Ahmed, A., Mam, B. and Sowdhamini, R. (2021). DEELIG: A deep learning approach to predict protein-ligand binding affinity. *Bioinformatics and Biology Insights, 15*, 11779322211030364.

Akella, L. B. and DeCaprio, D. (2010). Cheminformatics approaches to analyze diversity in compound screening libraries. *Current Opinion in Chemical Biology, 14*(3), 325–330.

Akter, S., Babu, M. M., Hani, U., Sultana, S., Bandara, R. and Grant, D. (2024). Unleashing the power of artificial intelligence for climate action in industrial markets. *Industrial Marketing Management, 117*, 92–113.

Aljalbout, V., Golkov, Y., Siddiqui, S. A. and Cremers, D. (2018). Clustering with deep learning: Taxonomy and new methods. *arXiv preprint arXiv:1801.07648.*

Alpaydin, E. (2010). *Introduction to machine learning* (2nd ed.). MIT Press.

Anghel, C. I. (2006). Artificial intelligence methods in the pollutant concentrations prediction. *Revista de Chimie-Bucharest-Original Edition, 57*(7), 773.

Aquilante, F., Autschbach, J., Baiardi, A., Battaglia, S., Borin, V. A., Chibotaru, L. F., et al. (2020). Modern quantum chemistry with [Open] Molcas. *The Journal of Chemical Physics, 152*(21), 214113.

Arnold, C. (2023). Inside the nascent industry of AI-designed drugs. *Nature Medicine, 29*, 1292–1295.

Ashenden, S. K. (2021). *The era of artificial intelligence, machine learning, and data science in the pharmaceutical industry.* Elsevier.

Atienza, R. (2018). *Advanced deep learning with Keras: Apply deep learning techniques, autoencoders, GANs, variational autoencoders, deep reinforcement learning, policy gradients, and more.* Packt Publishing.

Auslander, N., Gussow, A. B., Benler, S., Wolf, Y. I. and Koonin, E. V. (2020). Seeker: Alignment-free identification of bacteriophage genomes by deep learning. *Nucleic Acids Research, 48*(21), e121–e121.

Baek, M., DiMaio, F., Anishchenko, I., Dauparas, J., Ovchinnikov, S., Lee, G. R., et al. (2021). Accurate prediction of protein structures and interactions using a three-track neural network. *Science, 373*(6557), 871–876.

Balakrishnan, G., Zhao, A., Sabuncu, M. R., Guttag, J. and Dalca, A. V. (2019). VoxelMorph: A learning framework for deformable medical image registration. *IEEE Transactions on Medical Imaging, 38*(8), 1788–1800.

Bandyopadhyay, S. and Pal, S. K. (2007). *Classification and learning using genetic algorithms: Applications in bioinformatics and web intelligence.* Springer-Verlag.

Baskin, I. I., et al. (2016). A renaissance of neural networks in drug discovery. *Expert Opinion on Drug Discovery, 11*(8), 785–795.

Bateman, B., Jha, A. R. and Johnston, B. (2020). *The supervised learning workshop* (2nd ed.). Packt.

Baum, Z. J., Yu, X., Ayala, P. Y., Zhao, Y., Watkins, S. P. and Zhou, Q. (2021). Artificial intelligence in chemistry: Current trends and future directions. *Journal of Chemical Information and Modeling, 61*(7), 3197–3212.

Bazoobandi, A., Emamgholizadeh, S. and Ghorbani, H. (2022). Estimating the amount of cadmium and lead in polluted soil using artificial intelligence models. *European Journal of Environmental and Civil Engineering, 26*(3), 933–951.

Bellemare, Y., Naddaf, J., Veness, J. and Bowling, M. (2013). The arcade learning environment: An evaluation platform for general agents. *Journal of Artificial Intelligence Research, 47*, 253–279.

Bender, A., et al. (2006). Bayes affinity fingerprints improve retrieval rates in virtual screening and define orthogonal bioactivity space: When are multitarget drugs a feasible concept? *Journal of Chemical Information and Modeling, 46*(6), 2445–2456.

Bengio, Y. (2009). Learning deep architectures for AI. *Foundations and Trends in Machine Learning, 2*(1), 1–127.

Bhamare, D. and Suryawanshi, P. (2018). Review on reliable pattern recognition with machine learning techniques. *Fuzzy Information and Engineering, 10*(3), 362–377.

Bird, S., Klein, E. and Loper, E. (2009). *Natural language processing with Python: Analyzing text with the Natural Language Toolkit.* O'Reilly Media.

Bishop, C. (2006). *Pattern recognition and machine learning.* Springer.

Bishop, M. (1995). *Neural networks for pattern recognition.* Oxford University Press.

Bohlmann, A., Mostafa, J. and Kumar, M. (2021). Machine learning and medication adherence: A scoping review. *JMIRx Med, 2*(4), e26993.

Bohr, A. and Memarzadeh, K. (2020). *Artificial intelligence in healthcare.* Elsevier.

Bonet, J., Chen, M., Dabad, M., Heath, S., Gonzalez-Perez, A., Lopez-Bigas, N. and Lagergren, J. (2022). DeepMP: A deep learning tool to detect DNA base modifications on Nanopore sequencing data. *Bioinformatics, 38*(5), 1235–1243.

Bonnet, F., Mazari, J., Cinnella, P. and Gallinari, P. (2022). AirfRANS: High fidelity computational fluid dynamics dataset for approximating Reynolds-averaged Navier–Stokes solutions. *Advances in Neural Information Processing Systems, 35*, 23463–23478.

Bose, S., Das, C., Ghosh, K., Chattopadhyay, M. and Chattopadhyay, S. (2022). A framework for neighbourhood configuration to improve the KNN-based imputation algorithms on microarray gene expression data. *International Journal of Bioinformatics Research and Applications, 18*(3), 141–190.

Brandes, N., Ofer, D., Peleg, Y., Rappoport, N. and Linial, M. (2022). ProteinBERT: A universal deep-learning model of protein sequence and function. *Bioinformatics, 38*(8), 2102–2110.

Brindle, A. (1981). *Genetic algorithms for function optimization* (Doctoral dissertation). University of Alberta.

Butow, P. and Hoque, E. (2020). Using artificial intelligence to analyze and teach communication in healthcare. *The Breast, 50*, 49–55.

Bystrom, K. and Kozinsky, B. (2022). CIDER: An expressive, nonlocal feature set for machine learning density functionals with exact constraints. *Journal of Chemical Theory and Computation, 18*(4), 2180–2192.

Cannataro, M., Guzzi, P. H. and Millano, M. (2022). *Artificial intelligence in bioinformatics.* Elsevier. ISBN: 978-0-12-822952-1.

Cao, Y., Chen, Y. and Khosla, D. (2015). Spiking deep convolutional neural networks for energy-efficient object recognition. *International Journal of Computer Vision, 113*(1), 54–66.

Chang, Y., Park, H., Yang, H. J., Lee, S., Lee, K. Y., Kim, T. S., et al. (2018). Cancer drug response profile scan (CDRscan): A deep learning model that predicts drug effectiveness from cancer genomic signature. *Scientific Reports, 3*(1), 8857.

Chapman, B. and Chang, J. (2000). Biopython: Python tools for computational biology. *ACM SIGBIO Newsletter, 20*(2), 15–19.

Chen, C., Shi, H., Jiang, Z., Salhi, A., Chen, R., Cui, X. and Yu, B. (2021). DNN-DTIs: Improved drug-target interaction prediction using XGBoost feature selection and deep neural network. *Computers in Biology and Medicine, 136*, 104676.

Chen, K. T., Gong, E., de Carvalho Macruz, F. B., Xu, J., Boumis, A., Khalighi, M., et al. (2019). Ultra-low-dose 18F-florbetaben amyloid PET imaging using deep learning with multi-contrast MRI inputs. *Radiology, 290*(3), 649-656.

Chen, P., Huang, J. Z. and Gao, X. (2014, December). LigandRFs: Random forest ensemble to identify ligand-binding residues from sequence information alone. *BMC Bioinformatics, 15*(15), 1–12.

Chen, T., Carter, J., Mahmud, M. and Khuman, A. S. (2022). *Artificial intelligence in healthcare.* Springer International Publishing.

Chen, W., Liu, X., Zhang, S. and Chen, S. (2023). Artificial intelligence for drug discovery: Resources, methods, and applications. *Molecular Therapy - Nucleic Acids, 31*, 691–702.

Chen, X., Leng, S., He, J. and Zhou, L. (2020). Deep-learning-based intelligent intervehicle distance control for 6G-enabled cooperative autonomous driving. *IEEE Internet of Things Journal, 8*, 15180–15190.

Chklovski, A., Parks, D. H., Woodcroft, B. J. and Tyson, G. W. (2023). CheckM2: A rapid, scalable and accurate tool for assessing microbial genome quality using machine learning. *Nature Methods, 20*(8), 1203–1212.

Chollet, F. (2017). *Deep learning with Python.* Manning Publications.

Chollet, F. and Allaire, J. J. (2022). *Deep learning with R.* Manning Publications.

Choudhary, A., Fox, G. and Hey, T. (2023). *Artificial intelligence for science: A deep learning revolution.* Springer. ISBN: 978-981-12-6567-9.

Chris, A. (2018). *Machine learning with Python cookbook: Practical solutions from preprocessing to deep learning.* O'Reilly Media.

Christiansen, M. P., Garg, S. K., Brazg, R., Bode, B. W., Bailey, T. S., Slover, R. H., et al. (2017). Accuracy of a fourth-generation subcutaneous continuous glucose sensor. *Diabetes Technology & Therapeutics, 19*, 446–456.

Coates, B., Huval, T., Wang, D., Wu, A., Ng, A. and Catanzaro, B. (2013). Deep learning with COTS HPC systems. *Proceedings of the 30th International Conference on Machine Learning (ICML)*, 1337–1345.

Cortes, C. and Vapnik, V. N. (1995). Support-vector networks. *Machine Learning, 20*, 273–297.

Dahlgren, B. (2018). ChemPy: A package useful for chemistry written in Python. *Journal of Open Source Software, 3*(24), 565.

Dalai, T., Mishra, T. K. and Sa, P. K. (2024). Deep learning-based POS tagger and chunker for Odia language using pre-trained transformers. *ACM Transactions on Asian and Low-Resource Language Information Processing, 23*(2), 1–23.

Daphne, K. and Nir, F. (2009). *Probabilistic graphical models: Principles and techniques.* The MIT Press.

Das, A., Ben-Menachem, T., Cooper, G. S., Chak, A., Sivak, M. V., Gonet, J. A., et al. (2003). Prediction of outcome in acute lower-gastrointestinal hemorrhage based on an artificial neural network: Internal and external validation of a predictive model. *The Lancet, 362*, 1261–1266.

David, B. (2012). *Bayesian reasoning and machine learning.* Cambridge University Press.

Dedov, F. (2022). *Deep learning: Practical machine learning and artificial intelligence solutions with Python and TensorFlow.* Packt Publishing.

Deneubourg, J. L., Aron, S., Goss, S. and Pasteels, J. M. (1990). The self-organizing exploratory pattern of the Argentine ant. *Journal of Insect Behavior, 3*(2), 159–168.

Devijver, P. A. and Kittler, J. (1983). *Pattern recognition: A statistical approach.* Prentice-Hall.

Dhiman, H. S., Deb, D. and Balas, V. E. (2020). *Supervised machine learning in wind forecasting and ramp event prediction (Vol. 1).* Elsevier.

Dick, S. and Fernandez-Serra, M. (2020). Machine learning accurate exchange and correlation functionals of the electronic density. *Nature Communications, 11*(1), 3509.

Dorado-Díaz, P. I., Sampedro-Gómez, J., Vicente-Palacios, V. and Sánchez, P. L. (2019). Applications of artificial intelligence in cardiology: The future is already here. *Revista Española de Cardiología, 72*, 1065–1075.

Dorigo, M. (1992). *Optimization, learning, and natural algorithms* (Doctoral dissertation). Politecnico di Milano, Milan.

Dorigo, M. and Gambardella, L. M. (1997). Ant colonies for the traveling salesman problem. *BioSystems, 43*(2), 73–81.

Dorigo, M., Maniezzo, V. and Colorni, A. (1996). The ant system: Optimization by a colony of cooperating ants. *IEEE Transactions on Systems, Man, and Cybernetics - Part B, 26*(1), 29–42.

Draizen, E. J., Readey, J., Mura, C. and Bourne, P. E. (2024). Prop3D: A flexible, Python-based platform for machine learning with protein structural properties and biophysical data. *BMC Bioinformatics, 25*(1), 1–24.

Drew, C. and John, M. W. (2012). *Machine learning for hackers.* O'Reilly Media.

Dubes, R. C. and Jain, A. K. (1976). Clustering techniques: The user's dilemma. *Pattern Recognition, 8*, 247–290.

Duda, R. O. and Hart, P. E. (1973). *Pattern classification and scene analysis.* Wiley.

Duda, R. O., Hart, P. E. and Stork, D. G. (2000). *Pattern classification* (2nd ed.). Wiley-Blackwell. ISBN: 978-0471056690

Eglese, R. W. (1990). Simulated annealing: A tool for operational research. *European Journal of Operational Research, 56*, 271–281.

Eisenstein, J. (2018). *Natural language processing*. Retrieved from https://princeton-nlp.github.io/cos484/readings/eisenstein-nlp-notes.pdf

Emil, H. and Julia, S. (2021). *Supervised machine learning for text analysis.* CRC Press. ISBN: 978-0-367-55419-4

Esmaeilzadeh, H., Dhebar, Y. and Lethin, R. (2021). *Deep learning for computer architects.* Morgan & Claypool Publishers.

Fernández-Esparrach, G., Bernal, J., López-Cerón, M., Córdova, H., Sánchez-Montes, C.,

Fine, T. L. (2006). *Probability and probabilistic reasoning for electrical engineering.* Pearson. ISBN: 0-13-020591-5

Fukunga, K. (1972). *Introduction to statistical pattern recognition.* Academic Press. ISBN: 0-12-269851-7

Gainza, P., Sverrisson, F., Monti, F., Rodola, E., Boscaini, D., Bronstein, M. M. and Correia, B. E. (2020). Deciphering interaction fingerprints from protein molecular surfaces using geometric deep learning. *Nature Methods, 17*(2), 184–192.

Gardner, J., Pleiss, G., Weinberger, K. Q., Bindel, D. and Wilson, A. G. (2018). Gpytorch: Blackbox matrix-matrix Gaussian process inference with GPU acceleration. *Advances in Neural Information Processing Systems, 31*.

Gaur, A. S., Bhardwaj, A., Sharma, A., John, L., Vivek, M. R., Tripathi, N., et al. (2017). Assessing therapeutic potential of molecules: Molecular property diagnostic suite for tuberculosis (MPDS TB). *Journal of Chemical Sciences, 129*, 515–531.

Gaur, A. S., Nagamani, S., Tanneeru, K., Druzhilovskiy, D., Rudik, A., Poroikov, V. and Sastry, G. N. (2018). Molecular property diagnostic suite for diabetes mellitus (MPDSDM): An integrated web portal for drug discovery and drug repurposing. *Journal of Biomedical Informatics, 85*, 114–125.

Gautam, K., Sharma, P., Dwivedi, S., Singh, A., Gaur, V. K., Varjani, S., et al. (2023). A review on control and abatement of soil pollution by heavy metals: Emphasis on artificial intelligence in recovery of contaminated soil. *Environmental Research*, 115592.

Geem, Z. W., Kim, J. H. and Loganathan, G. V. (2001). A new heuristic optimization algorithm: Harmony search. *Simulation, 76*(2), 60–68.

Geman, S., Bienenstock, E. and Doursat, R. (1992). Neural networks and the bias/variance dilemma. *Neural Computation, 4*, 1–58.

Géron, A. (2019). *Hands-on machine learning with Scikit-Learn, Keras, and TensorFlow*. O'Reilly Media.

Géron, A. (2019). *Hands-on machine learning with Scikit-Learn, Keras, and TensorFlow: Concepts, tools, and techniques to build intelligent systems*. O'Reilly Media.

Gerstner, W. and Kristler, W. (2012). *Spiking neural networks*. Cambridge University Press. ISBN: 9780511815706.

Glover, F. (1989). Tabu search: Part I. *ORSA Journal on Computing, 1*(3), 190–206.

Glover, F. (1990). Tabu search: Part II. *ORSA Journal on Computing, 2*(1), 4–32.

Gnana Lakshmi, T. C. and Madeleine, S. (2020). *Hands-on supervised learning with Python: Learn how to solve machine learning problems with supervised learning algorithms using Python*. BPB Publications.

Goodfellow, I., Bengio, Y. and Courville, A. (2016). *Deep learning*. MIT Press.

Goyal, P., Pandey, S. and Jain, K. (2020). *Deep learning for natural language processing*. Apress.

Grüning, B., Dale, R., Sjödin, A., Chapman, B. A., Rowe, J., Tomkins-Tinch, C. H., et al. (2018). Bioconda: Sustainable and comprehensive software distribution for the life sciences. *Nature Methods, 15*(7), 475–476.

Gulli, A. and Pal, S. (2017). *Deep learning with TensorFlow: Explore neural networks, implement deep learning algorithms, and improve performance with TensorFlow*. Packt Publishing.

Günal, E., Budak, M., Kılıç, M., Cemek, B. and Sırrı, M. (2023). Combining spatial autocorrelation with artificial intelligence models to estimate spatial distribution and risks of heavy metal pollution in agricultural soils. *Environmental Monitoring and Assessment, 195*(2), 317.

Haghighatlari, M., Vishwakarma, G., Altarawy, D., Subramanian, R., Kota, B. U., Sonpal, A., et al. (2020). ChemML: A machine learning and informatics program package for the analysis, mining, and modeling of chemical and materials data. *Wiley Interdisciplinary Reviews: Computational Molecular Science, 10*(4), e1458.

Hahn, S., Yuan, D. K., Thompson, W. K., Owens, M., Allgaier, N. and Garavan, H. (2021). Brain Predictability toolbox: A Python library for neuroimaging-based machine learning. *Bioinformatics, 37*(11), 1637–1638.

Hajkowicz, S., Sanderson, C., Karimi, S., Bratanova, A. and Naughtin, C. (2021). Artificial intelligence adoption in the physical sciences, natural sciences, life sciences, social sciences, and the arts and humanities: A bibliometric analysis of research publications from 1960-2021. *Technology in Society, 74*, 102260.

Halcox, J. P. J., Wareham, K., Cardew, A., Gilmore, M., Barry, J. P., Phillips, C., et al. (2017). Assessment of remote heart rhythm sampling using the AliveCor heart monitor to screen for atrial fibrillation: The REHEARSE-AF study. *Circulation, 136*, 1784–1794.

Hand, D. J. (2014). *The improbability principle: Why coincidences, miracles, and rare events happen every day*. Scientific American.

Hapke, H., Howard, C. and Lane, H. (2019). *Natural language processing in action: Understanding, analyzing, and generating text with Python*. Simon & Schuster.

Haque, A., Chowdhury, M. N. U. R. and Soliman, H. (2023). Transforming chronic disease management with chatbots: Key use cases for personalized and cost-effective care. In *2023 Sixth International Symposium on Computer, Consumer and Control (IS3C)* (pp. 367–370). IEEE.

Hardeniya, N., Perkins, J., Chopra, D., Joshi, N. and Mathur, I. (2016). *Natural language processing: Python and NLTK*. Packt Publishing.

Hassanien, A. E. and Darwish, A. (Eds.). (2023). *The power of data: Driving climate change with data science and artificial intelligence innovations (Vol. 118)*. Springer Nature.

Hassoun, M. H. (2003). *Fundamentals of artificial neural networks*. MIT Press. ISBN: 9780262514675.

Hastie, T., Tibshirani, R. and Friedman, J. (2009). *Elements of statistical learning: Data mining, inference, and prediction*. Springer.

Heaton, J. (2015). *Artificial intelligence for humans*. Heaton Research, Inc.

Hennigh, O., Narasimhan, S., Nabian, M. A., Subramaniam, A., Tangsali, K., Fang, Z., et al. (2021, June). NVIDIA SimNet™: An AI-accelerated multi-physics simulation framework. In *International Conference on Computational Science* (pp. 447–461). Springer International Publishing.

Hernández-Lemus, E. (2021). Random fields in physics, biology, and data science. *Frontiers in Physics, 9*, 641859.

Hert, J., et al. (2006). New methods for ligand-based virtual screening: Use of data fusion and machine learning to enhance the effectiveness of similarity searching. *Journal of Chemical Information and Modeling, 46*, 462–470.

Himanen, L., Jäger, M. O., Morooka, E. V., Canova, F. F., Ranawat, Y. S., Gao, D. Z., et al. (2020). DScribe: Library of descriptors for machine learning in materials science. *Computer Physics Communications, 247*, 106949.

Holland, R. C., Down, T. A., Pocock, M., Prlić, A., Huen, D., James, K., et al. (2008). BioJava: An open-source framework for bioinformatics. *Bioinformatics, 24*(18), 2096–2097.

Hooke, R. and Jeeves, T. A. (1961). Direct search solution of numerical and statistical problems. *Journal of the ACM, 8*(2), 212–229.

Hope, T., Resheff, Y. S. and Lieder, I. (2017). *Learning TensorFlow: A guide to building deep learning systems*. O'Reilly Media.

Hornik, M., Stinchcombe, M. and White, H. (1989). Multilayer feedforward networks are universal approximators. *Neural Networks, 2*(5), 359–366.

Hu, X., Wang, K. and Dong, Q. (2016). Protein ligand-specific binding residue predictions by an ensemble classifier. *BMC Bioinformatics, 17*, 1–12.

Huang, Z., Chan, T. M. and Dong, W. (2017). MACE prediction of acute coronary syndrome via boosted resampling classification using electronic medical records. *Journal of Biomedical Informatics, 66*, 161–170.

Hyok, R. J., Chung, O. H. and Kim, C. H. (2023). Probability cost function-based weighted extreme learning machine. *Multimedia Tools and Applications*, 1–16.

Ichimasa, K., Kudo, S. E., Mori, Y., Misawa, M., Matsudaira, S., Kouyama, Y., et al. (2018). Artificial intelligence may help in predicting the need for additional surgery after endoscopic resection of T1 colorectal cancer. *Endoscopy, 50*, 230–240.

Inamuddin, A. T., Cruz, J. N. and Refat, M. S. E. (2022). *Drug design using machine learning*. Wiley Publishers.

Jackson, P. C. (2019). *Introduction to artificial intelligence*. Courier Dover Publications.

Jacoba, C. M. P., Celi, L. A. and Silva, P. S. (2021, May). Biomarkers for progression in diabetic retinopathy: Expanding personalized medicine through integration of AI with electronic health records. *Seminars in Ophthalmology, 36*(4), 250–257. Taylor & Francis.

Jain, A. K., Duin, R. P. W. and Mao, J. (2000). Statistical pattern recognition: A review. *IEEE Transactions on Pattern Analysis and Machine Intelligence, 22*(1), 4–37.

Jalili, V., Afgan, E., Gu, Q., Clements, D., Blankenberg, D., Goecks, J., et al. (2020). The Galaxy platform for accessible, reproducible and collaborative biomedical analyses: 2020 update. *Nucleic Acids Research, 48*(W1), W395–W402.

Jendele, L., Krivak, R., Skoda, P., Novotny, M. and Hoksza, D. (2019). PrankWeb: A web server for ligand binding site prediction and visualization. *Nucleic Acids Research, 47*(W1), W345–W349.

Jiménez, J., Skalic, M., Martinez-Rosell, G. and De Fabritiis, G. (2018). K deep: Protein–ligand absolute binding affinity prediction via 3D-convolutional neural networks. *Journal of Chemical Information and Modeling, 58*(2), 287–296.

Jiménez-Luna, J., Grisoni, F. and Schneider, G. (2020). Drug discovery with explainable artificial intelligence. *Nature Machine Intelligence, 2*, 573–584.

Jin, D., Guo, D., Ho, T. Y., Harrison, A. P., Xiao, J., Tseng, C. K. and Lu, L. (2021). Deep Target: Gross tumor and clinical target volume segmentation in esophageal cancer radiotherapy. *Medical Image Analysis, 68*, 101909.

John, L., Nagamani, S., Mahanta, H. J., Vaikundamani, S., Kumar, N., Kumar, A., et al. (2023). Molecular Property Diagnostic Suite Compound Library (MPDS-CL): A structure-based classification of the chemical space. *Molecular Diversity*, 1–17.

John, L., Soujanya, Y., Mahanta, H. J. and Narahari Sastry, G. (2022). Cheminformatics and machine learning approaches for identifying antiviral compounds. *Molecular Informatics, 41*(4), 2100190.

Jumper, J., Evans, R., Pritzel, A., Green, T., Figurnov, M., Ronneberger, O., et al. (2021). Highly accurate protein structure prediction with AlphaFold. *Nature, 596*(7873), 583–589.

Kaack, L. H., Donti, P. L., Strubell, E., Kamiya, G., Creutzig, F. and Rolnick, D. (2022). Aligning artificial intelligence with climate change mitigation. *Nature Climate Change, 12*(6), 518–527.

Kalyan, K. S., Rajasekharan, A. and Sangeetha, S. (2022). AMMU: A survey of transformer-based biomedical pretrained language models. *Journal of Biomedical Informatics, 126*, 103982.

Kandathil, S. M., Greener, J. G., Lau, A. M. and Jones, D. T. (2022). Ultrafast end-to-end protein structure prediction enables high-throughput exploration of uncharacterized proteins. *Proceedings of the National Academy of Sciences, 119*(4), e2113348119.

Kassem, L. M., Alhabib, B., Alzunaydi, K. and Farooqui, M. (2021). Understanding patient needs regarding adverse drug reaction reporting smartphone applications: A qualitative insight from Saudi Arabia. *International Journal of Environmental Research and Public Health, 18*(8), 3862.

Katoch, S., Chauhan, S. S. and Kumar, V. (2021). A review on genetic algorithm: Past, present, and future. *Multimedia Tools and Applications, 80*, 8091–8126.

Katubi, K. M., Saqib, M., Mubashir, T., Tahir, M. H., Halawa, M. I., Akbar, A., et al. (2023). Predicting the multiple parameters of organic acceptors through machine learning using RDkit descriptors: An easy and fast pipeline. *International Journal of Quantum Chemistry, 123*(23), e27230.

Kennedy, J. and Eberhart, R. (1995). Particle swarm optimization. *Proceedings of the International Conference on Neural Networks*, Perth, Australia, November 27 to December 1, Piscataway, NJ: Institute of Electrical and Electronics Engineers (IEEE), 1942–1948.

Khanfar, M. A. and Taha, M. O. (2013). Elaborate ligand-based modeling coupled with multiple linear regression and k nearest neighbor QSAR analyses unveiled new nanomolar mTOR inhibitors. *Journal of Chemical Information and Modeling, 53*, 2587–2612.

Kiewhuo, K., Gogoi, D., Mahanta, H. J., Rawal, R. K., Das, D. and Sastry, G. N. (2022). North East India medicinal plants database (NEI-MPDB). *Computational Biology and Chemistry, 100*, 107728.

Kiewhuo, K., Gogoi, D., Mahanta, H. J., Rawal, R. K., Das, D., Vaikundamani, S., et al. (2023). OSADHI–An online structural and analytics-based database for herbs of India. *Computational Biology and Chemistry, 102*, 107799.

Kim, S., Thiessen, P. A., Bolton, E. E., Chen, J., Fu, G., Gindulyte, A., et al. (2016).

Kirkpatrick, S., Gelatt, C. D. and Vecchi, M. P. (1983). Optimization by simulated annealing. *Science, 220*(4598), 671–680.

Kleine Deters, J., Zalakeviciute, R., Gonzalez, M. and Rybarczyk, Y. (2017). Modeling PM 2.5 urban pollution using machine learning and selected meteorological parameters. *Journal of Electrical and Computer Engineering*.

Kochmar, E. (2022). *Getting started with natural language processing*. Simon and Schuster.

Kosko, B. (1994). *Neural network and fuzzy system.* Prentice Hall.

Kottur, S. V. and Mantha, S. S. (2015). An integrated model using artificial neural network (ANN) and Kriging for forecasting air pollutants using meteorological data. *International Journal of Advanced Research in Computer and Communication Engineering, 4*(1), 146–152.

Krivák, R. and Hoksza, D. (2015). Improving protein-ligand binding site prediction accuracy by classification of inner pocket points using local features. *Journal of Cheminformatics, 7*(1), 1–13.

Krivák, R. and Hoksza, D. (2018). P2Rank: Machine learning-based tool for rapid and accurate prediction of ligand binding sites from protein structure. *Journal of Cheminformatics, 10*, 1–12.

Krohn, J. (2021). *Deep learning for predictive analytics: Time series, image, and text data predictive analytics*. Packt Publishing.

Kumar, S. (2012). *Neural networks: A classroom approach*. McGraw-Hill Education India. ISBN: 9781259006166.

Kumari, G., Bandyopadhyay, D., Ekbal, A., Pal, S., Chatterjee, A. and Vinutha, B. N. (2024). Let's all laugh together: A novel multitask framework for humor detection in internet memes. *IEEE Transactions on Computational Social Systems*.

Kurniawan, M. H., Handiyani, H., Nuraini, T., Sri Hariyati, R. T. and Sutrisno, S. (2024). A systematic review of artificial intelligence-powered (AI-powered) chatbot intervention for managing chronic illness. *Annals of Medicine, 56*(1), 2302980.

Kwan, J. K. M. and Cho, S.-Y. (2021). *Deep learning for healthcare*. CRC Press.

L. P., K. and K. E. (2005). *Artificial neural networks: An Introduction*. SPIE Press. ISBN: 9780819459879.

Lahner, E., Grossi, E., Intraligi, M., Buscema, M., Corleto, V. D., Delle Fave, G., et al. (2005). Possible contribution of artificial neural networks and linear discriminant analysis in recognition of patients with suspected atrophic body gastritis. *World Journal of Gastroenterology, 11*(37), 5867–5873.

Lambora, A., Gupta, K. and Chopra, K. (2019, February). Genetic algorithm—A literature review. In *2019 International Conference on Machine Learning, Big Data, Cloud and Parallel Computing (COMITCon)* (pp. 380–384). IEEE.

Lapan, M. (2018). *Deep reinforcement learning hands-on*. Packt Publishing.

Lawton, J., Blackburn, M., Allen, J., Campbell, F., Elleri, D., Leelarathna, L., et al. (2018). Patients' and caregivers' experiences of using continuous glucose monitoring to support diabetes self-management: Qualitative study. *BMC Endocrine Disorders, 18*, 12.

Lee, K. S. and Geem, Z. W. (2004). A new structural optimization method based on the harmony search algorithm. *Computers and Structures, 82*(9–10), 781–798.

Levesque, H. J. and Lakemeyer, G. (2001). *The logic of knowledge bases*. MIT Press.

Levy, W. and Baxter, R. (1996). Energy efficient neural codes. *Neural Computation, 8*(3), 531–543.

Lewis, N. D. (2020). *Deep learning for time series forecasting*. Packt Publishing.

Li, T., Liu, W., Zeng, Z. and Xiong, N. (2021). DRLR: A deep reinforcement learning-based recruitment scheme for massive data collections in 6G-based IoT networks. *IEEE Internet of Things Journal.*

Limin, F. (1994). *Neural networks in computer intelligence*. McGraw-Hill.

Liu, B., Wang, X. and Gao, L. (2021, May). Overview of the application of artificial intelligence in several key issues of water conservancy. In *2021 33rd Chinese Control and Decision Conference (CCDC)* (pp. 7458–7465). IEEE.

Liu, H., et al. (2003). QSAR study of ethyl 2-[(3-methyl-2, 5-dioxo (3-pyrrolinyl)) amino]-4-(trifluoromethyl) pyrimidine-5-carboxylate: An inhibitor of AP-1 and NF-kB mediated gene expression based on support vector machines. *Journal of Chemical Information and Computer Sciences, 43*, 1288–1296.

Liu, H., Li, Q., Yu, D. and Gu, Y. (2019). Air quality index and air pollutant concentration prediction based on machine learning algorithms. *Applied Sciences, 9*(19), 4069.

Liu, Y., Wang, X., Mei, J., Boudreau, G., Abou-Zeid, H. and Sediq, A. B. (2020). Situation-aware resource allocation for multi-dimensional intelligent multiple access: A proactive deep learning framework. *IEEE Journal on Selected Areas in Communications, 39*, 116–130.

Liu, Y., Zhang, C., Liu, Z., Truhlar, D. G., Wang, Y. and He, X. (2023). Supervised learning of a chemistry functional with damped dispersion. *Nature Computational Science, 3*(1), 48–58.

Lodhi, H. and Yamanishi, Y. (2010). *Chemoinformatics and advanced machine learning perspectives: Complex computational methods and collaborative techniques*.

Lourenço, H. R., Martin, O. C. and Stützle, T. (2003). Iterated local search. In *Handbook of Metaheuristics* (pp. 320–353). Springer US.

M., K. P. (2012). *Machine Learning: A Probabilistic Perspective*. The MIT Press.

Ma, Y., Mao, J., Liu, X., Dai, Z., Zhang, H., Zhang, X. and Li, Q. (2023). Deep learning-based internal gross target volume definition in 4D CT images of lung cancer patients. *Medical Physics, 50*(4), 2303–2316.

Maass, W., Natschlager, T. and Markram, H. (2002). Real-time computing without stable states: A new framework for neural computation based on perturbations. *Neural Computation, 14*(11), 2351–2560.

MacCuish, J. D. and MacCuish, N. E. (2014). Cheminformatics applications of cluster analysis. *Computational Molecular Sciences, 4*, 34–48.

MacKay, D. J. C. (2003). *Information theory, inference, and learning algorithms*. Cambridge University Press.

Madan, T., Sagar, S. and Virmani, D. (2020, December). Air quality prediction using machine learning algorithms–a review. In *2020 2nd International Conference on Advances in Computing, Communication Control and Networking (ICACCCN)* (pp. 140–145). IEEE.

Mahmud, S. H., Chen, W., Jahan, H., Dai, B., Din, S. U. and Dzisoo, A. M. (2020). DeepACTION: A deep learning-based method for predicting novel drug-target interactions. *Analytical Biochemistry, 610*, 113978.

Maji, P. and Pal, S. K. (2012). *Rough fuzzy pattern recognition: Application in bioinformatics and medical imaging*. John Wiley & Sons.

Mak, K. K. and Pichika, M. R. (2019). Artificial intelligence in drug development: Present status and future prospects. *Drug Discovery Today, 24*(3), 773–780.

Mani, G. and Viswanadhapalli, J. K. (2022). Prediction and forecasting of air quality index in Chennai using regression and ARIMA time series models. *Journal of Engineering Research, 10*(2A), 179–194.

Mardani, M., Gong, E., Cheng, J. Y., Vasanawala, S. S., Zaharchuk, G., Xing, L. and Pauly, J. M. (2018). Deep generative adversarial neural networks for compressive sensing MRI. *IEEE Transactions on Medical Imaging, 38*(1), 167–179.

Marill, K. A. (2004). Advanced statistics: Linear regression, part II: Multiple linear regression. *Acad. Emerg. Med., 11*, 94–102.

Marques, J. P. (2012). *Pattern recognition concepts, methods and applications*. Springer Berlin Heidelberg. ISBN: 978-3-540-42297-6.

Masci, U., Meier, D., Ciresan, D. and Schmidhuber, J. (2011). Stacked convolutional autoencoders for hierarchical feature extraction. *Artificial Neural Networks and Machine Learning, 52–59.*

McConkey, R., Yee, E. and Lien, F. S. (2021). A curated dataset for data-driven turbulence modelling. *Scientific Data, 8*(1), 255.

McCulloch, W. S. and Pitts, W. H. (1943). A logical calculus of the ideas immanent in nervous activity. *The Bulletin of Mathematical Biophysics, 5*(4), 115–133.

McKay, D. (2003). *Information theory, inference, and learning algorithms*. Cambridge University Press. ISBN-10: 052164298.

Mei, J., Wang, X., Zheng, K., Boudreau, G., Sediq, A. B. and Abou-Zeid, H. (2021). Intelligent radio access network slicing for service provisioning in 6G: A hierarchical deep reinforcement learning approach. *IEEE Transactions on Communications, 69*, 6063–6078.

Melo, M. C. R., Maasch, J. R. M. A. and Fuente-Nunez, C. d. I. (2022). *Machine learning for drug discovery*. American Chemical Society. eISBN: 9780841299238.

Milojevic-Dupont, N. and Creutzig, F. (2021). Machine learning for geographically differentiated climate change mitigation in urban areas. *Sustainable Cities and Society, 64*, 102526.

Minsky, M. and Papert, S. (1969). *Perceptrons: An introduction to computational geometry*. MIT Press.

Mitchell, T. M. (2017). *Machine learning* (1st ed.). Hill Education. ISBN-10: 1259096955.

Mitrofanov, A., Alkhnbashi, O. S., Shmakov, S. A., Makarova, K. S., Koonin, E. V. and Backofen, R. (2021). CRISPRidentify: Identification of CRISPR arrays using machine learning approach. *Nucleic Acids Research, 49*(4), e20-e20.

Mohri, M., Rostamizadeh, A. and Talwalkar, A. (2012). *Foundations of machine learning*. MIT Press. ISBN: 978-0-262-01825-8.

Montufar, G. (2014). Universal approximation depth and errors of narrow belief networks with discrete units. *Neural Computation, 26*(7), 1386–1407.

Morin, O., Vallières, M., Braunstein, S., Ginart, J. B., Upadhaya, T., Woodruff, H. C., et al. (2021). An artificial intelligence framework integrating longitudinal electronic health records with real-world data enables continuous pan-cancer prognostication. *Nature Cancer, 2*(7), 709–722.

Mortazavi, B. J., Downing, N. S., Bucholz, E. M., Dharmarajan, K., Manhapra, A., Li, S. X., et al. (2016). Analysis of machine learning techniques for heart failure readmissions. *Circulation Cardiovascular Quality and Outcomes, 9*, 629–640.

Motulsky, A., Nikiema, J. N. and Bosson-Rieutort, D. (2021). Artificial intelligence and medication management. In *Multiple perspectives on artificial intelligence in healthcare: Opportunities and challenges* (pp. 91–101). Springer International Publishing.

Müller, A. C. and Guido, S. (2016). *Introduction to machine learning with Python: A guide for data scientists.* O'Reilly Media.

Murthy, M. N. and Devi, V. S. (2011). *Pattern recognition: An algorithmic approach*. Co-publication with Universities Press (India) Pvt. Ltd. ISBN: 978-0-85729-494-4.

Musavi, W., Ahmed, K., Chan, K., Faris, D. and Hummels, D. (1992). On the training of radial basis function classifiers. *Neural Networks, 5*(4), 595–603.

Neumann, D., Reddy, A. S. and Ben-Hur, A. (2022). RODAN: A fully convolutional architecture for basecalling nanopore RNA sequencing data. *BMC Bioinformatics, 23*(1), 1–9.

Nirmal, K. B. and Ping, L. (1996). *Neural network fundamentals with graphs, algorithms, and applications*. McGraw-Hill. ISBN: 9780070066182.

Nti, E. K., Cobbina, S. J., Attafuah, E. A., Senanu, L. D., Amenyeku, G., Gyan, M. A., et al. (2023). Water pollution control and revitalization using advanced technologies: Uncovering artificial intelligence options towards environmental health protection, sustainability and water security. *Heliyon, 9*(7), e18170.

O'Boyle, N. M., Banck, M., James, C. A., Morley, C., Vandermeersch, T. and Hutchison, G. R. (2011). Open Babel: An open chemical toolbox. *Journal of Cheminformatics, 3*(1), 1–14.

Oguike, O. (2021). *A first course in artificial intelligence*. Bentham Science Publishers.

Olofsson, P. (2007). *Probabilities: The little numbers that rule our lives*. Wiley. ISBN: 978-0-470-04001-0.

Ouyang, J., Chen, K. T., Gong, E., Pauly, J. and Zaharchuk, G. (2019). Ultra□low□dose PET reconstruction using generative adversarial network with feature matching and task□specific perceptual loss. *Medical Physics, 46*(8), 3555–3564. https://doi.org/10.1002/mp.13740

Öztürk, H., Özgür, A. and Ozkirimli, E. (2018). DeepDTA: Deep drug–target binding affinity prediction. *Bioinformatics, 34*(17), i821–i829.

Pace, F., Buscema, M., Dominici, P., Intraligi, M., Baldi, F., Cestari, R., et al. (2005). Artificial neural networks are able to recognize gastro-oesophageal reflux disease patients solely on the basis of clinical data. *European Journal of Gastroenterology & Hepatology, 17*, 605–610.

Pal, J. K., Ray, S. S. and Pal, S. K. (2021). Identifying drug resistant miRNAs using entropy-based ranking. *IEEE/ACM Transactions on Computational Biology and Bioinformatics, 18*(3), 973–984.

Paolanti, M. and Frontoni, E. (2020). Multidisciplinary pattern recognition applications: A review. *Computer Science Review, 37*, 100276. https://doi.org/10.1016/j.cosrev.2020.100276

Paroubek, P., Chaudiron, S. and Hirschman, L. (2007). Principles of evaluation in natural language processing. In *Proceedings of the 11th conference of the European Chapter of the Association for Computational Linguistics* (pp. 269–276). Association for Computational Linguistics.

Pathak, Y., Saikia, S., Pathak, S., Patel, J. and Prajapati, B. G. (Eds.). (2022). *Artificial Intelligence in Bioinformatics and Chemoinformatics*. Taylor & Francis Group, CRC Press.

Paul, D., Sanap, G., Shenoy, S., Kalyane, D., Kaila, K. and Tekade, R. K. (2021). Artificial intelligence in drug discovery and development. *Drug Discovery Today, 26*(1), 80–93.

Peng, J. C., Ran, Z. H. and Shen, J. (2015). Seasonal variation in onset and relapse of IBD and a model to predict the frequency of onset, relapse, and severity of IBD based on artificial neural network. *International Journal of Colorectal Disease, 30*, 1267–1273.

Pestian, J. P., Deleger, L., Savova, G. K., Dexheimer, J. W. and Solti, I. (2012). Natural language processing—The basics. In *Pediatric Biomedical Informatics: Computer Applications in Pediatric Research* (pp. 149–172). Springer.

Peter, F. (2012). *Machine learning: The art and science of algorithms that make sense of data*. Cambridge University Press.

Pietron, M. and Michalewicz, Z. (2022). *Deep learning for industry: A comprehensive introduction*. World Scientific Publishing Company.

Pisetta, A. (2018). *Deep learning for NLP and speech recognition*. Apress.

Pouyanfar, N., Harofte, S. Z., Soltani, M., Siavashy, S., Asadian, E., Ghorbani-Bidkorbeh, F., et al. (2022). Artificial intelligence-based microfluidic platforms for the sensitive detection of environmental pollutants: Recent advances and prospects. *Trends in Environmental Analytical Chemistry, 34*, e00160.

Probst, D., Schwaller, P. and Reymond, J. L. (2022). Reaction classification and yield prediction using the differential reaction fingerprint DRFP. *Digital Discovery, 1*(2), 91–97.

PubChem substance and compound databases. (2016). *Nucleic Acids Research, 44*(D1), D1202–D1213.

Pumperla, M. and Ferguson, K. (2020). *Deep learning and the game of Go*. Manning Publications.

Pun, F. W., Ozerov, I. V. and Zhanvoronkov, A. (2023). AI-powered therapeutic target discovery. *Trends in Pharmacological Sciences, 44*(9), 561–572.

Quinlan, J. R. (1986). Induction of decision trees. *Machine Learning, 1*, 81–106.

Raja, J. M., Elsakr, C., Roman, S., Cave, B., Pour-Ghaz, I., Nanda, A., et al. (2019). Apple watch, wearables, and heart rhythm: Where do we stand? *Annals of Translational Medicine, 7*, 417.

Rajasekaran, S. and Pai, G. A. V. (2004). *Neural networks, fuzzy systems, and evolutionary algorithms: Synthesis and applications*. ISBN: 9788120353343

Rajkomar, A. and Dean, J. (2020). Machine learning in healthcare: A comprehensive review.

Ramachandra, R. and Gupta, P. (2019). *Deep learning for biometrics*. CRC Press.

Ramasubramanian, K. and J.M. (2019). *Applied Supervised Learning with R: Use machine learning libraries of R to build models that solve business problems and predict future trends*. ISBN-10: 1838556338.

Ramsundar, B. and Eastman, P. (2020). *Deep learning for the life sciences: Applying deep learning to genomics, microscopy, drug discovery, and more*. O'Reilly Media.

Ramsundar, B. and O'Reilly, S. (2019). *Deep learning for the life sciences: Applying deep learning to genomics, microscopy, drug discovery, and more*. O'Reilly Media.

Rasmussen, C. E. and Williams, C. K. I. (2005). *Gaussian processes for machine learning*. The MIT Press.

Ratcliff, L. E., Dawson, W., Fisicaro, G., Caliste, D., Mohr, S., Degomme, A., et al. (2020). Flexibilities of wavelets as a computational basis set for large-scale electronic structure calculations. *The Journal of Chemical Physics, 152*(19).

Renaud, N., Geng, C., Georgievska, S., Ambrosetti, F., Ridder, L., Marzella, D. F., et al. (2021). DeepRank: A deep learning framework for data mining 3D protein-protein interfaces. *Nature Communications, 12*(1), 7068.

Renaud, N., Jung, Y., Honavar, V., Geng, C., Bonvin, A. M. and Xue, L. C. (2020). iScore: An MPI-supported software for ranking protein–protein docking models based on a random walk graph kernel and support vector machines. *SoftwareX, 11*, 100462.

Richard, S. S. and Andrew, G. B. (2018). *Reinforcement learning: An introduction*. The MIT Press.

Ridder, D., Ridder, J. and Reinders, M. J. T. (2013). Pattern recognition in bioinformatics. *Briefings in Bioinformatics, 14*(5), 633–647.

Robert, J. S. (1997). *Artificial neural networks*. McGraw-Hill International Editions. ISBN: 9780070571181

Roberts, M. G. and Lawrence, R. (2020). Chapter 3: MedChemInformatics: An introduction to machine learning for drug discovery. In *RSC Publications*.

Rolnick, D., Donti, P. L., Kaack, L. H., Kochanski, K., Lacoste, A., Sankaran, K., et al. (2022). Tackling climate change with machine learning. *ACM Computing Surveys (CSUR), 55*(2), 1-96.

Rosenblatt, F. (1958). The perceptron: A probabilistic model for information storage and organization in the brain. *Psychological Review, 65*(6), 386.

Rowley, S., Baluja, S. and Kanade, T. (1998). Neural network-based face detection. *IEEE Transactions on Pattern Analysis and Machine Intelligence, 20*(1), 23–38.

Roy, C., Saha, R., Misra, S. and Dev, K. (2021). Micro-Safe: Microservices-and deep learning-based safety-as-a-service architecture for 6G-enabled intelligent transportation system. *IEEE Transactions on Intelligent Transportation Systems*.

Ruck, S., Rogers, K. and Kabrisky, M. (1990). Feature selection using a multilayer perceptron. *Journal of Neural Network Computing, 2*(2), 40–88.

Ruder, S. (2016). An overview of gradient descent optimization algorithms. *arXiv preprint arXiv:1609.04747*.

Rumelhart, G. H. and Williams, R. (1986). Learning internal representations by backpropagating errors. In *Parallel Distributed Processing: Explorations in the Microstructure of Cognition* (pp. 318–362).

Rumelhart, G., Hinton, G. and Williams, R. (1986). Learning representations by backpropagating errors. *Nature, 323*(6088), 533–536.

Rutz, A., Sorokina, M., Galgonek, J., Mietchen, D., Willighagen, E., Gaudry, A., et al. (2022). The LOTUS initiative for open knowledge management in natural products research. *eLife, 11*, e70780.

Ryan, M. (2021). *Deep learning with structured data: A complete guide for business analysts, data scientists, and machine learning engineers*. Packt Publishing.

S., K. (2013). *Artificial neural networks: Architectures and applications*. IntechOpen. ISBN: 978-953-51-0935-8.

Sadybekov, A. V. and Kartich, V. (2023). Computational approaches streamlining drug discovery. *Nature, 616*, 673–685.

Saka, M. P., Hasançebi, O. and Geem, Z. W. (2016). Metaheuristics in structural optimization and discussions on harmony search algorithm. *Swarm and Evolutionary Computation, 28*, 88–97.

Sami, H., Otrok, H., Bentahar, J. and Mourad, A. (2021). AI-based resource provisioning of IoE services in 6G: A deep reinforcement learning approach. *IEEE Transactions on Network and Service Management, 18*, 3527–3540.

Saraphian, A. (2022). *Applied deep learning with Keras and TensorFlow: Solve real-world machine learning problems with Google's TensorFlow and Keras frameworks*. Packt Publishing.

Sarkar, D., Bali, R. and Sharma, T. (2018). *Practical machine learning with Python: A problem-solver's guide to building real-world intelligent systems*. Apress.

Sastry, G. N., Priyadarsinee, L., Jamir, E., Nagamani, S., Mahanta, H. J., Kumar, N., et al. (2023). Molecular Property Diagnostic Suite for COVID-19 (MPDSCOVID-19): An open access disease-specific drug discovery portal. *bioRxiv*. https://doi.org/10.1101/2023-08

Sato, F., Shimada, Y., Selaru, F. M., Shibata, D., Maeda, M. and Watanabe, G., et al. (2005). Prediction of survival in patients with esophageal carcinoma using artificial neural networks. *Cancer, 103*, 1596–1605.

Sato, H. and Akiba, T. (2020). *TensorFlow 2 pocket reference: Your quick guide to the new TensorFlow APIs*. O'Reilly Media.

Schalkoff, R. J. (2014). *Pattern recognition: Statistical, structural, and neural approaches*. John Wiley & Sons Inc. ISBN: 978-0-471-52974-3

Schmidt, J. W. and Thanos, C. (Eds.). (2012). *Foundations of knowledge base management: Contributions from logic, databases, and artificial intelligence applications*. Springer Science & Business Media.

Schwenk, H. and Bengio, Y. (2000). Boosting neural networks. *Neural Computation, 12*(8), 1869–1887.

Sebastian, R. and Vahid, M. (2015). *Python machine learning*. Packt Publishing.

Sedghi, A., O'Donnell, L. J., Kapur, T., Learned-Miller, E., Mousavi, P. and Wells III, W. M. (2021). Image registration: Maximum likelihood, minimum entropy, and deep learning. *Medical Image Analysis, 69*, 101939.

Sengorur, B., Koklu, R. and Ates, A. (2015). Water quality assessment using artificial intelligence techniques: SOM and ANN—A case study of Melen River, Turkey. *Water Quality, Exposure and Health, 7*, 469-490.

Serey, J., Alfaro, M., Fuertes, G., Vargas, M., Duran, C., Ternero, R., Rivera, R. and Sabattin, J. (2023). Pattern recognition and deep learning technologies, enablers of Industry 4.0, and their role in engineering research. *Symmetry, 15*(2), 535.

Sergios, T. and Konstantinos. (2020). *Machine learning: A Bayesian and optimization perspective*. Academic Press.

Seth, W. (2019). *Deep learning from scratch*. O'Reilly Media.

Shaban-Nejad, A., Michalowski, M. and Buckeridge, D. L. (2020). *Explainable AI in healthcare and medicine*. Springer Cham.

Shah, H. A., Zhao, L. and Kim, I. (2021). Joint network control and resource allocation for space-terrestrial integrated network through hierarchical deep actor-critic reinforcement learning. *IEEE Transactions on Vehicular Technology, 70*, 4943–4954.

Shankar, T. N. (2008). *Neural network.* University Science Press. ISBN: 9788131804667.

Shanmugamani, R. (2018). *Deep learning for computer vision: Expert techniques to train advanced neural networks using TensorFlow and Keras*. Packt Publishing Ltd.

Shanmugamani, R. (2019). *Deep learning for computer vision*. Packt Publishing.

Shao, X., Chen, X., Qiang, Y., Zhong, C. and Zhang, Z. (2021). Feature-aided adaptive-tuning deep learning for massive device detection. *IEEE Journal on Selected Areas in Communications, 39*, 1899–1914.

Sietsma, J. and Dow, R. (1991). Creating artificial neural networks that generalize. *Neural Networks, 4*(1), 67–79.

Simon, S. H. (2005). *Neural networks: A comprehensive foundation*. Pearson. ISBN: 81-7808-300-0, 9th Indian Edition.

Simonovsky, M., Gutiérrez-Becker, B., Mateus, D., Navab, N. and Komodakis, N. (2016). A deep metric for multimodal registration. In *Medical Image Computing and Computer-Assisted Intervention-MICCAI 2016: 19th International Conference, Athens, Greece, October 17-21, 2016, Proceedings, Part III* (pp. 10-18). Springer International Publishing.

Singh, N. and Varshney, U. (2020). IT-based reminders for medication adherence: Systematic review, taxonomy, framework, and research directions. *European Journal of Information Systems, 29*(1), 84–108.

Sivanandam, S. N., Sumathi, S. and Deepa, S. N. (2006). *Introduction to neural networks using MATLAB*. McGraw Hill Edition. ISBN: 978-0-07-059112-7

Smith, T. (2019). *Supervised machine learning with Python*. Packt Publishing. ISBN-10: 838825665

Sorokina, M., Merseburger, P., Rajan, K., Yirik, M. A. and Steinbeck, C. (2021). COCONUT online: Collection of open natural products database. *Journal of Cheminformatics, 13*(1), 1–13.

Stajich, J. E., Block, D., Boulez, K., Brenner, S. E., Chervitz, S. A., Dagdigian, C., et al. (2002). The Bioperl toolkit: Perl modules for the life sciences. *Genome Research, 12*(10), 1611–1618.

Stevens, E., Antiga, L. and Viehmann, T. (2020). *Deep learning with PyTorch*. Manning Publications.

Strodthoff, N., Wagner, P., Wenzel, M. and Samek, W. (2020). UDSMProt: Universal deep sequence models for protein classification. *Bioinformatics, 36*(8), 2401–2409.

Stuart, R. and Peter, N. (2010). *Artificial intelligence: A modern approach* (3rd ed.). Prentice Hall.

Subramanian, M., Wojtusciszyn, A., Favre, L., Boughorbel, S., Shan, J., Letaief, K. B., et al. (2020). Precision medicine in the era of artificial intelligence: Implications in chronic disease management. *Journal of Translational Medicine, 18*(1), 1–12.

SuperNatural 3.0—A database of natural products and natural product-based derivatives. (2023). *Nucleic Acids Research, 51*(D1), D654–D659.

Sussman, J. L., Lin, D., Jiang, J., Manning, N. O., Prilusky, J., Ritter, O. and Abola, E. E. (1998). Protein Data Bank (PDB): Database of three-dimensional structural information of biological macromolecules. *Acta Crystallographica Section D: Biological Crystallography, 54*(6), 1078–1084.

Svetnik, V., et al. (2003). Random forest: A classification and regression tool for compound classification and QSAR modeling. *Journal of Chemical Information and Computer Sciences, 43*, 1947–1958.

Tangadpalliwar, S. R., Vishwakarma, S., Nimbalkar, R. and Garg, P. (2019). ChemSuite: A package for Cheminformatics calculations and machine learning. *Chemical Biology and Drug Design, 93*(5), 960–964.

Taulli, T. and Oni, M. (2019). *Artificial intelligence basics*. Apress.

Theodoridis, S. and Koutroumbas, K. (2009). *Pattern recognition* (4th ed.). Academic Press. ISBN-10: 1597492728.

Thurlemann, M., Boselt, L. and Riniker, S. (2023). Regularized by physics: Graph neural network parametrized potentials for the description of intermolecular interactions. *Journal of Chemical Theory and Computation, 19*(2), 562–579.

Tok, G. and Schmidhuber, J. (2021). *Deep learning: A comprehensive guide to neural networks, CNNs, and RNNs*. Packt Publishing.

Tou, J. T. and Gonzalez, R. C. (1974). *Pattern recognition principle*. Addison-Wesley Publishing Company. ISBN: 9780201075861.

Turakhia, M. P., Desai, M., Hedlin, H., Rajmane, A., Talati, N., Ferris, T., et al. (2019). Rationale and design of a large-scale, app-based study to identify cardiac arrhythmias using a smartwatch: The Apple Heart Study. *American Heart Journal, 207*, 66–75. https://doi.org/10.1016/j.ahj.2018.09.002

Umberto M. (2018). *Applied deep learning: A case-based approach to understanding deep neural networks*. Apress. ISBN: 978-1-4842-3790-8.

Valliappa, L. (2021). *Practical machine learning for computer vision*. O'Reilly Media.

Vamathevan, J., Clark, D., Czodrowski, P., Dunham, I., Ferran, E., Lee, G., Li, B., Madabhushi, A., Shah, P., Spitzer, M. and Zhao, S. (2019). Applications of machine learning in drug discovery and development. *Nature Reviews Drug Discovery, 18*, 463-477.

Van der Heijden, F., Duin, R. P. W., de Ridder, D. and Tax, D. M. J. (2004). *Classification, parameter estimation and state estimation*. Wiley.

Van, H. (1968). *Trees, detection, estimation, and modulation theory*. Wiley. ISBN: 471-89955-0.

Vapnik, V. N. (2000). *The nature of statistical learning theory*. Springer. ISBN: 978-1-4757-3264-1.

Vasilev, I. and Slater, D. (2019). *Python deep learning*. Packt Publishing.

Vasilev, I. and Slater, D. (2020). *Advanced deep learning with Python: A comprehensive guide to advanced deep learning techniques using Python*. Packt Publishing.

Vasiliev, Y. (2020). *Natural language processing with Python and spaCy: A practical introduction*. No Starch Press.

Vijayan, R. S. K., Kihlberg, J., Cross, J. B. and Poongavanam, V. (2022). Enhancing preclinical drug discovery with artificial intelligence. *Drug Discovery Today, 27*(4), 967-984.

Walpole, R. E., Myers, R. H., Myers, S. L. and Ye, K. (1993). *Probability and statistics for engineers and scientists* (Vol. 5). New York: Macmillan.

Wang, K., Zhou, R., Li, Y. and Li, M. (2021). DeepDTAF: A deep learning method to predict protein–ligand binding affinity. *Briefings in Bioinformatics, 22*(5), bbab072.

Wang, L., Chen, M., Feng, X., Zhang, Z., Yang, H., Zhang, J., Chen, Z., et al. (2024). A survey on large language model based autonomous agents. *Frontiers of Computer Science, 18*(6), 1–26.

Wang, L., Han, D., Zhang, M., Wang, D. and Zhang, Z. (2021). Deep reinforcement learning-based adaptive handover mechanism for VLC in a hybrid 6G network architecture. *IEEE Access, 9*, 87241–87250.

Wang, P., Yao, J., Wang, G., Hao, F., Shrestha, S., Xue, B., et al. (2019). Exploring the application of artificial intelligence technology for identification of water pollution characteristics and tracing the source of water quality pollutants. *Science of the Total Environment, 693*, 133440.

Wang, T., Shao, W., Huang, Z., Tang, H., Zhang, J., Ding, Z. and Huang, K. (2021). MOGONET integrates multi-omics data using graph convolutional networks allowing patient classification and biomarker identification. *Nature Communications, 12*(1), 3445.

Ward, J. H. (1963). Hierarchical grouping to optimize an objective function. *Journal of the American Statistical Association, 48*, 236–244.

Webb, A. (2002). *Statistical pattern recognition* (2nd ed.). Wiley International. ISBN: 0-470-84514-7.

Wilkinson, M. D., Dumontier, M., Aalbersberg, I. J., Appleton, G., Axton, M., Baak, A., et al. (2016). The FAIR Guiding Principles for scientific data management and stewardship. *Scientific Data, 3*(1), 1–9.

Witten, H. and Frank, E. (2008). *Data mining: Practical machine learning tools and techniques* (2nd ed.). Elsevier India. ISBN: 0-12-088407-0.

Woolfson, M. M. (2012). *Everyday probability and statistics* (2nd ed.). Imperial College. ISBN: 978-1-84816-761-2.

Wu, J. (2020). *Essentials of pattern recognition: An accessible approach.* Cambridge University Press. ISBN: 9781108650212.

Wu, Y., Ma, Y., Capaldi, D. P., Liu, J., Zhao, W., Du, J. and Xing, L. (2020). Incorporating prior knowledge via volumetric deep residual network to optimize the reconstruction of sparsely sampled MRI. *Magnetic Resonance Imaging, 66*, 93–103.

Wu, Z., Ramsundar, B., Feinberg, E. N., Gomes, J., Geniesse, C., Pappu, A. S., et al. (2018). MoleculeNet: A benchmark for molecular machine learning. *Chemical Science, 9*(2), 513–530.

Xie, Y., Lu, L., Gao, F., He, S. J., Zhao, H. J., Fang, Y., et al. (2021). Integration of artificial intelligence, blockchain, and wearable technology for chronic disease management: A new paradigm in smart healthcare. *Current Medical Science, 41*, 1123–1133.

Xu, H., Wu, J., Li, J. and Lin, X. (2021). Deep-reinforcement-learning-based cybertwin architecture for 6G IIoT: An integrated design of control, communication, and computing. *IEEE Internet of Things Journal, 8*, 16337–16348.

Yang, Y. J. and Bang, C. S. (2019). Application of artificial intelligence in gastroenterology. *World Journal of Gastroenterology, 25*, 1666–1683.

Yao, X. (1999). Evolving artificial neural networks. *Proceedings of the IEEE, 87*(9), 1423–1447.

Z, J. M. (2006). *Introduction to artificial neural systems*. JAICO Publishing House. ISBN: 9788172246501.

Zaccone, G., Rezaul Karim, M. and Menshawy, A. (2021). *Deep Learning with TensorFlow: Explore Neural Networks and Build Intelligent Systems with Python*. Packt Publishing.

Zafar, I., Tzanidou, G., Burton, R., Patel, N. and Araujo, L. (2018). *Hands-on Convolutional Neural Networks with TensorFlow: Solve Computer Vision Problems with Modeling in TensorFlow and Python*. Packt Publishing Ltd.

Zha, H., Ding, C., Gu, M., He, X. and Simon, H. D. (2001). Spectral relaxation for k-means clustering. *Neural Information Processing Systems, 14*, 1057–1064.

Zhang, B. X.-Y., Liu, C.-L. and Suen, C. Y. (2020). Towards robust pattern recognition: A review. *Proceedings of the IEEE, 108*(6), 894–922.

Zhang, L. (2019). *Deep Learning: A Visual Approach*. Springer.

Zhang, Q., Li, S., Chen, F., Zeng, R. and Tong, R. (2022). Targeted delivery strategy: A beneficial partner for emerging senotherapy. *Biomedicine & Pharmacotherapy, 155*, 113737.

Zhou, D., Nakamura, M., Mukumoto, N., Yoshimura, M. and Mizowaki, T. (2022). Development of a deep learning□based patient□specific target contour prediction model for markerless tumor positioning. *Medical Physics, 49*(3), 1382–1390.

# Index